Utilization-Focused Evaluation

4th Edition

To
Brandon, Quinn, and Charmagne
May you live to experience the vision of
an experimenting society
in which knowledge is used thoughtfully and astutely
to truly inform practice
and contribute to making the world a better place.

Utilization-Focused Evaluation

4th Edition

Michael Quinn Patton

Los Angeles • London • New Delhi • Singapore

For information:

SAGE Publications, Inc.
2455 Teller Road
Thousand Oaks, California 91320
E-mail: order@sagepub.com

SAGE Publications Ltd.
1 Oliver's Yard
55 City Road
London EC1Y 1SP
United Kingdom

SAGE Publications India Pvt. Ltd.
B 1/I 1 Mohan Cooperative Industrial Area
Mathura Road, New Delhi 110 044
India

SAGE Publications Asia-Pacific Pte. Ltd.
33 Pekin Street #02-01
Far East Square
Singapore 048763

Printed in the United States of America

Library of Congress Cataloging-in-Publication Data

Patton, Michael Quinn.
Utilization-focused evaluation / Michael Quinn Patton—4th ed.
        p. cm.
Includes bibliographical references and index.
ISBN 978-1-4129-5861-5 (pbk.)
    1. Evaluation research (Social action programs)—United States.
I. Title.

H62.5.U5P37 2008
361.6'1068—dc22   2007052936

This book is printed on acid-free paper.

08   09   10   11   12   10   9   8   7   6   5   4   3   2   1

Acquisitions Editor:	Vicki Knight
Associate Editor:	Sean Connelly
Editorial Assistant:	Lauren Habib
Production Editor:	Astrid Virding
Copy Editor:	QuADS Prepress (P) Ltd
Typesetter:	C&M Digitals (P) Ltd
Proofreader:	Dennis W. Webb
Indexer:	Molly Hall and Michael Quinn Patton
Cover Designer:	Candice Harman
Marketing Manager:	Stephanie Adams

Contents

Detailed
Table of Contents

About the Author

Michael Quinn Patton is an independent evaluation consultant with 35 years experience conducting evaluations, training evaluators, and writing about useful evaluation. He is former President of the American Evaluation Association and recipient of both the *Alva and Gunnar Myrdal Award* from the Evaluation Research Society for "outstanding contributions to evaluation use and practice" and the *Paul F. Lazarsfeld Award* for lifetime contributions to evaluation theory from the American Evaluation Association. The Society for Applied Sociology honored him with the *Lester F. Ward Award* for Outstanding Contributions to Applied Sociology.

In addition to *Utilization-Focused Evaluation*, he has written books on *Qualitative Research and Evaluation Methods*, *Creative Evaluation*, and *Practical Evaluation*. He has edited volumes on *Culture and Evaluation* and *Teaching Evaluation Using the Case Method*. He is coauthor of *Getting to Maybe: How the World Is Changed*, a book that applies complexity science to social innovation.

After receiving his doctorate in Organizational Sociology from the University of Wisconsin, Madison, he spent 18 years on the faculty of the University of Minnesota, including 5 years as Director of the Minnesota Center for Social Research. He received the University's Morse-Amoco Award for outstanding teaching. He is a regular trainer for the *International Program for Development Evaluation Training* sponsored by The World Bank each summer in Ottawa; *The Evaluators' Institute* annual courses in Chicago, San Francisco, and Washington, D.C.; and the American Evaluation Association's preconference professional development courses.

In his consulting practice, he brings an evaluation perspective to organizational development projects, strategic planning, policy analysis, board development, management consulting, and systems analysis. As a transdisciplinary evaluation generalist, his work has included a range of efforts at improving effectiveness, including programs in leadership development, education at all levels, human services, the environment, public health, medical education, employment, agricultural extension, arts, criminal justice, antipoverty programs, mental health, transportation, diversity initiatives, international development, managing for results, performance indicators, effective governance, and futuring. He has worked with organizations and programs at the international, national, state, and local levels, and with philanthropic, not-for-profit, private sector, and government programs. He has worked with peoples from many different cultures and perspectives in all parts of the globe.

Evaluating a wilderness education program in the United States Southwest introduced him to the magnificence of the Grand Canyon, where he has backpacked at least once a year for 25 years. The influence of those cumulative experiences can be found in this book, he says, "by those who know the Canyon." His creative nonfiction book, *Grand Canyon Celebration: A Father-Son Journey of Discovery*, was finalist for Minnesota book of the year.

He has three children, to whom this book is dedicated—a musician, an engineer, and an international development practitioner, "each doing a great deal of evaluation in their own distinctive ways," he says, "but, like much of the world, seldom officially calling it that."

Preface

Sufi stories are tales used to pass on ancient wisdom. One such story tells of a revered teacher, Mulla Nasrudin, who was asked to return to his home village to share his wisdom with the people there.

Mulla Nasrudin mounted a platform in the village square and asked rhetorically, "O my people, do you know what I am about to tell you?"

Some local rowdies, deciding to amuse themselves, shouted rhythmically, "NO . . . ! NO . . . ! NO . . . ! NO . . . !"

"In that case," said Mulla Nasrudin with dignity, "I shall abstain from trying to instruct such an ignorant community," and he stepped down from the platform.

The following week, having obtained an assurance from the hooligans that they would not repeat their harassment, the elders of the village again prevailed upon Nasrudin to address them. "O my people," he began again, "do you know what I am about to say to you?"

Some of the people, uncertain as to how to react, for he was gazing at them fiercely, muttered, "Yes."

"In that case," retorted Nasrudin, "there is no need for me to say more." He then left the village square.

On the third occasion, after a deputation of elders had again visited him and implored him to make one further effort, he stood before the people: "O my people! Do you know what I am about to say?"

Since he seemed to demand a reply, the villagers shouted, "Some of us do, and some of us do not."

"In that case," said Nasrudin as he withdrew, "Let those who know teach those who do not."

—Adapted from Shah (1964:80–81)

This book reports the things I have learned about doing program evaluation from those who know. The pages that follow represent an accumulation of wisdom from many sources: from research on use, from interviews with 40 federal decision makers and evaluators who participated in a study of the use of federal health evaluations, from conversations with hundreds of program staff and funders about their evaluation experiences, from evaluation colleagues and participation in evaluation conferences around the world, from participants in my evaluation workshops who struggle to conduct useful evaluations, and from 38 years of evaluation practice. From these diverse sources, this book connects theory with practice, research with practitioner wisdom, and aspirations for use with real examples of evaluations actually used.

The evaluation profession has developed dramatically since the last edition of this book, 10 years ago. Globalization of evaluation has been especially significant with more than 60 evaluation associations worldwide. Thus, this edition has more international examples and content. Updating this edition with recent evaluation research and thinking proved a formidable task because so much has happened on so many fronts as evaluation has become increasingly diverse. In particular, there has been a resurgence of research on evaluation use and new conceptual models providing both a broader and deeper understanding of utilization processes and impacts. I've added new material on innovative uses of evaluation, alternative roles for evaluators, and pressing concerns about ethics, including the increased politicalization of evaluation as heightened attention to accountability has put the spotlight on data-based decision making and evidence-based practice. More organizations aspire to become learning organizations, using evaluation for both learning and accountability—and generating tensions between these distinct and often-conflicting functions. Systems thinking and complexity science have altered how evaluators conceptualize interventions, challenging traditional logic models and making theories of change both more complex and more important. The ever increasing pace of change and new technologies, especially the ascendance of the Internet as a means of instant global communication, have pressured evaluators to produce findings faster, shortened feedback timelines, and exponentially expanded opportunities for

widely disseminating findings. Vociferous debate is going on around the world about how to judge evaluation quality and whether there is or ought to be a methodological gold standard. Running counter to the efforts to create universal and uniform standards are demands for greater contextual sensitivity and adapting evaluation to local conditions and constraints. The immensity of change shows no signs of slowing, yet through it all, *the central challenge to professional practice remains doing evaluations that are useful and actually used.*

The tone and substance of this new edition have been influenced by the fact that *Utilization-Focused Evaluation* is now more than 30 years old. The first edition, published in 1978 and based on research begun in 1975, had the tone of a toddler throwing a temper tantrum because no one seemed to be paying attention. The second edition, published in 1986, established *intended use by intended users* as the central tenet of utilization-focused evaluation, and added examples to clarify points of uncertainty and contention. By the third edition, the basic premise *of utilization-focused evaluation* had become widely accepted among professional evaluators. Joe Wholey, Harry Hatry, and Kathryn Newcomer (1994) observed in the *Handbook of Practical Program Evaluation* that "in recent years the watchword of the evaluation profession has been utilization-focused evaluation" (p. 5). In that context, the third edition book paid more attention to details and nuances of practice, and opened up the new territory of *process use*, examining the impacts of evaluation beyond findings to look at how stakeholders were affected by being involved in evaluation processes. The concept of *process use* called attention to the observation that those who go through an evaluation often experience changes in thinking, attitudes, and behavior that can have lasting effects on how programs and organizations go about their business. In the last decade, our understanding of these effects has deepened considerably and this edition reviews the latest evidence and provides more direction for how to enhance evaluation capacity in organizations by infusing evaluative thinking into organizational culture.

Today, evaluation generally, and utilization-focused evaluation in particular, face new challenges. The ideas for and research that formed utilization-focused evaluation emerged at a time when our major concern was that evaluations were largely ignored. In an article that has become a classic, distinguished evaluation pioneer Carol Weiss (1990) asked, "Is Anybody There? Does Anybody Care?" The answers turned out to be a resounding "Yes!" But just as I was looking forward to years spent resting on our profession's laurels, to my great surprise a major new concern has emerged that perhaps *too much attention* is being paid to evaluation—attention of the wrong kind—leading to expecting more than evaluation can deliver, high stakes decision making that goes beyond the evidence, politicalization and distortion of findings, misuse of evaluations, bloated rhetoric about accountability, huge expenditures on poorly done and useless studies, and a likely decline in quality as demand has outstripped the capacity for high-quality supply. As a result, this edition places more emphasis on *appropriate use* of evaluation and training intended users to be astute in what evaluation can—and cannot—deliver.

I hasten to add that evaluation can deliver a great deal. It can contribute mightily to increased effectiveness in meeting the needs of people in poverty, the homeless, the sick and afflicted, children in need of quality education, and wiser use of resources for the full range of hopeful human endeavors aimed at improving the human condition. But like any tool, evaluation can be used for harm as well as good, and in the last decade we have seen unprecedented examples of data corruption, suppression of findings to serve narrow political and partisan agendas, and distorting data to justify decisions already made in the interests of those with power and wealth. Increasingly, the evaluation profession is called on to contribute to the general public welfare, speak truth to power, and support critical thinking in this global age of widespread disinformation and misinformation. As politicians worldwide have adopted the language of evaluation—rhetoric about accountability, outcomes, benchmarks, evidence, impact, lessons learned—evaluators have the added role of assuring that the rhetoric matches reality, and that means working to ensure the *appropriate uses of evaluation*.

Why do you practice evaluation?

In January 2008, as I was completing this book, I was contacted by Eric De Muynck, Conseiller politique, Programme Régional Energie Pour La Réduction De La Pauvreté in Dakar, Senegal. He wrote that 20 years ago, the French newspaper *Libération* published in its literary supplement a set of short responses by 400 writers worldwide answering the question: *Why do you write?* Inspired by this, he was soliciting responses from evaluators to the question, "Why do you practice evaluation?" It struck me as the kind of question that might be appropriate to address in this preface for, in my case, both questions apply: Why do I practice evaluation and why do I write about it? The answer to both questions is the same:

(Continued)

(Continued)

I practice and write about evaluation because I believe that evaluative thinking can make more effective those who are deeply committed to and authentically engaged in making the world a better place. Evaluation, at its best, distinguishes *what works from what doesn't*, and helps separate effective change makers from resource wasters, boastful charlatans, incompetent meddlers, and corrupt self-servers. Through evaluation, I aspire to make my own small contribution toward realizing the vision of an *experimenting global community*, one characterized by commitment to reality-testing, respect for different perspectives, and open dialogue about evidence—a world in which ongoing learning is valued and practiced, and knowledge is generated and used.

Balancing concerns about evaluation misuse is a welcome crescendo of affirmation that evaluation can be and is used for learning and improvement, the theme of the 2007 national conference of the American Evaluation Association. In philanthropic institutions, not-for-profits, international aid agencies, government at all levels, and the private sector, there is unprecedented hunger for timely and relevant information that can support learning, increased effectiveness, and development. As I am writing this, the world's greatest golfer, Tiger Woods, began 2008 by once again winning the first tournament he entered, eight strokes ahead of his closest competitor. In his post-tournament interview, however, he said that he was still working to improve his game and that he had not yet played his best golf. If Tiger Woods can still make improvements and adjustments, based on feedback, learning, and adapting to new conditions, it seems likely that most programs *and evaluations* have some room for improvement. To support learning, evaluations must be conducted with that purpose in mind and geared to provide relevant and timely feedback to those who can benefit. That's not as easy and straightforward as it may sound. This edition of *utilization-focused evaluation* aspires to capture and communicate knowledge and lessons generated over the last decade to improve evaluators' performance and utility.

In this edition, I have sought the mature voice of the elder, which I find I've become. It has been said that life has three stages: youth, middle age, and "lookin' good" (spoken by those surprised to see that you're still alive and kicking). I've attained the "lookin' good" stage, which, fortunately, has nothing to do with actual looks. My professional development parallels the maturation of our profession. As a field of professional practice, we have reached a level where we know what we're doing and have a track record of important contributions to show. That knowledge and those contributions are the bedrock of this latest edition. I've built on that foundation with lots of new examples, illustrations, graphics, and exhibits, plus 16 original new cartoons by creative illustrators Susan Kropa and Jason Love. There's also new wisdom from Halcolm (pronounced "How come," as in Why), my internal philosophical alter ego and muse who pipes in every so often to remind us that evaluation methods, approaches, and decisions are grounded in fundamental philosophical underpinnings about how and why the world works as it does. Halcolm takes the form of a jester in the new cartoons in this edition. This edition, for the first time, also includes practice exercises at the end of each chapter.

While I have learned from and am indebted to many more people than I can acknowledge, the personal and professional contributions of a few special colleagues have been especially important to me in recent years, particularly in the writing of this edition. Gene Lyle, a Minnesota colleague of 30-plus years, retired from a long and distinguished career as an internal evaluator in Ramsey County Human Services (Saint Paul) just in time to read and provide feedback on this entire volume; I am deeply indebted to Gene for his generous effort and insights. Marv Alkin, Stan Capela, Tina Christie, Brad Cousins, Jean King, Karen Kirkhart, Mel Mark, and Hallie Preskill have been important fellow travelers on the journey to understand the many and complex dimensions of evaluation use and ways to enhance appropriate and meaningful use. Other colleagues whose writings and wisdom have informed not just this edition but my entire professional career include Eleanor Chelimsky, Huey Chen, Ross Connor, David Fetterman, Jennifer Greene, Mike Hendricks, Ernie House, Donna Mertens, Ricardo Millett, Sharon Rallis, Tom Schwandt, Michael Scriven, Midge Smith, Nick Smith, Bob Stake, Dan Stufflebeam, Bill Trochim, Abe Wandersman, Carol Weiss, and Joe Wholey. Minnesota provides a thriving evaluation community in which to work and an active local chapter of the American Evaluation Association where friends and colleagues share experiences. Among local evaluators who have been especially helpful to me in recent years are Glenda Eoyang, Jean Gornick, Meg Hargreaves, Jean King, Dick Krueger, Gene Lyle, Paul Mattessich, Diane Morehouse, Gayle Peterson, Stacey Stockdill, and Bill Svrluga. On the national scene, I have benefited greatly from evaluation discussions and collaborative projects with John Bare, Teresa Behrens, Deborah Bonnet, John Bryson, Don Compton, Malcolm Gray, Kippy King, Astrid Hendricks-Smith, Rodney Hopson, Jackie Williams Kaye, Penny McPhee, Patti Patrizi, Debra Rog, John Sherman, Kay Sherwood, Judith Stockdale, Karl Stauber, Hazel Symonette, and Ellen Taylor-Powell. This edition has been heavily influenced by the opportunity to dialogue and work with international colleagues, especially Michael Bamberger, Fred Carden, Tessie Tzavaras Catsambas, Brad Cousins, Jane Davidson, Sarah Earl, Sulley Gariba, Douglas Horton, Keiko Kuji-Shikatani, Saville Kushner, Arnold Love, Kate McKegg, Alexey Kuzmin, Linda Morra, John Mayne, Masafumi Nagao, Zenda Ofir, Mahesh Patel, Burt Perrin, Donna Podems, Ray Rist, Patricia Rogers, Andy Rowe, Jim Rugh, Craig Russon, Lawrence Salmen, Terry Smutylo, and Bob Williams. This revision delves much more deeply into *developmental evaluation* as an emergent evaluation approach grounded in complexity theory; colleagues who have been especially engaged with and helpful to me in applying systems thinking to the developmental evaluation alternative include Mark Cabaj, Jamie Gamble, Katharine Pearson, Patricia Rogers, Frances Westley, Bob Williams, Ricardo Wilson-Grau, and Brenda Zimmerman. Frances and Brenda are my coauthors of a book titled *Getting to Maybe: How the World Is Changed* (2006) that provides the broad framework for why developmental evaluation is an important utilization-focused evaluation option. Patricia Rogers has contributed to my elaboration of developmental evaluation through her extensive thinking about program theory, appropriate evaluation methods, and engagement internationally; I am especially appreciative of her feedback on this revision, including a list of issues regarding utilization-focused evaluation she felt needed to be clarified that pushed me to stop talking about doing a new edition and get down to the work of actually writing. Jean Gornick contributed not only important practitioner insights from her 20 years directing a community-based, antipoverty agency but also support and encouragement.

* * * * * * *

This book is both practical and theoretical. It tells readers how to conduct program evaluations and why to conduct them in the manner prescribed. Part I sets the context with chapters reviewing the challenges of and mandate for evaluation use, *defining utilization-focused evaluation*, elaborating the importance of the personal factor in *utilization-focused evaluation*, and looking in depth at various kinds of findings use and process use. Each chapter contains both a review of the relevant literature and actual case examples to illustrate major points. Exhibits summarize key points while *Utilization-Focused Menus* highlight options available to evaluators in working with intended users to make selections from the vast smorgasbord of evaluation approaches. Each chapter concludes with new follow-up exercises. Part II, on "Focusing Evaluations," presents and discusses the active-reactive-interactive-adaptive roles of the utilization-focused evaluator and discusses how to work with program goals, alternatives to goals-based evaluation, implementation evaluation, and logic models, including new systems and complexity approaches that are the basis for developmental evaluation. Part III examines evaluation methods and the ways in which making measurement and design decisions affects use, including ways to analyze findings and communicate results to enhance use.

Part IV examines the political and ethical realities of evaluation and utilization-focused strategies for dealing with those realities.

Utilization-focused evaluation emerged from the observation that much of what has passed for program evaluation has not been very useful. The fundamental premise of the book is that *evaluations ought to be useful*. Therefore, something different must be done if evaluation is to be useful. This book illuminates what should be different. Based on research and professional experience, and integrating theory and practice, this book provides both an overall framework and concrete advice for how to conduct useful evaluations that actually get used.

The following reviewers are gratefully acknowledged:

Eileen M. Harwood, University of Minnesota; Betty Malen, University of Maryland, College Park; Olin E. Myers Jr., Western Washington University; Sue Ann Savas, University of Michigan; Mary Kay Schleiter, University of Wisconsin-Parkside; Jackie D. Sieppert, University of Calgary; and John Sterlacci, Binghamton University.

—Michael Quinn Patton
Saint Paul, Minnesota

PARt 1

Toward More Useful Evaluations

In the beginning God created the heaven and the earth.

Then God stood back, viewed everything made, and proclaimed "Behold, it is very good." And the evening and the morning were the sixth day.

And on the seventh day God rested from all work.

God's archangel came then, asking, "God, how do you know that what you have created is 'very good'? What are your criteria? On what data do you base your judgment? Just what results were you expecting to attain? And aren't you a little close to the situation to make a fair and unbiased evaluation?"

God thought about these questions all that day and God's rest was greatly disturbed. On the eighth day God said, "Lucifer, go to hell."

Thus was evaluation born in a blaze of glory.

—From Halcolm's *The Real Story of Paradise Lost*

1

Evaluation Use

Both Challenge and Mandate

*T*he human condition: insidious prejudice, stultifying fear of the unknown, con-
tagious avoidance, beguiling distortion of reality, awesomely selective perception, stupefying self-deception, profane rationalization, massive avoidance of truth—all
marvels of evolution's selection of the fittest. Evaluation is our collective effort to outwit
these human propensities—when we choose to use it.

—Halcolm

On a cold November morning in Minnesota, some 15 coffee-clutching people in
various states of wakefulness have gathered to discuss evaluation of a county
welfare-to-work program. Citizen advisory board representatives are present; the
county board and state representatives have arrived; and the internal evaluator is
busy passing out handouts and setting up the PowerPoint presentation. We are
assembled at this early hour to review the past year's evaluation.

The evaluator begins by reviewing the problems getting started—fuzzy program
goals, uncertain funding, incomplete program files, and software inadequacies. Data
collection problems included staff resistance to doing additional paperwork, difficulty finding clients for follow-up interviews, and inconsistent state and county information systems. The evaluation was further hampered by management problems,
staff turnover, unclear decision-making hierarchies, political undercurrents, trying to
do too much, and an impossibly short timeline for reporting. Despite the problems,
the evaluation had been completed and, putting the best face on a difficult situation,

the evaluator explains that "the findings are tentative to be sure, but more than we knew a year ago."

Advisory board members are clearly disappointed. One says, "The data just aren't solid enough." A county commissioner explains why Board decisions have been contrary to evaluation recommendations: "We didn't really get the information we needed when we wanted it and it wasn't what we wanted when we got it." The room is filled with disappointment, frustration, defensiveness, cynicism, and more than a little anger. There are charges, countercharges, budget threats, moments of planning, and longer moments of explaining away problems. The chairperson ends the meeting in exasperation, lamenting: "What do we have to do to get evaluation results we can actually use?"

This book is an outgrowth of, and an answer to, that question.

Evaluation Use as a Critical Societal Issue

If the scene I have described were unique, it would merely represent a frustrating professional problem for the people involved. But if that scene is repeated over and over on many mornings, with many advisory boards, then the question of evaluation use would become what eminent sociologist C. Wright Mills called a critical public issue:

> Issues have to do with matters that transcend these local environments of the individual and the range of his inner life. They have to do with the organization of many such milieux into the institutions of an historical society as a whole. . . . An issue, in fact, often involves a crisis in institutional arrangements (Mills 1959:8–9).

In my judgment, the challenge of using evaluation in appropriate and meaningful ways represents just such a crisis in institutional arrangements. How evaluations are used affects the spending of billions of dollars to fight problems of poverty, disease, ignorance, joblessness, mental anguish, crime, hunger, and inequality. How are programs that combat these societal ills to

be judged? How does one distinguish effective from ineffective programs? And how can evaluations be conducted in ways that lead to use? How do we avoid producing reports that gather dust on bookshelves, unread and unused? These are the questions this book addresses, not just in general, but within a particular framework: *utilization-focused evaluation.*

But first, what are these things called "evaluations" that we hope to see used?

Evaluation as Defined in the *Encyclopedia of Evaluation*

Evaluation is an applied inquiry process for collecting and synthesizing evidence that culminates in conclusions about the state of affairs, value, merit, worth, significance, or quality of a program, product, person, policy, proposal, or plan. Conclusions made in evaluations encompass both an empirical aspect (that something is the case) and a normative aspect (judgment about the value of something). It is the value feature that distinguishes evaluation from other types of inquiry, such as basic science research, clinical epidemiology, investigative journalism, or public polling. (Fournier 2005a:140)

To evaluate something means determining its merit, worth, value, or significance. Program or project evaluations typically involve making the following kinds of judgments: How effective is the program? To what extent has the program been implemented as expected? Were the program's goals achieved? What outcomes and results were achieved by the program? To what extent and in what ways did program participants benefit, if at all? What needs of participants were met? What unanticipated consequences resulted from the program? What are the strengths and weaknesses of the program, and how can it be improved? What worked and what didn't work? What has been learned in this program that might be useful to other programs? To what extent do the benefits of the program provide sufficient value to justify the costs of the program? Should the program's funding be maintained as is, increased, or decreased? Evaluations, then, typically describe and assess what was intended (goals and objectives), what happened that was unintended, what was actually implemented, and what outcomes and results were achieved. The evaluator will then discuss the implications of these findings, sometimes including items for future action and recommendations. In the simplest terms, evaluations are said to answer three questions:

What?

So What?

Now What?

Sometimes these evaluation questions are answered in formal reports. Some evaluative judgments flow from analyzing and discussing data from a program's information system without producing a formal report; indeed, increasingly findings emerge as "the real-time production of streams of evaluative knowledge" (Rist 2006a:6–7; Stame 2006b:vii), rather than as discrete, stand-alone studies. Some evaluation reports are entirely internal to an organization for use by staff and administrators to support ongoing managerial decision making. Other evaluation reports are published or posted on the Internet to meet an obligation for public accountability or to share lessons learned.

The issue of evaluation use has emerged at the interface between science and action, between knowing and doing. It raises fundamental questions about human rationality, decision making, and knowledge applied to creation of a better world. And the issue is not just a concern of researchers. Sometimes it reaches the larger public as in this classic newspaper headline, "Agency Evaluation Reports Disregarded by Legislators Who Requested Them" (see Exhibit 1.1).

A Broader Perspective: Using Information in the Knowledge Age

The challenge of evaluation use epitomizes the more general challenge of knowledge use in our times. Our age—*the Age of Information, Knowledge, and Communications*—has developed the capacity to generate, store, retrieve, transmit, and instantaneously communicate massive amounts of information. Our problem is keeping up with, sorting out, absorbing, prioritizing, and *using* information. Our technological capacity for gathering and computerizing information now far exceeds our human ability to process and make sense out of it all. We're constantly faced with deciding what's worth knowing and what to ignore.

Evaluators are "knowledge workers," a term the great management scholar and consultant Peter Drucker introduced to

What? So What? Now What?

Glenda H. Eoyang, Executive Director of the Human Systems Dynamics Institute in Minnesota, describes how she uses this evaluative framework in managing her own organization.

At the Institute, we use three simple questions to help us distinguish emergencies from the merely emergent, to analyze multiple factors in the moment, and to align our diverse actions toward shared goals. These questions, though simple, are deeply powerful as we shape our work together toward adaptive action.

WHAT? What do we see? What does data tell us? What are the indicators of change or stability? What cues can we capture to see changing patterns as they emerge?

SO WHAT? So, what sense can we make of emerging data? What does it mean to us in this moment and in the future? What effect are current changes likely to have on us, our clients, our extended network, and our field of inquiry and action?

NOW WHAT? What are our options? What are our resources? When and how can we act—individually or collectively—to optimize opportunities in this moment and the next?

We and our clients have used these questions to move together toward decisive action.

A social service agency faced radical changes in public policy that would have a direct effect on their clients and the resources they had available to meet clients' needs. What? So what? Now what?

A medical technology company focused on getting processes under control and ensuring lean, high quality product development and deployment procedures. What? So what? Now what?

An organization in the midst of internal transformation faced backlash from disgruntled workers. What? So what? Now what?

A group of attorneys and their support staff recognized patterns of negative attitudes and disruptive relationships that sucked their energies and distracted them from productive work. What? So what? Now what?

In each of these cases, the three questions helped leadership focus on critical options and effective actions. What emerged was not a sophisticated and complicated plan for an unknowable future. No. What did emerge was a shared understanding of emerging challenges and clear focus on actions that could shift emergencies into emergent possibilities. (Eoyang 2006b)

SOURCE: Reprinted with permission of Glenda Eoyang.

describe anyone who produces knowledge, ideas, and information in contrast to more tangible products and services (Drucker 2003; Lowenstein 2006). The challenge we face is not just producing knowledge but the even greater challenge of getting people to use the knowledge we produce.

Getting people to use what is known has become a critical concern across the different knowledge sectors of society. A major specialty in medicine (compliance research) is dedicated to understanding why so many people don't follow their doctor's orders. Common problems of information use

EXHIBIT 1.1

Newspaper Column on Evaluation Use

Agency Evaluation Reports Disregarded by Legislators Who Had Requested Them

Minnesota lawmakers who mandated that state agencies spend a lot of employee hours and money developing performance evaluation reports pretty much ignored them. . . . The official word from the state legislative auditor's evaluation of the performance evaluation process: Legislators who asked for the reports did not pay much attention to them. They were often full of boring and insignificant details. . . .

Thousands of employee hours and one million taxpayer dollars went into writing the 21 major state agency performance evaluation reports. The auditor reports the sad results:

- Only three of 21 state commissioners thought that the performance reports helped the governor make budget choices regarding their agencies.
- Only seven of 21 agencies were satisfied with the attention given the reports in the House committees reviewing their programs and budgets. And only one agency was satisfied with the attention it received in the Senate.

Agency heads also complained to legislative committees this year that the 1993 law mandating the reports was particularly painful because departments had to prepare new two-year budget requests and program justifications at the same time. That "dual" responsibility resulted in bureaucratic paperwork factories running overtime.

"Our experience is that few, if any, legislators have actually read the valuable information contained in our report . . . ," one agency head told auditors. "The benefits of performance reporting will not materialize if one of the principal audiences is uninterested," said another.

"If the Legislature is not serious about making the report 'the key document' in the budget decision process, it serves little value outside the agency," said a third department head.

Mandating the reports and ignoring them looks like another misguided venture by the 201-member Minnesota Legislature. It is the fifth largest Legislature in the nation and during much of the early part of this year's five-month session had little to do. With time on their hands, lawmakers could have devoted more time to evaluation reports. But if the reports were dull and of little value in evaluating successes of programs, can they be blamed for not reading them?

Gary Dawson, "State Journal" column
Saint Paul Pioneer Press August 7, 1995: 4B

underlie trying to get people to use seat belts, quit smoking, begin exercising, eat properly, and pay attention to evaluation findings. In the fields of nutrition, energy conservation, education, criminal justice, financial investment, human services, corporate management, public administration, philanthropy, international development—the list could go on and on—a central problem, often *the* central problem, is getting people to apply what is already known.

In agriculture, a major activity of university extension services is trying to get farmers to adopt new scientific methods.

Experienced agricultural extension agents like to tell the story of a young agent telling a farmer about the latest food production techniques. As he begins to offer advice the farmer interrupts him and says, "No sense telling me all those new ideas, young man. I'm not doing half of what I know I should be doing now."

I remember talking with a time management trainer who had done a follow-up study of people who had taken her workshop series. Few were applying the time management techniques they had learned. When she compared the graduates of her time management training with a sample of nonparticipants, the differences were not in how people in each group managed their time. The time management graduates had quickly fallen back into old habits. The difference was *the graduates felt much guiltier about how they wasted time.*

Research on adolescent pregnancy illustrates another dimension of the knowledge use problem. In a classic study, adolescent-health specialist Michael Resnik (1984) interviewed teenagers who became pregnant. He found very few cases in which the problem was a lack of information about contraception, about pregnancy, or about how to avoid pregnancies. The problem was that teens just didn't apply what they knew. "There is an incredible gap between the knowledge and the application of that knowledge. In so many instances it's heartbreaking—they have the knowledge, the awareness, and the understanding, but somehow it doesn't apply to them" (p. 15).

Sometimes the stakes are incredibly high, as in using information to prevent genocide. Between April and June 1994, an estimated 800,000 Rwandans were killed in the space of 100 days. Lieutenant General Roméo Dallaire headed the small UN Peacekeeping Force in Rwanda. He filed detailed reports about the unspeakable horrors he and his troops witnessed. He documented the geographic scope of the massacre and the numbers of people being slaughtered. In reporting these findings to the UN officials and Western governments, Dallaire pleaded for more peacekeepers and additional trucks to transport his woefully ill-equipped force. He sought authority to seize Hutu arms caches, but the narrow UN mandate didn't allow him to disarm the militias. As bodies filled the streets and rivers, the general tried in vain to attract the world's attention to what was going on. In an assessment that military experts now accept as realistic, Dallaire argued that with 5,000 well-equipped soldiers and a free hand to fight Hutu power, he could bring the genocide to a rapid halt. The United Nations, constrained by the domestic and international politics of Security Council members, ignored him. He asked the United States to block the Hutu radio transmissions that were provoking and guiding the massacre. The Clinton administration refused to do even that.

Instead, following the deaths of 10 Belgian peacekeepers assigned to protect the President of Rwanda, Dallaire's forces were cut to a mere 500 men, far too few to make a difference as one of the most horrific genocides in modern history unfolded. Dallaire, frustrated and disheartened by the passive attitude of world leaders, repeatedly confronted his superiors, trying to get them to deal with the data about what was going on, all to no avail. The international community occupied itself with arguing about the definition of genocide, placing blame elsewhere, and finding reasons not to intervene.

The highly respected Danish international development agency, Danida, sponsored a major retrospective evaluation of the Rwanda genocide seeking to extract lessons that might help the world avoid future such tragedies (Danida 2005). The United Nations (1996) undertook its own investigation and Dallaire and Beardsley (2004) have provided their own account of what happened and why. The point, for our purposes, is that the Rwanda story included the refusal of international agencies and world leaders to take seriously and use the data they were given. Those who had the responsibility and capacity to act failed to pay attention to the evidence Dallaire provided them about the deteriorating situation and the consequences of a failure to act. While his efforts involved the highest stakes possible—saving human lives—evaluators across a broad range of sectors face the daily challenge of getting decision makers to take evidence of ineffectiveness seriously and act on the implications of the evidence. It was precisely this larger relevance of the Rwanda example that led to Dalliare being invited to keynote 2,330 evaluation professionals from 55 countries at the joint Canadian Evaluation Society and the American Evaluation Association (AEA) international conference in Toronto in 2005. Following the keynote, he was awarded the Presidents' Prize for *Speaking Truth to Power*. This award symbolizes one of the most important roles evaluators can be called on to play, a role that goes beyond technical competence and methodological rigor, a role that recognizes the inherently political nature of evaluation in a world where knowledge is power—the role of speaking truth to power.

The High Stakes of Evaluation Use

When the space shuttle Columbia disintegrated on February 1, 2002, killing all seven astronauts aboard, a comprehensive independent investigation ensued by a 13-member board of inquiry. While the direct mechanical problem was damage caused by a foam tile that came loose during liftoff, the more basic cause, investigators concluded, was the National Aeronautics and Space Administration's (NASA's) own culture, a culture of complacency nurtured by a string of successes since the 1986 Challenger disaster, which also killed seven. This led to a habit of relaxing safety standards to meet financial and time constraints, for example, defining a problem as insignificant so as not to require a fix that would cause delay. The Columbia Accident Investigation Board (2003) concluded in its 248-page report that the space agency lacked effective checks and balances, did not have an independent safety program, and had not demonstrated the characteristics of a learning organization.

In addition to detailing the technical factors behind Columbia's breakup just minutes before its scheduled landing at the end of a 16-day science mission, the board's report laid out the cultural factors behind NASA's failings. It said NASA mission managers fell into the habit of accepting as normal some flaws in the shuttle system and tended to ignore, not recognize, or *not want to hear about* such problems even though they might foreshadow catastrophe. Such repeating patterns meant that flawed practices embedded in NASA's organizational system continued for years and made substantial contributions to both accidents, the report concluded. During Columbia's last mission, NASA managers missed opportunities to evaluate possible damage to the craft's heat shield from a strike on the left wing by flying foam insulation. Such insulation strikes had occurred on previous missions and, the report said, engineers within NASA had documented the dangers involved, but the evidence they submitted and the accompanying warnings they sent up the chain-of-command were ignored. This attitude of ignoring data that led to conclusions they didn't like also contributed to the lack of interest among NASA managers in getting spy satellite photos of Columbia, images that might have identified the extent of damage on the shuttle. Over time, NASA managers had come to accept more and more risk in order to meet scheduled launch deadlines. But most of all, the report concluded, there was ineffective leadership that discouraged dissenting views on safety issues, ignored the evaluation findings of safety engineers, and ultimately created blind spots about the risk to the space shuttle of the foam insulation impact.

Sometimes, as in the examples of the Rwanda genocide and the Columbia shuttle disaster, important data are ignored. In other cases, the data-generating process itself is distorted and manipulated to create biased and distorted findings. Regardless of what one thinks of the U.S. invasion of Iraq to depose Saddam Hussein, both those who supported the war and those who opposed it have come to agree that the intelligence used to justify the invasion was deeply flawed and systematically distorted (U.S. Senate Select Committee on Intelligence 2004). Under intense political pressure to show sufficient grounds for military action, those charged with analyzing and evaluating intelligence data began doing what is sometimes called cherry-picking or stovepiping—selecting and passing on only those data that support preconceived positions and ignoring or repressing all contrary evidence (Hersh 2003). This is a problem of the *misuse of evaluation findings*, the shadow side of the challenge of increasing utility.

Getting evaluations used begins with having valid, accurate, relevant, and balanced findings *that are worth using*. Then, as the Rwanda example demonstrates, those with data have to get the attention of those who will make crucial decisions. As the NASA story shows, this is not just a matter of reaching individual decision makers but dealing with the whole culture of organizations to create a learning environment that is receptive to data-based decision making. And as the problem of Iraq prewar intelligence shows, evaluators committed to accurate and balanced reporting will have to deal with political obstacles and speak truth to power.

These are high-profile examples of evaluation neglect and misuse, but the challenges of getting evaluations used aren't limited to such obviously high stakes national and international initiatives. Look at today's local news. What decisions are being reported about programs and policies in your community—decisions by city councils, school boards, county commissions, legislative committees, not-for-profit agencies, philanthropic foundations, and businesses? What does the news story tell you about the data that informed those decisions? What evidence was used? What was the quality of that evidence? How were data generated and presented as part of the decision-making process?

Decisions abound. Policy choices are all around us. Programs aimed at solving problems exist in every sector of society. And behind every one of these decisions, policy choices, and program initiatives is an evaluation story. What evaluative evidence, if any, was used in the decision making? What was the quality of that evidence? Asking these questions is at the foundation of *utilization-focused evaluation.*

These questions also have relevance at the personal level. Some degree of evaluative thinking is inherently involved in every decision you make. How did you decide what computer to purchase? Or what course to take? How do you and those you know make decisions about dating, marriage, nutrition, exercise, lifestyle, where to live, what to do for leisure, who to vote for (and whether to vote at all), what movie to see (and whether you thought it was any good), what books or magazines to read, when to see a doctor, and so on. We are all evaluators. But we are not all good at it, not always systematic or thoughtful, careful about seeking out and weighing evidence, and explicit about the criteria and values that underpin our interpretations of whatever evidence we have. Thus, as we consider how to enhance program decision making through systematic evaluation, you may pause now and again to consider the implications of this way of thinking for decisions you make in your personal life. Or maybe not. How will you decide?

These examples of the challenges of putting knowledge to use are meant to set a general context for the specific concern of this book: generating high-quality and highly relevant evaluation findings and then actually getting those findings used for program decision making and improvement. Although the problem of information use remains central to our age, we are not without knowledge about what to do. We've learned a few things about overcoming our human resistance to new knowledge and change, and over the past three

decades of professional evaluation practice, we've learned a great deal about how to increase evaluation use. Before presenting what's been learned, let's set the context.

Historical Precedents

Today's professional evaluators stand on the shoulders of much earlier practitioners though they didn't necessarily call what they did evaluation. The emperor of China established formal proficiency testing for public officials some 4,000 years ago. The book of Daniel in the Old Testament of the *Bible* opens with the story of an educational program evaluation in which King Nebuchadnezzar of Babylon created a 3-year civil service training program for Hebrew youth after his capture of Jerusalem. When Daniel objected to eating the King's meat and wine, the program director, Melzar, agreed to an experimental comparison to evaluate how eating a kosher diet might affect the "countenance" of Daniel and his friends, Hananiah, Mishael, and Azariah. When they remained healthy after the pilot test period, he agreed to a permanent change for those who eschewed the Babylonian diet—the earliest documentation of using evaluation findings to change a program's design.

Once you start looking, you can turn up all kinds of historical precedents for evaluation.

The great Lewis and Clark expedition through the central and western American wilderness had as its purpose evaluating the suitability of the interior rivers for transportation and the value of the land for settlement. The Louisiana Purchase, which they would reconnoiter, covered more than 2 million square kilometers of land

Evaluating a Venture in Colonial America

In the 1730s, the settlement of the colony of Georgia by the English poor began as a philanthropic venture in colonial America complete with a detailed proposal ("blueprint"), grandiose goals, quite measurable outcomes, testable hypotheses about how to achieve outcomes (what we'd call today a "theory of change"), annual plans, internal evaluation reports from the staff to the Board of Trustees, independent site visits, multiple and conflicting stakeholders, divisive politics, bureaucratic ineptitude and micromanaging, pointed participant feedback about problems, a major problem with dropouts, ongoing efforts at project improvement, and ultimately, a judgment that the experiment failed, accompanied by a lofty explanation from the funders about why they were compelled to pull the plug, to wit:

"At first it was a trial, now it is an experiment; and certainly no man or society need be ashamed to own, that from unforeseen emergencies their hypothesis did misgive; and no person of judgment would censure for want of success where the proposal was probable; but all the world would exclaim against that person or society who, through mistaken notions of honor or positiveness of temper, would persist in pushing an experiment contrary to all probability, to the ruin of the adventurers." (Boorstin 1958:96)

extending from the Mississippi River to the Rocky Mountains, essentially doubling the size of the United States. They would travel all the way to the Pacific Ocean. On June 20, 1803, President Thomas Jefferson launched the exploration thusly:

> The Object of your mission is to explore the Missouri river & such principal streams of it as by its course and communication with the waters of the Pacific ocean, whether the Columbia, Oregon, Colorado or any other river may offer the most direct and practicable water communication across this continent for the purpose of commerce.

The reports Lewis and Clark sent back to Jefferson were, for all intents and purposes, evaluation reports addressing the objectives set forth and much, much more. In effect, President Jefferson needed to find out what he had purchased, what we might call a *retrospective evaluation*. The reports of Lewis and Clark went well beyond their narrow, stated mission and included extensive inventories of plants and animals, including many new species, details about

indigenous peoples, maps of the land, indeed, everything they did and all that they encountered over a 3-year period through lands that later became 11 states. They might be awarded a posthumous Guinness World Record for the evaluation that most exceeded its original scope of work. The impressive Saint Louis Gateway Arch on the banks of the Mississippi River, commemorating the Westward Expansion opened up by the Lewis and Clark Expedition, could be considered a monument to the impact of evaluation findings.

You get the idea. Just because something wasn't officially labeled an evaluation report doesn't mean it didn't serve an evaluative function. Lewis and Clark gathered and reported extensive data to judge the merit, worth, significance, and value of the Louisiana Territory. Their descriptive data and judgments affected congressional policy, executive directives, and federal appropriations. If it reads like an evaluation, serves evaluative functions, and gets used like an evaluation, we might call it an evaluation.

Thomas Jefferson was also among the recipients of another evaluation report, this one well before he became president, indeed, before the American Revolution. Jefferson and other founding fathers of the United States had become knowledge-able about and impressed with the Iroquois republic, a Native American people in the Northeastern part of North America, which had continuously existed since the fourteenth or fifteenth century. The Iroquois Constitution, known as "The Great Law of Peace," was an orally transmitted constitution for the union of five (later six) Indian nations: Mohawk, Onondagam Seneca, Oneida, Cayuga, and the Tscarora. Jefferson, Benjamin Franklin, John Adams, and George Washington were all familiar with the Iroquois polity and were influ-enced by its key ideas and processes in conceptualizing American government (Johansen 1998; 1987; Idarius 1998). In 1774, the Virginia Colony offered the Iroquois Confederacy scholarships to send six of their young men to Williamsburg College to be educated. The Iroquois Chiefs responded that they had already had some of their young men attend such a college and their evaluation of the results did not predispose them to accept the Virginia offer, which they, in fact, declined:

> Several of our Young People were formally brought up at the Colleges of the Northern Provinces; they were instructed in all of your Sciences; but, when they returned to us, they were bad runners, ignorant of every means of living in the Woods, unable to bear either Cold or Hunger, knew neither how to build a Cabin, take a Deer, or kill an Enemy, spoke our language imperfectly, were there-fore neither fit for Hunters, Warriors, nor Counsellors, they were totally good for nothing. (Hopkins 1898:240)

Now that's a clear, evidence-based, mince-no-words, evaluative judgment!

You never know where an evaluation report may turn up. Doing archival research in Tanzania, I found scores of reports by anthropologists, colonial managers, and English academics describing and assessing various and sundry failed attempts to settle the nomadic cattle-herding Wagogo people of the Dodoma Region in what had been central Tanganyika. My assignment was to wrestle lessons learned from the many failed settlement schemes spanning some 50 years of colonial rule so that the modern demo-cratic government under President Julius Nyerere could find a new, more humane, and effective approach. None of the reports were titled "evaluations," but all of them were fundamentally evaluative.

I stumbled across an explicit but still secret evaluation visiting the Hiroshima Museum while conducting evaluation training at Hiroshima University. One of the exhibits there describes how the American military's "Target Committee" selected Hiroshima for trying out the first atomic bomb. Allied forces were engaged in heavy bombing throughout Japan, espe-cially in and around Tokyo. Since the destructive power of the atomic bomb was unknown, a small number of major Japanese cities were excluded from routine bombing and carefully photographed with inventories of buildings, infrastructure, and industries. On August 6, 1945, the nuclear weapon *Little Boy* was dropped on Hiroshima by the *Enola Gay*, a U.S. Air Force B-29 bomber, which was altered specifically to hold the bomb, killing an estimated 80,000 people and heavily dam-aging 80 percent of the city. An American military team subsequently completed a full evaluation of the bomb's damage and impact but, according to the Museum display, that report has never been made public. Whether and how it was used is also, therefore, unknown.

Using Evaluative Thinking: A Transdisciplinary Perspective

Experience in thinking can be won, like all experience in doing something, only through practice.

—Philosopher Hannah Arendt (1963:4)

The historical examples of evaluations I have just reviewed provide some sense of the long and diverse history of evaluation reporting, but even more important, they illustrate the centrality of *evaluative thinking* in human affairs and inquiries of all kinds. Using evaluative thinking and reasoning is ultimately more important and has more far-reaching implications than merely using evaluation reports. This is why eminent philosopher and evaluation theorist Michael Scriven (2005b, 2004) has characterized evaluation as a *transdiscipline*, because every discipline, profession, and field engages in some form of evaluation, the most prominent example being, perhaps, evaluations of students taking courses and completing disciplinary programs of study, and refereed journals in which new research is evaluated by peers to determine if it is worthy of publication. Evaluation is a discipline that serves other disciplines even as it is a discipline unto itself; thus its emergent transdisciplinary status (Coryn and Hattie 2006). Statistics, logic, and evaluation are examples of transdisciplines in that their methods, ways of thinking, and knowledge base are used in other areas of inquiry, e.g., education, health, social work, engineering, environmental studies, and so on (Mathison

2005:422). In studying evaluation use, then, we will be looking at not only the use of evaluation findings and reports but also what it means to use evaluative thinking.

The Emergence of Program Evaluation as a Formal Field of Professional Practice

There is nothing more difficult to take in hand, more perilous to conduct, or more uncertain in its success, than to take the lead in the introduction of a new order of things. Because the innovator has for enemies all those who have done well under the old conditions and lukewarm defenders in those who may do well under the new.

—Advice from *The Prince* (1513) Niccolo Machiavelli (1469–1527)

While evaluative thinking, inquiry, and judgments are as old as and inherent to our human species, formal and systematic evaluation as a field of professional practice is relatively recent. Like many poor people, evaluation in the United States has grown up in the "projects"—federal projects spawned by the Great Society legislation of the 1960s. When the federal government of the United States began to take a major role in alleviating poverty, hunger, and joblessness during the Depression of the 1930s, the closest thing to evaluation was the employment of a few jobless academics to write program histories. Some important evaluations began to be done after World War II, for example, an evaluation of the First Salzberg Seminar conducted by distinguished anthropologist Margaret Mead for the W. K. Kellogg Foundation in 1947 (Russon and Ryback 2003; Greene 2003; Patton 2003). In 1959, the U.S. Department of Health, Education, and Welfare published guidelines for evaluation (Herzog 1959). Preeminent evaluation researcher and author Carol Weiss has recounted finding a number of published evaluation studies from the late 1950s and early 1960s that informed her own first evaluation effort (Weiss 2004:163). But it was not until the massive federal expenditures on an awesome assortment of programs during the 1960s and 1970s that accountability in government began to mean more than financial audits or political head counts of opponents and proponents. Demand for systematic empirical evaluation of the effectiveness of government programs grew as government programs grew (Shadish and Luellen 2005; Aucoin and Heinzman 2000; House 1993; Wye and Sonnichsen 1992). At the same time, fear of, resistance to, and a backlash against evaluation accompanied evaluation's growth as some program staff and agency managers looked on evaluation as a personal attack and feared that evaluation was merely a ruse for what was really a program termination agenda.

Educational evaluation accompanied the expansion of access to public schooling. Joseph Rue's comparative study of spelling performance by 33,000 students in 1897 was a precursor of educational evaluation, which remains dominated by achievement testing. During the cold war, after the Soviet Union launched Sputnik in 1957, calls for better educational assessments accompanied a critique born of fear that the education gap was even larger than the "missile gap." Demand for independent evaluation accelerated with the growing realization, in the years after the 1954 Supreme Court *Brown* decision requiring racial integration of schools, that "separate and unequal" was still the norm rather than the exception. Passage of the U.S. Elementary and Secondary Education Act in 1965 contributed greatly to more

comprehensive approaches to evaluation. The massive influx of federal money aimed at desegregation, innovation, compensatory education, greater equality of opportunity, teacher training, and higher student achievement was accompanied by calls for evaluation data to assess the effects on the nation's children: To what extent did these changes really make an educational difference?

But education was only one arena in the War on Poverty of the 1960s. Great Society programs from the Office of Economic Opportunity were aimed at nothing less than the elimination of poverty. The creation of large-scale federal health programs, including community mental health centers, was coupled with a mandate for evaluation, often at a level of 1 percent to 3 percent of program budgets. Other major programs were created in housing, employment, services integration, community planning, urban renewal, welfare, and so on—the whole of which came to be referred to as "butter" (in contrast to "guns") expenditures. In the 1970s, these Great Society programs collided head on with the Vietnam War, rising inflation, increasing taxes, and the fall from glory of Keynesian economics. All in all, it was what sociologists and social historians, with a penchant for understatement, would characterize as "a period of rapid social and economic change."

Program evaluation as a distinct field of professional practice was born of two lessons from this period of large-scale social experimentation and government intervention: first, the realization that there is not enough money to do all the things that need doing and, second, even if there were enough money, it takes more than money to solve complex human and social problems. As not everything can be done, there must be a basis for deciding which things are worth doing. Enter evaluation.

High Hopes for Evaluation

One of the most appealing ideas of our century is the notion that science can be put to work to provide solutions to social problems.

—Political Sociologist Hans Zetterman (quoted in Suchman [1967:1])

Evaluation and Rationality

The great sociologist Max Weber (1864–1920), founder of organizational sociology, predicted that modern institutions would be the foundation of ever-increasing rationality in human affairs. "Modernity, Weber said, is the progressive disenchantment of the world. Superstitions disappear; cultures grow more homogeneous; life becomes increasing rational" (Menand 2006:84). Evaluation epitomizes Weber's vision of rationality in the modern world. Donald Campbell (1917–1996) picked up the mantle of Weber's work on the sociology of science and rearticulated his vision of modernity, explicitly incorporating evaluation as a cornerstone of rationality, and expressed in the ideal of an "experimenting society":

> It would be an *active society* preferring exploratory innovation to inaction. . . . It will be an *evolutionary, learning society*. . . . It will be an *honest society*, committed to *reality testing*, to self-criticism, to avoiding self-deception. It will say it like it is, face up to the facts, be undefensive and open in self-presentation. (Campbell 1999:13)

The ascendance of applied social and behavioral sciences was driven by hope that knowledge could be used rationally to make the world a better place, that is, that social sciences would yield *practical knowledge* (Stehr 1992). In 1961, Harvard-educated President John F. Kennedy welcomed scientists to the White House as never before. Scientific perspectives were taken into account in the writing of new social legislation. Economists, historians, psychologists, political scientists, and sociologists were all welcomed into the public arena to share in the reshaping of modern postindustrial society. They dreamed of and worked for a new order of rationality in government—a rationality undergirded by social scientists who, if not exemplifying Plato's philosopher-kings themselves, were at least ministers to philosopher-kings. Carol Weiss has captured the optimism of that period:

> There was much hoopla about the rationality that social science would bring to the untidy world of government. It would provide hard data for planning . . . and give cause-and-effect theories for policy making, so that statesmen would know which variables to alter in order to effect the desired outcomes. It would bring to the assessment of alternative policies a knowledge of relative costs and benefits so that decision-makers could select the options with the highest payoff. And once policies were in operation, it would provide objective evaluation of their effectiveness so that necessary modifications could be made to improve performance. (Weiss 1977:4)

While pragmatists turned to evaluation as a commonsensical way to figure out what works and is worth funding, visionaries were conceptualizing evaluation as the centerpiece of a new kind of society: "the experimenting society." Donald T. Campbell gave voice to this vision in his 1971 address to the American Psychological Association:

> The experimenting society will be one which will vigorously try out proposed solutions to recurrent problems, which will make

hard-headed and multidimensional evaluations of the outcomes, and which will move on to other alternatives when evaluation shows one reform to have been ineffective or harmful.
> We do not have such a society today. (Campbell 1991:223)

Early visions for evaluation, then, focused on evaluation's expected role in guiding funding decisions and differentiating the wheat from the chaff in federal programs. But as evaluations were implemented, a new role emerged: helping improve programs as they were implemented. The Great Society programs floundered on a host of problems: management weaknesses, cultural issues, and failure to take into account the enormously complex systems that contributed to poverty. Wanting to help is not the same as knowing how to help; likewise, having the money to help is not the same as knowing how to spend money in a helpful way. Many War on Poverty programs turned out to be patronizing, controlling, dependency generating, insulting, inadequate, misguided, over-promised, wasteful, and mismanaged. Evaluators were called on not only to offer final judgments about the overall effectiveness of programs but also to gather process data and provide feedback to help solve problems along the way.

By the mid-1970s, interest in evaluation had grown to the point where two professional organizations were established: the academically oriented Evaluation Research Society and the practitioner-oriented Evaluation Network. In 1984, they merged as the American Evaluation Association. By that time, interest in evaluation had become international with establishment of the Canadian Evaluation Society and the Australasian Evaluation Society.

One manifestation of the scope, pervasiveness, and penetration of the high hopes for evaluation is the number of evaluation studies conducted. As early as 1976, the

Congressional Sourcebook on Federal Program Evaluations contained 1,700 citations of program evaluation reports issued by 18 U.S. executive branch agencies and the General Accounting Office (GAO) during fiscal years 1973 through 1975 (Office of Program Analysis, GAO 1976:1). In 1977, federal agencies spent $64 million on program evaluation and more than $1.1 billion on social research and development (Abramson 1978). The third edition of the Compendium of Health and Human Services Evaluation Studies (HHS 1983) contained 1,435 entries. The fourth volume of the U.S. Comptroller General's directory of Federal Evaluations (GAO 1981) identified 1,429 evaluative studies from various U.S. federal agencies completed in fiscal year 1980. While the large number of and substantial funding for evaluations suggested great prosperity and acceptance, under the surface and behind the scenes a crisis was building—a utilization crisis.

Reality Check:
Evaluations Largely Unused

By the end of the 1960s, it was becoming clear that evaluations of "Great Society" social programs were largely ignored or politicized. The utopian hopes for a scientific and rational society had somehow failed to be realized. The landing of the first human on the moon came and went, but poverty persisted despite the 1960s "war" on it—and research was still not being used as the basis for government decision making. While all types of applied social science suffered from underuse (Weiss 1977, 1972a), nonuse seemed to be particularly characteristic of evaluation studies. Ernest House (1972) put it this way: "Producing data is one thing! Getting it used is quite another" (p. 412). Williams and Evans (1969) wrote that "in the final analysis, the test of the effectiveness

of outcome data is its impact on implemented policy. By this standard, there is a dearth of successful evaluation studies" (p. 119). Wholey et al. (1970) concluded that "the recent literature is unanimous in announcing the general failure of evaluation to affect decision making in a significant way" (p. 46). They went on to note that their own study "found the same absence of successful evaluations noted by other authors" (Wholey et al. 1970:48). There was little evidence to indicate that government planning offices had succeeded in linking social research and decision making. Seymour Deitchman (1976), in his *Tale of Social Research and Bureaucracy*, did not mince words: "The impact of the research on the most important affairs of state was, with few exceptions, nil" (p. 390). Weidman et al. (1973) concluded that "on those rare occasions when evaluations studies have been used . . . the little use that has occurred [has been] fortuitous rather than planned" (p. 15). In 1972, the eminent evaluation scholar Carol Weiss viewed underutilization as one of the foremost problems in evaluation research: "A review of evaluation experience suggests that evaluation results have not exerted significant influence on program decisions" (Weiss 1972c:10–11).

This conclusion was echoed by four prominent commissions and study committees: the U.S. House of Representatives Committee on Government Operations, Research and Technical Programs Subcommittee (1967); the Young Committee report published by the National Academy of Sciences (1968); the Report of the Special Commission on the Social Sciences for the National Science Foundation (1968); and the Social Science Research Council's prospective on the Behavioral and Social Sciences (1969).

British economist L. J. Sharpe (1977) reviewed the European literature and commission reports on use of social scientific

An Evaluation Report Disappears into the Void—And an Area of Inquiry Is Born

Sociologist and Harvard professor Carol Weiss is recognized in the *Encyclopedia of Evaluation* as the "Founding Mother" of evaluation (Mathison 2005:449). She was also the first to give prominence to the issue of evaluation use, a deep-seated interest arising from her experience in the 1960s evaluating a government program that was part of the "War on Poverty."

"I was asked to evaluate a program in central Harlem. One of the program's goals was to bring black college students from universities in the south to work in central Harlem, to work in the schools, the hospitals and social agencies. They were trained and then they spent the year working in the community. When I finished my evaluation of the Harlem program, the report came out in 3 volumes. We sent copies of the report to Washington: I never heard a word from them! I had the feeling I could have just dumped it into the ocean and it would have made no difference. So, I asked myself: 'Why did they support and fund this evaluation if they were not going to pay any attention to it?' That's how I got interested in the uses of research: What was going on? What could researchers—or anyone else—do to encourage people to pay more attention to research?" (www.gse.harvard.edu/news/features/weiss09102001.html)

Weiss subsequently began studying and writing about knowledge utilization (Weiss 1977) and became one of the most influential contributors to our understandings of evaluation use, policy formulation, and organizational decision making (Alkin 2004). She has been one of the most visible and influential voices for the idea that cumulative evaluative evidence can contribute to significant program and policy changes expressed in the aphorism: *In Evidence Lies Change* (Graff and Christou 2001). Bottom line: "Utility is what evaluation is all about" (Weiss 2004:161).

knowledge and reached a decidedly gloomy conclusion:

> We are brought face to face with the fact that it has proved very difficult to uncover many instances where social science research has had a clear and direct effect on policy even when it has been specifically commissioned by government. (P. 45)

Ronald Havelock (1980) of the Knowledge Transfer Institute generalized that "there is a gap between the world of research and the world of routine organizational practice, regardless of the field" (p. 13). The same conclusions came forth time and again from different fields:

> At the moment there seems to be no indication that evaluation, although the law of the land, contributes anything to educational practice, other than headaches for the researcher, threats for the innovators and depressing articles for journals devoted to evaluation. (Rippey 1973:9)

More recent utilization studies continue to show low levels of research use in government decision making (Landry, Lamari, and Amara 2003)

It can hardly come as a surprise, then, that support for evaluation began to decline. During the Reagan Administration in the 1980s, the U.S. GAO found that federal evaluation received fewer resources and that "findings from both large and small studies have become less easily available for use by the Congress and the public" (GAO 1987:4). In both 1988 and 1992, the GAO prepared status reports on program evaluation to inform changing executive branch administrations at the federal level.

We found a 22-percent decline in the number of professional staff in agency program evaluation units between 1980 and 1984. A follow-up study of 15 units that had been active in 1980 showed an additional 12-percent decline in the number of professional staff between 1984 and 1988. Funds for program evaluation also dropped substantially between 1980 and 1984 (down by 37 percent in constant 1980 dollars). . . . Discussions with the Office of Management and Budget offer no indication that the executive branch investment in program evaluation showed any meaningful overall increase from 1988 to 1992. (GAO 1992a:7)

The GAO went on to conclude that its 1988 recommendations to enhance the federal government's evaluation function had gone unheeded: "The effort to rebuild the government's evaluation capacity that we called for in our 1988 transition series report has not been carried out" (GAO 1992a:7). Here, ironically, we have an evaluation report on evaluation going unused.

In 1995, the GAO provided another report to the U.S. Senate on Program Evaluation subtitled "Improving the Flow of Information to Congress." GAO analysts conducted follow-up case studies of three major federal program evaluations: the Comprehensive Child Development Program, the Community Health Centers Program, and the Chapter 1 Elementary and Secondary Education Act aimed at providing compensatory education services to low-income students. The analysts concluded that

> lack of information does not appear to be the main problem. Rather, the problem seems to be that available information is not organized and communicated effectively. Much of the available information did not reach the [appropriate Senate] Committee, or reached it in a form that was too highly aggregated to be useful or that was difficult to digest. (GAO 1995:39)

Many factors affect evaluation use in Congress, but politics is always a dominant factor (Chelimsky 2007; 2006a, 2006b; Julnes and Rog 2007; Mohan and Sullivan 2007). Evaluation use throughout the U.S. federal government continued its spiral of decline through the early 1990s (Popham 1995; Wargo 1995; Chelimsky 1992). In many federal agencies, the emphasis shifted from program evaluation to inspection, auditing, and investigations (Smith 1992; Hendricks, Mangano, and Moran 1990). Then came attention to and adoption of performance monitoring for accountability and the picture changed dramatically.

New Directions in Accountability: Reinventing Government

A predominant theme of the 1995 International Evaluation Conference in Vancouver was worldwide interest in reducing government programs and making remaining programs more effective and accountable. Decline in support for government programs was fueled by the widespread belief that such efforts were ineffective and wasteful. While the Great Society and War on Poverty programs of the 1960s had been founded on good intentions and high expectations, they came to be perceived as a failure. The "needs assessments" that had provided the rationales for those original programs had found that the poor, the sick, the homeless, and the uneducated—the needy of all kinds—needed services. So services and programs were created. Thirty years down the road from those original efforts, and billions of dollars later, most social indicators revealed little improvement. Poverty statistics, rates of homelessness, hard core unemployment and underemployment, multigenerational welfare recipients, urban degradation, and crime rates combined to raise questions about the effectiveness of services. Reports on effective programs (e.g., Guttmann and Sussman 1995; Kennedy School of Government 1995; Schorr 1988) received relatively little media attention compared with the relentless press about waste and ineffectiveness (Wortman 1995). In the 1990s, growing concerns about federal budget deficits and runaway entitlement costs intensified the debate about the effectiveness of government programs. Both conservatives and liberals were faced with public demands to know what had been achieved by all the programs created and all the money spent. The call for greater accountability became a watershed flowing at every level—national, state, and local; public sector, not-for-profit agencies, and the private sector (Mohan and Sullivan 2007; Chelimsky 2006a; Harvard Family Research Project 1996a, 1996b).

Clear answers were not forthcoming. Few programs could provide data on results achieved and outcomes attained. Internal accountability had come to center on how funds were spent (inputs monitoring), eligibility requirements (who gets services and client characteristics), how many people get services, what activities they participate in, and how many complete the program. These indicators of inputs, client characteristics, activities, and outputs (program completion) measured whether providers were following government rules and regulations rather than whether desired results were being achieved. Control had come to be exercised through audits, licensing, and service contracts rather than through measuring outcomes. The consequence was to make providers and practitioners compliance-oriented rather than results-focused. Programs were rewarded for doing the paperwork well

rather than making a difference in clients' lives.

Public skepticism turned to deep-seated cynicism. Polling data showed a widespread perception that "nothing works." As an aside, and in all fairness, this perception is not unique to the late twentieth century. In the nineteenth century, Spencer traced 32 acts of the British Parliament and discovered that 29 produced effects contrary to those intended (Edison 1983:5). Given today's public cynicism, three effective programs out of 32 might be considered a pretty good record.

More damning still, in modern times, the perception has grown that no relationship exists between the amount of money spent on a problem and the results accomplished, an observation made with a sense of despair by economist John Brandl in his keynote address to the AEA in New Orleans in 1988. Brandl, a professor in the Hubert H. Humphrey Institute of Public Affairs at the University of Minnesota (formerly its Director), was present at the creation of many human services programs during his days at the old Department of Health, Education and Welfare (HEW). He created the interdisciplinary Evaluation Methodology training program at the University of Minnesota. He later moved from being a policy analyst to being a policy formulator as a Minnesota state legislator. His opinions carried the weight of both scholarship and experience. In his keynote address to professional evaluators, he opined that no demonstrable relationship exists between program funding levels and impact, that is, between inputs and outputs; more money spent does not mean higher quality or greater results.

In a later article, Brandl updated his analysis. While his immediate focus was on Minnesota state government, his comments characterize general concerns about the effectiveness of government programs in the 1990s:

> The great government bureaucracies of Minnesota and the rest of America today are failing for the same reason that the formerly Communist governments in Europe fell a few years ago. . . . There is no systematic accountability. People are not regularly inspired to do good work, rewarded for outstanding performance, or penalized for not accomplishing their tasks.
>
> In bureaus, people are expected to do well because the rules tell them to do so. Indeed, often in bureaus here and abroad, able, idealistic workers become disillusioned and burned-out by a system that is not oriented to produce excellent results. No infusion of management was ever going to make operations of the Lenin shipyard in Gdansk effective.
>
> Maybe—I would say surely—until systematic accountability is built into government, no management improvements will do the job. (Brandl 1994:13A)

Similar indictments of government effectiveness became the foundation for efforts at Performance Monitoring, Total Quality Management, Reengineering Government, Management by Objectives (MBO), Reinventing Government, and Managing for Results. Such public sector initiatives made greater accountability and performance monitoring, and increased use of evaluation, central to reform in U.S. federal and state governments, as well as governments around the world, notably Australia, Canada, New Zealand, and the United Kingdom (Moynihan 2006; Rogers 2006; Sears 2006). In this vein, Exhibit 1.2 illustrates the premises for results-oriented government as promulgated by Osborne and Gaebler (1992) in their influential and best-selling book *Reinventing Government*.

In the United States, the Clinton/Gore Administration's effort to "reinvent government" led to the 1993 Government Performance and Results Act (GPRA). This major legislation aimed to shift the focus of government decision making and accountability away from a preoccupation with reporting on activities to a focus on the results of those activities, such as real gains in employability, safety, responsiveness, or program quality. Under GPRA, U.S. federal government agencies are required to

---

EXHIBIT 1.2
Premises of Reinventing Government

- What gets measured gets done.
- If you don't measure results, you can't tell success from failure.
- If you can't see success, you can't reward it.
- If you can't reward success, you're probably rewarding failure.
- If you can't see success, you can't learn from it.
- If you can't recognize failure, you can't correct it.
- If you can demonstrate results, you can win public support.

From Osborne and Gaebler (1992, chap. 5)

develop multiyear strategic plans, annual performance plans, and annual performance reports.

It is now an entrenched part of American politics that each new presidential administration will initiate new performance monitoring and accountability requirements. The Bush administration focused a good portion of its campaign rhetoric on performance, accountability, and results. To that end, in 2001, the Office of Management and Budget (OMB) began to develop a mechanism called the Program Assessment Rating Tool (PART) to help budget examiners and federal managers measure the effectiveness of government programs. A PART review aims to identify a program's strengths and weaknesses in order to inform funding and management decisions aimed at making the program more effective. The PART framework sets as its goal an evaluation of "all factors that affect and

reflect program performance including program purpose and design; performance measurement, evaluations, and strategic planning; program management; and program results" (www.whitehouse.gov/omb/part). PART aims to examine program improvements over time and allow comparisons between similar programs. William Trochim (2006a), Chair of the American Evaluation Association Public Affairs Committee, observed, "PART is one of the more significant evaluation-related items emerging from the US federal government in many years." In Chapter 4, we shall examine the utility of these accountability initiatives.

Seemingly endless administrative reforms with a focus on accountability are by no means limited to the U.S. government. It is indicative of the political power and public appeal of accountability-oriented government reforms that one of the first things

the newly elected Conservative government of Prime Minister Harper did in Canada was pass a 255-page "Accountability Act." In one review of the Act, political observer Robin Sears (2006) concluded that it was one more effort in a long tradition of trying "to tame the twin nightmares of every modern democracy: lousy management of public spending, and a broad conviction among voters that insiders get favours from government" (p. 19). Making government accountability meaningful, credible, and useful is one of the challenges facing all modern democracies (Chelimsky 2006a, 2006b).

> I was working with a major, long-established organization. In a meeting with senior management to get the evaluation off to a good start, I asked them to tell me about an evaluation that had been useful to them, to start exploring the features that make evaluation useful. There was a long, nervous silence until one of them said, "None, really."
>
> "Then I guess we'll have to do things quite differently," I said.
>
> —An experienced evaluator

Misuse of Evaluations

Utilization-focused evaluation can be located between two extremes. One extreme, as just discussed, is the oversimplified image of analyzing evaluation findings then mechanically making instantaneous decisions based on those findings, for example, the simplistic expectation that PART effectiveness scores (or any simple grading system that categorizes results) should nicely match budget allocations (high scores equal more funds, low scores mean program termination). Real-world evaluation

use, we shall find, is more complex, nuanced, and interpretative. Moving from data to action involves treading a path fraught with obstacles. Evaluators who successfully facilitate use of findings need technical skill, to be sure, but they also need to be good communicators, have political savvy, understand how organizations function, and know how to work with a variety of people with different learning and decision-making styles and competing interests.

If one extreme is an image of simple, mechanical, and immediate use, the other extreme is ignoring evaluation findings altogether, or worse, misusing them. Evaluation findings are not going to be methodologically or technically perfect. Debates about focus, measurement challenges, design weaknesses, sampling problems, and controversies about what the data mean are the rule rather than the exception. The world is a messy place. Programs are messy and complex. Studying the world and evaluating programs is difficult because, in doing so, we encounter what William James (1950) famously called "one great blooming, buzzing confusion" (p. 488). Clear, precise, certain, and noncontroversial findings are elusive, a modern chimera, especially on matters about which people have differing opinions and perspectives, which is just about everything. The imperfections of research designs and the difficulties of moving from evaluation findings to action are not, however, reasons to ignore evaluation findings altogether, or worse yet, manipulate the findings and interpretations to support preconceived positions and biases. Let's distinguish then, right here in the first chapter, between seriously taking evaluation findings into account as part of a complex and multifaceted process of deliberation versus ignoring findings altogether because the person getting the findings doesn't like how they came out, or that person manipulating the findings to make them come out the way he or she wants them to be.

Thus, we face not only the challenge of increasing evaluation use. We also must be concerned with misuse, deception, and abuse. Marv Alkin (1990, 2004), an early theorist of user-oriented evaluation, has long emphasized that evaluators must attend to appropriate use, not just amount of use, and be concerned about misuse (Christie and Alkin 1999; Alkin and Coyle 1988). Ernest House, one of the most astute observers of how the evaluation profession has developed, observed in this regard: "Results from poorly conceived studies have frequently been given wide publicity, and findings from good studies have been improperly used" (1990a:26). The field faces a dual challenge then: supporting and enhancing appropriate uses while also working to eliminate improper uses (Patton 2005b).

In 2004, Philip A. Cooney, chief of staff for the White House Council on Environmental Quality, repeatedly edited government climate reports to play down links between such emissions and global warming. Before joining the Bush White House, Cooney had been a lobbyist at the American Petroleum Institute, the largest trade group representing the interests of the oil industry, where he led the oil industry's fight against limits on greenhouse gases. He was trained as a lawyer with a bachelor's degree in economics, but with no scientific training. News accounts (e.g., *New York Times*, June 8, 2005) reported that Cooney removed or adjusted descriptions of climate research that government scientists and their supervisors had already approved. The dozens of changes, while sometimes as subtle as the insertion of the phrase "significant and fundamental" before the word

"uncertainties," tended to raise doubts about findings, despite a consensus among climate experts that the findings were robust. In one instance, he changed an October 2002 draft of a regularly published summary of government climate research, "Our Changing Planet," by adding the word "extremely" to this sentence: "The attribution of the causes of biological and ecological changes to climate change or variability is extremely difficult." In a section on the need for research into how warming might change water availability and flooding, he crossed out a paragraph describing the projected reduction of mountain glaciers and snowpack.

Such distortions don't just happen with politically motivated advisors protecting national policies. Evaluators at a local level regularly report efforts by program staff, administrators, and elected officials to alter their findings and conclusions. As I was working on this very section, I received a phone call from an evaluation colleague in a small rural community who had just received a request from an agency director to rewrite an evaluation report "with a more positive tone" and leave out some of the negative quotations from participants. She wanted help with language that would diplomatically but firmly explain that such alterations would be unethical.

There is irony here that, in a broad historical context, is worth noting. When the first edition of this book was published in 1978, just as the field of evaluation was emerging, the primary concern was getting anyone to pay any attention to evaluations and take findings seriously. In the last quarter century, a sea change has occurred in political rhetoric. Now, in the information and knowledge age, politicians, policymakers, business leaders, and not-for-profit advocates have learned that the public expects them to address problems through a research and evaluation lens. Public debates regularly include these questions: What do we actually know about this issue? What does the research show? What are evaluation findings about the effectiveness of attempted interventions and solutions? From 1981 to 2006, the frequency of articles about "accountability" in the *New York Times* increased some fivefold, from 124 to 624, a rate by 2006 of at least one per day (John Bare, Vice President, The Arthur M. Blank Foundation, Atlanta, Georgia, 2007 personal communication).

The irony is that as evaluation has become more prominent and more used, it has also become more subject to manipulation and abuse. Thus, critics of the Bush administration consider the Cooney manipulation of climate research to be business-as-usual in politics rather than an exception. The Centers for Disease Control, long the world's leading source for high-quality, credible research and evaluation, has been subject to such manipulation. Data about the ineffectiveness of abstinence-only sex education programs have been manipulated and suppressed; and clear evidence about the effectiveness of condoms in preventing HIV-AIDS has been denigrated. On the National Cancer Institute Web site, evidence about a correlation between abortions and cancer was fabricated and disseminated. There are a great many other examples, not least of which was the manipulation and distortion of intelligence about weapons of mass destruction to justify the Iraq invasion (Specter 2006). All political groups attempt to support their preferred ideological positions by championing empirical findings that support their beliefs and denigrating evidence that runs counter to their beliefs. In both the Clinton and the Bush administrations, findings about the effectiveness of needle exchanges to prevent HIV transmission were dismissed. Scholarship published by the National Society for the Study of Education has documented both the uses and the misuses of data for educational accountability, especially in the standards-based *No Child Left Behind* initiative of the U.S. federal government (Herman and Haertel 2005); misuses have resulted from lack of competence, inadequate resources, political pressures, and, in some cases, premeditation and corruption.

These examples illustrate some of the political and ethical challenges evaluators face in working to get evaluation findings taken seriously and used (Chelimsky 1995b). We'll look at these issues in depth in later chapters, especially how evaluators can meet their responsibility to assure the integrity and honesty of evaluations as called for in the Guiding Principles adopted by the AEA.

> Evaluators display honesty and integrity in their own behavior and attempt to ensure the honesty and integrity of the entire evaluation process. (AEA Task Force on Guiding Principles for Evaluators 1995; see Exhibit 1.3)

Standards of Excellence for Evaluation

Concerns about ethics, the quality of evaluations, and making evaluations useful undergirded an early effort by professional evaluators to articulate standards of practice. To appreciate the importance of the standards, let's begin with some context. Prior to adoption of standards, many researchers took the position that their responsibility was merely to design studies, collect data, and publish findings; what decision makers did with those findings was not their problem. This stance removed from the evaluation researcher any responsibility for fostering use and placed all the blame for nonuse or underutilization on decision makers.

EXHIBIT 1.3

Guiding Principles for Evaluators

Systematic Inquiry
Evaluators conduct systematic, data-based inquiries about what is being evaluated.

Competence
Evaluators provide competent performance to stakeholders.

Integrity/Honesty
Evaluators display honesty and integrity in their own behavior, and attempt to ensure the honesty and integrity of the entire evaluation process.

Respect for People
Evaluators respect the security, dignity, and self-worth of the respondents, program participants, clients, and other stakeholders with whom they interact.

Responsibilities for General and Public Welfare
Evaluators articulate and take into account the diversity of interests and values that may be related to the general and public welfare.

American Evaluation Association (AEA), 1995
Task Force on Guiding Principles for Evaluators
(See also Shadish, Newman, Scheirer, and Wye 1995)

For detailed elaboration and discussion of the specific Guiding Principles adopted by the American Evaluation Association, see www.eval.org/Publications/GuidingPrinciples.asp

Academic aloofness from the messy world in which research findings are translated into action has long been a characteristic of basic scientific research. Before the field of evaluation generated its own standards in the late 1970s, criteria for judging evaluations were based on the quality standards of traditional social and behavioral sciences, namely, technical quality and methodological rigor. Use was ignored. Methods decisions dominated the evaluation design process. Methodological rigor meant experimental designs, quantitative data, and sophisticated statistical analysis. Whether decision makers understood such analyses was not the researcher's problem. Validity, reliability, measurability, and generalizability were the dimensions that received the greatest attention in judging evaluation research proposals and reports (e.g., Bernstein and Freeman 1975). Indeed, evaluators concerned about increasing a study's usefulness often called for ever more methodologically rigorous evaluations to increase the validity of findings, thereby hoping to compel decision makers to take findings seriously.

By the late 1970s, however, it was becoming clear that greater methodological rigor was not solving the use problem. Program staff and funders were becoming openly skeptical about spending scarce funds on evaluations they couldn't understand and/or found irrelevant. Evaluators were being asked to be "accountable" just as program staff members were supposed to be accountable. The questions emerged with uncomfortable directness: Who will evaluate the evaluators? How will evaluation be evaluated? It was in this context that professional evaluators began discussing standards.

The most comprehensive effort at developing standards was hammered out over 5 years by a 17-member committee appointed by 12 professional organizations, with input from hundreds of practicing evaluation professionals. The standards published by the Joint Committee on Standards in 1981 dramatically reflected the ways in which the practice of evaluation had matured. Just prior to publication, Dan Stufflebeam, Chair of the Committee, summarized the committee's work as follows:

> The standards that will be published essentially call for evaluations that have four features. These are *utility, feasibility, propriety* and *accuracy*. And I think it is interesting that the Joint Committee decided on that particular order. Their rationale is that an evaluation should not be done at all if there is no prospect for its being useful to some audience. Second, it should not be done if it is not feasible to conduct it in political terms, or practicality terms, or cost effectiveness terms. Third, they do not think it should be done if we cannot demonstrate that it will be conducted fairly and ethically. Finally, if we can demonstrate that an evaluation will have utility, will be feasible and will be proper in its conduct, then they said we could turn to the difficult matters of the technical adequacy of the evaluation. (Stufflebeam 1980:90)

In 1994 and 2008, revised standards were published following extensive reviews spanning several years (Stufflebeam 2007; Patton 1994b). While some changes were made in the individual standards, the overarching framework of four primary criteria remained unchanged: *utility, feasibility, propriety,* and *accuracy* (see Exhibit 1.4). Specific standards have also been adapted to various international contexts (Russon and Russon 2004), but the overall framework has translated well cross-culturally. Taking the standards seriously has meant looking at the world quite differently. Unlike the traditionally aloof stance of purely academic researchers, professional evaluators are challenged to take responsibility for use. No more can we play the game of blaming the resistant decision maker. If evaluations are ignored or misused, we have to look at where our own practices and processes may have been inadequate. *Implementation of a utility-focused, feasibility-conscious, propriety-oriented, and accuracy-based evaluation requires situational responsiveness, methodological flexibility, multiple evaluator roles, political sophistication, and substantial doses of creativity, all elements of utilization-focused evaluation.*

Daniel Stufflebeam (2001), the guiding leader of the standards movement in evaluation, undertook a comprehensive, exhaustive, and independent review of how 22 different evaluation approaches stack up against the standards. No one was better positioned by knowledge, experience, prestige within the profession, and commitment to the standards to undertake such a challenging endeavor. He concluded, "Of the variety of evaluation approaches that emerged during the twentieth century, nine can be identified as strongest and most promising for continued use and development." Utilization-focused evaluation was among those nine, with the highest rating for adherence to the utility standards (p. 80).

EXHIBIT 1.4

Standards for Evaluation

UTILITY
The Utility Standards are intended to ensure that an evaluation will serve the practical information needs of intended users.

FEASIBILITY
The Feasibility Standards are intended to ensure that an evaluation will be realistic, prudent, diplomatic, and frugal.

PROPRIETY
The Propriety Standards are intended to ensure that an evaluation will be conducted legally, ethically, and with due regard for the welfare of those involved in the evaluation, as well as those affected by its results.

ACCURACY
The Accuracy Standards are intended to ensure that an evaluation will reveal and convey technically adequate information about the features that determine worth or merit of the program being evaluated.

(Joint Committee on Standards for Educational Evaluation 1994)

For the full set of detailed standards, see www.wmich.edu/evalctr/jc

Worldwide Surge in Demand for Evaluation

Interest in evaluation has surged in the new millennium, including a proliferation of different models and approaches (Stufflebeam and Shinkfield 2007). But no trend has been more important to evaluation in the last decade than its expanding global reach. In the 1970s and 1980s, professional evaluation associations began to appear: the Canadian Evaluation Society, the Australasian Evaluation Society, and the AEA. In 1995, evaluation professionals from 61 countries around the world came together at the first truly international evaluation conference in Vancouver, British Columbia. Ten years later, a second international conference in Toronto attracted 2,330 evaluation professionals from around the world. The 1990s also gave rise to the European Evaluation Society (founded in 1994 in the Hague) and the African Evaluation Association (founded in 1999 in Nairobi and having held its fourth continent-wide conference in Niamey, Niger, in 2007). Now there are more than 60 national evaluation associations around the world, including Japan, Malaysia, Sri Lanka, Mongolia, Russia, Brazil, Colombia, Peru, South Africa, Zimbabwe, Niger, and New Zealand, to name but a few examples. In 2003 in Lima, Peru, the inaugural meeting of the new International Organization for Cooperation in Evaluation (IOCE) was held as an umbrella networking and support initiative for national and regional evaluation associations around the world. The International Development Evaluation Association (IDEAS) was formed in Beijing in 2002 to support evaluators with special interests in developing countries; its first biennial conference was held in New Delhi in 2005. The Network for Monitoring, Evaluation, and Systematization of Latin America and the Caribbean (ReLAC) was formed in 2005 in Peru.

Commemorating 20 Years of Evaluation Scholarship

In 2005, the *Canadian Journal of Program Evaluation* (CJPE) published a special 20th anniversary issue (www.cjpe.ca). The volume featured articles on the state of the art of evaluation in Canada in a variety of domains of practice, including health, education, child welfare, social services, and government as well as two independent content analyses of CJPE since the publication of Volume 1, Number 1 in 1986. All issues are available online.

In 2007, the American Evaluation Association journal *New Directions for Evaluation* celebrated its 20th anniversary with a review of enduring issues: judging interpretations, theory-based evaluation, participatory evaluation, and cultural issues (Cousins and Whitmore 2007; Datta 2007a; King 2007b; Leviton 2007; Lipsey 2007c; Madison 2007; Mark 2007; Mathison 2007; Rogers 2007; Schwandt 2007a).

Evaluation capacity can be a crucial part of what the World Bank calls "the knowledge-based economy." The Bank's Knowledge Assessment Methodology (KAM 2006) is an interactive benchmarking tool aimed at helping countries identify the challenges and opportunities they face in making the transition to the knowledge-based economy. The World Bank, through its International Program for Development Evaluation Training, also offers annually, month-long evaluation training for people throughout the developing world (Cousins 2006a).

International agencies have developed comprehensive guidelines for the conduct of evaluation (e.g., United Nations Development Programme 2007; United Nations Evaluation Group 2007, 2005a, 2005b; Danida 2006; Independent Evaluation Group 2006; International Organization for Management 2006; Organisation for Economic Co-operation and Development 2006; World Food Programme 2006; International Fund for Agricultural Development

2002). Various national associations have reviewed and adapted the Joint Committee Standards to their own socio-political contexts as the African Evaluation Association (AfrEA) did in adopting African Evaluation Guidelines in 2007 (AfrEA 2007; Russon and Russon 2004). Evaluation texts and anthologies are available for specific countries and languages, e.g., Italy (Stame 2007), France (Ridde and Dagenais 2007, Japan (Patton and Nagao 2000), and New Zealand (Lunt, Davidson, and McKegg 2003).

Such globally interconnected efforts made it possible for evaluation strategies and approaches to be shared worldwide. Thus, the globalization of evaluation supports our working together to increase our international understanding about factors that support program effectiveness and evaluation use. International perspectives also challenge Western definitions and cultural assumptions about how evaluations ought to be conducted and how quality ought to be judged. As the evaluation standards are translated into different languages, national associations are adding their own cultural nuances and adapting practices to fit local political, social, organizational, economic, and cultural contexts (Stufflebeam 2004b).

Governments around the world are building new systems for monitoring and evaluation, aiming to adapt results-based management and performance measurement to support development (Rist and Stame 2006). International agencies have also begun using evaluation to assess the full range of development efforts under way in developing countries. Most major international organizations have their own evaluation units with guidelines, protocols, conferences, training opportunities, Web sites, and resource specialists. In his keynote address to the international conference in Vancouver, Masafumi Nagao (1995), a cofounder of Japan's evaluation society, challenged evaluators to think globally even as they evaluate locally, that is, to consider how international forces and trends affect project outcomes even in small and remote communities. This book will include attention to how utilization-focused evaluation offers a process for adapting evaluation processes to address multicultural and international issues and constituencies.

The International Evaluation Challenge

In 2005, distinguished international leaders meeting in Bellagio, Italy, committed their support for impact evaluations of social programs in developing countries. Participants noted that in 2005, donor countries committed $34 billion to aid projects addressing health, education, and poverty in the developing world, but evaluation of results was rare and inadequate. Developing countries themselves spent hundreds of billions more on similar programs. The leaders from international agencies, governments, research organizations, and philanthropic foundations endorsed five principles for action.

1. Impact studies are beneficial

2. Knowledge is a public good

3. A collective initiative to promote impact studies is needed

4. The quality of impact studies is essential

5. The initiative should be complementary, strategic, transparent, and independent

(Evaluation Gap Working Group 2006)

The challenges and opportunities for evaluation extend well beyond government-supported programming. Because of the enormous size and importance of government efforts, program evaluation is inevitably affected by trends in the public sector, but evaluation has also been growing in importance in the private and independent sectors. Corporations, philanthropic foundations, not-for-profit agencies, and nongovernmental organizations (NGOs) worldwide are increasingly turning to evaluators for help in enhancing their effectiveness.

All this ferment means that evaluation has become a many-splendored thing—a rich tapestry of models, methods, issues, approaches, variations, definitions, jargon, concepts, theories, and practices. And therein lies the rub. How does one sort through the many competing and contradictory messages about how to conduct evaluations? The answer in this book is to stay focused on the issue of use—conducting evaluations that are useful and actually get used. And as Carol Weiss (1998b) observed in her keynote address to the AEA annual conference, the challenge is not just increasing use, "but more effective utilization, use for improving daily program practice and also use for making larger changes in policy and programming" (p. 30).

From Problem to Solution: Toward Use in Practice

The future of evaluation is tied to the future effectiveness of programs. Indictments of program effectiveness are, underneath, also indictments of evaluation. The original promise of evaluation was that it would point the way to effective programming. Later, that promise broadened to include providing ongoing feedback for improvements during implementation. Evaluation cannot be considered to have fulfilled its promise if, as is increasingly the case, the general perception is that few programs have attained desired outcomes, that "nothing works."

As this introduction and historical overview closes, we are called back to the early morning scene that opened this chapter: decision makers lamenting the disappointing results of an evaluation, complaining that the findings did not tell them what they needed to know. For their part, evaluators complain about many things as well, but for a long time their most common complaint has been that their findings are ignored (Weiss 1972d:319). The question from those who believe in the importance and potential utility of evaluation remains: "What has to be done to get results that are appropriately and meaningfully used?" This question has taken center

stage as program evaluation has emerged as a distinct field of professional practice—and that is the question this book answers. In doing so, we recognize a lineage that extends much farther back than the more recent establishment of the evaluation profession.

> Scientists now calculate that all living human beings are related to a single woman who lived roughly 150,000 years ago in Africa, a "mitochondrial Eve." . . . all humanity is linked to Eve through an unbroken chain of mothers. (Shreeve 2006:62)

And, adds Halcolm, she was an evaluator.

Follow-Up Exercises

1. Scan recent issues of local and/or national newspapers. Look for articles that report evaluation findings. Write a critique of the press report. Can you tell what was evaluated? Are the methods used in the evaluation discussed? How clear are the findings from the evaluation? Can you tell how the findings have been or will be used? How balanced and comprehensive is the press report?

2. See if you can locate the actual evaluation report discussed in the newspaper (Question 1 above). Many evaluation reports are posted on the Internet. Write your own newspaper report based on what you consider important in the evaluation. How is your press report different from the one you found in the newspaper? Why? What does this tell you about the challenges of disseminating evaluation findings to the general public?

3. Find the Web site for one of the international or national evaluation associations. Review the site and its offerings.

4. Most major philanthropic foundations, federal agencies, and international

organizations have Web sites with access to evaluation policies, guidelines, and reports. Visit the evaluation sections of at least one government site and one nongovernmental site. Write a comparison of their information about and approaches to evaluation.

5. Review the full list of Program Evaluation Standards (www.wmich.edu/ evalctr/jc). (a) Conduct a cultural assumptions analysis of the standards. What specific standards, if any, strike you as particularly Western in orientation? (b) Select and discuss at least two standards that seem to you unclear, that is, you aren't sure what you would have to do in an evaluation to meet that particular standard.

2

What Is Utilization-Focused Evaluation?

How Do You Get Started?

*W*hen I was a child, I spake as a child, I understood as a child. I thought as a child: but when I became an adult, I put away childish things. I decided to become an evaluator. My only problem was, I didn't have the foggiest idea what I was getting into or how to begin.

—Halcolm

In Search of Impact

A modern version of an ancient Sufi story (adapted from Shah 1964:64) casts light on the challenge of searching for evaluation use.

A man found his neighbor down on his knees under a street lamp looking for something. "What have you lost, friend?"
"My key," replied the man on his knees.
After a few minutes of helping him search, the neighbor asked, "Where did you drop it?"
"In that dark pasture," answered his friend.
"Then why, for heaven's sake, are you looking here?"
"Because there is more light here."

The obvious place to look for use is in what happens after an evaluation is completed and there's something to use. What we shall find, however, is that the search for use takes us into the "dark pasture" of decisions made before any data are ever collected. The reader will find relatively little in this book about what to do when a study is over. At that point the potential for use has been largely determined. Utilization-focused evaluation emphasizes that what happens from the very beginning of a study will determine its eventual impact long before a final report is produced.

A Comprehensive Philosophy and Pragmatic Approach

The question of how to enhance the use of program evaluation is sufficiently complex that a piecemeal approach based on isolated prescriptions for practice is likely to have only a piecemeal impact. A number of excellent, comprehensive reviews of research and theory on evaluation use have been produced periodically; these reviews capture over a quarter-century of inquiry into the factors related to utilization, ways of conceptualizing use, and challenges in measuring how evaluations are used (e.g., Cousins and Shulha 2006; Alkin 2005; Alkin and Christie 2004; Hofstetter and Alkin 2003; Cousins 2003; Henry and Mark 2003; Kirkhart 2000; Caracelli and Preskill 2000; Lester and Wilds 1990; McLaughlin et al. 1988; Connor 1988; Smith 1988; Cousins and Leithwood 1986; Leviton and Hughes 1981). Considered cumulatively, they reveal the complexities of making evaluations useful and illustrate that the problems of underuse and inappropriate use will not be solved by compiling and following some clever list of evaluation axioms. It's like trying to live your life according to *Poor Richard's*

Almanac. At the moment of decision, you reach into your socialization and remember, "He who hesitates is lost." But then again, "Fools rush in where angels fear to tread." Advice to young evaluators is no less confusing: "Work closely with decision makers to establish trust and rapport," but "maintain distance to guarantee objectivity and credibility."

Real-world circumstances are too complex and unique to be routinely approached through the application of isolated pearls of evaluation wisdom. What is needed is a comprehensive framework within which to develop and implement an evaluation with attention to use built-in. In program evaluation, as in life, it is one's overall philosophy integrated into pragmatic principles that provides a guide to action. Utilization-focused evaluation offers both a philosophy of evaluation and a practical framework for designing and conducting evaluations.

Since original publication in 1978, *Utilization-Focused Evaluation* has been tested and applied in thousands of evaluations throughout the world. This reservoir of experience provides strong confirmation that evaluations will be used if the foundation for use is properly prepared. Evidence to that effect will be presented throughout this book. First, let me outline the utilization-focused approach to evaluation and indicate how it responds to the challenge of getting evaluations used.

Utilization-Focused Evaluation: A Synopsis

The watchword of the evaluation profession has been utilization-focused evaluation.

—Kathryn Newcomer, Harry Hatry, and Joseph Wholey *Handbook of Practical Program Evaluation* (2004:xxxix)

Utilization-focused evaluation is evaluation done for and with specific intended primary users for specific, intended uses. *Utilization-Focused Evaluation* begins with the premise that evaluations should be judged by their utility and actual use; therefore, evaluators should facilitate the evaluation process and design any evaluation with careful consideration for how everything that is done, from beginning to end, will affect use. Use concerns how real people in the real world apply evaluation findings and experience the evaluation process. Therefore, the focus in utilization-focused evaluation is on *intended use by intended users*.

> |Utilization-focused program evaluation is ✳ evaluation done for and with specific intended primary users for specific, intended uses. Utilization-focused evaluation begins with the premise that evaluations should be judged by their utility and actual use; therefore, evaluators should facilitate the evaluation process and design any evaluation with careful consideration for how everything that is done, from beginning to end, will affect use.)Use concerns how real people in the real world apply evaluation findings and experience the evaluation process. Therefore, the focus in utilization-focused evaluation is on *intended use by intended users.*

In any evaluation, there are many potential stakeholders and an array of possible uses. Utilization-focused evaluation requires moving from the general and abstract, i.e., possible audiences and potential uses, to the real and specific: actual primary intended users and their explicit commitments to concrete, specific uses. The evaluator facilitates judgment and decision making by intended users. Since no evaluation can be value-free, utilization-focused evaluation answers the question of whose values will frame the evaluation by working with clearly identified, primary intended users who have responsibility to apply evaluation findings and implement recommendations. In essence, I shall argue, evaluation use is too important to be left to evaluators.

Utilization-focused approach is personal and situational. The evaluation facilitator develops a working relationship with intended users to help them determine what kind of evaluation they need. This requires negotiation in which the evaluator offers a menu of possibilities within the framework of established evaluation standards and principles. While concern about utility drives a utilization-focused evaluation, the evaluator must also attend to the evaluation's accuracy, feasibility, and propriety (Joint Committee on Standards 1994). Moreover, as a professional, the evaluator has a responsibility to act in accordance with the profession's adopted principles of conducting systematic, data-based inquiries; performing competently; ensuring the honesty and integrity of the entire evaluation process; respecting the people involved in and affected by the evaluation; and being sensitive to the diversity of interests and values that may be related to the general and public welfare (see Exhibit 1.3, on p. 27).

Utilization-focused evaluation does not advocate any particular evaluation content, model, method, theory, or even use. Rather, it is a process for helping primary intended users select the most appropriate content, model, methods, theory, and uses for their particular situation. Situational responsive- ✳ ness guides the interactive process between evaluator and primary intended users. This book will present and discuss the many options now available in the feast that has become the field of evaluation. As we consider the rich and varied menu of evaluation, it will become clear that utilization-focused evaluation can include any evaluative purpose (formative, summative, developmental), any kind of data (quantitative, qualitative, mixed), any kind of design (e.g., naturalistic, experimental), and any kind of focus (processes, outcomes, impacts, costs, and cost-benefit, among many possibilities). Utilization-focused evaluation is a process for making decisions about these issues in collaboration with an identified group of primary users focusing on their intended uses of evaluation.

A psychology of use undergirds and informs utilization-focused evaluation. In essence, research and my own experience indicate that intended users are more likely to use evaluations if they understand and feel ownership of the evaluation process and findings; they are more likely to understand and feel ownership if they've been actively involved; and by actively involving primary intended users, the evaluator is training users in use, preparing the groundwork for use, and reinforcing the intended utility of the evaluation every step along the way. The rest of this chapter will offer some ways of working with primary intended users to begin the process of utilization-focused evaluation. Beyond the heuristic value of these examples, they are meant to illustrate how the philosophy of utilization-focused evaluation is translated into practice.

The First Challenge: Engendering Commitment

Utilization-focused evaluators begin their interactions with primary intended users by working to engender commitments to both evaluation and use. Even program funders and decision makers who request or mandate an evaluation often don't know what evaluation involves, at least not in any specific way. And they typically haven't thought much about how they will use either the process or the findings.

In working with program staff, administrators, and funders to lay the groundwork for an evaluation, I typically begin with a workshop. In the opening, I write the word "EVALUATE" on a flip chart and ask those present to free-associate with the word. They typically begin slowly with synonyms or closely related terms: *assess, measure, judge, rate, compare.* Soon someone calls out "*waste of time.*" Another voice from the back of the room yells: "*crap.*" The energy picks up and more associations follow in rapid succession: *budget cuts, downsize, politics, demeaning, pain, fear.* And inevitably, the unkindest cut of all: "*USELESS.*"

Clearly, evaluation can evoke strong emotions, negative associations, and genuine fear. To ignore such perceptions, past experiences, and feelings people bring to an evaluation is like ignoring a smoldering dynamite fuse in hope it will burn itself out. More likely, unless someone intervenes and extinguishes the fuse, it will burn faster and eventually explode. Many an evaluation has blown up in the face of well-intentioned evaluators because they rushed into technical details and methods decisions without establishing a solid foundation for the evaluation in clear purposes and shared understandings. To begin, both evaluators and those with whom we work need to develop a shared definition of evaluation and mutual understanding about what the process will involve.

What Is Program Evaluation?

As noted in the first chapter, to evaluate something means systematically determining its merit, worth, value, quality, or significance (Davidson 2005:1–2; Fournier 2005a:139–40; Stufflebeam 2001:11; Schwandt 2002:xi; House 1993:1; Scriven 1991a:39). This widely used definition emphasizes the value-based judgmental nature of evaluation.

I offer the people with whom I work a more expansive definition that emphasizes the uses of evaluation, not just the rendering of judgment:

Program evaluation is the systematic collection of information about the activities, characteristics, and results of programs to make judgments about the program, improve or further develop program effectiveness, inform decisions about future programming, and/or increase understanding. *Utilization-focused program evaluation* is evaluation done for and with specific intended primary users for specific, intended uses.

This definition emphasizes three things: (1) the systematic collection of information about (2) a potentially broad range of issues on which evaluations might focus (3) for a variety of possible judgments and uses. It is clear from this definition that the focus and uses of a particular evaluation will have to be determined by someone. The inclusion of the definition of utilization-focused evaluation answers how the focus will be determined: by specific intended users.

Stufflebeam (1994) warns against "obscuring the essence of evaluation—to assess value—by overemphasizing its constructive uses" (p. 323). However, for me, use is the essence, so I choose to include it in my definition, as a matter of emphasis, to reinforce the point that concern about use is a distinguishing characteristic of program evaluation, even at the point of defining what program evaluation is. I'm not interested in determining merit or worth as an end in itself. I want to keep before us these questions: Why is merit or worth to be judged? What will be done with whatever judgments are made?

This matter of defining evaluation is of considerable import because different evaluation approaches rest on different definitions. The use and user-oriented definition offered above contrasts in significant ways with other approaches. One traditional approach has been to define program evaluation as determining the extent to which a program attains its goals or intended outcomes. However, as we shall see, program evaluation can and does involve examining much more than goal attainment or outcomes measurement, for example, evaluations can focus on implementation, program processes, unanticipated consequences, and long-term impacts. Goal attainment, then, takes too narrow a focus to encompass the variety of ways program evaluation can be useful.

A different approach emphasizes evaluation as "applied research" (Weiss 2004:154). This emphasis is the focus of the widely used Rossi, Lipsey, and Freeman (2003) textbook *Evaluation: A Systematic Approach.* They define *evaluation research* as the systematic application of social research procedures in assessing social intervention programs. But note that they are defining evaluation research and their text emphasizes applying social science methods, so naturally they include that in their definition of evaluation. As Rossi has explained,

Evaluation is social research applied to answering policy-oriented questions. As such, an important criterion for judging evaluations is the extent to which they successfully apply the canons of social science. (Rossi 2004:127)

The definition of evaluation I've offered here emphasizes systematic data collection rather than applying social science methods. This is an important distinction in emphasis, one in keeping with the "Principle of Systematic Inquiry" adopted by the American Evaluation Association (AEA Task Force on Guiding Principles 1995:22). From my perspective, program evaluators may use research methods to gather information, but they may also use data from management information systems, program monitoring statistics, program files, clinical records, and other forms of systematic information that are not research-oriented.

This question of whether and how evaluation differs from research haunts the field. The AEA sponsors an Internet listserv called *EvalTalk* that attracts thousands of people seeking clarity about and resources for evaluation. A standing joke among long-time EvalTalk participants is that you can time the change of seasons by a posting from a novice participant asking, "Is evaluation different from research? I'm confused." Those who define evaluation as the application of social science methods argue that evaluation research is simply a specialization within social science. Those who emphasize judging merit or worth argue that evaluation is its own discipline, or transdiscipline (Scriven 2004). I emphasize that evaluation is different from research because the criteria for judging quality are different—and I find it useful to make the distinction. Let me explain.

Utilization-focused program evaluation differs fundamentally from research in the purpose of data collection and standards for judging quality. Basic scientific research is undertaken to discover new knowledge, test theories, establish truth, and generalize across time and space. Program evaluation is undertaken to inform decisions, clarify options, identify improvements, and provide information about programs and policies within contextual boundaries of time, place, values, and politics. The difference between research and evaluation has been called by Cronbach and Suppes (1969) the difference between conclusion-oriented and decision-oriented inquiry. Research aims to produce knowledge and truth. Useful evaluation supports action.

In early formulations, Stake (1981) and Cronbach and Associates (1980) emphasized that evaluation differs from research in the relative importance attached to making generalizations. An inquiry that is called "evaluation research" tends to focus on producing generalizable and theory-testing

findings. An inquiry labeled "program eval-uation" tends to focus on the effectiveness of a specific program. In any inquiry, the extent to which there is concern about gen-eralizability, scientific rigor, and relevance of the findings to specific users will vary. Each of these dimensions is a continuum. Because this book emphasizes meeting the information and decision needs of specific intended users, the focus will most often be on program evaluation within a particular context rather than evaluation research aimed at producing general knowledge. "Evaluation research differs from the more typical program evaluation in that it is more likely to be investigator initiated, theory based, and focused on evaluation as the object of study" (Bickman 2005:141). I hasten to add, however, that how one labels the process depends on who is involved and the evaluation's purpose. With staff in local-level, community-based pro-grams, the idea of conducting "research" may be intimidating, or grassroots practi-tioners may consider research "academic and irrelevant," and not part of their job. On the other hand, national programs or those staffed or funded by people with advanced degrees may attach positive asso-ciations to conducting "research," in which case they may prefer to call the process "evaluation research." *The language, like everything else in utilization-focused evalua-tion, depends on the program context and the explicit needs and values of primary intended users.* In short, how to define eval-uation and what to call a particular evalua-tion are matters for discussion, clarification, and negotiation. Therefore, I find it useful to distinguish research from evaluation to facilitate this very discussion.

What is not negotiable is that the evalua-tion be systematic, intentional, and data based. Both program evaluation and evaluation research bring an empirical perspective to bear on questions of policy and program

effectiveness. This *data-based approach* to evaluation stands in contrast to two alterna-tive and often competing ways of assessing programs: the charity orientation and pure pork barrel politics. I sometimes introduce these distinctions in working with clients to help them more fully appreciate the sine qua non nature of evaluation's commitment to systematic data collection.

Charitable Assessment

And now abideth faith, hope, charity, these three; but the greatest of these is charity.

—Paul's First Letter to the Corinthians 13:13

Modern social service and education programs are rooted in charitable and philanthropic motives: helping people. From a charity perspective, the main crite-rion for evaluation is the sincerity of funders and program staff; the primary measure of program worth is that the pro-gram organizers care enough to try their very best to help the less fortunate. As an agency director told me after an evalua-tion training session, "All I want to know is whether or not my staff are trying their best. When you've got a valid and reliable and all-that-other-stuff instrument for love and sincerity, come back and see me."

The limitation of a purely charitable frame of mind is nicely captured by an old German proverb: Charity sees the need, not the cause.

Sometimes religious motives can also be found in this mix. All the widely practiced religions of the world advocate charity. Reminding me of this, a United Way agency director once told me, "God has mandated our helping the less fortunate, so God alone will judge the outcomes and effectiveness of our efforts." The implica-tion was that God needed no assistance

Faith-Based Initiatives

President George W. Bush made "Faith-Based Initiatives" a centerpiece of his political strategy, a way of getting federal funds to churches and religious organizations for social, educational, and community programs. These initiatives were controversial and opposed by those who advocate a wall of separation between church and state. Shortly after President Bush created the White House Office for Faith-Based Initiatives, I happened to be giving a keynote speech on making evaluation useful at a national conference. When I finished the first question was, "What does evaluation show about the effectiveness of faith-based initiatives?"

I thought for a moment and responded, "From an evaluation perspective, all initiatives are faith-based until they've been evaluated."

from the likes of social scientists, with their impersonal statistics and objective analyses of human suffering.

Data-oriented evaluators have little to offer those who are fully ensconced in charitable assessment. Others, however (and their numbers are increasing), have come to believe that, even for the sincere, indeed especially for the sincere and caring, empirically-based program evaluations can be valuable. After all, if you're sincere and caring, you presumably want to make a difference—and that means being effective. The purpose of program evaluation is precisely that—to increase effectiveness and provide information on whether hopes are actually being realized. People who care deeply about their work are precisely the people who can benefit greatly from utilization-focused evaluation.

Pork Barrel Assessment

A second common approach to evaluating programs has been pork barrel politics, which takes as its main criterion the political power of a program's constituency: If powerful constituents want the program, or if more is to be gained politically by support for rather than opposition to the program, then the program is judged worthwhile; no other evidence of program effectiveness is needed, though data may be

sought to support this predetermined political judgment. Pork barrel evaluations are one reason it is so difficult to terminate government-funded programs and agencies. Programs rapidly develop constituencies whose vested interests lie in program continuation. The driving force of the pork barrel approach is to give out money where it counts politically, not where it will be used most effectively.

The pork barrel criterion is not unique to elected politicians and governmental bodies. The funding boards of philanthropic foundations, corporate boards, and service agencies have their own constituencies to please. Political debts must be paid so programs are judged effective as long as they serve powerful interests. Empirical evaluation findings are of interest only insofar as they can be manipulated for political and public relations purposes. (Later chapters will address in more depth the relationship, often healthy when properly approached, between politics and evaluation.)

Evidence-Based Evaluation: Developing a Commitment to Reality Testing

At the outset, then, evaluators work on engendering commitment to data-based evaluation and use. We want to get beyond

Pork Barrel Politics

The term *pork barrel* derives from a time when pork was stored in barrels; in politics, pork means money. Pork barrel politics is a derogatory phrase used to describe government spending that is intended to benefit constituents of a politician in return for their political support through campaign contributions, votes, or both. The term originated on Southern plantations where well-behaved slaves were placated with the unwanted remainder of slaughtered pigs, or the "pork barrel." Today "pork" means funding for government programs whose benefits are limited to favored constituents or a politician's home district while costs are borne by all taxpayers. In 2006, two powerful Alaska politicians with clout in Congress, Senator Ted Stevens and Representative Don Young, sponsored legislation that allocated $223 million to connect Ketchikan, Alaska (population 8,900) to Gravina Island (population 50). Dubbed "the bridge to nowhere" by opponents, the bridge was widely criticized as a classic pork barrel project and became a national symbol of *porkmania* in American politics (Safire 2006).

pure *are-you-sincere* charity assessments and corrupt *are-you-with-me-or-against-me* pork barrel assessments. Early research on "readiness for evaluation" (Smith 1992; Studer 1978; Mayer 1975, 1976) found that "valuing evaluation" is a necessary condition for evaluation use (see Exhibit 2.1). Valuing evaluation cannot be taken for granted. Nor does it happen naturally. Users' commitment to evaluation is typically fragile, often whimsical, and must be cultivated like a hybrid plant that has the potential for enormous yields, but only if properly cared for, nourished, and appropriately managed. More recent work by Taut (2007) highlights the importance of team and organizational readiness for the benefits of evaluation to be realized and sustained.

I find the idea of "reality testing" helpful in working with intended users to increase the value they attach to evaluation and, correspondingly, their willingness to be actively engaged in the work necessary to make the evaluation useful. I include in the notion of testing reality gathering varying perceptions of reality in line with the theorem that "what is perceived as real is real in its consequences." The phrase "reality testing" implies that being "in touch with reality" cannot simply be assumed. When individuals lose touch with reality, they become dysfunctional and, if the distortions of reality are severe, they may be referred for psychotherapy. Programs and organizations can also "lose touch with reality" in the sense that the people in those programs and organizations are operating on myths and behaving in ways that are dysfunctional to goal attainment and ineffective for accomplishing desired outcomes. Program evaluation can be a mechanism for finding out whether what's hoped for is, in fact, taking place—a form of reality testing.

Some people would just as soon not be bothered dealing with programmatic or organizational reality. They've constructed their own comfortable worlds built on untested assumptions and unexamined beliefs. Evaluation is a threat to such people. Evaluators who ignore the threatening nature of reality testing and plow ahead with their data collection in the hope that knowledge will prevail are engaged in their own form of reality distortion. Utilization-focused evaluators, in contrast, work with intended evaluation users to help them understand the value of reality testing and buy into the process, thereby reducing the threat of evaluation and resistance (conscious or unconscious) to evaluation use. One way to do this is to look for

EXHIBIT 2.1

Items on Belief in Program Evaluation
From Readiness for Evaluation Questionnaire

Rank Order By Factor	Item	Factor Loading
1.	Program evaluation would pave the way for better programs for our clientele.	.78
2.	This would be a good time to begin (or renew or intensity) work on program evaluation.	.73
3.	Installing a procedure for program evaluation would enhance the stature of our organization.	.72
4.	We don't need to have our program evaluated.	−.69
5.	The amount of resistance in the organization to program evaluation should not be a deterrent to pursuing a policy of program evaluation.	.69
6.	I have yet to be convinced of the alleged benefits of program evaluation.	.67
7.	Program evaluation would only increase the work load.	−.67
8.	"Program evaluation" and "accountability" are just fads that hopefully will die down soon.	−.65
9.	Program evaluation would tell me nothing more than I already know.	−.64
10.	I would be willing to commit at least 5% of the program budget for evaluation.	.62
11.	A formal program evaluation would make it easier to convince administrators of needed changes.	.62
12.	We could probably get additional or renewed funding if we carry out a plan for program evaluation.	.59
13.	Program evaluation might lead to greater recognition and rewards to those who deserve it.	.55
14.	It would be difficult to implement a procedure for program evaluation without seriously disrupting other activities.	−.52
15.	No additional time and money can be made available for program evaluation.	−.45
16.	Most of the objections one hears about program evaluation are really pretty irrational.	.44
17.	Some money could probably be made available to provide training to staff in program evaluation skills.	.38

SOURCE: Smith (1992:53–54).

NOTES: Factor analysis is a statistical technique for identifying questionnaire or test items that are highly intercorrelated and therefore may measure the same factor, in this case, belief in evaluation.

The positive or negative signs on the factor loadings reflect whether questions were worded positively or negatively; the higher a factor loading, the better the item defines the factor.

A Reality-Testing King

Canute the Great (994–1035) combined the thrones of England, Denmark, and Norway in medieval times. As a man of great power, he found himself surrounded by flatterers constantly telling him how great he was. Legend has it that he came increasingly to disdain this insincere and ingratiating praise. As his courtiers competed to outdo each other in adulation, he wondered aloud, "So, you think I can do anything."

"Yes, Sire, anything," his chief minister replied.

"There is nothing I cannot do?"

"Nothing, Sire," they replied as one. "You are the greatest king who ever lived. You can do anything."

"Let us see," he replied.

He had them follow him to the seaside where, in front of the entire assembled Court and in a booming voice, he commanded the waves to cease. When the sea failed to obey, he looked accusingly at the courtiers. Then he turned back to the sea and commanded in an even louder voice, "Waves, cease your rolling."

He waited. And waited. At length he turned to the Court and said, "Meaningless flattery and exaggerations of my power do not serve this kingdom. Those who would serve me can best do so with well-considered assessments of what a king can actually accomplish."

After that, he was no longer known as *Canute the Great* but *Canute the Wise.*

and use examples of good ideas that haven't worked out. Exhibit 2.2 presents an example I find quite powerful, the story of a thoughtfully designed program funded by the world's largest and most prestigious health foundation. The evaluation showed that the program didn't work and they had to go back to the drawing board.

As I work with intended users to agree on what we mean by evaluation and engender a commitment to use, I invite them to assess incentives for and barriers to reality testing and information use in their own program culture. Barriers typically include fear of being judged, cynicism about whether anything can really change, skepticism about the worth of evaluation, concern about the time and money costs of evaluation, and frustration from previous bad evaluation experiences, especially lack of use. As we work through these and related issues to "get ready for evaluation,"

the foundation for use is being built in conjunction with a commitment to serious and genuine reality testing.

Because evaluators have typically internalized the value of data-based reality testing, it is easy to assume that others share this perspective. But a commitment to examine beliefs and test actual goal attainment is neither natural nor widespread. People involved in program management and service delivery can become quite complacent about what they're doing and quite content with the way things are. Reality testing will only upset things. "Why bother?" they ask.

Nor is it enough that an evaluation is required by some funder or oversight authority. Indeed, under such conditions, evaluation often becomes an end in itself, something to be done because it is mandated, not because it will be useful or because important things can be learned. Doing an evaluation because it is required—operating on a *compliance*

EXHIBIT 2.2

Reality-Testing: Example of a
Good Idea That Didn't Work Out in Practice

The Robert Wood Johnson Foundation funded an eight-year effort to help doctors and patients deal with death in hospitals. Called SUPPORT (Study to Understand Prognoses and Preferences for Outcomes and Risks of Treatment), the project placed nurses in five teaching hospitals to facilitate communications between physicians and families facing the death of a family member. The idea was that by increasing doctors' understanding of what patients and their families wanted and didn't want, pain could be diminished, the appropriateness of care would increase, and fewer "heroic measures" would be used to prolong life for short periods.

The evaluation found that the culture of denial about death could not be overcome through better communication. Major gaps remained between what patients privately said they wanted and what doctors, dedicated to saving lives, did. Living wills didn't help. Half the patients still died in pain. Many died attached to machines, and died alone.

Dr. Joanne Lynn, a codirector of the project, expressed dramatically the importance of testing good ideas in practice to see if they really work: "We did what everyone thought would work and it didn't work at all, not even a quiver."

While the idea didn't work, important lessons were learned, she concluded. "This wasn't a group of doctors dedicated to finding the last possible date on the tombstone. What we learned was that the conspiracy of silence about death was stronger than we expected and the force of habit was also stronger than we expected. We are all involved in the dance of silence."

SOURCE: Lynn with Goodman (1995:17A).

---

mentality—is entirely different from doing it because one is committed to learning and grounding decisions in a careful assessment of reality. Ironically, mandated evaluations can actually undercut utility by making the motivation for the evaluation simply compliance with a funding requirement rather than genuine interest in being more effective. A career internal evaluator with 25 years experience once told me,

> The most pervasive problem we dealt with, particularly in our relations with state and federal agencies, was submitting mandated reports that no one cared about, no one read, and we never got any feedback on. It was constantly discouraging and frustrating.

A common error made by novice evaluators is believing that because someone has requested an evaluation or some group has been assembled to design an evaluation, the commitment to reality testing and use is already there. Quite the contrary, these commitments must be engendered (or revitalized if once they were present) and then reinforced throughout the evaluation process. Utilization-focused evaluation makes this a priority.

Overcoming Evaluation Anxiety and Fear

Whether evaluations are mandated or voluntary, those potentially affected by the evaluation may approach the very idea with trepidation, manifesting what has come to be recognized by experienced evaluations as "evaluation anxiety"—or what

I jokingly refer to with clients as a clinical diagnosis of *pre-evaluation stress syndrome.* But the fear is often serious and needs to be acknowledged and managed. Signs of extreme evaluation anxiety include "people who are very upset by, and sometimes rendered virtually dysfunctional by, any prospect of evaluation, or who attack evaluation without regards to how well conceived it might be" (Donaldson, Gooler, and Scriven 2002:262).

In proposing a "psychology of evaluation" for use in managing evaluation anxiety, Donaldson et al. (2002) identified a number of strategies for evaluators to consider, including working through "hangovers from bad evaluation experiences," assessing and acknowledging "legitimate opposition to bad evaluation," discussing why "honesty to the evaluator is not disloyalty to the group," being prepared to wear "your psychotherapy hat," and distinguishing the "blame game from the program evaluation game" (p. 265). Taut and Brauns (2003) gathered data from 21 experienced evaluation practitioners about strategies to address resistance to evaluation. They recommended high communication about the evaluation, working to increase interest among those affected, building a sense of ownership about the evaluation, paying attention to psychological issues such as self-esteem and anxiety, and getting knowledge about the organizational context to increase understanding of reasons for resistance. In their conclusion, Taut and Brauns stressed that "evaluators should see resistance not only as a burden but also as an importance source of information. Resistance is related to development and change, and its analysis helps the evaluator choose the most effective evaluation activities" (p. 259).

I would add appealing to what I presume with most people to be a desire to be effective. I don't encounter many people who get up in the morning wanting to do a bad job or devote their time to ineffective activities. Indeed, the desire to be effective is so strong that it is often the source of evaluation anxiety. What if I've been wasting my time? What if what we've been doing isn't helping people? What then?

What then, indeed? The evaluation answer: Change the program to become more effective. So engendering a commitment to evaluation use often involves engendering an openness to change. That openness can start with a commitment to do reality testing, to actually examine whether what they hope is going on is what is going on, whether what they hope to be accomplishing is what is being accomplished—and acknowledging that such inquiries can be scary.

Because evaluation use is so dependent on the commitment to reality testing, evaluators need ways to cultivate that commitment and enlarge the capacity of intended users to undertake the process. This means engaging program staff, managers, funders, and other intended users in examining how their beliefs about program effectiveness may be based on selective perception, predisposition, prejudice, rose-colored glasses, unconfirmed assertions, or simple misinformation. I often share evidence from psychology showing that we all tend to distort reality. Social scientist Yi-Fu Tuan (2000) has studied the human propensity toward escapism as a way of avoiding facing reality and even defines human beings as "animals congenitally indisposed to accept reality as it is" (p. 6). One way we distort reality is through the "confirmation bias," the tendency to look for evidence to confirm our preconceptions and biases. If a program director believes his program is effective, he'll look for evidence of effectiveness and discount or ignore evidence of ineffectiveness. If a philanthropic foundation executive believes she is doing good, she'll find evidence of doing good wherever she looks. "The brain looks for patterns," explains Meir Statman, a behavioral finance scholar. "And once you decide there is a pattern, you will look for confirming evidence and you will dismiss contradictory evidence as a fluke" (quoted by Clement 2006:D1). Systematic and balanced evaluation aims to counter that human tendency.

Study after study shows that we tend to be overconfident about our ability to make informed and objective decisions. For example, the work of Kahneman and Tversky (2000a) on "prospect theory" has established that people have an aversion to loss that is about twice the desire for gain; in essence, we fear bad news and failure twice as much as we hope for good news and success. Brain research is helping us understand these proclivities (e.g., Schwartz and Begley 2003), but culture and socialization also play key roles (Tuan 2000). The research of psychologists David Dunning and Justin Kruger (1999) brings irony to this picture of human reality distortion. They found that people who perform poorly are typically quite confident about their competence. In fact, they're often more confident than those who actually perform well. The title of their research report sums up the problem quite succinctly: "Unskilled and Unaware of It: How Difficulties in Recognizing One's Own Incompetence Lead to Inflated Self-Assessments." Incompetent people also lack the skill to recognize competence in others.

A classroom experiment by behavioral economist Richard Thaler provides yet another glimpse of common reality distortion. At the beginning of his course on decision making, he asks students to anonymously write down where they'll rank in the final grading. He reports that none of his 125 MBA students thought they would finish in the bottom half of the class. "Obviously, half of them were wrong," he adds. "We all think we are pretty good at sizing things up, just the same way we all think we are good judges of character. We should know that we really are all hopeless" (quoted in Peltz 1999:105).

In addition to our tendency to deceive ourselves and distort reality, the irony of living in the information age is that we are surrounded by so much misinformation (Stossel 2006) and act on so many untested assumptions. By putting intended users in touch with how little they really know, and how flimsy is the basis for much of what they think they know, we are laying the groundwork for use. We are, in fact, identifying that there are useful things to be found out, establishing that systematic inquiry processes are needed to counter our tendencies to distort reality, and creating the expectation that testing reality will be valuable, not just an academic or mandated exercise. In short, we are establishing psychological and organizational openness to and readiness for serious evaluation.

I should perhaps add that I am using the term *reality testing* in its common and ordinary connotation of finding out what is happening. While philosophers of science will rightly point out that the whole notion of "reality" is an epistemological and ontological quagmire, I find that the people I work with in the "real world"—their phrase—resonate to the notion of "reality testing." It is their own sense of reality I want to help them test, not some absolute, positivist construct of reality. The notion that reality is socially constructed doesn't mean it can't be tested and understood. At the 1995 International Evaluation Conference in Vancouver, Ernie House, Will Shadish, and I participated in a session on evaluation theory in which we agreed on the following two propositions, among

Truthiness

The challenge of engendering a commitment to reality testing is nicely captured by the word "*truthiness*," voted the 2005 word of the year by the American Dialect Society. Popularized on the satirical mock news show, the *Colbert Report* on Comedy Central television, *truthiness* refers to the quality of preferring concepts or facts one wishes to be true, rather than concepts or facts known to be true. When the Colbert Report debuted in October, 2005, comedian Stephen Colbert made clear that his mantra would be *truthiness*, a devotion to information that he wishes were true even if it's not. "I'm not a fan of facts," he asserted. "You see, facts can change, but my opinion will never change, no matter what the facts are" (Peyser 2006).

others: (1) Most theorists postulate a real physical world, though they differ greatly as to its knowability and complexity and (2) logical positivism is an inadequate epistemology that few theorists advocate anymore, either in evaluation or philosophy.

Generating Meaningful Questions

It is impossible for a man to learn what he thinks he already knows.

—Epictetus (AD 55–135),
Greek Stoic philosopher

One way of facilitating a program's readiness for evaluation is to take primary intended users through a process of generating meaningful evaluation questions. I find that when I enter a new program setting as an external evaluator, the people with whom I'm working typically expect me to tell them what the focus of the evaluation will be. They're passively waiting to be told by the evaluation expert—me— what questions the evaluation will answer. But I don't come with specific evaluation questions. I come with a process for determining what questions will be meaningful and what answers will be useful given the program's situation, priorities, and decision context. Taking them through the process

of formulating questions and determining evaluation priorities is aimed at engendering their commitment to data-based evaluation and use. Let me share an example.

The Frontier School Division in Manitoba, Canada, encompasses much of northern Manitoba—a geographically immense school district. The Deputy Minister of Education in Manitoba thought evaluation might be a way to shake things up in a district he considered stagnant, so he asked me to facilitate an evaluation process with district officials. The actual form and content of the evaluation was to be determined internally, by them. So I went to Winnipeg and met with the division administrators, a representative from the parents' group, a representative from the principals' group, and a representative from the teachers' union. I had asked that all constituencies be represented in order to establish credibility with all the people who might be involved in using the evaluation.

In as much as I had been brought in from outside by a superordinate official, it was not surprising that I encountered reactions ranging from defensiveness to outright hostility. They had not asked for the evaluation, and the whole idea sounded unsavory and threatening.

I began by asking them to tell me what kinds of things they were interested in evaluating. The superintendent frowned and responded, "We'd like to see the evaluation instruments you've used in assessing other school districts."

I replied that I would be happy to share such instruments if they should prove relevant, but it would be helpful to first determine the evaluation issues and priorities of Frontier School Division. They looked skeptical, and after a lingering silence, the Superintendent tried again: "You don't need to show us all the instruments you intend to use. Just show us one so we have an idea of what's going to happen."

I again replied that it was too early to talk about instruments. First, we had to identify their evaluation questions and concerns. Then we would talk about instruments. However, their folded arms and scowling faces told me that what they interpreted as my evasiveness was only intensifying their initial suspicions and fears. I was deepening their resistance by what they perceived as my secretiveness about the content of my evaluation scheme. The superintendent tried again: "How about just showing us one part of the evaluation, say the part that asks teachers about administrative effectiveness?" And he smiled sarcastically.

At that point, I was about to throw in the towel, give them some old instruments, and let them use what they wanted from other evaluations. But first, I made one more attempt to get at their issues. I said,

> Look, maybe your questions will be the same as questions elsewhere. Maybe other district's instrument will work here. Or maybe you don't need an evaluation. I certainly don't have any questions I need answered about your operations and effectiveness. Maybe you don't either. In which case, I'll tell the Deputy Minister that evaluation isn't the way to go. But before we decide to quit, let me ask you to participate in a simple little exercise. It's an old complete-the-blank exercise from grade school.

I then turned to the blackboard and wrote a sentence in capital letters.

I WOULD REALLY LIKE TO KNOW _____

ABOUT FRONTIER SCHOOL DIVISION.

I turned back to them and continued,

> I want to ask each of you, individually, to complete the blank 10 times. What are 10 things about Frontier School Division that you'd like to know, things you aren't certain about, that would make a difference in what you do if you had more information? Take a shot at it, without regard to methods, measurement, design, resources, precision—just 10 basic questions, real questions about this division.

After about 10 minutes, I divided them into three groups of four people each and asked them to combine their lists together into a single list of 10 things that each group wanted to know, in effect, to establish each group's priority questions. Then we pulled back together and generated a single list of 10 basic evaluation questions—answers to which, they agreed, could make a real difference to the operations of Frontier School Division.

The questions they generated were the kind an experienced evaluator could anticipate being asked in a district-wide educational evaluation because there are only so many things one can ask about a school division. But the questions were phrased in their terms, incorporating important local nuances of meaning and circumstance. Most important, they had discovered that they had questions they cared about—not my questions but their questions, because during the course of the exercise it had become their evaluation. The whole atmosphere had changed. This became most evident as I read aloud the final list of 10 items they had generated that morning. One item read, "How do teachers view the effectiveness of administrators and how often do they think administrators ought to come into classrooms?" One of the administrators who had been most hostile at the outset said, "That would be dynamite information. We have no idea at all what teachers think about us and what we do. I have no idea if they want me in their classrooms or not, or how often they think I ought to visit. That could turn my job around. That would be great to know." Another question concerned the relationship between the classroom and the community. Both the teacher and parent representatives said that nobody had ever thought about that in any real way: "We don't have any policy about that. We don't know what goes on in the different schools. That would be really helpful for us to know."

We spent the rest of the day refining questions, prioritizing, formalizing evaluation procedures, and establishing an agenda for the evaluation process. The hostility had vanished. By the end of the day, they were anxious to have me make a commitment to return. They had become excited about doing their evaluation. The evaluation had credibility because the questions were their questions. A month later they found out that budget shifts in the Ministry meant that the central government would not pay for the evaluation. The Deputy Minister told them that they could scrap the evaluation if they wanted to, but they decided to pay for it out of local division funds.

The evaluation was completed in close cooperation with the task force at every step along the way. The results were disseminated to all principals, teachers, and parent leaders. The conclusions and recommendations formed the basis for staff development conferences and division policy sessions. The evaluation process itself had an impact on the division. Over the next few years, Frontier School Division went through many changes. It became a very different place in terms of direction, morale, and activity than it was on my first visit. Not all those changes were touched on in the evaluation, nor were they simply a consequence of the evaluation. But generating a list of real and meaningful evaluation questions played a critical part in getting things started. Exhibit 2.3 offers criteria for good, utilization-focused questions.

Communicating Commitment to Use from the Beginning

The criterion I offered the primary intended users in Winnipeg for generating meaningful questions was, "Things you'd like to know that would make a difference to what you do." This criterion emphasizes knowledge for action—finding out things that can be used. But generating a list of potentially useful questions is only one way to start interacting with primary users. How one begins depends on what backgrounds, experiences, preconceptions, and relationships the primary users bring to the table. In Winnipeg, I needed to get the group engaged quickly in reframing how they were thinking about my role because their resistance was so palpable and because we didn't have much time.

With a seemingly more neutral group, one that is neither overtly hostile nor enthusiastic (Yes, some groups are actually enthusiastic at

EXHIBIT 2.3

Criteria for Utilization-Focused Evaluation Questions

1. Data can be brought to bear on the question; that is, it is truly an empirical question.

2. There is more than one possible answer to the question; that is, the answer is not predetermined by the phrasing of the question.

3. The primary intended users *want* to answer the question. They care about the answer to the question.

4. The primary users want to answer the question for themselves, not just for someone else.

5. The intended users can indicate how they would use the answer to the question; that is, they can specify the relevance of an answer for future action.

the beginning!), I may begin, as I noted earlier in this chapter, by asking participants to share words and feelings they associate with evaluation, then we explore how this "baggage" they've brought with them may affect their expectations about the evaluation's likely utility. As we work toward a shared definition of evaluation and a clear commitment to use, I look for opportunities to review the development of program evaluation as a field of professional practice and present the standards for and principles of evaluation (see Chapter 1). Sharing the standards and principles of evaluation communicates to primary intended users that evaluation has developed into an established profession—and that those engaged in evaluation have an obligation to act in accordance with professional standards and principles, including priority attention to utility.

Few nonevaluators are aware of the field's professional associations, conferences, journals, standards, and principles. By associating a particular evaluative effort with the larger profession, you can elevate the status, seriousness, and meaningfulness of the process you are facilitating, and help the primary intended users understand the

sources of wisdom you are drawing on and applying as you urge them to attend carefully to utilization issues from the start. In this same vein, the history of the profession, presented in the first chapter, can be shared with intended users to communicate the larger context within which any particular evaluation takes place and to show sophistication about the issues the profession has focused on over time. I consider this so important that I have students practice 10-minute minilectures on the development of evaluation as a field of professional practice, one guided by standards and principles (see Exhibits 1.3 and 1.4), so they can hold forth at a moment's notice, whether the opportunity be a workshop or a cocktail party.

Creative Beginnings

Authors of all races, be they Greeks, Romans, Teutons, or Celts, can't seem just to say that anything is the thing it is; they have to go out of their way to say that it is like something else.

—Ogden Nash

With easy-going, relaxed groups that seem open to having some fun, I'll often begin with a metaphor exercise. Metaphors, similes, and analogies help us make connections between seemingly unconnected things, thereby opening up new possibilities by unveiling what had been undetected. Bill Gephart, in his 1980 presidential address to evaluators, drew an analogy between his work as a watercolor artist and his work as an evaluator. Gephart compared the artist's efforts to "compel the eye" with the evaluator's efforts to "compel the mind." Both artist and evaluator attempt to focus the attention of an audience by highlighting some things and keeping other things in the background. He also examined the ways in which the values of an audience (of art critics or program decision makers) affect what they see in a finished piece of work.

Nick Smith directed a Research on Evaluation Program in which he and others thought about evaluators as poets, architects, photographers, philosophers, operations analysts, and artists (Smith 1981). They consciously and creatively used metaphors and analogies to understand and elaborate the many functions of program evaluation. Use of these forms of figurative speech can help evaluators communicate the nature and practice of evaluation. Many of the problems encountered by evaluators, much of the resistance to evaluation, and many failures of use occur because of misunderstandings and communications problems. What we often have, between evaluators and nonevaluators, is the classic "failure to communicate."

One reason for such failures is that the language of research and evaluation—the jargon—is alien to many laypersons, decision makers, and stakeholders. Language matters; jargon creates barriers; understandable language facilitates access to evaluative thinking (Hopson 2000; Patton 2000, 1975b). From my point of view, the burden for clear communications rests on the evaluator. It is the evaluator who must find ways of bridging the communications gap (Patton 2002a). Metaphors and analogies help because a

> metaphor uses a base domain, familiar domain, to achieve situation awareness, that is, to interpret and understand a new domain. . . . Metaphor does more than adorn our thinking. It structures our thinking. It conditions our sympathies and emotional reactions. It helps us achieve situation awareness. It governs the evidence we consider salient and the outcomes we elect to pursue. (Klein 1999:198–99)

To assist intended users and stakeholders understand the nature of evaluation, I like to ask them to construct metaphors and similes about evaluation. The exercise helps participants in the process discover their own values concerning evaluation while also giving them a mechanism to communicate those values to others. The exercise could be used with a program staff, an evaluation task force, evaluation trainees, workshop participants, or any group for whom it might be helpful to clarify and share perceptions about evaluation. The exercise opens like this.

> One of the things that we'll need to do during the process of working together is come to some basic understandings about what evaluation is and can do. In my experience, evaluation can be a very creative and energizing experience. In particular, interpreting and using evaluation findings for program improvement requires creativity and openness to a variety of possibilities. To help us get started on this creative endeavor, I'm going to ask you to participate with me in a little exercise.
>
> In this box, I have a bunch of toys, household articles, office supplies, tools, and other

miscellaneous gadgets and thingamajigs that I've gathered from around my house. I'm going to dump these in the middle of the table and ask each of you to take one of them and use that item to make a statement about evaluation. Evaluation is like _____ because. . . .

To illustrate what I want people to do, I offer to go first. I ask someone to pick out any object in the room that I might use for my metaphor. What follows are some examples from actual workshops.

Someone points to a coffee cup: "This cup can be used to hold a variety of things. The actual contents of the cup will vary depending on who is using it and for what purpose they are using it. Utilization-focused evaluation is a process like this cup; it provides a form, but is empty until the group of people working on the evaluation fill it with focus and content and substance. The potential of the cup cannot be realized until it holds some liquid. The potential of utilization-focused evaluation cannot be realized until it is given the substance of a concrete evaluation problem and situation. One of the things that I'll be doing as we work together is providing an evaluation framework like this cup. You will provide the substance."

Someone points to a chalkboard: "Evaluation is like a chalkboard because both are tools that can be used to express a variety of different things. The chalkboard itself is just an empty piece of slate until someone writes on it and provides information and meaning by filling in that space. The chalkboard can be filled up with meaningless figures, random marks, obscene words, mathematical formulas, or political graffiti—or the board can be filled with meaningful information, insights, helpful suggestions, and basic facts. The people who write on the chalkboard carry the responsibility for what it says. The people who fill in the blanks in the evaluation and determine its content and substance carry

the responsibility for what the evaluation says. The evaluation process is just a tool to be used—and how it is used will depend on the people who control the process—in this case, you."

I'll typically take a break at this point and give people about 10 minutes to select an item and think about what to say. If there are more than 10 people in the group, I will break the larger group into small groups of 5 or 6 for sharing analogies and metaphors so that each person is given an opportunity to make an evaluation statement. Below are some examples from actual workshops.

This empty grocery bag symbolizes my feelings about evaluation. When I think about our program being evaluated, I want to find someplace to hide. I can put this empty bag over my head so that nobody can see me and I can't see anything else, and it gives me at least the feeling that I'm able to hide. (She puts the bag over her head.)

Evaluation can be like this toothbrush. When used properly it gets out the particles between the teeth so they don't decay. If not used properly, if it just lightly goes over the teeth or doesn't cover all the teeth, then some of the gunk will stay on and cause the teeth to decay. Evaluation should help get rid of any things that are causing a program to decay.

Evaluation for me is like this rubber ball. You throw it down and it comes right back at you. Every time I say to my staff we ought to evaluate the program, they throw it right back at me and they say, "You do the evaluation."

Evaluation is like this camera. It lets you take a picture of what's going on, but it can only capture what you point it at, and only for a particular point in time. My concern about this evaluation is that it won't give the whole picture, that an awful lot may get left out.

Evaluation for me is like this empty envelope. You can use it to send a message to someone. I want to use evaluation to send a message to our funders about what we're doing in the program. They don't have any idea about what we actually do. I just hope they'll read the letter when they get it.

Evaluation for me is like this adjustable wrench. You can use this wrench to tighten nuts and bolts to help hold things together. If used properly and applied with the right amount of pressure, it holds things together very well. If you tighten the bolt too hard, however, you can break the bolt and the whole thing will fall apart. I'm in favor of evaluation if it's done right. My concern is that you can overdo it and the program can't handle it.

The process of sharing is usually accompanied by laughter and spontaneous elaborations of favorite metaphors. It's a fun process that offers hope the evaluation process itself may not be quite as painful as people thought it would be. In addition, participants are often surprised to find that they have something to say. They are typically quite pleased with themselves. Most important, the exercise serves to express very important thoughts and feelings that can be dealt with once they are made explicit.

Those participating are typically not even aware that they have these feelings. By providing a vehicle for discovering and expressing their concerns, it is possible to surface major issues that may later affect evaluation use. Shared metaphors can help establish a common framework for the evaluation, capturing its purpose, its possibilities, and the safeguards that need to be built into the process. Robert Frost once observed, "All thought is a feat of association: Having what's in front of you bring up something in your mind that you almost didn't know you knew." This exercise helps participants bring to mind things about evaluation they almost didn't know they knew.

By the way, I've used this exercise with many different groups and in many different situations, including cross-cultural settings, and I've never yet encountered someone who couldn't find an object to use in saying something about evaluation. One way of guaranteeing this is to include in your box of items some things that have a pretty clear and simple message. For example, I'll always include a lock and key so that a very simple and fairly obvious analogy can be made: "Evaluation is like a lock and key, if you have the right key you can open up the lock and make it work. If you have the right information, you can make the thing work." Or I'll include a light bulb so that someone can say "evaluation is like this light bulb, its purpose is to shed light on the situation."

The Cutting Edge of Metaphors

Metaphors can open up new understandings and enhance communications. They can also distort and offend. At the 1979 meeting of the Midwest Sociological Society, well-known sociologist Morris Janowitz was asked to participate in a panel on the question, "What is the cutting edge of sociology?" Janowitz, having written extensively on the sociology of the military, took offense at the "cutting edge" metaphor. He explained, "Cutting edge is a military term. I am put off by the very term, cutting edge, like the parallel term breakthrough: slogans which intellectuals have inherited from the managers of violence" (Janowitz 1979:592).

"Strategic planning" is a label with military origins and connotations as is "rapid reconnaissance," a phrase sometimes used to describe certain quick, exploratory evaluation efforts. Some stakeholder groups will object to such associations; others will relate positively. Evaluators, therefore, must be sensitive in their selection of metaphors to avoid offensive comparisons and match analogies to stakeholders' interests. Of particular importance, in this regard, is avoiding the use of metaphors with possible racist and sexist connotations, for example, "It's black and white" or "We want to get inside the Black Box of evaluation." As Minnich (1990) has observed in her important book *Transforming Knowledge*, our language and thinking can perpetuate "the old exclusions and devaluations of the majority of humankind that have pervaded our informal as well as formal schooling" (p. 1). She observed further that "even when we are all speaking the same languages, there are many 'languages' at play behind and within what the speakers mean and what we in turn understand . . . , levels and levels of different meanings in even the most apparently simple and accessible utterance" (p. 9). Minnich's point was nicely illustrated at a conference on educational evaluation where a women's caucus formed to express concerns about the analogies used in evaluation and to suggest some alternatives.

> To deal with diversity is to look for new metaphors. We need no new weapons of assessment—the violence has already been done! How about brooms to sweep away the attic-y cobwebs of our male/female stereotypes? The tests and assessment techniques we frequently use are full of them. How about knives, forks, and spoons to sample the feast of human diversity in all its richness and color? Where are the techniques that assess the delicious-ness of response variety, independence of thought, originality, uniqueness? (And lest you think those are female metaphors, let me do away with that myth—at our house everybody sweeps and everybody eats!) Our group talked about another metaphor—the cafeteria line versus the smorgasbord banquet styles of teaching/learning/assessing. Many new metaphors are needed as we seek clarity in our search for better ways of evaluating.

> To deal with diversity is to look for new metaphors. (Hurty 1976)

As we "look for new metaphors" in evaluation, we would do well to do so in the spirit of Thoreau, who observed, "All perception of truth is the detection of an analogy." The added point for utilization-focused evaluators is the admonition to be sensitive in selecting metaphors that are meaningful to specific intended users. The importance of such sensitivity stems from the centrality of "the personal factor" in evaluation use, the subject of the next chapter. First, however, a closing metaphor.

Navigating Evaluation's Rough Seas

Utilization-focused evaluation offers a philosophical harbor to sail toward when the often rough and stormy seas of evaluation threaten to blow the evaluator off course. With each new evaluation, the evaluator sets out, like an ancient explorer, on a quest for useful knowledge, not sure whether seas will be gentle, tempestuous, or becalmed. Along the way the evaluator will often encounter any number of challenges: political intrigues wrapped in mantles of virtue; devious and flattering antagonists trying to co-opt the evaluation in service of their own narrow interests and agendas; unrealistic deadlines and absurdly limited resources; gross misconceptions about what can actually be measured with precision and definitiveness; deep-seated fears about the evils-incarnate of evaluation, and therefore, evaluators; incredible exaggerations of evaluators' power; and insinuations about defects in the evaluator's genetic heritage. The observant evaluator is also likely to encounter tremendously dedicated staff working under difficult conditions for pitiable wages; program participants who have suffered grievous misfortunes and whose lives seem to hang by the most fragile of threads; administrators working feverishly to balance incredible needs against meager resources; funders and policymakers struggling to make sensible and rational decisions in a world that often seems void of sense and reason. The seas of evaluation offer encounters with discouraging corruption and inspiring virtue, great suffering and hopeful achievements, unmitigated programmatic disasters and solidly documentable successes, and an abundance of ambiguity between these poles of the human experience. The voyage is worth taking, despite the dangers and difficulties, because the potential rewards include making a meaningful difference in the effectiveness of important programs, and thereby improving the quality of people's lives. That only happens, however, if the evaluation process and findings are used.

Evaluation Is an Unnatural Act

This was the *double entendre* slogan an evaluator once wore on a tee shirt at an evaluation conference. Evaluation is not natural to managers, funders, policymakers, program staff, or program participants. That's why they need professional evaluation assistance, support, training, and facilitation.

Follow-Up Exercises

1. Explain, from your perspective, how research and evaluation are related. From what perspective is evaluation a specialization within research? From what perspective is research subsumed within evaluation? How are research and evaluation different? How do they overlap?

2. Write about a good idea that didn't work in practice. (See Exhibit 2.2 for inspiration.) What was the idea? What evidence was brought to bear showing that it didn't work? Your example could be a program idea or an idea from your own personal experience.

3. What's your favorite example or illustration of how humans distort reality? Perhaps you have an example from personal experience or a particularly informative example from research. Look for research examples in psychology, sociology, anthropology, and behavioral economics. If making a presentation to the staff of a program to stimulate interest in and commitment to evaluation, how would you use this example to explain the need for systematic and balanced evaluation?

4. Use a favorite activity of your own as a metaphor or analogy to illuminate some aspect of evaluation. Here's an example for inspiration. Fishing is the No. 1 participation sport in Minnesota, the land of 10,000 lakes. (That's the license plate slogan; the actual number of lakes is 11,842.) Suppose you are making an introductory evaluation presentation in Minnesota. How would use fishing as an analogy to introduce evaluation? Or pick your own favorite hobby, recreational activity, sport, or area of personal interest and use it to illuminate an evaluation issue.

3

Fostering Intended
Use by Intended Users

The Personal Factor

*T*here are five key variables that are absolutely critical in evaluation use. They
are, in order of importance: people, people, people, people, and people.

—Halcolm

A Setting

On a damp summer morning at Snow Mountain Ranch near Rocky Mountain National Park,
some 40 human service and education professionals have gathered from all over the country in a
small, dome-shaped chapel to participate in an evaluation workshop. The session begins like this:

*Instead of beginning by my haranguing you about what you should do in program
evaluation, we're going to begin with an evaluation exercise to immerse us immediately in the process. I'm going to ask you to play the dual roles of participants and
evaluators since that's the situation most of you find yourself in anyway in your own
agencies and programs, where you have both program and evaluation responsibilities. We're going to share an experience to loosen things up a bit . . . perhaps warm
you up, wake you up, and allow you to get more comfortable. The exercise will also
allow us to test your participant observer skills and provide us with a common experience as evaluators. We'll also generate some personal data about the process of
evaluation that we can use for discussion later.*

So, what I want you to do for the next five minutes is move around this space in any way you want to. Explore this environment. Touch and move things. Experience different parts of this lovely setting. And while you're observing the physical environment, watch what others do. Then, find a place where you feel comfortable to write down what you observe, and also to evaluate the exercise. Experience, explore, observe, and evaluate. That's the exercise.

At the end of the writing time, participants shared, on a voluntary basis, what they had written.

First Observer: People slowly got up. Everybody looked kind of nervous 'cause they weren't sure what to do. People moved out toward the walls, which are made of rough wood. The lighting is kind of dim. People sort of moved counterclockwise. Every so often there would be a nervous smile exchanged between people. The chairs are fastened down in rows so it's hard for people to move in the center of the room. A few people went to the stage area, but most stayed toward the back and outer part. The chairs aren't too comfortable, but it's a quiet, mellow room. The exercise showed that people are nervous when they don't know what to do.

Second Observer: The room is hexagon-shaped with a dome-shaped ceiling. Fastened-down chairs are arranged in a semicircle with a stage in front that is about a foot high. A podium is at the left of the small stage. Green drapes hang at the side. Windows are small and triangular. The floor is wood. There's a coffee table in back. Most people went to get coffee. A couple people broke the talking rule for a minute. Everyone returned to about the same place they had been before after walking around. It's not a great room for a workshop, but it's OK.

Third Observer: People were really nervous about what to do because the goals of the exercise weren't clear. You can't evaluate without clear goals so people just wandered around. The exercise shows you can't evaluate without clear goals.

Fourth Observer: I said to myself at the start, this is a human relations thing to get us started. I was kind of mad about doing this because we've been here a half hour already, and we haven't done anything that has to do with evaluation. I came to learn about evaluation, not to do touchy-feely group stuff. So I just went to get coffee. I didn't like wasting so much time on this.

Fifth Observer: I felt uneasy, but I told myself that it's natural to feel uneasy when you aren't sure what to do. But I liked walking around, looking at the chapel, and feeling the space. I think some people got into it, but we were stiff and uneasy. People avoided looking at each other. Sometimes there was a nervous smile when people passed each other, but by kind of moving in a circle, most people went the same direction and avoided looking at each other. I think I learned something about myself and how I react to a strange, nervous situation.

These observations were followed by a discussion of the different perspectives reported on the same experience and speculation on what it would take to produce a more focused set of observations and evaluations. Suggestions included establishing clear goals, specifying evaluation criteria, figuring out what was supposed to be observed in advance so everyone could observe it, giving clearer directions of what to do, stating the purpose of evaluation, and training the evaluation observers so that they all recorded the same thing.

Further discussion revealed that before any of these evaluation tasks could be completed, a prior step would be necessary: *determining who the primary intended users of the evaluation are.* This task constitutes the first priority in utilization-focused evaluation.

Identifying Primary Intended Users: The First Priority in Utilization-Focused Evaluation

Many decisions must be made in any evaluation. The purpose of the evaluation must be determined. Concrete evaluative criteria for judging program success will usually have to be established. Methods will have to be selected and timelines agreed on. All these are important issues in any evaluation. The question is, "Who will decide these issues?" The utilization-focused answer is *primary intended users of the evaluation.*

Clearly and explicitly identifying people who can benefit from an evaluation is so important that evaluators have adopted a special term for potential evaluation users: *stakeholders.* This term has been borrowed from management consulting where it was coined in 1963 at the Stanford Research Institute as a way of describing people who were not directly stockholders in a company but "without whose support the firm would cease to exist" (Mendelow 1987:177).

> Stakeholder management is aimed at proactive action—action aimed, on the one hand, at forestalling stakeholder activities that could adversely affect the organization and on the other hand, at enabling the organization to take advantage of stakeholder opportunities. . . . This can be achieved only through a conscious decision to adopt the stakeholder perspective as part of a strategy formulation process. (Mendelow 1987:177–78)

Evaluation stakeholders are people who have a stake—a vested interest—in evaluation findings. For any evaluation, there are multiple possible stakeholders: program funders, staff, administrators, and clients or program participants. Greene (2006) clusters stakeholders into four groups:

> (a) people who have decision authority over the program, including other policy makers, funders, and advisory boards; (b) people who have direct responsibility for the program, including program developers, administrators in the organization implementing the program, program managers, and direct service staff; (c) people who are the intended beneficiaries of the program, their families, and their communities; and (d) people disadvantaged by the program, as in lost funding opportunities. (Pp. 397–98)

BEHOLD the "STAKE-HOLDER"!

Others with a direct, or even indirect, interest in program effectiveness may be considered stakeholders, including journalists and members of the general public, or, more specifically, taxpayers, in the case of public programs, participants in "civil society" (Weiss 1998b:28–29). Ordinary people of all kinds who are affected by programs and policies can be thought of as stakeholders, what Leeuw (2002) has called the challenge of "bringing evaluation to the people" (pp. 5–6). Stakeholders include anyone who makes decisions or desires information about a program. However, stakeholders typically have diverse and often competing interests. No evaluation can answer all potential questions equally well. This means that some process is necessary for narrowing the range of possible questions to focus the evaluation. In utilization-focused evaluation, this process begins by narrowing the list of potential stakeholders to a much shorter, more specific group of primary intended users. Their information needs, that is, their intended uses, focus the evaluation.

The Stakeholder Idea

The word *stakeholder* originated in gambling in sixteenth-century England, where wagers were posted on wooden stakes. Later the term was broadened to refer to a neutral or trustworthy person who held a wager until the winner was decided. The term was brought into management and given visibility by R. Edward Freeman (1984) in his influential text *Strategic Management: A Stakeholder Approach.* He defined a stakeholder as any group or individual who can affect or is affected by the achievement of the organization's objectives. Following this formulation:

Evaluation stakeholders are individuals, groups, or organizations that can affect or are affected by an evaluation process and/or its findings.

Stakeholder analyses are now arguably more important than ever because of the increasingly interconnected nature of the world. Choose any public problem—economic development, poor educational performance, natural resources management, crime, AIDS, global warming, terrorism—and it is clear that "the problem" encompasses or affects numerous people, groups, and organizations. In this shared-power world, no one is fully in charge; no organization "contains" the problem. Instead many individuals, groups, and organizations are involved or affected or have some partial responsibility to act. Figuring out what the problem is and what solutions might work are actually part of the problem, and taking stakeholders into account is a crucial aspect of problem solving.

Failure to attend to the information and concerns of stakeholders clearly is a kind of flaw in thinking or action that too often and too predictably leads to poor performance, outright failure, or even disaster (Bryson 2004b:23–24). Paul Nutt in *Why Decisions Fail* (2002) conducted a careful analysis of 400 strategic decisions. He found that half of the decisions "failed"—that is, they were not implemented, only partially implemented, or otherwise produced poor results—in large part because decision makers failed to attend to interests and information held by key stakeholders.

The workshop exercise that opened this chapter illustrates the importance of clearly identifying primary intended users. The participants in that exercise observed different things in part because they were interested in different things. They "evaluated" the exercise in different ways, and many had trouble "evaluating" the exercise at all, in part because they didn't know for whom they were evaluating. There were several potential users of an evaluation of the "explore the environment" exercise:

1. As a workshop leader, I might want to evaluate the extent to which the exercise accomplished my objectives.

2. Each individual participant might conduct a personal evaluation according to his or her own criteria.

3. The group could establish consensus goals for the exercise, which would then serve as focus for the evaluation.

4. The bosses, agency directors, and/or funding boards who paid for participants to attend might want an assessment of the return on the resources they have invested for training.

5. The Snow Mountain Ranch director might want an evaluation of the appropriateness of the chapel for such a workshop.

6. The building architects might want an evaluation of how participants responded to the space they designed.

7. Professional workshop facilitators might want to evaluate the exercise's effectiveness for opening a workshop.

8. Psychologists or human relation trainers might want to assess the effects of the exercise on participants.

9. Experiential learning educators might want an assessment of the exercise as an experiential learning tool.

10. The janitors of the chapel might want an evaluation of the work engendered for them by an exercise that permits moving things around (which sometimes occurs when I've used the exercise in settings with moveable furniture).

This list of people potentially interested in the evaluation (stakeholders) could be expanded. The evaluation question in each case would likely be different. I would have different evaluation information needs as workshop leader than would the camp director; the architects' information needs would differ from the janitors' "evaluation" questions; the evaluation criteria of individual participants would differ from those reached by the total group through a consensus-formation process.

Beyond Audience

The preceding discourse is not aimed at simply making the point that different people see things differently and have varying interests and needs. I take that to be on the order of a truism. The point is that this truism is regularly and consistently ignored in the design of evaluation studies. To target an evaluation at the information needs of a specific person or a group of identifiable and interacting persons is quite different

---

Stakeholder Analysis Goes Global

The *Wall Street Journal* headline read

UNTRANSLATABLE WORD IN U.S. AIDE'S SPEECH LEAVES BEIJING BAFFLED: ZOELLICK CHALLENGES CHINA TO BECOME 'STAKEHOLDER'; WHAT DOES THAT MEAN? (December 7, 2005)

In September 2005, U.S. Deputy Secretary of State Robert Zoellick delivered a major policy speech to a large meeting of the National Committee on U.S.-China Relations in New York. His theme was, "We need to urge China to become a responsible stakeholder" in the international system.

The *Wall Street Journal* report emphasized that in the written version of the speech, the words were in italics and Mr. Zoellick gave them added emphasis while speaking. He used the word "stakeholder" seven times in all. But, it turned out that the Chinese language has no comparable word for "stakeholder."

In response to Chinese requests for a translation, the U.S. State Department offered the following on a Chinese-language U.S. government Web site: "liyi xiangguang de canyuzhe" or "participants with related interests."

The *Journal* went on to report that U.S. scholars traveling in China were inundated with requests for translation. Jeffrey Bader, a former U.S. trade official, was in Beijing soon after and said, "I ran into people all over the place who kept pulling out tattered copies of the speech. I must have spent eight hours in total helping people understand its meaning," much of the time devoted to the "s" word.

Chinese government academies sent scholarly delegations to Washington to decipher the new term. The *Journal* quoted Minxin Pei, a China scholar at the Carnegie Endowment for International Peace, a Washington think tank: "We hosted several in one week. They arrived and said, 'What does this word mean?' "

The *Journal* reported that some in China preferred a translation that brought out the downside to being a stakeholder, translating it as "participants with related benefits and drawbacks." That implied China's interests might suffer if it attempted to meet Mr. Zoellick's "responsible stakeholder" challenge. Other interpretations came out as "joint operator" or "partner," which connoted an important role for China in world affairs. The *Journal* reported that the Chinese Ministry of Foreign Affairs had not yet decided on an official Chinese translation of "stakeholder" (King, Jr. 2005:A1).

Evaluators Chime In

The *Journal* article, posted on EvalTalk, the listserv of the American Evaluation Association, prompted several responses throughout December 2005. Here are some summary highlights.

- Not only Chinese evaluators and policymakers have difficulties translating "stakeholder" into their language. The same is definitely true for German-speaking evaluators. There are a number of translations in use but they do not really capture the meaning the term *stakeholder* carries in English. In German, *"Beteiligte & Betroffene"* is an often used translation (meaning in English: people participating in or affected by something), although others are used as well, like *"Anspruchsgruppen"* (groups with claims or demands) or *"Interessengruppen"* (interest groups). Interestingly, the use of a specific terminology is highly indicative for the field people are working in. For example, in (quality or public) management, usually there are *Anspruchsgruppen*, in business *Interessengruppen*, in evaluation *Beteiligte & Betroffene*.
- In French, there are as well various translations: *"parties prenantes et concernees"* (parties involved or affected), *"protagonistes"* (protagonists).
- In Italian, the term *stakeholder* used to be translated either with *"parti interessate"* (interested parties), or with *"parti coinvolte"* (involved parties); very often it is kept in English, but I am not sure how precisely Italian non-English speakers can understand its meaning. After the discussion in social sciences on how to best involve stakeholders in policy decisions, the term *"parti coinvolte"* was somewhat abandoned (there are stakeholders that are not necessarily yet involved), and the preferred translation seems now *"parti interessate."*
- In the development of the United States and the movement West people "staked" a claim to land or mines or whatever. Literally, there were stakes in the ground indicating your "40 acres" or land identified as yours. I have always thought a stakeholder had much more than just interest or involvement—it implied ownership. This is important because we not only want to involve those people who have a stake, but also avoid NOT involving critical individuals or groups who have legitimate ownership in whatever we are doing. As we all know, failing to involve an important stakeholder is very likely to result in considerable difficulties down the road.
- Bob Williams of Aotearoa/New Zealand added, "I've just returned from the Australian and New Zealand Systems Conference (working with complexity was the theme). One of the speakers, involved in an extremely complex situation ("World Heritage" park, major fruit-growing industry, rich Sydneyites buying land at huge prices for weekend homes, major tourist attraction) stated that in his work he used the concept of "community of practice" rather than "stakeholder." His point was that "stakeholder" implies representing an "interest," whereas "community of practice" focuses primarily on what people "do."
- Which prompted Jane Davidson, also of Aotearoa/New Zealand, to recall, "It reminds me of my first class in evaluation at graduate school. I had just moved to the States and still wasn't quite used to how much North Americans drop h's in the middle of words. I spent an entire class listening to this mysterious word "stake'olders" wondering "Who ARE these people and just WHY do they have to stay cold?"
- Which prompted this posting: And, of course, there's the definition contained in the 2003 edition of the *Phonetic Dictionary for Carnivores*: "Stakeholder: One who routinely consumes charred slabs of meat without using utensils" (p. 535).

And that gives you a flavor of EvalTalk postings.

These contributions were posted under the subject heading The term *stakeholder*.

For the EvalTalk archives, go to this site: http://bama.ua.edu/archives/evaltalk.html

from *identifying the audience* for an evaluation. For example, Stufflebeam (2001) defines evaluation as "a study designed and conducted to assist some audience assess an object's merit and worth" (p. 11). But audiences are amorphous, largely anonymous entities. Audience connotes passive reception rather than the active engagement of specific users.

Nor is it sufficient to identify an agency or organization as a recipient of evaluation findings. Organizations are an impersonal collection of hierarchical positions. People, not organizations, use evaluation information. I shall elaborate these points later in this chapter. First, I want to present findings from a classic study of how federal health evaluations were used. Those results provide a research foundation for this first step in utilization-focused evaluation. In the course of presenting these data, it will also become clearer how one identifies primary intended users and why they are the key to specifying and achieving intended uses.

Studying Use

In the mid-1970s, as evaluation was emerging as a distinct field of professional practice, I undertook a study with colleagues and students of 20 federal health evaluations to assess how their findings had been used and to identify the factors that affected varying degrees of use. We interviewed the evaluators and those for whom the evaluations were conducted.[1] That study marked the beginning of the formulation of utilization-focused evaluation presented in this book. We asked respondents to comment on how, if at all, each of 11 factors extracted from the literature on utilization had affected use of their evaluation. These factors were methodological quality, methodological appropriateness, timeliness, lateness of report, positive or negative

findings, surprise of findings, central or peripheral program objectives evaluated, presence or absence of related studies, political factors, decision maker/evaluator interactions, and resources available for the study. Finally, we asked respondents to "pick out the single factor you feel had the greatest effect on how this study was used." From this long list of questions only two factors emerged as consistently important in explaining utilization: (1) political considerations, to be discussed in Chapter 14 and (2) a factor we called the *personal factor*. This latter factor was unexpected, and its clear importance to our respondents had, we believed, substantial implications for the use of program evaluation. None of the other specific literature factors about which we asked questions emerged as important with any consistency. Moreover, when these specific factors were important in explaining the use or nonuse of a particular study, it was virtually always in the context of a larger set of circumstances and conditions related to either political considerations or the personal factor.

The Personal Factor

The personal factor is the presence of an identifiable individual or group of people who personally care about the evaluation and the findings it generates. Where such a person or group was present, evaluations were used; where the personal factor was absent, there was a correspondingly marked absence of evaluation impact.

The personal factor represents the leadership, interest, enthusiasm, determination, commitment, assertiveness, and caring of specific, individual people. These are people who actively seek information to learn, make judgments, get better at what they do, and reduce decision uncertainties.

They want to increase their ability to predict the outcomes of programmatic activity and thereby enhance their own discretion as decision makers, policymakers, consumers, program participants, funders, or whatever roles they play. These are the primary users of evaluation.

Data on the Importance of the Personal Factor

The personal factor emerged most dramatically in our interviews when, having asked respondents to comment on the importance of each of our 11 utilization factors, we asked them to identify the single factor that was most important in explaining the impact or lack of impact of that particular study. Time after time, the factor they identified was not on our list. Rather, they responded in terms of the importance of individual people:

Item: I would rank as the most important factor this division director's interest, [his] interest in evaluation. Not all managers are that motivated toward evaluation. [DM353:17][2]

Item: [The single most important factor that had the greatest effect on how the study got used was] the principal investigator. . . . If I have to pick a single factor, I'll pick people any time. [DM328:20]

Item: That it came from the Office of the Director—that's the most important factor. . . . The proposal came from the Office of the Director. It had his attention and he was interested in it, and he implemented many of the things. [DM312:21]

Item: [The single most important factor was that] the people at the same level of decision making in [the new office] were not interested in making decisions of the kind that the people [in the old office] were, I think that probably had the greatest impact. The

fact that there was no one at [the new office] after the transfer who was making programmatic decisions. [EV361:27]

Item: Well, I think the answer there is in the qualities of the people for whom it was made. That's sort of a trite answer, but it's true. That's the single most important factor in any study now that's utilized. [EV232:22]

Item: Probably the single factor that had the greatest effect on how it was used was the insistence of the person responsible for initiating the study that the Director of _____ become familiar with its findings and arrive at judgment on it. [DM369:25]

Item: [The most important factor was] the real involvement of the top decision makers in the conceptualization and design of the study, and their commitment to the study. [DM268:9]

While these comments concern the importance of interested and committed individuals in studies that were actually used, studies that were not used stand out in that there was often a clear absence of the personal factor. One evaluator, who was not sure how his study was used, but suspected it had not been, remarked,

I think that since the client wasn't terribly interested and the whole issue had shifted to other topics, and since we weren't interested in doing it from a research point of view, nobody was interested. [EV264:14]

Another highly experienced evaluator was particularly adamant and articulate about the one factor that is most important in whether an evaluation gets used:

The most important factor is desire on the part of the managers, both the central federal managers and the site managers. I don't think there's [any doubt], you know, that evaluation should be responsive to their needs, and if they have a real desire to get on with whatever it is they're supposed to do, they'll apply it. And if the evaluations don't meet their needs, they won't. About as simple as you can get. I think the whole process is far more dependent on the skills of the people who use it than it is on the sort of peripheral issues of politics, resources. . . . Institutions are tough as hell to change. You can't change an institution by coming and doing an evaluation with a halo. Institutions are changed by people, in time, with a constant plugging away at the purpose you want to accomplish. And if you don't watch out, it slides back. [EV346:15–16]

His view had emerged early in the interview when he described how evaluations were used in the U.S. Office of Economic Opportunity:

In OEO it depended on who the program officer was, on the program review officials, on program monitors for each of these grant programs. Where there were aggressive program people, they used these evaluations whether they understood them or not. They used them to affect improvements, direct allocations of funds within the program, explain why the records were kept this way, why the reports weren't complete or whatever. Where the program officials were unaggressive, passive—nothing!

Same thing's true at the project level. Where you had a director who was aggressive and understood what the hell the structure was internally, he used evaluation as leverage to change what went on within his program. Those who weren't—nothing! [EV346:5]

The same theme emerged in his comments about each possible factor. Asked about the effects on use of methodological quality, positive or negative findings, the degree to which the findings were expected, he always returned eventually to the importance of managerial interest, competence,

and confidence. **The person makes the difference,** he insisted. All else follows.

Our sample included another rather adamant articulation of this premise. An evaluation of a pilot program involving four major projects was undertaken at the instigation of the program administrator. He made a special effort to make sure that his question (i.e., Were the pilot projects capable of being extended and generalized?) was answered. He guaranteed this by personally taking an active interest in all parts of the study. The administrator had been favorable to the program in principle, was uncertain what the results would be, but was hoping that the program would prove effective. The evaluation findings were, in fact, negative. The program was subsequently ended, with the evaluation carrying "considerable weight" in that decision [DM367:8]. Why was this study used in such a dramatic way? His answer was emphatic:

Look, we designed the project with an evaluation component in it, so we were committed to use it and we did. It's not just the fact that [evaluation] was built in, but the fact that we built it in on purpose. That is, the agency head and myself had broad responsibilities for this, wanted the evaluation study results and we expected to use them. Therefore, they were used. That's my point. If someone else had built it in because they thought it was needed, and we didn't care, I'm sure the use of the study results would have been different. [DM367:12]

The evaluator (an external agent selected through an open request for proposal process) independently corroborated the decision maker's explanation:

The principal reason [for use] was that the decision maker was the guy who requested the evaluation and used its results. That is, the organizational distance between the policymaker and the evaluator was almost zero in this instance. That's the most important reason it had an impact. It was the fact that the guy who was asking the question was the guy who was going to make use of the answer. [EV367:12]

Here, then, is a case in which a decision maker commissioned an evaluation knowing what information he needed; the evaluator was committed to answering the decision maker's questions; and the decision maker was committed to using the findings. The result was a high level of use in making a decision contrary to the director's initial personal hopes. In the words of the evaluator, the major factor explaining use was that "the guy who was going to be making the decision was aware of and interested in the findings of the study and had some hand in framing the questions to be answered; that's very important" [EV367:20].

The program director's overall conclusion gets to the heart of the personal factor:

Factors that made a positive contribution to use? One would be that the decision makers themselves want the evaluation study results. I've said that several times. If that's not present, it's not surprising that the results aren't used. [DM367:17]

One highly placed and widely experienced administrator offered the following advice at the end of a 4-hour interview:

Win over the program people. Make sure you're hooked into the people who're going to make the decision in six months from the time you're doing the study, and make sure that they feel it's their study, that these are their ideas, and that it's focused on their values. [DM283:40]

Presence of the personal factor increases the likelihood of long-term follow-through, that is, persistence in getting evaluation findings used. One study in particular stood out in this regard. It was initiated by a new

office director with no support internally and considerable opposition from other affected agencies. The director found an interested and committed evaluator. The two worked closely together. The findings were initially ignored because it wasn't a hot political issue at the time, but over the ensuing 4 years the director and evaluator personally worked to get the attention of key members of Congress. The evaluation eventually contributed to passing significant legislation in a new area of federal programming. From beginning to end, the story was one of personal human commitment to getting evaluation results used.

Although the specifics vary from case to case, the pattern is markedly clear: Where the personal factor emerges, where some individuals take direct, personal responsibility for getting findings to the right people, evaluations have an impact. Where the personal factor is absent, there is a marked absence of impact. Use is not simply determined by some configuration of abstract factors; it is determined in large part by real, live, caring human beings.

The Personal Factor

The personal factor is the presence of an identifiable individual or group of people who personally care about the evaluation and the findings it generates. Where such a person or group is present, evaluations are more likely to be used; where the personal factor is absent, there is a correspondingly lower probability of evaluation impact.

Supporting Research on the Personal Factor

Hofstetter and Alkin (2003) conducted a comprehensive review of research on evaluation use for the *International Handbook of Educational Evaluation*. They concluded,

"In sum, numerous factors influence use. The 'personal factor' appears to be the most important determinant of what impact as well as the type of impact of a given evaluation" (p. 216). And what does this mean in practice? They found that

> the evaluator could enhance use by engaging and involving intended users early in the evaluation, ensuring strong communications between the producers and users of evaluations, reporting evaluation findings effectively so users can understand and use them for their purposes, and maintaining credibility with the potential users. (P. 216)

Sridharan, Campbell, and Zinzow (2006) add to this list of recommendations the importance of developing with intended users a specific anticipated timeline of impact for the evaluation. Ghere et al. (2006) emphasize that such interactions with intended users require interpersonal skills to communicate effectively and engage in design and use negotiations.

Findings about the importance of the personal factor have been accumulating over a quarter century. Burry (1984) and Alkin (1985) of the UCLA Center for the Study of Evaluation synthesized research on factors that affect evaluation use, work that built on their own important empirical research (Alkin, Daillak, and White 1979). They organized factors affecting use into three major categories: human, contextual, and evaluation factors.

Human factors reflect evaluator and user characteristics with a strong influence on use. Included here are such factors as people's attitudes toward and interest in the program and its evaluation, their backgrounds and organizational positions, and their professional experience levels.

Context factors consist of the requirements and fiscal constraints facing the evaluation, and relationships between the program being evaluated and other segments of its broader organization and the surrounding community.

Evaluation factors refer to the actual conduct of the evaluation, the procedures used in the conduct of the evaluation, and the quality of the information it provides (Burry 1984:1).

The primary weakness of this framework is that the factors are not prioritized. At a conference where this synthesis was presented, I asked Jim Burry if his extensive review of the literature suggested any factors as particularly important in explaining use. He answered without hesitation:

> There's no question about it. The personal factor is far and away the most important explanatory variable in evaluation use. The research of the last five years confirms the primacy of the personal factor (personal conversation 1985).

R. Burke Johnson (1998) conducted a comprehensive review of empirical literature and major models of evaluation utilization. He examined and compared 17 different models of utilization and synthesized these into a "meta-model." He summarized what he found as follows:

> Evaluation utilization is a continual and diffuse process that is interdependent with local contextual, organizational and political dimensions. Participation by program stakeholders is essential and continual (multi-way) dissemination, communication and feedback of information and results to evaluators and users (during and after a program) help increase use by increasing evaluation relevance, program modification and stakeholder ownership of results. Evaluators, managers and other key stakeholders should collaboratively employ organizational design and development principles to help increase the amount and quality of participation, dissemination, utilization and organizational learning. (P. 104)

In a field parallel to program evaluation, Lester and Wilds (1990) conducted a comprehensive review of the literature on use of public policy analysis. Based on that review, they developed a conceptual framework to predict use. Among the hypotheses they found supported were these:

• The greater the interest in the subject by the decision maker, the greater the likelihood of utilization.

• The greater the decision maker's participation in the subject and scope of the policy analysis, the greater the likelihood of utilization (Lester and Wilds 1990:317).

Hypotheses linking stakeholder participation and utilization have found support in a quarter century of evaluation literature (e.g., Huberman 1995; Greene 1988a, 1988b; King 1982), especially in the American Evaluation Association (AEA) journal *New Directions for Evaluation.* Special issues of the journal have focused on *Promoting the Use of Government Evaluations in Policymaking* (Mohan and Sullivan 2007; Mohan, Tikoo, Capela, and Bernstein 2007); *Responding to Sponsors and Stakeholders in Complex Evaluation Environments* (Mohan, Bernstein, and Whitsett 2002); *The Expanding Scope of Evaluation Use* (Caracelli and Preskill 2000); *Legislative Program Evaluation: Utilization Driven Research for Decision Makers* (Jonas 1999); *Understanding and Practicing Participatory Evaluation* (Whitmore 1998); *Using Performance Measurement to Improve Public and Nonprofit Programs* (Newcomer 1997); *Evaluation Utilization* (McLaughlin et al. 1988); *The Client Perspective on Evaluation* (Nowakowski 1987); and *Stakeholder-Based Evaluation* (Bryk 1983).

Marvin Alkin, founder and former director of the Center for the Study of Evaluation at the University of California, Los Angeles, made the personal factor the basis for his *Guide for Evaluation Decision Makers* (1985). Jean King concluded from her research review (1988) and case studies (1995) that involving the right people is critical to evaluation use. In a major analysis of "Assessing the Feasibility and Likely Usefulness of Evaluation," Joseph Wholey (1994:16) has shown that involving intended users early is critical so that "the intended users of the evaluation results have agreed on how they will use the information" before the evaluation is conducted. Carol Weiss, one of the leading scholars of knowledge use, concluded in her keynote address to the AEA:

> First of all, it seems that there are certain participants in policymaking who tend to be "users" of evaluation. The personal factor—a person's interest, commitment, enthusiasm—plays a part in determining how much influence a piece of research will have. (Weiss 1990:177)

More recently, Cousins and Shulha (2006) reviewed a great volume of research on utilization of evaluation and knowledge; they found that "both social scientists and evaluators are learning that attention to the characteristics of knowledge users is a potent way to stimulate the utilization of findings" (p. 273).

You get the point. From the 1970s (Patton, Grimes et al. 1977; Weiss 1977) to the most updated comprehensive reviews of research on evaluation use (Cousins 2007; Mark 2006; Cousins and Shulha 2006; Alkin 2005), the evaluation profession has been deepening its understanding of how interactions with primary intended users affects actual use. Over that time, the evaluation literature has generated substantial evidence that attention to the personal factor—involving key stakeholders and working with intended users—can increase use.[3]

Primary Intended Users of an Evaluation

Primary intended users of an evaluation are those *specific* stakeholders selected to work with the evaluator throughout the evaluation to focus the evaluation, participate in making design and methods decisions, and interpret results to assure that the evaluation is useful, meaningful, relevant, and credible. Primary intended users represent key and diverse stakeholder constituencies and have responsibility for transmitting evaluation findings to those constituencies for use.

What we've learned harkens back to the influential insights of the Stanford Evaluation Consortium, one of the leading places of ferment and reform in evaluation during the late 1970s. Cronbach and associates in the Consortium identified major reforms needed in evaluation by publishing a provocative set of 95 theses, following the precedent of Martin Luther. Among them was this gem:

> Nothing makes a larger difference in the use of evaluations than *the personal factor*—the interest of officials in learning from the evaluation and the desire of the evaluator to get attention for what he knows. (Cronbach et al. 1980:6; italics added)

Issues of Scale and Scope: Connectors at All Levels

In local program settings, it's fairly easy to imagine the personal factor at work. Chapter 1 opened with a scene on a

November morning in Minnesota where 15 people gathered to discuss evaluation of a county welfare-to-work program. The primary intended users included the county commissioner who chaired the human services committee and another commissioner; state legislators from the county who served on the House and Senate welfare committees; the county administrator for human services and his deputy; an associate director from the state welfare office; two citizen advisory board representatives, one of whom had once been on welfare; the director of a welfare rights advocacy organization; the director of a local employment training program; a university public policy scholar; and the internal county evaluator. These people knew each other and, although they came with varying political perspectives and values, they could be counted on to behave in a congenial manner that has come to be called "Minnesota nice." The network and influence of these 15 people extended to a broad range of stakeholder constituencies. These are the people who Malcolm Gladwell (2002) in *The Tipping Point* called "connectors." In Gladwell's "Law of the Few," he identified connectors as people who know a lot of people and know the right people. *When connectors are the primary intended users, they get the evaluation findings out to a broad range of people.* They are hubs connected to spokes, and they make the wheels of change turn.

But does the personal factor work in larger, more complex settings like the federal government, international agencies, and national organizations? This has been a matter of some significant debate (Alkin 1990; Patton 1988b; Weiss 1988). The debate clarified that different political and decision contexts affect the answer to this question. Policy decisions are different from program decisions and involve different

political contexts. Policy change is subject to a broad range of influences that cumulate over time and can be subject to the vagaries and uncertainties of precipitous events. Hurricane Katrina hits New Orleans and suddenly there's all kinds of new legislation about natural disasters. The political party controlling Congress or the presidency changes, and a flurry of new policy possibilities are brought to the fore. The cast of characters is large, diverse, and subject to sudden change. Research and evaluation findings enter into this fray in diffuse and unpredictable ways. Thus, in a national policy context, evaluation findings may influence thinking and understanding but are unlikely to lead directly to specific decisions by specific decision makers (Weiss 1988, 1998b).

In short, *context matters*. The national policy context is different from the local program context, with different stakeholder configurations, and different utilization patterns and challenges. But what of a national *program* context? The question remains: Does the personal factor work in larger, more complex settings like the federal government, international agencies, and national organizations? Can targeting and working with key stakeholders enhance use in these broader contexts? Let's look at the evidence.

Wargo (1989) analyzed three unusually successful federal evaluations in a search for "characteristics of successful program evaluations"; he found that active involvement of key stakeholders was critical at every stage: during planning, while conducting the evaluation, and in dissemination of findings (p. 77). In 1995, the U.S. General Accounting Office (since renamed the Government Accountability Office [GAO]) studied the flow of evaluative information to Congress (GAO 1995) by following up three major federal programs:

the Comprehensive Child Development Program, the Community Health Centers Program, and the Chapter 1 Elementary and Secondary Education Act aimed at providing compensatory education services to low-income students. Analysts concluded that underutilization of evaluative information was a direct function of poor communications between intended users (members of the Senate Committee on Labor and Human Resources) and responsible staff in the three programs:

> Finally, we observed that communication between the Committee and agency staff knowledgeable about program information was limited and comprised a series of one-way communications (from the Committee to the agency or the reverse) rather than joint discussion. This pattern of communication, which was reinforced by departmental arrangements for congressional liaison, affords little opportunity to build a shared understanding about the Committee's needs and how to meet them. (GAO 1995:40)

The GAO report recommended that Senate Committee members have "increased communication with agency program and evaluation staff to help ensure that information needs are understood and that requests and reports are suitably framed and are adapted as needs evolve" (GAO 1995:41). This recommendation affirms the importance of personal interactions as a basis for mutual understanding to increase the relevance and, thereby, the utility of evaluation reports. In a similar vein, in its report on performance budgeting and program performance, the GAO (2006c) report headline summarized its overall conclusion: "*More Can Be Done to Engage Congress.*"

Patrick Grasso is a federal-level and international agency evaluator with extensive experience dealing with large-scale program contexts at the GAO and The World Bank. He has written about the importance of moving from vague and general audiences to "priority" and "key" evaluation users. He has observed that, even in broad evaluations with multiple potential audiences, evaluation

> efforts can be made more successful through up-front consultations with prospective users of the evaluation. Where possible, it is helpful to solicit from the identified potential users indications of what information they need and when they need to have it to meet any pending decision points.

He goes on to advocate that "the extent that all the potential audience groups can reach consensus on the 'what and when' issues, the likelihood of the evaluation actually being used is likely to expand significantly." But how is this done? He tells of the evaluation of a World Bank forestry policy that began with a "kick-off workshop" for interested parties to define the appropriate evaluation questions for the study, and frequent communications with this group throughout the evaluation helped ensure that it would meet the needs of these often-competing interests. He concluded, "An important side benefit is that the final report was accepted by virtually all the parties involved in this contentious area of Bank development work" (all quotes from Grasso 2003:510).

This epitomizes utilization-focused evaluation in a complex, dynamic, and conflict-laden international setting. My only quarrel with how my good friend and colleague Patrick Grasso has characterized this evaluation is that he describes the report's acceptance as a "side benefit." But the key stakeholder-involving process he describes is aimed explicitly and intentionally at such acceptance and use. It is not a side effect. It is the direct, intended outcome of a utilization-focused evaluation.

George Grob, another highly experienced evaluator at the federal level, has laid out how to get evaluations used at that level by actively engaging "gatekeepers" and "thought leaders" on the program or policy of interest. *Thought leaders* form a "community of experts" on a topic. They are akin to what Gladwell called connectors, with their expertise the basis of their connections. Grob (2003) advises,

> Once you start engaging the thought leaders in a field of interest to you, listen to them. They know what they are talking about. Answer their questions. Make practical recommendations. Tell them something they don't already know. Treat them with respect. (P. 503)

These are wise and effective utilization-focused strategies regardless of the context—local, national, or international.

Exhibit 3.1 summarizes important Canadian research on "drivers of effective evaluations" based on case studies of 15 national evaluations. These drivers emphasize the importance of targeting relevant information to specific intended users and involving those users in the evaluation process.

Evaluation Use Exemplars

Another place to learn what works in large, complex contexts is to examine evaluation exemplars. Each year the Awards Committee of the AEA gives an Outstanding Evaluation Award. In 1998, the outstanding evaluation was the Council for School Performance's "School and System Performance Reports" for the state of Georgia. The reports and reporting process garnered high accolades for their utility. Obviously, schools have a multitude of stakeholders and a statewide education system magnifies the number and diversity of vested interests and competing perspectives. There are lots of potential "audiences." Were there any primary intended users actually involved in the evaluation's design and use? In an interview for the *American Journal of Evaluation*, Gary Henry described how the evaluation unfolded.

> We knew that it would be important to engage superintendents, school board members, teachers, and principals. Our work was overseen by six Council members who were appointed by the Governor, Lieutenant Governor, the Speaker of the Georgia House of representatives and an ex-officio member, the State Superintendent of Schools. Members of the Council were emphatic about extending stakeholder status to members of the community in a highly inclusive way—including parents and others in the community. It took almost a year working with these groups to create the architecture of the accountability system. . . . Once we all got on the same page, there was a great deal of creativity and excitement. The process focused on identifying what indicators we would use. We met in four separate groups—principals, superintendents, teachers, and community members—to reduce the influence of pre-existing power relationships on the deliberations. At three points during the process and twice after the system was being implemented we brought all four groups together. Turnout at the meetings was very high. (Henry quoted in Fitzpatrick 2000:109)

Another exemplar and the 2002 Outstanding Evaluation Award recipient was the evaluation of the Colorado Healthy Communities Initiative. This was an 8-year study that involved community-based health promotion projects in 29 communities across the state. Ross Connor (2005), former president of the AEA and overall program evaluator, used what he called a "collaborative, community-based approach"

EXHIBIT 3.1
Research on Use: Drivers of Effective Evaluations

"Best practices" for useful evaluations were reported by the Treasury Board of Canada (2002) based on review of 15 major Canadian evaluations. The report identified "drivers of effective evaluations" that "were felt, by both the evaluation staff and the program staff, to have contributed significantly to making the evaluations useful and worthwhile."

Senior Management Support

Senior management support of the process and the evaluation results is extremely important. This can help in areas where processes are being stalled; relationships with clients and stakeholders are tenuous and require senior management involvement; disagreements exist on evaluation objectives, results or recommendations; or support is required to approve contentious recommendations.

Participatory Relationship between Evaluation Staff and Program Staff

Evaluations where programs staff were actively involved in the evaluation process contributed not only to a process that was focused, smooth, and problem-free but also to producing results that were relevant, timely, and defensible. The buy-in from programs is critical to increasing the likelihood that results and recommendations will be accepted and ultimately implemented.

Specific Best Practices Include

- Program participation: Involvement of the Program management in the planning of evaluation, including providing input to the evaluation Terms of Reference, interview lists, and data collection instruments. Involvement could be through membership on the evaluation governance body (e.g., Steering Committee), or frequent interaction and communication with the evaluation unit.
- Mutually agreed-on terms of reference and evaluation objectives: Mutual agreement on the objectives of the evaluation, including the measures of success, between the evaluation unit and the program staff will lessen the risk of the evaluation going off track and ensure that there are no last-minute surprises. For example, using very specific evaluation terms of reference and meeting to discuss and document evaluation objectives and expectations have helped ensure that all parties are working toward the same goal.
- Open and rapid communication throughout process: Examples of methods that have been used include making regular presentations to programs areas, steering committees, and client groups; maintaining an open process throughout the evaluation; and engaging in internal consultations to ensure that the evaluation was addressing managers' concerns.
- Engagement of program managers in the presentation of management response: Effective evaluation processes have included the program managers in developing and presenting the management response and action plan to the departmental senior management committee approving the evaluation. This provides an opportunity for program managers to be part of the process and promotes ownership of the action plan. It also ensures the development of a timely response to the evaluation by program management.

SOURCE: From Treasury Board of Canada (2002), *Case Studies on the Uses and Drivers of Effective Evaluations in the Government of Canada*, sect. 5.

that "involved a lot of different stakeholders" to design the evaluation and interpret findings. The evaluation brought together key stakeholders from different communities at various times to prioritize evaluation questions—people called the "primary question askers." Key stakeholders also participated in designing instruments (the evaluation used a variety of methods), overseeing implementation, and interpreting findings. Connor spent a lot of time in communities, and community people spent a lot of time working collaboratively on the evaluation. With so many people involved over a number of years, managing the stakeholder involvement process was a major activity of the evaluation—and that included managing inevitable conflicts. Lest we give the impression that involving primary intended users in evaluation is always a lovefest, consider this incident in the Colorado evaluation. In the process of involving community people in designing a survey, Connor reports,

> The discussion got so heated that I actually ended up having the sheriff come to the parking lot . . . There was a religious right segment of the community that was invited to participate. They attended, but they did not come to participate. They came to collect information to send to their attorney, they said, to sue these people because they were spending blood money—money that came from abortionists. (Quoted in Christie 2005:374)

The situation got resolved, but that group dropped out of the process. And this makes an important point about identifying primary intended users. Not everyone is interested in data for decision making. Not everyone is an information user. Not everyone will buy into evaluation. Some may participate for ulterior motives. Later in this chapter, we'll discuss how to locate and involve those who make good primary intended users.

A Long-Term Evaluation Partnership: The Colorado Community Trust Community-Based Collaborative Evaluation

This evaluation stretched over a long period of time [8 years]. People come and go. Reality happens. Life happens. It takes patience, and it takes an evaluation team that really wants to be partners with the communities and to follow the journey with them— through the good times and challenging ones. . . . It was a long process. And I'm still in touch with some of the people there.

—Evaluator Ross Connor
(quoted in Christie 2005:374)

In summary, the need for interactive dialogue at an interpersonal level applies to large-scale state, national, and international evaluations as well as in smaller scale, local evaluations.

Evaluation's Premier Lesson

The importance of the personal factor in explaining and predicting evaluation use leads directly to the emphasis in utilization-focused evaluation on working with intended users to specify intended uses. The personal factor directs us to attend to specific people who understand, value, and care about evaluation and further directs us to attend to their interests. This is the primary lesson the profession has learned about enhancing use, and it is wisdom now widely acknowledged by practicing evaluators, as evidenced by research on evaluators' beliefs and practices.

Brad Cousins and his colleagues surveyed a sample of 564 evaluators and 68 practitioners drawn from the membership lists of professional evaluation associations in the United States and Canada. The survey included a list of possible beliefs that respondents could agree or disagree with. Greatest consensus centered on the statement, "Evaluators should formulate recommendations from the study." (I'll discuss recommendations in a later chapter.) The item eliciting the next highest agreement was, "The evaluator's primary function is to maximize intended uses by intended users of evaluation data" (Cousins, Donohue, and Bloom 1996:215).

As part of a review of developments over the first 10 years of the AEA, Preskill and Caracelli (1997) conducted a survey of members of AEA's Topical Interest Group on Use. They found that 85 percent rated as extremely or greatly important "identifying and prioritizing intended users of the evaluation" (p. 216). The only item eliciting higher agreement (90 percent) was the importance of "planning for use at the beginning of the evaluation." Preskill and Caracelli also found that 80 percent of survey respondents agreed that *evaluators should take responsibility for involving stakeholders in the evaluation processes.* Fleischer (2007) asked the same question on a replication survey of AEA members in 2006 and found that *98 percent agreed with this assertion.* In rating the importance of eight different evaluation approaches, "user-focused" evaluation was rated highest. **Stakeholder involvement in evaluations has become accepted practice in the profession.**

In a review of models of evaluation use, Shulha and Cousins (1997) found significantly increased attention to the way in which context affects evaluation use, where context includes different kinds of stakeholder environments and varying relationships with intended users. They noted especially "the proliferation of collaborative modes of evaluation . . . [which] aspire to more equitable power relationships between evaluators and program practitioners leading to jointly negotiated decision making and meaning making" (p. 200).

> **Evaluators' Responsibility for Intended Use by Intended Users**
>
> In a 2006 online survey of members of the American Evaluation Association, 77 percent of 1,047 respondents agreed or strongly agreed with the following statement: Evaluators should take responsibility for *being accountable to intended users of the evaluation for intended uses of the evaluation.*
>
> SOURCE: Fleischer (2007).

Jody Fitzpatrick (2004) examined patterns in evaluations chosen as exemplary by the Awards Committee of the AEA and subsequently featured in the *American Journal of Evaluation.* She examined case studies of all eight exemplary evaluations and found that regardless of the evaluation model, methods, or theories guiding the evaluation, "stakeholder involvement is a central component in these exemplary evaluators' practice" (p. 552). Christina Christie (2003) examined the "practice-theory relationship in evaluation" by conducting research on the actual practices of prominent and influential evaluation theorists. She found,

> Regardless of the extent to which theorists discuss stakeholder involvement in their writing, results from this study show that all theorists involve stakeholders in the evaluation process. . . . This revelation is interesting, because not all theorists have traditionally been proponents of stakeholder involvement. . . . I offer as a plausible explanation of this finding that, in practice, the trend has turned toward increased stakeholder involvement, even across a broad theoretical spectrum. (Christie 2003:30)

Alkin (2003), House (2003), and King (2003), in commenting on this finding, concur that some degree of stakeholder involvement has become central to exemplary evaluation practice, but important differences remain in the depth, breadth, and nature of stakeholder involvement advocated and practiced by difference theorists. Of the theories examined, *utilization-focused evaluation came out on the high end in advocating and practicing active involvement of key stakeholders throughout all aspects, stages, and decisions in an evaluation* (Christie 2003:15–30).

In a simulation study of how different evaluation theories and theorists approach evaluation (Alkin and Christie 2005), a common theme was *stakeholder engagement*. Again, however, there were important differences in what stakeholder engagement meant.

In a major review of evaluation use in national not-for-profit organizations, the Independent Sector concluded that attending to "the human side of evaluation" makes all the difference. "Independent Sector learned that evaluation means task, process <u>and</u> people. It is the people side—the human resources of the organization—who make the 'formal' task and process work and will make the results work as well" (Moe 1993:19). The same emphasis is true in *practical* approaches to evaluation in government (Newcomer et al. 2004).

Attending to the personal factor also applies cross-culturally and internationally. Long-time Kiwi evaluator Bob Williams has conducted his own research on what he elegantly calls "getting the stuff used," uncovered the importance of "the personal effect" and has related it to how things work in New Zealand.

> In the interviews I conducted . . . , most people stressed the importance of personal relationships within and between government agencies. There are close and often personal relationships between ministers, policy advisors, politicians, programme providers, and clients of programmes. . . . Things happen here in New Zealand because of who knows whom and their particular reputations. Process matters—a lot. Evaluations and evaluation processes that sustain or improve these relationships are inevitably more welcome than those that undermine them. (Williams 2003:198–9)

Williams' description of how things happen in New Zealand applies to many countries and many localities. For example, Rosenström, Mickwitz, and Melanen (2006) and Mickwitz (2006:63–64) have documented the critical importance of involving influential local actors in the development of sociocultural indicators as part of an environmental evaluation framework in Finland. Maclure (2006) has described the pragmatic approach that led to successfully involving key stakeholders, including beneficiaries, in an evaluation of humanitarian aid in Sierra Leone. Salmen and Kane (2006) offer examples of the value of including beneficiary perspectives in designing and evaluating development projects throughout the world.

Given widespread agreement about the desired outcome of evaluation, namely, intended uses by intended users, let's now examine some of the practical implications of this perspective.

Practical Implications of the Personal Factor

1. *Find the right people.* It can be helpful to conduct a stakeholder analysis to distinguish different degrees of potential involvement for different stakeholders based on personal factor considerations: their interest, influence, importance, availability, connections, and capacity for contributing to the evaluation and its use. Bryson (2004), based on the work of

Eden and Ackermann (1998), offers a process for sorting stakeholders by degree of interest and amount of power. Those with high interest and considerable power can be excellent candidates to become primary intended users. Those with high power but low interest may become obstacles to use. Those with high interest but relatively little power may provide connections to those with power. Those with low interest and little power, for example, the program's intended beneficiaries are often in this category, may require extra attention and support to generate interest and enhance their capacity to participate in the evaluation. Exhibit 3.2 presents the "Power Versus Interest" grid from Eden and Ackermann (1998:122).

A more refined stakeholder analysis distinguishes five levels of stakeholder engagement: informing, consulting, involving, collaborating, and empowering. Each level of engagement involves a different promise from the evaluator and varying degrees of commitment. Menu 3.1 provides details of this approach to stakeholder analysis.

2. *Find and train information users.* To work with primary intended users to achieve intended uses, the evaluation process must surface people who want to know something. This means locating people who are able and willing to use information. The number may vary from one prime user to a fairly large group representing several constituencies, for example, a task force of program staff, clients, funders, administrators, board members, community representatives, and officials or policymakers (see Exhibit 3.3). Cousins et al. (1996) surveyed evaluators and found that they reported six stakeholders as the median

EXHIBIT 3.2
Stakeholder Analysis: Power versus Interest Grid

	Low-Power Stakeholders	High-Power Stakeholders
High-interest stakeholders	Support and enhance their capacity to be involved, especially when they may be affected by findings, as in the case of program participants. Their involvement increases the diversity of the evaluation.	High potential as primary intended users. These are often key "players" who are in a prime position to affect use, including using it themselves as well as drawing the attention of others.
Low-interest stakeholders	Inform them about the evaluation and its findings. Controversy can quickly turn this amorphous "crowd" of general public stakeholders into a very interested mob.	Need to cultivate their interest and be alert in case they pose barriers to use through their disinterest. They are "context setters" (Eden and Ackermann 1998:122).

MENU 3.1

Alternative Degrees and Kinds of Stakeholder Involvement

Types of involvement	Inform	Consult	Involve	Collaborate	Empower
Promise evaluator makes:	We will keep you informed of the evaluation's progress and findings.	We will keep you informed, listen to you, and provide feedback on how your input influenced the evaluation.	We will work with you to ensure your concerns are considered and reflected in options considered, make sure you get to review and comment on options, and provide feedback on how your input is used in the evaluation.	We will incorporate your advice and suggestions to the greatest extent possible, and give you meaningful opportunities to be part of the evaluation decision-making process.	This is your evaluation. We will offer options to inform your decisions. You will decide and we will support and facilitate implementing what you decide.
People especially important and useful to . . .	Disseminate findings and create interest in the results.	anticipate issues, identify landmines, suggest priorities, and enhance the credibility of the evaluation.	affirm the importance, appropriateness and utility of the evaluation, attracting attention to findings, and establish credibility.	serve as primary intended users because of their high interest, interpersonal style, availability, influential positions and/or connections, and sense of ownership of the evaluation.	capacity development, using the evaluation to build their capacity to engage in evaluative thinking and practice.

SOURCE: Inspired by and adapted from Bryson (2004b:33).

number typically involved in a project. While stakeholders' points of view may vary on any number of issues, what they should share is a genuine interest in using evaluation, an interest manifest in a willingness to take the time and effort to work through their information needs and interests. Thus, the first challenge in evaluation is to answer seriously and searchingly the classic question posed by Marvin Alkin (1975): "Evaluation: Who Needs It? Who Cares?" Answering this question, as we shall see, is not always easy, but it is always critical.

EXHIBIT 3.3
A Statewide Evaluation Task Force

The Personal Factor means getting key influentials together, face-to-face, to negotiate the evaluation. Here's an example.

In 1993, the Minnesota Department of Transportation created seven "Area Transportation Partnerships" to make decisions about roads and other transportation investments in a cooperative fashion between state and local interests. To design and oversee the evaluation of how well the partnerships were working, a "technical panel" was created to represent the diverse interests involved. Members of the technical panel included

- The District Engineer from District 1 (Northeast)
- The Planning Director from District 6 (Southeast)
- The District Planner from District 7 (South central)
- Planner for a Regional Development Council (Northwest)
- Department of Transportation Director of Economic Analysis and Special Studies, State Office of Investment Management
- An influential county commissioner
- Director of a regional transit operation
- Director of a regional metropolitan Council of Governments (Western part of the state)
- Member of the Metropolitan Council Transportation Advisory Committee (Greater Minneapolis/Saint Paul)
- A county engineer
- A private transportation consultant
- A city engineer from a small town
- A metropolitan planning and research engineer
- The State Department of Transportation Interagency Liaison
- A University of Minnesota researcher from the University's Center for Transportation Studies
- An independent evaluation consultant (not the project evaluator)
- Five senior officials from various offices of the State Department of Transportation
- The evaluator and two assistants

This group met quarterly throughout the evaluation. The group made substantive improvements in the original design, gave the evaluation credibility with different stakeholder groups, and laid the groundwork for use.

---

3. *Find tipping point connectors.* Formal position and authority are only partial guides in identifying primary users. Evaluators must find strategically located people who are enthusiastic, committed, competent, interested, and connected—*tipping point* connectors, people who are looked to by others for information (Gladwell 2002). Our data suggest that more may sometimes be accomplished by working with a lower-level person displaying these characteristics than by working with a passive, disinterested person in a higher position. However, the lower-level person needs to be able to connect with, have credibility with, and be able to

influence higher-level people. Evaluation use is clearly facilitated by having genuine support from the program and organizational leadership. Those people are not always the best for detailed, hands-on engagement along the way, but reaching them with findings remains important.

4. *Facilitate high quality interactions.* Quality, quantity, and timing of interactions with intended users are all important—but quality is most important. A large amount of interaction between evaluators and users with little substance may backfire and actually reduce stakeholder interest. Evaluators must be strategic and sensitive in asking for time and involvement from busy people and be sure they're interacting with the right people around relevant issues. Increased contact by itself is likely to accomplish little. Nor will interaction with the wrong persons (i.e., people who are not oriented toward use) help much. It is the nature and quality of interactions between evaluators and decision makers that are at issue. My own experience suggests that where the right people are involved, the amount of direct contact can sometimes be reduced because the interactions that do occur are of such high quality. Later, when we review the decisions that must be made in the evaluation process, we'll return to the issues of quantity, quality, and timing of interactions with intended users.

5. *Nurture interest and develop capacity in evaluation.* Evaluators will typically have to work to build and sustain interest in evaluation use. Identifying intended users is part selection and part nurturance. Potential users with low opinions of or little interest in evaluation may have had bad prior experiences or just not have given much thought to the benefits of evaluation. The second chapter discussed ways

of cultivating interest in evaluation and building commitment to use. Even people initially inclined to value evaluation will still often need training and support to become effective information users.

6. *Develop facilitation skills.* Evaluators need skills in building relationships, facilitating groups, managing conflict, walking political tightropes, and effective interpersonal communications to capitalize on the importance of the personal factor. Technical skills and social science knowledge aren't sufficient to get evaluations used. People skills are critical. Ideals of rational decision making in modern organizations notwithstanding, personal and political dynamics affect what really happens. Evaluators without the savvy and skills to deal with people and politics will find their work largely ignored or, worse yet, used inappropriately. Jean King and colleagues have paid special attention to the interpersonal and other competences that evaluators need to make evaluations useful (Ghere et al. 2006; Stevahn et al. 2005, 2006; King et al. 2001).

7. *Strategize about appropriate involvement.* A particular evaluation may have multiple levels of stakeholders and, therefore, need multiple levels of stakeholder involvement. For example, funders, chief executives, and senior officials may constitute the primary users for overall effectiveness results, while lower level staff and participant stakeholder groups may be involved in using implementation and monitoring data for program improvement. Exhibit 3.4 provides an example of such a multiple level structure for different levels of stakeholder involvement and evaluation use.

8. *Demonstrate cultural sensitivity and competence.* Involvement of stakeholders and primary intended users has to be adapted to cultural and contextual factors (Madison 2007; Kirkhart 2005, 1995;

Riddle 2005; Connor 2004; Hood 2004; Symonette 2004; King, Nielsen, and Colby 2004; SenGupta, Hopson, and Thompson-Robinson 2004; Patton 1999c, 1985). Clayson et al. (2002) examined negotiations between evaluation stakeholders in Latino communities and found that they had to be especially attentive to power inequalities and a dynamic environment. Along the way they had to play a variety of roles, including interpreters, translators, mediators, and storytellers. Relationships among people in evaluation situations are affected by larger societal issues, including the challenges of involving people with disabilities (Gill 1999; Lee 1999), racism, sexism, and other forms of prejudice that engender conflict and misunderstandings (Hopson 1999; House 1999; Patton 1999a; Stanfield 1999). Moreover, the norms for and challenges to stakeholder involvement and evaluation practice vary greatly across cultures and geographies (Laperrière 2006; Stern 2004; Lunt et al. 2003; Williams 2003; Leeuw 2002; Patton 1985).

Culturally Competent and Responsive Evaluators

Diversity, in its many dimensions and manifestations, is increasingly acknowledged as a necessary prerequisite for excellence.... Diversity fires and fuels creativity, innovation, and generative engagement in all sectors of life and living.... Multicultural development requires moving beyond tolerance, accommodation, and pressure to fit in toward a focus on changes in policies, processes, and practices in order to genuinely invite and engage the full spectrum of diverse voices, perspectives, experiences, and peoples.

Clearly, evaluative judgments are, by their very nature, inextricably bound up with culture and context. So, where there is sociocultural diversity, there very likely is some diversity in the expected and preferred evaluative processes and practices that undergird judgments of merit, worth, value, quality, significance, congruence. Maximizing accuracy, appropriateness, respect, and excellence calls for an openness to the decentering realities and complexities of difference and diversity.

SOURCE: "Walking Pathways toward Becoming a Culturally Competent Evaluator." Hazel Symonette (2004:96, 107).

In beginning an evaluation training program with Native Americans, I started off by asking them, as part of introducing themselves, to mention any experiences with and perceptions of evaluation they cared to share. With 15 participants, I expected the process to take no more than a half hour. But deep feelings surfaced and a dialogue ensued that took over 2 hours. Here is some of what they said.

• "I'm frustrated that what constitutes 'success' is always imposed on us by somebody who doesn't know us, doesn't know our ways, doesn't know me."

• "By white standards I'm a failure because I'm poor, but spiritually I'm rich. Why doesn't that count?"

• "I have a hard time with evaluation. We need methods that are true to who we are."

• Said through tears by a female elder: "All my life I've worked with grant programs and evaluation has been horrible for us—horribly traumatic. Painful. Made us look bad, feel bad. We've tried to give the funders what they want in numbers but we know that those numbers don't capture what is happening. It's been demeaning. It's taken a toll. I didn't want to come here today."

• Spoken in his native language by a spiritual leader who had opened the session with a smudge ceremony and blessing, translated by his son: "Everything I do is connected to who I am as an Oglala Lakota elder, to our way as a people, to what you call our culture. Everything is connected. Evaluation will have to be connected if it is to have meaning. That's why I brought my son, and my neighbor, and my friend, and my granddaughter. They aren't signed up for this thing we're here to do. But they are connected, so they are here."

Respecting and honoring culture is a significant dimension of the personal factor. As these quotations show, culture is personal. Everyone who comes to the evaluation table brings culture with them. To ignore it is to disrespect those present and imperil use.

9. *Anticipate turnover of intended users.* One implication of the personal factor concerns the problem of turnover. An experienced, utilization-focused evaluator recently wrote me,

> I've very nearly finished all the revisions to the final reports for a 4 year national evaluation and none of the people I'm now working with were involved in the evaluation design. During the project, there were SEVEN different people in the position of signing-off on critical stages of the evaluation. This is quite a typical experience and has obvious effects on utilization. How can evaluators deal with the more usual turnover issue, apart from trying to do more rapid cycles of planning, implementing and reporting evaluations before the next round of musical chairs?

Turnover in primary intended users can be the Achilles' heel of utilization-focused evaluation unless evaluators watch for, anticipate, and plan for turnover. The longer the timeframe for the evaluation, the more important it is to engage with multiple intended users, build in some overlap, and, when turnover happens, bring the new people up to speed quickly. This will sometimes involve making some later-stage design changes, if possible, to get their buy-in and increase their sense of ownership of the evaluation.

10. *Strategize about different levels of evaluation influence.* Henry and Mark (2003) have called attention to different mechanisms through which evaluation produces influences at the individual, interpersonal, and collective (organizational) level. "Because the influence of a single evaluation can transpire through numerous outcome chains, there are multiple possible pathways of influence" (p. 305).

Menu 3.2 summarizes these 10 practical implications of the personal factor for use.

Diversions Away from Primary Intended Users

To appreciate some of the subtleties of the admonition to focus on intended use by intended users, let's consider a few of the temptations that evaluators face that lure them away from the practice of utilization-focused evaluation.

First, and most common, evaluators are tempted to make themselves the major decision makers for the evaluation. This can happen by default (no one else is willing to do it), by intimidation (clearly, the evaluator is the expert), or simply by failing to think about or seek primary users (Why make life difficult?). The tip-off that evaluators have become the primary intended users (either by intention or default) is that the evaluators are answering their own questions according to their

EXHIBIT 3.4

A Multilevel Stakeholder Structure and Process

The Saint Paul Foundation formed a Donor Review Board of several philanthropic foundations in Minnesota to fund a project "Supporting Diversity in Schools" (SDS). The project established local school-community partnerships with communities of color: African Americans, Hispanics, Native Americans, and Southeast Asian-Americans. The evaluation had several layers based on different levels of stakeholder involvement and responsibility.

Stakeholder Group	Evaluation Focus	Nature of Involvement
Donor Review Board (executives and program interim officers from contributing foundations and school superintendent)	Overall effectiveness policy implications; sustainability.	Twice-a-year meetings to review the design and evaluation results. Final report directed to this group.
District Level Evaluation Group (representatives from participating schools, social service agencies, community organizations, and project staff)	Implementation monitoring in early years; district level outcomes in later years.	An initial full-day retreat with 40 people from diverse groups; annual retreat sessions to update, refocus, and interpret interim findings.
Partnership Level Evaluation Teams (teachers, community representatives, and evaluation staff liaisons)	Documenting activities and outcomes at the local partnership level: one school, one community of color.	Annual evaluation plan. Completing evaluation documents for every activity. Quarterly review of progress to use findings for improvement.

own interests, needs, and priorities. Others may have occasional input here and there, but what emerges is an evaluation by the evaluators, for the evaluators, and of the evaluators. Such studies are seldom of use to other stakeholders, whose reactions are likely to be, "Great study. Really well done. Shows lots of work, but, honestly, it doesn't tell us anything *we* want to know."

A less innocent version of this scenario occurs when academics pursue their basic research agendas under the guise of evaluation research. The tip-off here is that the evaluators insist on designing the study in such a way as to test some theory they think is particularly important, whether or not people involved in the program see any relevance to such a test.

A second temptation is to fall prey to the seemingly stakeholder-oriented "identification of audience" approach. Audiences turn out to be relatively passive groups of largely anonymous faces: the "feds," state officials, the legislature, funders, clients, the program

MENU 3.2

Attending to the Personal Factor to Plan for Use

- Conduct a stakeholder analysis with attention to variations in interest and power. Distinguish and determine appropriate types and degrees of involvement in the evaluation for different stakeholders (see Menu 3.1).
- Find and cultivate people who want to learn.
- Find strategically located people who are enthusiastic, committed, competent, interested, and connected. Formal position and authority are only partial guides in identifying primary users.
- Focus on quality interactions with primary intended users. The quality and timing of interactions are more important than the amount of interaction.
- Nurture stakeholder interest. Evaluators will typically have to work to build and sustain interest in evaluation use. Building effective relationships with intended users is part selection, part nurturance, and part training.
- Hone facilitation and communication skills. Evaluators need people skills in how to build relationships, facilitate groups, manage conflict, walk political tight ropes, and communicate effectively.
- Strategize about different levels and types of stakeholder involvement. A particular evaluation may have multiple levels of stakeholders and therefore need multiple levels and different types of stakeholder involvement.
- Be sensitive to cross-cultural and international factors that affect stakeholder participation, especially inequalities in power, status, and education.
- Watch for, anticipate, and plan for turnover in primary intended users. Bring new users up to speed quickly and, when possible, add design features that increase their interest in the evaluation.
- Strategize about different levels of evaluation influence: individual, interpersonal, and collective (organizational).

staff, the public, and so forth. If specific individuals are not identified from these audiences and organized in a manner that permits meaningful involvement in the evaluation process, then, by default, the evaluator becomes the real decision maker and stakeholder ownership suffers, with a corresponding threat to utility. This is my critique of "responsive evaluation" as advocated by Stake (1975) and Guba and Lincoln (1981). Responsive evaluation "takes as its organizer the *concerns and issues of stakeholding audiences*" (Guba and Lincoln 1981:23). The evaluator interviews

and observes stakeholders, then designs an evaluation that is responsive to stakeholders' issues. The stakeholders, however, are no more than sources of data and an audience for the evaluation, not real partners in the evaluation process. That, at least, has been the classic approach to responsive evaluation. More recent conceptualizations and applications, for example, Abma (2006), include face-to-face interactions and dialogue among stakeholders as a central element in responsive evaluation.

The 1994 revision of the Joint Committee Standards for Evaluation moved to language about "intended users" and "stakeholders" in place of earlier references to "audiences." Thus, in the new version, "the Utility Standards are intended to ensure that an evaluation will serve the information needs of *intended users* [italics added]," as opposed to "given audiences" in the original 1981 version (Joint Committee 1981, 1994). The first standard was changed to "Stakeholder Identification" rather than the original "Audience Identification." Such changes in language are far from trivial. They indicate how the knowledge base of the profession has evolved. The language we use shapes how we think. The nuances and connotations reflected in these language changes are fundamental to the philosophy of utilization-focused evaluation.

A third diversion from intended users occurs when evaluators target organizations rather than specific individuals. Targeting organizations appears to be more specific than targeting general audiences, but really isn't. Organizations as targets can be strangely devoid of real people. Instead, the focus shifts to positions and the roles and authority that attach to positions. Since Max Weber's seminal essay on bureaucracy gave birth to the study of organizations, sociologists have viewed the interchangeability of people in organizations as the hallmark of institutional rationality in modern society. Under ideal norms of bureaucratic rationality, it doesn't matter who's in a position, only that the position be filled using universalistic criteria. Weber argued that bureaucracy makes for maximum efficiency precisely because the organization of role-specific positions in an unambiguous hierarchy of authority and status renders action calculable and rational without regard to personal considerations or particularistic criteria. Such a view ignores the personal factor. Yet it is just such a view of the world that has permeated the minds of evaluators when they say that their evaluation is for

"the federal government," "the state," "the agency," the "foundation," or any other organizational entity. Organizations do not consume information; people do—individual, idiosyncratic, caring, uncertain, searching people. Who is in a position makes all the difference in the world to evaluation use. To ignore the personal factor is to diminish utilization potential from the outset. To target evaluations at organizations is to target them at nobody in particular—and, in effect, not to really target them at all.

A fourth diversion away from intended users is to focus on decisions instead of on decision makers. This approach is classically epitomized by Mark Thompson (1975:26, 38), who defined evaluation as "marshalling of information for the purposes of improving decisions," and makes the first step in an evaluation "identification of the decision or decisions for which information is required." The question of who will make the decision remains implicit. The decision-oriented approach stems from a rational social scientific model of how decision making occurs:

1. A clear-cut decision is expected to be made.

2. Information will inform the decision.

3. A study supplies the needed information.

4. The decision is then made in accordance with the study's findings.

The focus in this sequence is on data and decisions rather than people. But people make decisions and, it turns out, most "decisions" accrete gradually and incrementally over time rather than get made at some concrete, decisive moment (Weiss 1990, 1977; Allison 1971; Lindblom 1965). It can be helpful, even crucial, to orient evaluations toward future decisions, but identification of such decisions, and the implications of those decisions for the evaluation, are best made in conjunction with intended users who come together to decide what data will be needed for what purposes, including, but not limited to, decisions. This important nuance means that *utilization-focused evaluation is always user-oriented* (Alkin 1995) *but only sometimes decision-oriented.* User-focused evaluation involves an evaluation process for making decisions about the content of an evaluation—but the content itself is not specified or implied in advance, including whether the primary focus is a decision.

A fifth temptation is to assume that the funders of the evaluation are the primary intended users, that is, those who pay the fiddler call the tune. In some cases, this is accurate. It is hoped that funders are among those most interested in using evaluation. But there may be additional important users. Moreover, evaluations are funded for reasons other than their perceived utility, for example, wanting to give the appearance of supporting evaluation; because legislation or licensing requires evaluation; or because someone thought it had to be written into the budget. Those who control evaluation purse strings may not have any specific evaluation questions. Often, they simply believe that evaluation is a good thing that keeps people on their toes. They do not care about the content of a specific evaluation, they only care that evaluation—any evaluation—takes place. They mandate the process but not the substance. Under such conditions (which are not unusual), there is considerable opportunity for identifying and working with additional interested stakeholders to formulate relevant evaluation questions and a correspondingly appropriate design.

A sixth temptation is to put off attending to and planning for use from the beginning. It's tempting to wait until findings are in to worry about use, essentially not planning for use by waiting to see what happens. But experienced evaluator Bob Williams (2003) warns, "Evaluation use is not something to think about at the end of an evaluation. The initial conditions, the negotiations, the development of the evaluation design, the implementation of the reporting phases all influence the use of an evaluation" (p. 212). In short, use has to be planned for and anticipated. Planned use occurs when the intended use by intended users is identified at the beginning. Unplanned use can occur in any evaluation, but relying on the hope that something useful will turn up is a risky strategy. Eleanor Chelimsky (1983:160) has asserted that the most important kind of accountability in evaluation is use that comes from "designed tracking and follow-up of a predetermined use to predetermined user." She calls this a "closed-looped feedback process" in which "the policy maker wants information, asks for it, and is interested in and informed by the response" (1983:160). This perspective solves the problem of defining use, addresses the question of who the evaluation is for, and builds in evaluation accountability since the predetermined use becomes the criterion against which the success of the evaluation can be judged. Such a process has to be planned.

A seventh temptation is to convince oneself that it is unseemly to enter the fray and

> **Fundamentally Changing the Evaluator's Role to Enhance Learning**
>
> From a distant, research-oriented person trying to systematise the known and unearth the hidden, she or he will become a process facilitator whose greatest skill is to design and organise others' learning effectively. Stakeholder analysis, communication knowledge and skills become increasingly important as well as managing group dynamics.
>
> SOURCE: Engel and Carlsson (2002). European Evaluation Society (2002:13).

thereby run the risks that come with being engaged. I've heard academic evaluators insist that their responsibility is to assure data quality and design rigor in the belief that the scientific validity of the findings will carry the day. The evidence suggests this seldom happens. An academic stance that justifies the evaluator standing above the messy fray of people and politics is more likely to yield scholarly publications than improvements in programs. Fostering use requires becoming engaged in building relationships and sorting through the politics that enmesh any program. In so doing, the evaluator runs the risks of getting entangled in changing power dynamics, having the rug pulled out by the departure of a key intended user, having relationships go bad, and/or being accused of bias. Later, we'll discuss strategies for dealing with these and other risks, but the only way I know to avoid them altogether is to stand

aloof; that may provide safety but at the high cost of utility and relevance.

An eighth and final temptation is to allow oneself to be co-opted by acquiescing to powerful stakeholders who ask for or demand subtle or significant changes in the evaluation after it is underway (this can happen up front during design but it's easier to deal with then), or who become gradually more resistant as time goes by as it becomes apparent that they will not be able to control findings. Particularly powerful stakeholders will sometimes act in ways that undermine the involvement of less powerful stakeholders. This is a particular danger for less-experienced evaluators or those who lack the skill to deal with powerful stakeholders. Chapter 14 will discuss in greater depth dealing with such political interference.

Menu 3.3 summarizes these eight use-deadly temptations that divert evaluators

MENU 3.3

Temptations Away from Being User-Focused: Use-Deadly Sins

1. Evaluators make themselves the primary decision makers and, therefore, the primary users.

2. Identifying vague, passive audiences as users instead of real people.

3. Targeting organizations as users (e.g., "the feds") instead of specific persons.

4. Focusing on decisions instead of decision makers.

5. Assuming the evaluation's funder is automatically the primary stakeholder.

6. Waiting until the findings are in to identify intended users and intended uses.

7. Taking a stance of standing above the fray of people and politics. That just makes you irrelevant.

8. Being co-opted by powerful stakeholders.

9. Identifying primary intended users but not involving them meaningfully in evaluation decision making.

from clearly specifying and working with intended users.

User-Focused Evaluation in Practice

Lawrence Lynn Jr., Professor of Public Policy at the Kennedy School of Government, Harvard University, has provided excellent evidence for the importance of a user-focused way of thinking in policy analysis and evaluation. Lynn was interviewed by Michael Kirst for *Educational Evaluation and Policy Analysis*. He was asked, "What would be a test of a 'good policy analysis'?"

> One of the conditions of a good policy analysis is that it is helpful to a decision maker. A decision maker looks at it and finds he or she understands the problem better, understands the choices better, or understands the implications of choice better. The decision maker can say that this analysis helped me. (Lynn 1980a:85)

Note here that the emphasis is on informing the decision maker, not the decision. Lynn argues in his authoritative and still-relevant casebook on policy analysis (Lynn 1980b) that a major craft skill needed by policy and evaluation analysts is the ability to understand and make accommodations for specific decision maker's cognitive style and other personal characteristics. His examples are exemplars of the user-focused approach.

> Let me take the example of Eliot Richardson, for whom I worked, or Robert MacNamara, for that matter. These two individuals were perfectly capable of understanding the most complex issues and absorbing details—absorbing the complexity, fully considering it in their own minds. Their intellects were not limited in terms of what they could handle. . . . On the other hand, and I do not want

to use names, you will probably find more typical the decision makers who do not really like to approach problems intellectually. They may be visceral, they may approach issues with a wide variety of preconceptions, they may not like to read, they may not like data, they may not like the appearance of rationality, they may like to see things couched in more political terms, or overt value terms. And an analyst has got to take that into account. There is no point in presenting some highly rational, comprehensive piece of work to a Secretary or an Assistant Secretary of State who simply cannot or will not think that way. But that does not mean the analyst has no role; that means the analyst has to figure out how he can usefully educate someone whose method of being educated is quite different. The analyst needs to see and understand things in a different style. (Lynn 1980a:85–86)

Lynn studied the Carter administration's handling of welfare reform issues, especially the role that his different analysts played. Joe Califano, a senior presidential advisor, dealt with information through a political lens. Califano was a political animal with a relatively short attention span—highly intelligent but an action-oriented person. When his analysts attempted to educate him in a purely logical and rational manner, without reference to political priorities, communication problems arose. Califano's cognitive style and his analyst's approach just did not match.

Lynn also used the example of Jerry Brown, former Governor of California. Brown liked policy analyses framed as a debate—thesis, antithesis—because he had been trained in the Jesuitical style of argument. The challenge for a policy analyst or evaluator, then, becomes grasping the decision maker's cognitive style and logic. President Ronald Reagan, for example, liked *Reader's Digest* style stories and anecdotes. From Lynn's perspective, an analyst presenting to Reagan would have to figure out how to communicate policy issues through stories. He admonished analysts and evaluators to "discover those art forms by which one can present the result of one's intellectual effort" in a way that can be heard, appreciated, and understood:

> In my judgment, it is not as hard as it sounds. I think it is not that difficult to discover how a Jerry Brown or a Joe Califano or a George Bush or a Ted Kennedy thinks, how he reacts. All you have got to do is talk to people who deal with them continuously, or read what they say and write. And you start to discover the kinds of things that preoccupy them, the kinds of ways they approach problems. And you use that information in your policy analyses. I think the hang-up most analysts or many analysts have is that they want to be faithful to their discipline. They want to be faithful to economics or faithful to political science and are uncomfortable straying beyond what their discipline tells them they are competent at dealing with. The analyst is tempted to stay in that framework with which he or she feels most comfortable.
>
> And so they have the hang-up, they cannot get out of it. They are prone to say that my tools, my training do not prepare me to deal with things that are on Jerry Brown's mind, therefore, I cannot help him. That is wrong. They can help, but they have got to be willing to use the information they have about how these individuals think and then begin to craft their work, to take that into account. (Lynn 1980a:86–87)

Lynn's examples document the importance of the personal factor at the highest levels of government. Differences among people matter just as much at state and local levels and in communities around the world. Focusing on the personal factor provides direction about what to look for and how to proceed in planning for use.

Beyond Just Beginning

This chapter has emphasized that utilization-focused evaluators begin by identifying and organizing primary intended evaluation users. They then interact with these primary users throughout the evaluation to nurture and sustain the commitment to use.

Use as a Two-Way Interaction

Far from being a one-way process of knowledge flow, as many traditional texts would indicate, evaluation utilization needs to be understood as a complex, dynamic transaction. The stakeholders or users cannot be construed as passive receptacles of information. Evaluation utilization is an _active process_ in terms of which meaning is shaped by both the evaluator and those involved in evaluation.

SOURCE: _New Zealand Evaluator,_ Kate McKegg (2003: 222).

For there is _a ninth deadly-use sin:_ identifying primary intended users at the outset of the study, then ignoring them until the final report is ready.

Involving specific people who can and will use information enables them to establish direction for, commitment to, and ownership of the evaluation every step along the way from initiation of the study through the design and data collection stages right through to the final report and dissemination process. If decision makers have shown little interest in the study in its earlier stages, our data suggest that they are not likely to suddenly show an interest in using the findings at the end. They won't be sufficiently prepared for use.

The remainder of this book examines the implications of focusing on intended use by intended users. We'll look at the implications for how an evaluation is conceptualized and designed (Chapters 4 through 10), methods decisions (Chapters 11 and 12), and analysis approaches (Chapter 13). We'll also look at the political and ethical implications of utilization-focused evaluation (Chapter 14).

Throughout, we'll be guided by attention to the essence of utilization-focused evaluation: *focusing on intended use for specific intended users.* Focus and specificity are ways of coming to grip with the fact that no evaluation can serve all potential stakeholders' interests equally well. As Spanish baroque philosopher Baltasar Gracian observed in 1647 in *The Art of Worldly Wisdom:* "It is a great misfortune to be of use to nobody; scarcely less to be of use to everybody."

Follow-Up Exercises

1. Find a published evaluation. Does the report identify the primary intended users? If so, can you identify their degree of participation in the evaluation? If intended users are not identified, what can you infer about who determined the focus and methods of the evaluation?

2. Conduct a stakeholder analysis for a program or policy issue. Identify any well known program or a program with which you are personally familiar. List the various stakeholder groups in one column, and next to each stakeholder group, identify as best you can what you think the priority evaluation issues would be given their "stake" in the program.

3. Think about some people you know well who process information differently. Identify at least four different people with varying information-processing styles.

Perhaps one person likes to always see both sides of an issue. Perhaps another likes stories to understand things. Yet another may prefer numbers. Still another may be highly opinionated with little attention to facts. Use these examples to discuss how differences in learning styles and information-processing preferences would affect how you, as an evaluator, would work with these different people.

4. Interview a program director in your area about his or her views about and uses of evaluation. Conduct your own utilization study of a particular agency or a specific evaluation that has been done.

Notes

1. At the time of the study, in 1976, I was Director of the Evaluation Methodology Program in the Humphrey Institute of Public Affairs, University of Minnesota. The study was conducted through the Minnesota Center for Social Research, University of Minnesota. Results of the study were first published under the title, "In Search of Impact: An Analysis of the Utilization of Federal Health Evaluation Research" (Patton et al., 1977). For details on the study's design and methods, see Patton (1986:30–39). The 20 cases in the study included 4 mental health evaluations, 4 health training programs, 2 national assessments of laboratory proficiency, 2 evaluations of neighborhood health center programs, 2 studies of health services delivery systems programs, a training program on alcoholism, a health regulatory program, a federal loan forgiveness program, a training workshop evaluation, and 2 evaluations of specialized health facilities. The types of evaluations ranged from a 3-week program review carried out by a single internal evaluator to a 4-year evaluation that cost $1.5 million. Six of the cases were internal evaluations and 14 were external.

Because of very limited resources, it was possible to select only three key informants to be contacted and intensively interviewed about the utilization of each of the 20 cases in the final sample. These key informants were (1) the government's internal project officer (PO) for the study, (2) the person identified by the project officer as being either the decision maker for the program evaluated or the person most knowledgeable about the study's impact, and (3) the evaluator who had major responsibility for the study. Most of the federal decision makers interviewed had been or now are office directors (and deputy directors), division heads, or bureau chiefs. Overall, these decision makers represented more than 250 years of experience in the federal government.

The evaluators in our sample were a rather heterogeneous group. Six of the 20 cases were internal evaluations, so the evaluators were federal administrators or researchers. In one case, the evaluation was contracted from one unit of the federal government to another, so the evaluators were also federal researchers. The remaining 13 evaluations were conducted by private organizations or nongovernment employees, although several persons in this group either had formerly worked for the federal government or have since come to do so. Evaluators in our sample represented more than 225 years of experience in conducting evaluative research.

2. Citations for quotes taken from the interview transcripts use the following format: [DM367:13] refers to the transcript of an interview with a decision maker about evaluation study number 367; this quote was taken from page 13 of the transcript. The study numbers and page numbers have been systematically altered to protect the confidentiality of the interviewees. EV201:10 and PO201:6 refer to interviews about the same study, the former being an interview with the evaluator, the latter an interview with the project officer.

3. Examples from a quarter century of research reported in the evaluation literature that supports the importance of the personal factor, working with primary intended users, and involving stakeholders to enhance use: Mohan, Tikoo, Capela, and Bernstein (2007); King (2007a, 2007b); Sridharan et al. (2006);

Cousins and Shulha (2006); Nance (2005); Weaver and Cousins (2004); Christie (2003); Christie and Alkin (2003); Leviton (2003); Feinstein (2002); Morris (2002); Cousins (2001); Michalski and Cousins (2001); Brandon (1998); Johnson, Willeke, and Steiner (1998); Johnson (1995); Cooley and Bickel (1985); Lawler et al. (1985); Siegel and Tuckel (1985); Bedell et al. (1985); Dawson and D'Amico (1985); King (1985); Cole (1984); Evans and Blunden (1984); Hevey (1984); Rafter (1984); Glaser, Abelson, and Garrison (1983); Campbell (1983); Bryk (1983); Lewy and Alkin (1983); Stalford (1983); Saxe and Koretz (1982); Beyer and Trice (1982); King and Pechman (1982); Barkdoll (1982); Canadian Evaluation Society (1982); Leviton and Hughes (1981); Dickey and Hampton (1981); Braskamp and Brown (1980); Alkin and Law (1980); and Studer (1978).

4

Intended Uses of Findings

I f you don't know where you're going, you'll end up somewhere else.

—Yogi Berra

Evaluation Wonderland

When Alice encounters the Cheshire Cat in Wonderland, she asks, "Would you tell me, please, which way I ought to walk from here?"
"That depends a good deal on where you want to get to," said the Cat.
"I don't much care where—" said Alice.
"Then it doesn't matter which way you walk," said the Cat.
"—so long as I get somewhere," Alice added as an explanation.
"Oh, you're sure to do that," said the Cat, "if you only walk long enough."

—Lewis Carroll

This story carries a classic evaluation message: To evaluate how well you're doing, you must have some place you're trying to get to. For programs, this has meant having goals and evaluating goal attainment. For evaluators, this means clarifying the intended uses of a particular evaluation.

In utilization-focused evaluation, the primary criterion by which an evaluation is judged is *intended use by intended users*. The previous chapter discussed identifying primary intended users. This chapter will offer a menu of intended uses.

Identifying Intended Uses from the Beginning

The last chapter described a follow-up study of 20 federal health evaluations that assessed use and identified factors related to varying degrees of use. A major finding from that study was that *none of our interviewees had carefully considered intended use prior to getting the evaluation's findings.* We found that decision makers, program officers, *and* evaluators typically devoted little or no attention to intended uses prior to data collection. The goal of those evaluations was to produce findings; then they'd worry about how to use whatever was found. Findings would determine use, so until findings were generated, no real attention was paid to use.

Utilization-focused evaluators, in contrast, work with intended users to determine priority uses early in the evaluation process. The agreed-on, intended uses then become the basis for subsequent design decisions. This increases the likelihood that an evaluation will have the desired impact. Specifying intended uses is evaluation's equivalent of program goal setting.

Let me emphasize this point with an analogy. Once a year, I hike the Grand Canyon and have written a book about my experiences there (Patton 1999a). Once I was unloading my backpack at the Lodge on the North Rim when a young couple approached and said, "We want to hike down into the Canyon for a couple of days. Can you tell us what we have to do and where to get equipment?" I explained that the Grand Canyon is 217 miles long; you have to apply for overnight backcountry permits for specific areas and trails 4 months in advance; the terrain is steep and rugged, so it's wise, indeed essential, to have trained for a hike to the bottom, including carrying a heavy pack with enough water because it's a desert environment. And you have to bring your own equipment. It turned out that they had long dreamed of coming to the Grand Canyon, but had never thought about what they'd do once they got there. Now their options were quite limited—a short day hike, visiting some vistas, taking some photos. But it was too late to undertake a significant inner Canyon hike or join a rafting expedition on the Colorado River, which takes a minimum of a week to complete and a reservation months in advance. Their lack of advance planning is like deciding to do an evaluation but having given no real thought about what you really want to do with it until you get to the end. Then, you'll find, your options are quite limited. Using an evaluation to inform a specific decision, for example, requires advance planning and preparation so that the evaluation provides the needed information in time to be useful. You have to know the terrain of that decision, what the decision environment is like, and what the challenges are likely to be.

Baseline Data on Evaluation Use

In the 1970s, as the profession of evaluation was just emerging, those of us interested in use began by trying to sort out the influence of evaluations on decisions about programs. At the time, that seemed a reasonable place to begin. Much of the early literature on program evaluation defined use as immediate, concrete, and observable influence on specific decisions and program activities resulting *directly* from evaluation findings. For example, Carol Weiss (1972c), one of the pioneers in studying use, stated, "Evaluation research is meant for immediate and direct use in improving the quality of social programming" (p. 10). It was with reference to immediate and direct use that Weiss (1972c) was speaking when she concluded that "a review of evaluation experience suggests that evaluation results have generally not exerted significant influence on program decisions" (p. 11). Weiss (1990) reaffirmed this conclusion in her 1987 keynote address at the American Evaluation Association: "The influence of evaluation on program decisions has not noticeably increased" (p. 7). The evaluation literature reviewed in the first chapter was likewise overwhelming in concluding that evaluation studies exert little influence in decision making.

King and Pechman (1982, 1984) defined use as "intentional and serious consideration of evaluation information by an individual with the potential to act on it." This definition lowers the stakes for use—the evaluation has to be taken seriously—but doesn't necessarily have to lead to action. But even evidence of evaluations being taken seriously seemed hard to come by at the time.

It was in this gloomy context that I set out with a group of students in search of evaluations that had actually been used to help us identify factors that might enhance use in the future. (Details about this follow-up study of the use of federal health evaluations were presented in Chapter 3 and in Patton, Grimes et al. 1977.) Given the pessimistic picture of most writings on use, we began our study fully expecting our

major problem would be finding even one evaluation that had had a significant impact on program decisions. What we found was considerably more complex and less dismal than our original impressions had led us to expect. Our results provide guidance in how to work with intended users to set *realistic* expectations about how much influence an evaluation will have. After reviewing these baseline results on use, we'll look at developments in studying and conceptualizing utilization in recent years.

Views from the Field on Evaluation Impact

Our major question on use to project managers, program directors, and evaluators was this:

We'd like to focus on the actual impact of this evaluation study . . . , to get at any ways in which the study may have had an impact—an impact on program operations, on planning, on funding, on policy, on decisions, on thinking about the program, and so forth. From your point of view, what was the impact of this evaluation study on the program we've been discussing?

After coding responses for the nature and degree of impact (Patton 1986:33), we found that 78 percent of responding decision makers and 90 percent of responding evaluators felt that *the evaluation had had an impact on the program.*

We asked a follow-up question about the nonprogram impacts of the evaluations:

We've been focusing mainly on the study's impact on the program itself. Sometimes studies have a broader impact on things beyond an immediate program, things like general thinking on issues that arise from a study, or position papers, or legislation. To what extent and in what ways did this evaluation have an impact on any of these kinds of things?

We found that 80 percent of responding decision makers and 70 percent of responding evaluators felt these specific evaluation studies had had identifiable nonprogram impacts.

The positive responses to the questions on impact were quite striking considering the predominance of the impression of nonuse in the evaluation literature. The main difference here, however, was that *the actual participants in each specific evaluation process were asked to define impact in terms that were meaningful to them and their situations.* None of the evaluations we studied led directly and immediately to the making of a major, concrete program decision. The more typical impact was one in which the evaluation provided additional pieces of information in the difficult puzzle of program action, permitting some reduction in the uncertainty within which any decision maker inevitably operates. In most such cases, though the use was modest, those involved considered the evaluation worthwhile.

The most dramatic example of use reported in our sample was evaluation of a pilot program. The program administrator had been favorable to the program in principle, was uncertain what the evaluation results would be, but was "hoping the results would be positive." The evaluation proved to be negative. The administrator was "surprised, but not alarmingly so. . . . We had expected a more positive finding or we would not have engaged in the pilot studies" [DM367:13]. The program was subsequently ended, with the evaluation carrying "about a third of the weight of the total decision" [DM367:8]. Thus, the evaluation served the purpose of contributing to a final decision, but was one of only several factors (politics, impressions already held, competing priorities and commitments) that influenced the decision.

Contrast such use with the experiences of a different decision maker we interviewed, one who had 29 years' experience in the federal government, much of that time directing research. He reported the impact of the evaluation about which he was interviewed as follows:

It served two purposes. One is that it resolved a lot of doubts and confusions and misunderstandings that the advisory committee had . . . and the second was that it gave me additional knowledge to support facts that I already knew, and, as I say, broadened the scope more than I realized. In other words, the perceptions of where the organization was going and what it was accomplishing were a lot worse than I had anticipated . . . but I was somewhat startled to find out that they were worse, yet it wasn't very hard because it partly confirmed things that I was observing. [DM232:17]

He went on to say that, following the evaluation,

we changed our whole functional approach to looking at the identification of what we should be working on. But again I have a hard time because these things, *none of these things occurred overnight, and in an evolutionary process it's hard to say, you know, at what point it made a significant difference or did it merely verify and strengthen the resolve that you already had.* [DM232:17]

As in this example, respondents frequently had difficulty assessing the degree to which an evaluation actually affected decisions made after completion of the evaluation. This was true, for example, in the case of a large-scale evaluation conducted over several years' at considerable cost. The findings revealed some deficiencies in the program, but, overall, were quite positive. Changes corresponding to those recommended in the study occurred when the report was published, but those changes could not be directly and simply attributed to the evaluation:

> A lot of studies like this confirmed what close-by people knew and they were already taking actions before the findings. *So you can't link the finding to the action, that's just confirmation. . . . The direct link between the finding and the program decision is very diffuse.* [DM361:12, 13]

In essence, we found that evaluations provided some additional information that was judged and used in the context of other available information to help reduce the unknowns in the making of incremental program changes. The impact ranged from "it sort of confirmed our impressions . . . , confirming some other anecdotal information or impression that we had" [DM209:7, 1] to providing a new awareness that carried over to other programs.

This kind of use to stimulate thinking about what's going on and reduce uncertainty emerged as highly important to decision makers. In some cases, it simply made them more confident and determined. On the other hand, where a need for change was indicated, an evaluation study could help speed up the process of change or provide a new impetus for finally getting things rolling. Reducing uncertainty, speeding things up, and getting things finally started are real impacts—not revolutionary—but real, important impacts in the opinion of the people we interviewed. We found few major, direction-changing decisions in most programs. Rather, evaluation findings were used as one piece of information that fed into a slow, evolutionary process of program development. Program development is, typically, a process of "muddling through" (Allison 1971; Lindblom 1965), and program evaluation is

part of that muddling. Or, as Weiss (1980) has observed, even major decisions typically accrete gradually over time through small steps and minor adjustments rather than getting decided all at once at some single moment at the end of a careful, deliberative, and rational process.

The impacts of evaluation have most often been felt as ripples, not waves. The question is whether such limited impact is sufficient to justify the costs of evaluation. The decision makers and evaluators we interviewed were largely satisfied with the type and degree of use they experienced. But times have changed. The stakes are higher. There's more sophistication about evaluation and higher expectations for accountability. However, the point of a utilization-focused approach is not to assume either high or low expectations. The point is to find out what the expectations of intended users are and negotiate a shared understanding of realistic, intended use—a mutual commitment that can be met. In negotiating the nature and degree of evaluation use, that is, setting goals for the evaluation, it is important to challenge intended users to be both optimistic and realistic—the twin tensions in any goal-setting exercise. Whether the expected type and degree of use hoped for actually occurs can then be followed up as a way of evaluating the evaluation. The question utilization-focused evaluation asks is, "What are the expected uses by intended users before and during the evaluation?" To work with intended users in clarifying intended uses, the evaluator needs to offer a menu of options and possibilities. The options have grown considerably based on considerable research on use and theoretical work in recent years. After looking at these developments, I'll offer a framework that distinguishes six primary purposes evaluations can serve. First, however, the results from research and theory.

Conceptualizing Use Options: Distinctions from Research

Inquiries into utilization show that intended uses vary from evaluation to evaluation, greatly affected by the context within which the evaluation occurs. There can be no generic or absolute ideal of evaluation use because "use" depends in part on the values and goals of primary users. As Eleanor Chelimsky (1983) observed, "The concept of usefulness . . . depends upon the perspective and values of the observer. This means that one person's usefulness may be another person's waste" (p. 155). To help intended users deliberate on and commit to intended uses, evaluators need a menu of potential uses to offer. Utilization-focused evaluation is a menu-oriented approach. *It's a process for matching intended uses and intended users.*

Let's begin this consideration of options by looking at classic distinctions. Early on, three types emerged as important: instrumental use, conceptual use, and symbolic use

(Leviton and Hughes 1981)—and these remain the major distinctions informing discussions of use (Cousins and Shulha 2006; Alkin 2005; Weiss, Murphy-Graham, and Birkeland 2005). *Instrumental use* refers to evaluation findings directly informing a decision or contributing to solving a problem; the findings are linked to some subsequent action and in that sense become an *instrument* of action. An example of instrumental use would be an evaluation of the Drug Abuse Resistance Education (D.A.R.E.) program in a school district that showed no effects on student drug use so the School Board decides to no longer fund the program (Weiss et al. 2005; Government Accountability Office [GAO] 2003). In the international arena, an evaluation finds that broken solar water pumps in African villages go without needed repairs because, after initial installation, no follow-up maintenance program was put in place. Based on the evaluation findings, the international agency that funded the installation decides to establish a maintenance program. That is instrumental use.

An Exemplar of Instrumental Use by the U.S. Congress

Laura Leviton, a former president of the American Evaluation Association and long-time contributor to research and theory on evaluation use, reviewed the state of our knowledge about evaluation use in the *American Journal of Evaluation*. She concluded that article by citing an outstanding example of instrumental evaluation use and the characteristics of the evaluator and evaluation that contributed to such a high degree of utilization. She wrote,

> For me the most consummate evaluation practitioner in terms of identifiable policy impact is still Paul Hill, who conducted a major evaluation mandated by the U.S. Congress on behalf of the National Institute of Education (NIE) in the late 1970s. As Boruch and I documented (Leviton and Boruch 1984), this work led to a great many specific changes in amendments to federal education law. In retrospect I believe Hill employed some of the [following] principles.
>
> - He was expert in the ways of Congress, having been on the Congressional staff.
> - Hill had the substantive education policy expertise as well.
> - The NIE study provided, not a stand-alone data collection effort, but a body of evidence . . . : the study was a collection of syntheses, pre-existing material, and some new, highly targeted primary data collection.

- The evaluation questions already had been sharply framed by years of Congressional debate on the relevant issues.
- Some debates had long ago turned into hardened positions. Hill sought findings in areas where there was still room for cross-party negotiation.
- Congressional stakeholders were heavily consulted in planning the study, during the course of the study, and in interpretation. Hill therefore understood the mental models of his stakeholders and was effective in translating findings into action, most notably when his team provided the legislative language needed for the amendments. (Leviton 2003:533)

Conceptual use occurs when an evaluation influences how key people think about a program or policy; they understand it better in some significant way, but no action or decision flows from the findings. We found conceptual use to be widespread in our follow-up study of federal health evaluations. As one project manager reported,

> The evaluation led us to redefine some target populations and rethink the ways we connected various services. This rethinking happened over a period of months as we got a better perspective on what the findings meant. But we didn't so much change what we were doing as we changed how we thought about what we were doing. That has had big pay-offs over time. We're just a lot clearer now. [DM248:19]

An international example of conceptual use is the Inter-American Development Bank evaluation of initiatives in six Latin American countries aimed at decentralization of government services to increase effective citizen participation. The evaluation revealed complex and diverse understandings of and experiences with decentralization. What seemed on the surface to be a straightforward administrative process of decentralizing government services turned out to be deeply intertwined with political, cultural, social, and economic conditions and factors. The findings conceptually distinguished "deconcentration" from decentralization, a situation in which "citizens are told

that they have new decision-making power to help gain their support for a program" but the central government retains actual responsibility for the service and control of the financial resources. Deconcentration describes "cases where a certain obeisance is shown to decentralization and popular participation, but where the power structure retains control" (Inter-American Development Bank 2001:9–10). The report also reviewed privatization as a popular approach to decentralization and concluded,

> Privatization does not necessarily mean decentralization. It means, rather, that more actors are participating in the economic life of the country. Whether they are participating in the political life is more a matter of political parties, organizations for representation, and the enabling environment. (Inter-American Development Bank 2001:5)

Such findings provide important conceptual insights for future planning but are not directed at a particular decision for a specific program at a concrete point in time (instrumental use).

In one of the first studies comparing instrumental use with conceptual use, Shea (1991) did a follow up of 332 Canadian program evaluations and found that 55 percent reported instrumental use while 65 percent reported conceptual use. He also found an inverse relationship between the two: the greater the instrumental use, the less the conceptual use, and vice versa. In addition, he found that (1) evaluators who identified specific decision makers who would take responsibility for utilization reported significantly more instrumental use and (2) he found a significant relationship between the extent of instrumental use and the number of contact hours that the evaluator spent in working with program personnel during the planning, implementation, and dissemination stages of the evaluation.

Weiss (2004) has added a time dimension to conceptual use in what she has called "enlightenment" use and defines as

> the longer term percolation of ideas from evaluation into organizational discourse. . . . Evaluations not infrequently change decision makers' perceptions about what is important, they cast doubt on assumptions that had long been taken for granted, they evoke new ideas, and they alter priorities. (P. 161)

> Generalizations from evaluation can percolate into the stock of knowledge that participants draw on. Empirical research has confirmed this. . . . [D]ecision makers indicate a strong belief that they are influenced by the ideas and arguments that have their origins in research and evaluation. Case studies of evaluations and decisions tend to show that generalizations and ideas that come from research and evaluation help shape the development of policy. The phenomenon has come to be known as "enlightenment" . . . , an engaging idea. The image of evaluation as increasing the wattage of light in the policy arena brings joy to the hearts of evaluators. (Weiss 1990:176–77)

Owen and Rogers (1999:110) link instrumental use with enlightenment in a model that conceives of enlightenment as sometimes an end in itself, but also as the first stage leading to more instrumental use. First, enlightenment and understanding, then application and decision making.

Symbolic use refers to token or rhetorical support for an evaluation process or findings but with no real intent to take either the process or findings seriously. Symbolic use has become more prevalent as research and evaluation findings have become increasingly prominent in political dialogue. In the knowledge age, politicians and decision makers have to at least appear to be basing their views on data. This distinction carries a warning to evaluators not to believe naively easily expressed rhetoric about interest in evaluation. Look for evidence of and specific actions in support of evaluation processes and findings; a reasonable evaluation budget and time devoted to the evaluation are prime types of such evidence.

Symbolic use constitutes a shrewd political use of evaluation to give the appearance of being an evidence-based decision maker. Other political uses distinguish specific intents. *Persuasive use* refers to using evaluation findings, often quite selectively, to support one's position in political debates. So, for example, a police chief testifying before a School Board in support of funding for D.A.R.E. would emphasize findings that students feel more trusting of police after classes about the dangers of drug use taught by police and ignore the findings that the program has no effect on students' subsequent drug use (GAO 2003). Weiss et al. (2005) caution against judging such persuasive use as necessarily inappropriate. "When evaluation supports a course of action that already has advocates, there does not seem to be anything wrong with using evaluation evidence to strengthen the case" (pp. 13–14).

Another type of politically oriented use is "legitimative utilization" (Alkin 2005:435; Leviton 2003:533; Owen and

Rogers 1999) in which evaluation findings are used to support a decision that was actually made before the evaluation was ever conducted or was made without regard to evaluative evidence. This is what the critics of the Iraq War argue happened, namely, that President Bush and his neo-conservative advisors had already decided immediately after the 9/11 terrorist attack on the World Trade Center that they would use the attack as justification for invading Iraq and deposing Saddam Hussein. They then set about gathering and presenting selective "evidence" to legitimate that pre-determined decision (U.S. Senate Select Committee on Intelligence 2004; Hersh 2003). This happens in a program context when a decision is made to terminate a program and then an evaluation is commissioned for the purpose of legitimating the decision after the fact. Program staff is often fearful of just such an agenda when internal evaluations are commissioned in a time when resources are known to be constrained and some cuts somewhere will have to be made. To the extent that legitimative use is intentionally manipulative and deceptive, it becomes misuse.

Misuse of Evaluations

Studies of evaluation use have generated examples of and raised concerns about misuse. Evaluation processes and findings can be misrepresented and abused. The profession recognizes a critical distinction between *misevaluation*, in which an evaluator performs poorly or fails to adhere to standards and principles, and *misuse*, in which users manipulate the evaluation in ways that distort the findings or corrupt the inquiry.

Sources of misuse include hard-core politics, asking the wrong questions, pressures on internal evaluators to present only positive findings, petty self-interest, and ideology (Stevens and Dial 1994; Dial 1994; Duffy 1994; Mowbray 1994; Posavac 1994; Vroom, Columbo, and Nahan 1994; Alkin and Coyle 1988). Misuse, like use, is ultimately situational. Consider, for example, the case of an administrator who blatantly squashes several negative evaluation reports to prevent the results from reaching the general public. On the surface, such an action appears to be a prime case of misuse. Now consider the same action (i.e., suppressing negative findings) in a situation where the reports were invalid due to poor data collection. Thus, misuse in one situation may be conceived of as appropriate nonuse in another. Intentional nonuse of poorly conducted studies can be viewed as appropriate and responsible. Here are some premises with regard to misuse.

1. Misuse is *not* at the opposite end of a continuum from use. Two dimensions are needed to capture the complexities of real-world practice. One dimension is a continuum from appropriate nonuse to appropriate use. A second is a continuum from inappropriate nonuse to intentional misuse. Studying or avoiding misuse is quite different from studying or facilitating use.

2. Having conceptualized two separate dimensions, it is possible to explore the relationship between them. Consider the following proposition: *As use increases, misuse will also increase.* When people ignore evaluations, they ignore their potential uses as well as abuses. As evaluators successfully focus greater attention on evaluation data and increase actual use, there may be a corresponding increase in abuse, often within the same evaluation experience. Donald T. Campbell (1988:306) formulated a discouraging law along these lines that the more any social indicator is used for important societal decision

making, the more likely is that indicator to be corrupted.

3. Misuse can be either intentional or unintentional. Unintentional misuse can be corrected through the processes aimed at increasing appropriate and proper use. Intentional misuse is an entirely different matter that invites active intervention to correct whatever has been abused, either the evaluation process or findings. As with most problems, correcting misuse is more expensive and time-consuming than preventing it in the first place.

4. Working with multiple users who understand and value an evaluation is one of the best preventatives against misuse. Allies in use are allies against misuse. Indeed, misuse can be mitigated by working to have intended users take so much ownership of the evaluation that they become the champions of appropriate use, the guardians against misuse, and the defenders of the evaluation's credibility when misuse occurs.

5. Policing misuse is sometimes beyond the evaluator's control, but to the extent possible and realistic, professional evaluators have a responsibility to monitor, expose, and prevent misuse (Patton 2005a).

Evaluators' Perceptions of Nonuse and Misuse

Rated by evaluators as "a great problem"

Nonuse of evaluation results	68 percent
Intentional misuse of evaluation results	21 percent
Unintentional misuse of evaluation results	22 percent

SOURCE: Results of a 2006 online survey of members of the American Evaluation Association with 1,014 respondents (Fleischer 2007).

Appropriate versus Inappropriate Nonuse

The utility standards of the profession make it clear that a good evaluation is one that is used. Some use is good; more use is better. Appropriate and intended use by intended users is best. Misuse is bad. And nonuse? From a utilization-focused evaluation perspective, nonuse represents some kind of failure in the evaluation process. We often lay that failure at the feet of resistant or unappreciative stakeholders, but it can also be the evaluator's fault. *Nonuse due to misevaluation* (Patton 2005b:254), or justified nonuse (Cousins and Shulha 2006:282) refers to appropriate nonuse because of weak evidence, a late report, poor evaluator performance, or other failures of the evaluator to adhere to the profession's standards and principles (see Chapter 1). In contrast, *political nonuse* occurs when the findings are ignored because they conflict with a potential user's values, prejudices, preferences, and predisposition—so the evaluation is just simply ignored. Utilization-focused evaluation attempts to reduce political nonuse by creating a climate and process in which those involved are willing and prepared to examine their basic assumptions and incorporate evidence into their understandings, even when they had hoped for, or would have preferred, different results.

Aggressive nonuse, or calculated resistance, refers to situations where an evaluation or evaluator is attacked and use undermined because the results conflict with or raise questions about a preferred position. Resistance to evaluation findings can be a specific example of the more general phenomenon of resistance to change. A major reason for identifying and involving primary intended users in the evaluation is to anticipate and short-circuit inappropriate and specious attacks, or at least to have allies among informed and credible intended users in fending off such politically motivated attacks.

Most resistance to evaluations is behind the scenes, but occasionally political reports grab media attention and the whole world gets to watch the circus of attacks and counterattacks. A prominent example was the May 2005 release of a report by the human rights organization Amnesty International on conditions in the U.S. military prison at Guantanamo Bay in Cuba where alleged terrorists were being held. The report, citing interviews with prisoners and people who had been inside the prison, concluded that prisoners had been mistreated and called for the prison to be shut down. The report got considerable international media attention. Amnesty International has an explicit agenda and its recommendation to close the Guantanamo facility could be expected, but the cases cited and interview results were viewed as credible by some reporters, so the Bush Administration needed to make a response. The tone of the response gives a flavor of the rhetoric that can accompany an aggressive attack on disputed and unwelcome evaluation conclusions. President Bush, addressing a news conference at the White House on May 31, 2005, said the Amnesty document was an "absurd report. It's absurd. It's an absurd allegation. The United States is a country that promotes freedom around the world." He went on to attack the investigation's methods and resulting data asserting that the Amnesty allegations were based on interviews with detainees who hated America and were trained to lie. President Bush's remarks were echoed by Vice President Dick Cheney, who said that same day in a video-taped interview with CNN's Larry King, "Frankly, I was offended by it. For Amnesty International to suggest that

somehow the United States is a violator of human rights, I frankly just don't take them seriously."

In the early 1970s, I was involved in an independent survey of teachers in Kalamazoo, Michigan with funds from the local and national education associations. The School District refused to cooperate with the study and when the results came in showing very low morale, widespread complaints about working conditions, a dysfunctional accountability system, and allegations of administrative abuses, the Superintendent publicly attacked the findings, calling them "absurd." He attacked my integrity, saying I was an out-of-state paid-gun-for-hire, and further asserted that the teachers association instructed teachers how to respond. He dismissed the results out of hand. Fortunately, the school board members actually read the report, including pages of in-depth quotations from teachers and documented cases of problems. The school board made instrumental use of the report by requiring major administrative changes in the District and, subsequently, the superintendent "resigned." (For details, see Patton 2002a:17–20.)

The point: Evaluation is a political activity and as the varieties of use, nonuse, and misuse illustrate, utilization is also a political activity—and sometimes the politics gets rough. This work is not for the faint of heart; it's not just an academic exercise. The stakes can get very high, very fast. Some more recent use distinctions further reinforce this caution.

More Recent Use Distinctions

The classic three types of use—instrumental, conceptual, and symbolic—have long framed inquiries into evaluation use and led to concerns about misuse. Over time, as the field has matured and inquiries into utilization have broadened and deepened, additional distinctions have emerged from research and theory. Weiss et al. (2005), based on case studies of the use of D.A.R.E. evaluations, have identified *imposed use* that occurs when those with the power to do so mandate an action based on evaluative judgments; in essence, those at a higher level of authority require a prescribed use by those at a lower level. For example, a federal requirement that to receive funding a school district curriculum must be on an approved list of "evidence-based" or evaluated programs. In the case of D.A.R.E., administrators in some districts felt forced to drop the program, despite local support, because it did not qualify as a preapproved, evidence-based program by the federal authorities.

I have become concerned about *overuse*, which occurs when too much emphasis is placed on evaluation findings. For example, weak evaluation results are overused when treated as if they are definitive, or imposed use becomes overuse when there is insufficient evidence to generalize findings and justify the top-down mandate for compliance, or there is lack of attention to local conditions. This latter overuse can occur when supposed "best practices" are universally mandated (Patton 2001). Concern about overuse is ironic since, as the first chapter documented, the profession has been dominated by concern about underuse and nonuse. But as in much of life, you can have too much of a good thing. An unintended consequence of all the focus on increasing use may have contributed to overuse and misuse.

Mechanical use (Patton 2006) is another emergent distinction of increasing concern. Mechanical, or compliance, use refers to going through the motions to meet an evaluation requirement. The evaluation is required, so it is done, but the motivation is compliance and the implementation is mechanical. A number of colleagues who do evaluations in the federal government have encountered this approach, as have I, especially with regard to mandated Program Assessment Rating Tool (PART) reviews, a process mandated by the U.S. Office of Management and Budget (OMB) for all federal programs. PART was developed to help budget examiners and federal managers measure the effectiveness of government programs. It is a 25-item questionnaire divided into four sections: program purpose and design (5 questions); strategic planning (8 questions); program management (7 questions); and program results/accountability (5 questions). Based on answers to these questions, a score is generated and a program is rated as Effective, Moderately Effective, Adequate, or Results Not Generated. The stakes are high. Results are made public and can affect program budgets and status. So how does mechanical use come into play? A director of a program preparing for a PART says to the evaluator, "Just tell me what I have to do to increase my PART score." Such a director isn't looking to improve the program or make a decision. The object is just to get a decent, acceptable score. The same phenomenon happens in not-for-profit programs when they go mechanically through the motions of complying with a funder's mandated evaluation.

Process Use

Now we turn to a quite different type of use. *Process use* has emerged as one of the most important distinctions in the last decade (Cousins and Shulha 2006; Alkin 2005). Process use refers to cognitive, behavioral, program, and organizational changes resulting, either directly or indirectly, from engagement in the evaluation process and learning to think evaluatively (e.g., goals clarification, conceptualizing the program's logic model, identifying evaluation priorities, struggling with measurement issues, participation in design and interpretation). Process use occurs when those involved in the evaluation learn from the evaluation process itself or make program changes based on the evaluation process rather than findings—as, for example, when those involved in the evaluation later say "the impact on our program came not just from the findings but also from going through the thinking process that the evaluation required." Process use also includes the effects of evaluation procedures and operations, for example, the premise that "what gets measured gets done," so establishing measurements and setting targets affects program operations and management focus. These are uses of the evaluation process to affect programs, not use of findings. Process use has become so important that the entire next chapter is devoted to it. I mention it here to be sure it is on the menu when considering use options.

Utilization versus Use versus Influence: The Terminology Debate

Words are loaded pistols.

—Jean Paul Sartre,
philosopher (1905–1980)

The evaluation language we choose and use, consciously or unconsciously, necessarily and inherently shapes perceptions, defines "reality," and affects mutual understanding. Whatever issues in evaluation we seek to understand—types of evaluation, methods, relationships with stakeholders, power, use—a full analysis will lead us to consider the words and concepts that undergird our understandings and actions because language matters (Patton 2000). Deciding on terminology is complicated

because two people can infer different connotations from the same word. Early on Carol Weiss (1980, 1981) expressed a preference for *use* rather than *utilization*. She went so far as to propose abandoning the term *utilization* "because of its overtones of instrumental episodic application. People do not utilize research the way that they utilize a hammer." She preferred use instead of utilization to capture the sense that findings "penetrate" decision making through "processes of understanding, accepting, reorienting, adapting, and applying research results to the world of practice." She wanted a more "fluid and diffuse" connotation (Weiss 1981:18). Yet I have quite the opposite reaction to the two terms. Use seems to me more instrumental and episodic in connotation. Taking her analogy, I would argue that people use hammers; they don't "utilize" hammers. But they do utilize evaluations, which connotes to me *a process* of precisely the kind Weiss describes—understanding, accepting, reorienting, adapting, and applying. Use sounds to me more direct, specific, concrete, and moment-in-time. Utilization evokes for me a dynamic process that occurs over time. So I continue to prefer utilization-focused evaluation over use-focused evaluation.

Others have expressed a preference for use instead of utilization simply because the longer word sounds more academic, like jargon, and is too highfalutin (pompous or pretentious). For that reason, I much prefer the verb use instead of utilize, but I make use of both nouns—use and utilization—varying my usage by audience and context.

Karen Kirkhart (2000) wants to abandon both the terms *use* and *utilization* in order to construct an "integrated theory" of evaluation's consequences using the concept of "evaluation influence" as a unifying construct. She defines influence as "the capacity or power of persons or things to produce effects on others by intangible or indirect means." Kirkhart posits three dimensions of evaluation influence: source of influence (evaluation process or results), intention (intended or unintended), and time (immediate, end-of-cycle, long-term). She is especially anxious to capture effects that are "multidirectional, incremental, unintentional, and instrumental" (p. 7).

Unintended uses are any applications of evaluation findings or processes that were not planned, not predictable, or unforeseen. Kirkhart (2000) cites as an example a program advisory committee that intends to use evaluation results to improve the program, but "the data had unexpected policy implications that led them to initiate a community coalition to advocate for legislative change" (p. 13). I evaluated a leadership program for a philanthropic foundation, and the foundation liked the approach so much they supported me to train others in development-oriented utilization-focused evaluation and made it a centerpiece of their evaluation philosophy. Such influence was beyond the scope of anything imagined at the beginning of the process.

Kirkhart's influence framework has influenced, quite rightly, how research on evaluation's effects are conceptualized and studied (e.g., Christie 2007; Mark and Henry 2004; Henry 2003; Henry and Mark 2003), especially in calling attention to the importance of looking for unintended effects; examining long-term, incremental, and unanticipated uses of findings; and investigating diverse forms of influence. But the framework is less useful, in my judgment, for informing practice. Alkin (2005) has cogently explained why this is the case.

> Evaluation use typically refers to the impact of the evaluation (findings or process) within the context of the program being evaluated, within some reasonable time frame. Evaluation influence refers to the impact on an external program, which may or may not be related to the program evaluated, or to the impact of the evaluation at some future time. An important distinction between evaluation influence and evaluation use is that evaluators who are concerned with evaluation use can actively pursue a course of action to potentially enhance utilization by recognizing the evaluation factors and attempting to be responsive to them, but evaluation influence is more difficult to predict or to control. (P. 436)

Utilization-focused evaluation is focused on *intended use by intended users.* The emphasis is on intentionality and harnessing that intentionality to enhance utilization. In contrast, evaluation influence emphasizes the indirect aspects of evaluation's effects over time and outside the program evaluated, things that are largely beyond the evaluator's control. Utilization-focused evaluators, however, can conduct evaluations in ways that increase use, especially by being intentional about the evaluation's primary purpose, which is the focus of the next section. Exhibit 4.1 reviews and summarizes the use distinctions discussed above. We turn now to a menu of six distinct evaluation purposes based on varying uses for evaluation *findings*. In the next chapter, we'll add to this menu a variety of uses of evaluation *processes*.

Six Alternative Evaluation Purposes

The purpose of an evaluation conditions the use that can be expected of it.

—Eleanor Chelimsky (1997)

You don't get very far in studying evaluation before realizing that the field is characterized by enormous diversity. From

large-scale, long-term, international comparative designs costing millions of dollars to small, short evaluations of a single component in a local agency, the variety is vast. Contrasts include internal versus external evaluations; outcomes versus process evaluation; experimental designs versus case studies; mandated accountability systems versus voluntary management efforts; academic studies versus informal action research by program staff; and published, polished evaluation reports versus oral briefings and discussions where no written report is ever generated. Then there are combinations and permutations of these contrasting approaches. In the midst of such splendid diversity, any effort to reduce the complexity of evaluation options to a few major categories will inevitably oversimplify. Yet some degree of simplification is needed to make

the evaluation design process manageable and facilitate interactions with primary intended users about priority purposes. So let us attempt to heed Thoreau's advice:

> Simplicity, simplicity, simplicity! I say, let your affairs be as two or three, and not a hundred or a thousand.
>
> —Walden (1854)

A Menu of Intended Uses Based on Alternative Purposes

The previous edition of this book highlighted three primary purposes for evaluation: rendering judgments, facilitating improvements, and generating knowledge. In this edition, I have added three additional purposes based on evolution of the field, feedback from readers, and trends in evaluation practice: accountability, monitoring,

EXHIBIT 4.1
Use Distinctions

Direct Intended Uses

Instrumental use occurs when evaluation findings are used to directly inform a decision, improve a program or policy, develop new directions, or contribute to solving a problem; the findings are linked to some subsequent, identifiable action. (Menu 4.2 in this chapter elaborates types of instrumental use.)

Conceptual use occurs when an evaluation influences how key people think about a program or policy, and understand it better in some significant way, but no action or decision flows from the findings. This use is often anticipated and intended by including in the scope of work the expectation of generating "lessons learned" or, more generally, contributing to knowledge.

Process use refers to changes resulting from engagement in the evaluation process and learning to think evaluatively. Process use occurs when those involved in the evaluation learn from the evaluation process itself or make program changes based on the evaluation process rather than findings. Process use also includes the effects of evaluation procedures and operations, for example, the premise that "what gets measured gets done," so establishing measurements and setting targets affects program operations and management focus. (See Chapter 5, Menu 5.1, for different types of process use.)

Longer Term, More Incremental Influences

Influence intentionally broadens thinking about evaluation impacts by attending to "the capacity or power of persons or things to produce effects on others by intangible or indirect means" (Kirkhart 2000:7). Influence draws attention to effects of an evaluation over time and beyond the specific program evaluated. Influence can be intended or unintended, and can flow from either results or the evaluation process.

Enlightenment adds a longer time dimension and connotes a broader policy scope to conceptual use. It involves the gradual percolation of ideas from evaluation into policy discourse, changing understandings, questioning assumptions, evoking new ideas, and altering priorities (Weiss 2004).

Primarily Political Uses

Symbolic use refers to token support for an evaluation process or findings but with no real intent to take either the process or findings seriously. Symbolic use can be helpful when it creates a supportive environment for others to make serious use of evaluation processes and findings.

Legitimative use occurs when evaluation findings are used to support and justify a decision that was already made before the evaluation was ever conducted.

Persuasive use refers to using evaluation findings, often quite selectively, to support one's position in funding decisions and political debates. This is not necessarily inappropriate, for instance, when evaluation results support a course of action that already has advocates and they appropriately use findings to support their position (Weiss et al. 2005).

Imposed use occurs when those with the power to do so mandate a particular form of evaluation use, usually when those at a higher level of authority require a prescribed use by those at a lower level. For example, a federal requirement that to receive funding a school district curriculum must be on an approved list of "evidence-based" or evaluated programs (Weiss et al. 2005).

Mechanical use, or compliance use, refers to going through the motions to meet an evaluation requirement. The evaluation is required, so it is done, but the motivation is compliance and the implementation is mechanical.

Misuses

Mischievous misuse includes the calculated and intentional suppression, misrepresentation, or unbalanced use of evaluation findings to influence opinions and decisions.

Inadvertent misuse, also called mistaken misuse, occurs when those using findings lack the background or competence to appropriately interpret findings; spend too little time with the results to fully understand them; are swayed by the evaluator's status, expertise, or personality rather than the findings; or simply lack the sophistication needed for appropriate use.

Overuse occurs when too much emphasis is placed on evaluation findings. For example, weak evaluation results are overused when treated as if they are definitive, or imposed use (see above) occurs with insufficient evidence or lack of attention to local conditions. This latter overuse can occur when supposed "best practices" are universally mandated (Patton 2001).

Nonuses

Nonuse due to misevaluation (Patton 2005b:254), or justified nonuse (Cousins and Shulha 2006:282), refers to appropriate nonuse because of weak evidence, a late report, poor evaluator performance, or other failures of the evaluator to adhere to the profession's standards and principles (see Chapter 1).

Political nonuse occurs when the findings are ignored because they conflict with a potential user's values, prejudices, preferences, and predisposition—so the evaluation is just simply ignored.

Aggressive nonuse, or calculated resistance, refers to situations where an evaluation or evaluator is attacked and use undermined because the results conflict with or raise questions about a preferred position. Resistance to evaluation findings can be a specific example of the more general phenomenon of resistance to change.

Unintended Effects

Unintended uses are any applications of evaluation findings or processes that were not planned, not predictable, or unforeseen.

and development. I'll explain these additions and their importance as we go along. Different purposes lead to different uses, and that has implications for every aspect of evaluation—design, measurements, analysis, interpretation, reporting, dissemination, and criteria for judging quality.

Summative, Judgment-Oriented Evaluation

Evaluations aimed at determining the overall merit, worth, significance, or value of something are judgment oriented. Merit refers to the intrinsic value of a program, for example, how effective it is in meeting the needs of those it is intended to help. Worth refers to extrinsic value to those outside the program, for example, to the larger community or society. A welfare program that gets jobs for recipients has *merit* for those who move out of poverty and *worth* to society by reducing welfare costs. Judgment-oriented evaluation approaches include summative evaluations aimed at deciding if a program is sufficiently effective to be continued or replicated and comparative ratings or rankings of programs as done by *Consumer Reports*. These judgments are used to inform decisions. In the case of programs, the decisions concern whether to continue a program, expand it, or change it in some major way. In the case of consumer products, the judgments inform decisions about whether to purchase a particular item.

The first clue that intended users are seeking an overall, summative judgment is when you hear the following kinds of questions: Did the program work? Did it attain its goals? Should the program be continued, ended, or expanded to other sites? Did the program provide good value for money? Can the outcomes measured be attributed to the program? Answering these kinds of evaluative questions requires a data-based judgment that some need has been met, some goal attained, or some standard achieved.

In judgment-oriented evaluations, specifying the criteria for judgment is central and critical. Different stakeholders will bring different criteria to the table. During design discussions and negotiations, evaluators may offer additional criteria for judgment beyond those initially thought of by intended users. Clarifying the values that will be the basis for judgment is a central role for evaluators. The standard to be met in this regard has been articulated in the Joint Committee Program Evaluation Standards: "*Values Identification:* The perspectives, procedures, and rationale used to interpret the findings should be carefully described, *so that the bases for value judgments are clear* [italics added]" (Joint Committee 1994:U4).

Summative evaluation constitutes an important purpose distinction in any menu of intended uses. Summative evaluations judge the *overall effectiveness of a program* and are particularly important in making decisions about continuing or terminating

an experimental program or demonstration project. As such, summative evaluations are often requested by funders. Summative evaluation contrasts with *formative evaluation*, which focuses on ways of improving and enhancing programs rather than rendering definitive judgment about effectiveness. Michael Scriven (1967:40–43) introduced the summative-formative distinction in discussing evaluation of educational curriculum. The distinction has since become a fundamental evaluation typology.

With widespread use of the summative-formative distinction has come misuse, so it is worth examining Scriven's own definition:

> Summative evaluation of a program (or other evaluand) is conducted *after* completion of the program (for ongoing programs that means after stabilization) and *for* the benefit of some *external* audience or decision-maker (for example, funding agency, oversight office, historian, or future possible users). . . . The decisions it services are most often decisions between these options: export (generalize), increase site support, continue site support, continue with conditions (probationary status), continue with modifications, discontinue. . . . The aim is to report *on* it [the program], not to report *to* it. (Scriven 1991b:340)

Summative evaluation provides data to support a judgment about the program's worth so that a decision can be made about the merit of continuing the program. While Scriven's definition focuses on a single program, summative evaluations of multiple programs occur when, like the products in a *Consumer Reports* test, programs are ranked on a set of criteria such as effectiveness, cost, sustainability, quality characteristics, and so forth.

Such data support judgments about the comparative merit or worth of different programs. Exhibit 4.2 provides an example of a summative evaluation.

When decisions are made using evaluative judgments, evaluation results are combined with other considerations to support decision making. Politics, values, competing priorities, the state of knowledge about a problem, the scope of the problem, the history of the program, the availability of resources, public support, and managerial competence all come into play in program and policy decision processes. Evaluation findings, if used at all, are usually one piece of the decision-making pie, not the whole pie. Rhetoric about "data-based decision making" and "evidence-based practice" can give the impression that one simply looks at evaluation results and a straightforward decision follows. *Erase that image from your mind.* That is seldom, if ever, the case. Evaluation findings typically have technical and methodological weaknesses; data must

EXHIBIT 4.2
A Judgment-Oriented Summative Exemplar: Evaluating Home Visitation

The David and Lucile Packard Foundation employed an evaluation-focused grant-making strategy over more than a decade in funding the home visitation approach to supporting child development. The Foundation's rigorous evaluation of the home visitation model over many years was selected as a featured case for teaching evaluation published by *New Directions for Evaluation* (Sherwood 2005). The Packard Foundation first got involved with home visitation because of a grant request in 1987 from a group of school districts in the Salinas Valley of Monterey County, California, to adapt and implement a child development model called Parents as Teachers (PAT). The program provides education to parents about effective interaction with their children for learning and developmental screening for children in the first 3 years of life. PAT was also planned as an extension of school services that would be available to all parents within the community. As a result, the service population was predominantly low-income and Hispanic parents in the Salinas Valley.

At the time of the program proposal, there was increasing interest nationally in the 0 to 3 age group, early intervention programs to prevent child abuse and neglect, developmental delays among children in high-risk groups, and programs to enhance school readiness. Home visiting as an intervention model crosscut this broad range of child development activity. The general public and policymakers were paying attention to brain development research that highlighted the lasting effects of early childhood experiences.

The Packard Foundation funded a demonstration project of PAT that included evaluation of the PAT model. The highly regarded SRI International conducted the evaluation, which concluded that there were "consistent and strong beneficial effects from PAT participation on virtually all measures included in the evaluation. . . . Clearly PAT is an effective intervention for improving parenting knowledge, attitudes, and behaviors and for supporting positive child development" (quoted in Sherwood 2005:64). Based on the evaluation results, the Foundation decided to go forward with a full-scale program and a more comprehensive random assignment evaluation.

be interpreted; other contextual factors must be taken into consideration. In short, evaluation use is a complex process. Utilization-focused evaluation acknowledges and deals with those complexities to increase the likelihood that evaluation findings are appropriately and meaningfully used.

Understanding the Decision Contexts of Potential Users

Those who study evaluation use would be well advised to focus on the decision contexts of the potential users. The reasons include the need to fit evaluation findings into the users' existing construction of reality and the expertise that the potential users bring to the context. High payoff evaluations are likely to be those for which the questions have been framed by a structured process. These are likely to reduce uncertainty about important issues and test assumptions about policy, programs, social needs, and service delivery. To control legitimation: Provide a good enough product, control the spin, and seek utilization where positions have not yet hardened (Leviton 2003:533–34).

In summative, judgment-oriented evaluations, what Scriven (1980) has called "the logic of valuing" rules. Four steps are necessary: (1) Select criteria of merit; (2) set standards of performance; (3) measure performance; and (4) synthesize results into a judgment of value (Shadish, Cook, and Leviton, 1991:73, 83–94). Selecting criteria for judging success can be a complicated and time-consuming process when large numbers of stakeholders are involved. Gary Henry (2002) used a values inquiry approach to identify criteria for success of a public preschool program by surveying four groups of stakeholders: teachers, administrators, parents, and the public. Different values preferences and varying

criteria lead to different judgments about success. Jane Davidson (2005) in her "nuts-and-bolts" approach describes six strategies for determining judgment criteria (pp. 105–28). See Exhibit 4.3.

Improvement-Oriented, Formative Evaluation

Using evaluation results to improve a program turns out, in practice, to be fundamentally different from rendering judgment about overall effectiveness, merit, or worth. Improvement-oriented forms of evaluation include formative evaluation, quality enhancement, learning organization approaches, and continuous quality improvement (CQI), among others. What these approaches share is a focus on improvement—making things better—rather than rendering summative judgment. Judgment-oriented evaluation requires preordinate, explicit criteria and values that form the basis for judgment. Improvement-oriented approaches tend to be more open-ended, gathering varieties of data about strengths and weaknesses with the expectation that both will be found and each can be used to inform an ongoing cycle of reflection and innovation. Program management, staff, and sometimes participants tend to be the primary users of improvement-oriented findings, while funders and external decision makers tend to use judgmental evaluation, though I hasten to add that these associations of particular categories of users with specific types of evaluations represent utilization tendencies, not definitional distinctions; any category of user may be involved in any kind of use.

Improvement-oriented evaluations ask the following kinds of questions: What are the program's strengths and weaknesses? To what extent are participants progressing toward the desired outcomes? Which types of participants are making good progress

EXHIBIT 4.3

Six Strategies for Determining
the Importance of the Evaluative Criteria

1. Having stakeholders or consumers "vote" on importance

2. Drawing on the knowledge of selected stakeholders

3. Using evidence from the literature

4. Usually specialist judgment

5. Using evidence from the needs and values assessments

6. Using program theory and evidence of causal linkages

SOURCE: Davidson (2005:105–28).

and which types aren't doing so well? What kinds of implementation problems have emerged and how are they being addressed? What's happening that wasn't expected? How are staff and clients interacting? What are staff and participant perceptions of the program? What do they like? Dislike? Want to change? What are perceptions of the program's culture and climate? How are funds being used compared with initial expectations? How is the program's external environment affecting internal operations? Where can efficiencies be realized? What new ideas are emerging that can be tried out and tested?

The flavor of these questions—their nuances, intonation, feel—communicate improvement rather than judgment. Bob Stake's metaphor explaining the difference between summative and formative evaluation can be adapted more generally to the distinction between judgmental evaluation and improvement-oriented evaluation: "When the cook tastes the soup, that's formative; when the guests taste the soup, that's summative" (quoted in Scriven 1991b:169). More generally, anything done to the soup during preparation in the kitchen is improvement oriented; when the soup is served, judgment is rendered, including judgment rendered by the cook that the soup was ready for serving (or at least that preparation time had run out).

The metaphor also helps illustrate that one must be careful to stay focused on intent rather than activities when differentiating purposes. Suppose that those to whom the soup is served are also cooks, and the purpose of their tasting the soup is to offer additional recipe ideas and consider potential variations in seasoning. Then, the fact that the soup has moved from kitchen to table does not mean a change in purpose. Improvement remains the primary agenda. Final judgment awaits another day, a different serving—unless, of course, the collection of cooks suddenly decides that the soup as served to them is already perfect and no further changes should be made. Then, what was supposed to be formative would suddenly have turned out to be summative. And thusly

EXHIBIT 4.4

Formative and Summative Evaluation of The Saint Paul
Technology for Literacy Center (TLC): A Utilization-Focused Model

TLC was established as a 3-year demonstration project to pilot test the effectiveness of an innovative, computer-based approach to adult literacy. The pilot project was funded by six Minnesota Foundations and the Saint Paul Schools at a cost of $1.3 million. The primary intended users of the evaluation were the school superintendent, senior school officials, and School Board Directors who would determine whether to continue and integrate the project into the district's ongoing community education program. School officials and foundation donors participated actively in designing the evaluation. The evaluation cost $70,300.

After 16 months of formative evaluation, the summative evaluation began. The formative evaluation, conducted by an evaluator hired to be part of the TLC staff, used extensive learner feedback, careful documentation of participation and progress, and staff development activities to specify the TLC model and bring implementation to a point of stability and clarity where it could be summatively evaluated. The summative evaluation, conducted by two independent University of Minnesota social scientists, was planned as the formative evaluation was being conducted.

The summative evaluation began by validating that the specified model was, in fact, being implemented as specified. This involved interviews with staff and students, and observations of the program in operation. Outcomes were measured using the Test of Adult Basic Education administered on a pre-post basis to participant and control groups. The test scores were analyzed for all students who participated in the program for a 3-month period. Results were compared with data available on other adult literacy programs. An extensive cost analysis was also conducted by a University educational economist. The report was completed 6 months prior to the end of the demonstration, in time for decision makers to use the results to determine the future of the program. Retention and attrition data were also analyzed and compared with programs nationally.

are purposes and uses often confounded in real-world evaluation practice.

Formative evaluation typically connotes collecting data for a specific period of time, usually during the start-up or pilot phase of a project, to improve implementation, solve unanticipated problems, and make sure that participants are progressing toward desired outcomes. Often the purpose of formative evaluation is to get ready for summative evaluation, that is, to get the program's early implementation bugs worked out and the model stabilized so that it can be evaluated summatively to judge merit and worth. Exhibit 4.4 provides an example of how formative evaluation can prepare a program for summative evaluation by connecting these separate and distinct evaluation purposes to separate and distinct stages in the program's development. As the example also shows, the information needed for improvement is typically different from the data needed for summative judgment.

Accountability

Accountability is a state of, or process for, holding someone to account to someone else for something—that is, being required to justify or explain what has been done. Although accountability is frequently given as a rationale for doing evaluation, there is considerable variation in who is required to answer to whom, concerning what, through what means, and with what consequences. More important, within this range of options, the ways in which evaluation is

Comparisons showed significant gains in reading comprehension and math for the participant group versus no gains for the control group. Adult learners in the program advanced an average of one grade level on the test for every 52.5 hours spent in TLC computer instruction. However, the report cautioned that the results showed great variation: high standard deviations, significant differences between means and medians, ranges of data that include bizarre extremes, and very little correlation between hours spent and progress made. The report concluded, "Each case is relatively unique. TLC has created a highly individualized program where learners can proceed at their own pace based on their own needs and interests. The students come in at very different levels and make very different gains during their TLC work . . . , thus the tremendous variation in progress" (Council on Foundations 1993:142).

Several years after the evaluation, the Council on Foundations commissioned a follow-up study on the evaluation's utility. The Saint Paul Public Schools moved the project from pilot to permanent status. The Superintendent of Schools reported that "the findings of the evaluation and the qualities of the services it had displayed had irrevocably changed the manner in which adult literacy will be addressed throughout the Saint Paul Public Schools" (Council on Foundations 1993:148). TLC also became the basis for the District's new Five Year Plan for Adult Literacy. The evaluation was so well-received by its original philanthropic donors that it led the Saint Paul Foundation to begin and support an Evaluation Fellows program with the University of Minnesota. The independent Council on Foundations follow-up study concluded, "Everyone involved in the evaluation—TLC, funding sources, and evaluators—regards it as a utilization-focused evaluation. . . . The organization and its founders and funders decided what they wanted to learn and instructed the evaluators accordingly" (Council on Foundations 1993:154–55). The formative evaluation was used extensively to develop the program and get it ready for the summative evaluation. The summative evaluation was then used by primary intended users to inform a major decision about the future of computer-based adult literacy. Ten years later, Saint Paul's adult literacy effort continues to be led by TLC's original developer and director.

SOURCES: Turner and Stockdill (1987); Council on Foundations (1993:129–55).

used for accountability are frequently so poorly conceived and executed that they are likely to be dysfunctional for programs and organizations. (Rogers 2005a:2)

This astute conclusion by Australian Patricia Rogers, the first international recipient of the American Evaluation Association's prestigious Myrdal Award for contributions to evaluation use, frames the challenge of bringing utility to the very political undertaking of supporting accountability. More than a quarter century ago, in positing 95 theses for reform of evaluation, Lee J. Cronbach and associates (1980) at Stanford posited,

A call for accountability is a sign of pathology in the political system. . . . Accountability emphasizes looking back in order to assign praise or blame; evaluation is better used to

understand events and processes for the sake of guiding future activities. (P. 4)

Cronbach's distinction between the uses of accountability and evaluation continues to be debated today. Are accountability systems really evaluative or are they primarily political and managerial? In the last edition of this book, I incorporated accountability within judgment-oriented evaluation. However, in practice, these involve significantly different uses. One important reason for distinguishing and separating judgmental/summative evaluation from accountability is articulated by Rogers (2005a):

Accountability systems focus on reporting discrepancies between targets and performance to funders, the assumption being that they will use this information in future funding and policy decisions. However,

Formative-Summative Confusions

Common misconceptions about the formative-summative distinction

- Formative focuses on process, summative on outcomes. *Not true.* Formative evaluation often gives an early picture of what progress is being made toward desired outcomes and what unanticipated outcomes are emerging. Summative evaluation must describe implementation and processes to discuss and judge the relationship between what was done and what was accomplished.
- Formative is more qualitative while summative is more quantitative. *Not true.* Formative and summative are purpose distinctions, not methods distinctions. The nature and combination of methods used depends on what questions are being asked and what evidentiary criteria are preferred by evaluators and primary intended users as they negotiate the design.
- Summative is judgmental while formative is descriptive. *Not true.* The difference is a matter of degree. Summative evaluation involves a definitive, conclusive judgment of *overall* merit, worth, and value, if possible, and the data support such a definitive judgment. Providing formative feedback about what works and doesn't work involves some degree of judgment against criteria related to the notion of what it means for a program to "work," but formative judgments tend to be directed at specific aspects of a program (rather than the overall program) and involve lower stakes decisions than does overall summative judgment. Because of the focus on learning and improvement, formative evaluation typically *feels* less judgmental to staff and participants.
- Summative is definitive while formative is tentative. *Not true.* This depends on the nature of the evidence. While a summative evaluative aims to be definitive, the evidence may not be sufficient to support a definitive judgment. On the other hand, formative evidence about the need for improvement can be quite definitive.
- The formative versus summative distinction is context dependent. *True.* This means that a certain type of evaluation, for example, an impact evaluation, cannot be considered intrinsically summative. An impact evaluation can be used to improve the next stage in the life of a program. Qualitative feedback from participants and in-depth case studies can be used summatively when the results show little or no value from the perspective of intended beneficiaries. Scriven, originator of the distinction, emphasizes that the distinction is "not intrinsic, it's contextual — *mainly a matter of the use to which the evaluation is put* [italics added]. . . . In introducing the distinction between formative and summative, I stressed that this was a difference in roles, not of intrinsic nature. And roles are defined by context" (Scriven 1996:153).

accountability systems rarely provide sufficient information to make it possible for funders to decide if such discrepancies should be followed by decreased funding (as a sanction), increased funding (to improve the quality or quantity of services being provided), or termination of the function. (Pp. 3–4)

The accountability function includes *oversight and compliance:* "the assessment of the extent to which a program follows the directives, regulations, mandated standards or any other formal expectations" (Mark, Henry, and Julnes 2000:13).

Performance measurement is a common approach to oversight, compliance, and accountability. Burt Perrin (2002, 1998) has long been a leader in studying the "effective use and misuse of performance measurement." He has been especially adamant about the limitations of performance indicator approaches for evaluation asserting that such data are "useless for decision making and resource allocation" (1998:374). Why? Because a performance

The Utility of an Accountability System

The utility of an accountability system depends on who is held accountable, by whom, for what—and how they are held accountable, that is, the extent to which results can be determined and explained, and that there are consequences for failure and rewards for success. The credibility of an accountability system, which greatly affects its utility, depends on the extent to which those held accountable actually have the capacity to achieve those things over which they are held accountable, within the time frames expected, and that the consequences are proportionately and reasonably aligned with that capacity and those time frames.

indicator alone doesn't tell a decision maker why the results are at a certain level and without knowing why, informed action is problematic. In essence, accountability systems serve the purpose of providing *an account of how things are going* but not enough information to inform decisions or solve problems. Those actions require deeper evaluative data than accountability systems usually provide (Bemelmans-Videc, Lonsdale, and Perrin 2007; Mayne 2007a; Owen 2007; Perrin 2007).

A comprehensive accountability approach involves both description—What was achieved?—and explanation—How and why was it achieved at the levels attained? To describe is not to explain, and to explain is not to excuse or diminish responsibility. Ideally, description, explanation, and responsibility can be combined to produce an effective and useful accountability system. Description, however, comes first. Having an accurate account of how things are going, including what results are being attained, is essential. Explaining those results and assigning responsibility follow. And that's where it all becomes very political.

Accountability is like a red cape in front of a bull in the political arena where politicians fancy themselves as matadors braving the horns of waste and corruption. Funders and politicians issue shrill calls for accountability (notably for others, not for themselves), and "managing for accountability" (Kearns 1996) has become a rallying cry in both private and public sectors. In its extreme bean-counting manifestation, this can become what Weinberger (2007) has called "The Folly of Accountabalism."

Program and financial audits are aimed at assuring compliance with intended purposes and mandated procedures. The program evaluation units of legislative audit offices, offices of comptrollers and inspectors, and federal agencies such as the OMB have government oversight responsibilities to make sure programs are properly implemented and effective. Reflecting the increased emphasis on accountability in government, in 2004, the legal name of the Congressional oversight agency, GAO, changed its name to the Government Accountability Office instead of the General Accounting Office, a designation it had had for 83 years. The U.S. Government Performance and Results Act of 1993 requires annual performance measurement to "justify" program decisions and budgets. Political leaders in Canada, the United Kingdom, and Australia have been active and vocal in attempting to link performance measurement to budgeting for purposes of accountability (Auditor General of Canada 1993), and these efforts greatly influenced the United States federal approach to accountability (Breul 1994).

Accountability concerns are driven by the following kinds of questions: Are funds being used for intended purposes? Are goals and targets being met? Are indicators showing improvement? Are resources being efficiently allocated? Are problems being handled? Are staff qualified? Are

Accountability for Utilization

GAO, as the largest internal, independent evaluation unit in existence, has a distinguished history of paying attention to how its evaluations are used. Every recommendation in its numerous reports is followed to find out whether its findings are adopted. In 2004, for example, GAO made 1,950 recommendations. In its own internal utilization study, GAO found that 80 percent of its recommendations to improve government operations were implemented from 2000 to 2004 (Mathison 2005:168).

only eligible participants being accepted into the program? Is implementation following the approved plan? Are quality control mechanisms in place and being used?

The varying contexts within which such questions are asked matter a great deal. In government, accountability issues inevitably find their way into debates between those in power and those out of power. In philanthropy, accountability "satisfies the fiduciary responsibility of a foundation to oversee the use of money and to ensure that grant funds were spent according to its terms. Evaluation, therefore, provides the evidence for both grantee and foundation accountability" (Kramer and Bickel 2004:53). For not-for-profit agencies and nongovernmental organizations, accountability is part of good management. In all these contexts, accountability-oriented evaluation is manifesting one of the major historical streams that flow into the large ocean of evaluation: the audit stream (Wisler 1996).

In the public sector, rhetoric about accountability can become particularly strident in the heat of political campaigns. Everyone campaigns against ineffectiveness, waste, and fraud. Yet one person's waste is another's jewel. For years, U.S.

Senator William Proxmire of Wisconsin periodically held press conferences in which he announced *Golden Fleece Awards* for government programs he considered especially wasteful. I had the dubious honor of being the evaluator for one such project ridiculed by Proxmire, a project to take higher education administrators into the wilderness to experience, firsthand, experiential education. The program was easy to make fun of: Why should taxpayer dollars be spent for college deans to hike in the woods? Outrageous! What was left out of Proxmire's press release was that the project, supported by the Fund for the Improvement of Postsecondary Education, had been selected in a competitive process and funded because of its innovative approach to rejuvenating burned-out and discouraged administrators, and that many of those administrators returned to their colleges to spearhead curriculum reform. There was lots of room for debate about the merit or worth of the program *depending on one's values and priorities*, but our evaluation found that the funds were spent in accordance with the agency's innovative mandate and many, though not all, participants followed through on the project's goal of providing leadership for educational change. The funding agency found sufficient value that the project was awarded a year-long dissemination grant.

Some criteria, such as fraud and gross incompetence, are sufficiently general and agreed-on that when uncovered and given media attention, they inevitably raise the crescendo of voices lamenting the offending program's lack of accountability. One of my favorite examples comes from a program audit of a weatherization program in Kansas as reported in the newsletter of Legislative Program Evaluators.

Kansas auditors visited several homes that had been weatherized. At one home, workers had installed 14 storm windows to cut down on air filtration in the house. However, one could literally see through the house because some of the siding had rotted and either pulled away from or fallen off the house. The auditors also found that the agency had nearly 200 extra storm windows in stock. Part of the problem was that the supervisor responsible for measuring storm windows was afraid of heights; he would "eyeball" the size of second-story windows from the ground. . . . If these storm windows did not fit, he ordered new ones. (Hinton 1988:3)

The auditors also found fraud. The program bought windows at inflated prices from a company secretly owned by a program employee. A kickback scheme was uncovered. "The workmanship on most homes was shoddy, bordering on criminal. . . . [For example], workers installing a roof vent used an ax to chop a hole in the roof." Some 20 percent of beneficiaries didn't meet eligibility criteria. Findings such as these are thankfully rare, but they grab headlines when they become public, and they illustrate why accountability will remain a central purpose of many evaluations.

The extent to which concerns about accountability dominate a specific study varies by the role of the evaluator. For auditors, accountability is always primary. Public reports on performance indicators for government programs are accountability driven. Performance measurement follows the mantra that "what gets measured gets done." But for an accountability system to have integrity and credibility, there needs to be some separation between the measuring and the doing, or at least some independent way of verifying the accuracy of internally generated accountability data. Burt Perrin, in a presentation on accountability at the

European Evaluation Society annual conference, Seville, Spain, called attention to an article in *Nature* about how statistics reported by China regarding the fish catches by its fishery had been grossly distorted. "Apparently, under the Communist system of matching results with plan, the same bureaucrats were responsible for not only counting the catch but also meeting targets to increase it—so they simply exaggerated the count to match their allotted goals" (*International Herald Tribune* 2001).

> **What Gets Measured Gets Done**
>
> In Poland, as manufacturing shifted from communism to capitalism, performance incentives were introduced and the performance of furniture factories was measured by the tons of furniture shipped. Responding to this incentive system—what gets measured gets done—Poland came to have the heaviest furniture in the world (Perrin 2002:368).

Elliot Stern, former president of the International Organization for Cooperation in Evaluation, has long expressed concern that "most accountability systems encourage a blame culture." He sees this as part of "the wider preoccupation with regulation and control as part of public management today."

> When programmes do not achieve their targets or when policy instruments appear not to work, a first reflex is to identify the guilty party and remove or relocate him. Accountability is after all one of the acknowledged main purposes of evaluation. (Stern 2004:12)

Accountability systems, then, pose special challenges for evaluation, especially in implementing high-quality systems that are useful and credible, and overcoming the tendencies of such systems to become politicized and corrupted. Canada has had some success with such systems (Fraser 2006; Mayne 2006; Schwartz and Mayne 2004). The situation at the federal level in the United States is more problematic as the Bush administration instigated a new accountability system alongside and on top of the existing Clinton administration system. See Exhibit 4.5.

To be useful beyond providing meat for political dog fights, accountability systems need to be designed with utility in mind. Rogers has identified critical characteristics of such a useful system, what she calls *smart accountability:*

Accountability requires a much more comprehensive explanation of performance, an incentive system that encourages improvement of performance rather than misreport and distortion of it, and a commitment to address learning as well as accountability. In other words, accountability systems need to be a tool for informed judgment and management rather than a substitute. This is the smart accountability that is being increasingly advocated.

Smart accountability includes demonstrating responsible, informed management; including appropriate risk management, such as cautious trials of difficult or new approaches; and a commitment to identify and learn from both successes and mistakes. The incentive system for accountability needs to reward *intelligent failure* (competent implementation of something that has since been found not to work), discourage setting easy targets, discourage simply reporting compliance with processes or targets, and encourage seeking out tough criticism.

The acid test of a good accountability system is that it encourages responsibility and promotes better performance. (Rogers 2005a:4)

Performance Measurement Challenges

Many activities are in the public sector precisely because of measurement problems: If everything was so crystal clear and every benefit so easily attributable, those activities would have been in the private sector long ago.

SOURCE: Mintzberg (1996:76), Strategic Management Scholar

Performance Measurement: A View from the Trenches

I have been working now for about 20 years in the area of evaluation and performance measurement, and I am so discouraged about performance measurement and results reporting and its supposed impact on accountability that I am just about ready to throw in the towel. So I have had to go right back to the basics of reporting and democracy to try to trace a line from what was intended to what we have ended up with . . . .

Performance measurement has been oversold - it makes promises that are not easily kept, and I honestly believe now that it has become a paper exercise for departments, and is too boring and technical for the public or Legislators to have the time or interest to read. What ever happened to good old monitoring?

Karyn Hicks *EvalTalk* posting
Programs Advisor July 28, 2006, Government of the Northwest Territories. Yellowknife, Canada
Used with permission

EXHIBIT 4.5

Accountability: Too Much of a Good Thing?

GPRA and PART as Dueling Banjos

The Clinton/Gore Administration's effort to "reinvent government" led to the 1993 Government Performance and Results Act (GPRA). This major legislation aimed to shift the focus of government decision making and accountability away from a preoccupation with reporting on activities to a focus on the results of those activities, such as real gains in employability, safety, responsiveness, or program quality. Under GPRA, U.S. federal government agencies are required to develop multiyear strategic plans, annual performance plans, and annual performance reports.

In 2001, the U.S. Government Accountability Office (GAO) initiated major reviews of how GPRA was being implemented (www.gao.gov/new.items/gpra/gpra.htm). GAO has continued issuing annual reviews (www.gao.gov/pas/2005) as part of its Performance and Accountability Series. At the beginning of each new Congress, based on its audits and evaluations, GAO identifies federal programs and operations that are "*high risk*" due to their vulnerabilities to fraud, waste, abuse, and mismanagement. GAO has increasingly focused on the need for broad-based transformations to address major economy, efficiency, and effectiveness challenges (GAO 2006a). Those agencies identified as *high risk* receive increased scrutiny both inside and outside government. Follow-up reviews show that GAO's *high risk* evaluations are used to bring about significant change. "Lasting solutions to high-risk problems offer the potential to save billions of dollars, dramatically improve service to the American public, strengthen public confidence and trust in the performance and accountability of our national government, and ensure the ability of government to deliver on its promises" (GAO 2005, Highlights).

Immediately following election in 2000, the Bush administration reiterated a commitment to performance, accountability, and results. To that end, in 2001, the Office of Management and Budget (OMB) began to develop a mechanism called the Program Assessment Rating Tool (PART) to help budget examiners and federal managers measure the effectiveness of government programs. A PART review aims to identify a program's strengths and weaknesses to inform funding and management decisions aimed at making the program more effective. The PART framework aims to evaluate "all factors that affect and reflect program performance including program purpose and design; performance measurement, evaluations, and strategic planning; program management; and program results" (www.whitehouse.gov/omb/part). PART intends to examine program improvements over time and allow comparisons between similar programs. Bill Trochim, Chair of the American Evaluation Association Public Affairs Committee, observed, "PART is one of the more significant evaluation-related items emerging from the US federal government in many years" (Trochim 2006a).

In 2006, OMB launched a Web site (www.ExpectMore.gov) that reports on federal program performance and what is being done to improve results. It opened with nearly 800 PART program assessments. GAO evaluated how federal agencies responded to PART. Their findings focused on implementation rather than evaluation use.

Several agencies struggled to identify appropriate outcome measures and credible data sources before they could evaluate program effectiveness. Evaluation typically competed with other program activities for funds, so managers may be reluctant to reallocate funds to evaluation. Some agency officials thought that evaluations should be targeted to areas of policy significance or uncertainty. However, all four agencies indicated that the visibility of an OMB recommendation brought agency management attention—and sometimes funds—to get the evaluations done. Moreover, by coordinating their evaluation activities, agencies met these challenges by leveraging their evaluation expertise and strategically prioritizing their evaluation resources to the studies that they considered most important (GAO 2006b:3).

(Continued)

(Continued)

Both GPRA and PART involve massive amounts of staff time, money, and paperwork. Both are federal government efforts to increase accountability, evaluate effectiveness, and demonstrate results. How do they relate to each other? Not very well, it turns out. Integration is, at best, a work in progress. They are parallel, often redundant, efforts. The promulgation of competing and redundant government performance measurement systems goes well beyond GPRA and PART and has become a widespread problem stemming from the many different performance measurement approaches and systems introduced at all levels of government (Nicholson-Crotty et al. 2006). Both legislative and executive improvements are proposed regularly, often in recognition that the sheer volume of information reported reduces utility because there is too much to sort through and make sense of. Compliance with mandated reporting trumps meaningfulness. Nor is this simply an American problem. Around the world new performance monitoring systems get created with little sense of what is already in place, with little evaluation of the strengths, weakness, and uses of current information systems, and with inadequate attention to the accuracy, credibility, timeliness, and utility of new systems (Rogers 2006).

The GAO (2004) evaluated how GPRA and PART were being used—an excellent example of a utilization study—and concluded that PART had emerged as a parallel and competing approach with GPRA's Performance Management Framework. Many federal agency officials, they found, viewed PART's program measures as detrimental to and in conflict with their GPRA planning and reporting processes. The relationship between the PART and GPRA was not well-defined, was often confusing to program officials and agency managers, and, ironically, undermined the efforts of both to promote efficiency and accountability, thus defeating the purpose of each, which is, pointedly, to increase efficiency and accountability.

Distinguished public administration scholar Paul Light (2006) reviewed the last six decades of major administrative reforms enacted by the U.S. Congress. He found acceleration in both the number and the variety of reforms attempted, fueled in part by heightened public distrust toward government. Ironically, from an evaluation perspective, part of what drives constant reform, Light found, is a lack of hard evidence about what actually works to improve government performance. New systems are put in place before existing systems have a chance to work, much less be evaluated. Meanwhile, critiques and ideas for still more reforms abound (e.g., Caiden 2006; Kettl et al. 2006; Shipman 2003).

Monitoring: Evaluation's Global Partner

Monitoring is another purpose distinction that is new to this edition. Sometimes, monitoring is subsumed under accountability since both use performance indicators. But that's like treating formative and summative evaluation as the same because they both use data. In fact, performance indicators can serve different purposes, and this is a chapter on purpose distinctions, so it seems to me worth calling attention to the facts that (1) performance indicators can be used for either accountability or ongoing management purposes and (2) these purposes are often in conflict because they involve different primary intended users. Accountability is driven by attention to external stakeholders, those to whom the program is responsible and those who have funded it. Ongoing monitoring serves managers, providing those internal to the program with the information they need to know where their managerial attention will do the most good.

The other reason for highlighting monitoring as a distinct purpose is that this has become the international norm. In the United States, we talk about evaluation and performance measurement as virtually distinct endeavors. But in developing countries, the standard reference is to "M&E"—monitoring and evaluation. These are close siblings, always together. There are "M&E handbooks," "M&E" conferences, "M&E" workshops. As serendipity would have it, on the very day I was writing this section, an international participant on EvalTalk, the AEA listserv, posted a request for resources on building "M&E capacity." The very first response from an American

participant was, "What's M&E?" That sealed the deal. Readers of this book will not have to ask that question.

But there are different approaches to M&E. Ray Rist, coauthor with Jody Zall Kusek (2004) of *Ten Steps to a Results-Based Monitoring and Evaluation System* (see Exhibit 4.6), created the International Program for Development Evaluation Training (IPDET) with his World Bank colleague Linda Morra. That program has trained more development evaluators than any other in the world and the graduates of IPDET, with support and inspiration from Ray, Linda, and others in the international community, have provided the leadership for the International Development Evaluation Association (IDEAS) (www.ideas-int.org).

EXHIBIT 4.6

Ten Steps to a Results-Based Monitoring and Evaluation System

1. Conducting a readiness assessment

2. Agreeing on outcomes to monitor and evaluate

3. Selecting key indicators to monitor outcomes

4. Baseline data on indicators—where are we today?

5. Planning for improvement—selecting results targets

6. Monitoring for results

7. Planning the role of evaluations

8. Reporting findings

9. Using findings

10. Sustaining the M&E system within the organization

SOURCE: Kusek and Rist (2004:25).

Rist, now president of IDEAS, travels the world advocating for and training people in a particular kind of M&E system:

A theoretical distinction needs to be drawn between traditional M&E and results-based M&E. Traditional M&E focuses on the monitoring and evaluation of inputs, activities, and outputs, that is, project or program implementation. Governments have over time tracked their expenditures and revenues, staffing levels and resources, program and project activities, numbers of participants, goods and services produced, etc. Indeed, traditional efforts at monitoring have been a function of many governments for many decades or longer. In fact, there is evidence that the ancient Egyptians (5000 B.C.) regularly tracked their government's outputs in grain and livestock production.

Results-based M&E, however, combines the traditional approach of monitoring implementation with the assessment of results. . . . It is this linking of implementation progress (performance) with progress in achieving desired objectives or goals (results) of government policies and programs that makes results-based M&E most useful as a tool for public management. (Rist 2006a:4–5)

Most approaches to designing M&E systems intend them to serve both accountability and managerial functions. And therein lies the rub. Policymakers and funders want global, big picture data, what is sometimes called the view from 40,000 feet. Managers need detailed data, the view from 10,000 feet. Aggregating detailed indicators into big picture patterns is one of the major challenges of a performance monitoring system that tries to serve both sets of stakeholders equally well. Still, major texts, while distinguishing between managerial and accountability uses, tend to play down these different uses. Consider how Theodore Poister presents performance monitoring in the influential *Handbook of Practical Program Evaluation* (Wholey, Hatry, and Newcomer 2004):

Performance monitoring systems are designed to track selected measures of program, agency, or system performance at regular time intervals and report them to managers and other specified audiences on an ongoing basis. Their purpose is to provide objective information to managers and policy makers in an effort to improve decision making and thereby strengthen performance, as well as to provide accountability to a range of stakeholders, such as higher-level management, central executive agencies, governing bodies, funding agencies, accrediting associations, clients and customers, advocacy groups, and the public at large. Thus, performance monitoring systems are critical elements in a variety of approaches to results-oriented management." (Poister 2004:99)

A utilization-focused approach to M&E is less cavalier about such laundry lists of stakeholders and multiple intended uses. Any system will have to set priorities for intended uses by intended users at some point, or risk serving everyone poorly.

The "monitoring and tailoring" approach of Cooley and Bickel (1985) illustrates an approach where school administrators and teachers are the primary intended users. They built a classroom-based information system aimed at systematically tracking daily attendance patterns for individuals, classrooms, and schools. Teachers and administrators could quickly identify attendance problems and intervene before the problems became chronic or overwhelming. Attendance could also be treated as an early warning indicator of other potential problems.

Most monitoring systems look internally (Owen, 1999:239–62). How is program implementation unfolding? What is progress toward desired results? Are we reaching the target population? Are we maintaining quality? Indeed, continuous quality improvement systems (CQI) are one common form of monitoring (Colton 1997). But monitoring systems that include periodic environmental scanning can be especially useful as early warning systems that something in the environment has changed, something that might threaten performance. During a training workshop in South Africa, participants found an M&E metaphor in the vineyards outside Cape Town. The fields of grapevines nestled beneath the green hills are surrounded by fence rows of white roses. Each day the growers inspect the roses. Anything, disease or pest, that might harm the vines will show up on the roses first. They monitor the roses to decide if action is needed to protect the grapes.

At the policy and resource allocation level, a major challenge has been to connect monitoring to planning and budget cycles (Joyce 1997; Newcomer 1997). Influencing how money is spent may be the ultimate instrumental use for a monitoring system. One long-time dream has been to tie performance results to the budget process, thus increasing attention to results and, hopefully, utility, by increasing the stakes. This is a program-level application of the idea of pay-for-performance in personnel evaluation in which executives and staff who excel get bonuses and special recognition while poor performers get weeded out. This sounds reasonable, even ideal, but proves quite complicated in practice. See Exhibit 4.7 for a review of how the federal PART system has approached the connection to budget.

As evidenced by periodic discussions on the *EvalTalk*, the American Evaluation Association listserv, evaluators disagree about how monitoring and in-depth evaluation studies are related. Hatry et al. (2004) have looked closely and thoughtfully at this issue, bringing great expertise and experience to consider what works. They acknowledge that

> performance monitoring seeks primarily to assess the outcomes of a program without any in-depth examination of the program. . . . In-depth evaluations are considerably more informative and provide considerably more information for major policy and program decisions. . . . We believe these processes are complementary. We believe that performance monitoring can and should be considered an important subset of program evaluation. (p. 676)

The phrase M&E makes the marriage of monitoring and evaluation explicit. In particular, findings from monitoring data can generate questions to be answered by evaluation through more in-depth inquiry, helping to focus and increase the utility of scare evaluation resources. Kusek and Rist (2004) emphasize the integration of monitoring and evaluation in a well-designed, well-implemented, and results-oriented M&E system:

> We want to stress the complementarity of evaluation to monitoring. Each supports the other—even as each asks different questions and will likely make different uses of information and analyses. The immediate implication is that moving to a results-based M&E system requires building an information and analysis system with two components—monitoring and evaluation. Either alone, in the end, is not sufficient. (p. 114)

As always we return to the issue of use. Ongoing and continuous monitoring systems, like all useful evaluation approaches, must be designed to meet the specifiable information needs of identifiable users. A system designed by software, technology, and data experts with little or no serious input and pilot-testing with intended users can be a wonderful system—for the experts who designed it, but not for the intended users.

EXHIBIT 4.7
Follow the Money

A performance monitoring system shows weak results. What are the budget implications of such a finding? Often a primary reason a program has poor results is that it has inadequate resources to achieve quite grandiose goals. If a program is producing poor results, do you kill it or increase its resources so it can improve? Answering this question involves more than a simple report-card grade that the program is good or bad. You need to know why the program is struggling and whether increased resources could be well used.

Consider the situation of a student struggling in a course. Do you just flunk the student or try to provide tutoring and extra help? Does the student have special needs? What else is going on in the student's life? Is the problem in this course part of a long-term pattern of underachievement or is the student's poor performance new? The decision to fail the student or provide extra help will depend, then, on why the student is struggling and an assessment of whether tutoring will help. What does this have to do with government performance monitoring and evaluation?

In the United States, the President's fiscal year 2006 budget elevated the importance of federal PART accountability reviews (see Exhibit 4.5) and increased their visibility by asserting that the budget process was influenced by measures of the success of programs in meeting goals and "identifies which are achieving their intended results and which are not . . . and helps the Administration to reward only those [programs] that succeed" (White House 2006:4). Based on this analysis, the President's budget identified a list of 154 programs slated for deep cuts or elimination because those programs were "not getting results." That sounds straightforward, even laudatory, but here's where the story gets interesting.

OMB Watch is an independent, not-for-profit organization founded in 1983 to increase transparency in the policy-making process. It is funded primarily by philanthropic foundations and has been a thorn in the side of both Republican and Democratic administrations as it has analyzed and evaluated the details of policies and budgets. *OMB Watch* analyzed the list of programs to be cut in the President's 2006 budget and compared program funding requests with the ratings received under the PART. Here is what they found:

> Out of the list of 154 programs to be cut or eliminated, supposedly for lack of results, more than two-thirds have never even been reviewed by the PART. It is unclear what kinds of determinations, if any, the administration used to identify these failing programs when the White House budget staff had yet to assess them.

- Of the 85 programs receiving a top PART score in 2006, the president proposed cutting the budgets of more than 38 percent, including the National Center for Education Statistics.
- Of all the programs reviewed on the list of 154, nearly 20 percent of programs receiving an "effective" or "moderately effective" PART score—the two highest ratings—were targeted for elimination. Further, 46 percent of programs receiving the middle rating of "adequate" were proposed to be eliminated.
- Some programs receiving the lowest score were not cut. For instance, the Substance Abuse Prevention and Treatment Block Grant, a program that provides grants to states to address addiction problems, was given the lowest possible rating of "ineffective" but received no reduction in funding. Moreover, the Earned Income Tax Credit Compliance Program—which targets poor people who have claimed the EITC and double-checks their eligibility for the credit—was rated ineffective, yet it received a funding increase. (Hughes and Shull 2005:4)

The analysis of all programs rated under PART since its inception revealed no logical or consistent connections with budget requests. On the face of it, this judgment sounds like strong criticism. But it is only a negative finding when interpreted in the context of the promise to base budget decisions on PART ratings of program performance. As noted earlier, there is good reason to be skeptical about the wisdom of any such simple and mechanical approach to budgeting: highly rated programs get more funds; poorly rated programs get cuts. Performance ratings can and should be one factor in budget decisions, but not the only factor. Those ratings must be interpreted and used within a larger context taking into account factors such as what alternatives are available, what the program has learned about what works and doesn't work that could improve future performance, the track record of managerial competence, how much support the program has among important political constituencies, overall state of the economy and the federal budget, and competing program priorities, to name but a few factors.

Knowledge-Generating Evaluation

Whoever undertakes to set himself up as a judge of Truth and Knowledge is shipwrecked by the laughter of the gods.

—Albert Einstein

In the knowledge age, what could be more useful than contributing to knowledge? Despite Einstein's caution, the evaluation profession has set its sights on knowledge generation, in part because of the great potential for use. The instrumental uses of summative and formative evaluation concern judgments about and improvements for specific programs. Accountability and monitoring also focus typically on performance indicators for a particular program. Knowledge generation, however, changes the unit of analysis as evaluators look across findings from different programs to identify general *patterns of effectiveness*. Knowledge generation, then, has emerged as one of the principal purposes of evaluation (Chelimsky 1997).

As the field of evaluation has matured and a vast number of evaluations has accumulated, the opportunity has arisen to look beyond and across findings about specific programs to formulate generalizations about processes and interventions that make a difference. This involves synthesizing findings from different studies, a strategy the GAO has found useful in providing accumulated wisdom to Congress about how to formulate effective policies and programs (GAO 1992c). A classic example was GAO's report (1992b) on "Adolescent Drug Use Prevention: Common Features of Promising Community Programs." See Exhibit 4.8.

An excellent and important example of synthesis evaluation is Lisbeth Schorr's (1988) *Within Our Reach*, a study of programs aimed at breaking the cycle of poverty. She identified "the lessons of successful programs" as follows (pp. 256–83):

- offering a broad spectrum of services;
- regularly crossing traditional professional and bureaucratic boundaries, i.e., organizational flexibility;
- seeing the child in the context of family and the family in the context of its surroundings, i.e., holistic approaches;

EXHIBIT 4.8

Example of a Knowledge-Oriented Evaluation Synthesis: Common Features of Promising Community Programs Engaged in Adolescent Drug Use Prevention

Six features associated with high levels of participant enthusiasm and attachment:

1. a comprehensive strategy,

2. an indirect approach to drug abuse prevention,

3. the goal of empowering youth,

4. a participatory approach,

5. a culturally sensitive orientation, and

6. highly structured activities.

Six common program problems:

1. maintaining continuity with their participants,

2. coordinating and integrating their service components,

3. providing accessible services,

4. obtaining funds,

5. attracting necessary leadership and staff, and

6. conducting evaluation.

SOURCE: GAO (1992b).

- coherent and easy-to-use services;
- committed, caring, results-oriented staff;
- finding ways to adapt or circumvent traditional professional and bureaucratic limitations to meet client needs;
- professionals redefining their roles to respond to severe needs; and
- overall, intensive, comprehensive, responsive and flexible programming.

These kinds of "lessons" constitute accumulated wisdom—principles of effectiveness—that can be adapted, indeed, must be adapted, to specific programs, organizations,

or even broader initiatives like community change (Auspos and Kubisch 2004).

Earlier in this chapter, in reviewing judgment-oriented use, Exhibit 4.2 offered an example of a summative evaluation of a Packard Foundation grant for home visitation. The evaluation reached a positive conclusion that led to additional funding. It also led to a significant knowledge-building effort that spanned several years as results from multiple home visitation grants, project evaluations, and independent research findings accumulated. As findings from various evaluations and other home-visiting experiments were coming in during the 1996–1998 period, a pattern was emerging of mixed or no significant effects. "The bottom line was small positive effects on a few measures of child development and parenting outcomes for participants who received the expected intensity of service, but very few effects for the overall enrollee groups" (Sherwood 2005:67). What had looked like a promising intervention in the early 1990s had become a disappointment by the end of the decade. Ann Segal, then a senior official in the U.S. Department of Health and Human Services Office of the Assistant Secretary for Planning and Evaluation, examined the cumulative evidence and concluded that there was no solid evidence that early intervention, via home visiting, with pregnant and parenting teenagers was effective by itself. The lesson she drew was that such programs had been overpromised and that what they set out to accomplish would not work without other, complementary interventions.

> Most home visiting programs promised to do everything—get mothers working, reduce child abuse and neglect, increase literacy, and more. A common sense reading is that these programs aren't going to get you where you want to go. I take away that the evaluation answer is right—there's nothing there. *But,* these programs shouldn't be out there by themselves. You have to hook them onto something stronger. (Segal quoted in Sherwood 2005:70)

This journey from a single program that seemed to have promising outcomes to cumulative evidence that the model is not generally effective is a common evaluation story. Yet the accumulating evidence also shows the importance and value of early childhood interventions (Karoly, Kilburn, and Cannon 2005), for there are models

that consistently work, those with better trained home visitors and greater intensity of services. Cronbach and Associates (1980) observed in their 95 theses that "an evaluation of a particular program is only an episode in the continuing evolution of thought about a problem area" (p. 2). And "in project-by-project evaluation, each study analyzes a spoonful dipped from a sea of uncertainties" (p. 8).

In the philanthropic world, the strategy of synthesizing results from several studies has come to be called "cluster evaluation" (Connor et al. 2004; Millett 1996; Council on Foundations 1993:232–51). A cluster evaluation team visits a number of different grantee projects with a similar focus (e.g., grassroots leadership development) and draws on individual grant evaluations to identify patterns across and lessons from the whole cluster (Sanders 1997; Barley and Jenness 1993; Kellogg Foundation n.d.). The McKnight Foundation commissioned a cluster evaluation of 34 separate grants aimed at aiding families in poverty. One lesson learned was that "effective programs have developed processes and strategies for learning about the *strengths* as well as the needs of families in poverty" (Patton, 1993:10). This "lesson" takes on added meaning when connected with the finding of Independent Sector's review of "Common Barriers to Effectiveness in the Independent Sector":

> The deficits model holds that distressed people and communities are "needy"; they're a collection of problems, pathologies and handicaps; they need doctoring, rehabilitation and fixing of the kind that professionalized services are intended to provide.
>
> The assets model holds that even the most distressed person or community has strengths, abilities and capacities; with investment, their strengths, abilities and capacities can increase. This view is only

barely allowed to exist in the independent sector, where organizations are made to compete for funds on the basis of "needs" rather than on the basis of "can-do."

The deficit model—seeing the glass half empty—is a barrier to effectiveness in the independent sector. (Mayer 1993:7–8)

The McKnight Foundation cluster evaluation and the Independent Sector study reached similar conclusions concurrently and independently. Such triangulated evaluation findings about principles of effective programming have become the knowledge base of the evaluation profession. Being knowledgeable about patterns of program effectiveness allows evaluators to provide guidance about development of new initiatives, policies, and strategies for implementation. Such contributions constitute the conceptual use of evaluation findings. Efforts of this kind may be considered *research* rather than evaluation, but such research is ultimately evaluative in nature and important to the profession.

Some synthesis evaluations look at large numbers of cases. The World Bank's report on *Reducing Poverty on a Global Scale: Learning and Innovating for Development* draws on more than 100 case studies of poverty reduction worldwide. World Bank analysts identified the main factors that help or hurt in reducing poverty at scale. A whole chapter of the report assesses China's experiences in promoting economic growth and reducing poverty over the past 25 years, noting that China has achieved the most rapid large-scale poverty reduction in human history (World Bank 2006).

In a report published by the Knowledge for Development (K4D) Program of The World Bank Institute, Zeng (2006) studied *Knowledge, Technology and Cluster-based Growth in Africa* by synthesizing findings from 11 case studies of enterprise clusters in Africa.

These clusters are able to survive and succeed, mainly because they are able to upgrade their business activities towards more diversity and sophistication and reach a certain scale, through building up a supply-production-distribution value chain, acquiring knowledge and technology (both domestic and foreign) and disseminating and adapting them, building a relatively educated labor force, achieving collective efficiency through joint actions and cooperation, gaining government and institutional support as well as international support (such as EU, World Bank and UN) in some cases. (Pp. 8–9)

"Theory-driven evaluation" is an approach to evaluation that places a priority on testing and contributing to social science theory (Chen 1990, 1989; Chen and Rossi 1987). While theory-driven evaluations can provide program models for summative judgment or ongoing improvement, the connection to social science theory tends to focus on increasing knowledge about how effective programs work in general. Shadish (1987), in this vein, has argued that the understandings gleaned from evaluations ought to contribute to "macrotheories" about "how to produce important social change" (p. 94). Such knowledge-generating efforts focus beyond the effectiveness of a particular program to future program designs and policy formulation in general.

Synthesis evaluations also help us generate knowledge about conducting useful evaluations. The premises of utilization-focused evaluation featured in this book originally emerged from studying 20 federal evaluations (Patton, Grimes et al. 1977). Those premises were affirmed by Alkin et al. (1979) in the model of evaluation use they developed by analyzing evaluations from different education districts in California and by Wargo (1989) in his "characteristics of successful program evaluations" identified by studying three "unusually successful evaluations of national food and nutrition programs" (p. 71). Alkin, Hofstetter, and Ai (1998, pp. 109–11) identified "Lessons Learned from Stakeholder Approaches" based on their review of research and theory. The Council on Foundations commissioned a synthesis evaluation based on nine case studies of major foundation evaluations to learn lessons about "effective evaluating." (A summary of one of those case studies is presented as Exhibit 4.4 in this chapter.) Among the Council's 35 key lessons learned is this utilization-focused evaluation premise: "Key 6. Make sure the people who can make the most use of the evaluation are involved as stakeholders in planning and carrying out the evaluation" (Council on Foundations 1993:255). Carlsson et al. (1999) studied evaluation use in nine Swedish development project evaluations and concluded, among other lessons, that in developing countries where oral communications are especially important, overreliance on written evaluation reports reduces use and broad dissemination of findings.

Knowledge Generation and High-Quality Lessons Learned

Do not be proud of your knowledge. Listen to the ignorant and the wise. Truth may lie as hidden in the earth as copper, or it may be found at play upon the lips of maidens bent above their grindstones.

—Ptah-hotep, Egyptian teacher, 2540 BCE

As the knowledge-generating purpose of evaluation has become more prominent, it has become common practice for evaluation reports to include a section on "lessons learned." A common problem when some idea becomes highly popular, in this case the

search for lessons learned, is that the idea loses its substance and meaning. Ricardo Millett, former Director of Evaluation at the W. K. Kellogg Foundation, and I reviewed together the kinds of "lessons learned" that were offered in cluster evaluation reports. We found that the items included under these umbrella labels were so broad and inclusive that the phrases lacked any consistent meaning. As "lessons" became widely valued, the word "lesson" began to be applied to any kind of insight, evidentially based or not. We began thinking about what would constitute "high-quality lessons learned" and decided that one's confidence in the transferability or extrapolated relevance of a supposed lesson learned would increase to the extent that it was supported by multiple sources and types of learning. Exhibit 4.9 presents a list of kinds of evidence that could be accumulated to support a proposed lesson learned, making it more worthy of application and adaptation to new settings if it has independent triangulated support from a variety of perspectives. Questions for generating "lessons learned" are also listed.

High-quality lessons learned, then, represent principles extrapolated from multiple sources and independently triangulated to increase transferability as cumulative knowledge working hypotheses that can be adapted and applied to new situations, a form of pragmatic utilitarian generalizability, if you will. The internal validity of any single source of knowledge would need to be judged in terms of the criteria appropriate for that type of knowledge. Thus, practitioner wisdom and evaluation studies may be internally validated in different ways. However, when these various types and sources of knowledge cohere, triangulate, and reinforce each other, that very coalescence increases the likelihood of generalizability, perhaps sufficient to justify designation as a *triangulated better practice*, or a *high-quality lesson learned*.

EXHIBIT 4.9

High-Quality Lessons Learned

High-quality lessons learned: triangulated knowledge confirmed from multiple sources that can be applied to inform future action.

Sources for triangulation

1. evaluation findings—patterns across programs
2. basic and applied research findings
3. triangulation of multiple and mixed methods
4. practice wisdom and experience of practitioners
5. experiences reported by program participants/clients/intended beneficiaries
6. expert opinion
7. cross-disciplinary findings and patterns
8. theory as an explanation of the lesson and its mechanism of impact

Assessment criteria

- assessment of the importance of the lesson learned
- strength of the evidence connecting an intervention lesson to desired outcomes attainment
- consistency of findings across sources, methods, and types of evidence

The idea is that the greater the number of supporting sources for a "lesson learned," the more rigorous the supporting evidence, and the greater the *triangulation of supporting sources*, the more confidence one has in the significance and meaningfulness of a lesson learned. Lessons learned with only one type of supporting evidence would be considered a "lessons learned hypothesis." Nested within and cross-referenced to lessons learned should be the actual cases from which practice wisdom and evaluation findings have been drawn. A critical principle here is to maintain the contextual frame for lessons learned, that is, to keep lessons learned grounded in their context. For ongoing learning, the trick is to follow future supposed applications of lessons learned to test their wisdom and relevance over time in action in new settings.

Discussion Questions for Generating High-Quality Lessons Learned

1. What is meant by a "*lesson*"?
2. What is meant by "*learned*"?
3. By whom was the lesson learned?
4. What's the evidence supporting each lesson?
5. What's the evidence the lesson was learned?
6. What are the contextual boundaries around the lesson (i.e., under what conditions does it apply)?
7. Is the lesson specific, substantive, and meaningful enough to guide practice in some concrete way?
8. Who else is likely to care about this lesson?
9. What evidence will they want to see?
10. How does this lesson connect with other "lessons"?

Boruch and Petrosino (2004) have observed that

> part of the value of high-end systematic reviews, meta-analyses, and research and syntheses lies in determining where good evidence has been produced on the effects of interventions, where good evidence is absent, and where the evidence is ambiguous—respectively, the dry land, the water, and swamp. (P. 178)

They cited as an example examining hundreds of evaluations of *Scared Straight* evaluations, a program aimed at reducing juvenile delinquency by, among other interventions, scaring young people about what prison life is like. They found that most evaluations concluded that the program successfully reduced delinquent behavior, but most, in their judgment, were also not well designed.

> The authors discovered some dry land by focusing on randomized trials in this assemblage of studies. They found clear evidence that such programs have no discernible positive effect and in some cases even increase the likelihood that you will commit crime. That is, the programs effects are negative despite claims, based on untrustworthy evaluations, to the contrary. (P. 178)

They go on to note that "the value of some systematic reviews lies in establishing that no high-quality evaluations have been carried out on a particular topic." They provide detailed guidance for conducting high-quality syntheses.

One of the challenges facing the profession of evaluation going forward will be to bring some degree of rigor to such popular notions as "lessons learned" and "best practices." Such rigor takes on added importance as, increasingly, the substantive contribution of evaluation includes not only how to conduct high-quality evaluations but also generating knowledge based on having learned how to synthesize cross-program findings about patterns of effective interventions, that is, better practices in program design and lessons learned about effective programming generally. The future status and utility of evaluation may depend on the rigor and integrity we bring to these challenges. In the meantime, a little humility might be in order, as we proffer lessons learned.

Developmental Evaluation

> *Whosoever desires constant change must change his conduct with the times.*
>
> —Nicolò Machiavelli (1469–1527)

The last of the six purposes that can affect intended uses of evaluation is program and organizational development. Improvement-oriented, formative evaluation focuses on making an intervention or model better. Developmental evaluation, in contrast, involves changing the intervention, adapting it to changed circumstances, and altering tactics based on emergent conditions. Developmental evaluation is designed to be congruent with and nurture developmental, emergent, innovative, and transformative processes.

Summative judgment about a stable and fixed program intervention is traditionally the ultimate purpose of evaluation. Summative evaluation makes an overall judgment of merit or worth based on efficient goal attainment, replicability, clarity of causal specificity, and generalizability. *None of these traditional criteria are appropriate or even meaningful for highly volatile environments, systems-change-oriented interventions, and emergent social innovations.* Developmentally oriented leaders in organizations and programs don't expect (or even want) to reach the state of "stabilization" required for summative evaluation. Staff in such efforts doesn't aim for a steady state of programming because they're constantly tinkering as participants, conditions, learnings, and context change. They don't aspire to arrive at a fixed model that can be generalized and disseminated. At most, they may discover and articulate principles of intervention and development, but not a replicable model that says, "Do X and you'll get Y." Rather, they aspire to continuous progress, ongoing adaptation, and rapid responsiveness. No sooner do they articulate and clarify some aspect of the process than that very awareness becomes an intervention and acts to change what they do. They don't value traditional characteristics of summative excellence such as standardization of inputs, consistency of treatment, uniformity of outcomes, and clarity of causal linkages. They assume a world of multiple causes, diversity of outcomes, inconsistency of interventions, interactive effects at every level—and they find such a world exciting and desirable. They never expect to conduct a summative evaluation because they don't expect the change initiative—or world—to hold still long enough for summative review. They expect to be forever developing and changing—and they want an evaluation approach that supports development and change. That approach is developmental evaluation.

Moreover, they don't conceive of development and change as necessarily improvements. In addition to the connotation that formative evaluation (improvement-oriented evaluation) is ultimately meant to lead to summative evaluation (Scriven, 1991a, 1991b), formative evaluation carries a bias about making something better rather than making it different. From a developmental perspective informed by complexity science and systems thinking, you do something different because something has changed—your understanding, the characteristics of participants, technology, or the world. Those changes are dictated by your latest understandings and perceptions, but the commitment to change doesn't carry a judgment that what was done before was inadequate or less effective. Change is not necessarily progress. Change is adaptation. Assessing the cold reality of change, social innovators can be heard to say:

> At each stage we did the best we could with what we knew and the resources we had. Now we're at a different place in our development—doing and thinking different things. *That's development.* That's change. That's more than just making a few improvements. (Jean Gornick, former Director of Damiano, a not-for-profit working on poverty alleviation in Duluth, Minnesota; quoted in Westley, Zimmerman, and Patton 2006:179)

Developmental evaluation combines findings use with process use, the focus of the next chapter, so we will continue our discussion of it there. Chapter 8, on alternative ways of engaging in evaluation, will provide several examples of developmental evaluations. I have introduced it in this chapter to include it on the menu of alternative purposes for using findings, all six of which are summarized in Menu 4.2. For each distinct purpose, this menu shows the priority questions asked, common evaluation approaches associated with that purpose, and key factors affecting evaluation use. Menu 4.1 identifies the primary intended users and political stakes for each purpose.

MENU 4.1

Evaluation Purpose	Primary Intended Users	What's at Stake?
Overall Summative Judgment	Funders; those charged with making major decisions about the program's future (e.g., a board of directors); policymakers; those interested in adopting the model.	*Very high stakes*—the future of the program can be at stake, though evaluation findings are rarely the only or even primary basis for such decisions.
Formative Improvement and Learning	Program administrators, staff, and participants; those immediately involved day-to-day in the program.	*Moderate stakes*—make adjustments, act on participant feedback; enhance implementation and outcomes. Small changes involve low stakes; major improvements increase the stakes.
Accountability	Those with executive, managerial, legislative, and funding authority and responsibility to make sure that scarce resources are well-managed.	*High stakes*—the more visible the program, the more political the environment, and the more controversial the intervention, the higher the stakes.
Monitoring	Program managers are primary of a management information system: internal accountability as the priority.	*Low stakes*—ongoing, routine management, alert for bottlenecks and blips in indicators that require attention. *Becomes high stakes* when used for external accountability.
Developmental	Social innovators: those involved in bringing about major systems change in dynamic environments.	*Low stakes day-to-day* as tactical, incremental changes are made; *high stakes longer term* and strategically because social innovators aspire to have major impacts.
Knowledge generating	Program designers, planners, modelers, theorists, scholars, and policymakers.	*Moderate to low stakes*—knowledge is accumulated incrementally and cumulatively over time; no single study carries great weight; lessons learned are often principles to inform general practice and design rather than concrete recommendations to be implemented immediately.

MENU 4.2

Primary Uses of Evaluation Findings

Purpose	Priority Questions	Common Evaluation Approaches	Key Factors Affecting Use
Judgment of *overall* value to inform and support major decision making: Determine the value and future of the program and model.	Does the program meet participants' needs? To what extent does the program have merit? Worth? Does it add value for money? How do outcomes and costs compare with other options? To what extent can outcomes be attributed to the intervention? Is the program theory clear and supported by findings? Is this an especially effective practice that should be funded and disseminated as a model program?	–Summative evaluation –Impact evaluation –Cost-benefit analysis –Theory-driven evaluation	Independence and credibility of the evaluator. Rigor of the design: validity, generalizability. Significance of the findings to decision makers. Timeliness.
Learning: Improve the program.	What works and what doesn't? Strengths and weaknesses? Participant reactions? How do different subgroups respond, that is, what works for whom in what ways and under what conditions? How can outcomes and impacts be increased? How can costs be reduced? How can quality be enhanced?	–Formative evaluation –Quality enhancement –Learning reviews –Reflective practice –Participant feedback –Capacity building –Appreciative inquiry	Creating a learning climate, openness to feedback and change. Trust. Evaluator's skill in facilitating learning. Relevance of findings; actionable.
Accountability: Demonstrate that resources are well-managed and efficiently attain desired results.	Are funds being used for intended purposes? Are goals and targets being met? Are indicators showing improvement? Are resources being efficiently allocated? Are problems being handled? Are staff qualified? Are only eligible participants being accepted into the program? Is implementation following the approved plan? Are quality control mechanisms in place and being used?	–Government and funder mandated reporting –Program audits and inspections –Performance measurement and monitoring –Accreditation and licensing –End of project reports –Scorecards	Transparency. Validity of indicators. Integrity and credibility of the system and those reporting. Balance. Consistency of reporting. Fairness of comparisons.

Purpose	Priority Questions	Common Evaluation Approaches	Key Factors Affecting Use
Monitoring: Manage the program, routine reporting, early identification of problems.	Are inputs and processes flowing smoothly? What are participation and drop-out rates? Are these changing? Are outputs being produced as anticipated and scheduled? Where are bottlenecks occurring? What are variations across subgroups or sites?	–Management information systems –Quality control systems and CQI (continuous quality improvement) –Routine reporting and record keeping –Performance indicators	Timeliness, regularity, relevance, and consistency of reporting; incentives to input data at field levels and incentives to use the data at management levels; capacity and resources to maintain the system. Appropriate links to accountability system.
Development: Adaptation in complex, emergent, and dynamic conditions.	What's happening at the interface between what the program is doing/accomplishing and what's going on in the larger world around it? How is the program as an intervention system connected to and affected by larger systems in its environment? What are the trends in those larger systems? What does feedback show about progress in desired directions? What can we control and not control, predict and not predict, measure and not measure, and how do we respond and adapt to what we cannot control, predict, or measure? How do we distinguish signal from noise to determine what to attend to?	–Developmental evaluation –Complexity systems –Emergent evaluation –Real-time evaluation –Rapid assessment, rapid feedback –Environmental scanning	Openness. Adaptive capacity. Tolerance for ambiguity and uncertainty ("getting to maybe"). Balancing quality and speed of feedback. Nimble. Integrate and synthesize multiple and conflicting data sources.
Knowledge generation: Enhance general understandings and identify generic principles about effectiveness.	What are general patterns and principles of effectiveness across programs, projects, and sites? What lessons are being learned? How do evaluation findings *triangulate* with research results, social science theory, expert opinion, practitioner wisdom, and participant feedback? What principles can be extracted across results to inform practice?	–Cluster evaluation –Meta-analyses –Synthesis evaluation –Lessons learned –Effective practices studies	Quality and comparability of sources used; quality of synthesis; capacity to extrapolate. Rigor of triangulation. Identifying principles that can inform practice.

NOTE: Menu 5.1 (Chapter 5) presents a corresponding menu, "Uses of Evaluation Logic and Processes," where the impact on the program comes primarily from application of evaluation thinking and engaging in an evaluation process in contrast to impacts that come from using the content of evaluation findings, the focus of this menu.

Applying Purpose and Use Distinctions

By definition, the six different purposes we've examined—making summative judgments, offering formative improvements, accountability reporting, monitoring systems, generating generic knowledge, and developmental evaluation—can be distinguished fairly clearly. In practice, these purposes can become interrelated, parallel, and simultaneous processes as when internal government evaluators are engaged in ongoing monitoring while also preparing periodic summative reports for annual budget decisions. Or internal evaluators may be working on formative evaluation while external evaluators are conducting a summative evaluation. Many such combinations occur in real-world practice, some of them appropriate, but some of them entangling and confusing what should be distinct purposes, and those entanglements and confusions can affect use. Let me illustrate with an evaluation of an innovative educational program.

Some years ago, the Northwest Regional Educational Laboratory contracted with the Hawaii State Department of Education to evaluate Hawaii's experimental "3-on-2 Program," a team teaching approach in which three teachers worked with two regular classrooms of primary-age children, often in multiage groupings. Walls between classrooms were removed so that three teachers and 40 to 60 children shared one large space. The program was aimed at greater individualization, increased cooperation among teachers, and making more diverse resources available to students.

The Northwest Lab proposed an advocacy-adversary model for summative evaluation (Northwest Regional Educational Laboratory, 1977). Two teams

were created; by coin toss one was designated the advocacy, the other the adversary team. The task of the advocacy team was to gather and present data supporting the proposition that Hawaii's 3-on-2 Program was effective and ought to be continued. The adversaries were charged with marshalling all possible evidence demonstrating that the program ought to be terminated.

The advocacy-adversary model was a combination debate/courtroom approach to evaluation (Wolf 1975; Kourilsky 1974; Owens 1973). I became involved as a resource consultant on fieldwork as the two teams were about to begin site visits to observe classrooms. When I arrived on the scene, I immediately felt the exhilaration of the competition. I wrote in my journal,

> No longer staid academic scholars, these are athletes in a contest that will reveal who is best; these are lawyers prepared to use whatever means necessary to win their case. The teams have become openly secretive about their respective strategies. These are experienced evaluators engaged in a battle not only of data, but also of wits. The prospects are intriguing.

As the two teams prepared their final reports, a concern emerged among some about the narrow focus of the evaluation. The summative question concerned whether the Hawaii 3-on-2 program should be continued or terminated. Some team members also wanted to offer findings about how to change the program or how to make it better without terminating it. Was it possible that a great amount of time, effort, and money was directed at answering the wrong question? Two participating evaluators summarized the dilemma in their published *post mortem* of the project:

As we became more and more conversant with the intricacies, both educational and political, of the Hawaii 3-on-2 Program, we realized that Hawaii's decision-makers should not be forced to deal with a simple save-it-or-scrap-it choice. Middle ground positions were more sensible. Half-way measures, in this instance, probably made more sense. But there we were, obliged to do battle with our adversary colleagues on the unembellished question of whether to maintain or terminate the 3-on-2 Program. (Popham and Carlson 1977:5)

In the course of doing fieldwork, the evaluators had encountered many stakeholders who favored a formative evaluation purpose. These potential users wanted an assessment of strengths and weaknesses with ideas for improvement. Many doubted that the program, given its popularity, could be terminated. They recognized that changes were needed, especially cost reductions, but that fell in the realm of formative not summative evaluation. I had a conversation with one educational policymaker that highlighted the dilemma about appropriate focus. He emphasized that, with a high rate of inflation, a declining school-age population, and reduced federal aid, the program was too expensive to maintain. "That makes it sound like you've already made the decision to terminate the program before the evaluation is completed," I suggested.

"Oh, no!" he protested. "All we've decided is that the program has to be changed. In some schools the program has been very successful and effective. Teachers like it; parents want it; principals support it. How could we terminate such a program? But in other schools it hasn't worked very well. The two-classroom space has been re-divided into what is essentially three self-contained classrooms. We know that. It's the kind of program that has some strong political opposition and some strong political support. So there's no question of

terminating the program and no question of keeping it the same."

I felt compelled to point out that the evaluation was focused entirely on whether the program should be continued or terminated. "And that will be very interesting," he agreed. "But afterwards we trust you will give us answers to our practical questions, like how to reduce the size of the program, make it more cost-effective, and increase its overall quality."

Despite such formative concerns from some stakeholders, the evaluation proceeded as originally planned with the focus on the summative evaluation question. But was that the right focus? The evaluation proposal clearly identified the primary intended users as state legislators, members of the State Board of Education, and the superintendent. In a follow-up survey of those education officials (Wright and Sachse 1977), most reported that they got the information they wanted. But the most important evidence that the evaluation focused on the right question came from actions taken following the evaluation when the decision makers decided to eliminate the program.

After it was all over, I had occasion to ask the director of the evaluation whether a shift to a formative focus would have been appropriate. He replied,

We maintained attention to the information needs of the *true* decision makers, and adhered to those needs in the face of occasional counter positions by other evaluation audiences. . . . If a lesson is to be learned it is this: an evaluator must determine who is making the decisions and keep the information needed by the decision makers as the highest priority. In the case of the Hawaii "3 on 2" evaluation, the presentation of program improvement information would have served to muddle the decision making process. (Nafziger 1979, personal communication)

Choosing among Alternatives

As the Hawaii case illustrates, the formative-summative distinction can be critical. Formative and summative evaluations involve significantly different data collection foci. The same data seldom serve both purposes well. Nor will either a specific formative or summative evaluation necessarily yield generic knowledge (lessons learned) that can be applied to effective programming more generally. It is thus important to identify the primary purpose of the evaluation at the outset: overall judgment of merit or worth, ongoing improvement, or knowledge generation? Is a management information system and/or accountability reporting needed? Is the program poised for significant development in adapting to changed conditions rather than improving within a predetermined and fixed model framework? Decisions about what to do in the evaluation can then be made in accordance with how best to support the evaluation's primary purpose. But this is easier said than done. One frequent reaction to posing alternatives is, "We want to do it all." A comprehensive evaluation, conducted over time and at different levels, may include variations on all six purposes, but for any given evaluation activity, or any particular stage of evaluation, it's critical to have clarity about the priority use of findings.

Consider the evaluation of a leadership program run by a private philanthropic foundation. The original evaluation contract called for 3 years of formative evaluation followed by 2 years of summative evaluation. The program staff and evaluators agreed that the formative evaluation would be for staff and participant use; however, the summative evaluation would be addressed to the foundation's board of directors. The formative evaluation helped shape the curriculum,

brought focus to intended outcomes, and became the basis for the redesign of follow-up activities and workshops. As time came to make the transition from formative to summative evaluation, the foundation's president got cold feet about having the evaluators meet directly with the board of directors. The evaluators insisted on interacting directly with these primary users to lay the groundwork for genuinely summative decision making. Senior staff decided that no summative decision was imminent, so the evaluation continued in a formative mode and the design was changed accordingly. As a matter of ethics, the evaluators made sure that the chair of the board was involved in these negotiations and that the board agreed to the change in focus. There really was no summative decision on the horizon because the foundation had a long-term commitment to the leadership program. However, the program was facing some major new challenges in dealing with a large influx of immigrants in the area it served, and with major economic and political changes that affected the training leaders needed. Thus, the program moved from formative to developmental evaluation to create a substantially new approach based on changing conditions.

Now, consider a different case, the evaluation of an innovative school, the Saturn School, in Saint Paul, Minnesota. Again, the original evaluation design called for 3 years of formative evaluation followed by 2, final years with a summative focus. The formative evaluation revealed some implementation and outcome problems, including lower-than-desired scores on district-mandated standardized tests. The formative evaluation report, meant only for internal discussion to support program improvement, got into the newspapers with glaring headlines about problems and low test scores. The evaluation's visibility and public reporting put pressure on senior district officials to make summative decisions about the program despite earlier assurances that the program would have a full 5 years before such decisions were made. The formative evaluation essentially became summative when it hit the newspapers and district decision makers felt a need to make major decisions to show they were on top of things (accountability thus coming to the fore). Much to the chagrin of staff and program supporters, including many parents, the shift in purpose led to personnel changes and top-down, forced program changes. Many of those involved in openly and honestly sharing concerns in what they thought was an internal, formative process felt betrayed by the changed use from formative to summative, with heavy accountability overtones.

Sometimes, however, program staff like such a reversal of intended use as when, for example, evaluators produce a formative report that is largely positive and staff want to disseminate the results as if they were summative, even though the methods of the formative evaluation were aimed only at capturing initial perceptions of program progress, not at rendering an overall judgment of merit or worth. Keeping formative evaluations formative, and summative evaluations summative, is an ongoing challenge, not a one-time decision. When contextual conditions merit or mandate a shift in focus, evaluators need to work with intended users to fully understand the consequences of such a change. We'll discuss these issues again in the chapter on situational responsiveness and evaluator roles.

A knowledge-generating evaluation can also experience tugs and pulls into other purposes. A national foundation funded a cluster evaluation in which a team of evaluators would assemble data from some 30 different projects and identify lessons for effective community-based health programming— essentially a knowledge-generating evaluation.

The cluster evaluation team had no responsibility to gather data to improve specific programs or make summative judgments. Each separate project had its own evaluation for those purposes. The cluster evaluation was intended to look for patterns of effectiveness (and barriers to same) across projects. Yet during site visits, individual projects provided cluster evaluators with a great deal of formative feedback that they wanted communicated to the foundation, and individual grantees were hungry for feedback and comparative insights about how well they were doing and ways they might improve. As the evaluation approached time for a final report, senior foundation officials and trustees asked for summative conclusions about the overall effectiveness of the entire program area as part of rethinking funding priorities and strategies. They also asked the evaluators to design a routine reporting and monitoring system for the cluster grantees. Thus, a knowledge-generating evaluation got caught up in pressures to adapt to meet demands for formative, summative, and monitoring uses.

In results-oriented M&E systems, the relationship of monitoring to evaluation is often ambiguous. Rist (2006a, 2006b) argues that we are moving from "studies to streams," by which he means that organizations are increasingly relying on systems, not individual evaluators, to produce evaluative knowledge. Episodic and stand-alone evaluations, which dominated the early days of the profession, are becoming a thing of the past, he argues. He sees monitoring and evaluation as merging as evaluations increasingly integrate multiple streams of information, using information produced by nonevaluators, and drawing on databases that are continuous and virtual. With managers faced with time frames that are immediate, analysis is continuous, and data collection goes on at multiple levels by multiple stakeholders. He foresees partnerships being dominant in collecting, analyzing, and sharing evaluative knowledge (rather than evaluators acting alone and controlling the evaluation process) and the Internet becoming the new information glue in support of increased transparency of evaluative knowledge. M&E can then support continuous organizational adaptation and improvement (Rist and Stames 2006). In this vision of M&E, monitoring systems will generate evaluation questions which, as they are answered with specific inquires, will feed back into and improve monitoring, yielding a continuous cycle of improvements, the results of which can be documented to meet accountability needs and demands. It's an inspiring vision. Thus far, as I read the evidence and listen to evaluators describe their experiences from around the world, it's a vision that is far from being realized. More often, as soon as accountability mandates are introduced, and they're introduced early and authoritatively, the tail wags the dog, and everyone focuses on meeting accountability demands, effectively undercutting the learning and improvement agenda, and limiting managerial willingness and capability to take risks that might attract opposition or resistance. It's not enough to create results-oriented monitoring systems. An organizational culture and climate must be created to support the appropriate and effective use of such systems. That gets us into one form of process use, organizational development, which is the focus of the next chapter.

Evaluation Use and Decision Making

We began this chapter by noting that early in the emergence of the profession, evaluators aspired to have their findings used to inform decision making. While the development of the profession has yielded more—and more nuanced—distinctions about types of evaluation uses and the alternative purposes they serve, the aspiration to inform and influence decisions remains alluring. To find out whether such potential use might be realistic, evaluators need to push intended users to be clear about what, if any, decisions are expected to be influenced by an evaluation. It is worth repeating that none of the federal health decision makers we interviewed about evaluation use, the results of which were reported at the beginning of this chapter, had been involved in a utilization-focused process. That is, none of them had carefully considered how the evaluation would be used in advance of data collection. My experiences in pushing decision makers and intended users to be more intentional and prescient about evaluation use *during the design phase* have taught me that it is possible to significantly increase the degree of influence evaluations have. Doing so, however, requires persistence in asking the following kinds of questions: What decisions, if any, is the evaluation expected to influence? What is at stake? When will decisions be made? By whom? What other factors (values, politics, personalities, promises already made) will affect the decision making? How much influence do you expect the evaluation to have? What needs to be done to achieve that level of influence? How will we know afterward if the evaluation was used as intended? (In effect, how can use be measured?) Exhibit 4.10 highlights questions to use in determining an evaluation's potential for concrete and specific instrumental use in informing decision making.

EXHIBIT 4.10

Questions to Ask of Intended Users to Establish an Evaluation's Intended Influence on Forthcoming Decisions

What decisions, if any, are the evaluation findings expected to influence?
(There may not be any, in which case the evaluation's purpose may be simply to generate knowledge for conceptual use and future enlightenment. If, however, the evaluation is expected to influence decisions, clearly distinguish summative decisions about program funding, continuation or expansion from formative decisions about program improvement, and ongoing development.)

When will decisions be made? By whom? When, then, must the evaluation findings be presented to be timely and influential?

What is at stake in the decisions? For whom? What controversies or issues surround the decisions?

What's the history and context of the decision-making process?

What other factors (values, politics, personalities, promises already made) will affect the decision making? What might happen to make the decision irrelevant or keep it from being made? In other words, how volatile is the decision-making environment?

How much influence do you expect the evaluation to have—*realistically*?

To what extent has the outcome of the decision already been determined?

What data and findings are needed to support decision making?

What needs to be done to achieve that level of influence?
(Include special attention to which stakeholders to involve for the evaluation to have the expected degree of influence.)

How will we know afterwards if the evaluation was used as intended?
(In effect, how can use be measured?)

Making Menu Selections: Connecting Decisions to Uses

Where the answers to the evaluator's questions indicate that a major decision about program merit, worth, continuation, expansion, dissemination, and/or funding is at stake, then the evaluation should be designed to render overall judgment—summative judgment. The design should be sufficiently rigorous and the data collected should be sufficiently credible that a summative decision can be made. The findings must be available in time to influence this kind of major decision.

Where the dialogue with primary intended users indicates an interest in identifying strengths and weaknesses, clarifying the program's model, and generally working at increased effectiveness, the evaluation should be framed to support improvement-oriented decision making. Skills in offering formative feedback and creating an environment of mutual respect and trust between the evaluator and staff will be as important as actual findings.

Where the intended users are more concerned about generating knowledge for formulating future programs than with making decisions about current programs, then some form of synthesis or cluster evaluation will be most appropriate to discover generic principles of effectiveness.

Likewise, the evaluator can review accountability concerns, the potential role of a monitoring system, and the degree of interest in developmental evaluation.

The six options I've presented are by no means inherently conflicting purposes, and some evaluations strive to incorporate aspects of different approaches, as in M&E. But in my experience, one purpose is likely to become the dominant motif and prevail as the *primary* purpose informing design decisions and priority uses; or else, different aspects of an evaluation are designed, compartmentalized, and sequenced to address these contrasting purposes. I also find that confusion among these quite different purposes, *or failure to prioritize them*, is often the source of problems and misunderstandings along the way, and can become disastrous at the end when it turns out that different intended users had different expectations and priorities.

In helping intended users select from the evaluation purposes menu, and thereby focus the evaluation, evaluators may encounter some reluctance to make a commitment. I worked with one director who proudly displayed this sign on his desk: "My decision is maybe—and that's final." Unfortunately, the sign was all too accurate. He wanted me to decide what kind of evaluation should be done. After several frustrating attempts to narrow the evaluation's focus, I presented what I titled a "MAYBE DESIGN." I laid out cost estimates for an all-encompassing evaluation that included formative, summative, knowledge-generating, accountability, monitoring, and developmental components looking at all aspects of the program. Putting dollars and timelines to the choices expedited the decision making considerably. He decided not to undertake any evaluation "at this time."

I was relieved. I had become skeptical about the potential for doing anything useful. Had I succumbed to the temptation to become the decision maker, an evaluation would have been done, but it would have been my evaluation, not his. I'm convinced he would have waffled over using the findings as he waffled over deciding what kind of evaluation to do.

Thus, in utilization-focused evaluation, the choice of not dining at all is always on the menu. It's better to find out before preparing the meal that those invited to the banquet are not really hungry. Take your feast elsewhere, where it will be savored.

Follow-Up Exercises

1. Identify an actual program. Describe the program and its context. Specify the specific primary evaluation questions that would guide an evaluation endeavor under each of the six purposes in Menu 4.1.

2. For the program identified in Question 1, or another program, use Menu 4.2 to identify the specific intended users by name and position in the center column, "primary intended users." Then, assess the stakes (Column 3) for those intended users. How do the stakes for the primary intended users you've identified compare with the norms described in Column 3 of Menu 4.2?

3. Search the news, the Internet, evaluation journals, and other sources to find

(a) an example of instrumental use of an evaluation, (b) an example of conceptual use of an evaluation, and (c) example of persuasive use. Describe each use and its context. To what extent and in what ways do you consider the use as appropriate and meaningful? Explain the basis for your judgments.

4. Search the news, the Internet, evaluation journals, and other sources to find what you consider an example of misuse of an evaluation. Describe the misuse, the context, and the consequences. What, if anything, might have been done, in your judgment, to prevent or reduce the misuse?

5. Use Exhibit 4.10, Questions to Ask of Intended Users to Establish an Evaluation's Intended Influence on Forthcoming Decisions, to interact with a real-life program manager. Approach that manager as a simulation of a real evaluation consultation in which you will be assisting in designing a decision-oriented evaluation. Record the highlights of the interaction and comment on what it reveals about decision-oriented, instrumental use.

6. Conduct your own utilization study. Use the inquiry questions on use at the beginning of this chapter (page 99). Identify at least two different evaluations to follow up. Interview both a program person and the evaluator, if possible. Find out how those evaluations were used. Compare your findings with those presented from the federal health evaluation and more recent distinctions of types and degrees of use.

5

Intended Process Uses
Impacts of Evaluative Thinking and Experiences

*U*tility is in the eye of the user.

—Halcolm

The Medium Is the Message

In the past, the search for use has often been conducted like the search for contraband in the famous Sufi story about Nasrudin the smuggler.

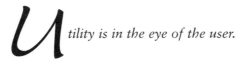

Nasrudin used to take his donkey across a frontier every day with the panniers loaded with straw. Since he admitted to being a smuggler, when he trudged home every night, the frontier guards searched him carefully. They searched his person, sifted the straw, steeped it in water, and even burned it from time to time. Meanwhile, he was becoming visibly more and more prosperous.

Eventually, he retired to another country, very wealthy. Years later, one of the customs officials encountered him there. "You can tell me now, Nasrudin," he said. "Whatever was it that you were smuggling, that we could never catch you at?"

"Donkeys," replied Nasrudin grinning (adapted from Shah 1964:59).

Process as Outcome

In this chapter, we'll consider ways in which being engaged in the processes of evaluation can be useful quite apart from the findings that may emerge from those processes. Reasoning processes are evaluation's donkeys; they carry the load. Reasoning like an evaluator and operating according to evaluation's values have impacts.

When I refer to "process use," then, I mean using the logic, employing the reasoning, and being guided by the values that inform our practice. One way of thinking about process use is to recognize that evaluation constitutes a culture, of sorts. We, as evaluators, have our own values, our own ways of thinking, our own language, and our own reward system. When we engage other people in the evaluation process, we are providing them with a cross-cultural experience. They often experience evaluators as imperialistic, that is, as imposing

the evaluation culture on top of their own values and culture—or they may find the cross-cultural experience stimulating and friendly. But in either case, and all the spaces in-between, it is a cross-cultural interaction. Those new to the evaluation culture may need help and facilitation in coming to view the experience as valuable. One of the ways I sometimes attempt to engage people in the value of evaluation is to suggest that they may reap personal and professional benefits from learning how to operate in an evaluation culture. Many funders are immersed in that culture. Knowing how to speak the language of evaluation and conceptualize programs logically are not inherent goods, but can be instrumentally good in helping people get the things they want, not least of all, to attract resources for their programs and make their work more effective. They may also develop skills in reality testing that have application in other areas of professional and even personal life.

This culture of evaluation that we evaluators take for granted can be quite alien to many of the folks with whom we work. Like people living daily inside any culture, our way of thinking, shaped by the research culture, seems natural and easy to us. However, to practitioners, decision makers, and policymakers, our logic can be hard to grasp and quite unnatural. I'm talking about what appear to be very simple notions that have profound effects on how one views the world. Thinking in terms of what's clear, specific, concrete, and observable does not come easily to people who thrive on, even depend on, vagueness, generalities, and untested beliefs as the basis for action. They're in the majority. Practitioners of evaluation logic are a small minority. The good news is that our way of thinking, once experienced, is often greatly valued. That's part of what creates demand for our services. Exhibit 5.1 provides examples of evaluation logic and values, ways of thinking that undergird evaluation practice (Mark, Greene, and Shaw 2006a:1–3; Fournier 2005a, 2005b, 1995; Scriven 2005a, 1995; Schwandt 2002:59–74; House 1980).

Process use is distinct from use of the substantive findings in an evaluation report. It's equivalent to the difference between learning how to learn versus learning substantive knowledge about something. Learning how to think evaluatively is learning how to learn and think critically, and those who become involved in an evaluation learn by doing. Facilitating evaluative thinking opens up new possibilities for impact that organizations and funders are coming to value because the capacity to engage in this kind of thinking can have more enduring value than a delimited set of findings. This especially resonates for organizations interested in becoming what has come to be called popularly "learning organizations." Learning to see the world

as an evaluator sees it often has a lasting impact on those who participate in an evaluation—an impact that can be greater and last longer than the findings from that same evaluation. Findings have a very short "half-life"—to use a physical science metaphor; they deteriorate very quickly as the world changes rapidly. Specific findings typically have a small window of relevance. In contrast, learning to think and act evaluatively can have an ongoing impact. The experience of being involved in an evaluation, then, for those stakeholders actually involved, can have a lasting impact on how they think, on their openness to reality testing, and on how they view the things they do.

How do I know this? Because that's often what intended users tell me when I follow up the evaluations I conduct. Months after an evaluation, I'll talk with clients (intended users) to get their assessments of whether the evaluation achieved its intended uses and to find out what other impacts may have resulted. They often say some version of the following, a response from an experienced and wise program director:

> We used the findings to make some changes in our intake process and improvements in the treatment program. We reorganized parts of the program and connected them together better. But, you know, the big change is in our staff's attitude. They're paying more attention to participant reactions on a daily basis. Our staff meetings are more outcomes oriented and reflective. Staff exchanges about results are more specific and data based. We're more focused. And the fear of evaluation is gone. Doing the evaluation had a profound impact on our program culture. It really did.

Any evaluation can, and often does, have these kinds of effects. What's different about utilization-focused evaluation is that

EXHIBIT 5.1

Evaluative Thinking

The Logic and Values of Evaluation
That Can Have Impact on Participants in Evaluation Processes

The logic and values of evaluation derive from principles of systematic inquiry, logical reasoning, and effective communications. The admonitions below constitute a "logic" in the sense that they represent a particular mode of reasoning viewed as valid within the culture of evaluation. They are values in the sense that they are what evaluators generally ascribe value to and believe contribute to effective action. The guidelines and principles below are meant to be illustrative rather than exhaustive of all possibilities.

Be clear	Be clear about goals and purposes; be clear about what's being evaluated, what data will be collected, what judgments are to be made, how results will be used—indeed, be as clear as possible about everything.
Be intentional	Know what you want to do and why. Plan your work and work your plan. Think through what you're doing. Consider contingencies.
Be accountable	Systematically examine the extent to which your intentions and hopes work out as planned and accomplish what you wanted to accomplish.
Be specific	A favorite evaluation clarifying question: "What exactly do you mean by that?"
Focus and prioritize	You can't do or look at everything. Be purposeful in deciding what's worth doing and knowing. Make decisions and own their consequences.
Be systematic	Create a system that covers all priorities. Carefully document what occurs at every stage of decision making and data collection.
Make assumptions explicit	Determine what can and cannot be subjected to empirical test.
Operationalize program concepts, ideas, and goals	The fundamental evaluation challenge is determining how to measure and observe, quantitatively or qualitatively, what is important. Know and specify, operationally, what success will look like—and what constitutes failure. Reality testing becomes real at this point.
Distinguish inputs and processes from outcomes	Confusing processes with outcomes is common. Evaluative thinking looks at the connections between processes and outcomes, and that means distinguishing them and measuring both.
Draw conclusions	Have data to support allegations of fact; provide empirical support based on data and logical explanations for conclusions. This means a commitment to reality testing in which logic and evidence are valued over strength of belief and intensity of emotions.
Separate data-based statements of fact from interpretations and judgments	Interpretations go beyond the data and must be understood as what they are: interpretations. Judgments involve values about what is desirable or undesirable.
Make criteria and standards for judgments explicit	The logical mandates to be clear and specific apply to making criteria and standards explicit.
Limit generalizations and causal explanations to what data support	Overgeneralizations and overly definitive attributions of causality are epidemic outside the culture of research and evaluation.
Cultural sensitivity and cultural competence	Cultural variations and factors are critical to understanding.

the process of actively involving intended users increases these kinds of evaluation impacts. Furthermore, the possibility and desirability of building an organization's capacity to learn from evaluation processes as well as findings can be made intentional and purposeful. In other words, instead of treating process use as an informal off-shoot, explicit and up-front attention to the potential impacts of evaluation logic and processes can increase those impacts and make them a planned purpose for undertaking the evaluation. In that way, the evaluation's overall utility is increased.

Process Use Defined

Process use refers to and is indicated by individual changes in thinking, attitudes, and behavior, and program or organizational changes in procedures and culture that occur among those involved in evaluation as a result of the learning that occurs during the evaluation process. Evidence of process use is represented by the following kind of statement after an evaluation: "The impact on our program came not just from the findings but from going through the thinking process that the evaluation required." As always, the most convincing evidence that learning has occurred is subsequent translation into action. Exhibit 5.2 provides a complete definition of process use. Process use has come to be recognized as an important contribution to evaluation practice and a significant focus of inquiry for research on utilization (Amo and Cousins 2007; Carden and Earl 2007; Cousins 2007, 2003; Cousins and Whitmore 2007; Fleischer 2007; Harnar and Preskill 2007; King 2007a; Lawrenz, Huffman, and McGinnis 2007; Patton 2007, 1999b, 1998; Podems 2007; Cousins and Shulha 2006; Preskill 2005b; Fetterman 2003; Hofstetter and Alkin 2003; Preskill, Zuckerman, and Matthews 2003; Forss, Rebien, and Carlsson 2002; Morabito 2002; Russ-Eft, Atwood, and Egherman 2002; Kirkhart 2000; Preskill and Caracelli 1997).

An Analogy

Before looking in detail at how evaluation processes can affect users, let me suggest an analogy to clarify the distinction between process use and findings use. I hike the Grand Canyon annually. During the days there, my body hardens and my thoughts soften. I emerge more mellow, peaceful, and centered. It doesn't matter which part of the Canyon I hike: the South Rim or North; whether I descend all the way to the Colorado River or stay on the Tonto to explore a side canyon; whether I push strenuously to cover as much territory as possible or plan a leisurely journey; whether I ascend some interior monument like Mount Huethawali or traverse the Supai platform that runs the length of the Canyon—I return different from when I entered. Not always different in the same way. But different.

Let me suggest that the specifics of place are like the findings of an evaluation report. The different places provide different content. From the rim one can view magnificent vistas. Deep within a side canyon, one can see little and feel completely alone. Much of the Canyon is desert, but rare streams and even rarer waterfalls offer a stark contrast to the ancient, parched rock. Each place offers different content for reflection. The substantive insights one receives may well vary by place, time, and circumstance. But quite beyond those variations is the impact that comes from *the very act of reflection*—regardless of content and place. The impacts of reflection and meditation on one's inner sense of self are, for me, analogous to the impacts of engaging in the processes of evaluation, quite apart from the content of the evaluation's findings. In this same sense, for certain

EXHIBIT 5.2
Process Use Defined

Process use occurs when those involved in the evaluation learn from the evaluation process itself or make program changes based on the evaluation process rather than just the evaluation's findings. Process use, then, includes cognitive, attitudinal, and behavior changes in individuals, and program or organizational changes resulting, either directly or indirectly, from engagement in the evaluation process and learning to think evaluatively (e.g., increased evaluation capacity, integrating evaluation into the program, goals clarification, conceptualizing the program's logic model, setting evaluation priorities, improving outcomes measurement). An example of or evidence for process use is when those involved in the evaluation later say something like this: "The impact on our program came not just from the findings but also from going through the thinking process that the evaluation required." As always, the most convincing evidence that learning has occurred is subsequent translation into action. Process use includes the effects of evaluation procedures and operations, for example, the premise that "what gets measured gets done," so establishing measurements and setting targets affects program operations and management focus. These are uses of evaluation processes that affect programs, different from use of specific findings generated by an evaluation.

Process Use as a Usefulism

Process use is best understood and used as a sensitizing concept, or "usefulism" (Safire 2007). A usefulism is an idea or concept that calls our attention to something, but that something takes its meaning from and must be defined within a particular context, like being "middle aged" or manifesting "wisdom." A sensitizing concept, in the tradition of qualitative research (Patton 2007, 2002a), raises consciousness about a possibility and alerts us to watch out for it within a specific context. That's what the concept of "process use" does. The concept process use says, things are happening to people and changes are taking place in programs and organizations as evaluation takes place, especially when stakeholders are involved in the process. Watch out for those things. Pay attention. Something important may be happening. The process may be producing outcomes quite apart from findings. Think about what's going on. Help the people in the situation pay attention to what's going on, if that seems appropriate and useful. In that way, process use can become a matter of intention (Patton 2007).

For variations in operationalizing process use in research on evaluation, see Amo and Cousins (2007) and Cousins (2007).

---

capacity-building purposes—staff development, program development, organization development (OD)—it doesn't matter so much what the focus of an evaluation is, or the substance of its findings, some impact will come from engaging thoughtfully and seriously in the processes of reflection.

Valuing Process Use

> *Data use leads to data valuing.*
>
> —Cousins, Goh, and Clark (2006)

In working with intended users, it's important to help them think about the potential and desired impacts of how the evaluation will be conducted. Questions about who will be involved take on a different degree of importance when considering that those most directly involved will not only play a critical role in determining the content of the evaluation, and therefore the focus of findings, but they also will be the people most affected by exposure to evaluation logic and processes. The degree of internal involvement, engagement, and ownership will affect the nature and degree of impact on the program's culture, as will the capacity of the program or organization to engage in evaluation for learning (Harnar and Preskill 2007; King 2007a, 2002; Taut 2007; Baizerman, Compton, and Stockdill 2005; Compton, Baizerman, and Stockdill 2002). How funders and users of evaluation think about and calculate the costs and benefits of evaluation are also affected. The cost-benefit ratio changes on both sides of the equation when the evaluation produces not only findings but also serves immediate programmatic needs like staff development or participant empowerment.

I differentiate six primary uses of evaluation processes: (1) infusing evaluative thinking into an organization's culture; (2) enhancing shared understandings; (3) supporting and reinforcing the program through intervention-oriented evaluation; (4) instrumentation effects (what gets measured gets done); (5) increasing participants' engagement, sense of ownership, and self-determination (participatory and empowerment evaluation); and (6) program or organizational development. Menu 5.1 summarizes these six types of process use. I'll elaborate each, with examples, then consider the challenges and controversies engendered by using evaluation in these ways.

Variety of Process Uses

Infusing Evaluative Thinking into Organizational Culture: Building Evaluation Capacity

> *What we think, we become.*
>
> —Hindu Prince Gautama
> Siddharta (563–483 BCE),
> the founder of Buddhism

When evaluation first emerged as a distinct profession in the 1960s and 1970s, the emphasis was on conducting specific evaluation studies for specific purposes. Correspondingly, research on utilization focused on how the findings from those studies were used. Now evaluation use has evolved to include facilitating *evaluative thinking* and building evaluation capacity. Building the evaluation capacity of an organization to support staff in thinking evaluatively means integrating evaluation into the organization's culture. This goes well beyond a focus on using the results of isolated studies. It takes us into the arena of organizational culture, looking at how decision makers and staff incorporate evaluative thinking into everything they do as part of ongoing attention to mission fulfillment and continuous improvement. In his 2001 presidential address at the American Evaluation Association (AEA) annual conference, James Sanders called integrating evaluation into organizational culture "mainstreaming evaluation."

> Mainstreaming refers to the process of making evaluation an integral part of an organization's everyday operations. Instead of being put aside in the margins of work, evaluation becomes a routine part of the organization's work ethic if it is mainstreamed. It is part of the culture and job responsibilities at all levels of the organization. . . . Mainstreaming depends on evaluation being internalized as a value throughout the organization and on an infrastructure that supports and maintains evaluation. (Sanders 2002:254)

Evaluation Capacity Building

Building evaluation capacity goes beyond conducting specific evaluation studies, though conducting specific evaluations by involving program staff can contribute to the organization's evaluation capacity, a premiere example of process use. Evaluation capacity building involves "working intentionally and continuously to create and sustain overall organizational processes that make quality evaluation and its uses routine" (Baizerman, Compton, and Stockdill 2005:39). "The Art, Craft, and Science of Evaluation Capacity Building" is one of the *New Directions for Evaluation* (Compton, Baizerman, and Stockdill 2002).

MENU 5.1

Process Uses

Uses that derive from engaging in an evaluation process in contrast to using evaluation findings

Uses	Examples
Infusing evaluative thinking into the organizational culture	Becoming an authentic learning organization
	Incorporating evaluative questioning into routine decision making
	Integrating monitoring and evaluation, and linking both to budget and planning cycles
	Incentives and rewards for evaluation use
	Building support for evaluation throughout the organization, ongoing capacity development and training in evaluation
Enhancing shared understandings	Agreeing on the program's model and expected outcomes as a result of evaluation questions and determining evaluation priorities
	Evaluability assessment, in which the program gets ready for evaluation by clarifying goals and the program's logic model
	Managing staff meetings or the program's plan of work around evaluation issues and explicit outcomes
	Giving voice to different perspectives and valuing diverse experiences
Supporting and reinforcing the program intervention	Building evaluation into program delivery processes in such a way that desired program outcomes are achieved in part through the effects of data collection
	Participants monitoring their own progress
	Specifying and monitoring outcomes as integral to working with program participants

Nowhere are evaluative thinking and mainstreaming evaluation as integral to organizational culture better illustrated than in the Corporate Assessment Framework of the International Development Research Centre (IDRC) headquartered in Ottawa, Canada.

IDRC is a public corporation created by the Parliament of Canada in 1970 to help developing countries use science and technology to find practical, long-term solutions to the social, economic, and environmental problems they face. Support is directed toward developing an "indigenous research capacity" to sustain policies and technologies that developing countries need to build healthier, more equitable, and more prosperous societies. IDRC's mission

MENU 5.1 (Continued)

Uses	Examples
Instrumentation effects and reactivity	What gets measured gets done so resources and staff efforts are aligned with performance measures and evaluation priorities
	Using interview protocols to enhance reflection
	Data collection processes affect program participants and staff intentionally or unintentionally
	Participants learn from and are affected by evaluation tests, surveys, and interviews
	Using the data collection process to enhance organizational communications
Increasing engagement, self-determination, and ownership	Participatory and collaborative evaluation
	Empowerment evaluation
	Reflective practice
	Self-evaluation
	Building evaluation capacity
	Learning evaluation by doing evaluation
Program and organizational development	Developmental evaluation (See Chapter 8)
	Making the organization the unit of analysis and organizational effectiveness the focus
	Looking at the connections between program effectiveness and organizational effectiveness to enhance understanding and support realignment
	Evaluability assessment and logic modeling used for program design

NOTE: Menu 4.1 (Chapter 4) presents a corresponding menu, "Uses of Evaluation Findings."

is "Empowerment Through Knowledge" (IDRC 2006).

In 1993, IDRC established an Evaluation Unit to support the conduct of evaluations (Carden and Earl 2007). The unit oversees various evaluation and monitoring functions and produces an annual overview of each year's evaluations, synthesizing significant findings for senior management and the Board of Governors. During a retreat in 2001, IDRC's Senior Management Committee expanded the organization's evaluation commitment to include a framework for mission assessment at the overall corporate level. This involved the systematic collection of performance data regarding IDRC's strategic goals and operating principles. To do this, senior managers had to identify those principles, or fundamental ways of doing business, that were expected to permeate all their work in accomplishing their two overall strategic goals: *Indigenous*

Capacity Building and *Policy and Technology Influence.* They committed the organization to monitoring and evaluating not only results in these two strategic goal areas but also the extent to which they were employing their fundamental operating principles. This is where it gets interesting from our point of view because one of those operating principles was *evaluative thinking.* This was the first organization I had encountered that made infusing evaluative thinking into the organizational culture an explicit dimension for performance measurement. (The five other performance areas were Devolution to the South, Regional Presence, Gender, Canadian Partnerships, and Donor Partnerships.)

IDRC's shift in emphasis is a premiere example of process use. In essence, the senior management committed not only to supporting the conduct and use of specific high-quality evaluation studies and management information system data, they made *evaluative thinking* a fundamental way of doing business, infused throughout the culture. What did they mean? Here's what they committed to monitoring as expressed in their working papers operationalizing evaluative thinking.

> Evaluative thinking permeates our work so that we consciously and constantly reflect on project, program, regional, and corporate experience with a view to implementing improvements based on what is learned. Evaluative thinking is evident in the way we clarify goals and design, and conduct and interpret evaluations throughout the organization.

> Within programs, evaluative thinking is demonstrated in the implementation of well-focused programs and in the use of high-quality project and program evaluations that feed into program and project decision making. Time and resources are allocated for reflection on evaluation findings and for documenting use of the findings.

> In program management, evaluative thinking is evident in our systematic use of evaluation to inform program design and implementation decisions.

> Senior management demonstrates evaluative thinking in its support for the adoption of evaluation processes, in its routine demand for the generation of outcomes-based data, and in the use of this and other feedback to expand management viewpoints and inform decisions.

> IDRC's partners in the South share our commitment to learning-based evaluation; they exhibit mastery over their own evaluation activities; they serve with competence as external and internal evaluators; and they support and promote advances in the science and art of performance assessment.

> The Board of Governors will request and use outcomes-based data in their governance of the Centre.

> Senior management will request and use outcomes-based evaluation information in its decision-making processes; engage in the Corporate Assessment Framework processes to reflect on past experiences, analyze empirical data related to the performance areas, and revise actions appropriately to improve performance; share learnings among themselves and with others in the organization; and foster an organizational environment conducive to learning.

> Program staff will implement and use the results of high-quality evaluations to improve project and program performance; establish regular processes of reflection (on both successes and failures) at the program level to share lessons and improve future performance; and support the building of capacity in evaluative thinking among partners.

Resources Branch will develop reporting systems to facilitate reflective processes.

Partners will develop effective evaluation systems directed to their own needs and purposes, collaborate with the Centre on implementing evaluations of relevance to both their and our needs, and have the capacity to operate as evaluators.

Evaluation Thinking in Practice

At the same time that IDRC was making evaluative thinking a priority area for overall organizational assessment, senior management was having to face a concrete reality at the most basic level: Project managers were not completing required end-of-project reports. Indeed, they had accumulated a backlog of hundreds of unfinished project completion reports. A variety of carrot-and-stick efforts to get reports completed had failed. Evaluating these efforts, they found that the reports were viewed as an arduous paperwork requirement with no real utility. Project managers didn't get

feedback when they did do reports and, given other workload priorities, there were no incentives to complete a report on work already done. All the energy was going into new initiatives rather than recording the details of yesterday's news.

As a part of rethinking the reporting function in the organization with an emphasis on creating opportunities for shared learning, they conducted an inquiry into how and when learning occurs in projects. Project staff said that the most learning takes place at the start of or during a project's life, while the least learning occurs at the end of a project, and different kinds of learning take place throughout a project's varying stages. Drawing on staff at different levels from throughout the organization, a working group was formed to redesign the project-reporting process.

They developed a three-stage process dubbed the "Rolling Project Completion Report" (rPCR) and changed the format, timing, and information input approach. The new system emphasized

The Importance of Evaluative Thinking

Distinguished philosopher Hannah Arendt was especially attuned to the importance of critical thinking as a foundation of democracy. Having experienced totalitarianism in Nazi Germany, then having fled it, she devoted much of her life to studying totalitarianism and its opposite, democracy. Totalitarianism is built on and sustained by deceit and thought control. To resist efforts by the powerful to deceive and control thinking, Arendt believed that people needed to practice thinking. Toward that end she developed "exercises in political thought" (Arendt 1963). She wrote that "experience in thinking . . . can be won, like all experience in doing something, only through practice, through exercises" (p. 4).

From this point of view, might we consider every evaluation an opportunity for those involved to practice thinking? Every evaluation is an opportunity to engage people in thinking evaluatively. In this regard, we might aspire to have evaluation do what Arendt hoped her exercises in political thought would do, namely, "to gain experience in how to think." Her exercises "do not contain prescriptions on what to think or which truths to hold," but rather on the act and process of thinking itself.

learning rather than paperwork account-ability. The new approach was pilot tested on a sample of projects from different units throughout the organization. Early in the life of a project, a junior staff member interviews a project officer to gather data about project design, start-up lessons, and issues that will need attention going forward. In the middle of a project, team leaders interview project officers to capture lessons about implementation and interim outcomes, as well as update work on key issues. After the end of a project, senior managers interview project officers to complete the project reports, identify results, and capture any final learnings. Major learnings are highlighted at an Annual Learning Forum. This new rPCR process replaces the old paperwork requirement with an interview process that has people at different levels in the organization talking to each other, learning about each other's work, and sharing lessons. All those involved went through formal interview training, including senior managers, so people share language and understandings about quality interviewing and what kind of cross-organization learning is being sought. The process is designed so that interview responses are entered into the learning system in real time, as the interview takes place, with subsequent opportunities for project managers to make corrections and append supporting documentation and cross-reference information sources (Carden and Earl 2007).

The project report backlog was completely cleared, and feedback about the process is highly positive. The organization-wide process of involving people in reflection and learning reinforces evaluative thinking as a core operating principle while also meeting accountability demands to get

reports done in a timely and meaningful fashion. The capacity of staff to engage in evaluation thinking has been systematically enhanced, including deepening their interviewing skills, pattern recognition capabilities, and data interpretation skills. The attention garnered for projects featured at the Annual Learning Forum and the direct involvement of senior management provides additional incentives to take the process seriously and document both learning and results. The Project Completion Reports, long disdained, became a source of energy and enlightenment, and a manifestation of evaluative thinking infused into the organizational culture. This redesign of IDRC's reporting process illustrates nicely the insight of *Future Shock* author Alvin Toffler (1970) who observed, "The illiterate of the 21st century will not be those who cannot read and write, but those who cannot learn, unlearn, and relearn."

Using Evaluation to Enhance Shared Understandings

Evaluation both depends on and facilitates clear communications. Shared understandings emerge as evaluation logic pushes the senders of messages to be as specific as possible and challenges listeners to reflect on and feed back to senders what they think they've heard. Shared understandings are especially important with regard to expected results. For example, board members and program staff often have different notions of what an agency or program is supposed to accomplish. The processes of clarifying desired ends and focusing staff efforts on accomplishing those ends by evaluating actual accomplishments ought to be primary board functions, but few boards fulfill these functions effectively (Carver 1997).

I'm often asked to facilitate board or staff retreats to help them apply the logic and discipline of evaluation to formulating the organization's mission and goals. The feedback I get is that the questions I pose as an evaluator (e.g., What *specific* results are you committed to achieving and how would you know if you accomplished them? What would success look like?) are different from what they are asked by nonevaluators. It's not so much that other facilitators don't ask these questions, but they don't ask them with the same seriousness and pursue the answers with the same rigor and intensity. The very process of formulating a mission and goals *so they can be evaluated* will usually have an impact on how people think about what they're trying to accomplish, long before data are actually collected to measure results.

A parallel use of evaluation is to increase shared understandings between program managers and line staff. Managers can work with staff under the guidance of an evaluator to establish a monitoring system to help everyone involved stay focused on desired outcomes. While the data from such a system may ultimately support decision making, in the short run, the impact is to focus staff attention and energy on priority outcomes. The process needs to be facilitated in such a way that staff can speak openly about whether board and administrative expectations are meaningful, realistic, and attainable. In other words, done properly, evaluation facilitates shared commitments to results from top to bottom *and* bottom to top for enhanced communication between staff at different levels of program implementation.

The logic and principles of evaluation also can be useful in negotiations between parties with different perspectives. For example, a major foundation was interested in funding an effort to make schools more racially equitable through a process that would engage the community. The school district expressed great interest in such funding but resisted committing to involving community people in schools in any ways that might undermine building-level autonomy or intrude into personnel evaluations of principals. Over a period of several months, the funder and school officials negotiated the project. The negotiations centered on defining what was meant by "greater racial equity." Was the only criterion closing the gap in test scores between students of different races? Should other criteria, like parental involvement, attendance rates, and graduation rates, be included? The funder and school district eventually agreed to focus the project and evaluation on community-based, school-specific action plans, activities, and outcomes rather than a standardized and prescribed set of district-wide, uniform indicators. Part of the reason was to increase the buy-in of teachers and community people on a school-by-school basis since different schools had quite different racial profiles and varying equity challenges. The design of the entire project was changed and made more focused as a result of these negotiations. Applying the logic of evaluation had a major impact on the project's design before any data collection was done, or before findings and a report were produced. Everyone came out of the negotiations clear about what was to happen in the project and how it would be evaluated.

Inadequate specification of desired results reduces the likelihood of attaining those results. Consider how adding a results orientation changed the Request for Proposals announcement of a major environment-oriented philanthropic foundation. In the initial announcement, the foundation wanted to cast the net wide, so it issued a general invitation:

"We seek grant proposals that will enhance the health of specific ecosystems."

The responses varied greatly with many completely missing the mark in the opinion of the foundation staff. But what was the mark? A great deal of time and effort was wasted by hopeful proposal writers who didn't know what criteria to address, and staff spent a lot of time sifting through proposals that had no hope of being funded. The process created frustration on both sides. After a planning session focused on specifying desired results and explicit evaluation criteria, the second announcement was quite a bit more focused:

"We seek grant proposals that will enhance the health of specific ecosystems." Proposals will be judged on the following criteria:

- Clarity and meaningfulness of ecosystem definition
- Private-public sector cooperation
- Action orientation and likelihood of demonstrable impact
- Incorporation of a prevention orientation
- Regional coordination

This set of criteria eliminates basic research proposals, of which a large number were received from universities in the first round, and makes it clear that those seeking grants must submit as cooperative groups rather than as single individuals or entities, also characteristic of a large number of initial proposals. Subsequent announcements became even more specific when focused on specific action priorities, such as pollution prevention. The staff, with training and facilitation, learned to use evaluation logic to articulate desired results and enhance communications with potential grant applicants.

A different use of evaluation to enhance mutual understanding involves designing the evaluation to "give voice" to the disenfranchised, underprivileged, poor, and others outside the mainstream (Weiss and Greene 1992:145). In the evaluation of a diversity project in the Saint Paul Schools, a major part of the design included capturing and reporting the experiences of people of color. Providing a way for African American, Native American, Chicano-Latino, and Hmong (from Laos) parents to tell their stories to mostly white, corporate funders was an intentional purpose of the design, one approved by those same white corporate funders. Rather than reaching singular conclusions, the final report was a multivocal, multicultural presentation of different experiences with and perceptions of the program's impacts. The medium of the report carried the message that multiple voices needed to be heard and valued as a manifestation of diversity (Stockdill et al. 1992). The findings were used for both formative and summative purposes, but the parents and many of the staff were most interested in using the evaluation processes to make themselves heard by those in power. *Being heard was an end in itself, quite separate from use of the findings.*

Russ-Eft et al. (2002) found that in the initial stages of an environmental evaluation, the discussion about the program among diverse program stakeholders "contributed to the organization by enhancing communications" (p. 27). Wadsworth (1995) has reported that evaluation processes can facilitate interactions between service providers and service users in a way that leads to "connectedness" and "dialogue across difference" (p. 9). Each learns to see the service through the other's eyes. In the process, what began as opposing groups with opposing truths is transformed into "an affinity-based community of inquiry" with shared understandings.

Using evaluation to enhance shared understandings is a relatively traditional use of evaluation logic. Let's turn now to a different and more controversial use of evaluation processes: intervention-oriented evaluation.

Evaluation as Integral to the Program Intervention

Textbooks on measurement warn that measuring the effects of a treatment (e.g., a social program) should be independent of and separate from the treatment itself. For example, participants who take a pretest may perform better in the program than those who do not take the pretest because the pretest increases awareness, stimulates learning, and/or enhances preparation for program activities (instrumentation effects). To account for such test effects, evaluation researchers in the past have been advised to use experimental designs that permit analysis of differences in performance for those who took the pretest compared with a group that did not take the pretest. Integrating data collection into program implementation would be considered a problem—a form of treatment contamination—under traditional rules of research.

Departing from defining evaluation as application of social science methods opens a different direction in evaluation, one that supports integration of evaluation into program processes. Making data collection integral rather than separate can reinforce and strengthen the program intervention. Such an approach also can be cost-effective and efficient since, when evaluation becomes integral to the program, its costs aren't an add-on. This enhances the sustainability of evaluation because, when it's built in rather than added on, it's not viewed as a temporary effort or luxury that can be easily dispensed with when cuts are necessary.

To illustrate this approach, consider the case of a one-day workshop. A traditional evaluation design, based on standard social science standards of rigor, would typically include a pretest and posttest to assess changes in participants' knowledge, skills, and attitudes. Let's suppose you are participating in such a workshop. As the workshop opens, you are told,

> Before we begin the actual training, we want you to take a pretest. This will provide a baseline for our evaluation so we can find out how much you already know and then measure how much you've learned when you take the posttest.

At the end of the day, you are given the same instrument as a posttest. You are told, "Now the workshop is over, but before you leave, we need to have you take the posttest to complete the evaluation and find out how much you have benefited from the training."

The most rigorous design for high internal validity would include, *in addition* to the pre-post treatment group, (1) a control group that takes the pre- and posttests without experiencing the workshops, (2) a control group that gets the posttest only, and (3) a treatment group that gets the posttest only. All groups, of course, should be randomly selected and assigned, and the administration of the test should be standardized and take place at the same time. Such a design would permit measurement of and control for instrumentation effects.

Let me now pose a contrary example of how the evaluation might be handled, a design that fully integrates the evaluation data collection into the program delivery, that is, a design that makes the data collection part of the workshop rather than separate from and independent of the workshop. In this scenario, the workshop begins as follows:

> The first part of the workshop involves your completing a self-assessment of your knowledge, skills, and attitudes. This will help you prepare for and get into thinking about the things we will be covering today in your training.

The workshop then proceeds. At the end of the day, the workshop presenter closes as follows:

> Now the final workshop activity is for you to assess what you have learned today. To that end, we are going to have you retake the self-assessment you took this morning. This will serve as a review of today and let you see how much you've learned.

In this second scenario, the word *evaluation* is never mentioned. The pre- and post assessments are explicitly and intentionally part of the workshop in accordance with adult learning principles (Brookfield 1990; Knox 1987; Schön 1987; Knowles et al. 1985). We know, for example, that when participants are told what they will learn, they become prepared for the learning; learning is further enhanced when it is reinforced both immediately and over the long term. In the second scenario, the self-assessment instrument serves *both* the function of preparing people for learning and as baseline data. The posttest serves the dual functions of learning reinforcement and evaluation. Likewise, a 6-month follow-up to assess retention can serve the dual functions of learning reinforcement and longitudinal evaluation.

The methodological specialist will note that the second scenario is fraught with threats to validity. However, the purpose of data collection in this second scenario is not only assessment of the extent to which change has occurred, but increasing the likelihood that change will occur. It does not matter *to these particular intended users (the workshop instructors)* how much of the measured change is due to pretest sensitization versus actual learning activities, or both, as long as the instrument items are valid indicators of desired outcomes. Moreover, in the second scenario, the data collection is so well integrated into the program that there are no separate evaluation costs except for the data analysis itself. Under the second scenario, the administration of the pretest and posttest is a part of the program such that *even if the data were not analyzed for evaluation purposes, the data collection would still take place,* making evaluation data collection highly cost-effective.

Principles of Intervention-Oriented Evaluation

I have called this process *intervention-oriented evaluation* to make explicit the direct and integral connection between data collection and program results. A program is an intervention in the sense that it is aimed at changing something. The evaluation becomes part of the programmatic intervention to the extent that the way it is conducted supports and reinforces accomplishing desired program goals.

The primary principle of *intervention-oriented evaluation* is to build a program delivery model that logically and meaningfully interjects data collection in ways that enhance achievement of program outcomes, while also meeting evaluation information needs. We followed this principle in evaluating a wilderness program that aimed to transform traditional college administrators into leaders in *experiential education*. Participants were university presidents, college deans, and department heads with no previous wilderness experience. They hiked 10 days in the Gila Wilderness of New Mexico in the fall, climbed the Kofa Mountains of Arizona in the winter, and rafted the San Juan River in Utah in the spring. During these trips, participants kept journals for reflection. The program's philosophy was, "One doesn't just learn from experience; one learns from *reflection* on experience." The process of journaling was part of the program intervention, but also a prime source of qualitative evaluation data capturing how participants reacted to and were changed by project participation. In addition, participants were paired together to interview each other before, during, and after each wilderness experience. These interviews were part of the project's reflection process, but also a source of case data for evaluation. The evaluation process thus became part of the intervention in providing participants with experiences in *reflective practice* (Schön 1987, 1983). Indeed, it was on this project that I first learned how profoundly in-depth interviews can affect people. Such personal, intensive, and reflective data collection is an intervention. In intervention-oriented evaluation, such data collection is designed to reinforce and strengthen the program's impact.

Another quite different example comes from an intervention-designed evaluation of an international development effort called the Caribbean Agricultural Extension Project, funded by the U.S. Agency for International Development. The project aimed to improve national agricultural extension services in eight Caribbean countries. The project began with a rapid reconnaissance survey to identify the farming systems in each participating island. This involved an interdisciplinary team of agricultural researchers, social scientists, and extension staff doing fieldwork and interviewing farmers for a period of 10 days to identify extension priorities for a specific agro-ecological zone. This process served as the basis for needs assessment and program development. It was also, quite explicitly and intentionally, an intervention in and of itself in that the process garnered attention from both farmers and agricultural officials, thereby beginning the extension mobilization process. In addition, the rapid reconnaissance survey served the critical evaluation function of establishing baseline data. Subsequent data on the effects of extension and agricultural development in the zone were compared against this baseline for evaluation purposes. Yet it would have been much too expensive to undertake this kind of intensive team fieldwork simply for purposes of evaluation. Such data collection was practical and cost-effective because it was fully integrated into other critical program processes.

Once the various farming systems were identified and the needs of farmers had been specified within those systems, the extension staff began working with individual farmers to assess their specific production goals. This process included gathering data about the farmer's agricultural enterprises and household income flows. With these data in hand, extension agents worked with farmers to set realistic goals for change and to help farmers monitor the effects of recommended interventions. The program purpose of using this approach, called a *farm management approach*, was to individualize the work of extension agents with farmers so that the agent's recommendations were solidly grounded in knowledge of the farm and household situation, including labor availability, land availability, income goals, and past agricultural experiences. These data were necessary for the extension agent to do a good job of advising farm families about increasing their productivity.

These same data were the baseline for measuring the program's impact on individual farmers for evaluation purposes.

The collection of such data for farm management purposes required training of agents and a great deal of time and effort. It would have been enormously expensive to collect such data independently, solely for purposes of evaluation. However, by establishing a record-keeping system for individual farmers that served a primary extension purpose, the project also established a record-keeping system for evaluation purposes. By aggregating the data from individual households, it was possible to analyze system-level impact over time. The data aggregation and comparative analysis were above and beyond the main program purpose of collecting the data. However, without that program purpose, the data would have been much too expensive to collect solely for evaluation of the system.

The program staff also used the evaluation design formulated by the external evaluators as the framework for their plan of work, which set the agenda for monthly staff meetings and quarterly staff reports (an example of using evaluation to enhance and focus communications). In this way, the evaluation priorities were kept before the staff at all times. As a result, the evaluation process improved program implementation from the very beginning by focusing staff implementation efforts.

Still another powerful example of intervention-oriented evaluation comes from the Hazelden Foundation, a chemical dependency treatment program in Minnesota. Part of the program intervention includes helping clients and their significant others identify their chemical abuse patterns. A self-assessment instrument serves this purpose while also providing baseline data on chemical use. After residency treatment, all clients and significant others receive follow-up surveys at 6 months, 1 year, and 2 years. The follow-up surveys not only provide outcome data on program effectiveness but they also remind clients and their significant others to assess their current chemical use behaviors. Clients who have relapsed into drugs or alcohol abuse are invited to contact Hazelden for support, assessment, and possible reentry into treatment. Thus, the follow-up survey is a mechanism for reinforcing treatment and extending an offer of new help. Many clients respond to this contact and seek additional help. For that reason, the survey is sent to all former clients, not just the small random sample that would be sufficient if the survey provided only evaluation data.

In my experience, program funders, managers, and staff can become very excited about the creative possibilities for integrating evaluation into a program in such a way that it supports and reinforces the program intervention. Not only does this make the evaluation process more useful, but it also often makes the evaluation findings more relevant, meaningful, accessible, and useful. Yet this approach can be controversial because the evaluation's credibility may be undercut by concerns about whether the data are sufficiently independent of the treatment to be meaningful and trustworthy; the evaluator's independence may be suspect when the relations with staff and/or participants become quite close; and the capacity to render an independent, summative judgment may be diminished. These are considerations to discuss with intended users and evaluation funders in deciding the relative priority of different potential uses of evaluation and in reviewing the principles of intervention-oriented evaluation (see Exhibit 5.3). It is also helpful to examine data or other information resources that already exist within a program that can be used in a different way in support of the program.

EXHIBIT 5.3

Principles of Intervention-Oriented Evaluation

- The evaluation is designed to support, reinforce, and enhance attainment of desired program outcomes.
- Evaluation data collection and use are integrated into program delivery and management. Rather than being separate from and independent of program processes, the evaluation is an integral part of those processes.
- Program staff and participants know what is being evaluated and know the criteria for judging success.
- Feedback of evaluation findings is used to increase individual participant goal attainment as well as overall program goal attainment.
- There are no or only incidental add-on costs for data collection because data collection is part of program design, delivery, and implementation.
- Evaluation data collection, feedback, and use are part of the program model, that is, evaluation is a component of the intervention.

Instrumentation Effects and Reactivity

Intervention-oriented evaluation as a form of intended process use occurs when evaluation data collection is *intentionally* made integral to the program treatment as in the Hazelden follow-up assessments described above. Process use can also be unintentional, especially where those participating in evaluation data collection react to completing tests or filling out evaluation questionnaires or are affected by interviews. Instrumentation effects, or reactivity, call attention to the ways in which people are affected by taking tests, completing surveys, or being interviewed.

In-depth, open-ended interviews, for example, can have a powerful effect on people (Patton 2002a:chap. 7). An intensive, probing interview that invites a program participant or staff member to reflect on and share experiences and perspectives can affect him or her in unexpected and unpredictable ways. Emotions may be aroused, assumptions examined, and changes in behavior stimulated. A good interview often opens up or brings to the surface thoughts, feelings, knowledge, and experience, not only to the evaluator conducting the interview but also to the person being interviewed. The process of being taken through a directed, reflective process can leave interviewees realizing things about themselves that they were not fully aware of before the interview. Two hours or more of thoughtfully reflecting on a program experience can evoke a lot of thoughts and feelings, even stimulate commitment to change some behavior pattern. Such a change would be *an instrumentation effect*—an effect of the interview process and experience.

The purpose of an evaluation interview is first and foremost to gather data, not change people. Skilled interviewers take a nonjudgmental stance and communicate neutrality so that the person being interviewed feels comfortable saying what they really think and feel. The evaluator's job is to judge the program not the program participants who provide evaluative reflections. Neither is an evaluation interviewer a therapist. Staying focused on the purpose of the interview is critical to gathering high-quality data. Still, it is common for program participants being interviewed to ask for advice, approval, or confirmation. This is a clue that the evaluation process—both the interview and, perhaps, the evaluator—is stimulating a reaction.

While the evaluation interviewer strives to present a stance of neutrality, that same interviewer is also attempting to establish rapport and show empathy, that is, understanding as opposed to sympathy. In so doing, the evaluation interviewer is not a cold slab of granite—unresponsive to revelations of great suffering, fear, and pain that may unfold during an interview. Let me take you inside this dilemma. In a major farming needs assessment project to develop agricultural extension programs for distressed farm families during the Midwestern farm crisis of the mid-1980s, I was part of a team of 10 interviewers (working in male-female pairs) who interviewed 50 farming couples. Many of these couples were struggling economically and emotionally. They were losing their farms. Their children had left for the city. Their marriages were under stress. The 2-hour interviews traced their family history, their farm situation, their community relationships, and their hopes for the future. Sometimes questions would lead to husband-wife conflict. The interviews would open old wounds, lead to second-guessing decisions made long ago, or bring forth painful memories of dreams never fulfilled. People reacted to the reflective process of the interview. Because we were university sponsored and clearly well educated, people often asked for advice—what to do about their finances, their children, government subsidy programs, even their

marriages. But we were not there to give advice. Our task was to get information about needs that might, or might not, lead to new programs of assistance. Could we do more than just ask our questions and leave? Yet as researchers, could we justify in any way intervening? Yet again, our interviews were already an intervention, stimulating people to think about past choices and future options. Such are the ethical dilemmas that can derive from the power of evaluation data collection, especially in-depth interviewing.

What we decided to do was leave each family a packet of information about resources and programs of assistance, everything from agricultural referrals to financial and family counseling. To avoid having to decide which couples really needed such assistance, we left the information with all couples—separate and identical packages for both husband and wife. When interviewees asked for advice during the interview, we could tell them that we would leave them referral information at the end of the interview. This was also a way of offering them something for giving us their time in participating in the needs assessment.

While interviews may be intrusive in reopening old wounds, they can also be healing. In doing follow-up interviews with families who had experienced child sexual abuse, we found that most mothers appreciated the opportunity to tell their stories, vent their rage against the system, and share their feelings with a neutral, but interested, listener. Our interviews with elderly residents participating in a program to help them stay in their homes and avoid nursing home institutionalization typically lasted much longer than planned because the elderly interviewees longed to have company and talk. When interviewees are open and willing to talk, the power of interviewing poses new risks. People will tell you things they never intended to tell you. This can be true even with reluctant or hostile interviewees, a fact depended on by journalists. Indeed, it seems at times that the very thing someone is determined *not* to say is the first thing they tell, just to release the psychological pressure of secrecy or deceit. Interviews can become confessions, particularly under the promise of confidentiality. All these are *reactions to the process of being interviewed.*

These reactions can affect the participants' understanding of a program. People being interviewed learn things from the questions asked. If you ask a mother in an early childhood education program whether she is engaging with other mothers outside the formal sessions, she may respond, as one quite shy mother once did to me, "No, but that's a good idea. I'd like to do that." Then, looking quizzical, "Are we supposed to be doing that? I get it. That's why we all exchanged phone numbers." She was learning about the program from the evaluation interview.

This is a qualitative example of a classic concern about pre-post knowledge tests in which participants learn from taking the test, an issue raised earlier.

Learning from being interviewed or taking a test is an instrumentation effect. Questionnaires can also affect people, solidifying attitudes about a program or stimulating discussions among those who complete the questionnaires: "How did you answer that question about how the program can be improved?" Such exchanges of views can affect how a group of participants engage with staff going forward.

The performance measurement mantra, "What gets measured gets done," is a recognition of process use and measurement reactivity. When a teacher announces a test and says, "Here's what will be on the test and here's what I'll be looking for," that teacher is manifesting the performance measurement principle that *what gets measured gets done.* Some weight loss programs have participants set goals and then weigh in weekly in front of other participants as a way of increasing commitment to losing weight. Weighing oneself is a measurement. It is also feedback about progress aimed at encouraging goal achievement. Weighing oneself in front of other participants increases the likelihood of reacting to the measurement process. That's why it is done, to harness the desire to avoid shame and embarrassment in service of goal attainment. Such regular monitoring becomes part of the intervention.

In program performance monitoring, what gets measured gets done means that program resources and staff efforts are meant to be focused on moving the indicators. Staff, therefore, is expected to react to what is being measured. In the chapter on goals-based evaluation, we'll look in greater depth at the challenges of choosing and using performance indicators, including concerns about goal displacement (doing what is measurable rather than what's important) and corruption of indicators. The point here is that process use occurs when the measurement process itself affects what people do and when the evaluation data collection instruments—tests, questionnaires, interviews, journals—affect how participants experience a program and what outcomes they attain.

The interview-based project completion report process developed by IDRC, described earlier in this chapter, exemplifies intentional instrumentation effects. The IDRC staff being interviewed are supposed to become reflective as a result of the interviews. Indeed, the interviews are designed to increase reflectivity—a form of intentional and desired instrument reactivity. The IDRC staff conducting the interviews are also supposed to be affected in that they are learning from the people they are interviewing. The data collection

What Gets Measured Gets Done—For Better or Worse

Examples of "what gets measured gets done"—if you measure the wrong thing, you do the wrong thing:

If a highway department measures the number of potholes filled as a performance indicator for street repair it may reward quickly done, temporary pothole filling to show "good numbers" versus the more time-intensive and time-consuming repairs that result in a longer-term fix.

If an office manager insists that front line staff answer every call within three rings, the results may be a lot of answered calls where most of the callers are put on hold for excessive amounts of time. Answering the phone and actually responding to a call involve different outcomes and different measures.

"We found that fewer measures, but measures that were developed in collaboration with the people doing the work being measured, were more successful."

Theresa N. Westover, Ph.D.
California Department of Education
Policy & Evaluation Division
EvalTalk listserv posting, July 31, 2006

process is designed to enhance communications and learning throughout IDRC, including across divisions and up and down the hierarchy of staff responsibility. While the interview content generates findings about projects, the interview *process* enhances communications and facilitates organizational learning. Thus, the IDRC project completion report design includes both findings use and process use.

Now, let's examine the intentional use of entire evaluation processes, not just data gathering, to engage participants more fully, empower them, and build their capacity to think evaluatively.

Supporting Engagement, Self-Determination, and Ownership: Participatory, Collaborative, and Empowerment Evaluation

Early in my career, I was commissioned by a Provincial Deputy Minister in Canada to undertake an evaluation in a school division he considered mediocre. I asked what he wanted the evaluation to focus on. "I don't care what the focus is," he replied.

> I just want to get the people engaged in some way. Education has no life there. Parents aren't involved. Teachers are just putting in time. Administrators aren't leading. Kids are bored. I'm hoping evaluation can stir things up and get people involved again.

That's how the evaluation of the Frontier School Division, described in Chapter 2, began.

The processes of participation and collaboration have an impact on those who participate beyond whatever tasks they may accomplish by working together. In the *process* of participating in an evaluation, participants are exposed to and have the opportunity to learn the logic of evaluation and the discipline of evaluation reasoning. Skills are acquired in problem identification, criteria specification, and data collection, analysis, and interpretation. Acquisition of evaluation skills and ways of thinking can have a

What Gets Measured Gets Measured

"What gets measured gets done."

Management speak. Baloney. Nonsense.

Hopeful, to be sure. Visionary, perhaps.

Desirable, maybe. Consultant's promise, surely.

Nice PowerPoint slide.

Also a lie.

The causal link is problematic at best.

What gets measured gets measured.

What gets done gets done.

What gets measured may get done

and what gets done may get measured.

But don't confuse measuring with doing,

or doing with measuring.

Measuring something does not assure it gets done.

any more than

counting how many times you cast a fishing line

assures that you will catch a fish.

—Halcolm

longer-term impact than the use of findings from a particular evaluation study.

Moreover, people who participate in creating something tend to feel more ownership of what they have created, make more use of it, and take better care of it. Active participants in evaluation, therefore, are not only more likely to feel ownership of their evaluation findings but also of the evaluation process itself. Properly, sensitively, and authentically done, it becomes *their* process.

Participants and collaborators can be staff and/or program participants (e.g., clients, students, community members). Sometimes administrators, funders, and others also participate, but the usual connotation is that the primary participants are "lower down" in the hierarchy. In that sense, participatory evaluation is bottom-up.

In 1995, evaluators interested in "Collaborative, Participatory, and Empowerment Evaluation" formed a Topical Interest Group within the AEA. What these approaches have in common is a style of evaluation in which the evaluator becomes a facilitator, collaborator, and teacher in support of program participants and staff engaging in their own evaluation. While the findings from such a participatory process are intended to be used for program improvement, the more immediate impact is to use the evaluation process to increase participants' sense of being in control of, deliberative about, and reflective on their own lives and situations.

The labels "participatory evaluation" and "collaborative evaluation" mean different things to different evaluators. Some use these phrases interchangeably or as mutually reinforcing concepts (e.g., Dugan 1996; Powell et al. 1989; Whitmore and Kerans 1988). Wadsworth (1993) distinguishes "research on people, for people, or with people" (p. 1). Whitmore (1988) has defined the participatory approach as combining "social investigation, education, and action with the ultimate purpose of engendering broad community and social change" (p. 3). Whitmore worked with a community-based team and contended that, through the evaluation process, participants gained not only new knowledge and skills but also created a support network among themselves and gained a greater sense of self-efficacy. In a seminal article, Cousins and Whitmore (2007) distinguish three separate dimensions of participation and collaboration: (1) who controls the evaluation process (a researcher-practitioner continuum), (2) stakeholder selection for participation (a continuum from all legitimate groups to just primary intended users), and (3) depth of participation (a continuum from consultation to deep participation).

In the mid-1980s, several international grassroots development organizations advocated participatory evaluation as a tool for community and local leadership development in addition to being a management tool (PACT 1986). In advocating for participatory evaluation, the Evaluation Sourcebook of the American Council of Voluntary Agencies for Foreign Service asserted, "Participation is what development is about: gaining skills for self-reliance" (ACVAFS 1983:12). Thus, in developing countries, participatory monitoring and evaluation (M&E) has been linked to community development and capacity building (e.g., Salmen and Kane 2006; PREVAL 2006; Wageningen International UR 2006; Kuzmin 2005; Vernooy, Qui, and Jianchu 2003). More industrialized countries, where notions of "value-free" social science have long been dominant, have come to this idea of linking evaluation participation with empowerment more slowly, and, as we shall see later, the notion remains controversial.

Norman Uphoff (1991) published *A Field Guide for Participatory Self-Evaluation* aimed at grassroots community development projects. After reviewing a number of such efforts, he concluded,

> If the process of self-evaluation is carried out regularly and openly, with all group members participating, the answers they arrive at are in themselves not so important

---

The Global Movement toward More Participatory Approaches

As the World Bank task team leader starts her long flight from Washington to Accra, perhaps she reflects on how much the concept of development has changed over the past 25 years, and what the changes mean for how she does her work. It has been a long time since anyone in development could work only with governments and technical experts to create and implement plans for a country or sector. Now, she knows that social and cultural factors often carry as much or more weight than economic ones. Local stakeholders' concerns and insights are valued, indeed are often critical, in planning and carrying out development programs. Her work and that of her country government partners must include those stakeholders' views now that international development agencies, governments, and civil society organizations are clear that stakeholders have rights and roles in development, and that their involvement is critical, both technically and morally.

SOURCE: Lawrence Salmen and Eileen Kane (2006:7). *Bridging Diversity: Participatory Learning for Responsive Development.*

as what is learned from the discussion and from the process of reaching consensus on what questions should be used to evaluate group performance and capacity, and on what answers best describe their group's present status. (P. 272)

Here is clear support for the central premise of this chapter: *The process of engaging in evaluation can have as much or more impact than the findings generated.* It was not a group's specific questions or answers that Uphoff found most affected the groups he observed. It was the process of reaching consensus about questions and engaging with each other in the meaning of the answers turned up. The process of participatory self-evaluation, in and of itself, provided useful learning experiences for participants.

Since no definitive definitions exist for "participatory" and "collaborative"

evaluation, these phrases must be defined and given meaning in each setting where they're used. Exhibit 5.4 presents what I consider the primary principles of participatory evaluation. This list can be a starting point for working with intended participants to decide what principles they want to adopt for their own process.

Cousins and Earl (1995) examined how participatory and collaborative approaches contribute to increased use of findings: "Unlike emancipatory forms of action research, the rationale for participatory evaluation resides not in its ability to ensure social justice or to somehow even the societal playing field but in the utilization of systematically collected and socially constructed knowledge" (p. 10). They then ventured beyond increased use of findings when they discussed how participation helps create a learning organization. Viewing participatory

EXHIBIT 5.4
Principles of Participatory Evaluation

- The evaluation process involves participants in learning evaluation logic and skills, for example, goal setting, establishing priorities, focusing questions, interpreting data, data-based decision making, and connecting processes to outcomes.
- Participants in the process *own* the evaluation. They make the major focus and design decisions. They draw and apply conclusions. Participation is real, not token.
- Participants focus the evaluation on process and outcomes they consider important and to which they are committed.
- Participants work together as a group, and the evaluation facilitator supports group cohesion and collective inquiry.
- All aspects of the evaluation, including the data, are understandable and meaningful to participants.
- Internal, self-accountability is highly valued. The evaluation, therefore, supports participants' accountability to themselves and their community first, and external accountability secondarily, if at all.
- The evaluator is a facilitator, collaborator, and learning resource; participants are decision makers and evaluators.
- The evaluation facilitator recognizes and values participants' perspectives and expertise and works to help participants recognize and value their own and each other's expertise.
- Status differences between the evaluation facilitator and participants are minimized.

evaluation as a means of creating an organizational culture committed to ongoing learning has become an important theme in literature linking evaluation to learning organizations and capacity building (e.g., Harnar and Preskill 2007; King 2007a, 2007b, 2002, 1995; PREVAL 2006; Fetterman and Wandersman 2005; Kuzmin 2005; Owen 2005; Podems 2005; Preskill 2005a, 2005b; Preskill and Russ-Eft 2005; Cousins 2004; Baker and Sabo 2004; Preskill and Torres 1999; Sonnichsen 1993; Leeuw et al. 1993; Aubel 1993). "The goal of a participatory evaluator is eventually to put him or herself out of work when the research capacity of the organization is self-sustaining" (King 1995:89). Indeed, "the self-evaluating organization" (Wildavsky 1985) constitutes an important direction in the institutionalization of evaluation logic and processes.

Cousins (2001) studied and reported perspectives on collaborative evaluation from 67 pairings of North American evaluators and nonevaluator program practitioners who had participated together on a specific evaluation project. The results highlighted

> the benefits of evaluation process as a distinct source of impact on programs and, in particular, stakeholders associated with them. . . . Emerging evidence suggests that the logic of evaluation and systematic inquiry can be integrated into program, organizational, and community culture, but that such eventualities are most likely to occur within sustained evaluation activities that involve evaluators working in collaboration with non-evaluator stakeholder participants." (Pp. 127–28)

And just what does Cousins (2001) mean by "sustained evaluation activities" that involve collaboration?

> In our approach to collaborative evaluation (called practical participatory evaluation) primary users of evaluation data participate directly in the evaluation process from start to finish, including many of the technical activities such as instrument development, data collection, processing, and interpretation and reporting. We suggest that engagement in such activities engenders deep levels of understanding, by evaluators and program practitioners alike. . . . Collaborative evaluation of this sort is consistent with a utilization-oriented, problem-solving approach. (Pp. 115–16)

Participatory evaluation involves a partnership between the evaluator and those who participate in the evaluation (McGarvey 2007; Baker and Sabo 2004). These partnerships can be at the organizational level or with entire communities, as in a community development process (Cabaj 2007; Ridde 2006). As with any partnerships in any arena, building and maintaining a partnership is not easy, despite the best of intentions. Participatory evaluation partnerships can be particularly challenging in part because of underlying fears, bad past experiences with evaluation, resistance to reality testing, and cultural norms that undercut openness and questioning (Podems 2005). Facilitating participatory processes adds layers of complexity to the already complex tasks of evaluation. Nor do all evaluators have the skills and temperament to successfully engage in and facilitate a participatory evaluation. Some evaluators can't imagine anything more horrific than spending time with a group of untrained, nonresearch-oriented laypeople designing an evaluation. "Why would I want to do that?" A colleague once asked me after a panel on the topic, his face filled with disdain. "I can't imagine a bigger waste of time." Such evaluators resonate with the sentiment of Canadian piano virtuoso Glenn Gould who suffered from such horrible stage fright that he abandoned public performing completely.

"To me," he said, "the ideal artist-to-audience relationship is one to zero" (Lahr 2006:38). Many evaluators feel similarly about the desired ratio between the evaluator and those participating in the evaluation process: The ideal evaluator-to-participant relationship is one to zero.

Utilization-focused evaluation is inherently participatory and collaborative in actively involving primary intended users in all aspects of the evaluation. Evidence presented in earlier chapters has demonstrated the effectiveness of this strategy for increasing use of findings. The added emphasis of this chapter is how participation and collaboration can lead to an ongoing, longer-term commitment to using evaluation logic and building a culture of learning in a program or organization. Making this kind of process use explicit enlarges the menu of potential evaluation uses. How important this use of evaluation should be in any given evaluation is a matter for negotiation with intended users. The practical implication of an explicit emphasis on creating a learning culture as part of the process will mean building into the evaluation attention to and training in evaluation logic and skills.

When designing and negotiating participatory evaluations, one can use the three dimensions discussed earlier (Cousins 2003) that define important variations in the degree of participation and collaboration between evaluators and nonevaluators: (1) the control of the process—how much is practitioner controlled versus researcher controlled; (2) the scope of participation—many diverse stakeholders versus select primary intended users; and (3) depth of participation—great and deep participation by nonevaluator practitioners versus a more consultative, advice-giving, and perspective-sharing role. There are not right places to be on these three dimensions.

Rather, the depth and nature of participation depend on the situation, the purpose of the evaluation, the skills of those involved, and the degree to which participant learning is a major intended outcome of the evaluation. Suzanne Callahan (2005) has provided excellent "case studies in the art of evaluation" that take us inside participatory evaluation in real-world practice.

Not all references to "participatory" or "collaborative" evaluation make the link to participant learning—and the labels are sometimes misused. I have seen evaluations described as "participatory" simply because the evaluator surveyed program participants to get feedback about the program. That does *not* qualify as participatory evaluation, which requires some degree of interaction with and involvement of participants in the evaluation design itself, not just filling out the evaluator's survey questions or responding to interviews.

Levin (1993) distinguished three purposes for collaborative research: (1) the pragmatic purpose of increasing use, (2) the philosophical or methodological purpose of grounding data in practitioner's perspectives, and (3) the political purpose of mobilizing for social action. A fourth purpose, identified here, is teaching evaluation logic and skills, or more generally, *building evaluative capacity.* Cousins et al. (2004) found an empirical relationship between evaluation capacity and organizational learning in schools. Preskill and Russ-Eft (2005) have identified and described 72 activities that can be used in *Building Evaluation Capacity.* Empowerment evaluation makes capacity building a priority of collaboration.

Empowerment Evaluation

The theme of the 1993 AEA national conference was "Empowerment Evaluation."

Factors Affecting Learning from an Evaluation

The theme chosen by President Hallie Preskill for the 2007 Annual Conference of the American Evaluation Association was "Learning to evaluate . . . evaluating to learn."

Several factors appear to influence the likelihood that those involved in evaluation processes will learn from their participation. These include factors related to the following:

1. *How evaluation meetings are facilitated.* This involves the intentionality of learning from the evaluation process, the amount and quality of dialogue and reflection, the meeting facilitators' group process skills, the degree of trust among participants, and how much time is given to discussing various issues.

2. *The extent to which, and the ways in which, management and leadership support participants' involvement in the evaluation process.* This involves expectations managers have for participants to share their learning with others in the organization or community, and how they are rewarded for sharing and using what they have learned.

3. *Participants' personal characteristics and experiences with evaluation in the program being evaluated.* These include participants' motivation to engage in the evaluation process, their position, their rank, their previous training in evaluation, and the belief that evaluation findings will be used.

4. *The frequency, methods, and quality of communications between and among stakeholder participants.*

5. *Organizational characteristics.* These include the extant degree of organizational stability, external demands, constraints, and threats in the extent to which the organization supports evaluation work.

If process use is supported, nurtured, and studied, it may lead not only to individual learning but also to team and organizational learning.

SOURCES: Preskill (2005b: 328, 2007).

David Fetterman (1993), AEA President that year, defined empowerment evaluation as "the use of evaluation concepts and techniques to foster self-determination. The focus is on helping people help themselves" (p. 115).

Self-determination, defined as the ability to chart one's own course in life, forms the theoretical foundation of empowerment evaluation. It consists of numerous interconnected capabilities that logically follow each other . . . : the ability to identify and express needs, establish goals or expectations and a plan of action to achieve them, identify resources, make rational choices from various alternative courses of action, take appropriate steps to pursue objectives, evaluate short- and long-term results (including reassessing plans and expectations and taking necessary detours), and persist in pursuit of those goals. (Fetterman 1994a:2)

These skills are used to realize the group's own political goals; through self-assessment and a group's knowledge of itself it achieves accountability unto itself as well as to others (Fetterman, Kaftarian, and Wandersman 1996; Fetterman 1994b). With experience and reflection, empowerment evaluation has come to focus on 10 principles (Fetterman and Wandersman 2005):

1. Improvement

2. Community ownership

3. Inclusion

4. Democratic participation

5. Social justice

6. Community knowledge

7. Evidence-based strategies

8. Capacity building

9. Organizational learning

10. Accountability

Fetterman (2005a) explains that there is no absolute ranking or ordering of these principles. "However, there is a logical flow of the principles in practice" (p. 4). The principles are interdependent.

> As a general rule, the quality [of an empowerment evaluation] increases as the number of principles are applied, because they are synergistic. Ideally each of the principles should be enforced at some level. However, specific principles will be more dominant than others in each empowerment evaluation. The principles that dominate will be related to the local context and purpose of evaluation. Not all principles will be adopted equally at any given time or for any given project. (P. 9)

One of the conceptual developments in empowerment evaluation has been recognizing its impacts on individuals, organizations, and communities as a form of process use. As an example, in one evaluation Fetterman (2005b) reports the following process uses:

> A culture of evidence evolved from the discussions and self-assessments. The community of learners engaged in a dialogue about the status of their efforts. This engagement helped them build and refine skills in discourse and reasoning. The skills were generalizable to many other facets of their life. It also contributed to building a trusting relationship in the process. (P. 102)

Empowerment evaluation is most appropriate where the goals of the program include helping participants become more self-sufficient and personally effective. In such instances, empowerment evaluation is also intervention-oriented in that the evaluation is designed and implemented to support and enhance the program's desired outcomes. Weiss and Greene (1992) have shown how "empowerment partnerships" between evaluators and program staff were particularly appropriate in the family support movement because that movement emphasized participant and community empowerment. Orthner et al. (2006) conducted a cross-national experimental design comparison and found that organizational learning, staff empowerment, and program outcomes were related, and that it was especially important to focus the learning on program outcomes for, in this case, improved lives of children in the program.

As with the label "participatory evaluation," merely labeling an evaluation an empowerment evaluation does not make it empowering. Miller and Campbell (2006) studied 47 published studies labeled empowerment evaluations. They found wide variation in what was done and which principles were followed, including a case of an evaluation that was designed and executed solely by an evaluator with no input or involvement from stakeholders. . . . In this particular case, the evaluator indicated that the project was an empowerment evaluation because by allowing a disenfranchised population to respond to a survey, the population was afforded a voice. (P. 306)

I facilitated a cluster team evaluation of 34 programs serving families in poverty (Patton 1993). A common and important outcome of those programs was "increased intentionality"—having participants end up with a plan, a sense of direction, taking responsibility for their lives, and a commitment to making progress. Increased intentionality began with small first steps. Families in poverty often feel stuck where they are or are experiencing a downward spiral of worsening conditions and ever-greater hopelessness. These programs commonly reported that it was a major achievement to give people a sense of hope manifest in a concrete plan that participants had developed, understood, and believed they could accomplish. "Increased intentionality" is a commitment to change

---

Evaluating Empowerment Evaluations

Robin Lin Miller and Rebecca Campbell (2006) systematically examined 47 case examples of evaluations labeled "empowerment evaluation" published from 1994 through June 2005. They found wide variation among practitioners in adherence to empowerment evaluation principles and weak emphasis on the attainment of empowered outcomes for program beneficiaries.

The larger picture that emerges from these data suggests that although many evaluation projects get labeled (and relabeled) as empowerment evaluations, frequently, these evaluations do not embody the core principles that are supposed to undergird empowerment evaluation practice . . . . Although empowerment evaluation advocates for the inclusion of program consumers in the evaluation, and it is they who ultimately are to be empowered, program recipients were seldom part of the empowerment evaluations, relative to what one might expect . . . Interpretations of empowerment evaluation in practice seem more narrowly focused on benefiting those who run and deliver programs. The goal of empowering citizens who are the beneficiaries of social programs has become less salient in cases of empowerment evaluation practice than has increasing the self-determining status of program staff members and managers and holding the program staff members accountable to funding institutions (Miller and Campbell 2006:314).

---

for the better and a belief that such a change is possible. Thus, the programs collectively placed a great deal of emphasis on developing such skills as goal setting, learning to map out strategies for attaining goals, and monitoring progress in attaining personal goals. The programs' evaluations were built around these family plans and supported them. Developing family plans was not an end in itself, but the ability and willingness to work on a plan emerged as a leading indicator of the likelihood of success in achieving longer-term outcomes. Creating and taking ownership of a plan became milestones of progress. The next milestone was putting the plan into action.

Another empowering outcome of participatory evaluation is forming effective groups for collective action and reflection. For example, social isolation is a common characteristic of families in poverty. Isolation breeds a host of other problems, including family violence, despair, and alienation. Bringing participants together to establish mutual goals of support and identifying ways of evaluating (reality testing) goal attainment is a process of community development. The very process of working together on an evaluation has an impact on the group's collective identity and skills in collaborating and supporting each other. Participants also learn to use expert resources, in this case, the facilitating evaluator, but inquiry is democratized (IQREC 1997). One poverty program director explained to me the impact of such a process as she observed it:

> It's hard to explain how important it is to get people connected. It doesn't sound like a lot to busy middle class people who feel their problem is too many connections to too many things. But it's really critical for the people we work with. They're isolated. They don't know how the system works. They're discouraged. They're intimidated by the system's jargon. They don't know where to begin. It's just so critical that they get connected, take action, and start to feel effective. I don't know how else to say it. I wish I could communicate what a difference it makes for a group of poor people who haven't had many years of formal education to share the responsibility to evaluate their own program experiences, learn the language of evaluation, deal with data, and report results. It's very empowering.

Empowerment and Social Justice

The phrase "empowerment evaluation" can bridle. It comes across to some like a trendy, buzz word. Others experience it as oxymoronic or disingenuous. Still others find the phrase offensive and condescending. Few people, in my experience, react neutrally. Like the strategic planning term *proactive,* the word *empowerment* can create hostile reactions and may fall on hard times.

Empowerment carries an activist, social change connotation, as does a *related idea,*

using evaluation for social justice. Vera, the main character in Nadine Gordimer's (1994) novel, *None to Accompany Me,* exclaims after a lengthy exchange about empowerment of South African blacks: "Empowerment, what is this new thing? What happened to what we used to call justice?" (p. 285). Perhaps Vera would have been pleased by the theme chosen by President Karen Kirkhart for the American Evaluation Association national conference in 1994 (the year after Empowerment Evaluation was the theme): "Evaluation and Social Justice."

The first prominent evaluation theorist to advocate valuing based on principles of social justice was Ernest House (1990b, 1980). He has consistently voiced concern for democratizing decision making (House 2004; House and Howe 2000). In that context, he has analyzed the ways in which evaluation inevitably becomes a political tool in that it affects "who gets what" (distributive justice). Evaluation can enhance fair and just distribution of benefits and responsibilities, or it can distort such distributions and contribute to inequality. In rendering judgments on programs, the social justice evaluator is guided by principles such as equality, fairness, and concern for the common welfare (Sirotnik 1990).

"Deliberative democratic evaluation" is an approach that attends to social justice by engaging the full range of stakeholder perspectives (the principle of inclusion) in dialogue and deliberation (House and Howe 2000, 1999; Ryan and DeStefano 2000). House has emphasized that such an inclusive and deliberative process reduces bias in findings:

> To be unbiased, evaluators might obtain stakeholder opinions from all relevant parties and process these values, views, and interests in systematic ways, thus balancing bias against bias in arriving at (relatively)

unbiased conclusions. The process is analogous to enlisting different perspectives on panels to secure a balanced outcome or collecting diverse facts to obtain a correct perspective. (House 2004:222)

While House has emphasized the way in which deliberative democratic evaluation produces balanced results and reduces bias in findings, those stakeholders who participate in such deliberative and dialogic processes are learning to think evaluatively (Patton 2002b; Torres et al. 2000).

Feminist evaluation is another approach that emphasizes participatory, empowering, and social justice agendas (Podems 2005; Bamberger and Podems 2002; Seigart and Brisolara 2002). Feminist, social justice, and empowerment evaluations change the role of the evaluator from the traditional judge of merit or worth to a social change agent—or advocate (Greene 1997). Many evaluators surveyed by Cousins et al. (1996) were hostile to or at least ambivalent about whether participatory evaluation can or should help bring about social justice. Certainly, evaluators undertaking such an approach need to be comfortable with and committed to it, and such an activist agenda must be explicitly recognized by, negotiated with, and formally approved by primary intended users.

From a utilization-focused perspective, the important point about using evaluation processes to support social change is this: *Using evaluation to mobilize for social action, empower participants, and support social justice are options on the menu of evaluation process uses.* Since how these options are labeled will affect how they are viewed, when discussing these possibilities with primary intended users, evaluation facilitators will need to be sensitive to the language preferences of those involved.

Now, we turn to a conceptually different use of evaluation processes, evaluation for program and organizational development.

Evaluation for Program and Organization Development: Developmental Evaluation

The profession of program evaluation has developed parallel to the professions of management consulting and OD (organizational development) consultants advise on and facilitate a variety of change processes (Rothwell and Sullivan 2005; Carnevale 2002; Patton 1999a), including solving communications problems (Miller 2005); conflict resolution (Miall, Ramsbotham, and Woodhouse 2005; Angelica 1999); strategic planning (Bryson 2004a); leadership development (Crosby and Bryson 2005; Terry 2001; Schein 1985); organizational learning (Senge 2006; Hamilton et al. 2006; Preskill and Torres 1999); teamwork (Parker, Zielinski, and McAdams 2000); human resources (Dessler 2004); diversity training (Wildermuth 2005); shaping organizational culture (Schein 1989); and defining mission, to name but a few OD arenas of practice. Sometimes their methods include organizational surveys and field observations, and they may facilitate *action research* as a basis for problem solving (Whyte 1991; Schön 1987; Argyris, Putnam, and Smith 1985; Wadsworth 1984) or even evaluation (Patton 2002a; King 1995; Wadsworth 1993).

Program evaluation can be viewed as one approach on the extensive menu of organization and program development approaches. *Capacity building in evaluation can be a core part of more general organizational development initiatives and processes* (ECDG 2006; Kuzmin 2005; Horton and Mackay 2003; Horton et al. 2003). Evaluation's niche is defined by its emphasis on reality testing based on systematic data collection for improvement, rigorous assessment of outcomes, judging merit and worth, and generating knowledge about effectiveness. The processes of evaluation support change in organizations by getting people engaged in reality testing, that is, helping them think empirically, with emphasis on specificity and clarity, and teaching them the methods and utility of data-based decision making.

For example, *evaluability assessment* (Wholey 1994; Smith 1989) has emerged as a process for evaluators to work with program managers to help them get ready for evaluation. It involves clarifying goals, finding out various stakeholders' views of important issues, and specifying the model or intervention to be assessed. From my perspective, this is really a fancy term that gives evaluators a credible niche for doing program and organizational development. Time and time again, evaluators are asked to undertake an evaluation only to find that goals are muddled, key stakeholders have vastly different expectations of the program, and the model that the program supposedly represents, that is, its intervention, is vague at best. In other words, the program has been poorly designed, conceptualized, or developed. To do an evaluation, the evaluator has to make up for these deficiencies. Thus, by default, the evaluator becomes a program or organizational developer. Rog (1985) studied the use of evaluability assessments and found that many of them precipitated substantial program change but did not lead to a formal evaluation. The programs realized, through the process of evaluability assessment, that they had a lot more development to do before they could or should undertake a formal evaluation, especially a summative evaluation. In such cases, the processes and logic of evaluation have impact on program staff quite beyond the use of findings from the assessment.

Mission-oriented evaluation is an organizational development approach that involves assessing the extent to which the various units and activities of the organization are consistent with its mission. For example, I evaluated the extent to which 550 grants made by the Northwest Area Foundation over 5 years were congruent with its mission. The board used that assessment at a retreat to review and then revise the organization's mission. The process of clarifying the foundation's mission with staff and board directors had at least as much impact as the findings (Hall 1992). I noted earlier in this chapter the very process of formulating a mission and goals so they can be evaluated will usually have an impact long before data are actually collected to measure effectiveness. In this way, evaluative questioning and facilitation can be understood as an organizational development activity.

Mission-oriented evaluation changes the unit of evaluation (unit of analysis) from the program to the organization. Many program and project evaluators have been self-limiting and missed organizational development opportunities by defining the primary unit of analysis for evaluation as the program or project. The question of organizational effectiveness can be quite different from program or project effectiveness. Let's look at some of the implications of changing the unit of analysis.

The Organization as the Unit of Analysis

First, the evaluation situation typically becomes more complex at the organizational level. There may be more stakeholders to deal with, more levels of stakeholders, and therefore greater challenges in sorting through various interests, interpersonal dynamics, and organizational politics. The environment surrounding and influencing an organization may also be more complex and dynamic compared with the environment of a single program. On the other hand, operating at the organization level may increase the possibility of having impact by being able to deal directly with those who have the power to make changes.

Second, because programs and projects are usually embedded in larger organizational contexts, improving programs and projects may be linked to and even dependent on changing the organizations of which they are a part. For example, when evaluating the effectiveness of government programs, evaluators may need to examine, understand, and assess the ways in which being part of larger bureaucracies affect program and project effectiveness. Factors that can affect effectiveness include staff motivation, efficiency of program processes, and incentives to achieve outcomes, all of which are more determined at the organizational level than at the program or project level. Thus, improving programs may mean developing greater organizational effectiveness. This point deserves elaboration through an example and review of supporting data.

Systems Interconnections Between Levels and Units of Analysis

I once directed a knowledge-generating evaluation synthesis in search of overarching themes, patterns, and lessons learned that cut across the diverse experiences and evaluations of 34 separate Aid to Families in Poverty (FIP) programs supported by The McKnight Foundation in Minneapolis. The synthesis team consisted of five analysts. I had overall thematic integration responsibility while my four evaluation colleagues focused on integrating findings from the four cluster areas of the FIP initiative: employment, effective parenting/family stability, child care, and comprehensive poverty programs.

Our analytical process began with review of specific evaluation findings from separate projects. Then, we began looking for patterns across projects. We examined patterns of participant outcomes and project implementation. We found that effective projects shared some common characteristics, including the following:

- Effective staff are highly *responsive* to individual participants' situations, needs, capabilities, interests, and family context. In being responsive and respectful, they work to raise hopes and empower participants by helping them make concrete, intentional changes.

- Effective projects support staff responsiveness by being *flexible* and giving staff discretion to take whatever actions assist participants to climb out of poverty.

- Flexible, responsive projects affect the larger systems of which they are a part by *pushing against boundaries,* arrangements, rules, procedures, and attitudes that hinder their capability to work flexibly and responsively—and therefore effectively—with participants.

What is of interest for our purposes here is the extent to which we found an interconnectedness of these patterns at project, program, and organizational levels. An important breakthrough in our synthesis came when we understood that project and agency-wide organizational cultures were systemically interrelated. Systems consist of interdependent parts such that a change in one part affects other parts and the entire system. In examining FIP patterns across projects and host agencies, we found *that how people are treated affects how they treat others*:

responsiveness reinforces responsiveness,

flexibility supports individualization, and

empowerment breeds empowerment.

Effective projects emphasized the importance of individualized, responsive, and respectful work with families in poverty. But we also found that staff generally could not (or would not) be individually responsive and supportive if they were part of organizational environments that were rigid and bureaucratic. We found that staff tended to treat participants the way they were treated as professionals within their organizations. If the program administration and environment were rigid, rules oriented, and punitive, the staff tended to be rigid, rules oriented, and blaming with participants. If the program environment and administration were flexible, responsive, nurturing, and supportive, the staff in that environment was more likely to interact with participants in ways that were responsive, nurturing, and supportive.

The systems connection between projects, programs, and organizations operated in both directions, however. Programs developed cultures that affected entire agencies and systems of which they were a part. The receipt of prestigious and relatively flexible philanthropic funding gave projects a certain degree of power, confidence, and autonomy such that they could make demands on their host organizations and cooperating units of government to be responsive and flexible. In many cases, when projects began implementation, they found that they could not do what needed to be done to assist participants because of agency or government rules and restrictions. Ordinarily, project leaders lacked the power or confidence to challenge system barriers to effectiveness. Many project leaders, however, with the open support of the independent philanthropic foundation funding the project, formulated strategies to overcome system barriers and thereby create a more flexible and responsive environment for their projects. Even as project

staff were often called on to be advocates for families in poverty and help those families become assertive in overcoming system barriers they encountered, so also staff became assertive in working to change organizational and system barriers to program effectiveness. In some cases, then, projects changed the agencies in which they were housed, moving those host agencies toward greater flexibility and responsiveness. The evaluation synthesis, by highlighting these interconnections, led to further organizational development efforts. More directly related to the focus of this chapter, as our findings emerged in collaboration with leadership from these different organizations, their discussions, interactions, and reflections led many of them to change how they managed programs and projects. Well before we had produced formal findings and written a report, the processes of being engaged in the evaluation synthesis led those involved to begin thinking in different ways about how projects and programs related to their overall organizational cultures. In other words, being involved in the evaluation process, especially interpreting findings through interaction with leaders from other organizations, stimulated organizational development—a *process use* of the synthesis evaluation.

Overlapping Dimensions of Process Use: Organizational Development and Evaluative Thinking

The various kinds of process use discussed in this chapter are often found together. For example, infusing evaluative thinking into an organization's culture is one specific approach to overall organizational development and often involves participatory and collaborative evaluation as the

Organizational Development and Evaluative Thinking

The Five Most Important Questions You Will Ever Ask About Your Nonprofit Organization:

Peter Drucker died in 2005 at the age of 95. He invented the field of management consulting and after a highly successful career advising multinational corporations, he turned his attention to the challenges of increasing the effectiveness of not-for-profit organizations. While the bottom line for a business was monetary profit, he considered the bottom line for educational and nonprofit organizations to be changed lives. He founded the Drucker Foundation to promote increased effectiveness of not-for-profit organizations of all kinds. This led him to an organizational development framework that invited organizations to seriously engage with fundamentally evaluative questions. His classic work in this regard was a workbook entitled *"The Five Most Important Questions You Will Ever Ask About Your Nonprofit Organization."* Note the evaluative thinking that permeates his organizational development framework.

1. *What is our business (mission)?*

    What are we trying to achieve?

    What specific results are we seeking?

    What are our major strengths?

    What are our weaknesses?

2. *Who is our customer?*

    Who are our primary customers?

    Who are our supporting customers?

    Have our customers changed?

    Should we add or delete some customers?

3. *What does the costumer consider value?*

    How well are we providing what our customers consider value?

    How can we use what our customers consider value to become more effective?

    What additional information do we need?

4. *What have been our results?*

    How do we define results for our organization?

    To what extent have we achieved these results?

    How well are we using our resources?

5. *What is our plan?*

    What have we learned and what do we recommend?

    Where should we focus our efforts?

    What, if anything, should we do differently?

    What is my plan to achieve results for my group/responsibility area?

    What is our plan to achieve results for the organization?

SOURCE: Peter Drucker (1993).

mechanism of development. Nowhere is this better illustrated than in the pacesetting organizational effectiveness initiative of the Bruner Foundation called the Evaluative Thinking in Organizations (ETHOS) project (Baker and Bruner 2006). Founded in 1963, the Bruner Foundation has made nonprofit evaluation methodologies and organizational effectiveness a major focus of its grant making. In 1996, the Bruner Foundation launched the Rochester Effectiveness Partnership (REP) in Rochester, New York, a pioneering project aimed at building evaluation capacity in local not-for-profit agencies through skill training, technical assistance, and participatory evaluation demonstration efforts. The initiative was founded on the premise that organizations that valued and used evaluation would become more effective, but that for organizations to learn to value and use evaluation, they would need guidance, training, technical assistance, and financial support. Between 1996 and 2003, 14 funding organizations and 32 social service provider organizations focused together on using evaluation to increase program and organizational effectiveness. The evaluations of this evaluation capacity-building effort showed substantial variation in the nature, quality, and utility of the program evaluations undertaken. Early on it became apparent that increasing the use of evaluation would require a supportive organizational culture and that building such a culture would necessitate organizational development and leadership support. Some organizations were open to this; others were not. It was clear that where program evaluation came to be valued, there were ripple effects within the larger organizations in which those programs resided. Thus, as the 7 years of the original capacity-building commitment

was coming to an end, Beth Bruner and her colleagues turned their attention to this larger issue:

> While we had documented the spread or "ripple" of REP evaluation skills, we were curious to understand more about a possible relationship between increased evaluation capacity and the use of that capacity beyond the program level. In other words, could evaluation skills be applied to human resources, governance, communications and marketing as well as other organizational management areas? (Baker and Bruner 2006:xix)

This led, in 2004, to a new initiative, the ETHOS project, in which service provider partners in Rochester joined with funders and evaluators to inquire into the relationships between evaluation capacity, evaluative thinking, and organizational effectiveness.

> Evaluative Thinking was defined as a type of reflective practice that incorporated use of systematically collected data to inform organizational decisions and other actions. . . . The partners also clarified that evaluative thinking could be applied to many organizational functions (e.g., mission development/revision, human resources decision making) in addition to program development and service delivery. (Baker and Bruner 2006:34)

To support their inquiry, the evaluation and organizational partners reviewed various organizational assessment tools to develop an instrument that could be used to measure evaluative thinking practices within key organizational areas. The "ETHOS Assessment Tool" included multiple indicators in 15 organizational capacity areas, including Mission, Strategic Planning, Executive Leadership, Management Leadership, Governance,

Inquiry Question for Evaluative Thinking in Organizations (ETHOS) Project

1. What does evaluative thinking look like within various organizational capacity areas?

2. How are evaluative thinking and organizational effectiveness related?

3. What is needed to enhance and broaden evaluative thinking?

SOURCE: Baker and Bruner (2006:32).

Fund Development/Fund Raising, Evaluation, Program Development, Client Relationships, Communication and Marketing, Technology Acquisition and Training, Staff Development, Human Resources, Business Venture Development, and Alliances and Collaborations. The assessment tool was completed through site visits in which key decision makers from each organization were interviewed, for example, the executive director, representatives from upper- and mid-level management, line staff, representatives from the board of directors, and others as appropriate.

> Review of cross-site evaluative thinking findings showed that the partners' combined scores for each capacity area were relatively high. Respondents confirmed the presence of many indicators of evaluative thinking in their regular practices. There were some differences, however, in the scores. For example, the lowest combined score was 78 for Management Leadership and the highest combined score was 94 for Strategic Planning. This tells us that respondents saw more evidence of evaluative thinking in the way their organizations planned their actions than in the way they administered them. (Baker and Bruner 2006:40)

What is especially important for our purposes is that this Bruner Foundation initiative,

for the first time, operationalized "evaluative thinking" and measured its manifestation in a variety of organizational functions across several organizations. Moreover, by using a participatory partnership research strategy, their inquiry into evaluative thinking offered evidence of cumulative process use, for the organizations that collaborated in the inquiry could point to ways that evaluative thinking had become more deeply infused in their organization's culture, could document specific changes they had made based on evaluation findings, could identify areas of enhanced organizational development, and reported increased understanding of and commitment to evaluative thinking for organizational effectiveness (Baker and Bruner 2006, especially pp. 49–57).

The combination of the Rochester Effectiveness Project followed by the ETHOS initiative took place over a decade with substantial financial support, training, technical assistance, and ongoing reinforcement. This contrasts dramatically with most such organizational learning and change initiatives that have a faddish, flavor-of-the-month feel, and lack sustainability and long-term commitment. Most organizational change initiatives fail precisely because they lack long-term commitment and follow through and prove unsustainable (Senge 1999). The successful case examples of infusing evaluative thinking into organizational culture we have presented in this chapter, IDRC and ETHOS, were both long-term, full-organization, leadership-engaged, and well-supported initiatives.

Intentional and Planned Process Use as an Option in Utilization-Focused Evaluations

Menu 5.1, presented earlier, summarizes the six primary uses of evaluation logic and processes discussed in this chapter. As

I noted in opening this chapter, any evaluation can, and often does, have these kinds of effects unintentionally or as an offshoot of using findings. *What's different about utilization-focused evaluation is that the possibility and desirability of using and learning from evaluation processes, as well as from findings, can be made intentional and purposeful—an option for intended users to consider building in from the beginning.* In other words, instead of treating process use as an informal ripple effect, explicit and up-front attention to the potential impacts of using evaluation logic and processes can increase those impacts and make them a planned purpose for undertaking the evaluation. In this way, the evaluation's overall utility is increased.

The six kinds of process use identified and discussed here—(1) infusing evaluative thinking into organizational culture, (2) enhancing shared understandings, (3) reinforcing interventions, (4) instrumentation effects and reactivity, (5) supporting participant engagement, and (6) developing programs and organizations—have this in common: They all go beyond the traditional focus on findings and reports as the primary vehicles for evaluation impact. As such, these new directions have provoked controversy.

Concerns, Caveats, and Controversies: Objections to and Abuses of Process Use

Just as evaluation findings can be misused, so too evaluation processes can be misused. Too much time can be spent worrying about evaluation to the detriment of direct service delivery. Evaluation can support interventions, but can also interfere with programs, as when so many forms have to be filled out or so much testing is done that time for direct work with those in need is significantly reduced.

Resources and staff time devoted to evaluation are resources and staff time not available for working with clients (as staff, in frustration, will often readily point out). Indeed, evaluation can become its own source of goal displacement in which an organization becomes so enamored with its evaluation system that it's devoting more attention to that than to meeting client needs. One major foundation invited me in to look at its sophisticated process for capturing lessons. The foundation was, indeed, seriously engaged in analyzing and reflecting on what was working and not working; evaluative thinking clearly permeated the foundation's documents, plans, staff meetings, and governance sessions. The problem was that it was all thinking and no doing. They were congratulating themselves for openly acknowledging failures, but they have been documenting the same failures over and over again for several years and nothing seemed to have significantly changed. They were heavy into process use—*but had neglected findings use.* They were thinking and talking a lot about evaluation, but, in fact, they weren't adept at actually using findings. All the attention to and rhetoric about evaluation, and their precious status as a knowledge-generating learning organization, had disguised the fact that they were quite ineffective in actually using evaluation findings. *Process use is no substitute for findings use. Process use should enhance findings use.*

In addition to the classic concern that too much attention to process may undercut attention to outcomes (in this case, findings use), six other objections—closely interrelated, but conceptually distinct—arise most consistently when process use is proposed as an evaluation option.

1. *Definitional objection.* Evaluation should be narrowly and consistently defined

in accordance with the "common sense meaning of evaluation," namely, "the systematic investigation of the merit or worth of an object" (Stufflebeam 1994:323). Anything other than that isn't evaluation. Adding terms such as empowerment or collaborative to evaluation changes focus and undermines the essential nature of evaluation as rendering judgment.

2. *Goals confusion objection.* The goal of evaluation is to render judgment. "While . . . 'helping people help themselves' is a worthy goal, it is not the fundamental goal of evaluation" (Stufflebeam 1994:323). Goals such as organizational development, evaluation capacity building, and infusing evaluative thinking into the organization's culture are worthy undertakings, but are not evaluation.

3. *Role confusion objection.* Evaluators as people may play various roles beyond being an evaluator, such as training clients or helping staff develop a program, but in taking on such roles, one moves beyond being an evaluator and should call the role what it is, for example, trainer or developer, not evaluator.

> While one might appropriately assist clients in these ways, such services are not evaluation. . . . The evaluator must not confuse or substitute helping and advocacy roles with rendering of assessments of the merit and/or worth of objects that he/she has agreed to evaluate. (Stufflebeam 1994:324)

Scriven (1991a) has been emphatic in arguing that being able to identify that something is or is not working (an evaluator's role) is quite different from knowing how to fix it or improve it (a designer's role).

4. *Threat to data validity objection.* Quantitative measurement specialists teach that data collection, for the results to be valid, reliable, and credible, should be separate from the program being evaluated. Integrating data collection in such a way that it becomes part of the intervention contaminates both the data and the program. Designing instruments to contribute to learning and reflection undercut their validity to measure program processes and outcomes accurately.

5. *Loss of independence objection.* Approaches that depend on close relationships between evaluators and other stakeholders undermine the evaluator's neutrality and independence. "It's quite common for younger evaluators to 'go native,' that is, psychologically join the staff of the program they are supposed to be evaluating and become advocates instead of evaluators" (Scriven 1991a:41). This can lead to overly favorable findings and an inability to give honest, negative feedback.

6. *Corruption and misuse objection.* Evaluators who identify with and support program goals, and develop close relationships with staff and/or participants, can be inadvertently co-opted into serving public relations functions or succumb to pressure to distort or manipulate data, hide negative findings, and exaggerate positive results. Even if they manage to avoid corruption, they may be suspected of it, thus undermining the credibility of the entire profession. Or these approaches may actually serve intentional misuse and foster corruption, as Stufflebeam (1994) worries,

> What worries me most about . . . empowerment evaluation is that it could be used as a cloak of legitimacy to cover up highly corrupt or incompetent evaluation activity. Anyone who has been in the evaluation

business for very long knows that many potential clients are willing to pay much money for a "good, empowering evaluation," one that conveys the particular message, positive or negative, that the client/interest group hopes to present, irrespective of the data, or one that promotes constructive, ongoing, and nonthreatening group process. . . . Many administrators caught in political conflicts would likely pay handsomely for such friendly, nonthreatening, empowering evaluation service. Unfortunately, there are many persons who call themselves evaluators who would be glad to sell such service. (P. 325)

Exhibit 5.5 summarizes contributions and concerns about different kinds of process use. The concerns have sparked vigorous debate (e.g., Fetterman 1995). In Chapter 14 on the politics and ethics of utilization-focused evaluation, I'll address these concerns with the seriousness they deserve. For the purpose of concluding this chapter, it is sufficient to note that the utilization-focused evaluator who presents to intended users options that go beyond narrow and traditional uses of findings has an obligation to disclose and discuss objections to such approaches. As evaluators explore new and innovative options, they must be clear that *dishonesty, corruption, data distortion, and selling out are not on the menu*. Where primary intended users want and need an independent, summative evaluation, that is what they should get. Where they want the evaluator to act independently in bringing forward improvement-oriented findings for formative evaluation, that is what they should get. But those are no longer the only options on the menu of evaluation uses. New participatory, collaborative, intervention-oriented, and developmental approaches

are already being used. The utilization-focused issue is not whether such approaches should exist. They already do. The issues are understanding when such approaches are appropriate and helping intended users make informed decisions about their appropriateness.

Crossing Borders, Crossing Boundaries

The theme of the 2006 International Evaluation Conference in Toronto was "Crossing Borders, Crossing Boundaries." In the spirit of that theme, I close this chapter by updating the Sufi story with which this chapter began. Nasrudin had fooled customs officials by smuggling donkeys, which were in plain sight, when they were forever searching him for presumed contraband not in plain sight. Having retired wealthy from smuggling donkeys, he encountered a former customs officials to whom he confessed what he had been smuggling. The man then asked, "And what are you doing these days?"

"Smuggling ideas and new ways of thinking across closed borders," Nasrudin replied. "I get paid more for a good idea than I ever got paid for a donkey. Though good ideas are harder to come by, they're easier to carry across borders." (See illustration on the next page.)

The idea that evaluation can be useful as a way of thinking is not always a welcome or credible idea. Sometimes it has to be introduced to closed minds and rigid compliance-based organizations with cunning and stealth. And sometimes not. Knowing the difference is the challenge of situational responsiveness, the topic of Chapter 6.

Follow-Up Exercises

1. Identify a real program. Describe the program's activities, intended outcomes, and its context. Choose one kind of *Process Use* from Menu 5.1 and describe how that process could be applied to an evaluation of this program. What would be the benefits of such evaluation process use? What disadvantages or difficulties can be anticipated?

2. Locate someone who has experienced a powerful learning experience or a major change in their life and is willing to be interviewed. Interview that person about the major change experienced and how that change has affected the person's current life—actions, behaviors, attitudes, feelings, and priorities. Probe about the nature of the change or learning experience, the situation that led to the change or learning, and the factors that affected what happened. At the end of the interview, ask questions about the experience of being interviewed. Did the person come to any new understandings about the learning experience or change that was the focus of

the interview? Probe for reactions to being interviewed and reflecting on the questions asked. Analyze those reactions as instrumentation effects and discuss this kind of reactivity as an example of process use.

3. Conduct an Internet search of the term *participatory evaluation*. Examine the variations in what is meant by and described as "participatory evaluation." Discuss the implications of these variations for evaluation practice. How does utilization-focused evaluation deal with such variations in definition, meaning, and practice?

4. Write out a script for explaining *process use* and process use options to a philanthropic foundation funder who might be interested in funding evaluations. In your own words, with a specific person in mind, tell them about process use.

5. Find your own analogy for describing and explaining process use. This chapter opened and closed with a Sufi tale that illustrated aspects of process use. I also offered hiking the Grand Canyon as an analogy for process use (see page 155). Come up with your own analogy for process use.

EXHIBIT 5.5

Process Use Contributions and Concerns

Type of Process Use	Contributions	Concerns, Challenges, and Caveats
1. Infusing *evaluative thinking* into the organizational culture	Evaluation becomes part of the organization's way of doing business, contributing to all aspects of organizational effectiveness. People speak the same language, share meanings, and priorities. Reduces resistance to evaluation.	Requires consistent leadership, ongoing training, and reinforcement (rewards). The rhetoric is easy, but actually internalizing evaluative thinking is difficult. Can increase conflict between those who "get it" and those who don't.
2. Enhancing shared understandings	Gets everyone on the same page; supports alignment of resources with program priorities.	Can force premature closure before alternatives are fully considered; those with the most power may impose their perspective on the less powerful.
3. Supporting and reinforcing the program intervention	Enhances outcomes and increases impact; increases the value of evaluation	Complicates attribution; the effects of the program become intertwined with the effects of the evaluation, in effect making the evaluation part of the intervention.
4. Instrumentation	What gets measured gets done. Focuses program resources on priorities. Measurement contributes to participant learning.	Measure the wrong things, the wrong things gets done. Goal displacement, where what can be measured becomes the program's goals. Corruption of indicators, especially where the stakes become high.
5. Increasing engagement, self-determination, and ownership	Makes evaluation especially meaningful and understandable to participants; empowering.	Can reduce the credibility of the evaluation to external stakeholders; comingles evaluation purposes with empowerment agendas, potentially undermining both.
6. Program and organizational development	Capacity building; long-term contribution beyond specific findings; enhances ongoing adaptability.	Evaluator serves multiple purposes and plays multiple roles, potentially confusing the evaluation role; evaluator develops a close relationship with program decision makers, raising questions about the evaluator's independence.

PART 2

Focusing Evaluations:
Choices, Options, and Decisions

Desiderata for the Indecisive and Complacent

G o placidly amid the noise and haste, and remember what peace there may be in avoiding options. As far as possible, without surrender, be on good terms with the indecisive. Avoid people who ask you to make up your mind; they are vexations to the spirit. Enjoy your indecisiveness as well as your procrastinations. Exercise caution in your affairs lest you be faced with choices, for the world is full of menus. Experience the joys of avoidance.

You are a child of the universe, no less than the trees and the stars; you have a right to do and think absolutely nothing. And if you want merely to believe that the universe is unfolding as it should, avoid evaluation, for it tests reality. Evaluation threatens complacency and undermines the oblivion of fatalistic inertia. In undisturbed oblivion may lie happiness, but therein resides neither knowledge nor effectiveness.

—Halcolm's *Indesiderata*

6

Situational Evaluation
Being Active-Reactive-Interactive-Adaptive

uman propensities in the face of evaluation; feline curiosity; stultifying fear; beguiling distortion of reality; ingratiating public acclamation; inscrutable selective perception; profuse rationalization; and apocalyptic anticipation. In other words, the usual run-of-the-mill human reactions to uncertainty.

Once past these necessary initial indulgences, it's possible to get on to the real evaluation issues: What's worth knowing? How will we get it? How will it be used?

Meaningful evaluation answers begin with meaningful questions.

—Halcolm

A young hare, born to royal-rabbit parents in a luxury warren, showed unparalleled speed. He won races far and wide, training under the world's best coach. He boasted that he could beat anyone in the forest.

The only animal to accept the hare's challenge was an old tortoise. This first amused, then angered the arrogant hare, who felt insulted. The hare agreed to the race, ridiculing the tortoise to local sports columnists. The tortoise said simply, "Come what may, I will do my best."

A course was created that stretched all the way through and back around the forest. The day of the race arrived. At the signal to start, the hare sped away, kicking dust in the tortoise's eyes. The tortoise slowly meandered down the track.

Halfway through the race, rain began falling in torrents. The rabbit hated the feel of cold rain on his luxuriously groomed fur, so he stopped for cover under a tree. The tortoise pulled his head into his shell and plodded along in the rain.

When the rain stopped, the hare, knowing he was well ahead of the meandering tortoise and detesting mud, decided to nap until the course dried. The track, however, was more than muddy; it had become a stream. The tortoise turned himself over, did the backstroke, and kept up his progress.

By and by, the tortoise passed the napping hare and won the race. The hare blamed his loss on "unfair and unexpected conditions," but observant sports columnists reported that the tortoise had beaten the hare by adapting to conditions as he found them. The hare, it turned out, was only a "good conditions" champion.

Evaluation Conditions

What are good evaluation conditions? Here's a wish list (generated by some colleagues over drinks late one night at the annual conference of the American Evaluation Association). The program's goals are clear, specific, and measurable. Program implementation is standardized and well managed. The project involves 2 years of formative evaluation working with open, sophisticated, and dedicated staff to improve the program; this is followed by a summative evaluation for the purpose of rendering independent judgment to an interested and knowledgeable funder. The evaluator has ready access to all necessary data and enthusiastic cooperation from all necessary people. The evaluator's role is clear and accepted. There are adequate resources and sufficient time to conduct a comprehensive and rigorous evaluation. The original evaluation proposal can be implemented as designed. No surprises turn up along the way, like departure of the program's senior executive or the report deadline moved up 6 months.

How often had this experienced group of colleagues conducted an evaluation under such ideal conditions? Never. (Bring on another round of drinks.)

The real world doesn't operate under textbook conditions. Effective evaluators learn to adapt to inevitable constraints. There is never enough time, resources, expertise, or control to design and conduct an ideal evaluation. And contrary to the belief that such constraints are limited to the government and not-for-profit sectors, a survey of evaluators working in the for-profit sector found the same challenges (Fawson, Moss-Summers, and May 2004). Rapid change is the norm rather than the exception.

> The pace of today's modern corporation is a barrier to evaluation. Time is measured in months rather than years. Corporate sponsors for projects come and go. Managers are moved around, groups re-organized, and new products and processes are introduced daily. Control of variables is virtually impossible and time to wait for the impact of an intervention to be demonstrated is a rare luxury. (P. 340)

Doing evaluations under such conditions requires situational responsiveness and

Adapting to the Situation

Marathon runner Steve Spence arrived in Tokyo in August 1991 to run for the world championship. The hot and humid conditions were aggravated by air pollution so heavy that he had trouble taking a deep breath. Dr. David Martin, an exercise physiologist, said that they were "the most challenging conditions that have ever been reported for world championships."

At dawn on race day, the temperature was already in the 70s. Spence decided to moderate his usual pace given the difficult conditions, so he ran slower than usual, hoping he would be able to speed up at the end if leading runners faded. In an interview reported in the *New York Times*, he recalled that when the starting gun went off, the other runners quickly pulled ahead. "You begin to wonder, 'Where am I?'" he recalled. "The leaders are so far ahead of me that I'll never catch up."

But his strategy worked. The faster runners wilted; indeed, 40 percent dropped out. Spence finished third, just 40 seconds behind the winner, with an average pace of 5 minutes 11 seconds per mile. He became one of the few American marathoners to win a medal in a world championship.

"Was I the third most fit person in that race? Absolutely not," Spence said looking back. "Was I the third most talented? Absolutely not." What made the difference, he concluded, was adapting to the conditions of the day (Kolata 2006a).

strategic, contingency thinking—what I've come to call being active-reactive-interactive-adaptive in working with primary intended users.

Situational Evaluation

There is no one best way to conduct an evaluation.

This insight is critical. The design of a particular evaluation depends on the people involved and their situation. Situational evaluation follows in the tradition of classic frameworks such as situational leadership (Blanchard 1986; Hersey 1985), situational ethics (Fletcher 1966), situational crime prevention (Clarke 1998), and *situated learning*: "Action is grounded in the concrete situation in which it occurs" (Anderson et al. 1996:5). The standards and principles of evaluation provide overall direction, a foundation of ethical guidance, and a commitment to

professional competence and integrity, but there are no absolute rules an evaluator can follow to know exactly what to do with specific users in a particular situation. As an evaluation unfolds, evaluators and primary intended users must work together to identify the evaluation that best fits their information needs and the program's context and situation. This means *negotiating* the evaluation's intended and desired uses, and adapting the design to financial, political, timing, and methodological constraints and opportunities.

Every evaluation situation is unique. A successful evaluation (one that is useful, practical, ethical, and accurate) emerges from the special characteristics and conditions of a particular situation—a mixture of people, politics, history, context, resources, constraints, values, needs, interests, and chance. Despite the rather obvious, almost trite, and basically commonsense nature of this observation, it is not at all obvious to most stakeholders, who worry a great deal about whether an evaluation is being done "right." Indeed, one common objection both evaluators and stakeholders make to active involvement of nonevaluators in designing an evaluation is that they lack the knowledge to *do it right*. In his classic best-selling book on creativity, Roger von Oech, founder and president of Creative Think, identified the search for "the one right answer" as the number one barrier to creative thinking and problem solving.

> Much of our educational system is geared toward teaching people *the one right answer*. By the time the average person finishes college, he or she will have taken over 2,600 tests, quizzes, and exams. . . . Thus, the "right" answer approach becomes deeply ingrained in our thinking. This may be fine for some mathematical problems where there is in fact only one right answer. The difficulty is that most of life doesn't present itself in this way. Life is ambiguous; there are many right answers—all depending on what you are looking for. But if you think there is only one right answer, then you will stop looking as soon as you find one. (von Oech 1983:21)

The notion that there is one right way to do things dies hard. The right way, from a utilization-focused perspective, is the way that will be meaningful, credible, and useful to the specific intended users involved, and finding that way requires interaction, negotiation, situational analysis, and ongoing *situational awareness*. Indeed, the evaluator needs to tap the situation understandings of primary intended users to fit the evaluation to their specific situation. In so doing, the evaluator may need to cultivate the situation awareness of intended users. *Situational analysis* is one of the "Essential Competencies for Program Evaluators" (Ghere et al. 2006; King et al. 2001).

Essential Competencies for Program Evaluators

Jean King, a recipient of the American Evaluation Association's prestigious Alva and Gunnar Myrdal Practice Award, has worked for a number of years with colleagues and students conducting research on and developing a framework for Essential Competencies for Program Evaluators (Ghere et al. 2006; King et al., 2001). The final product is a taxonomy of essential program evaluator competencies organized into six primary categories.

1. *Professional Practice*: knowing and observing professional norms and values, including evaluation standards and principles.

2. *Systematic Inquiry*: expertise in the technical aspects of evaluations, such as design, measurement, data analysis, interpretation, and sharing results.

3. *Situational Analysis*: understanding and attending to the contextual and political issues of an evaluation, including determining evaluabiity, addressing conflicts, and attending to issues of evaluation use.

4. *Project Management*: the nuts and bolts of managing an evaluation from beginning to end, including negotiating contracts, budgeting, identifying and coordinating needed resources, and conducting the evaluation in a timely manner.

5. *Reflective Practice*: an awareness of one's program evaluation expertise as well as the needs for professional growth.

6. *Interpersonal Competence*: the people skills needed to work with diverse groups of stakeholders to conduct program evaluations, including written and oral communication, negotiation, and cross-cultural skills.

An apt metaphor for the challenge of *situational awareness* comes from aviation. Craig (2001) analyzed case studies of airline crashes and crashes avoided. With all the technological advances in flight control and the precise instruments available for navigation, he found that it's easy for pilots to become "fat, dumb, and happy," a phrase that paints a picture of a pilot who has become complacent, flying with dull senses, and inadequate attention to what is going on (p. 5). They still take in the data from flight instruments, they see the changing indicators, but the changing situation displayed before them doesn't register. When pilots fly without situation awareness, the result can be catastrophic.

Situation recognition affects decision making. Substantial research has focused on how people make decisions, including the influential works of Economics Nobel Prize recipient Daniel Kahneman (Kahneman and Tversky 2000a, 2000b; Tversky and Kahneman 2000). How we decide what to do is far from rational (Tversky and Fox 2000; Gigerenzer, Todd, and ABC Research Group 1999; Inbar 1979). Our rationality is "bounded" (Simon 1978, 1957). We rely on routine "heuristics"—rules of thumb, standard operating procedures, practiced behaviors, and selective perception (Groopman 2007:37). Consider, for example, the *confidence heuristic* that operates as we obtain more and more information about a situation or problem. The more information we obtain, the more confident we are about our judgments. But experimental evidence shows that "the level of accuracy does not vary significantly with increased information" (Inbar 1979:85). We tend to force the new information to fit initial judgments while steadily increasing our confidence in those judgments.

Another heuristic is the *representativeness heuristic*. On entering a new situation, we make sense out of that situation, that is,

we categorize and label it, by focusing on those aspects of the situation that are most familiar to us and those elements that are most similar to our previous experiences. We thus force the new problem or situation to be *representative* of things we already know, selectively ignoring information and evidence that is unfamiliar or that doesn't fit our preconceptions developed through past experiences. This can lead to systematic distortions and errors in analyzing the situation.

Still another heuristic that can readily affect our ability to engage in a creative situational evaluation process is the *availability heuristic*. When facing a new situation, things that happened to us recently or information that we come across frequently is more readily available for retrieval. We thus carry into new situations probability estimates about the likelihood of a new situation falling into a certain category based on our previously available experiences with that category. For example, an evaluator trained in survey research is likely to have available a large repertoire of cases where conducting a survey was the preferred evaluation method. This increases the probability of defining any new situation as one appropriate for doing a survey.

Scholars of decision making and expertise have found that what distinguishes people with great expertise is not that they have more answers than others, but they are more adept at situational recognition and more intentional about their decision-making processes (Klein 1999). We can, in fact, come to recognize our heuristic tendencies.

People are rarely aware of the basis of their impressions and they have little deliberate control over the processes by which these impressions are formed. However, they can learn to identify the heuristic processes that determine their impressions, and to make appropriate allowances for the biases to which they are liable. (Tversky and Kahneman 1974:1124–25)

The Challenge of Situation Analysis in Designing and Conducting Evaluations

How complicated can it be to design an evaluation to fit the program's situation? Very. Consider the analogy to playing a game of chess. Bruce Pandolfini (1998), a world-class chess master, consults with major corporate leaders to teach them the mindset of a chess master so that they can become more skilled at strategic analysis and thinking. He points out that there are some 85 billion ways of playing just the first four moves in a game of chess. Deciding what moves to make requires both strategy and tactics grounded in an analysis of the situation presented by a particular game and opponent within an overall framework of fundamental chess ideas and concepts, understanding what the different pieces do, how they can be moved, and how they relate to each other. Once the game starts, subsequent moves are contingent on and must be adapted to what one's opponent does and the unfolding situation.

To become more sophisticated and intentional about situational analysis in evaluation, one needs a framework to decide what to pay attention to because you can't track everything. Alkin (1985), in an influential framework, identified some 50 factors associated with use. He organized them into four categories:

1. *Evaluator characteristics,* such as commitment to make use a priority, willingness to involve users, political sensitivity, and credibility

2. *User characteristics,* such as interest in the evaluation, willingness to commit time and energy, and position of influence

3. *Contextual characteristics,* such as size of organization, political climate, and existence of competing information

4. *Evaluation characteristics,* such as nature and timing of the evaluation report, relevance of evaluation information, and quality of the data and evaluation

Mark and Henry (2004), building on three decades of utilization research and theory, and focusing on "the *underlying mechanisms* through which evaluation may have its effects" (p. 37), conceptualized a comprehensive theory of evaluation influence. They differentiated individual, interpersonal, and collective levels of analysis, and hypothesized four kinds of mechanisms: "general influence processes, cognitive and affective (or attitudinal) processes, motivational processes, and behavioral processes" (pp. 40–41). Their comprehensive framework identified and organized 50 factors that can affect an evaluation's influence (p. 46).

Now, the practical problem: How does an evaluator analyze a real-world situation taking into account 50 factors? Those who study decision making say it can't be done, so let's try simplifying. Exhibit 6.1 lists just 20 of the situational variables that can affect how an evaluation is designed and conducted, things like number of stakeholders to be dealt with, the evaluation's purpose, staff attitudes toward evaluation, the budget and timeline for evaluation, and the program's prior experience with evaluation. These variables are presented in no particular order. Most of them could be broken down into several additional dimensions. If we conceive of just three points (or situations) on each of these dimensions—the two endpoints and a midpoint, for example, low budget, moderate budget, substantial budget—then the possible combinations of these 20 dimensions represent 8,000 unique situational configurations for evaluation.

Nor are these static situations. The program you thought was new at the first session turns out to have been created out of and to be a continuation of another program; only the name has been changed to protect the guilty. You thought you were dealing with only one primary decision maker at the outset, and suddenly you have stakeholders coming out your ears, or vice versa. With some programs, I've felt like I've been through all 8,000 situations in the first month of design negotiations.

Now, just in case 8,000 situations to analyze, be sensitive to, and design evaluations for doesn't seem challenging enough, add two more points to each dimension—a point between each endpoint and the midpoint. Now, combinations of the five points on all 20 dimensions yield 3,200,000 potentially different situations. Perhaps such complexity helps explain why the slogan that won the hearts of evaluators in attendance at the pioneering 1978 Evaluation Network conference in Aspen, Colorado, was the lament,

Evaluators do IT under difficult circumstances.

Of course, one could make the same analysis for virtually any area of decision making. Life is complicated, so what's new? First, let's look at what's old. *The evidence from social and behavioral science is that in other areas of decision making, when faced with complex choices and multiple situations, we fall back on a set of rules and standard operating procedures that predetermine what we will do, that effectively short-circuit situational adaptability.* The evidence is that we are running most of the time on preprogrammed tapes. That has always been the function of rules of thumb and scientific paradigms. Faced with a new situation, the evaluation researcher (unconsciously) turns to old and comfortable patterns. This may help explain why so many evaluators who have rhetorically embraced

the philosophy of situational evaluation find that the approaches in which they are trained and with which they are most comfortable *just happen* to be particularly appropriate in each new evaluation situation they confront—time after time after time. Sociologists just happen to find doing a survey appropriate. Economists just happen to feel the situation needs cost-benefit analysis. A psychologist studies the situation and decides that—surprise!—pre- and posttesting with an experimental design would be appropriate. And so it goes. This is like a mouse "choosing" to eat cheese or a "bear" making a decision to "prefer" honey.

The point of this analysis is to raise a fundamental question: How can evaluators prepare themselves to deal with a lot of different people and a huge variety of situations? The research on decision making says we can't systematically consider every possible variable, or even 50 variables, or even 20 variables. What we need is a framework for making sense of situations, for telling us what factors deserve priority based on research and desired results. Such a framework, rather than providing narrow, specific prescriptions, should offer questions to force us to think about and analyze the situation. The evaluation standards, fine-tuned through the lens of utilization-focused evaluation, provide such a framework. Exhibit 6.2 presents this framework.

Basically, the *utilization heuristic* for managing situational complexity in utilization-focused evaluation is to *stay focused on use.* For every issue that surfaces in evaluation negotiations, for every design decision, for every budget allocation, and for every choice among alternatives, keep asking, "How will this affect use in this situation?"

Utilization-focused evaluation is a problem-solving approach that calls for creative

EXHIBIT 6.1

Examples of Situational Factors in Evaluation That Can Affect Users' Participation and Use

One primary decision maker	1. *Number of stakeholders to be dealt with*	Large number
Formative purpose (improvement)	2. *Purpose of the evaluation*	Summative purpose (funding decision)
New program	3. *History of the program*	Long history
Enthusiasm	4. *Staff attitude toward evaluation*	Resistance
Knows virtually nothing	5. *Staff knowledge about evaluation*	Highly knowledgeable
Cooperative	6. *Program interaction patterns (administration-staff, staff-staff, staff-client)*	Conflict laden
First time ever	7. *Program's prior evaluation experience*	Seemingly endless experience
High	8. *Staff and participants education levels*	Low
Homogeneous groups	9. *Staff and/or participants' characteristics (pick any 10 you want)*	Heterogeneous groups
One site	10. *Program location*	Multiple sites

No money to speak of	11. *Resources available for evaluation*	Substantial funding
One funding source	12. *Number of sources of program funding*	Multiple funding sources
Simple and singular	13. *Nature of the program treatment*	Complex and multidimensional
Highly standardized and routine	14. *Standardization of treatment*	Highly individualized and nonroutine
Horizontal, little hierarchy, little stratification	15. *Program organizational decision-making structure*	Hierarchical, long chain of command, stratified
Well articulated, specifically defined	16. *Clarity about evaluation purpose and function*	Ambiguous, broadly defined
Operating information system	17. *Existing data on program*	No existing data
External	18. *Evaluator(s)' relationship to the program*	Internal
Voluntary, self-initiated	19. *Impetus for the evaluation*	Required, forced on program
Long timeline, open	20. *Time available for the evaluation*	Short timeline, fixed deadline

EXHIBIT 6.2

Framework for Utilization-Focused Situational Analysis

Joint Committee Standard: High-Quality Evaluation	Utilization-Focused Questions for Situation Analysis: Intended Use by Intended Users
1. *Utility:* Ensure that an evaluation will serve the information needs of intended users.	Who are the primary intended users for this evaluation? (personal factor) What are the intended uses for this evaluation: uses of findings? Uses of evaluation processes?
2. *Feasibility:* Ensure that an evaluation will be realistic, prudent, diplomatic, and frugal.	What political considerations will affect use? (power issues) What resources are available for the evaluation? What timelines must be met to ensure the evaluation is useful?
3. *Propriety:* Ensure that an evaluation will be conducted legally, ethically, and with due regard for the welfare of those involved in the evaluation, as well as those affected by its results.	Given the focus on intended use by intended users, what specific ethical issues must be kept before the intended users? How are diverse interests taken into account, including the interests of those intended to benefit from the program, those with less power, and the general public interest? (fairness issues)
4. *Accuracy:* Ensure that an evaluation will reveal and convey technically adequate information about the features that determine worth or merit of the program being evaluated.	What technical and methodological issues must be dealt with to make the evaluation credible, informative, meaningful, balanced, and accurate? What are the methodological options that will enhance use?

adaptation to changed and changing conditions. Creative problem-solving approaches focus on what works and what makes sense in the situation. Lawrence Lynn's (1980a) ideal policy analyst bears a striking resemblance to my ideal of a creative and responsive utilization-focused evaluator.

Individuals really do have to be interdisciplinary; they have to be highly catholic in their taste for intellectual concepts and ideas and tools. I do not think we are talking so much about acquiring a specific kind of knowledge or a specialist's knowledge in order to deal with environmental issues or energy issues. One does not have to know what a petroleum engineer knows, or what an air quality engineer knows, or what a chemist knows. Rather, *one simply has to be able to ask questions of many disciplines and many professions and know how to use the information.* And what that says is, I think, *one has to be intellectually quite versatile* [italics added].

It is not enough to be an economist . . . , an operations research specialist, [or] statistician. One has to be a little bit of all of those things. One has to have an intuitive grasp of an awful lot of different intellectual approaches, different intellectual disciplines or traditions so that one can range widely in doing one's job of crafting a good analysis, so that you are not stuck with just the tools you know. I think, then, the implication is versatility and an intuitive grasp of a fairly wide range of different kinds of skills and approaches. (P. 88)

As the professional practice of evaluation has become increasingly diverse, the potential roles and relationships have multiplied. Menu 6.1 offers a range of dimensions to consider in defining the evaluator's relationship to intended users. Menu 6.2 presents options that can be considered in negotiations with intended users. The purpose of these menus is to elaborate the multiple roles now available to evaluators and the kind of strategic, contingency thinking involved in making role decisions.

Being Active-Reactive-Interactive-Adaptive

Versatility, flexibility, creativity, and responsiveness underpin utilization-focused evaluation design negotiations. In the title of this chapter, I used the phrase *active-reactive-interactive-adaptive* to suggest the nature of the consultative interactions that go on between evaluators and intended users. The phrase is meant to be both descriptive and prescriptive. It describes how real-world decision making actually unfolds—act, react, interact, and adapt. Yet it is prescriptive in alerting evaluators to consciously and deliberately act, react, interact, and adapt to increase their effectiveness in working with intended users.

Utilization-focused evaluators are, first of all, active in deliberately and calculatedly identifying intended users and focusing useful questions. They are reactive in listening to intended users and responding to what they learn about the particular situation in which the evaluation unfolds. They are adaptive in altering evaluation questions and designs in light of their increased understanding of the situation and changing conditions. Active-reactive-interactive-adaptive evaluators don't impose cookbook designs. They don't do the same thing time after time. They are genuinely immersed in the challenges of each new setting and authentically responsive to the intended users of each new evaluation.

It is the paradox of decision making that effective action is born of reaction. Only when organizations and people take in information from the environment and react to changing conditions can they act on that same environment to reduce uncertainty and increase discretionary flexibility. The same is true for the individual decision maker or for a problem-solving group. Action emerges through reaction and interaction and leads to adaptation. The imagery is familiar: thesis-antithesis-synthesis; stimulus-response-change. Exhibit 6.3 depicts this adaptive cycle.

The strategic approach of adaptive management offers parallel understandings (Wysocki and McGary 2003; Dawid et al. 2002). In a rapidly changing environment, quick adaptation is one of the crucial tasks for modern management and ongoing situation analysis and responsiveness are key to successfully coping with dynamic situations. Adaptive management consultants advise observing a system for a while to determine its natural tendencies before intervening. They may even try out some things on a small scale to learn how the system reacts. The focus is on learning

MENU 6.1

Dimensions Affecting Evaluator and User Engagement

1. Relationship with primary intended users

Distant from/noninteractive   Close to/highly interactive

2. Control of the evaluation process

Evaluator directed and controlled; evaluator as primary decision maker

Directed by primary intended users; evaluator consults

3. Scope of intended user involvement

Very narrow; primarily as audience for findings

Involved in some parts (usually focus but not methods or analysis)

Involved in all aspects of the evaluation from start to finish

4. Number of primary intended users and/or stakeholders—engaged

None   One   A few   Many   All constituencies represented

5. Variety of primary intended users engaged

Homogeneous   Heterogeneous

Dimensions of heterogeneity:

(a) Position in program (funders, board executives, staff, participants, community members, media, onlookers)
(b) Background variables: cultural/racial/ethnic/gender/social class
(c) Regional: geographically near or far
(d) Evaluation: sophistication and experience
(e) Ideology (political perspective/activism)

6. Timeline for the evaluation

Tight deadline; little time for processing with users

Long developmental timeline; time for processing with users

EXHIBIT 6.3

Working with Primary Intended Users: Adaptive Cycle

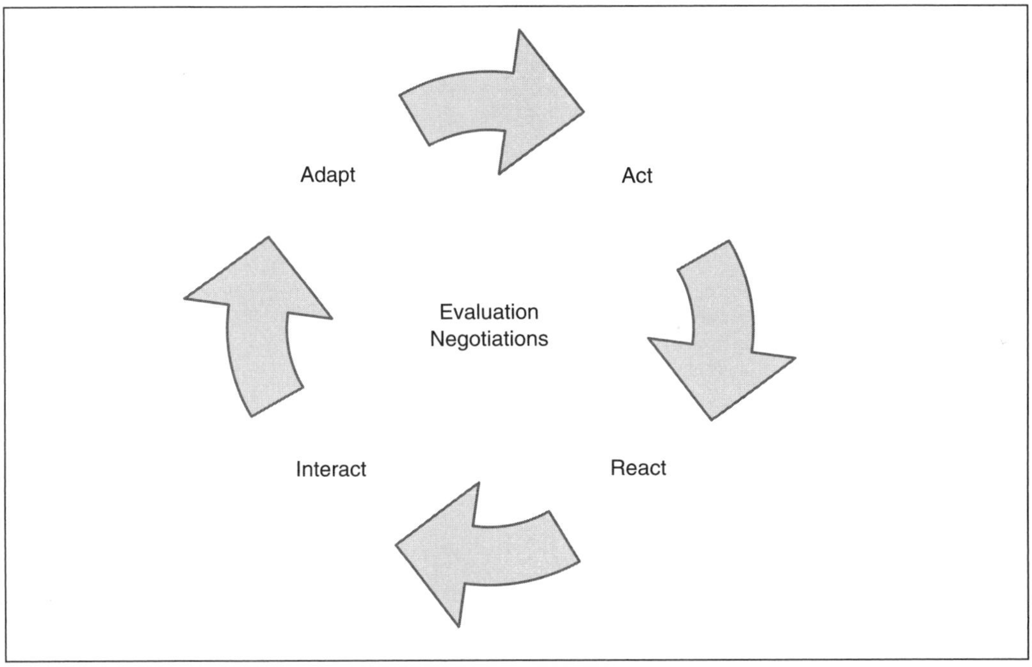

Adapt

Act

Evaluation
Negotiations

Interact

React

through interaction, not just standing outside the system and observing it. In tracking strategies and their implementation, it becomes critical to follow emergent "streams of actions" rather than looking for discrete and formal decisions (Mintzberg 2007:2).

This active-reactive-interactive-adaptive stance characterizes all phases of evaluator-user interactions, from initially identifying primary intended users to focusing relevant questions, choosing methods, and analyzing results. All phases involve collaborative processes of action-reaction-interaction-adaptation as evaluators and intended users consider their options. The menu of choices includes a broad range of design options, various methods, and diverse reporting possibilities—evaluation ingredients from bland to spicy. Throughout the remainder of this book, we'll be looking at those options. The point of this chapter is to lay the foundation for the utilization-focused evaluator to be prepared to facilitate evaluation negotiations under varying circumstances. Having emphasized the desirability of situational responsiveness, let's look at some of the challenging situations evaluators can find themselves facing.

MENU 6.2

Matching Primary Users, Evaluation Purposes, and Evaluator Roles

Most Likely Primary Users	Primary Evaluator Roles	Dominant Style of Evaluator	Most Likely Evaluation Purpose	Primary Evaluator Characteristics Affecting Use
1. Funders Officials Decision makers	Judge	Authoritative	Summative determination of overall merit or worth	Perceived independence Methodological expertise Substantive expertise Perceived neutrality
2. Funders Policymakers Board members	Auditor Inspector Investigator	Independent	Accountability Compliance Adherence to rules	Independence Perceived toughness Detail oriented Thoroughness
3. Academics Planners Program designers Policy specialists	Researcher	Knowledgeable	Generate generalizable knowledge; truth	Methodological expertise Academic credentials Scholarly status Peer review support
4. Program staff Program executives and administrators Participants	Consultant for program improvement	Interactive Perceptive Insightful	Program improvement	Perceived understanding of program Rapport Insightfulness
5. Diverse stakeholders	Evaluation facilitator	Available Balanced Empathic	Facilitate judgments and recommendations by nonevaluators	Interpersonal skills Group facilitation skills Evaluator knowledge Trust Consensus-building skills
6. Program design team	Team member with evaluation perspective	Participatory Questioning Challenging	Program development	Contribution to team Insightfulness Ability to communicate evaluation perspective Flexibility Analytical leadership

Matching Primary Users, Evaluation Purposes, and Evaluator Roles

Most Likely Primary Users	*Primary Evaluator Roles*	*Dominant Style of Evaluator*	*Most Likely Evaluation Purpose*	*Primary Evaluator Characteristics Affecting Use*
7. Program staff and participants	Collaborator	Involved Supportive Encouraging	Action research and evaluation on groups' own issues; participatory evaluation	Accepting of others Mutual respect Communication skills Enthusiasm Perceived genuineness of collaborative approach
8. Program participants/ community members	Empowerment facilitator	Resource person	Participatory self-determination; pursuit of political agenda	Mutual respect Participation Engagement Enabling skills Political savvy
9. Ideological adherents	Supporter of cause	Coleader Committed	Social justice	Engagement Commitment Political expertise Knowledge of "the system" Integrity Values
10. Future evaluation planners and users	Synthesizer Meta-evaluator Cluster leader	Analytical	Synthesize findings from multiple evaluations Judge quality of evaluations	Professionalism Analytical insightfulness Conceptual brilliance Integrity Adherence to standards

Learning to Be Situationally Responsive

To be situationally responsive, one must understand the situation. Exhibit 6.4 provides some fundamental questions to guide a situation analysis.

A generic situation analysis based on fundamental questions (Exhibit 6.4) should

elucidate the special conditions that will affect a particular evaluation design and its utility. This chapter opened by recounting the story of the race between the turtle and the hare in which the hare lost because he was unable to adapt to a sudden thunderstorm. Evaluation thunderstorms include highly charged political debates, public controversies about programs, thunderous

EXHIBIT 6.4
Beginning Situation Analysis

Understand the program

What is the program's history? What situation gave rise to the program?

What are the program's primary goals? To what extent are these goals clear, specific, and measurable?

What are the strategies for attaining these goals?

Who are the intended beneficiaries of the program's intervention? What are their characteristics?

What are staff characteristics?

What's the program's budget?

For existing programs, how has the program changed over time? What led to those changes?

Identify primary stakeholders and their interests

Where do stakeholders' interests align?

Where do their interests conflict?

What's the political context for the evaluation?

Who will be the primary intended users of the evaluation?

Evaluation history

What prior experiences, if any, has the program had with evaluation?

What are current monitoring and evaluation approaches, if any? How are monitoring and evaluation data currently used, if at all? What factors affect current uses?

What capacities does the program have to engage in evaluation (staff skills, budget for evaluation, information systems, a culture of inquiry, data management, and interpretation capacity)?

Decision and action context

What's the primary intended purpose of the evaluation?

What decisions, if any, is the program facing? What are the timelines for any such decisions?

What uncertainties does the program face? Externally? Internally?

conflicts among divergent stakeholders, and attacks on the evaluator's integrity or the evaluation's credibility. Menu 6.3 presents several examples of situations that pose special challenges to evaluation use and the special evaluator skills needed to manage those situations.

Handling these diverse situations involves much more than technical and methodological knowledge. Evaluation practice needs to be grounded in what Tom Schwandt calls "practical knowledge."

> This kind of knowledge is shown or demonstrated via . . . one's ability to be present in and handle a situation, and one's capacity to exercise judgment of when to apply, or not apply, a particular kind of understanding of a situation . . . . The fundamental distinction between instrumental reason as the hallmark of technical knowledge and judgment as the defining characteristic of practical knowledge is instinctively recognizable to many practitioners . . . "good" practice depends in a significant way on the experiential, existential knowledge we speak of as perceptivity, insightfulness, and deliberative judgment. (Schwandt 2008:31, 37)

Multiple Evaluator Roles and Individual Style

The challenging situations highlighted in Menu 6.3 call attention to special evaluator skills that go beyond methodological and technical expertise. Evaluator roles vary: collaborator, trainer, group facilitator, technician, politician, organizational analyst, internal colleague, external expert, methodologist, information broker, communicator, change agent, diplomat, problem solver, and creative consultant. Some of these roles may be combined and the roles of evaluation and program development

may be integrated (Symonette 2007). The roles played by an evaluator in any given situation will depend on the evaluation's purpose, the unique constellation of conditions with which the evaluator is faced, *and the evaluator's own personal knowledge, skills, style, values, and ethics.*

> **Reflection on Evaluator Roles**
>
> Stephen Morabito (2002) has described an educational evaluation in which the evaluator at various times, in addition to being the evaluator, played the roles of educator (about evaluation), organizational development consultant, group facilitator, and counselor. He concluded, "An evaluator should explore his/her own knowledge, skills, abilities, and personal characteristics to develop and implement appropriate roles that have the potential to foster an enhanced evaluation process influence. It is unlikely that an evaluator could succeed in the implementation of an evaluation by selecting one role" (p. 328).

The mandate to be active-reactive-interactive-adaptive in role playing provokes protest from those evaluators and intended users who advocate only one narrow role, namely, that the evaluator renders judgment about merit or worth— *nothing else* (Stufflebeam 1994; Scriven 1991a). Clearly, I have a more expansive view of an evaluator's role possibilities and responsibilities. Keeping in mind that the idea of multiple evaluator roles is controversial, let's turn to look at what the evaluator brings to the utilization-focused negotiating table.

The evaluator as a person in his or her own right is a key part of the situational mix. Each evaluation will be unique in part

MENU 6.3

Examples of Situations That Pose Special Challenges to Evaluation Use and the Evaluator's Role

Situation	Challenge	Special Evaluator Skills Needed
1. Highly controversial issue	Facilitating different points of view	Conflict resolution skills
2. Highly visible program	Dealing with publicity about the program; reporting findings in a media-circus atmosphere	Public presentation skills Graphics skills Media-handling skills
3. Highly volatile program environment	Rapid change in context, issues, and focus	Tolerance for ambiguity Being a "quick study" Rapid responsiveness Flexibility
4. Cross-cultural or international	Including different perspectives, values Being aware of cultural blinders and biases	Cross-culture sensitivity Skills in understanding and incorporating different perspectives
5. Team effort	Managing people	Identifying and using individual skills of team members; team-building skills
6. Evaluation attacked	Preserving credibility	Calm; staying focused on evidence and conclusions
7. Corrupt program	Resolving ethical issues/upholding standards	Integrity Clear ethical sense Honesty

because individual evaluators are unique. Evaluators bring to the negotiating table their own style, personal history, and professional experience. All the techniques and ideas presented in this book must be adapted to the style of the individuals using them.

Cousins, Donohue, and Bloom (1996) surveyed North American evaluators to find out what variables correlated with a collaborative style of practice. Organizational affiliation, gender, and primary job

responsibility did not differentiate practice and opinion response. Canadian evaluators reported greater depth of stakeholder involvement than Americans. Most telling, however, were years and depth of experience with collaborative approaches. More experienced evaluators expected and attained more use of their evaluations, and reported a greater sense of satisfaction from the collaborative process and greater impacts of the resulting evaluations. In essence, evaluators get better at the active-reactive-adaptive process the more they experience it; and the more they use it, the more they like it and the more impact they believe it has.

Being active-reactive-interactive-adaptive explicitly recognizes the importance of the individual evaluator's experience, orientation, and contribution by placing the mandate to be active first in this dynamic framework. Situational responsiveness does not mean rolling over and playing dead (or passive) in the face of stakeholder interests or perceived needs. Just as the evaluator in utilization-focused evaluation does not unilaterally impose a focus and set of methods on a program, so too, the stakeholders are not set up to impose their initial predilections unilaterally or dogmatically. Arriving at the final evaluation design is a negotiated process that allows the values and capabilities of the evaluator to intermingle with those of intended users.

The utilization-focused evaluator, in being active-reactive-interactive-adaptive, is one among many at the negotiating table. At times there may be discord in the negotiating process; at other times harmony. Whatever the sounds, and whatever the themes, the utilization-focused evaluator does not sing alone. He or she is part of a choir made up of primary intended users. There are solo parts, to be sure, but the climatic theme song of utilization-focused evaluation is not Frank Sinatra's "I Did It My Way." Rather, it's the full chorus joining in a unique, situationally specific rendition of "We Did It Our Way."

User Responsiveness and Technical Quality

User responsiveness should not mean a sacrifice of technical quality. Later chapters will discuss in detail the utilization-focused approach to ensuring technical quality.

A beginning point is to recognize that standards of technical quality vary for different users and varying situations. The issue is not meeting some absolute research standard of technical quality but, rather, making sure that methods and measures are *appropriate* to the validity and credibility needs of a particular evaluation purpose and specific intended users.

Jennifer Greene (1990) examined in depth the debate about technical quality versus user responsiveness. She found general agreement that both are important but disagreement about the relative priority of each. She concluded that the debate is really about how much to recognize and deal with evaluation's political inherency:

> Evaluators should recognize that tension and conflict in evaluation practice are virtually inevitable, that the demands imposed by most if not all definitions of responsiveness and technical quality (not to mention feasibility and propriety) will characteristically reflect the competing politics and values of the setting. (P. 273)

She then recommended that evaluators "explicate the politics and values" that undergird decisions about purpose, audience, design, and methods. Her recommendation is consistent with utilization-focused evaluation.

Variations in technical difficulty require contingency thinking in evaluation. Technical decisions cannot be made in isolation from other factors that affect an evaluation design and, ultimately, utility. Bryson and Cullen (1984) conducted research on evaluation decision making through simulations in which participants were asked to design an evaluation process to achieve a specific goal in a specific context. Participants were faced with eight different evaluation situations that varied in whether or not a formative or summative evaluation was to be undertaken, whether the situation was easy or difficult politically, and whether it was easy or difficult technically. Technical difficulty was presented as the degree to which accepted methods and valid measures were available; in half the scenarios, technical difficulty was low while in half the situations there was major disagreement about appropriate methods and measures. Eight panels of 10 people each participated in the simulated evaluation exercises. Panel participants were members of the faculty and administration or advanced doctoral students from several major colleges of education. Each participant was at least on occasion an evaluator or user of evaluations, and all were familiar with the educational issues involved in the evaluation scenario. The scenarios included realistic budget and time constraints.

The simulation revealed contingent thinking in which participants changed their strategies and tactics as the evaluation situation changed. Panelists tried to assure that technical concerns were thoroughly addressed but did so taking into account political difficulties and whether the purpose of evaluation was formative or summative. Bryson and Cullen (1984) concluded their analysis with comments on the relationship between contingency thinking and rationality.

> The role of "rationality" in the processes designed by participants deserves special attention. The processes are not strictly rational, if by that one means they are focused on technical matters and free of politics and competing values. They are rational, however, in a broader sense. Besides attending to technical concerns, participants were politically savvy and emphasized organizational learning. The implication is that in most situations evaluations aren't "planned" so much as negotiated, processed, politicked, hassled, and haggled in a structured, goal-oriented fashion. (P. 287)

Respect for Intended Users

One central value that should undergird the evaluator's active-reactive-interactive-adaptive role is respect for all those with a stake in a program or evaluation. In their classic article on evaluation use, Davis and Salasin (1975) asserted that evaluators were involved inevitably in facilitating change and that "any change model should . . . generally *accommodate* rather than *manipulate* the view of the persons involved" (p. 652). Respectful utilization-focused evaluators do not use their expertise to intimidate or manipulate intended users. Egon Guba (1977) has described in powerful language an archetype that is the antithesis of the utilization-focused evaluator:

> It is my experience that evaluators sometimes adopt a very supercilious attitude with respect to their clients; their presumptuousness and arrogance are sometimes overwhelming. We treat the client as a "childlike" person who needs to be taken in hand; as an ignoramus who cannot possibly understand the tactics and strategies that we will bring to bear; as someone who doesn't appreciate the questions he *ought* to ask until we tell him—and what we tell him often reflects our own biases and interests rather than the problems with which the client is actually beset. The phrase "Ugly American" has emerged in international settings to describe the person who enters into a new culture, immediately knows what is wrong with it, and proceeds to foist his own solutions onto the locals. In some ways I have come to think of evaluators as "Ugly Americans." And if what we are looking for are ways to manipulate clients so that they will fall in with our wishes and cease to resist our blandishments, I for one will have none of it. (P. 1)

For others who "will have none of it," there is the alternative of undertaking a utilization-focused evaluation process based on mutual respect between evaluators and intended users.

Internal and External Evaluators

One of the most fundamental issues in considering the role of the evaluator is the location of the evaluator inside or outside the program and organization being evaluated, what has sometimes been called the "in-house" versus "outhouse" issue. The early evaluation literature was aimed primarily at external evaluators, typically researchers who conducted evaluations under contract to funders. External evaluators come from universities, consulting firms, and research organizations or work as independent consultants. The defining characteristic of external evaluators is that they have no long-term, ongoing position within the program or organization being evaluated. They are therefore not subordinated to someone in the organization and not directly dependent on the organization for their job and career.

External evaluators are valuable precisely because they are outside the organization. It is typically assumed that their external status permits them to be more independent, objective, and credible than internal evaluators. Internal evaluations are suspect because, it is presumed, they can be manipulated more easily by administrators to justify decisions or pressured to present positive findings for public relations purposes. Of course, external evaluators who want future evaluation contracts are also subject to pressure to produce positive findings. In addition, external evaluators are also typically more costly, less knowledgeable about the nuances and particulars of the local situation, and less able to follow through to facilitate the implementation of recommendations. When external evaluators complete their contract, they may take with them a great deal of knowledge and insight that is lost to the program. That knowledge stays "in-house" with internal evaluators. External evaluators have also been known to cause difficulties in a program through insensitivity to organizational relationships and norms, one of the reasons the work of external evaluators is sometimes called "outhouse" work.

Internal Evaluation

One of the major trends in evaluation during the 1980s was a transition from external to internal evaluation, with Canadian Arnold Love (2005, 1991, 1983) documenting and contributing to the development of internal evaluation. At the beginning of the 1970s, evaluation was just emerging as a profession. There were fewer distinct evaluation units within government bureaus, human service agencies, and private sector organizations than there are now. School districts had research and evaluation units, but even they contracted out much of the evaluation work mandated by the landmark 1965 Elementary and Secondary Education Act in the United States. As evaluation became more pervasive in the 1970s, as the mandate for evaluation was added to more and more legislation, and as training for evaluators became more available and widespread, internal evaluation units became more common. Studies of internal evaluation approaches emerged (Winberg 1991; Lyon 1989; Huberty 1988; Kennedy 1983). Now, most federal, state, and local agencies have internal evaluation units to fulfill accountability mandates. International organizations also have internal evaluation divisions with comprehensive guidelines (e.g., International Organization for Migration [IOM] 2006; Organisation for Economic Co-operation and Development [OECD] 2006; World Food Programme [WFP] 2006; International Fund for Agricultural Development [IFAD] 2002). It has become clear that internal evaluators can produce evaluations of high quality and high impact while still performing useful service to administrators if they work diligently to establish an image of an independent but active voice in the organizational structure and take a pragmatic approach to helping solve management problems (Sonnichsen 2000, 1987). In recent years, ongoing performance monitoring has become a major activity of internal evaluation systems (Mohan et al. 2007; Rist and Stame 2006; Poister 2004) and internal evaluation units support both accountability and learning (Wholey, Hatry, and Newcomer 2004; Leeuw, Rist, and Sonnichsen 1999).

Over the years, I have had extensive contact with internal evaluators through training and consulting, working closely with several of them to design internal monitoring and evaluation systems. I interviewed 10 internal evaluators who I knew used a utilization-focused approach. Their comments about how they have applied utilization-focused principles offer insights into the world of the internal evaluator and illuminate research findings about effective approaches to internal evaluation.

Themes From Internal Evaluators

1. *Actively involving stakeholders within the organization can be difficult* because evaluation is often perceived by both superiors and subordinates as the job of the evaluator. The internal evaluator is typically expected to *do* evaluations, not

---

Advice from a Seasoned Internal Evaluator

Stan Capela, an internal evaluator with 28 years in human services and a leader in the American Evaluation Association, offers this advice on making internal evaluations useful to people in the organization.

I have found that talking their language helps. When you explain evaluation use, give examples that are real to the people you are trying to communicate with. You have to show how the evaluation will help them. Basically, individuals want to know just a few things. What's the problem? What caused the problem? How can you help them solve the problem?

One key is spending time with people and asking them what they need to know. Then find the best source of information to help them. But you have to know what they want to know and how they want you to present the information to them. Then present what you find in a way that gets the point across to the people who need the information. When providing findings, the report should be short and to the point. If you can, present a picture so that when a person looks at it, their eyes go directly to the information they are looking for.

Always strive to show how evaluation is there to help them and not there to expose them.

When people view evaluation as punitive, they go into their CYA mode and nothing gets accomplished.

One last point: You need to help people understand that evaluation does not solve management problems. Some managers try to use evaluation as a way to fire someone. These managers try to make the evaluator the bad guy instead of dealing with the management problem directly themselves. So, as an internal evaluator, my mantra is always: If it's a management problem, you don't need evaluation. Evaluation will only exacerbate the problem.

Stan Capela
Senior Director, Quality Improvement
HeartShare Human Services of New York

facilitate an evaluation process involving others. Internal evaluators who have had success involving others have had to work hard at finding special incentives to attract participation in the evaluation process. One internal evaluator commented,

> My director told me he doesn't want to spend time thinking about evaluations. That's why he hired me. He wants me to "anticipate his information needs." I've had to find ways to talk with him about his interests and information needs without explicitly telling him he's helping me focus the evaluation. I guess you could say I kind of involve him without his really knowing he's involved.

2. *Internal evaluators are often asked by superiors for public relations information rather than evaluation.* The internal evaluator may be told, "I want a report for the legislature proving our program is effective." It takes clear conviction, subtle diplomacy, and an astute understanding of how to help superiors appreciate evaluation to keep internal evaluation responsibilities from degenerating into public relations. One mechanism used by several internal evaluators to increase support for real evaluation rather than public relations is establishing an evaluation advisory committee, *including influential people from outside the organization*, to provide independent checks on the integrity of internal evaluations.

3. *Internal evaluators get asked to do lots of little data-gathering and report-writing tasks* that are quite time-consuming but too minor to be considered meaningful evaluation. For example, if someone in the agency wants a quick review of what other states are doing about some problem, the internal evaluator is an easy target for the task. Such assignments can become so pervasive that it's difficult to have time for longer-term, more meaningful evaluation efforts.

4. *Internal evaluators are often excluded from major decisions* or so far removed from critical information networks that they don't know about new initiatives or developments in time to build in an evaluation perspective up front. One internal evaluator explained,

> We have separate people doing planning and evaluation. I'm not included in the planning process and usually don't even see the plan until it's approved. Then they expect me to add on an evaluation. It's a real bitch to take a plan done without any thought of evaluation and add an evaluation without screwing up or changing the plan. They think evaluation is something you do at the end rather than think about from the start. It's damn hard to break through these perceptions. Besides, I don't want to do the planners' job, and they don't want to do my job, but we've got to find better ways of making the whole thing work together. That's my frustration. . . . . It takes me constantly bugging them, and sometimes they think I'm encroaching on their turf. Some days I think, "Who needs the hassle?" even though I know it's not as useful just to tack on the evaluation at the end.

5. *Getting evaluation used takes a lot of follow-through.* One internal evaluator explained that her job was defined as data gathering and report writing without consideration of following up to see if report recommendations were adopted. That's not part of her job description, and it takes time and some authority. She commented,

> How do I get managers to use a report if my job is just to write the report? But they're above me. I don't have the authority to ask them in six months what they've done. I wrote a follow-up memo once reminding managers about recommendations in an evaluation and some of them didn't like it at all, although a couple of the good ones said they were glad I reminded them.

Another internal evaluator told me he had learned how to follow up informally. He has 7 years' experience as an internal human services evaluator. He said,

At first I just wrote a report and figured my job was done. Now, I tell them when we review the initial report that I'll check back in a few months to see how things are going. I find I have to keep pushing, keep reminding, or they get busy and just file the report. We're gradually getting some understanding that our job should include some follow-up. Mostly it's on a few things that we decide are really important. You can't do it all.

What's in a Name?

Part of defining the role of an internal evaluation unit is labeling it in a meaningful way. Consider this reflection from internal school district evaluator Nancy Law whose office was renamed from Research and Evaluation Department to Accountability Department.

This title change has become meaningful for me personally. It was easy to adopt the name, but harder to live up to it. . . . Now, I am learning that I am the one accountable—that my job doesn't end when the report is finished and presented. My role continues as I work with others outside research to create changes that I have recommended. Oh, yes, we still perform the types of research/evaluation tasks done previously, but there is a greater task still to be done—that of convincing those who need to make changes to move ahead! Put simply, when we took a different name, we became something different and better (Law 1996:1).

Internal Role Definitions

The themes from internal evaluators indicate the importance of carefully defining the job to include attention to use. When and if the internal evaluation job is defined primarily as writing a report and filling out routine reporting forms, the ability of the evaluator to influence use is quite limited. When and if the internal evaluator is organizationally separated from managers and planners, it is difficult to establish collaborative arrangements that facilitate use. Thus, a utilization-focused approach to internal evaluation will often require a redefinition of the position to include responsibility for working with intended users to develop strategies for acting on findings.

In research on the differences between internal and external evaluators with regard to communicating and reporting, Torres, Preskill, and Piontek (1997) found that internal evaluators less frequently engaged in many formal practices commonly expected to facilitate use—namely, developing evaluation and reporting plans, writing executive summaries, making formal verbal presentations, writing interim reports, and holding planned personal discussions. Internal evaluators . . . also cited lack of planning for communicating and reporting as an impediment to success. (P. 120)

One of the most effective internal evaluation units I've encountered was in the U.S. Federal Bureau of Investigation (FBI). This unit reported directly to the bureau's deputy director. The evaluation unit director had direct access to the director of the FBI in both problem identification and discussion of findings. The purpose of the unit was program improvement. Reports were written *only* for internal use; there was no public relations use of reports because public relations was the function of a different unit. The internal evaluation staff was drawn from experienced FBI agents. They thus had high credibility with agents in the field. They also had the status and authority of the director's office behind them. The evaluation unit had an operations handbook that clearly delineated responsibilities and procedures. Evaluation proposals and designs were planned and reviewed with intended users. Multiple methods were used. Reports were written with use in mind. Six months after the report had been written and reviewed, follow-up was formally undertaken to find out if recommendations had been implemented. The internal evaluators had a strong commitment to improving FBI programs and clear authority to plan, conduct, and report evaluations in ways that would have an impact on the organization, including follow-up to make sure recommendations approved by the director were actually implemented.

Based on his experience directing the FBI's internal evaluation unit, Dick Sonnichsen (1988) formulated what he has called *internal advocacy evaluation* as a style of organizational development:

> Internal evaluators have to view themselves as change agents and participants in policy formulation, migrating from the traditional position of neutrality to an activist role in the organizational decision-making process. The practice of *Advocacy Evaluation* positions internal evaluators to become active participants in developing and implementing organizational improvements. Operating under an advocacy philosophy, evaluation becomes a tool for change and a vehicle for evaluators to influence the organization. (P. 141)

An evaluation advocate is not a cheerleader for the program, but rather a champion of evaluation use in which "advocates work actively in the politics of the organization to get results used" (Caracelli and Preskill 1996).

> The new evaluator is a program advocate— not an advocate in the sense of an ideologue willing to manipulate data and to alter findings to secure next year's funding. The new evaluator is someone who believes in and is interested in helping programs and organizations succeed. At times the program advocate evaluator will play the traditional critic role: challenging basic program assumptions, reporting lackluster performance, or identifying inefficiencies. The difference, however, is that criticism is not the end of performance-oriented evaluation; rather, it is part of a larger process of program and organizational improvement, a process that receives as much of the evaluator's attention and talents as the criticism function. (Bellavita, Wholey, and Abramson 1986:289)

The roles of champion, advocate (Greene 1997), activist (Scriven 2007a), and change agent (Sonnichsen 1994) are just some of the many roles open to internal evaluators. Love (1991) has identified a number of both successful and unsuccessful roles for internal evaluators (see Exhibit 6.5). Carefully defining the role of internal evaluator is a key to effective and credible internal evaluation use.

One increasingly important role is as a resource for infusing evaluative thinking into and throughout the entire organization as discussed in Chapter 5. This means that rather than only or primarily conducting evaluations, the internal evaluator becomes a trainer, a resource to other units, a facilitator of meetings where evaluative thinking is needed, and an evaluator of the organization's progress in learning and applying those learnings to its work. "The key to successful internal consulting in organizations

EXHIBIT 6.5

Successful and Unsuccessful Roles of Internal Evaluators

Successful Roles	Unsuccessful Roles
Management consultant	Spy
Decision support	Hatchet carrier
Management information resource	Fear-inspiring dragon
Systems generalist	Number cruncher
Expert troubleshooter	Organizational conscience
Advocate for/champion of evaluation use	Organizational memory
Systematic planner	Public relations officer

SOURCE: Adapted and expanded from Love (1991:9).

is to develop the image of the evaluation office as an organizational problem-solving asset with a diversity of knowledge and skills to employ in a variety of situations" (Sonnichsen 2000:168). In this role, the internal evaluator plays a leadership role in "mainstreaming" evaluation into the organizational culture and infrastructure (Sanders 2002). The example of the International Development Research Centre's internal evaluation unit, described in Chapter 5, is an exemplar in this regard.

Internal-External Evaluation Combinations

In workshops, I am often asked to compare the relative advantages and disadvantages of internal versus external evaluations. After describing some of the differences along the lines of the preceding discussion, I like to point out that the question is loaded by implying that internal *and* external approaches are mutually exclusive. Actually, there are a good many possible combinations of internal and external evaluations that may be more desirable and more cost-effective than either a purely internal *or* purely external evaluation. Exhibit 6.6 describes some of the points along the internal-external continuum.

Accreditation processes are a good example of an internal-external combination. The internal group collects the data and arranges them so that the external group can come in, inspect the data collected by the internal group, sometimes collect additional information on their own, and pass judgment on the program.

There are many ways in which an evaluation can be set up so that some external group of respected professionals and evaluators guarantees the validity and fairness of the evaluation process while the people

EXHIBIT 6.6

A Continuum of Internal/External Evaluation Relationships

1. *Entirely External.* None of the evaluations of the organization's programs or projects are being completed by internal staff members. No other evaluation activities (e.g., developing program logic models, creating evaluation plans) are performed by staff. When evaluation occurs in the organization, it is in response to funders' demands for accountability and is conducted by external evaluation consultants.

2. *Minimal Ad Hoc Internal Evaluation.* Program staff have conducted the evaluation of only a minority of the organization's programs and projects. Those evaluations were ad hoc, that is, they occurred in response to requests from individual managers or funders. Usually, the focus and questions for these evaluations were set by external stakeholders (e.g., providing required performance indicators to funders, accreditation demands).

3. *Occasional Internal Evaluation.* When staff perform evaluations of programs or projects, they usually focus on questions about outputs and processes (e.g., What services were delivered to which clients?). These internal evaluations are conducted by managers or staff who are temporarily given evaluation responsibilities. Core evaluation activities such as having staff create logic models only occur rarely.

4. *Part-Time Internal Evaluator.* The organization has assigned one staff member to perform evaluation tasks on a part-time basis. This person gets their assignments from the Executive Director (or a similar senior manager). Internal evaluations often focus on whether or not the program or project is doing what both the organization and its funders want it to do (e.g., Is the program meeting the goals stated in the program proposal?).

5. *Full-Time Internal Evaluator.* Evaluations performed by internal staff are fairly common in the organization with at least one staff member assigned to evaluation duties on an ongoing basis. Program managers participate in identifying priority evaluation questions and planning evaluations. These internal evaluations often include questions of program outcome (e.g., How effective was the program? Did clients benefit? To what extent did the program produce its intended outcomes?).

6. *Routine Internal Evaluation.* Evaluation occurs on a regular basis. Several internal staff members have evaluation skills and plan/manage internal evaluations on a regular basis. The organization has policies that require that certain evaluation tasks must occur throughout the organization (e.g., all programs must have a logic model, all programs must collect data on client satisfaction). Results from internal evaluations are routinely reported to managers and staff. These evaluation results are used to inform decisions about the development of the program that was evaluated. Internal evaluations often focus on issues of program costs. Program managers decide which evaluation questions will get asked. The organization has an Evaluation Coordinator or Manager and several staff who have evaluation responsibilities.

7. *Fully Integrated and Highly Valued Internal Evaluation.* Evaluation of all programs and projects is an organizational requirement. An Evaluation Manager leads an internal Evaluation Team. Evaluation staff provide evaluation training and coaching to managers and staff, including how to use findings in their work. Findings are used to improve both individual programs and the entire organization's structures and processes in an ongoing way. Results from internal evaluations are shared with the Board, with partners, and with key stakeholders. Summaries of evaluation findings appear in the newsletter and Annual Report. Evaluation is viewed as central to organizational effectiveness and is an integral part of the organization's culture.

SOURCE: Adapted from Shea and Love (2007).

internal to the program actually collect and/or analyze the evaluation data. The cost savings of such an approach can be substantial while still allowing the evaluation to have basic credibility and legitimacy through the blessing of the external review committee.

I worked for several years with one of the leading chemical dependency treatment centers in the country, the Hazelden Foundation of Minnesota. The foundation has established a rigorous evaluation process that involves data collection at the point of entry into the program and then follow-up questionnaires 6 months, 12 months, and 24 months after leaving the program. Hazelden's own research and evaluation department collects all the data. My responsibility as an external evaluator was to monitor that data collection periodically to make sure that the established procedures were being followed correctly. I then worked with the program decision makers to identify the kind of data analysis that was desirable. They performed the data analysis with their own computer resources. They sent the data to me, and I wrote the annual evaluation report. They participated in analyzing, interpreting, and making judgments about the data, but for purposes of legitimacy and credibility, the actual writing of the final report was done by me.

This internal-external combination is sometimes extended one step further by having still another layer of external professionals and evaluators pass judgment on the quality and accuracy of the evaluation final report through a *meta-evaluation* process—evaluating the evaluation based on the profession's standards and principles. Indeed, the revised standards for evaluation (Joint Committee 1994:A12) prescribe meta-evaluation so that stakeholders have an independent credible review of an evaluation's strengths and weaknesses. Such an effort will be most meaningful and cost-beneficial for large-scale summative evaluations of major policy importance.

When orchestrating an internal-external combination, one danger to watch for is that the external group may impose unmanageable and overwhelming data collection procedures on the internal people. I saw this happen in an internal-external model with a group of school districts in Canada. The external committee recommended the following specifications for conducting a "comprehensive" evaluation at the local school level: data on learning outcomes, staff morale, quality of facilities, curriculum, the school lunch program, the library, parent reactions, the perceptions of local businesspeople, analysis of the school bus system, and on and on. After listening to all the things the external committee thought should be done, the internal folks dubbed it the Internal-External-*Eternal* model of evaluation.

The point is that a variety of internal-external combinations are possible to combine the lower costs of internal data collection with the higher credibility of external review. In working out the details of internal-external combinations, care will need to be taken to achieve an appropriate and mutually rewarding balance based on a collaborative commitment to the standards of utility, feasibility, propriety, and accuracy.

Evaluation as a Leadership Function

Most writings about internal evaluation assume a separate unit or specialized position with responsibility to conduct evaluations. An important new direction in evaluation is to treat evaluation as a leadership function of all managers and program directors in the organization, including, especially, the Executive Director. The person responsible for internal evaluation then plays facilitative, resource, and training functions in support of managers and leaders rather than spending time actually conducting

EXHIBIT 6.7

Four Functions of Results-Oriented, Reality-Testing, Learning-Focused Leadership

- Create and nurture a results-oriented, reality-testing, learning-focused culture.
- Lead in deciding what outcomes to commit to and hold yourselves accountable for.
- Make measurement of outcomes thoughtful, meaningful, and credible.
- Use the results—and model for others serious use of results.

evaluations. The best example of this approach I've worked with and observed up close was the position of Associate Administrator for Performance Measurement and Evaluation in Hennepin County, Minnesota (Minneapolis). The county had no internal evaluation office. Rather, this senior position, as part of the County Executive team, had responsibility to infuse evaluation thinking and systems throughout the county, in every department and program. Every manager in the county received training in how to build outcomes evaluation into ongoing program processes and use data for decision making and budgeting. What made this approach to internal evaluation work, in my judgment, was threefold: (1) Results-oriented evaluation was defined as a leadership function of every county manager, not just a technical reporting function delegated to data nerds; (2) the overall responsibility for evaluation resided at the highest level of the organization, in the executive team, with direct access to the County Board of Commissioners backed up by public commitments to use evaluation for decision making and budgeting; and (3) because of the prior two commitments, a person of great competence and dedication was selected to fill the position of Associate Administrator

for Performance Measurement and Evaluation position, after a national search.

These patterns of effectiveness stand out because so often internal evaluation is delegated to the lowest level in an organization and treated as a clerical or technical function. Indeed, being given an evaluation assignment is often a form of punishment, or a way of giving deadwood staff something meaningless to occupy themselves with. It is clear that for internal evaluators to be useful and credible, they must have high status in the organization and real power to make evaluation meaningful. And even when this occurs, as in the case of Hennepin County, just reviewed, it can be difficult to sustain. After a few years, when the County Executive changed, the Associate Administrator for Performance Measurement and Evaluation was lost in a reorganization, and the system reverted to treating evaluation as a separate support unit and function.

Elevating the status of evaluation to that of a leadership function may require leadership development. Indeed, as an example of reaching primary intended users, I participated in developing a leadership development workshop that focused on evaluative thinking and practice. We didn't promote it as an evaluation workshop because leaders would not come to such a workshop; they would send lower-level technical staff. To reach the leadership level of organizations with the message and promise of evaluation use, we had to promote the effort as leadership development and embed the evaluation training in that framework. Exhibit 6.7 presents the four functions of results-oriented, reality-testing, learning-focused leadership we used for the leadership training workshop. In this framework, evaluation becomes an executive leadership responsibility focused on decision-oriented use rather than a data-collection task focused on routine internal reporting. Evaluation *of* leadership development (Hannum, Martineau, and Reinelt 2007) and evaluation *for* leadership development (a form of process use) intersect in training leaders to think evaluatively and infuse evaluation into their organizational cultures.

Balancing Task and Relationship Demands

One of the most fundamental and oft-replicated findings from early research on group effectiveness is that high-performing groups attend to both task completion and relationship building (Bales 1951; Lewin 1948). In an evaluation context, *the task focus* concerns the primary intended uses of the evaluation and how those uses will be achieved. *The relationship focus* concerns how the evaluator works with and relates to primary intended users to enhance the likelihood of use. Embedded in the utilization-focused evaluation goal of *intended use by intended users* is attention to both tasks and relationships.

Chapter 3 focused on the importance of identifying primary intended users and building a relationship with them. Chapter 4 focused on deciding among

different possible intended uses (the task side of evaluation). Chapter 5, on *process use*, explored how the way the evaluation is conducted (which includes the evaluator's relationship with intended users) affects what is accomplished (the impacts of the evaluation). Situational responsiveness involves ongoing assessment of the balance between task completion and quality of relationship. While internal and external evaluators face some different dynamics in this regard, what they share is a need to analyze the situation they face to determine what kind of relationship and process for conducting the evaluation will support task completion and lead to use.

Some evaluators focus only on getting the evaluation designed, the data collected and analyzed, and the report written. They are entirely task focused and want no part of relationship building. Indeed, they wear their independence as a badge of pride, justifying their inattention to relationships and process as fundamental to their credibility. In this approach to evaluation, independence, neutrality, distance, and credibility are the cornerstones of utility.

At the other end of the continuum are evaluation consultants who make regular interaction with clients a priority and give at least as much attention to relationship building as getting the work done. Such a consultant once told me, "Building a strong relationship with the client is the task." This evaluator viewed trust, in-depth knowledge, shared values, and close connection to the client as the pillars that support utility.

These two evaluators defined the situational challenge differently. For our purposes, these examples raise questions that can only be answered within the context of a particular situation.

- What kind of relationship to specific intended users will enhance use given the purpose of the evaluation?

- How much distance is needed to establish credibility? How much closeness is appropriate to assure relevance and trust?

- How much ongoing interaction with intended users supports mutual understanding and keeping everyone informed? When does regular communication become burdensome and overdone? What constitutes too little communication to maintain an appropriate degree of interest and engagement?

- How does the relationship with intended users change over the course of an evaluation as the tasks change (from design to data collection, to analysis, to reporting, to use of findings)?

- To what extent is it appropriate for an evaluator to have different relationships with different intended users? Some stakeholders are likely to be more interested in both task and process while others are less so. How does an evaluator deal with these variations, by having different relationships with different intended users, without creating conflicts and distrust in the group as a whole?

There can be no standardized, recipe-like answers to these questions. The answers flow from the situational and stakeholders analyses that inform the entire evaluation process. The answer to these questions is, in that sense, to ask them—seriously, thoughtfully, astutely, and pragmatically—and then let what you come to understand guide your engagement. And, of course, you don't just ask these questions once at the beginning. As the evaluation unfolds, it's important to evaluate how well the tasks are getting done (quality of work being completed) and how the relationships are unfolding. Feedback from intended users along the way provides critical guidance about whether more or less interaction and communication are needed to enhance use.

Risk Assessment and Contingency Thinking

Contingency thinking inevitably involves some degree of risk assessment. Designing an evaluation involves some kind of informal cost-benefit analysis in which potential benefits, e.g., using results to improve the program, are considered in relationship to costs, which include financial resources, evaluator and staff time, and opportunity costs (what else could have been done with the money spent on evaluation?).

Introducing the notion of risk into evaluation design and relationship decisions is a way of acknowledging that things seldom turn out exactly the way they are planned. We have many adages to remind us that human endeavors inherently involve risks: "Even the best laid plans . . . ." "Many a slip between cup and lip." And the bumper sticker: "Stuff Happens" (or a more emphatic version that replaces "stuff" with a certain popular four-letter word).

Explicitly introducing risk into conversations and negotiations between evaluators and primary intended users begins by asking the following kinds of questions:

1. What can go wrong in this evaluation?

2. What is the likelihood that it would go wrong?

3. What are the consequences and how bad would they be?

The intent of such front-end risk assessment is *not* to deepen the illusion that one can anticipate and thereby prevent all difficulties. Rather, it is to lay the foundation for contingency thinking as a basis for evaluator-user negotiations and revisions as the evaluation unfolds. Risk analysis should push evaluators and intended users to be prepared for contingencies. Contingency thinking and planning acknowledges the reality that every design will run into execution problems. What distinguishes one evaluation from another is not the absence of problems but the preparation for and ability to solve them. Examining what can go wrong should include thoughtful consideration of what can really be accomplished with available resources.

Risk analysis requires evaluators and stakeholders to become explicit about different scenarios and how they might behave in each. Risk is traditionally defined as the probability of an occurrence multiplied by the severity of the consequences associated with the hazard.

Three Types of Risk

In dialogues with intended users, it can be helpful to break the "what can go wrong?" question into three interdependent categories: idea risk, implementation risk, and evidence risk (Patton, Bare and Bonnet 2004; Bare 2002). Two of these three types of risk—idea risk and implementation risk—derive from classic program risks. The premise here is that the more risky the intervention (either because of idea risk or implementation risk, or both), the more uncertain may be the evaluation situation and therefore the more risk that could be entailed in conducting the evaluation due to those uncertainties. The third type of risk, evidence risk, is a fundamental evaluation issue. However, this is a risk shared by the program and the evaluation because the harder it is to evaluate a program, the more that program may be at risk of losing funding or other support. Exhibit 6.8 compares the three kinds of risk for programs and evaluations.

EXHIBIT 6.8
Risk Assessment

Nature of Risk	Program Risk Assessment	Evaluation Risk Assessment
Idea/design risk	How clear, well tested, and logical is the intervention idea?	How routine is the evaluation design? How accepted and valid are the measurement approaches?
Implementation risk	What are the challenges to implementing the idea?	What are the challenges to implementing the evaluation design?
Evidence risk	How difficult will it be to evaluate the effectiveness of the idea and/or its implementation?	What are the threats to the evaluation's credibility, utility, feasibility, accuracy, and propriety?

The process of risk analysis should reveal instances in which what is at risk is not just wasted money or useless findings but includes the relationship between the evaluator and intended users by failing to converse openly and honestly about actual and potential problems.

What's Worth Knowing

Focusing an evaluation involves figuring out *what's worth knowing*. What's worth knowing depends on the situation, especially the priority information needs of the primary intended users. This chapter has explored how situation analysis helps an evaluator engage in strategic contingency thinking and be active-reactive-interactive-adaptive as a foundation for situational responsiveness and determining what's worth knowing.

Distinguishing informational wheat from chaff requires determining what's important. The challenge of making such a distinction is nicely illustrated by a story about the founder of the Ford Motor Company. A visitor to Ford's factory encountered the famous Henry Ford himself while being given a tour of the factory. Looking at a car being built, Ford told the visitor authoritatively, "There are exactly 4,719 parts in that model." The visitor was subsequently introduced to the engineer who oversaw production and, having been impressed that the president had a grasp of such details, reported what Henry Ford had said. The engineer shrugged, clearly unimpressed, and said, "I don't know if that's true, but I can't think of a more useless piece of information" (Fadiman and Bernard 2000:210).

Figuring out what information will be useful and then delivering that information to the people who can use it is the challenge of utilization-focused evaluation.

Follow-Up Exercises

1. Situation analysis. Identify a program for which you might design an evaluation. Use Exhibit 6.4 to conduct a beginning situation analysis. Use Menu 6.3 to identify any special conditions for the evaluation.

2. Optional evaluator roles. Select three different roles from Menu 6.2. Describe a particular program (see the preceding exercise) and examine how three different evaluator roles would play out in that program situation.

3. Being active-reactive-interactive-adaptive explicitly recognizes the importance of the individual evaluator's experience, orientation, and contribution. Assess your readiness to engage in utilization-focused evaluation. What assets and strengths do you bring to this approach to evaluation? What are your weaknesses? To what extent are your values and philosophy congruent with utilization-focused evaluation? What optional evaluator roles (see Menu 6.2) can you play well? What roles are problematic for you?

4. Write a job description for an internal evaluator. First, describe an organization that you know (or fabricate an organization). Specify the organization's mission, staff size, organizational structure (e.g., different units or program areas), and the challenges the organization is currently facing. Now, write a job description for an internal evaluator in this organization. Include specification of where the internal evaluator will be located, what the evaluation priorities will be, what relationship qualities will be important, and what tasks must get done. Give a rationale for your job description by explaining how the job description is attuned to and appropriate for the organizational situation.

5. Evaluation risk assessment. Identify an example of an innovative program that has been evaluated or that has an evaluation design. Use Exhibit 6.8 to discuss evaluation risks in relation to program risks. Elucidate the relationship between program risks and evaluation risks using a concrete program example.

6. Here is a situation for situational analysis. Your assignment is to elucidate the evaluation relevance of the following story repeated from generation to generation by school children.

A man walking along the street notices another man on the other side with bananas in his ears. He shouts, "Hey, mister, why do you have bananas in your ears?" Receiving no response, he pursues the man, calling again as he approaches, "Pardon me, but why have you got bananas in your ears?" Again there is no response.

He catches up to the man, puts his hand on his shoulder, and says, "Do you realize you have bananas in your ears?"

The gentleman in question stops, looks puzzled, takes the bananas out of his ears, and says, "I'm sorry, what did you ask? I couldn't hear you because I have bananas in my ears."

Now for the situational analysis. Part 1 analysis: How might you use this story with a group of intended users to make a point about the nature of evaluation? What point(s) could the story be used to illustrate (metaphorically)?

Part 2 analysis: What are the implications of the story for evaluation under four different conditions:

a. If the man with the bananas in his ears is a stakeholder and the man in pursuit is an evaluator;

b. if the banana man is an evaluator, and the man in pursuit is a stakeholder;

c. if both are primary stakeholders and the evaluator observes this scene; and

d. if both are evaluators observed by a stakeholder.

7

Focusing on Outcomes

Beyond the Goals Clarification Game

M *ulla Nasrudin was a Sufi guru. A king who enjoyed Nasrudin's company, and also liked to hunt, commanded him to accompany him on a bear hunt. Nasrudin was terrified.*

When Nasrudin returned to his village, someone asked him: "How did the Hunt go?"

"Marvelously!"

"How many bears did you see?"

"None."

"How could it have gone marvelously, then?"

"When you are hunting bears, and you are me, seeing no bears at all is a marvelous experience."

—Shah 1964:61

Evaluation of the Bear Project

If this tale were updated by means of an evaluation report, it might read something like this:

Under the auspices of His Majesty's Ministry of the Interior, Department of Natural Resources, Section on Hunting, Office of Bears, field observers studied the relationship between the number of bears sighted on a hunt and the number of bears shot on a hunt. Having hypothesized a direct, linear relationship between the sighting of bears and killing of bears, data were collected on a recent royal hunting expedition.

The small sample size limits generalizability, but the results support the hypothesis at the 0.001 level of statistical significance. Indeed, the correlation is perfect. The number of bears sighted was zero and the number killed was zero. In no case was a bear killed without first being sighted. We therefore recommend new Royal regulations requiring that bears first be sighted before they are killed.
Respectfully submitted,

—The Incomparable Mulla Nasrudin
Royal Evaluator

BEAR HUNTING

Whose Goals Will Be Evaluated?

Although Nasrudin's evaluation bears (and bares) certain flaws, it shares one major trait with almost all other reports of this genre: It is impossible to tell whether it answers anyone's question. Who decided that the goal evaluated should be the number of bears killed? Perhaps the hunt's purpose was a heightened sensitivity to nature, or a closer relationship between Nasrudin and the king, or reducing Nasrudin's fear of bears, or increasing the king's power over Nasrudin. It may even be possible (likely!) that different participants in the hunt had different goals. Nasrudin perceived a "marvelous" outcome. Other stakeholders, with different goals (e.g., bagging a bear), might have concluded otherwise.

In utilization-focused evaluation, the primary intended users determine whose goals will be evaluated if they decide that evaluating goal attainment will be the focus of the evaluation. There are other ways of focusing an evaluation, as we'll see in the next chapter, but first, let's review the traditional centrality of goal attainment in evaluation.

The Centrality of Goals in Evaluation

Traditionally, evaluation has been synonymous with measuring goal attainment (Morris and Fitz-Gibbon 1978). The basic logic of goals-based evaluation involves, at a minimum, three points of comparison: (1) a starting point, or baseline; (2) a goal or target (the ideal); and (3) the ending point, or actual result. It doesn't get any simpler than that. Exhibit 7.1 depicts this fundamental ideal-actual goals-based logical comparison.

Distinguished evaluation methodologist Peter Rossi (1972) asserted that "a social welfare program (or for that matter any program) which does not have clearly specified goals cannot be evaluated without specifying some measurable goals. This statement is obvious enough to be a truism" (p. 18). In a major review of the evaluation literature in education, Worthen and Sanders (1973) concluded that "if evaluators agree on anything, it is that program objectives written in unambiguous terms are useful information for any evaluation study" (p. 231). Carol Weiss (1972b) observed that

> the traditional formulation of the evaluation question is: To what extent is the program succeeding in reaching its goals?. . . . The goal must be clear so that the evaluator knows what to look for. . . . Thus begins the long, often painful process of getting people to state goals in terms that are *clear*, *specific*, and *measurable*. (Pp. 74–76)

EXHIBIT 7.1

Most Fundamental Goals-Based Logic of Evaluation: Ideal-Actual Comparison

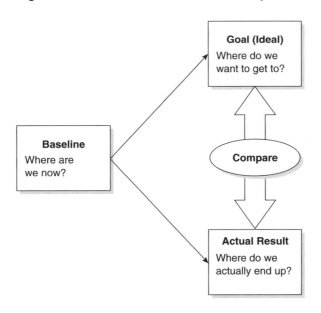

Stating Goals Can Be Tricky

A Youth Center highlighted the following goal in its funding proposal to a philanthropic foundation:

We strive hard for every participant to achieve their goals and dreams by nurturing their self esteem as they grow up. It is our goal that 85% will feel motivated or good about themselves and 15% will not.

As the preceding quotes illustrate, the evaluation literature is replete with serious entreaties on the centrality of program goals, and this solemnity seems to carry over into evaluators' work with program staff. There may be no more deadly way to begin an evaluation effort than assembling program staff to identify and clarify program goals and objectives. If evaluators are second only to tax collectors in the hearts of program staff, I suspect that it is not because staff fear evaluators' judgments about program success but because they hate constant questioning about goals.

The Goals Clarification Game

Evaluators frequently conduct goals clarification meetings as if playing the Twenty Questions party game. Someone thinks of an object in the room and then the players are allowed 20 questions to guess what it is. In the goals clarification game, the evaluator has an object in mind (a clear, specific, and measurable goal). Program staff are the players. The game begins with the staff generating some statement they think is a goal. The evaluator scrutinizes the statement for clarity, specificity, and measurability, usually judging the staff's effort inadequate. This process is repeated in successive tries

until the game ends in one of three ways: (1) The staff gives up (so the evaluator wins and writes the program goals for staff); (2) the evaluator gives up (so the staff gets by with vague, fuzzy, and unmeasurable goals); or (3) in rare cases, the game ends when staff actually stumbles on a statement that reasonably approximates what the evaluator had in mind.

Why do program staff typically hate this game so much?

1. They have played the game hundreds of times, not just for evaluators, but for funders and advisory boards, in writing proposals, and even among themselves.

2. They have learned that when playing the game with an evaluator, the evaluator almost always wins.

3. They come out of the game knowing that they appear fuzzy-minded and inept to the evaluator.

4. It is a boring game.

5. It is an endless game because each new evaluator comes to the game with a different object in mind. (Clarity, specificity, and measurability are not clear, specific, and measurable criteria, so each evaluator can apply a different set of rules in the game.)

Among experienced program staff, evaluators may run into countering strategies like the goals clarification shuffle. Like many dance steps (e.g., the Harlem shuffle, the hustle), this technique has the most grace and style when executed simultaneously by a group. The goals clarification shuffle involves a sudden change in goals and priorities after the evaluator has developed measuring instruments and a research design. The choreography is dazzling. The top-priority program goal is moved two spaces to either the right or left and four spaces backward. Concurrently, all other goals are shuffled with style and subtlety, the only stipulation being that the first goal end up somewhere in the middle, with other goals reordered by new criteria.

The goals clarification shuffle first came into national prominence in 1969 when it was employed as a daring counterthrust to the Westinghouse-Ohio State University Head Start Evaluation. That study evaluated cognitive and affective outcomes of the Head Start Program and concluded that Head Start was largely ineffective (Cicarelli 1971; Westinghouse Learning Corporation 1969). However, as soon as the final report was published, the goals clarification shuffle was executed before enthusiastic Congressional audiences, showing that Head Start's health, nutrition, resource redistribution, cultural, and community goals ought to have been in the spotlight (see Evans 1971:402; Williams and Evans 1969). Thus, despite negative evaluation findings, Congress expanded the Head Start program, and the evaluators were thrown on the defensive. (It was about this same time that serious concerns over nonuse of evaluation findings started to be heard on a national scale.)

Conflicts Over Goals

Not all the goals clarification exercises resemble dances. Often, the more fitting metaphor is competition. Conflict over program goals among different stakeholder groups is common. For example, in criminal justice programs, battles are waged over whether the purpose of a program is punitive (punish criminal offenders for wrongdoing), custodial (keep criminal offenders off the streets), or rehabilitative (return offenders to society after treatment). In education and training programs, conflicts often emerge over whether the priority goal is attitude change or behavior change. In welfare agencies, disagreements can be found over whether the primary purpose is to get clients off welfare or out of poverty, and whether the focus should be long-term change or short-term crisis intervention (Conte 1996). In health settings, staff dissension may emerge over the relative emphasis to be placed on preventive versus curative medical practice. Chemical dependency programs are often enmeshed in controversy over whether the desired outcome is sobriety or responsible use. Even police and fire departments can get caught in controversy about the purpose and actual effects of sirens, with critics arguing that they're more a nuisance than a help (Perlman 1996). Virtually any time a group of people assemble to determine program goals, conflict can emerge, resulting in a lengthy, frustrating, and inconclusive meeting.

For inexperienced evaluators, conflicts among stakeholders can be unnerving. Once, early in my career, a goals clarification session erupted into physical violence between a school board member and the district's internal evaluator. The novice evaluator can lose credibility by joining one side or the other. More experienced evaluators have learned to remain calm

EXHIBIT 7.2

Conceptualizing goals involves identifying a gap between what people have and what they want. This gap or discrepancy can take several forms. Fred Nickols (2003) developed *The Goals Grid* to help people clarify goals. In some cases, people want things they don't have and in others they have things they don't want. This generates two questions: "Do we have it?" and "Do we want it?" The four goal categories then become

1. Achieve (we don't have it and we want it)

2. Preserve (we have it and we want to keep it)

3. Avoid (we don't have it and we don't want it)

4. Eliminate (we have it and we don't want it)

This Goals Grid is a useful tool for thinking about different kinds of program and participant goals and objective.

The Goals Grid

		Do We Want It?	
		Yes	**No**
Do We Have It?	**No**	*1* *Achieve*	*3* *Avoid*
	Yes	*2* *Preserve*	*4* *Eliminate*

SOURCE: Reprinted with permission of Fred Nickols.

and neutral, sometimes suggesting that multiple goals be evaluated, thereby finessing the need for consensus about program priorities.

In some instances, an evaluator may encounter intense fighting over goals and values. A "goals war" usually occurs when two or more strong coalitions are locked in battle to determine which group will control the future direction of some public policy or program. Such conflicts involve highly emotional issues and deeply held values, such as conflicting views on abortion or sex education for teenagers.

Evaluation of school busing programs to achieve racial balance offers an example rich with conflict. By what criteria ought busing programs be evaluated? Changed

racial attitudes? Changed interracial behaviors? Improved student achievement? Degree of parent involvement? Access to educational resources? All are candidates for the honor of primary program goal. Is school busing supposed to achieve desegregation (representative proportions of minority students in all schools) or integration (positive interracial attitudes, cooperation, and interaction)? Many communities, school boards, and school staffs are in open conflict over these issues. Central to the battles fought are basic disagreements about what evaluation criteria to apply.

Classic Goals Conflicts

Prisons:	rehabilitation versus punishment
Chemical dependency:	sobriety versus responsible drinking
Homelessness:	adequate shelters versus low-income housing
Sex education:	abstinence versus responsible safe sex
Affirmative action:	equal opportunity versus equal results
Welfare reform:	off welfare versus out of poverty
Transportation:	more freeways for cars versus public transportation
Abortion:	restrictions on choice versus informed choice and access
Health care:	treatment versus prevention
School desegregation:	racial integration versus equal achievement

Evaluability Assessment and Goals Clarification

Evaluators have gotten heavily involved in goals clarification because, when we are invited in, we seldom find a statement of clear, specific, prioritized, and measurable goals. This can take novice evaluators by surprise if they think that their primary task will be formulating an evaluation design for already established goals. Even where goals exist, they are frequently unrealistic, having been exaggerated to secure funding—what are called *BHAGs* (big hairy audacious goals). One reason evaluability assessment has become an important preevaluation tool is that by helping programs get ready for evaluation, it acknowledges the frequent need for a period of time to work with program staff, administrators, funders, and participants on clarifying goals—making them realistic, meaningful, agreed on, and evaluable (Wholey 1994; Smith 1989). Evaluability assessment often includes fieldwork and interviews to determine how much consensus there is among various stakeholders about goals and to identify where differences lie. Based on this kind of contextual analysis, an evaluator can work with primary intended users to plan a strategy for goals clarification.

When an evaluability assessment reveals broad aims and fuzzy goals, it's important to understand what role goals are understood to play in the program. Fuzzy goals actually characterize much human cognition and reasoning (Ragin 2000; Zadeh et al. 1975). Classic laboratory experiments found that fuzzy conceptualizing may be typical of half the population (Kochen 1975:407). No wonder evaluators have so much trouble getting clear, specific, and measurable goals! Carol Weiss (1972b) has commented in this regard:

> Part of the explanation [for fuzzy goals] probably lies in practitioners' concentration on concrete matters of program functioning and their pragmatic mode of operation. They often have an intuitive rather than an analytical approach to program development. But there is also a sense in which ambiguity serves a useful function; it may mask underlying divergences in intent . . . glittering generalities that pass for goal statements are meant to satisfy a variety of interests and perspectives. (P. 27)

Thus, evaluators have to figure out if administrators and staff are genuinely fuzzy about what they're attempting to accomplish, or if they're simply being shrewd in not letting the evaluator (or others) discover their *real* goals, or if they're trying to avoid conflict through vagueness. Fuzzy goals, then, may be a conscious strategy for avoiding conflict among competing interests. In such instances, the evaluation may be focused on important questions, issues, and concerns without resort to clear, specific, and measurable objectives. However, more often than not in my experience, the difficulty turns out to be a conceptual problem rather than deviousness.

From a utilization-focused point of view, the challenge is to calculate how early interactions in the evaluation process will affect later use. Typically, it's not useful to ignore goals conflict, accept poorly formulated or unrealistic goals, or let the evaluator assume responsibility for writing clear, specific, and measurable goals. Primary intended users need to be involved in assessing how much effort to put into goals clarification. In doing so, both evaluators and primary intended users do well to heed the *evaluation standard on political viability:*

> The evaluation should be planned and conducted with anticipation of the different positions of various interest groups, so that their cooperation may be obtained, and so that possible attempts by any of these groups to curtail evaluation operations or to

bias or misapply the results can be averted or counteracted. (Joint Committee on Standards 1994:F2)

There are alternatives to goals-based evaluation, alternatives we'll consider in the next chapter. First, let's examine how to work with intended users who want to focus on goals and results.

Communicating about Goals and Results

Part of the difficulty, I am convinced, is the terminology *goals and objectives*. These very words can intimidate staff. Goals and objectives have become daunting weights that program staff feel around their necks, burdening them, slowing their efforts, and impeding rather than advancing their progress. Helping staff clarify their purpose and direction may mean avoiding use of the term goals and objectives.

I've found program staff quite animated and responsive to the following kinds of questions: What are you trying to achieve with your clients? If you are successful, how will your clients be different after the program than they were before? What kinds of changes do you want to see in your clients? When your program works as you want it to, how do clients *behave* differently? What do they say differently? What would I see in them that would tell me they are different? Program staff can often provide quite specific answers to these questions, answers that reveal their caring and involvement with the client change process, yet when the same staff are asked to specify their goals and objectives, they freeze.

Questions for Clarifying Goals and Intended Outcomes

What are you trying to achieve with your program participants?

If you are successful, how will participants be different after the program than they were before?

What kinds of changes do you want to see in program participants? When your program works as you want it to, how do participants *behave* differently?

What do they say differently? What would I see in them that would tell me they are different?

After querying staff about what results they hope to accomplish with program participants, I may then tell them that what they have been telling me constitutes their goals and objectives. This revelation often brings considerable surprise. They often react by saying, "But we haven't said anything about what we would count." This, as clearly as anything, I take as evidence of how widespread the confusion is between the conceptualization of goals and their measurement. Help program staff and other intended users be realistic and concrete about goals and objectives, but don't make them hide what they are really trying to do because they're not sure how to write a formally acceptable statement of goals and objectives, or because they don't know what measurement instruments might be available to get at some of the important things they are trying to do. Instead, *take them through a process that focuses on achieving outcomes and results rather than writing goals*. The difference, it turns out, can be huge.

Focusing on Outcomes and Results

In the minds of many program people, from board members to frontline staff and participants, goals are abstract statements of ideals written to secure finding—meant to inspire but never achieved. Consider this poster on the wall of the office of a program I evaluated:

The greatest danger is not that we aim too high and miss, but that our goal is too low and we attain it.

For the director of this program, goals were something you put in proposals and plans, and hung on the wall, then went about your business.

Let me illustrate the difference between traditional program goals and a focus on participant outcomes with plans submitted by county units to a state human services agency. The plans required statements of outcomes. Each statement below promises something, but that something is not a change in client functioning, status, or well-being. These statements reveal how people in social services have been trained to think about program goals. My comments, following each goal, are meant to illustrate how to help program leaders and other intended evaluation users reframe traditional goals to focus on participant outcomes.

Problematic Outcome Examples

1. To continue implementation of a case management system to maintain continued contact with clients before, during, and after treatment.

Comment: Continued implementation of the system is the goal. And what is promised for the client? "Continued contact."

2. Case management services will be available to all persons with serious and persistent mental illness who require them.

Comment: This statement aims at availability—a service delivery improvement. Easily accessible services could be available 24 hours a day, but with what outcomes?

3. To develop needed services for chronically chemically dependent clients.

Comment: This statement focuses on program services rather than the client outcomes. My review of county plans revealed that most managers focus planning at the program delivery level, that is, the program's goals, rather than how clients' lives will be improved.

4. To develop a responsive, comprehensive crisis intervention plan.

Comment: A plan is the intended outcome. I found that many service providers confuse planning with getting something done. The characteristics of the plan—"responsive, comprehensive"—reveal nothing about results for intended beneficiaries.

5. Develop a supportive, family-centered empowering, capacity-building intervention system for families and children.

Comment: This goal statement has lots of human services jargon, but, carefully examined, the statement doesn't commit to empowering any families or actually enhancing the capacity of anyone receiving services through the system.

6. Expand placement alternatives.

Comment: More alternatives is the intended results, but to what end? Here is another system-level goal that carries the danger of making placement an end in itself rather than a means to client improvement.

7. County clients will receive services that they value as appropriate to their needs and helpful in remediating their concerns.

Comment: Client satisfaction can be an important outcome, but it's rarely sufficient by itself. Especially in tax-supported programs, taxpayers and policymakers want more than happy clients. They want clients to have jobs, be productive, stay sober, parent effectively, and so on. Client satisfaction needs to be connected to other desired outcomes.

8. Improve ability of adults with severe and persistent mental illness to obtain employment.

Comment: Some clients remain for years in programs that enhance their ability to obtain employment—without ever getting a job.

9. Adults with serious and persistent mental illness will engage in a process to function effectively in the community.

Comment: Engaging in the process is as much as this aims for, in contrast to clients actually functioning effectively in the community.

10. Adults with developmental disabilities will participate in programs to begin making decisions and exercising choice.

Comment: Program participation is the stated focus. This leads to counting how many people show up rather than how many make meaningful decisions and exercise real choice. A client can participate in a program aimed at teaching decision-making skills, and can even learn those skills, yet never be permitted to make real decisions.

11. Each developmentally disabled consumer (or their substitute decision maker) will identify ways to assist them to remain connected, maintain, or develop natural supports.

Comment: This goal is satisfied, as written, if each client has a list of potential connections. The provider, of course, can pretty much guarantee composition of such a list. The actual important outcome: Clients who are connected in a meaningful way to a support group of people.

12. Adults in training and rehab will be involved in an average of 120 hours of community integration activities per quarter.

Comment: Quantitative and specific, but the outcome stated goes only as far as being involved in activities, not actually being integrated into the community.

13. Key indicators of intended results and client outcomes for crisis services:

- Number of patients served
- Number of patient days and the average length of stay
- Source of referrals to the crisis unit and referrals provided to patient at discharge

Comment: Participation numbers, not client outcomes.

14. Minimize hospitalizations of people with severe and persistent mental illness.

Comment: This is a system-level outcome that is potentially dangerous. One of the premises of results-oriented management is that "what gets measured gets done." An easy way to attain this desired outcome is simply not to refer or admit needy clients to the hospital. That will minimize hospitalizations (a system-level outcome) but may not help people in need. A more appropriate outcome would be that these clients function effectively. If that outcome is attained, they won't need hospitalizations.

15. Improve quality of child protection intervention services.

Comment: I found a lot of outcome statements aimed at enhancing quality. Ironically, quality can be enhanced by improving services without having an impact on client outcomes. Licensing and accrediting standards often focus on staff qualifications and site characteristics (indicators of quality), but seldom require review of what program participants achieve.

The point of reviewing these examples has been to show the kinds of goal statements an evaluator may encounter when beginning to work with a program. A utilization-focused evaluator can help intended users review plans and stated goals to see if they include an outcome focus. There's nothing wrong with program-level goals (e.g., improve access or quality) or system-level goals (e.g., reduce costs), but such goals ought to connect to outcomes for clients. An evaluator can facilitate discussion of why, in the current political environment, one hears increased demand for "outcomes-based" management and accountability (e.g., Nolan and Mock 2005). Given that increased focus, there are helpful guides for working with outcomes in evaluation, such as the excellent GrantCraft guide

Making Measures Work for You: Outcomes and Evaluation, supported by the Ford Foundation (McGarvey 2006), the Bruner Foundation capacity-building resources (Baker 2008), and *Getting to Outcomes with Developmental Assets* (Fisher, Chinman, and Wandersman 2006). Evaluators need to provide technical assistance in helping program planners, managers, and other potential evaluation users understand the difference between a participant outcomes approach and traditional program or system goals approaches. In particular, they need assistance understanding the difference between service-focused goals versus client-focused outcome goals. Exhibit 7.3 compares these two kinds of goals. Both can be useful, but they place emphasis in different places.

EXHIBIT 7.3

Service-Focused Versus Outcome-Focused Goals: Examples From Parenting Programs

Service-Focused Goals	Outcome-Focused Goals
Provide coordinated case management services with public health to pregnant adolescents	Pregnant adolescents will give birth to healthy babies and care for the infants and themselves appropriately
Improve the quality of child protection intervention services	Children will be safe; they will not be abused or neglected
Develop a supportive, family-centered, capacity-building intervention system for families and children	Parents will adequately nurture and provide necessities for their children
Provide assistance to parents to make employment-related child care decisions	Parents who wish to work will have adequate child care

Leading a Horse to Water versus Getting It to Drink

The shift from service goals to outcomes often proves difficult in programs and agencies that have a long history of focusing on services and activities. But even where the difference is understood and appreciated, some fear or resistance may emerge. One reason is that service providers are well schooled in the proverbial wisdom that "you can lead a horse to water, but you can't make it drink."

This familiar adage illuminates the challenge of committing to outcomes. The desired outcome is that the horse drink the water. Longer-term outcomes are that the horse stays healthy and works effectively. But because program staff know they can't make a horse drink water, they focus on the things they can control: leading the horse to water, making sure the tank is full, monitoring the quality of the water, and keeping the horse within drinking distance of the water. In short, they focus on the *processes* of water delivery rather than the outcome of water drunk. Because staff can control processes but cannot guarantee attaining outcomes, government rules and regulations get written specifying exactly how to lead a horse to water. Funding is based on the number of horses led to water. Licenses are issued to individuals and programs that meet the qualifications for leading horses to water. Quality awards are made for improving the path to the water—and keeping the horse happy along the way. Whether the horse drinks the water gets lost in all this flurry of lead-to-water-ship. Most reporting systems focus on how many horses get led to the water, and how difficult it was to get them there, but never quite get around to finding out whether the horses drank the water and stayed healthy. And they seem unaware of the parallel wisdom that "you may have to lead a horse to water but it will run on its own to oats." Or this, sometimes called Murphy's 12th law: "You can't lead a cavalry charge if you think you look funny on a horse." But enough with horses already. Back to evaluation and accountability.

One point of resistance to outcomes accountability, then, is the fear among providers and practitioners that they're being asked to take responsibility for, and will be judged on, something over which they have little control. The antidote to this fear is involving staff in determining how to measure outcomes and establishing a results-oriented culture in an organization or agency. Evaluators have a role to play in such efforts by facilitating a process that helps staff, administrators, and other stakeholders think about, discuss the implications of, and come to understand both the advantages and limitations of an outcomes approach. There's a lot of managerial and political rhetoric about being results oriented, but not much expertise in how to set up a results-oriented system. The next section presents a framework for conceptualizing outcomes that are meaningful and measurable for use in facilitating an outcomes-oriented management, monitoring, and evaluation system.

Utilization-Focused Outcomes Framework

This framework distinguishes six separate elements that need to be specified for focusing an evaluation on participant or client outcomes:

- A specific participant or client target group
- The desired outcome(s) for that target group
- One or more indicators for each desired outcome
- Details of data collection
- How results will be used
- Performance targets

I'll discuss each of these elements and offer illustrations from actual programs to show how they fit together. Evaluators can use this framework to work with primary intended users.

Identifying Specific Participant or Client Target Groups

I'll use the generic term *client* to include program participants, consumers of services, beneficiaries, students, and customers, as well as traditional client groups. The appropriate language varies, but for every program, there is some group that is expected to benefit from and attain outcomes as a result of program participation. However, the target groups identified in enabling legislation or existing reporting systems typically are defined too broadly for meaningful outcomes measurement. Intended outcomes can vary substantially for subgroups within general eligible populations. The trick is to be as specific as necessary to conceptualize meaningful outcomes. Some illustrations may help clarify why this is so.

Consider a program aimed at supporting the elderly to continue living in their homes, with services ranging from "meals on wheels" to home nursing. Not all elderly people can or want to stay in their homes. Therefore, if the desired outcome is "continuing to live in their own home," it would be inappropriate to specify that outcome for all elderly people. A more appropriate target population, then, would be people above the age of 65 who want to and can remain safely in their homes. For this group, it is appropriate to aim to keep them in their homes. It is also clear that some kind of screening process will be necessary to identify this subpopulation of the elderly.

A different example comes from programs serving people with developmental disabilities (DD). Many programs exist to prepare DD clients for work and then support them in maintaining employment. However, not all people with DD can or want to work. In cases where funding supports the right of DD clients to choose whether to work, the appropriate subpopulation becomes people with DD who can and want to work. For that specific subpopulation, then, the intended outcome could be that they obtain and maintain satisfying employment.

There are many ways of specifying subpopulation targets. Outcomes are often different for young, middle-aged, and elderly clients in the same general group (e.g., persons with serious and persistent mental illness). Outcomes for pregnant teens or teenage mothers may be different from outcomes for mothers receiving welfare who have completed high school. Outcomes for first-time offenders may be different from those for repeat offenders. The point is that categories of funding eligibility often include subgroups for which outcomes appropriately vary. Similarly, when identifying groups by services received, for example, counseling services or jobs training, the outcomes expected for generic services may vary by subgroups. It is important, then, to make sure an intended outcome is meaningful and appropriate for everyone in the identified target population.

Specifying Desired Outcomes

The choice of language varies under different evaluation approaches. Some models refer to *expected outcomes* or *intended outcomes*. Others prefer the language of *client goals* or *client objectives*. What is important is not the phrase used but that there be a clear statement of the targeted change in circumstances, status, level of functioning, behavior, attitude, knowledge, or skills. Other outcome types include maintenance and prevention. Exhibit 7.4 provides examples of outcomes.

EXHIBIT 7.4

Outcome Examples

Type of Change	Illustration
Change in circumstances	Children safely reunited with their families of origin from foster care
Change in status	Unemployed to employed
Change in behavior	Truants will regularly attend school
Change in functioning	Increased self-care; getting to work on time
Change in attitude	Greater self-respect
Change in knowledge	Understand the needs and capabilities of children at different ages
Change in skills	Increased reading level; able to parent appropriately
Maintenance	Continue to live safely at home (e.g., the elderly)
Prevention	Teenagers will not use drugs

Outcome Indicators: Operationalizing

An indicator is just that, an indicator. It's not the same as the phenomenon of interest but only an indicator of that phenomenon. A score on a reading test is an indicator for reading capability but should not be confused with a particular person's true ability. All kinds of things affect a test score on a given day. Thus, indicators are inevitably approximations. They are imperfect and vary in validity and reliability.

Figuring out how to measure a desired outcome is called *operationalizing* the outcome. In selecting a measurement, the desired outcome becomes more than a concept; it becomes something that can be operated. Indeed, the common dictionary definition of operational is that it makes it *"ready for use"* (American Heritage Dictionary 2006). A desired outcome isn't ready for use in evaluation until it is operationalized.

The resources available for measurement will greatly affect the kinds of data that can be collected for indicators. For example, if the desired outcome for abused children is that there be no subsequent abuse or neglect, regular in-home visitations and observations, including interviews with the child, parent(s), and knowledgeable others, would be desirable, but such data collection is expensive. With constrained resources, one may have to rely on routinely collected data and mandated reporting, that is, official substantiated reports of abuse and neglect over time. Moreover, when using such routine data, privacy and confidentiality restrictions may limit the indicator to aggregate results quarter by quarter rather than one that tracks specific families over time. In contemporary child protection services, tracking substantiated abuse, while desirable and required, is not considered enough and systems that enable much more detailed data collection have been and are being used. Risk assessment protocols not only attempt to establish risk of re-abuse but actually may be used to determine the frequency of agency contact with families.

As resources change, the indicator may change. Routine statistics may be used by an agency until a philanthropic foundation funds a focused evaluation to get better data for a specific period of time. In such a case, the indicator would change, but the desired outcome would not. This is the advantage of clearly distinguishing the desired outcome from its indicator. *As the state of the art of measurement develops or resources change, indicators may improve without changing the desired outcome.*

Time frames also affect indicators. The ultimate goal of a program for abused children would be to have them become healthy, well-functioning, and happy adults, but policymakers cannot wait 10 to 15 years to assess the outcomes of a program for abused children. Short-term indicators must be relied on, things such as school attendance, school performance, physical health, and the psychological functioning of a child, as well as any redeterminations of abuse. These short-term indicators provide sufficient information to make judgments about the likely long-term results. It takes 30 years for a forest to grow, but you can assess the likelihood of ending up with a forest by evaluating how many saplings are still alive, 1 year and 3 years after the trees are planted.

Another factor affecting indicator selection is the demands data collection will put on program staff and participants. Short-term interventions such as food shelves, recreational activities for people with developmental disabilities, drop-in centers, and one-time community events do not typically engage participants intensely enough to justify collection of much, if any, data. Many programs can barely collect data on end-of-program status, much less follow-up data 6 months after program participation.

In short, a variety of factors influence the selection of indicators, including the importance of the outcome claims being made, resources available for data collection, the state of the art of measurement of human functioning, the nature of decisions to be made with the results, and the willingness of staff and participants to engage in assessment. Some kind of indicator is necessary, however, to measure degree of outcome attainment. *The key is to make sure that the indicator is a reasonable, useful, and meaningful measure of the intended client outcome.*

The framework offered here will generate outcome statements that are *clear, specific,* and *measurable,* but getting clarity and specificity is separated from selecting measures. The reason for separating the identification of a desired outcome from its measurement is to ensure the utility of both. This point is worth elaborating. The following is a classic goal statement:

> Student achievement test scores in reading will increase one grade level from the beginning of first grade to the beginning of second grade.

Such a statement mixes together and potentially confuses the (1) specification of a desired outcome with (2) its measurement and (3) the desired performance target. The desired outcome is increased student achievement. The indicator is the score on a norm-referenced standardized achievement test. The performance target is one year's academic gain on the test. These are three separate decisions that primary intended evaluation users need to discuss. For example, there are ways other than standardized tests for measuring achievement, such as student portfolios or competency-based tests. The desired outcome should not be confused with its indicator. In the framework offered here, outcome statements are clearly separated from operational criteria for measuring them.

Another advantage of separating outcomes identification from indicator selection is to encourage program staff to be serious about the process. A premature focus on indicators may be heard as limiting a program to attempt only those things that staff already know how to measure. Such a limitation is too constraining. It is one thing to establish a purpose and direction for a program. It is quite another thing to say how that purpose and direction are to be measured. By confusing these two steps and making them one, program goals can become detached from what program staff and funders are actually working to accomplish. Under such a constraint, staff begin by figuring out what can be measured. Given that they seldom have much expertise in measurement, they end up counting fairly insignificant behaviors and attitudes that they can somehow quantify.

When I work with groups on goals clarification, I have them state intended outcomes *without regard to measurement*. Once they have stated as carefully and explicitly as they can what they want to accomplish, then it is time to figure out

what indicators and data can be collected to monitor outcome attainment. They can then move back and forth between conceptual level statements and operational (measurement) specifications, attempting to get as much precision as possible in both.

To emphasize this point, let me overstate the trade-off. *I prefer to have less-than-ideal or rough measures of important goals rather than highly precise measures of goals that no one much cares about.* In too many cases, evaluators focus on the later (meaningless but measurable goals) instead of on the former (meaningful goals with less-than-ideal measures).

Of course, this trade-off, stated in stark terms, is only relative. It is desirable to have as much precision as possible. By separating the process of goals clarification from the process of selecting indicators, it is possible for program staff to focus first on what they are really trying to accomplish and to state their goals and objectives as explicitly as possible *without regard to measurement*, and then to worry about how one would measure actual attainment of those goals and objectives.

SMART Indicators

SMART is a widely used mnemonic for helping people remember the characteristics of a good indicator.

Specific

Measurable

Achievable

Relevant

Timebound

Performance Targets

A performance target specifies the amount or level of outcome attainment that is expected, hoped for, or, in some kinds of performance contracting, required. What percentage of participants in employment training will have full-time jobs 6 months after graduation: 40 percent? 65 percent? 80 percent? What percentage of fathers failing to make child support payments will be meeting their full child support obligations within 6 months of intervention? 15 percent? 35 percent? 60 percent?

The best basis for establishing future performance targets is past performance. "Last year we had 65 percent success. Next year we aim for 70 percent." Lacking data on past performance, it may be advisable to wait until baseline data have been gathered before specifying a performance target. Arbitrarily setting performance targets without some empirical baseline may create artificial expectations that turn out unrealistically high or embarrassingly low. One way to avoid arbitrariness is to seek norms for reasonable levels of attainment from other, comparable programs, or review the evaluation literature for parallels.

As indicators are collected and examined over time, from quarter to quarter, and year to year, it becomes more meaningful and useful to set performance targets. The relationship between resources and outcomes can also be more precisely correlated longitudinally, with trend data, all of which increases the incremental and long-term value of an outcomes management approach.

The challenge is to make performance targets meaningful. Chapter 13, on interpreting data, includes further discussion on performance targets and establishing standards of desirability that can be developed with primary intended users as a framework for interpreting outcomes data.

In a political environment of outcomes mania, meaningfulness and utility are not necessarily priorities. Consider this example and judge for yourself. The 1995 Annual Management Report from the Office of the New York City Mayor included this performance target: The average daytime speed of cars crossing from one side of midtown Manhattan to the other will increase from 5.3 to 5.9 miles per hour. Impressed by this vision of moving from a "brisk 5.3" to a "sizzling 5.9," *The New Yorker* magazine interviewed Ruben Ramirez, Manhattan's Department of Transportation Traffic Coordinator, to ask how such a feat could be accomplished in the face of downsizing and budget cuts. Ramirez cited better use of resources. Asked what he could accomplish with adequate resources, he replied, "I think we could do six or seven, and I'm not being outrageous." *The New Yorker* found such a performance target a "dreamy future," one in which it might actually be possible to drive across midtown Manhattan faster than you can walk ("Speed" 1995:40).

Is such a vision visionary? Is a performance increase from 5.3 to 5.9 miles per hour meaningful? Is 6 or 7 worth aiming for? For a noncommuting Minnesotan, such numbers fail to impress. But, converted into annual hours and dollars saved for commercial vehicles in Manhattan, the increase may be valued in hundreds of thousands of dollars, perhaps even millions. It's for primary stakeholders in Manhattan, not Minnesota, to determine the meaningfulness of such a performance target.

Trade-Offs in Setting Performance Targets

In 2007, the United States Internal Revenue Service (IRS) began auditing income tax returns less deeply and more broadly, amounting to a change in its performance targets. Formerly the IRS target was collecting "every last dime" in an audit to maximize the amount collected in each individual audit. The new performance target is collecting 80 percent of what might be available in an audit but, at the same time, conducting a greater number of audits.

What's the rationale for this change? It involves a trade-off based on yet another version of an 80/20 rule. The IRS has found that its agents can collect 80 percent of the tax recoverable in an audit within the first 20 percent of the time it would take to collect the whole amount. So it is more cost efficient for the IRS to be satisfied with the 80 percent from individual audits while using the time saved to conduct a larger number of audits. This is expected to prove less annoying to those individuals who are audited, while the larger number of audits is intended to deter tax cheating due to the increased risk of being audited (Brown 2007).

Details of Data Collection: The Evaluation Design

The details of data collection are a distinct part of the framework; they must be attended to, but they shouldn't clutter the focused outcome statement. Unfortunately, I've found that people can get caught up in the details of refining methods and lose sight of the outcome. The details typically get worked out after the other parts of the framework have been conceptualized. Details include answering the following kinds of questions:

• What existing data will be used and how will they be accessed? Who will collect new indicators data?

• Who will have oversight and management responsibility for data collection?

• How often will indicators data be collected? How often reported?

• Will data be gathered on all program participants or only a sample? If a sample, how selected?

• How will findings be reported? To whom? In what format? When? How often?

These pragmatic questions put flesh on the bones of the outcomes framework. They are not simply technical issues, however. How these questions get answered will ultimately determine the credibility and utility of the entire approach. Primary intended users need to be involved in making decisions about these issues to ensure that they feel ownership of and responsibility for all aspects of the evaluation.

How Results Will Be Used

The final element in the framework is to make sure that the data collected on the outcomes identified will be useful. One way to do this is to engage intended users in a simulation exercise in which the evaluator fabricates some potential results and intended users practice interpreting and using those results. The evaluation facilitator asks, "If the results came out this way, what would you do? If the findings came out this other way, what would that tell you, and what actions would you take? Given what you want the evaluation to accomplish, have we focused on the right outcomes and useful indicators?"

(Chapter 13 will discuss this simulation approach in greater depth.) At every stage of a utilization-focused evaluation, the evaluator facilitator pushes intended users to think seriously about the implications of design and measurement decisions for use.

Interconnections among the Distinct Parts of the Framework

The utilization-focused outcomes framework, as just reviewed, consists of six parts: a specific participant target group, a desired outcome for that group, one or more outcome indicators, a performance target (if appropriate and desired), details of data collection, and specification of how findings will be used. While these are listed in the order in which an evaluation typically

facilitates the work with intended users, the conceptualization process is not linear. Groups often go back and forth in iterative fashion. The target group may not become really clear until the desired outcome is specified or an indicator designated. Sometimes formulating the details of data collection will give rise to new indicators, and those indicators force a rethinking of how the desired outcome is stated. The point is to end up with all elements specified, consistent with each other, and mutually reinforcing. That doesn't necessarily mean marching through the framework lockstep, but it does mean eventually determining all six elements.

Exhibit 7.5 provides an example of all the elements specified for a parenting program aimed at high school–age mothers.

EXHIBIT 7.5

Example of a Fully Specified Utilization-Focused Outcomes Framework

Target subgroup:	Teenage mothers at Central High School
Desired outcome:	Appropriate parenting knowledge, behaviors, and practices
Outcome indicator:	Score on Parent Practice Inventory (knowledge and behavior measures)
Data collection:	Pre- and post-test, beginning and end of program; 6-month follow-up; district evaluation office will administer and analyze results
Performance target:	75 percent of entering participants will complete the program and attain a passing score on both the knowledge and behavior scales
Use:	The evaluation advisory task force will review the results (principal, two teachers, two participating students, one agency representative, one community representative, an associate superintendent, one school board member, and the district evaluator). The task force will decide if the program should be continued at Central High School and expanded to other district high schools. A recommendation will be forwarded to the superintendent and school board.

Completing the framework often takes several tries. Exhibit 7.6 shows three versions of the utilization-focused outcomes framework as it emerged from the work of a developmental disabilities staff group.

Their first effort yielded a service-oriented goal. They revised that with a focus on skill enhancement. Finally, they agreed on a meaningful client outcome: functioning independently.

EXHIBIT 7.6

Three Versions of an Outcome-Focused Framework

	Target Population: Children with Development Disabilities		
	Desired Outcome	*Outcome Indicator*	*Method*
First draft (Service-oriented)	Children with developmental disabilities will receive supportive services for improved functioning in basic daily living skills	Track hours of supportive services received, and levels and amounts of client participation in training	Case records monitoring services and participation will be aggregated quarterly
Revised (Skills-focused; interim outcome)	Children with developmental disabilities will increase their skills for functioning independently	Changes in skills on a staff assessment form	Quarterly administration of skills assessment form as part of ongoing training
Final version (Primary desired outcome)	Children with developmental disabilities will function independently in their activities of daily living	Activities of Daily Living (ADL) behavioral assessment instrument	Quarterly administration of ADL to all children in the program. Compare scores over time. Do both individual case profiles and aggregate results by categories of severity and age

A Utilization-Focused Process for Developing Outcomes

A central issue in implementing an outcomes evaluation approach is who will be involved in the process of developing the outcomes. When the purpose is ongoing management by outcomes, the program's executives and staff must buy into the process. Who else is involved is a matter of political judgment. Those involved will feel the most ownership of the resulting system.

Some processes involve only managers and directors. Other processes include advisory groups from the community. Collaboration between funders and service providers in determining outcomes is critical where contracts for services are involved. Advice from some savvy foundation funders is to match outcomes evaluation to the stage of a program's development (Daniel 1996), keep the context long term (McIntosh 1996) and "turn outcome 'sticks' into carrots" (Leonard 1996:46).

Exhibit 7.7 shows the stages of a utilization-focused approach to developing an outcomes-based management system for a program. Critical issues and parallel activities are shown for each stage. Those to be involved will need training and support. I've found it helpful to begin with an overview of the purpose of an outcomes-focused programming approach: history, trends, the political climate, and potential benefits. Then I have participants work in small groups working on the elements of the utilization-focused outcomes framework (see Exhibit 7.5) for an actual program with which they're familiar. Facilitation, encouragement, and technical assistance are needed to help such groups successfully complete the task. Where multiple groups are involved, I like to have them share their work and the issues that emerged in using the outcomes framework.

Dealing with Concerns

It's important that those involved get a chance to raise their concerns openly. There's often suspicion about political motives. Service providers worry about funding cuts and being held accountable for things they can't control. Administrators and directors of programs worry about how results will be used, what comparisons will be made, and who will control the process. Line staff worry about the amount of time involved, paperwork burdens, and the irrelevancy of it all. State civil servants responsible for reporting to the Legislature worry about how data can be aggregated at the state level. These and other concerns need to be aired and addressed. Having influential leaders visibly involved in the process enhances their own understanding and commitment while also sending signals to others about the importance being placed on outcomes.

Ten Principles for Meaningful and Useful Goals

With the utilization-focused outcomes framework as background, here are 10 principles for working with intended users to identify meaningful and useful goals.

1. *Identify outcomes that matter to those who do the work.* Outcomes and performance measures often look and feel like academic exercises to those involved. They think they're involved in a paperwork process to please some funder. But a meaningful outcomes statement articulates fundamental values. This means asking program stakeholders not only what their goals are but *why* they care about those goals (Friedman, Rothman, and Withers 2006). Goals should remind practitioners why they get up in the morning and go to work: to protect children, feed the hungry, fight disease, reduce the ravages of poverty, and house the homeless. It should be inspirational. As the great management guru Peter Drucker (2000) said when asked about the bottom line for not-for-profit organizations, "The end results are people with changed lives." Outcomes should specify how lives will be changed.

EXHIBIT 7.7

Developing a Utilization-Focused System for Managing Outcomes: Stages, Issues, and Activities

	1	2	3	4	5	6	7	8	9	10	11	12	13
Stages	Identify and engage key actors whose commitment and support will be needed for transition to management and accountability based on client outcomes	Key actors and leaders: Commit to establish a client outcome approach. Understand principles, purposes, and implications of change	Agree on intended use by intended users	Conceptualize client outcomes; select indicators; set targets	Engage line staff: Facilitate their understanding and buy-in	Design data collection system; finalize methods; pilot; establish baselines	Implement data collection; train staff and managers for data collection and use	Prepare for use: Determine management uses; potential actions; decision options and parameters, and accountability report format	Analyze results: Compare results to baseline and targets	Involve key stakeholders in processing the findings	Judge performance and effectiveness	Make management decisions. Report results	Review and evaluate the outcome-based management system
Issues	Who are the key actors and leaders who must buy in? How widespread should initial involvement be?	What level of commitment and understanding is needed? By whom? How to distinguish real commitment from mere rhetoric?	What uses are possible? What uses are doable?	What target groups? How many outcomes? What are the really important bottomline outcomes?	What are staff's perspective/history/concerns/incentives?	What can be done with existing data? What new data will be needed? How can the system be integrated?	What resources will be available to support data collection? How will validity and reliability be addressed?	What incentives exist for managers to participate? How will managers be brought along? Trained? Rewarded? Who determines accountability reporting approaches?	Who will do the analysis? What additional data are needed to interpret the outcome results (e.g., demographics)	How do you keep key stakeholders engaged?	How clear are the data to support solid judgments?	What are the links between internal and external uses and audiences?	What should the system accomplish? Who determines success?
Activities	Establish leadership group	Leadership group makes strategic decision about how best to proceed and who to involve	Map out users and uses. Set priorities	Establish work team to determine outcomes; involve advisory to bring them along	Conduct staff workshops/training	Work team to make design decisions	Collect data; pilot-test and monitor data collection	Conduct training and management team sessions based on data use and simulations and mock scenarios	Analyze data; prepare graphics	Facilitate meeting of key stakeholders	Facilitate key stakeholders in judging and interpreting	Write report; present data; facilitate management decision making	Assemble a review team of management system users and key stakeholders

253

2. *Distinguish between outcomes and activities.* Outcomes describe desired impacts of the program on participants: Students will read with understanding. Participants will stop smoking. Activity goals describe *how* outcome goals will be achieved: Students will read 2 hours a day. Participants will openly discuss their dependence on cigarettes. People in the program will be treated with respect.

Outcome goals should clearly state how people will be different as a result of a program. Program staff may write goals describing intended activities thinking that they have stated desired outcomes. An agricultural extension agent told me his goal was "to get 50 farmers to participate in a farm tour." But what, I asked, did he want to result from the farm tour? After some dialogue, it became clear that the desired outcome was this: "Farmers will adopt improved milking practices in their own farm operations, and thus have more income."

A corporation stated one of its goals for the year as "establishing a comprehensive energy conservation program." After we discussed that it was perfectly possible to establish such a program without ever saving any energy, they rewrote the goal: "The corporation will significantly reduce energy consumption."

3. *Specificity matters. More specific outcomes are more powerful.* Some goal statements are amazingly adept at saying nothing. I worked with a school board whose overall goal was, "Students will learn." There is no way *not* to attain this goal. It is the nature of the species that young people learn. Fortunately, they can learn in spite of the schools. The issues are *what* and *how much* they will learn from schooling.

Another favorite is "increasing awareness." It's fairly difficult to put people through 2 weeks of training on some topic (e.g., chemical dependency) and *not* increase awareness. Under these conditions, the goal of "increasing awareness of chemical dependency issues" is hardly worth aiming at. Further dialogue revealed that the program staff wanted to change knowledge, attitudes, and behaviors. Specific outcomes identify what knowledge, what attitudes, and what behaviors.

4. *Each goal should contain only one outcome.* There is a tendency in writing goal statements to overload the content. "Our program will help parents with employment, nutrition, health, and parenting needs so that their children do well in school and reach their full potential, and families are integrated into neighborhoods feeling safe and connected, and being productive." Now there's a goal written by committee with a little bit for everyone. Ten different possible outcomes are implied for three different target populations in that statement. For evaluation purposes, they must be separated.

5. *Outcome statements should be understandable.* Goals should communicate a clear sense of direction. Avoid difficult grammatical constructions and complex interdependent clauses. Goal statements should also avoid internal program or professional jargon. The general public should be able to make sense of goals. Consider these two versions of goal statements for what amount to the *same* outcome:

(a) To maximize the capabilities of professional staff and use taxpayer resources wisely while engaging in therapeutic interventions and case management processes so that children's development capacities are unencumbered by adverse environmental circumstances or experiences.

(b) Children will be safe from abuse and neglect.

Now, see if you can make sense of this beauty from the National Council of Teachers of English and the International Reading Association: "Students employ a wide range of strategies as they write and use different writing process elements appropriately to communicate with different audiences for a variety of purposes." The *New York Times* (1996) found this goal less than inspiring or user-friendly, and editorialized: "a fog of euphemism and evasion" (p. A24). Bumper sticker: Honk if you use *writing process elements* appropriately.

6. *Formal goals statements should focus on the most important program outcomes.* Writing goals should not be a marathon exercise in seeing how long a document one can produce. As human beings, our attention span is too short to focus on long lists of goals and objectives. Limit them to outcomes that matter and for which the program intends to be held accountable.

7. *State intended outcomes separately from how they are to be attained.* An agricultural extension program posited this goal: "Farmers will increase yields through the education efforts of extension, including farm tours, bulletins, and related activities." Everything after the word *yields* describes how to goal is to be attained. Keep the statement clear and crisp—focused on the intended outcome.

8. *Separate goals from indicators.* Advocates of *management by objectives* and *behavioral objectives* often place more emphasis on measurement than on establishing a clear sense of direction (e.g., Combs 1972). *Desired outcome:* All children will be immunized against polio. Indicator: Health records when children enter school show that they received 4 doses of IPV: a dose at 2 months; at

4 months; at 6 to 18 months; and a booster dose at 4 to 6 years.

9. *Thou shalt not covet thy neighbor's goals and objectives.* Goals and objectives don't travel very well. They often involve matters of nuance. It is worth taking the time for primary stakeholders to construct their own goals so that they reflect their own values, expectations, and intentions in their own language. Buy-in happens through engagement.

10. *Help all involved keep their eyes on the prize. Use outcome statements to stay focused on achieving results.* Goals clarification should be an invigorating process of prioritizing what those involved care about and hope to accomplish (see Item 1 above). Goals should not become a club for assaulting staff but a tool for helping staff focus and realize their ideals. Too often outcomes are written into proposals and reports, then forgotten. Make monitoring outcomes attainment part of staff meetings. Find out if it's true that what gets measured gets done. Orient new staff members to the program's outcome commitments. Staff should share intended outcomes with participants so that everyone knows what's expected and envisioned. Report outcomes in newsletters and other program communications. Revisit outcomes at annual retreats. An informative and revealing exercise can be to conduct an outcomes communications audit: Where in the life and work of the program are priority outcomes shared and used?

There are exceptions to all these guidelines. For example, contrary to the ninth principle, one option in working with groups is to have them review the goals of other programs, both as a way of helping stakeholders clarify their own goals and to get ideas about format and content. From this beginning point, those in a particular situation can fine-tune others' goals to fit their values and context.

Where there is the time and inclination, then, I prefer to have key program people work on their own outcomes framework, including identifying indicators and uses of monitoring data, so that participants feel ownership and understand what commitments have been made. This can be part of the training function served by evaluators, increasing the likelihood that staff will internalize the evaluative thinking embedded in a utilization-focused outcomes framework (see Exhibit 7.5).

African Standards as an Example of Adapted Outcomes

An example of adapting goals to fit specific values and a particular context in evaluation are reviews being undertaken by national evaluation associations around the world to examine the Joint Committee Standards for Evaluation, originally formulated for educational evaluation in the United States, and adapt the standards to their own cultural contexts. The standards are, in a sense, the desired outcomes for evaluation. The utility standards, for example, "are intended to ensure that an evaluation will serve the information needs of intended users" (Joint Committee 1994:U). Here's an example of how the African Evaluation Association (AfrEA) adapted the standards to African concerns. One of the U.S. accuracy standards reads,

> **Justified Conclusions** The conclusions reached in an evaluation should be explicitly justified, so that stakeholders can assess them. (A10)

The African Evaluation Association adopted revised standards at its conference in Niamey, Niger, in January 2007. They revised the "Justified Conclusions" standard into two parts:

> A10a. **Relevant Conclusions.** The conclusions of an evaluation should result from methods and analysis so that stakeholders can appreciate them in full objectivity.

> A10b. **Realistic recommendations reached by consensus.** The recommendations of an evaluation should be validated by stakeholders, feasible and linked to expected results. (AfrEA 2007:A10a, A10b)

The original Joint Committee Standards didn't address recommendations. The African evaluators sought input from evaluators and national evaluation associations throughout Africa and determined that they needed a standard regarding recommendations. In this way, they made the standards their own while also affirming and adopting the rest of the Joint Committee framework and standards. They also wrote an important contextual introduction to the standards to delineate their relevance to and importance for Africa.

Performance Indicators

As we have seen in this chapter, discussions of goals quickly turn to how to measure attainment of goals and that leads to performance indicators. Performance indicators have become so important and widely used that they deserve some additional consideration, including how they relate to broader evaluation concerns. Chapter 4 discussed monitoring as one use of data in monitoring and evaluation (M&E) systems. Performance indicators have become central to such approaches. Ongoing monitoring of indicators against desired target levels may be called performance measurement or performance monitoring. Because of the increased importance of performance monitoring in the United Kingdom, the British Commonwealth, and the European Union, the Royal Statistical Society (2003) created a special group to review the quality of the United Kingdom's system. In a report titled *Performance Indicators: Good, Bad, and Ugly,* the reviewers began by examining the multiple purposes of performance monitoring: (1) to assess the impact of government policies on services, (2) to identify well-performing or underperforming institutions and public servants, and (3) for public accountability. Hence, government is in the position of both monitoring public services and being monitored, itself, by performance indicators. This makes the political stakes quite high. "Performance monitoring done well is broadly productive for those concerned. Done badly, it can be very costly and not merely ineffective but harmful and indeed destructive" (Royal Statistical Society 2003:2).

The potential positive contribution of performance monitoring is captured in the mantra that *what gets measured gets done.* Well-developed and appropriate indicators both focus attention on priority outcomes and provide accountability for achieving those outcomes. The shadow side of performance indicators is that measuring the wrong thing means the wrong thing gets done. Consider the goal of protecting children in child protection agencies. Children who are neglected or abused are removed and placed in foster homes. One common goal of such agencies, in an effort to support families and as a matter of public policy, is to reunite children with their natural families. In many states, this is monitored through a reunification rate. When comparative data are made public for accountability purposes, counties or agencies with low reunification rates

experience pressure to raise their rates. That's where the problem arises. It's an easy rate to manipulate. More children can simply be reunited with their natural families. But the real goal is to *safely* reunite children with their families. That involves a different indicator.

The Royal Statistical Society report recommends that before introducing performance monitoring in any public service, a performance monitoring (PM) protocol should be established. This is an orderly record not only of decisions made but also of the reasoning or calculations that led to those decisions. A PM protocol should cover objectives, design considerations, and the definition of performance indicators, sampling versus complete enumeration, the information to be collected about context, the likely perverse behaviors or side effects that might be induced as a reaction to the monitoring process, and also the practicalities of implementation. Procedures for data collection, analysis, presentation of uncertainty and adjustment for context, together with dissemination rules, should be explicitly defined and reflect good statistical practice. Because of their usually tentative nature, performance indicators should be seen as "screening devices" and not overinterpreted. If quantitative performance targets are to be set, they need to have a sound basis, take account of prior (and emerging) knowledge about key sources of variation, and be integral to the PM design (p. 2).

The report emphasizes the importance of education and training in the appropriate use and interpretation of performance indicators. Special emphasis is given to the importance of *independent scrutiny* as a safeguard of public accountability, methodological rigor, and to be fair to individuals and/or institutions being monitored. "The scrutineers' role includes checking that the objectives of Performance Monitoring are being achieved without disproportionate burden, inducement of counterproductive behaviours, inappropriate setting or revision of targets, or interference in, or over-interpretation of, analyses and reporting" (p. 4).

Concerns about the misuse of performance indicators follow from Campbell's Law, formulated by Donald Campbell, one of evaluation's most distinguished pioneers: "The more any quantitative social indicator is used for social decision-making," he posited, "the more subject it will be to corruption pressures and the more apt it will be to distort and corrupt the social processes it is intended to monitor" (Campbell 1988:360). Consider this example:

> Police officers in New Orleans manipulated crimes statistics to make it look like the crime rate was going down stimulated by the Department's policy of handing out awards to leaders of districts with the lowest crime statistics. Five police officers were fired over the scandal. (Associated Press, October 23, 2003)

Sometimes the "corruption" (or at least distortion) begins in the definition and labeling of indicators. In the U.S. Senate debate over whether to allow drilling for oil in the Alaskan wilderness, the issue arose about what it means for an area to be a wilderness. The traditional definition has included that a wilderness is "roadless." The Bush Administration's U.S. Department of Interior revised the definition of roadless as follows: "The term 'roadless' does not mean an absence of roads. Rather, it indicates an attempt to minimize the construction of permanent roads." Thus, gravel roads constructed for drilling and logging don't count and areas with such roads remain counted in the

statistics on how much of the wilderness is "roadless" (Barringer 2005:16).

Such examples make "the performance movement" controversial and in need of ongoing evaluation itself (Radin 2006).

Campbell's Law

"The more any quantitative social indicator is used for social decision-making, the more subject it will be to corruption pressures and the more apt it will be to distort and corrupt the social processes it is intended to monitor."

—Donald Campbell (1988:360)

Performance Indicators and Evaluation

Performance monitoring based on *key performance indicators* (KPIs) has become part of the political culture. Governments and politicians are expected to set targets and report on progress as a basis for public accountability. The usefulness of performance indicators depends on their credibility, relevance, validity, transparency, and meaningfulness—and an appropriate and fair process for interpreting them. The Royal Statistical Society (2003) report provides excellent guidance in this regard. What it does not do is distinguish monitoring from evaluation.

Performance indicators are one tool in a very large evaluation toolkit that includes a wide variety of methods, data collection techniques, measures, and models. Given the rapid and widespread proliferation of performance-monitoring approaches, there is the danger that many will think that performance measurement is sufficient for or equivalent to evaluation. But performance measurement merely portrays trends and directions. Indicators tell us whether something is increasing, declining, or staying the same. Evaluation takes us deeper into asking why indicators are moving in the direction they are, how the movement of indicators are related to specific interventions, what is driving the movement of indicators, and what values should guide interpretation of indicators in making judgments. Utilization-focused performance measurement adds the importance of being clear about the primary intended users and intended uses of performance indicators.

Burt Perrin has been one of evaluation's most thoughtful theorists about the relationship between performance monitoring and evaluation. Exhibit 7.8 presents his principles and strategies for effective use of performance measures. Given the increasing importance of performance measurement in the public sector around the world, evaluators, policymakers, and the general public need to understand both the strengths and limitations of key performance indicators.

EXHIBIT 7.8

Strategies for Effective Use of Performance Measures

- Recognize that performance indicators are most appropriate for use in planning and monitoring, not for evaluation.
- Performance measures can serve as a means of identifying where more comprehensive evaluation approaches would be most useful, in this way, help in responsible allocation of resources for evaluation.
- Recognize that every evaluation method, including performance indicators, has limitations that can only be overcome by using a combination of methods . . . . It is usually necessary to balance quantitative data from performance indicators with qualitative forms of information for balance.
- Be strategic, recognizing that performance indicators are appropriate for some activities and not for others.
- Be realistic about the context, such as political or organizational requirements for performance indicators, irrespective of their appropriateness, and help programs work around these realities.
- Make sure the measurements are at the right level. The logic model can help identify what forms of outcomes may be realistically expected given the status of the program. Do not hold programs accountable for impacts that are unrealistic.
- Always test indicators in advance.
- Anticipate misapplications.
- Review, revise, and update measures frequently. Don't expect that new measures will be perfect the first time around.
- Actively involve stakeholders, including program staff and consumers, in developing, reviewing, and revising measures and actively involve them in interpreting findings and identifying implications.
- Use multiple indicators, in order to examine a variety of program aspects, including process as well as outputs and outcomes.

—Burt Perrin (1998:375–76)

Levels of Goal Specification

From Overall Mission to Specific Objectives

To facilitate framing evaluation questions, evaluators may have to work with primary stakeholders to clarify purposes at three levels: (1) the overall mission of the program or organization, (2) the goals of specific programmatic units (or subsystems), and (3) the specific objectives that specify desired outcomes. The mission statement describes the general direction of the overall program or organization in long-range terms. The peacetime mission of the U.S. Army is simply "Readiness." A mission statement may specify a target population and a basic problem to be attacked. For example, the mission of the Minnesota Comprehensive Epilepsy Program was to "improve the lives of people with epilepsy."

The terms *goals* and *objectives* have been used interchangeably up to this point, but it is useful to distinguish between them as representing different levels of generality. Goals are more general than objectives and encompass the purposes and aims of program subsystems (i.e., research, education, and treatment in the epilepsy example). Objectives are narrow and specific, stating what will be different as a result of program activities, that is, the concrete outcomes of a program. (Note: In some parts of the world, objectives are more general and goals are more specific.) To illustrate these differences, a simplified version of the mission statement, goals, and objectives for the Minnesota Comprehensive Epilepsy Program is presented in Exhibit 7.9. This outline was developed after an initial discussion with the program director. The purpose of the outline was to establish a context for later discussions aimed at more clearly framing specific evaluation questions. In other words, we used this goals clarification and objectives *mapping exercise* as a means of focusing the evaluation question rather than as an end in itself.

The outline of goals and objectives for the Epilepsy Project (Exhibit 7.9) illustrates several points. First, the only dimension that consistently differentiates goals and objectives is the relative degree of specificity of each: Objectives narrow the focus of goals. There is no absolute criterion for distinguishing goals from objectives; the distinction is always a relative one.

Second, this outline had a specific evaluation purpose: to facilitate priority setting as I worked with primary intended users to focus the evaluation. Resources were insufficient to fully evaluate all three component parts of the program. Moreover, different program components faced different contingencies. Treatment and research had more concrete outcomes than education. The differences in the specificity of the objectives for the three components reflected real differences in the degree to which the content and functions of those program subsystems were known at the beginning of the evaluation. Thus, with limited resources and variations in goal specificity, it was necessary to decide which aspects of the program could best be served by evaluation.

Third, the outline of goals and objectives for the Comprehensive Epilepsy Program is not particularly well written. I constructed the outline from notes taken during my first meeting with the director. At this early point in the process, the outline was a tool for posing this question to evaluation decision makers: *Which program components, goals, and objectives should be evaluated to produce the most useful information for program improvement and decision making?* That is the question. To answer it, one does not need technically perfect goal

EXHIBIT 7.9

Minnesota Comprehensive Epilepsy Program: Mission Statement, Goals, and Objectives

Program Mission: Improve the lives of people with epilepsy

Research Component

Goal 1: Produce high-quality, *scholarly research* on epilepsy

Objective 1: Publish research findings in high-quality, refereed journals

Objective 2: Contribute to knowledge about

   a. neurological aspects of epilepsy
   b. pharmacological aspects of epilepsy
   c. epidemiology of epilepsy
   d. social and psychological aspects of epilepsy

Goal 2: Produce interdisciplinary research

Objective 1: Conduct research projects that *integrate* principal investigators from different disciplines

Objective 2: Increase meaningful *exchanges* among researchers from different disciplines

Education Component

Goal 3: Health professionals will know the nature and effects of epilepsy behaviors

Objective 1: Increase the *knowledge* of health professionals who serve people with epilepsy so that they know

   a. what to do if a person has a seizure
   b. the incidence and prevalence of epilepsy

Objective 2: Change the attitudes of health professionals so that they

   a. are sympathetic to the needs of people with epilepsy
   b. believe in the importance of identifying the special needs of people with epilepsy

Goal 4: Educate persons with epilepsy about their disorder

Goal 5: Inform the general public about the nature and incidence of epilepsy

Treatment Component

Goal 6: Diagnose, treat, and rehabilitate persons with severe, chronic, and disabling seizures

Objective 1: Increase seizure control in treated patients

Objective 2: Increase the functioning of patients

statements. Once the evaluation is focused, relevant goals and objectives can be reworked as necessary. The point is to avoid wasting time in the construction of grandiose, complicated models of program goals and objectives just because the folklore of evaluation prescribes such an exercise. In comprehensive, multidimensional programs, evaluators can spend so much time working on goals statements that considerable momentum is lost.

Establishing Priorities: Importance versus Utility

Let me elaborate the distinction between writing goals for the sake of writing goals and writing them to use as tools in narrowing the focus of an evaluation. In utilization-focused evaluation, goals are prioritized in a manner quite different from that usually prescribed. The classic criterion for prioritizing goals is ranking or rating in terms of *importance* (Edwards, Guttentag, and Snapper 1975; Gardiner and Edwards 1975). The reason seems commonsensical: Evaluations ought to focus on important goals. But from a utilization-focused perspective, what appears to be most sensible may not be most useful.

The most important goal may not be the one that decision makers and intended users most need information about. In utilization-focused evaluation, goals are also prioritized on the basis of what information is most needed and likely to be most useful, given the evaluation's purpose. For example, a final end-of-project summative evaluation would likely evaluate goals in order of overall importance, but a formative (improvement-oriented) evaluation might focus on a goal of secondary importance because it is an area being neglected or proving particularly troublesome.

Ranking goals by importance is often quite different from ranking them by the utility of evaluative information needed at a particular time. Exhibit 7.10 provides an example from the Minnesota Comprehensive Epilepsy Program, contrasting goals ranked by importance and utility. Why the discrepancy? The staff did not feel they needed a formal, external evaluation to monitor attainment of the most important program goal. The publishing of scholarly research in refereed journals was so important that the director was committed to personally monitor performance in that area. Moreover, he was relatively certain about how to achieve and measure that outcome, and he had no specific evaluation question related to that goal that he needed answered. In contrast, the issue of comprehensiveness was quite difficult to assess. It was not at all clear how comprehensiveness could be facilitated, although it was third on the importance list. Data on comprehensiveness had high formative utility, and this became the priority focus for the formative evaluation.

The education goal, second on the usefulness list, does not even appear among the top four goals on the importance list. Yet information about educational impact was ranked high on the usefulness list because it was a goal area about which the program staff had many questions. The education component was expected to be a difficult, long-term effort. Information about how to increase the educational impact of the Comprehensive Epilepsy Program had high use potential. In a utilization-focused approach, the primary intended users make the final decision about evaluation priorities.

In my experience, the most frequent reason for differences in importance and usefulness rankings is variation in the degree to which decision makers already have what

EXHIBIT 7.10

Minnesota Comprehensive Epilepsy Program: Goals Ranked by Importance to Program versus Goals Ranked by Utility of Evaluative Information Needed by Primary Users

Ranking of Goals by Program Importance	*Ranking Goals by Need for and Usefulness of Evaluative Information to Primary Intended Users*
1. Produce high-quality scholarly research on epilepsy	1. Integrate the separate program components into a comprehensive whole that is greater than the sum of its parts
2. Produce interdisciplinary research	2. Educate health professionals about epilepsy
3. Integrate the separate components into a whole	3. Diagnose, treat, and rehabilitate people with chronic and disabling seizures
4. Diagnose, treat, and rehabilitate people with chronic and disabling seizures	4. Produce interdisciplinary research

they consider good information about performance on the most important goal and the overall purpose of the evaluation (formative vs. summative vs. developmental vs. knowledge-generating). At the program level, staff members may be so involved in trying to achieve their most important goal that they are relatively well informed about performance on that goal. Performance on less important goals may involve less certainty for staff; information about performance in that goal area is therefore more useful for improvement because it tells staff members something they do not already know. On the other hand, for summative evaluations aimed at funders, they will typically want to know about attainment of the most important goals.

What I hope is emerging through these examples is an image of the evaluator as an active-reactive-adaptive problem solver. The evaluator actively solicits information about program contingencies, organizational dynamics, environmental uncertainties, and decision makers' goals in order to focus the evaluation on questions of real interest and utility to primary intended users at a particular stage in the life of the program and for a specific evaluation purpose.

Evaluation of Central versus Peripheral Goals

Prioritizing goals on the basis of perceived evaluative utility means that an evaluation might focus on goals of apparent peripheral importance rather than more central program goals. This is a matter of some controversy. In her early work, Weiss (1972b) offered the following advice to evaluators:

> The evaluator will have to press to find out priorities—which goals the staff sees as critical to its mission and which are subsidiary. But since the evaluator is not a mere technician for the translation of a program's stated aims into measurement instruments, he has a responsibility to express his own interpretation of the relative importance of goals. *He doesn't want to do an elaborate study on the attainment of minor and innocuous goals* [italics added], while some vital goals go unexplored. (Pp. 30–31)

Contrast that advice with the perspective of an evaluator from our study of use of federal health evaluations:

> I'd make this point about minor evaluation studies. If you have an energetic, conscientious program manager, he's always interested in improving his program around the periphery, because that's where he usually can. And an evaluation study of some minor aspect of his program may enable him to significantly improve. [EV52:171]

In our study, we put the issue to decision makers and evaluators as follows:

> Another factor sometimes believed to affect use has to do with whether the central objectives of a program are evaluated. Some writers argue that evaluations can have the greatest impact if they focus on major program objectives. What happened in your case?

The overwhelming consensus was that, at the very least, central goals ought to be evaluated and, where possible, both central and peripheral goals should be studied. As they elaborated, nine decision makers and eight evaluators said that

utilization had probably been increased by concentrating on *central issues*. This phrase reflects an important shift in emphasis. As they elaborated their answers about evaluating central versus peripheral goals, they switched from talking about goals to talking about "issues." Utilization is increased by focusing on central issues. *And what is a central issue? It is an evaluation question that someone really cares about.* The subtle distinction here is critical. Evaluations are useful to decision makers if they focus on central *issues*—which may or may not include evaluating attainment of central goals.

The Personal Factor Revisited

Different people will have different perceptions of what constitutes central program goals or issues. Whether it is the evaluator's opinion about centrality, the funder's, some special interest group's perspective, or the viewpoints of program staff and participants, the question of what constitutes central program goals and objectives remains an intrinsically subjective one. It cannot be otherwise. The question of central versus peripheral goals cannot really be answered in the abstract. The question thus becomes central from whose point of view? The personal factor (Chapter 3) intersects the goals clarification process in a utilization-focused evaluation. Increasing use is largely a matter of matching: getting information about the right questions, issues, and goals to the right people.

Earlier in this chapter, I compared the goals clarification process with the party game of Twenty Questions. Research indicates that different individuals behave quite differently in such a game (and, by extension, in any decision-making process).

In a classic experiment, Worley (1960) studied subjects' information-seeking endurance in the game under laboratory conditions. Initially, each subject was presented with a single clue and given the option of guessing what object the experimenter had in mind or of asking for another clue. This option was available after each new clue, but a wrong guess would end the game. *Worley found large and consistent individual differences in the amount of information players sought.* Such research provides evidence that decision-making and problem-solving behavior is dynamic, highly variable, and contingent on both situational and individual characteristics. This does not make the evaluator's job any easier. It does mean that the personal factor remains the key to evaluation use. The careful selection of knowledgeable, committed, and information-valuing people makes the difference. The goals clarification game is most meaningful when played by people who are searching for information because it helps them focus on central issues without letting the game become an end in itself or turning it into a contest between staff and evaluators.

Global Political Goals

The languages of goals and performance indicators have become part of the global political culture. The Kyoto Climate Treaty set specific targets for reduction of greenhouse gases. Most industrialized nations are required to cut emissions below 1990 levels (although some will be allowed to increase emissions by up to 10 percent over 1990 levels). In general, developing nations have no obligation to cut emissions now, but may be asked to make future cuts. Overall, the protocol's goal is to reduce carbon emissions by 5 percent below 1990 levels by 2008–2012, with further reductions to be negotiated in the future. No one expects these goals to be met. Their purpose and use is to focus the international political dialogue. The goals are important symbols that call attention to global warming and provide a basis for monitoring as the political dialogue continues.

In July 2007, international organizations, public officials, statistical agencies, academics, leaders of civil society, business representatives, and media gathered in Istanbul for a World Forum on Measuring and Fostering the Progress of Societies sponsored by the Organisation for Economic Cooperation and Development. The purpose of the conference was to focus worldwide attention on how societies can better use indicators to support dialogue and debate about what "progress" means. Participants affirmed the importance of measuring and fostering the progress of societies in all their dimensions, not just economic, but also social well-being, health status, and environmental quality. The conference called for producing high-quality, evidence-based information that can be used to form a shared view of societal well-being and its improvement over time.

Likewise the UN Millennium Development Goals serve the purpose of focusing international development efforts and providing a shared platform and language for political dialogue. Substantial resources have been committed to data collection for monitoring progress toward the goals. The World Bank and other international agencies have built strategic plans around the goals. Yet no one can realistically expect these goals to be achieved—not even close.

These are examples of the *process use* of goals on the global stage. They are used to provide a framework for communications and bring focus to widely disparate development efforts. They reinforce the

The UN Millennium Development Goals

Goal 1: Eradicate extreme poverty and hunger
- Reduce by half the proportion of people living on less than a dollar a day
- Reduce by half the proportion of people who suffer from hunger

Goal 2: Achieve universal primary education
- Ensure that all boys and girls complete a full course of primary education

Goal 3: Promote gender equality and empower women
- Eliminate gender disparity in primary and secondary education, preferably by 2005, and at all levels by 2015

Goal 4: Reduce Child mortality
- Reduce by two thirds the mortality rate among children under five

Goal 5: Improve maternal health
- Reduce by three quarters the maternal mortality ratio

Goal 6: Combat HIV/AIDS, malaria, and other diseases
- Halt and begin to reverse the spread of HIV/AIDS
- Halt and begin to reverse the incidence of malaria and other major diseases

Goal 7: Ensure environmental sustainability
- Integrate the principles of sustainable development into country policies and programmes; reverse loss of environmental resources
- Reduce by half the proportion of people without sustainable access to safe drinking water
- Achieve significant improvement in lives of at least 100 million slum dwellers, by 2020

Goal 8: Develop a global partnership for development
- Develop further an open trading and financial system that is rule based, predictable, and non-discriminatory, includes a commitment to good governance, development, and poverty reduction—nationally and internationally
- Address the least developed countries' special needs. These include tariff-and quota-free access for their exports; enhanced debt relief for heavily indebted poor countries; cancellation of official bilateral debt; and more generous official development assistance for countries committed to poverty reduction
- Address the special needs of landlocked and small island developing States
- Deal comprehensively with developing countries' debt problems through national and international measures to make debt sustainable in the long term
- In cooperation with the developing countries, develop decent and productive work for youth
- In cooperation with pharmaceutical companies, provide access to affordable essential dugs in developing countries
- In cooperation with the private sector, make available the benefits of new technologies—especially information and communications technologies

idea that we are all part of a global community with a common vision, shared goals, and mutual accountability. They illustrate the way in which evaluative thinking has become embedded in the global political culture.

Legislating BHAGs (Big Hairy Audacious Goals)

In 2006, the California legislature passed a bill that included the goal of *eliminating all childhood poverty in California in 20 years* (Assembly Bill 2556). It was ultimately vetoed by the governor. Such grandiose goals are controversial.

Professor Deborah Kerr, a senior lecturer at the Bush School of Government and Public Service, Texas A&M University, commented on this approach to goal-setting for *Governing Magazine*. Based on years having studied goals and the ways in which they do and don't work, she said,

> If you do goal-setting right, you'll get improvements, but you need to have a goal that's specific, measurable, achievable and there has to be a time element to it. I call goals like this—and you see them throughout government—"snap goals," because people snap under the pressure of pursuing something they can't accomplish.

Governing Magazine commentators Katherine Barrett and Richard Greene added,

> These are different from so-called "stretch goals," which encourage people to work their hardest to achieve something they have some hope of actually accomplishing. Human Resource experts believe that people like being challenged, as long as there's a chance of success. But when you stretch people until they're ready to snap, there's a good chance they'll either ignore the goal altogether or grow increasingly frustrated as they face failure on a daily basis. (Barrett and Greene 2006)

However, it is important to distinguish the effects of large-scale community and national goals, such as the proposed California commitment, from goals at the program and project level, which is what Kerr, Barrett, and Greene seem to be aiming at. These are different units of analysis and serve different purposes. Program and project outcomes focus on a more direct and immediate accountability with some hoped-for direct connection between the intervention and results. National and global goals involve the accumulation and aggregate effects of numerous separate but ultimately interdependent projects, programs, initiatives, and policies. Cumulative and aggregate societal outcomes are what former U.K. Prime Minister Tony Blair had in mind when he committed to end child poverty by 2020 (Minoff 2005).

The Goals Paradox

This chapter began with an evaluation of Nasrudin's hunting trip in search of bears. For Nasrudin, that trip ended with the "marvelous" outcome of seeing no bears. Our hunting trip in search of the role of goals in evaluation has no conclusive ending because the information needs of primary intended users will vary from evaluation to evaluation and situation to situation. Focusing an evaluation on program goals and objectives is clearly not the straightforward, logical exercise depicted by the classical evaluation literature because decision making in the real world is not purely rational and logical. This is the paradox of goals. They are rational abstractions in nonrational systems. Statements of goals emerge at the interface between the ideals of human rationality and the reality of diverse human values and ways of thinking. Therein lies their strength and their weakness. Goals provide direction for action and evaluation, but only for those who share in the values expressed by the goals.

Evaluators live inside that paradox. One way out of the paradox is to focus the evaluation without making goal attainment the central issue. The next chapter considers alternatives to goals-based evaluation.

Follow-Up Exercises

1. Locate the goals and objectives of a program in your area. Review them against the criteria in this chapter. Has the program identified indicators for monitoring goal attainment? If so, assess the quality and appropriateness of the indicators. If indicators have not been identified, develop your own examples of appropriate indicators for this program's goals and objectives.

2. This exercise involves analyzing goals conflict among different stakeholders. The example that follows is aimed at helping you find and discuss *your own example* of goals conflict.

In 1980, Candy Lightner's 12-year-old daughter, Cari, was killed by a drunk driver—a repeat offender. Brought to trial, the driver was given a slap on the wrist and released. Outraged, Lightner founded Mothers Against Drunk Drivers (MADD). During the 8 years she headed MADD, she built the organization from a one-woman crusade into a worldwide movement. The goal of MADD was to reduce drunk driving traffic fatalities, and the organization has been highly effective in raising public disapproval of drunk driving. The proportion of traffic fatalities that are alcohol-related has dropped 40 percent over the past quarter century. Most observers give substantial credit for that decline to the efforts of MADD. Today MADD's effect is felt with chapters in all 50 states, all Canadian provinces, and many international affiliates. Its goals are to educate, prevent, deter,

and punish. MADD helps victims, monitors the courts, and works to pass stronger antidrunk driving legislation.

But Candy Lightner has become alienated from MADD. She left in a highly visible and widely publicized display of anger and disgust from the organization that she herself created and served as founding president. Officially, she left because MADD changed its goals. "It has become far more neo-prohibitionist than I ever wanted or envisioned," she has explained. "I didn't start MADD to deal with alcohol. I started MADD to deal with the issue of drunk driving" (Westley, Zimmerman, and Patton 2006:195). She believed that if MADD really wanted to save lives, it would focus on going after the most chronic problem drunk drivers. Instead, some charge, MADD has become a prohibitionist organization, trying to completely outlaw driving after even one drink—a zero tolerance approach for everyone. Those who oppose this prohibitionist focus, including Candy Lightner, argue that it is misguided and ultimately ineffective. MADD is no longer a safety-promotion organization, they complain, but an antialcohol organization. Thus do committed stakeholders in an organization sometimes do battle with supporters and opponents about what their mission and goals are.

With this example in mind, find your own example of an issue on which major stakeholders are in conflict about priority goals and objectives. Identify and discuss the competing stakeholder positions. Discuss the evaluation implications of these different positions.

3. Find an example of a prominently publicized community indicator (such as crime statistics, test scores in school, immunization rates, employment rates, poverty rates, HIV/AIDS infection rates,

etc.) Find news media examples where changes in these rates are linked in some way to accountability. Analyze the use of such indicators in public policy discussions and political debates. Assess the appropriateness of the indicators you have identified for evaluation purposes.

4. There are eight UN Millennium Development Goals (see section Global Political Goals). A number of organizations are monitoring progress on these goals including regular reports from the United Nations. Select one of the goals and find, through a Web search, the latest indicators data on progress toward the goal you have selected. Analyze the commentary you find from experts about this goal. What is your assessment of the role such goals play in the international arena. Present and discuss the pros and cons of such global goal setting.

8

Evaluation Focus Options

Developmental Evaluation and Other Alternatives

Creative thinking may mean simply the realization that there's no particular virtue in doing things the way they always have been done.

—Rudolf Flesch

If you can see in any given situation only what everybody else can see, you can be said to be so much a representative of your culture that you are a victim of it.

—S. I. Hayakawa

More Than One Way to Manage a Horse

Here is a story about the young Alexander, later to become *Alexander the Great*, as recorded by the ancient Greek historian and biographer Plutarch.

There came a day when Philoneicus the Thessalian brought King Philip a horse named Bucephalus, which he offered to sell for 13 talents. The king and his friends went down to the plain to watch the horse's trials and came to the conclusion that he was wild and quite unmanageable, for he would allow no one to mount him, nor would he endure the shouts of Philip's grooms, but reared up against anyone who approached. The king became angry at being offered such a vicious unbroken animal and ordered it led away. But Alexander, who was standing close by, remarked, "What a horse they are losing, and all because they don't know how to handle him, or dare not try!"

King Philip kept quiet at first, but when he heard Alexander repeat these words and saw that he was upset, he asked him: "Do you think you know more than your elders or can manage a horse better?"

"I could manage this one better," retorted Alexander.

"And if you cannot," said his father, "what penalty will you pay for being so impertinent?"

"I will pay the price of the horse," answered the boy. At this, the whole company burst out laughing. As soon as the father and son had settled the terms of the bet, Alexander went quickly up to Bucephalus, took off his bridle, and turned him towards the sun, for he had noticed that the horse was shying at the sight of his own shadow, as it fell in front of him and constantly moved whenever he did. He ran alongside the animal for a little way, calming him down by stroking him, and then, when he saw he was full of spirit and courage, he quietly threw aside his cloak and with a light spring vaulted safely onto his back. For a little while, he kept feeling the bit with the reins, without jarring or tearing his mouth, and got him collected. Finally, when he saw that the horse was free of his fears and impatient to show his speed, he gave him his head and urged him forward, using a commanding voice and touch of the foot.

King Philip held his breath in an agony of suspense until he saw Alexander reach the end of his gallop, turn in full control, and ride back triumphant, exulting in his success. Thereupon the rest of the company broke into loud applause, while his father, we are told, actually wept for joy. When Alexander had dismounted, he kissed him and said: "My boy, you must find a kingdom big enough for your ambitions. Macedonia is too small for you." (Adapted from Plutarch 2001:139–45)

More Than One Way to Focus an Evaluation

Young Alexander showed that there was more than one way to manage a horse. What I like most about this story, as a metaphor for managing an evaluation, is that he based his approach to the horse on careful observations of the horse and situation. He noticed that the horse was afraid of its shadow, so he turned him toward the sun. He established a relationship with the wild animal before mounting it. He was sensitive to the horse's response to the bit and reins. Alexander exemplified being active, reactive, interactive, and adaptive. Chapter 6 explored how these traits can serve an evaluator in being situationally responsive. This chapter goes farther with situational responsiveness and contingency thinking by presenting a broad range of evaluation options and identifying the factors that affect choosing a specific evaluation approach to match the priority information needs of primary intended users.

The last chapter focused on goals and outcomes as traditional ways to focus an evaluation. A program with clear, specific, and measurable goals is like a horse already trained for riding. Programs with multiple, conflicting, and still developing or ever-changing goals can feel wild and risky to an evaluator whose only experience is with seasoned and trained horses. Just as there's more than one way to manage a horse, depending on its characteristics, there's more than one way to manage evaluation of a program, depending on the program's characteristics and the environment in which it operates. This chapter will examine why goals-based evaluation may not be as useful as some other options and offer alternatives for focusing an evaluation.

Problems with Goals-Based Evaluation

One can conduct useful evaluations without ever seeing an objective.

—Smith 1980:39

Alternatives to goals-based evaluation have emerged because of the problems evaluators routinely experience in attempting to focus on goals. In addition to fuzzy goals and conflicts over goals—problems addressed in the previous chapter—a longstanding concern has been that too much attention to measurable goals can distort a program's priorities. Lee J. Cronbach and Associates (1980) at the Stanford Evaluation Consortium, in their classic treatise on reforming evaluation, warned

> It is unwise for evaluation to focus on whether a project has "attained its goals." Goals are a necessary part of political rhetoric, but all social programs, even supposedly targeted ones, have broad aims. Legislators who have sophisticated reasons for keeping goal statements lofty and nebulous unblushingly ask program administrators to state explicit goals. Unfortunately, whatever the evaluator decides to measure tends to become a primary goal of program operators. (P. 5)

In other words, what gets measured gets done. An example is when teachers focus on whether students can pass a reading test rather than on whether they learn to read. The result can be students who pass mandated competency tests but are still functionally illiterate. There are, then, two sides to the goals sword: (1) a powerful focusing purpose (what gets measured gets done) and (2) a potentially distorting consequence (doing only what can be quantitatively measured, which is dependent on the state of the art of measurement and limited by the complexities of the real world).

Reification: Are Goals Real?

Another critique of goals is that they're not real. Since evaluation is grounded in reality testing, it behooves us to examine the reality of goals. To "reify" is to treat an abstraction as if it is real. Goals have long been a special target of social scientists concerned with concept reification. For example, Cyert and March (1963:28) asserted that *individual people have goals, collectiveness of people do not.* They likewise asserted that only individuals can act; organizations or programs, as such, cannot be said to take action, a matter of ongoing debate among sociologists (Fuchs 2007; Greenwood 2007). The future state desired by an organization (its goals) is nothing but a function of individual aspirations. In brief, *social scientists who study program goals are not quite sure what they are studying.* Organizational goals analysis is controversial and confusing. In the end, most researchers follow the traditionally pragmatic logic of pioneer organizational sociologist Charles Perrow (1970):

> For our purposes we shall use the concept of an organizational goal as if there were no question concerning its legitimacy, even though we recognize that there are legitimate objections to doing so. Our present state of conceptual development, linguistic practices, and ontology (knowing whether something exists or not) offers us no alternative. (P. 134)

Like Perrow, funders, program staff, and evaluators are likely to come down on the side of practicality. The language of goals will continue to dominate evaluation. By introducing the issue of goals reification, I have hoped merely to induce a modicum of caution and compassion among evaluators before they impose goals clarification exercises on program staff. Given the way organizational sociologists have gotten themselves tangled up in the question of whether program-level goals actually exist, it is just possible that *difficulties in clarifying a program's goals may be due to problems inherent in the notion of goals rather than staff incompetence, intransigence, or opposition to evaluation.* Failure to appreciate these difficulties and proceed with sensitivity and patience can create staff resistance that is detrimental to the entire evaluation process.

Turbulent Environments and Changing Goals

A half-century ago, organizational sociologists discovered that the clarity and stability of goals are contingent on the degree of stability or turbulence in an organization's environment (Emery and Trist 1965). Evaluators, having traditionally defined their task as measuring goal attainment, have been slow to incorporate this understanding by adapting what we do to different conditions. Uncertainty includes things like funding instability, changes in governmental rules and regulations, mobility and transience of clients and suppliers, technological innovation, and political, economic, or social turbulence. What is important about classic works in organizational sociology (e.g., Azumi and Hage 1972; Hage and Aiken 1970) from an evaluation perspective is the finding that the degree of uncertainty facing an organization directly affects *the degree to which goals and strategies for attaining goals can be made concrete and stable.* The less certain the environment, the less stable and concrete will be the organization's goals. Effective organizations in turbulent environments adapt their goals to changing demands and conditions.

I have also hoped that reviewing the conceptual and operational problems with goals would illuminate why utilization-focused evaluation does not depend on clear, specific, and measurable objectives as the sine qua non of evaluation. Clarifying goals is neither necessary nor appropriate in every evaluation. Nowhere is this premise clearer than in goal-free evaluation.

Goal-Free Evaluation

Philosopher-evaluator Michael Scriven, a strong critic of goals-based evaluation, has offered an alternative: *goal-free evaluation.* Goal-free evaluation involves gathering data on a broad array of *actual effects* and evaluating the importance of these effects in meeting demonstrated needs. The evaluator makes a deliberate attempt to avoid all rhetoric related to program goals. No discussion about goals is held with staff and no program brochures or proposals are read; only the program's actual outcomes and measurable effects are studied, and these are judged on the extent to which they meet *demonstrated participant needs.*

Scriven (1972b) offered four reasons for doing goal-free/needs-based evaluation:

1. To avoid the risk of narrowly studying the stated program objectives and thereby missing important unanticipated outcomes

2. To remove the negative connotations attached to the discovery of unanticipated

effects, because "the whole language of 'side-effect' or 'secondary effect' or even 'unanticipated effect' tended to be a put-down of what might well be the crucial achievement, especially in terms of new priorities" (pp. 1–2)

3. To eliminate the perceptual biases and tunnel vision introduced into an evaluation by knowledge of goals

4. To maintain evaluator objectivity and independence through goal-free conditions

In Scriven's (1972b) own words,

It seemed to me, in short, that consideration and evaluation of goals was an unnecessary but also a possibly contaminating step. . . . The less the external evaluator hears about the goals of the project, the less tunnel vision will develop, the more attention will be paid to *looking* for *actual* effects (rather than checking on *alleged* effects). (P. 2)

Scriven (1972b) distrusted the grandiose goals of most projects. Such great and grandiose proposals "assume that a gallant try at Everest will be perceived more favorably than successful mounting of molehills. That may or may not be so, but it's an unnecessary noise source for the evaluator" (p. 3). He saw no reason to get caught up in distinguishing alleged goals from real goals: "Why should the evaluator get into the messy job of trying to disentangle that knot?" He would also avoid goals conflict and goals war: "Why try to decide which goal should supervene?" He even countered the goals clarification shuffle:

Since almost all projects either fall short of their goals or overachieve them, why waste time rating the goals, which usually aren't what is achieved? Goal-free evaluation is unaffected by—and hence does not legislate against—the shifting of goals midway in a project. (P. 3)

Scriven (1991b) also dealt with the fuzziness problem: "Goals are often stated so vaguely as to cover both desirable and undesirable activities, by almost anyone's standards. Why try to find out what was really intended—if anything?" Finally, he has argued that "if the program *is* achieving its stated goals and objectives, then these will show up" in the goal-free interviews with and observations of program participants done to determine actual impacts (p. 180).

Goal-Free Evaluation: Bizarre Idea?

Contrary to a common argument that Goal-Free Evaluation (GFE) is a bizarre idea, most consumer product evaluation is done in GF mode. No one buying a car, for example, asks for a statement of the design team's goals; the buyer usually has the family climb into each one under consideration, drives it around a bit, and haggles for the best price. In other words, one is driven by one's own (perceived) needs assessment, not by matching goals to performance. GFE simply brought us back from the world of managerial values to that of consumer product evaluation (Scriven, personal communication).

For all its virtues, goal-free evaluation carries the danger of substituting the evaluator's goals for those of the project, as evaluation theorist Marvin Alkin (1972) has posited.

This term "Goal-Free Evaluation" is not to be taken literally. The Goal-Free Evaluation *does* recognize goals (and not just idiosyncratic ones), but they are to be wider context goals rather than the specific *objectives* of a program. . . . By "goal-free" Scriven simply means that the evaluator is free to choose a wide context of goals. By his description, he implies that a goal-free evaluation is always free of the goals of the specific program and *sometimes* free of the goals of the program sponsor. In reality, then, goal-free evaluation is not really goal-free at all, but is simply directed at a different and usually wide decision audience. The typical goal-free evaluator must surely think (especially if he rejects the goals of the sponsoring agency) that his evaluation will extend at least to the level of "national policy formulators." The question is whether this decision audience is of the highest priority. (P. 11)

Here, then, Alkin raises the question of who the primary intended users are for a goal-free evaluation. In that regard, it should be noted that Scriven's goal-free proposal assumes both internal and external evaluators. Thus, part of the reason the external evaluators can ignore program staff and local project goals is because the internal evaluator takes care of all that. Thus, goal-free evaluation is only partially goal free. Someone has to stay home and mind the goals while the external evaluators search for any and all effects. As Scriven (1972b) has stated

Planning and production require goals, and formulating them in testable terms is absolutely necessary for the manager as well as the internal evaluator who keeps the manager informed. That has nothing to do with the question of whether the external evaluator needs or should be given any account of the project's goals. (P. 4)

In later reflections, Scriven (1991b:181) proposed "hybrid forms" in which one part of a comprehensive evaluation includes a goal-free evaluator working parallel to a goals-based evaluator. For our purposes, Scriven's critique of goals-based evaluation is useful in affirming why evaluators need more than one way of focusing an evaluation.

Evaluation will not be well served by dividing people into opposing camps: progoal versus antigoal evaluators. I am reminded of an incident at the University of Wisconsin during the student protests over the Vietnam War. Those opposed to the war were often labeled communists. At one demonstration, both antiwar and

prowar demonstrators got into a scuffle, so police began making arrests indiscriminately. When one of the prowar demonstrators was apprehended, he began yelling, "You've got the wrong person. I'm *anticommunist!*" To which the police officer replied, "I don't care what kind of communist you are, you're going to jail."

Well, I don't care what kind of evaluator you are, to be effective you need the flexibility to evaluate with or without goals. *The utilization-focused evaluation issue is what information is needed by primary intended uses, not whether goals are clear, specific, and measurable.* Let's consider, then, some other alternatives to traditional goals-based evaluation.

> **Avoiding Posttraumatic Goal Nonattainment Syndrome**
>
> Your program's goals you need a way of knowing.
>
> You're sure you've just about arrived,
>
> But where have you been going?
>
> So, like the guy who fired his rifle at a 10-foot curtain
>
> And drew a ring around the hole to make a bull's eye-certain,
>
> It's best to wait until you're through
>
> And then see where you are:
>
> Deciding goals before you start is riskier by far.
>
> So, if you follow my advice in your evaluation,
>
> You'll start with certainty
>
> And end with self-congratulation.
>
> SOURCE: McIntyre (1976:39).

Developmental Evaluation

The only man who behaves sensibly is my tailor; he takes my measurements anew every time he sees me, while all the rest go on with their old measurements and expect me to fit them.

—George Bernard Shaw (1856–1950)

Developmental Evaluation (DE) is an approach to evaluation in innovative settings where goals are emergent and changing rather than predetermined and fixed. Innovative initiatives are characterized by a state of continuous development and adaptation, and they often unfold within dynamic and unpredictable conditions. DE supports such innovative initiatives by bringing data to bear to inform and guide emergent choices. I introduced DE in Chapter 4 as one kind of intended use (see Menu 4.1). DE is also listed in Menu 5.1 on *process use* (Chapter 5) as an approach to program and organizational development in which evaluative thinking is infused into and made integral to the development process. In this chapter, we'll look at DE as a major alternative for conceptualizing what evaluation can contribute and how an evaluator can work, an approach informed by insights from complexity science and the particular characteristics of complex, dynamic systems (see Exhibit 8.1).

I originally conceptualized DE as an alternative to formative and summative evaluation (Patton 2005a, 1996, 1994a). The formative-summative distinction was first conceptualized by Scriven (1967) in discussing evaluation of a school curriculum. Summative evaluations were those conducted after completion of the program and for the benefit of some external audience or decision maker to determine whether to continue, expand, or disseminate

EXHIBIT 8.1
Developmental Evaluation Defined

Developmental evaluation supports program and organizational development to guide adaptation to emergent and dynamic realities from a complex systems perspective. Developmental evaluation differs from typical program improvement evaluation (making a program better) in that it involves changing the program model itself as part of innovation and response to changed conditions and understandings. Developmental evaluation doesn't render overall judgments of effectiveness (traditional summative evaluation) because the program never becomes a fixed, static, and stable intervention. Developmental evaluation supports social innovation and adaptive management. Evaluation processes include asking evaluative questions, applying evaluation logic, and gathering real-time data to guide program, product, and/or organizational development. The evaluator is often part of a development team whose members collaborate to conceptualize, design, and test new approaches in a long-term, on-going process of continuous improvement, adaptation, and intentional change. The evaluator's primary function in the team is to infuse team discussions with evaluative questions, data, and thinking to facilitate data-based reflection and decision making in the developmental process.

the program or curriculum (Scriven 1991a, 1991b). Formative evaluations, in contrast, served the purpose of getting ready for summative evaluation by helping work through implementation problems and get the program (or curriculum) sufficiently stabilized to be ready for a summative assessment. Over time, formative evaluation came to refer to any evaluation aimed at improving an intervention or model, but the implication has remained that such improvements are supposed to lead to a stable, fixed model that can be judged as worthy or unworthy of continued funding and dissemination.

But suppose an innovative intervention is being tried out in a highly dynamic environment where those involved are engaged in ongoing trial and error experimentation, figuring out what works, learning lessons, adapting to changed circumstances, working with new participants—*and they never expect to arrive at a fixed, static, and stable model.* They are interested in and committed

to ongoing development. As I explained in Chapter 4, it was precisely this situation that gave rise to DE. I had a 5-year contract with a community leadership program that specified 3 years of formative evaluation to be followed by 3 years of summative evaluation. During the formative evaluation, the program made major changes in all aspects of how it operated, from recruitment through program activities and on to follow-up with graduates. At the end of this highly innovative phase of engagement, I pronounced, "From now on, you can't make any more changes in the program because we need it to stay stable so we can conduct the summative evaluation. Only with a fixed intervention, carefully implemented the same for each new group of leaders, can we attribute the measured outcomes to your program intervention in a valid and credible way."

Staff were aghast. They protested, "We don't want to implement a fixed model. In fact, what we've learned is that we need to keep adapting what we do to the particular needs of new groups. Communities vary. The backgrounds of our participants vary. The economic and political context keeps changing. No. No. No. We can't fix the model. We don't want to do summative evaluation."

Since the purpose of the formative evaluation was to get the program ready for summative evaluation, not doing summative evaluation also meant not doing formative evaluation. It meant doing something else. But what? The answer became *Developmental Evaluation*. DE involved ongoing changes in the program, adapting it to changed circumstances, and altering tactics based on emergent conditions. My two evaluation colleagues and I became part of the design team for the program, which included a sociologist, a couple of psychologists, a communications specialist, some adult educators, a philanthropic funder, and program staff. The design team represented a range of expertise and experiences. Our evaluation role was to bring evaluative thinking and data to bear as the team developed new approaches for new groups, including immigrants, Native Americans, people from distressed rural communities, elected officials, and young people.

The relationship lasted more than 6 years and involved different evaluation designs each year including participant observation, several different surveys, field observations, telephone interviews, case studies of individuals and communities, cost analyses, theory of change conceptualizations, futuring exercises, and training participants to do their own self-evaluations and community-based evaluations. Each year the program changed in significant ways and new evaluation questions emerged. Program goals and strategies evolved. The evaluation evolved. No final report was ever written. The

> **Summative-Formative-Developmental Evaluation Metaphors**
>
> It is said that formative evaluation occurs when the cook tastes the soup and decides if it needs more ingredients or simmering, while summative evaluation occurs when the guests taste the finished soup (Stake, quoted in Scriven 1991b:169). Developmental evaluation occurs when, before cooking, the chef goes to the market to see what vegetables are freshest, what fish has just arrived, and meanders through the market considering possibilities, thinking about who the guests will be, what they were served last time, what the weather is like, and considers how adventurous to be with this meal.

program continues to evolve—and continues to rely on DE.

Complexity Science and Developmental Evaluation

Complexity science offers insights into the changed role that evaluation can usefully play in highly innovative and dynamic circumstances characterized by uncertainty. Studying how living systems organize, adapt, evolve, and transform challenges the largely mechanistic models of most programs—and most evaluations. Complexity science reveals that the real world is not a machine. Complex systems are too dynamic, emergent, and, yes, complex, to be reduced to simple cause-effect predictions and controls. I had the opportunity to become part of a Think Tank on Social Innovation that examined the implications of complexity science for social change and evaluation. What we found is that social innovators are driven not by concrete goals but by possibilities, often ill-defined possibilities expressed as values, hopes, and visions. In the early days of innovation, when ideas about possibilities are just being formed, the innovative process can actually be damaged by forcing too much concreteness and specificity. That's why brainstorming exercises outlaw criticism, because premature critiques and demand for specificity stifle the imagination. Yet what do evaluators typically bring to these situations? Evaluators are trained to insist that hoped-for changes and visions be specified as clear, specific, and measurable goals. That is typically all the evaluator has to offer, the only conceptual tool in the evaluator's toolkit. That's the moral of the story of Alice's encounter with the Cheshire Cat in Wonderland, the sarcastic observation that if you don't know where you're going, any road will get you there.

In the Social Innovations Think Tank, we called that way of thinking "Getting to Yes" where "Yes" represented clear, specific, and measurable outcomes. As we studied real cases of innovation and social transformation, however, we were struck by the liberating effects of open-ended aspiration, belief in possibility, and visionary commitment. Partly tongue in cheek, we came to understand that social transformation begins not with a plan for "getting to yes" as much as a commitment to undertake a journey aimed at "getting to maybe." That phrase, *Getting to Maybe,* became the title of our book on how the world is changed (Westley, Zimmerman, and Patton 2006). And what does evaluation have to offer people on their journey to *maybe?* One answer is DE.

Getting to Maybe: The Case of Hope

One of the cases we examined in *Getting to Maybe* described the uncertain journey of the Hope Community in Minneapolis. I'm going to include part of that story here with particular attention to evaluation implications *for this situation* and what DE offers under these kinds of circumstances.

In 1977, three Roman Catholic nuns started St. Joseph's House in the inner city of Minneapolis. Over the years, thousands of women and kids found compassionate shelter, dozens of volunteers came to the inner city, women and children who were and had been homeless built a community around St. Joe's hospitality, and the sisters

---

Incremental Development over Time

Have you ever been in one of those old houses in a small town in a place like Ontario or Iowa that seem to have grown rather than being built? The house begins as a single-room structure, with, of course windows and a door. Then, as the years pass and prosperity increases, a second, much more gracious room is added, connected to the first by an arched door. That seems a much more welcoming way to enter the house, so this room also adds a door. But this is rather grand so when a kitchen is added in the back, the "real" door is built there. Later, a second wing is added and there too there must be a door. Each room has a door; each room is different—a unique space; all rooms are interconnected into one house.

Social innovation is much like that house, with recognizable rooms, each with its own character and each connected to each other through numerous doors. Whatever room you find yourself in, it is helpful to know that the other rooms exist and that you are likely to pass through them, sometimes repeatedly as you engage the demands of social innovation.

SOURCE: From *Getting to Maybe: How the World Is Changed* (Westley, Zimmerman, and Patton 2006:220).

became leaders in fighting against violence and injustice. But by the early 1990s, their environment had changed. The block surrounding St. Joe's had become the center of a crack cocaine epidemic, drug dealers had claimed the streets, and landlords had abandoned many buildings. St. Joe's guests and families living on the block hid their children inside, police regularly ran through the block with guns drawn, and drug dealers and prostitutes (desperate themselves) broke into abandoned buildings. At the north end of the block where two major Minneapolis streets intersected, once-thriving small businesses (a gas station and grocery store) were abandoned.

When Deanna Foster and Mary Keefe took over the leadership of St. Joe's (now Hope Community, Inc.), they brought a vision of a vital, engaged community and decided to attempt a housing revitalization project. In keeping with their community organizing values, they began by trying to talk with local residents. But they found people afraid to talk, afraid of the drug dealers and perpetrators of violence. They decided to start with some concrete changes. They built a playground at their center and renovated a duplex that shared a driveway with the largest drug house. They put fences around the yard and then added fences around the porch because the drug dealers would run through the porch to get around the fences. The drug house was a triplex filled with little children who were terribly neglected and abused. Those little kids were so desperate for something to do that they would climb onto the garage or climb over the fence, anything to try and get to the playground. They cut a hole in the fence and put a tube through it so that the little kids had their own doorway into the playground. The drug dealers would have to embarrass themselves to crawl through the tube, though some did.

One day in desperation they contacted several donors and raised the money to buy that house. They built a duplex where once there had been a crack house.

When Foster and Keefe tell this story, they don't portray the purchase of the drug house as part of some strategic plan. It was an emergent reaction to what they faced on a daily basis.

Based on their early success in ridding the community of one major drug house and their long-term commitment to that area, the leaders and community came together to shape a new vision and found support for that vision when a door suddenly opened. They garnered unexpected support from a major philanthropic donor in the form of a $500,000 check. Those funds became the core funding for what is, today, a revitalized neighborhood and a Children's Village.

Foster and Keefe know a lot about traditional planning and evaluation approaches, but those approaches didn't fit them, their fluid and dynamic situation, and how they wanted to engage the community.

> We almost had to do it, not backwards, but in alternate order. Normally, when an organization gets half a million dollars they have spent a lot of time in a more linear process thinking through what they are going to do. What is the goal? What is the work plan? What will it cost? Who is the staff? You get the community input, all that stuff, and then have this whopping proposal, right? But it didn't happen that way at all. It was "Here's the vision, here's the money, now, make it happen."

And that very absence of a traditional linear planning process became a source of criticism and complaint.

> One of the criticisms we get is that we don't have a linear, goal-directed approach. We don't assume where we are going. We ask: Who's here? What are people experiencing?

What are they believing and hoping? What is their understanding of community? And what is our understanding of all the things we've done? We keep trying things, we keep building understanding and building community around ourselves. We are about uncovering, discovering, and creating. It really unfolds itself. It grows organically. It's just such a natural process.

But it's more complex than that because, at the same time, there's a whole set of strategic thinking that's going on. We also have to ask: Where is the land out there? Where's the money? What are the opportunities? Where are the potential partners? What are the potential pitfalls? How could all this fit together? What would happen if we did this? (Quotations from Westley, Zimmerman, and Patton 2006:173–74; see also Foster and Keefe 2004)

Summative evaluation would not be appropriate for Hope Community because there is no model being created for replication. They are learning and generating principles to inform future action, but that is a far cry from a "best practices" model that can be faithfully replicated in one community after another. The questions Foster and Keefe were asking also differed from familiar formative evaluations, which are focused on establishing programs' strengths and weaknesses, and progress, relative to intended outcomes, as the program unfolds. Instead, Hope's leadership pursued an open-ended approach to data gathering, where the questions and concerns were emergent, and where trial and error experiences were continuously mined for learning.

The Hope Community reality was messy, not orderly; emergent, not controlled; and social innovation was an iterative process of experimentation, learning, and adaptation. The Hope Community leadership was immersed in a complexity perspective. They monitored both the big picture and the whole picture—national housing, community development, and real estate patterns; interest rates and international finance; government policies, philanthropic funding trends and priorities; research on community revitalization. They had a keen sense of the history of the community. And, at the same time, they were fully enmeshed in the day-to-day reality of work in the community, engaging with residents as well as local government inspectors, city planners, social service agencies working in the community, local businesses, and local funders.

In these kinds of complex situations of rapid change, ongoing adaptation, and shifting priorities, and with these kinds of social innovators who eschew a command-and-control approach to change in favor of engagement and emergence, DE offers a way to infuse systematic evaluative thinking and real-time data into the generative processes of change.

Understanding Evaluation Niches

Utilization-focused evaluation aims to adapt evaluation to the needs of particular information users and decision makers within the specific set of circumstances they face. As the Hope Community case illustrates, one category of primary intended user consists of social innovators who make up what they're doing as they go along. They are engaged in what management guru Tom Peters (1996) advocated in his book *Liberation Management* as

Ready. Fire. Aim.

Instead of Ready. Aim. Aim. Aim. . . .

This runs counter to the conventional wisdom that extensive planning (aiming) should precede action. But planning only

I evaluate; therefore, I am.

DEVELOPMENTAL EVALUATION

works where you have control and know what the critical factors are. Under conditions of high innovation, uncertainty rules and control freaks perish. Indeed, one of the advantages of *Ready, Fire, Aim* is, paradoxically, its high and rapid failure rate, facilitating fast learning and speedy moving on (Shirky 2007). Traditionally, goal-based evaluation operates under conditions of *Ready. Aim. Fire.* Then, the evaluator determines whether the target was hit. But what is the role for evaluation when the innovator's mode of operating is *Ready. Fire. Aim.* The developmental evaluator still figures out what was hit (if anything), but the analysis is not a comparison of what was hit to a preconceived target. In providing feedback about what the innovator has "hit" (what immediate outcomes are emerging), the developmental evaluator engages the innovator in the following kind of dialogue: What's your

reaction to what you've hit so far? And what you've missed? What does this "hit" tell you? How does what you've done so far align with your values and vision? What does this "hit" (or "miss") suggest about what to do next?

Let me give a concrete example. Some years ago I was invited to join a design team to bring an evaluative perspective to their vision of creating an innovative program aimed at helping chronically unemployed and disadvantaged men of color get living wage, sustainable jobs in established companies with good benefits. The team had been working on a comprehensive plan for a pilot effort. I had just completed a cluster evaluation of 34 projects aimed at supporting families in poverty to improve their lives. All those projects had been carefully planned by savvy advocates and experienced community development professionals, usually with participation of people in

The *Ontario Science Centre* in Toronto asked the question: What if Canada could become a world leader in innovation? From this question, an idea was born. What if a science centre could reconceptualize what it meant to be a visitor? What if visitors were participants whose experience would engage visitors directly in scientific experimentation and the gathering of data to take on problems with real-world applications? What if, as in actual engineering and science, participants could guide their research activities without certainty of the results, and have leeway to innovate in their approaches?

These questions led to the development of the Agents of Change initiative. A bold and creative experiment aimed at fostering the development of visitor's thinking about innovation, risk, collaboration, and creativity. What would it take to do this? How would the science centre need to think differently?

Developmental evaluation supported this process as the Agents of Change initiative moved forward with an ambitious time frame. Planning, acting, and adapting were simultaneous; as new elements were designed they were immediately tested on the floor and, with rapid observation and feedback, modifications were made daily. At the same time, the developmental evaluation helped in shaping the goal of fostering innovation in visitors.

SOURCE: Gamble (2007).

the communities they were serving. They had written detailed proposals as required by their philanthropic funder. *And not one of those 34 projects had unfolded as planned.* All experienced serious implementation difficulties and most had to substantially revise what they had planned to do, significantly adapting their model to the realities of the people in poverty with whom they were working. The funder supported, indeed, encouraged, those changes despite the delays and mishaps involved. Based on those findings I told design team I had just joined, "It won't make much difference what you plan, it won't be right, so just start doing it and make corrections as you go." What really mattered, I suggested, was experience on a small-scale with constant reengineering.

That innovative program, called *Twin Cities Rise!,* has now been operating for over a decade. Along the way, virtually every aspect of what they do has changed substantially. Their recruitment and orientation processes have developed—not just improved, but fundamentally changed. (They began with an in-depth selection

process trying to select for success. When that didn't work, they went to a more open recruitment process followed by a probation period before full, contractual enrollment in the program.) Their target populations have changed (more immigrants and women), partly in response to changed welfare-to-work legislation. The political and economic environment has changed. Their objectives and immediate outcomes have changed as they came to better understand what prospective employers wanted. Their "model" today looks nothing like the original "model" they had in mind, though *the fundamental principles and values that led to the program have not changed at all.* It is a values-driven program characterized by constant adaptation. What they disseminate are principles, values, and lessons, not a fixed model of specific practices (Rothschild forthcoming).

In our Social Innovations Think Tank meetings, we examined cases like the Hope Community and *Twin Cities Rise!* to learn about how change had occurred in those cases and to consider evaluation implications. Inevitably, questions arose: How solid are the data on results and impacts? Can the causal chain between intervention and outcomes be substantiated or even traced? What things didn't work along the way, and how did those involved learn from failure as well as success? How do complexity science concepts illuminate these change processes? We also looked at what the profession of evaluation had to offer in light of complexity theory. That led to a further refinement of DE and the contrasts between traditional evaluation and DE listed in Exhibit 8.2.

EXHIBIT 8.2

Evaluation Niche Contrasts

Traditional Summative Evaluations	*Developmental Evaluations*
Measure success against predetermined goals	Develop new measures and monitoring mechanisms as goals emerge and evolve
Based on linear cause-effect modeling	Based on complex systems thinking, nonlinear, emergent dynamics, and interdependent interconnections
Render judgments of success or failure	Provide rapid feedback, generate learnings, support direction, or affirm changes in direction
Position the evaluator outside to assure independence and objectivity	Position the evaluator as a design team member integrated into developmental decision making
Aim to produce generalizable findings so that effective practices can be applied elsewhere	Aim to produce context-specific understandings that inform ongoing innovation; innovative principles are generalizable
Accountability focused on and directed to external authorities and funders	Accountability centered on the innovators' deep sense of fundamental values and commitments
Accountability aimed at control and locating source of failures	Learning to respond to lack of control and staying in touch with what's unfolding and thereby responding strategically
Evaluation often a compliance function delegated down in the organization	Evaluation a leadership function: reality-testing, results-focused, learning-oriented leadership
Evaluator determines the design based on the evaluator's perspective about what is important. The evaluator controls the evaluation	Evaluator collaborates with those engaged in the change effort to design an evaluation process that matches the innovation philosophically and organizationally
Evaluation focuses on bottom line success or failure	Evaluation focuses on learning and adaptation

The Role of the Developmental Evaluator

In Hemmingway's *The Sun Also Rises*, the main character is asked how he went bankrupt. He replies in what has become a famous literary line, "Gradually, then suddenly." Developmental evaluators help monitor what is happening gradually to help anticipate sudden changes.

In DE, the evaluator is incorporated into the program or organizational development decision-making process because those involved value the logic and conceptual rigor of evaluation thought and engagement with data. Moreover, experienced evaluators have accumulated knowledge about patterns of effective programming that can inform options and facilitate discussion of the possible implications of actions as they are considered. My role as developmental evaluator has been to ask evaluative questions of the innovators and hold their feet to the fire of reality testing. Evaluation data are collected and interpreted as part of the feedback process, to be sure, but quite above and beyond the use of findings, these development-oriented decision makers want to have their ideas examined in the glaring light of evaluation logic. *Honing ideas on the whetstone of evaluative thinking is an example of process use.*

Keep in mind we are talking about working with social innovators here: action-oriented, change-obsessed, push-the-envelope, do-it-now people. As I noted in Chapter 4 when I first introduced DE on the menu of possible uses, many such innovators eschew clear, specific, and measurable goals up-front because clarity, specificity, and measurability are limiting. They've identified an issue or problem about which they are passionate and they want to explore potential solutions or interventions.

They realize that where they end up will be different from what they imagined in the beginning. Where innovative programming is involved, they expect different participants will want different outcomes (an individualized approach as a matter of principle) and that participants themselves should play a major role in setting individualized goals for themselves. This process often includes elements of participatory evaluation, for example, engaging staff and participants in setting personal goals and monitoring goal attainment, but those goals aren't fixed—they're milestones for assessing progress, subject to change as learning occurs. It is in this respect that the primary purpose is program and organizational *development*. As the evaluation unfolds, program designers observe where they end up and make adjustments based on dialogue about what's possible and what's desirable, though the criteria for what's "desirable" may be quite situational and always subject to change.

Social Innovators and Developmental Evaluation

Developmental evaluation is especially appropriate for social innovators who don't value traditional characteristics of summative excellence, such as standardization of inputs, consistency of treatment, uniformity of outcomes, and clarity of causal linkages. They assume a world of multiple causes, diversity of outcomes, inconsistency of interventions, interactive effects at every level—and they find such a world exciting and desirable. They never expect to conduct a summative evaluation because they don't expect the program—or world—to hold still long enough for summative review. They expect to be forever developing and changing—and they want an evaluation approach that supports development and change.

Development-focused relationships can go on for years and, in many cases, never involve formal, written reports. Here are some examples from my own evaluation consulting practice.

Three Examples of Developmental Evaluation

1. *Supporting Diversity in Schools.* A group of foundations agreed to support multicultural education in the Saint Paul Public Schools for 10 or more years. Community members identified the problem as low levels of success for children of color on virtually every indicator they examined, e.g., attendance, test scores, and graduation. The "solution" called for a high degree of community engagement, especially by people of color, in partnering with schools. The nature of the partnering and interim outcomes were to emerge from the process. Indeed, it would have been "disempowering" to local communities to predetermine the desired strategies and outcomes prior to their involvement. Moreover, different communities of color—African Americans, Native Americans, Hispanics, and Southeast Asians—could be expected to have varying needs, set differing goals, and work with the schools in different ways. All these things had to be *developed*.

The evaluation-documented developments, provided feedback at various levels from local communities to the overall district, and facilitated the process of community people and school people coming together to develop evaluative criteria and outcome claims. Both the program design and evaluation changed at least annually, sometimes more often. In the design process, lines between participation, programming, and evaluation were ignored as everyone worked together to develop the program. The evaluation reports took the form of multiple voices presenting multiple perspectives. These voices and perspectives were facilitated and organized by the evaluation team, but the evaluator's voice was simply one among many. No summative evaluation was planned or deemed appropriate though a great deal of effort went into publicly communicating the developmental processes and outcomes (see Exhibit 8.3).

2. *Children's and Families Community Initiative.* A local foundation made a 20-year commitment to work with two inner city neighborhoods to support a healthier environment for children and families. The communities are poor and populated by people of diverse ethnic and racial backgrounds. The heart of the commitment was to provide funds for people in the community to set their own goals and fund projects they deemed worthwhile. A community-based steering committee became, in effect, a decision-making group for small community grants. Grantmaking criteria, desired outcomes, and evaluation criteria all had to be developed by the local community. The purpose of the developmental process was to support internal, community-based accountability (as opposed to external judgment by the affluent and distant board of the sponsoring foundation). My role, then, was facilitating sessions with local community leaders to support their developing their own evaluation process and sense of shared accountability. The evaluation process had to be highly flexible and responsive. Aspects of participatory and empowerment evaluation also were incorporated. Taking a 20-year developmental perspective, where the locus of accountability is community based rather than funder based, changed all the usual parameters of evaluation.

EXHIBIT 8.3

Reflective Practice and Developmental Evaluation

For several years, I facilitated a monthly reflective practice process with innovative staff in a suburban adult and community education program. No specific problems or goals were addressed. Instead, they were committed to ongoing program development and organizational change. That meant going wherever their inquiries took them.

They met monthly to share their action research observations for the last month. Their observations focused on whatever issue the group had chosen the previous month. The reflective practice process involved

1. Identifying an issue, interest, or concern

2. Agreeing to try something

3. Agreeing to observe some things about what was tried

4. Reporting back to the group their individual observations with detailed descriptions

5. Identifying patterns of experience or themes across the separate reports (facilitated by the developmental evaluator)

6. Deciding what to try next, i.e., determining the action implications of the findings, and

7. Repeating the process with the new commitment to action

Over several years, this process supported major curricular and organizational change. Evaluation was ongoing and feedback was immediate. The process combined staff and organizational development with evaluative thinking and facilitated reflection. My role, as facilitator, was to keep them focused on data-based observations and help them interpret and apply findings. There were no formal reports and no formative or summative judgments in the usual evaluation sense. Instead, they engaged in an ongoing developmental process of incremental change, informed by data and judgment, which led to significant cumulative evolution of the entire program. They became a learning organization.

3. *Wilderness Education for College Administrators*. In evaluating a wilderness education program, my evaluation partner and I engaged in participant observation and provided daily feedback to program staff about issues that surfaced in our interviews and observations. Over the course of a year involving three 10-day wilderness experiences, staff used our feedback to shape the program, not just in the formative sense of improvement, but in a developmental way, actually conceptualizing and designing the program as it unfolded. The two leaders of the program expected different participants to take away different things and didn't have pre-set goals or outcomes in mind. Indeed, they wanted to find out what diverse outcomes emerged for those involved and which experiences seemed to support various outcomes for participants. We became part of the decision-making team that

conceptualized the program. Our evaluative questions, quite apart from the data we gathered and fed back, helped shape the program.

An example will illustrate our developmental role. Early in the first trip in the Gila Wilderness of New Mexico, we focused staff attention on our observation that participants were struggling with the transition from city to wilderness. After considerable discussion and input from participants, staff decided to have evening discussions on this issue. Out of those discussions a group exercise evolved in which, each morning and evening, everyone threw their arms about, shook their legs, and tossed their heads in a symbolic act of casting off the toxins that had surfaced from hidden places deep inside. The fresh air, beauty, quiet, fellowship, periods of solitude, and physical activity combined to "squeeze out the urban poisons." Participants left the wilderness feeling cleaner and purer than they had felt in years. They called that being "detoxified." Like the drunk who is finally sober, they took their leave from the wilderness committed to staying clear of the toxins.

No one, however, was prepared for the speed of *retoxification*. Follow-up interviews revealed that participants were struggling with reentry. As evaluators, we worked with staff to decide how to support participants in dealing with reentry problems. When participants came back together 3 months later, in the Kofa Mountains of Arizona, they came with the knowledge that detox faded quickly and enduring "purification" couldn't be expected. Then, the wilderness again salved them with its cleansing power. Most left the second trip more determined than ever to resist retoxification on reentering their urban environments, but the higher expectations only made the subsequent falls more distressing. Many came to the third trip skeptical and resistant.

It didn't matter. The San Juan River in Utah didn't care whether participants embraced or resisted it. After 10 days rowing and floating, participants, staff, *and* evaluators abandoned talking about "detox" as an absolute state. We came to understand it as a matter of degree and a process: an ongoing struggle to monitor the "poisons" around us, observe carefully their effects on our minds and bodies, and have the good sense to get to the wilderness when being poisoned started to feel normal. This understanding became part of the program model developed jointly by participants, staff, and evaluators. As evaluators, we led the discussions and pushed for conceptual clarity beyond what staff and participants would likely have been able to do without an evaluation perspective.

Cautions about Developmental Evaluation

It will be clear to the reader, I trust, that my evaluation role in each of the programs just reviewed involved a degree of engagement that went beyond the independent data collection and assessment that have traditionally defined evaluation functions. Lines between evaluation and development became blurred as we worked together collaboratively in teams. I have found these relationships to be substantially different from the more traditional evaluations I conducted earlier in my practice. My role has become more *developmental*.

But once again, a note of caution about language. The term *development* carries negative connotations in some settings. Miller (1981), in *The Book of Jargon*, defines development as "a vague term used to euphemize large periods of time in which nothing happens" (p. 208). Evaluators are well-advised to be attentive to what specific words mean in a particular context to specific intended users—and to choose their terms accordingly.

One reaction I've had from colleagues is that the examples I've shared above aren't "evaluations" at all but rather organizational development efforts. I won't quarrel with that. There are sound arguments for defining evaluation narrowly to distinguish genuinely evaluative efforts from other kinds of organizational mucking around. But, in each of the examples I've shared, and there are many others, *my participation, identity, and role were considered evaluative by those with whom I was engaged (and by whom I was paid)*. There was no pretense of external independence. My role varied from being evaluation facilitator to full team member. In no case was my role primarily *external* reporting and accountability. When reporting to funders, my developmental role and its implications were made clear.

DE certainly involves a role beyond being solely an evaluator, but I include it among the things we evaluators can do because program and organizational development are legitimate uses of evaluation processes. What we lose in conceptual clarity and purity with regard to a narrow definition of evaluation (independently judging merit or worth), we gain in appreciation for evaluation expertise. When Scriven (1995) cautions against crossing the line from rendering judgments to offering advice, I think he underestimates the valuable role evaluators can play in design and program improvement based on cumulative knowledge. Part of my value to a design team is that I bring a reservoir of knowledge (based on many years of practice and having read a great many evaluation reports) about what kinds of things tend to work and where to anticipate problems. Young and novice evaluators may be well-advised to stick fairly close to the data. However, experienced evaluators have typically accumulated a great deal of knowledge and wisdom about what works and what doesn't work. More generally, as

---

Is Developmental Evaluation Really Evaluation?

Developmental evaluation is fundamentally evaluative because it focuses on

Identifying/negotiating/deciding *evaluative criteria*—knowing that our understanding of these will change over time and new criteria may emerge as things change (e.g., new challenges, opportunities, imperatives, such as global warming) and that different people and groups will have different views on what these should be.

Identifying/negotiating/deciding *standards of performance*—knowing that our understanding of these will change over time and the standards may also need to change as things change and that different people and groups will have different views on what these should be.

Identifying/negotiating/deciding what would constitute *credible evidence of performance* and getting it—knowing that our understanding of the best way to do this within ubiquitous limitations will change, and that different people and groups will have different views on what these should be.

Identifying/negotiating/deciding *methods for synthesis of performance information*—knowing that our understanding of the best way to do this will change and the weightings may need to change as things change and that different people and groups will have different views on what these should be.

Personal communications from Patricia J. Rogers, Professor in Public Sector Evaluation, Founder of CIRCLE (Collaborative Institute for Research, Consulting and Learning in Evaluation), Royal Melbourne Institute of Technology, Australia.

a profession, we know a lot about patterns of effectiveness—and will know more over time. For example, we know that new initiatives will experience implementation problems, that original program (and evaluation) designs will need to be adapted to real, on-the-ground realities, and that the excitement of new, innovative efforts creates halo effects that cannot be sustained over time. That knowledge makes us valuable partners in the design process. Crossing that line, however, can reduce independence of judgment. The costs and benefits of such a role change must be openly acknowledged and carefully assessed with primary intended users and evaluation funders.

Balancing Critical and Creative Thinking

Evaluation requires critical thinking. Development involves creative thinking. These two types of thinking are often seen as mutually exclusive. *Developmental Evaluation* is about holding them in balance. What developmental evaluation does is bring the rigor of evaluation (evidence-based, reality-testing questioning) together with organizational development coaching (change oriented, relational, visionary).

A Menu Approach to Focusing Evaluations

DE offers an approach appropriate for a particular set of contingencies, one where social innovators (the primary intended users) want to use both evaluation processes and findings to support *development* (the primary intended use of the evaluation). Exhibit 8.4 provides a checklist of the contingency variables and situational factors for which DE is especially appropriate. Historically,

lacking the DE option, evaluators have tried to force such situations into formative or summative boxes, often, I believe, constraining or even doing damage to the very process of innovation they were meant to inform.

Evaluation is not benign. Like any powerful tool that is misused, the wrong evaluation approach can do harm despite the intention to do good. Likewise, it would be inappropriate to impose DE on a situation where primary intended users want a rigorous answer to the summative question of whether a specific, well-defined model should be disseminated; under those conditions, the evaluation judges whether evidence supports the proposition that the intervention can reliably and consistently produce desired and prescribed outcomes. The challenge, then, is to match the evaluation to the situation, which in utilization-focused evaluation is determined by the information needs and intended evaluation uses of primary intended users.

There are a variety of ways of focusing evaluations. The transdiscipline of evaluation has become a many-splendored thing, rich with options, alternatives, models, and approaches (e.g., Stufflebeam and Shinkfield 2007). Menu 8.1 at the end of this chapter offers an extensive list of alternative ways of focusing an evaluation. I'll elaborate on only a few of these here. I'm highlighting here alternatives to the traditional goal-based approach to evaluation. These options engage intended users in other ways, always with the purpose of providing useful findings to inform actions, decisions, and understandings.

Focusing on Future Decisions. An evaluation can be focused on information needed to inform future decisions. Proponents and opponents of school busing for

EXHIBIT 8.4

Developmental Evaluation (DE) Checklist: Ten Situational Contingencies Indicating DE Would Be Appropriate

1. Situation is characterized by systems complexity: multiple interacting variables and factors interacting dynamically, interdependently, and unpredictably.

2. Working with innovators who are guided by strong values and vision, want to tackle a problem or issue, but aren't yet sure what needs to be done or what specific outcomes they are aiming at, in part because the situation is so complex. (These innovators are the primary intended users of the evaluation.)

3. Innovators want to *develop a solution* through experimentation, trial and error, and seeing what responses they get to what they try. *Development* is the intended use for the evaluation process and findings.

4. Solutions are expected to emerge from engagement and action (not advance planning).

5. The innovation is being tried in a highly dynamic environment, subject to rapid and unpredictable changes and demands.

6. Uncertainty abounds. There is little agreement among people about what should be done. There is little knowledge about the real nature of the problem or what potential interventions will yield.

7. There is a high likelihood of unanticipated *and* unanticipatable consequences.

8. Innovators are open to, indeed, *want to* use evaluative questioning and data to inform their understandings about what is happening and guide their next steps on the indeterminate journey. They can deal with critical questioning and data-based feedback about their creative impulses and "let's try it out and see what happens" approach to change.

9. Developmental evaluator has high tolerance for ambiguity, can react and adapt quickly, and communicate effectively with hyperactive, short-attention-span, action-oriented innovators. (Not all innovators are like that, but it's helpful to be prepared. Developmental evaluation is not an academic exercise. The evaluator will often be engaged in the trenches where the action is happening while it's happening.)

10. Those funding the innovation and evaluation understand the unique niche, constraints, and deliverables of DE.

---

desegregation may never agree on educational goals, but they may well agree on what information is needed to inform future debate, for example, data about who is bused, at what distances, from what neighborhoods, and with what effects.

Focusing on Critical Issues or Concerns. When the Minnesota Legislature first initiated Early Childhood Family Education programs, some legislators were concerned about what advice was being given to parents. The evaluation focused on this issue, and the evaluators became the eyes and ears for the Legislature and general public at a time of conflict about "family values" and anxiety about values indoctrination. The evaluation, based on descriptions of what actually occurred and data on parent reactions, helped put this issue to rest. Over time new issues arose. For example, universal access became a matter of contentious debate. Should the program be targeted to low-income parents or continue to be available to all parents, regardless of income? What are the effects on parents of a program that integrates people of different socioeconomic backgrounds? An evaluation was commissioned to inform that policy debate and examine programming implications (Mueller 1996). These Early Childhood and Parent Education program evaluations, done for the State Legislature, were issue based more than goals based, although attention to differential parent outcomes was subsumed within the issues.

The "Responsive Approach" to Evaluation. Stake (1975) advocates incorporating into an evaluation the various points of view of constituency groups under the assumption that "each of the groups associated with a program understands and experiences it differently and has a valid perspective" (Stecher and Davis 1987:56–57). The focus, then, is on informing each group of the perspective of other groups and providing data on each group's goals.

Focusing on Questions. In Chapter 2, I described focusing an evaluation in Canada in which primary intended users generated questions that they wanted answered— without regard to methods, measurement, design, resources, precision, goals—just 10 basic questions, real questions that they considered important. After working individually and in small groups, we pulled back together and generated a single list of 10 basic evaluation questions—answers to which, they agreed, could make a real difference to the operations of the school

division. The questions were phrased in *their* terms, incorporating important local nuances of meaning and circumstance. Most important, they had discovered that they had questions they cared about—not my questions but their questions, because during the course of the exercise it had become their evaluation. Generating a list of real and meaningful evaluation questions played a critical part in getting things started. Exhibit 2.4 in Chapter 2 offers criteria for good utilization-focused questions.

It is worth noting that formulating an appropriate and meaningful question involves considerable skill and insight. In her novel, *The Left Hand of Darkness*, science fiction author Ursula K. Le Guin (1969) reminds us that questions and answers are precious resources, not to be squandered or treated casually. She shows us that how one poses a question frames the answer one gets—and its utility. In the novel, the character Herbor makes an arduous journey to fortune-tellers who convene rarely and, when they do, permit the asking of only a single question. His mate is obsessed with death, so Herbor asks them how long his mate will live. Herbor returns home to tell his mate the answer that Herbor will die before his mate. His mate is enraged:

> You fool! You had a question of the Foretellers, and did not ask them when I am to die, what day, month, year, how many days are left to me—you asked how long? Oh you fool, you staring fool, longer than you, yes, longer than you!
>
> And with that his mate struck him with a great stone and killed him, fulfilling the prophecy and driving the mate into madness. (Pp. 45–46)

Testing Assumptions. The Greek Stoic philosopher Epictetus observed, "It is impossible for a man to learn what he thinks he already knows." With a group that has some trust and is willing to dig deeply into tougher issues, the evaluation can draw on organizational development and action research techniques for questioning assumptions (Dick and Dalmau 1999) and surfacing the "undiscussables"—what is sometimes called naming the elephant in the organization (Hammond and Mayfield 2004). Much of evaluation is framed as finding out what is not known or filling the knowledge gap. But deeper problems go beyond what is not known to what is known but not true (false assumptions) or known to be untrue, at least by some, but not openly talked about (undiscussable). In doing a cluster evaluation for a group of antipoverty programs, the undiscussable was that the staff was almost all white while the clients were virtually all African American. The unexamined assumptions were that there weren't enough "qualified" black staff and that clients didn't care about the race of staff anyway, so it wasn't really an issue or factor. In fact, racism was an undiscussable. It wasn't until the third year of the evaluation, after trust had been built, some appreciation of evaluative thinking had been established, and those involved were ready to dig more deeply into tougher issues that the group moved inquiry into the effects of racial differences to the top of the list of issues for evaluative inquiry.

When I offer a group the option of testing assumptions and opening up the undiscussable, I ask them if they're ready to take on the evaluation challenge of American humorist Mark Twain who famously observed: "It ain't what you don't know that gets you into trouble. It's what you know for sure that just ain't so." This is hard core reality-testing. I'm not inclined to start there with a group.

I find it's better to start a new group with less threatening issues and build capacity for evaluative inquiry before taking on more challenging and threatening questions.

A "Seat-of-the-Pants" Approach. In our follow-up study of how federal health evaluations were used, we came across a case example of using issues and questions to focus an evaluation. The decision makers in that process, for lack of a better term, called how they focused the evaluation a "seat-of-the-pants" approach. I would call it focusing on critical issues. The results influenced major decisions about the national Hill-Burton Hospital Construction Program. This evaluation illustrates some key characteristics of utilization-focused evaluation.

The evaluation was mandated in federal legislation. The director of the national Hill-Burton program established a permanent committee on evaluation to make decisions about how to spend evaluation funds. The committee included representatives from various branches and services in the division: people from the state Hill-Burton agencies, the Comprehensive Health Planning agencies, and the health care industry, and regional Hill-Burton people. The committee met at regular intervals to "kick around" evaluation ideas. Everyone was free to make suggestions. Said the director, "If the committee thought a suggestion was worthwhile, we would usually give the person that suggested it an opportunity to work it up in a little more detail" [DM159:3]. The program officer commented that the final report *looked* systematic and goals based, but

> that's not the kind of thinking we were actually doing at that time . . . We got started by brainstorming: "Well, we can look at the funding formula and evaluate it." And someone said, "Well, we can also see what state agencies are doing." See? And it was this kind of seat-of-the-pants approach. That's the way we got into it. [PO159:4]

The evaluation committee members were carefully selected on the basis of their knowledge of central program issues. While this was essentially an internal evaluation, the committee also made use of outside experts. The director reported that the committee was the key to the evaluation's use: "I think the makeup of the committee was such that it helped this study command quite a lot of attention from the state agencies and among the federal people concerned" [DM159:18].

Here, then, we have a case example of the first two steps in utilization-focused evaluation: (1) identifying and organizing primary intended users of the evaluation and (2) focusing the evaluation on their interests and what they believe will be useful. And how do you keep a group like this working together?

Program Director: Well, I think this was heavily focused toward the major aspects of the program that the group was concerned about.

Interviewer: Did the fact that you focused on major aspects of the program make a difference in how the study was used?

Director: It made a difference in the interest with which it was viewed by people. . . . I think if we hadn't done that, if the committee hadn't been told to go ahead and proceed in that order, and given the freedom to do that, the committee itself would have lost interest. The fact that they felt that they were going to be allowed to pretty well free-wheel and probe into the most important things *as they saw them*, I think that had a lot to do with the enthusiasm with which they approached the task. [DM159:22]

The primary intended users began by brainstorming issues ("seat-of-the-pants approach") but eventually framed the evaluation question in the context of major policy concerns that included, but were not limited to, goal attainment. They negotiated back and forth—until they determined and agreed on the most relevant focus for the evaluation.

Changing Focus over Time: Stage Models of Evaluation

Evaluate no program until it is proud.

—Donald Campbell (1983)

Important to focusing an evaluation can be matching the evaluation to the program's stage of development, what Tripodi, Felin, and Epstein (1971) called *differential evaluation*. Evaluation priorities can vary at

the *initiation stage* (when resources are being sought), the *contact stage* (when the program is just getting under way), and the full implementation stage.

In a similar vein, Jacobs (1988) has conceptualized a "five-tier" approach: (1) the preimplementation tier focused on needs assessment and design issues; (2) the accountability tier served to document basic functioning to funders; (3) the program clarification tier focused on improvement and feedback to staff; (4) the "progress toward objectives" tier focused on immediate, short-term outcomes and differential effectiveness among clients; and (5) the "program impact" tier, which focused on overall judgments of effectiveness, knowledge about what works, and model specification for replication.

The logic of these stage models of evaluation is that, not only do the questions evolve as a program develops, but the stakes go up. When a program begins, all kinds of things can go wrong, and, as we'll see in the next chapter on implementation evaluation, all kinds of things typically do go wrong. It is rare that a program unfolds as planned. Before committing major resources to overall effectiveness evaluation, then, a stage model begins by making sure the groundwork was carefully laid during the needs assessment phase; then basic implementation issues are examined and formative evaluation for improvement becomes the focus; if the early results are promising, then *and only then,* are the stakes raised by conducting rigorous summative evaluation. It was to this kind of staging of evaluation that Donald Campbell (1983), one of the most distinguished social scientists of the twentieth century, was referring when he implored that no program should be evaluated before it is "proud." Only when program staff have reached a point where they and others close to the program believe that they're on to something, "something special that we know works here and we think others ought to borrow," should rigorous summative evaluation be done to assess the program's overall merit and worth (Schorr 1988:269–270).

An example may help clarify why it's so important to take into account a program's stage of development. The Minnesota State Department of Education funded a "human liberation" course in the Minneapolis public schools aimed at enhancing communication skills around issues of sexism and racism. Funding was guaranteed for 3 years, but a renewal application with evaluation findings had to be filed each year. To ensure rigorous evaluation, an external, out-of-state evaluator was hired. When the evaluator arrived on the scene, virtually everything about the program was uncertain: curriculum content, student reaction, staffing, funding, relationship to the school system, and parent support. The evaluator insisted on beginning at what Jacobs (1988) called the fourth of

five tiers: assessing progress toward objectives. He forced staff, who were just beginning course development (so they were at the initiation or preimplementation stage, tier one) to articulate clear, specific, and measurable goals in behavioral terms. The staff had no previous experience writing behavioral objectives, nor was program conceptualization sufficiently advanced to concretize goals, so the evaluator formulated the objectives for the evaluation.

To the evaluator, the program seemed chaotic. How can a program operate if it doesn't know where it's going? How can it be evaluated if there are no operational objectives? His first-year evaluation rendered a negative judgment with special emphasis on what he perceived as the staff's failure to seriously attend to the behavioral objectives he had formulated. The teaching staff reacted by dismissing the evaluation as irrelevant. State education officials were also disappointed because they understood the problems of first-year programs and found the evaluation flawed in failing to help staff deal with those problems. The program staff refused to work with the same evaluator the second year and faced the prospect of a new evaluator with suspicion and hostility.

When a colleague and I became involved the second year, the staff made it clear that they wanted nothing to do with behavioral objectives. The funders and school officials agreed to a DE with staff as primary users. The evaluation focused on the staff's need for information to inform ongoing, adaptive decisions aimed at program development. This meant confidential interviews with students about strengths and weaknesses of the course, observations of classes to describe interracial dynamics and student reactions, and beginning work on measures of racism and sexism. On this latter point, program staff were undecided as to whether they were really trying to change student attitudes and behaviors or just make students more "aware." They needed time and feedback to work out satisfactory approaches to the problems of racism and sexism.

By the third year, uncertainties about student reaction and school system support had been reduced by the evaluation. Initial findings indicated support for the program. Staff had become more confident and experienced. They decided to focus on instruments to measure student changes. They were ready to deal with program outcomes as long as they were viewed as experimental and flexible.

The results of the third-year evaluation showed that students' attitudes became more racist and sexist because the course experience inadvertently reinforced students' prejudices and stereotypes. Because they helped design and administer the tests used, teachers accepted the negative findings. They abandoned the existing curriculum and initiated a whole new approach to dealing with the issues involved. By working back and forth between specific information needs, contextual goals, and focused evaluation questions, it was possible to conduct an evaluation that was used for continuous development of the program. The key to use was matching the evaluation to the program's stage of development and the information needs of designated users as those needs changed over time.

Focusing an Evaluation

Focusing an evaluation is an interactive process between evaluators and the primary intended users of the evaluation. It can be a difficult process because deciding what will be evaluated means deciding what will not be evaluated. Programs are so complex and have so many levels,

goals, and functions that there are always more potential study foci than there are resources to examine them. Moreover, as human beings, we have a limited capacity to take in data and juggle complexities. We can deal effectively with only so much at one time. The alternatives have to be narrowed and decisions made about which way to go. That's why I've emphasized the menu metaphor throughout this book. The utilization-focused evaluation facilitator is a chef offering a rich variety of choices, from full seven-course feasts to fast-food preparation (*but never junk*). The stage approach to evaluation involves figuring out whether, in the life of the program, it's time for breakfast, lunch, a snack, a light dinner, or a full banquet.

This problem of focus is by no means unique to program evaluation. Management consultants find that a major problem for executives is focusing their energies on priorities. The trick in meditation is learning to focus on a single mantra, koan, or image. Professors have trouble getting graduate students to analyze less than the whole of human experience in their dissertations. Time-management specialists find that people have trouble setting and sticking with priorities in both their work and personal lives. And evaluators have trouble getting intended users to focus evaluation issues.

Focusing an evaluation means dealing with several basic concerns. What is the purpose of the evaluation? How will the information be used? What will we know after the evaluation that we don't know now? What actions will we be able to take based on evaluation findings? These are not simply rote questions answered once and then put aside. The utilization-focused evaluator keeps these questions front and center throughout the design process. The answers to these and related questions will determine everything else that happens in the evaluation. As evaluators and primary users interact around these questions, the evaluation takes shape.

The challenge is to find those "vital few" facts among the "trivial many" that are high in payoff and information load (MacKenzie 1972). The 20-80 rule expresses the importance of focusing on the right information. The 20-80 rule states that, in general, 20 percent of the facts account for 80 percent of what's worth knowing (Anderson 1980:26).

In working with intended users to understand the importance of focus, I often do a short exercise. It goes like this:

Let me ask you to put your right hand out in front of you with your arm fully extended and the palm of your hand open. Now, focus on the center of the palm of your hand. Really look at your hand in a way that you haven't looked at it in a long time. Study the lines—some of them long, some short; some of them deep, some shallow; some relatively straight, some nicely curved, and some of them quite jagged and crooked. Be aware of the colors in your hand: reds, yellows, browns, greens, blues, different shades and hues. And notice the textures, hills and valleys, rough places and smooth. Become aware of the feelings in your hand, feelings of warmth or cold, perhaps tingling sensations.

Now, keeping your right hand in front of you, extend your left arm and look at your left palm in the same way, not comparatively, but just focus on the center of your left palm, studying it, seeing it, feeling it. . . . Really allow your attention to become concentrated on the center of your left palm, getting to know your left hand in a new way. (Pause.)

Now, with both arms still outstretched I want you to focus, with the same intensity that you've been using on each hand, I want you to focus on the center of both palms at the same time. (Pause while they try.) Unless you have quite unusual vision, you're not able to do that. There are some animals *who* can move their eyes independently of each other, but humans do not have that capability. We can look back and forth between the two hands, or we can use peripheral vision and glance at both hands at the same time, but we can't focus intensely on the center of both palms simultaneously.

Focusing involves a choice. The decision to look at something is also a decision not to look at something. A decision to see something means that something else will not be seen, at least not with the same acuity. Looking at your left hand or looking at your right hand, or looking more generally at both hands, provides you with different information and different experiences.

The same principle applies to evaluation. Because of limited time and limited resources, it is never possible to look at everything in great depth. Decisions have to be made about what's worth looking at. Choosing to look at one area in depth is also a decision not to look at something else in depth. Utilization-focused evaluation suggests that the criterion for making those choices of focus be the likely utility of the resulting information. Findings that would be of greatest use for program improvement, decision making, and/or development focus the evaluation.

A Cautionary Note and Conclusion

Making use the focus of evaluation enhances the likelihood of, but does not guarantee, actual use. There are no guarantees. All one can really do is increase the likelihood of use. Utilization-focused evaluation is time-consuming, frequently frustrating, and occasionally exhausting. The process overflows with options, ambiguities, and uncertainties. When things go wrong, as they often do, you may find yourself asking a personal evaluation question: How did I ever get myself into this craziness?

But when things go right; when decision makers care; when the evaluation question is important, focused, and on target; when you begin to see programs changing even in the midst of posing questions—then evaluation can be exhilarating, energizing, and fulfilling. The challenges yield to creativity, perseverance, and commitment as those involved engage in that most splendid of human enterprises—the application of intellect and emotion to the search for answers that will improve human effort and activity. It seems a shame to waste all that intellect and emotion studying the wrong issues. That's why it's worth taking the time to carefully focus an evaluation for optimum utility.

Follow-Up Exercises

1. Conduct a goal-free inquiry with two or three participants in a program. Interview them about what has brought them to the program, what they feel they need, and what they think they are getting through program participation. Conduct the interview without reference to the program's stated and official goals. Analyze the results. After the interviews, compare participants' needs and reported results with the program's goals. Comment on similarities and differences. Reflect on your experience doing goal-free evaluation interviews with participants.

2. In 2006, Muhammad Yunus won the Nobel Peace Prize for his innovative microcredit work, which began in Bangladesh and became the Grameen Bank with 2.5 million borrowers worldwide, most of them women and all of them poor. It's easy to locate the story on the Internet. Imagine that you were a developmental evaluator working alongside Yunus. Describe how you, as an evaluator, would have supported his innovation with developmental evaluation. What kinds of data could you have provided him? What kinds of decisions would you have helped him with? What role would you have played?

Or pick another social innovation as your case study. Consider the case of Candy Lightner and the founding of Mothers Against Drunk Driving; or Bob Geldof and his work on Live Aid concerts; or any example of major social innovation. Put yourself into an example of social innovation as a developmental evaluator. Describe your role and the data you would provide to inform and guide the innovative process.

3. Review Menu 8.1 in this chapter. Select three quite different approaches, types, or areas of focus. Compare and contrast them emphasizing what factors, circumstances, and contingencies would lead you, as an evaluator, to recommend each one because of its particular suitability and utility for an evaluation situation and challenge you describe.

4. Review the section beginning on page 295 titled "Changing Focus Over Time: Stage Models of Evaluation." Use an example of an actual program that has been in existence for some time. Learn about the stages of that program's development and match evaluation questions and data to those different stages.

MENU 8.1

Alternative Ways of Focusing Evaluations

Different types of evaluations ask different questions and focus on different purposes. This menu is meant to be illustrative of the many alternatives available. These options by no means exhaust all possibilities. Various options can be and often are used together within the same evaluation, or options can be implemented in sequence over a period of time, for example, doing implementation evaluation before doing outcomes evaluation, or formative evaluation before summative evaluation.

Focus or Type of Evaluation	Defining Question or Approach
Accountability focus	Have resources have been appropriately used to accomplish intended results? Key issue: Who is accountable to whom for what? (Rogers 2005a)
Accreditation focus	Does the program meet minimum standards for accreditation or licensing? (Hughes and Kushner 2005)
Appreciative inquiry	What is best about the program? (Preskill 2005a)
Artistic evaluation (evaluation as art)	Emphasize the artistic and creative elements of evaluation design. (Callahan 2005; Donmoyer 2005a; Lincoln 1991; Patton 1981)
Attribution focus (also causal focus)	Determine the relationship between the program (as a treatment) and resulting outcomes: To what extent can the program be said to have caused the documented outcomes?
Beneficiary assessment	The perspective of intended beneficiaries about what they have experienced, both processes and outcomes (Salmen and Kane 2006).
Capacity-building focus	Doing evaluation in a way that enhances the long-term capacity to engage in evaluation more systematically. (Baizerman, Compton, and Stockdill 2005; McDonald, Rogers, and Kefford 2003)
CIPP Model	Evaluation of an entity's context, inputs, processes, and products. (Stufflebeam 2005)
Cluster evaluation	Synthesizing overarching lessons and/or impacts from a number of projects within a common initiative or framework. (Russon 2005)
Collaborative approach	Evaluators and intended users work together on the evaluation.
Comparative focus	How do two or more programs rank on specific indicators, outcomes, or criteria?

Focus or Type of Evaluation	Defining Question or Approach
Compliance focus	Are rules and regulations being followed?
Connoisseurship approach	Specialists or experts apply their own criteria and judgment, as with a wine or antiques connoisseur. (Donmoyer 2005b)
Context focus	What is the environment within which the program operates politically, socially, economically, culturally, and scientifically? How does this context affect program effectiveness?
Cost-benefit analysis	What is the relationship between program costs and program outcomes (benefits) expressed in dollars? (Levin 2005a)
Cost-effectiveness analysis	What is the relationship between program costs and outcomes where outcomes are *not* measured in dollars? (Levin 2005b)
Criterion focused	By what criteria (e.g., quality, cost, client satisfaction) should the program be evaluated?
Critical issues focus	Critical issues and concerns of primary intended users focus the evaluation.
Culturally responsive	Focusing on the influences of cultural context and factors on program processes and outcomes. (Hood 2005)
Decisions focus	What information is needed to inform specific future decisions?
Deliberative democratic approach	This approach uses concepts and procedures from democracy to arrive at justifiable conclusions through inclusion, dialogue, and deliberation. (House 2005a; MacDonald and Kushner 2005; House and Howe 2000)
Descriptive focus	What happens in the program? (No "why" question or cause-effect analysis)
Developmental evaluation	The purpose is program or organizational development and rapid response to emergent realities in highly dynamic and complex systems under conditions of uncertainty.
Diversity focus	The evaluation gives voice to different perspectives on and illuminates various experiences with the program. No single conclusion or summary judgment is considered appropriate.
Effectiveness focus	To what extent is the program effective in attaining its goals? How can the program be more effective?
Efficiency focus	Can inputs be reduced and still obtain the same level of output or can greater output be obtained with no increase in inputs?

(Continued)

MENU 8.1 (Continued)

Focus or Type of Evaluation	Defining Question or Approach
Effort focus	What are the inputs into the program in terms of number of personnel, staff/client ratios, and other descriptors of levels of activity and effort in the program?
Empowerment evaluation	The evaluation is conducted in a way that affirms participants' self-determination and political agenda. (Fetterman and Wandersman 2005)
Equity focus	Are participants treated fairly and justly?
Ethnographic focus	What is the program's culture?
Evaluability assessment	Is the program ready for formal evaluation? What is the feasibility of various evaluation approaches and methods?
Extensiveness focus	To what extent is the program able to deal with the total problem? How does the present level of services and impacts compare to the needed level of services and impacts?
External evaluation	The evaluation is conducted by specialists outside the program and independent of it to increase credibility
Feminist evaluation	Evaluations conducted for the explicit purpose of addressing gender issues, highlighting the needs of women, and promoting change through increased social justice. (Seigart 2005; Seigart and Brisolara 2002)
Formative evaluation	How can the program be improved?
Goals-based focus	To what extent have program goals and intended outcomes been attained?
Goal-free evaluation	To what extent are actual needs of program participants being met (without regard to stated program goals)?
Horizontal evaluation	Evaluation, knowledge sharing, and program development within a horizontal network (Thiele et al. 2007)
Inclusive evaluation	Emphasizes stakeholder inclusiveness, dialogical data collection methods, social justice, cultural pluralism, and transformation. (Mertens 2005)
Impact evaluation	What are the direct and indirect program impacts, over time, not only on participants, but also on larger systems and the community? Impact evaluation often includes a focus on determining the extent to which results can be attributed to the intervention.

Focus or Type of Evaluation	Defining Question or Approach
Implementation focus	To what extent was the program implemented as designed? What issues surfaced during implementation that need attention in the future?
Inputs focus	What resources (money, staff, facilities, technology, etc.) are available and/or necessary?
Internal evaluation	Program employees conduct the evaluation.
Intervention-oriented evaluation	Design the evaluation to support and reinforce the program's desired results.
Judgment focus	Make an overall judgment about the program's merit, worth, and/or significance (see also summative evaluation).
Judicial model	Two evaluation teams present opposing views of whether the program was effective, like a legal trial (Datta 2005).
Knowledge focus (or lessons learned)	What can be learned from this program's experiences and results to inform future efforts?
Learning-oriented evaluation	Focusing the evaluation on practice improvement and organizational learning. (Rogers and Williams 2006)
Logical framework	Specify goals, purposes, outputs, and activities and connecting assumptions: for each, specify indicators and means of verification.
Longitudinal focus	What happens to the program and to participants over time?
Metaevaluation	Evaluation of evaluations: Was the evaluation well done? Is it worth using? Did the evaluation meet professional standards and principles? (Scriven 2005b).
Mission focus	To what extent is the program or organization achieving its overall mission? How well do outcomes of departments or programs within an agency support the overall mission?
Monitoring focus	Routine data collected and analyzed routinely on an ongoing basis, often through a management information system.
M&E (Monitoring and evaluation)	M&E: Integrating monitoring and evaluation. (Jackson 2005; Kusek and Rist 2004)

(Continued)

MENU 8.1 (Continued)

Focus or Type of Evaluation	Defining Question or Approach
Needs assessment	What do clients need and how can those needs be met? (Altschuld and Kumar 2005)
Needs-based evaluation	(See Goal-free evaluation.)
Norm-referenced approach	How does this program population compare with some specific norm or reference group on selected variables?
Outcomes evaluation	To what extent are desired client/participant outcomes being attained? What are the effects of the program on clients or participants?
Participatory evaluation	Intended users, usually including community members, program participants, and/or staff, are directly involved in the evaluation. (Salmen and Kane 2006; King 2005)
Personalizing evaluation	Portrayal of people's lives and work as contexts within which to understand a program. (Kushner 2005, 2000)
Personnel evaluation	How effective are staff members in carrying out their assigned tasks and in accomplishing their assigned or negotiated goals?
Process focus	Evaluating the activities and events that occur as part of implementation: What do participants experience in the program? What are strengths and weaknesses of day-to-day operations? How can these processes be improved?
Product evaluation	What are the costs, benefits, and market for a specific product?
Program theory evaluation	Making explicit and testing the program's theory of change: What is the program's theory of change and to what extent do empirical findings support the theory in practice? (Rogers et al. 2000; Rogers 2000a, 2000b)
Quality assurance	Are minimum and accepted standards of care being routinely and systematically provided to patients and clients? (Williams 2005a)
Questions focus	What do primary intended users want to know that would make a difference to what they do? The evaluation answers questions instead of making judgments. (Russ-Eft 2005)
Realist evaluation (also realistic evaluation)	What are the underlying mechanisms (possible mediators) of program effects? What values inform the application of findings for social betterment? What works for whom in what circumstances and in what respects, and how? The result is a context-mechanism-outcome configuration. (Pawson and Tilley 2005; Mark, Henry, and Julnes 2000)

Focus or Type of Evaluation	Defining Question or Approach
Real-world evaluation	How can evaluation be done under budget, time, data, and political constraints? (Bamberger, Rugh, and Mabry 2006)
Reputation focus	How the program is perceived by key knowledgeables and influentials. Ratings of the quality of universities are often based on reputation among peers.
Responsive evaluation	What are the various points of view of different constituency groups and stakeholders? The responsive evaluator works to capture, represent, and interpret these varying perspectives under the assumption each is valid and valuable. (Stake and Abma 2005)
Social and community indicators	What routine social and economic data should be monitored to assess the impacts of this program? What is the connection between program outcomes and larger-scale social indicators, for example, crime rates?
Social justice focus	How effectively does the program address social justice concerns? (House 2005b)
Success case method	Compares highly successful participants with unsuccessful ones to determine primary factors of success. (Brinkerhoff 2005, 2003)
Summative evaluation	Should the program be continued? If so, at what level? What is the overall merit and worth of the program?
Systems focus	Using systems thinking, concepts, perspectives, and approaches as the framework for evaluation. (Williams and Iman 2006; Williams 2005b)
Theory-driven evaluation	On what theoretical assumptions and model is the program based? What social scientific theory is the program a test of and to what extent does the program confirm the theory? (Rogers 2007; Chen 2005a, 2005b)
Theory of change approach	What are the linkages and connections between inputs, activities, immediate outcomes, intermediate outcomes, and ultimate impacts?
Transformative evaluation	Diverse people are included in the evaluation in a way that is genuinely and ethically respectful of their culture, perspectives, political and economic realities, language, and community priorities? (Mertens 2007)
Utilization-focused evaluation	*Intended use by intended users*: What information is needed and wanted by primary intended users that will actually be used for program improvement and decision making? (Utilization-focused evaluation can include any of the other types above.)

9

Implementation Evaluation

What Happened in the Program?

If your train's on the wrong track, every station you come to is the wrong station.

—Bernard Malamud
American writer (1914–1986)

An old story is told that through a series of serendipitous events, much too convoluted and incredible to sort out here, four passengers found themselves together in a small plane—a priest; a young, unemployed college dropout; the world's smartest person; and the President of the United States. At 30,000 feet, the pilot suddenly announced that the engines had stalled, the plane was crashing, and he was parachuting out. He added as he jumped, "I advise you to jump too, but I'm afraid there are only three parachutes left. . . ." With that dire news, he was gone.

The world's smartest person did the fastest thinking, grabbed a parachute, and jumped. The President of the United States eyed the other two, put on a parachute, and said as he jumped, "You understand, it's not for myself but for the country."

The priest looked immensely uneasy as he said, "Well, my son, you're young, and after all I am a priest, and, well it seems only the right thing to do, I mean, if you want, um, just, um, go ahead, and um, well. . . ."

The college dropout smiled and handed the priest a parachute. "Not to worry, Reverend. There's still a parachute for each of us. The world's smartest person grabbed my backpack when he jumped."

Checking the Inventory

Programs, like airplanes, need all their parts to do what they're designed to do and accomplish what they're supposed to accomplish. Programs, like airplanes, are supposed to be properly equipped to carry out their assigned functions and guarantee passenger (participant) safety. Programs, like airplanes, are not always so equipped. Regular, systematic evaluations of inventory and maintenance checks help avoid disasters in both airplanes and programs.

Implementation evaluation focuses on finding out if the program has all its parts, if the parts are functional, and if the program is operating as it's supposed to be operating. Implementation is how people "translate vision into practice" (Bodley-Scott and Brache 2005). Implementation evaluation can be a major evaluation focus. Most fundamentally, it means answering the question: *What is the program?* This involves finding out what actually happens in the program. What are its key characteristics? Who is participating? What does staff do? What do participants experience? What's working and not working? Answering such questions is essential "because implementation problems are a common cause of program failure" (Smith 2005b:195). Nor does implementation evaluation only apply to programs as the unit of analysis. Anything that requires implementation may benefit from implementation evaluation, including such mammoth endeavors as the structural adjustment policies and mechanisms of the European Community (Lion, Martini, and Volpi 2006).

The *IT* Question

Perhaps the most basic evaluation question asked by policymakers, philanthropic funders, and journalists is, "Does it work?" But what's the *IT*? There's the rub. What is this *IT* that works or doesn't work? The evaluation jargon for the *IT* is *evaluand:* "any object of an evaluation . . . , a person, program, idea, policy, product, object, performance, or any other entity being evaluated" (Mathison 2005:139). *Evaluand* works well enough in academic encyclopedia explanations of evaluation's focus (e.g., Sanders 2007), but it's not exactly user-friendly language. People don't ask, "Does the evaluand work?" They ask, "Does *IT* work?"

Implementation evaluation unpacks, figures out, describes, elucidates, illuminates, takes apart, looks into, explicates, clarifies, explains, and otherwise demystifies the *evaluand*. Excuse me. The *IT*.

A Beginning Point: Does the Program Exist?

Our follow-up study of federal health evaluations turned up one quite dramatic case of evaluation use with important implementation lessons. A state legislature established a program to teach welfare recipients the basic rudiments of parenting and household management. Under this mandate, the state welfare department was charged with conducting workshops, distributing brochures, showing films, and training caseworkers on how low-income people could better manage their meager resources and become better parents. A single major city was selected for pilot-testing the program, with a respected independent research institute contracted to evaluate the program. Both the state legislature and the state welfare department committed

themselves publicly to using the evaluation findings for decision making.

The evaluators interviewed a sample of welfare recipients before the program began, collecting data about parenting, household management, and budgetary practices. Eighteen months later, they interviewed the same welfare recipients again. The results showed no measurable change in parenting or household management behavior. The evaluators judged the program ineffective, a conclusion they reported to the state legislature and the newspapers. Following legislative debate and adverse publicity, the legislature terminated funding for the program—a dramatic case of using evaluation results to inform a major decision.

Now suppose we want to know why the program was ineffective. The evaluation as conducted shed no light on what went wrong because it focused entirely on measuring the attainment of intended program outcomes: changed parenting and household management behaviors of welfare recipients. As it turns out, there is a very good reason why the program didn't attain the desired outcomes. It was never implemented.

When funds were allocated from the state to the city, the program immediately became embroiled in the politics of urban welfare. Welfare rights organizations questioned the right of government to tell poor people how to spend their money or rear their children: "You have no right to tell us we have to run our houses like the white middle-class parents. And who's this Frenchman Piaget who's going to tell us how to raise American kids?"

These and other political battles delayed program implementation. Procrastination the better part of valor, no parenting brochures were ever printed; no household management films were ever shown; no workshops were held; and no caseworkers were ever hired or trained.

In short, the program was never implemented. But it was evaluated! It was found to be ineffective—and was killed.

The Importance of Implementation Analysis: Distinguishing Theory Failure from Implementation Failure

It is important to know the extent to which a program attains intended outcomes and meets participant needs, but to answer those questions it is essential to know what occurred in the program that can reasonably be connected to outcomes. The classic primer *How to Assess Program Implementation* puts it this way:

> To consider only questions of program outcomes may limit the usefulness of an evaluation. Suppose the data suggest emphatically that the program was a success. You can say, "It worked!" But unless you have taken care to describe the details of the program's operations, you may be unable to answer a question that logically follows such a judgment of success: "*What worked?*" If you cannot answer that, you will have wasted the effort measuring the outcomes of events that cannot be described and therefore remain a mystery.... Few evaluation reports pay enough attention to describing the processes of a program that helped participants achieve its outcomes. (King, Morris, and Fitz-Gibbon 1987:9)

Not knowing enough about implementation limits the usefulness of findings about effective programs and contributes to confusion about why programs succeed or fail. At the most simple level, programs may fail for two fundamental reasons: (1) failure of implemented programs to attain desired outcomes, which is called *theory failure*, that is, the idea didn't work as hoped, versus (2) failure to actually implement the idea (or theory), which is *implementation failure*, and means the idea (program) was never really tested for effectiveness because it was not implemented adequately or sufficiently. For an evaluation to support decision making, it is critical to be able to distinguish theory failure (ideas that don't work) from implementation failure (ideas that haven't been appropriately tested). This distinction goes on at fever pitch in political debates. Was the War in Iraq a bad idea, ill-conceived from the start? Or did it fail because it was badly executed, poorly managed, and incompetently led? Or was it both a bad idea and poorly implemented? Such debates are about theory failure versus implementation failure. At the program level, such debates tend to be less shrill but are no less important for interpreting findings and making decisions about what programmatic actions should follow from the findings.

Execution

In the world of business the social services language of implementation gives way to an emphasis on *execution*. Best-selling corporate management coach Stephen R. Covey has emphasized:

In business, survival depends on meeting objectives. Most failures in organizations today are not the result of a lack of smarts, they are caused by a lack of execution—things just don't get done. Defining a clear strategy and setting goals is one thing, sticking to strategy is quite another. Execution means getting critical things accomplished. (Covey and Colosimo 2004: training audiotape)

Larry Bossidy, CEO of Honeywell International, Inc., and Ram Charan, advisor to corporate executives, coauthored a best-selling business book titled *Execution: The Discipline of Getting Things Done*. They argue that while things such as strategy, leadership, being results-oriented, and innovation get the most attention, knowing how to actually get things done is the ultimate difference between a company and its competitors. Getting ideas implemented means having the capacity to *execute*. They describe execution as "the missing link between aspirations and results." While failure in business is attributed to many causes, Bossidy and Charan (2002) argue that the biggest obstacle to success is the absence of execution.

Focus on Utility: Information for Action and Decisions

The problem with pure outcomes evaluation is that the results give decision makers little information to guide action. Simply learning that outcomes are high or low doesn't tell decision makers much about what to do. They also need to understand the nature of the program. In the example that opened this chapter, legislators learned that targeted welfare parents showed no behavioral changes, so they terminated the program. The evaluators failed to include data on implementation that would have revealed the absence of any of the mandated activities that were supposed to bring about the desired changes. By basing their decision only on outcomes information, the legislators terminated a policy approach that had never actually been tried. This was not a unique case. Historical examples abound:

Federal agencies are often inclined to assume that, once a cash transfer has taken place from a government agency to a program in the field, a program exists and can be evaluated. Experienced evaluation researchers know that the very existence of a program cannot be taken for granted, even after large cash transfers have taken place. Early evaluations of Title I programs in New York City provide an illustration of this problem. (Guttentag and Struening 1975b:3–4)

Terminating a policy inappropriately is only one possible error when outcomes data are used without data about implementation. Expanding a successful program inappropriately can also occur when decision makers lack information about the basis for the program's success. In one instance, a number of drug addiction treatment centers in a county were evaluated based on rates of re-addiction for treated patients. All had relatively mediocre success rates except one program that reported a 100 percent success rate over 2 years. The county board immediately voted to triple the budget of that program. Within a year, the re-addiction rates for that program had fallen to the same mediocre level as other centers. By enlarging the program, the county board had eliminated the key elements in the program's success—its small size and dedicated staff. It had been a six-patient halfway house with one primary counselor who ate, slept, and lived that program. He established such a close relationship with each addict that he knew exactly how to keep each one straight. When the program was enlarged, he became administrator of three houses and lost personal contact with the clients. The successful program became mediocre. A highly effective program, though small in scale, was lost because the county board acted without understanding the basis for the program's success.

Renowned global investor and philanthropist George Soros tells a similar story. Through a foundation he established in Moscow when the Cold War thawed, he funded a successful program aimed at transforming the education system. "I wanted to make it bigger, so I threw a lot of money at it—and in so doing, I destroyed it, effectively. It was too much money" (quoted by Buck 1995:76–77).

The Politics of Effective Implementation

The importance of effective implementation and delivery has been highlighted in the United Kingdom since the General Election of 2001, *when the reform and delivery of public services became the defining theme of the second Blair administration* [italics added]. . . . There is a very strong need for more and better implementation studies that can identify the particular conditions under which successful implementation and delivery takes place, or fails to take place, as well as those conditions that are more generalizable (Davies, Newcomer, and Soydan 2005: 178–79).

In many cases, in keeping with the developmental nature of new initiatives, implementation evaluation should precede

outcomes evaluation. For example, Leonard Bickman (1985) has described a statewide evaluation of early childhood interventions in Tennessee that began by asking stakeholders in state government what they wanted to know. The evaluators were prepared to undertake impact studies, and they expected outcomes data to be the evaluation priority. However, interviews with stakeholders revealed a surprising sophistication about the difficulties and expenses involved in getting good, generalizable outcomes data in a timely fashion. Moreover, it was clear that key policymakers and program managers "were more concerned about the allocation and distribution of resources than about the effectiveness of projects" (p. 190). They wanted to know whether every needy child was being served. What services were being delivered to whom? State agencies could use this kind of implementation and service delivery information to "redistribute their resources to unserved areas and populations or encourage different types of services" (p. 191). They could also use descriptive information about programs to increase communications among service providers about what ideas were being tried and to assess gaps in services. Before "the more sophisticated (and expensive) questions about effectiveness" were asked, "policymakers wanted to know simpler descriptive information. . . . If the currently funded programs could not even be described, how could they be improved?" (Bickman 1985:190–91).

Unless one knows that a program is operating according to design, there may be little reason to expect it to produce the desired outcomes. Furthermore, until the program is implemented and a "treatment" is believed to be in operation, there is little reason to evaluate outcomes. This is another variation on Donald Campbell's (1983) famous admonition to *evaluate no program until it is proud*, by which he meant that demanding summative outcomes evaluation should await program claims and supporting evidence that something worth rigorous evaluation is taking place.

Ideal Plans versus Actual Implementation

Putting ideals into practice can be difficult and frustrating as evidenced by a widely distributed case study about a community development effort in Oakland, California. The title of the study was,

IMPLEMENTATION

How Great Expectations in Washington Are Dashed in Oakland; Or, Why It's Amazing That Federal Programs Work at All, This Being a Saga of the Economic Development Administration as Told by Two Sympathetic Observers Who Seek to Build Morals on a Foundation of Ruined Hopes.

(Pressman and Wildavsky 1984)

Why is implementation so difficult? And so frustrating? Part of the answer may lie with how programs are legislated and planned. Policymakers seldom seem to analyze the feasibility of implementing their ideas during decision making. The tasks of both implementing a program and evaluating it are made all the more difficult when the feasibility of implementation has not been thoughtfully considered in advance. As a result, either as part of evaluability assessment or in early interactions with primary intended users, the evaluator will often have to facilitate discussion of what the program should look

like before it can be said to be fully implemented and operational. Criteria for evaluating implementation may have to be developed at the beginning of the evaluation when implementation plans are vague or benchmarks are absent.

Different stakeholders will often hold different views of what implementation should include. In the Food Stamps Program for poor people in the United States, there was a vociferous debate about whether program implementation should include active recruitment of needy people. Advocates for the poor argued that access depended on vigorous outreach. Antiwelfare interests argued that it was not part of the program design to actively recruit those who might be eligible and that to do so would increase the costs of the program and might even put it in jeopardy.

Evaluating Implementation Feasibility

Evaluations can be influential—not only by demonstrating the *consequences* of a program or other intervention, as causal methods can—but also by demonstrating the *feasibility of its implementation.* For example, early studies of welfare reform in the United States were highly influential, not so much because of what they found regarding the effectiveness of alternatives to the then-standard welfare system; rather, these evaluations were influential because they demonstrated it was feasible, in practice, to implement alternative welfare practices (Mark and Henry 2006:320).

Understanding the politics of and some of the well-documented barriers to implementation can help evaluators ask appropriate questions and generate useful information for program adaptation and improvement. For example, organizational conflict and disequilibrium often increase dramatically during the implementation stage of organizational change. No matter how much planning takes place, "people problems" will arise.

> The human element is seldom adequately considered in the implementation of a new product or service. There will be mistakes that will have to be corrected. . . . In addition, as programs takes shape power struggles develop. The stage of implementation is thus the stage of conflict, especially over power. . . . Tempers flare, interpersonal animosities develop, and the power structure is shaken. (Hage and Aiken 1970:100, 104)

Odiorne (1984:190–94) dissected "the anatomy of poor performance" in managing change and found gargantuan human obstacles, including staff members who give up when they encounter trivial obstacles, people who hang onto obsolete ideas and outmoded ways of doing things, emotional outbursts when asked to perform new tasks, muddled communications, poor anticipation of problems, and delayed action when problems arise so that once manageable problems become major management crises.

Meyers (1981:37–39) observed that much implementation fails because program designs are "counterintuitive"—they just don't make sense. He added to the litany of implementation hurdles the following: undue haste, compulsion to spend all allotted funds by the end of the fiscal year, personnel turnovers, vague legislation, severe understaffing, racial tensions, conflicts between different levels of government, and the divorce of implementation from policy.

The difference between the ideal, rational model of program implementation and the day-to-day, conflict-laden realities of dealing with unanticipated crises in program implementation is illuminated without resort to jargon in this notice found during an evaluation site visit by Jerome Murphy (1976) in the office of a state education agency:

NOTICE

The objective of all dedicated
department employees should
be to thoroughly analyze
all situations, anticipate all problems
prior to their occurrence,
have answers for these problems,
and move swiftly to solve these
problems when called upon. . . .
However . . .
When you are up to your ass in
alligators, it is difficult to remind
yourself that your initial objective
was to drain the swamp. (P. 92)

The Case of Project Follow Through

The national evaluation of Follow Through has become a widely studied and discussed cautionary tale of failing to give sufficient attention to implementation in a very high stakes evaluation. Though this national evaluation occurred years ago, its lessons remain germane and are worthy of thoughtful review.

Follow Through was begun in 1967 as an extension of *Head Start* for disadvantaged children in primary school (whereas *Head Start* was a preschool program). Follow Through was implemented as a "planned variation experiment" in compensatory education featuring 22 different models of education to be tested in 158 school districts on 70,000 children throughout the nation. The evaluation employed 3,000 people to collect data on program effectiveness. You begin to see why the findings attracted a lot of attention. This evaluation was a big deal.

The evaluation started down the path to trouble when the designers "simply assumed in the evaluation plan that alternative educational models could and would be implemented in some systematic, uniform fashion" (Alkin 1970:2). That assumption quickly proved fallacious.

> Each sponsor developed a large organization, in some instances larger than the entire federal program staff, to deal with problems of model implementation. Each local school system developed a program organization consisting of a local director, a team of teachers and specialists, and a parent advisory group. The more the scale and complexity of the program increased, the less plausible it became for Follow Through administrators to control the details of program variations, and the more difficult it became to determine whether the array of districts and sponsors represented "systematic" variations in program content. (Williams and Elmore 1976:108)

The Follow Through results revealed greater variation within models than between them; that is, the 22 models did not show systematic treatment effects as such. Most effects were null, some were negative, but "of all our findings, the most pervasive, consistent, and suggestive is probably this: *The effectiveness of each Follow Through model depended more on local circumstances than on the nature of the model*" (Anderson 1977:13). In reviewing these findings, Eugene Tucker (1977) of the U.S. Office of Education suggested that, in retrospect, the Follow Through evaluation should have begun as a formative effort with greater focus on implementation strategies:

> It is safe to say that evaluators did not know what was implemented in the various sites. Without knowing what was implemented, it is virtually impossible to select valid effectiveness measures. . . . Hindsight is a marvelous

teacher and in large-scale experimentations an expensive one. (Pp. 11–12)

Comparing Program Approaches: Implementation Differences Can Affect Development Outcomes

When comparing programs or policies, it is critical to know in what ways they have been implemented differently:

One project may use participatory planning and management in which stakeholders were actively involved in program design, implementation, and monitoring, while another uses top-down planning with design and management by client or funding agency. Similarly one microcredit project might open an office in a community, while another might require women to travel to the nearest town to apply for loans (Bamberger, Rugh, and Mabry 2006:177).

Ideals and Discrepancies

Malcolm Provus (1971) had warned against the design used in the Follow Through evaluation at a 1966 conference on educational evaluation of national programs:

> An evaluation that begins with an experimental design denies to program staff what it needs most: information that can be used to make judgments about the program while it is in its dynamic stages of growth. . . Evaluation must provide administrators and program staff with the information they need and the freedom to act on that information. . . .
>
> We will not use the antiseptic assumptions of the research laboratory to compare children receiving new program assistance with those not receiving such aid. We recognize that the comparisons have never been productive, nor have they facilitated corrective action. The overwhelming number of evaluations conducted in this way show no significant differences between "experimental" and "control" groups. (Pp. 11–12)

Instead, Provus (1971) advocated "discrepancy evaluation," an approach that compares the actual with the ideal and places heavy emphasis on implementation evaluation. He argued that evaluations should begin by establishing the degree to which programs are actually operating as desired. Conceptualization of ideals "may arise from any source, but under the Discrepancy Evaluation Model they are derived from the values of the program staff and the client population it serves" (p. 12). Data to compare actual practices with ideals would come from local fieldwork "of the process assessment type" in which evaluators systematically collect and weigh data descriptive of ongoing program activity (p. 13).

Given the reality that actual implementation will typically look different from original ideals, a primary evaluation challenge is to help identified decision makers determine how far from the ideal the program can deviate, and in what ways it can deviate, while still constituting the original idea (as opposed to the original ideal). In other words, a central evaluation question is, *"How different can an actual program be from its ideal and still be said to have been implemented?"* The answer must be clarified between primary intended users and evaluators as part of the process of specifying criteria for assessing implementation.

> At some point, there should be a determination of the degree to which an innovation has been implemented successfully. What should the implemented activity be expected to look like in terms of the underlying decision? For a complex treatment package put in different local settings, decision makers usually will not expect—or more importantly, not want—a precise reproduction of every detail of the package. The objective is performance, not conformance. To enhance the probability of achieving the basic program or policy objectives, implementation

should consist of a realistic development of the underlying decision in terms of the local setting. In the ideal situation, those responsible for implementation would take the basic idea and modify it to meet special local conditions. There should be a reasonable resemblance to the basic idea, as measured by inputs and expected outputs, incorporating the best of the decision and the best of the local ideas. (Williams and Elmore 1976:277–78)

Adaptation versus Fidelity

How closely must implementation of a program in new localities follow an original blueprint? How much can implementation vary from the original ideal and still be considered the same program? These questions point to one of the central issues in implementation: *adaptation versus fidelity as a premier evaluation criterion of excellence.*

Consider the case of JUMP Math, an approach to teaching developed by mathematician John Mighton in 1998. Although originally conceived as an after-school supplement for inner-city students struggling with math, by 2003 JUMP programs ran in 12 Toronto inner-city elementary schools involving more than 1,600 students. It has evolved into a classroom curriculum with a complete package of materials intended to cover all elementary school grades. The program has been adopted in schools throughout North America and other regions of the world. With such widespread adoption, there will be variations in implementation. For teachers and students to realize the full benefits of the approach, those who are supporting dissemination of the program want *high fidelity implementation.* This is true for any model that gets identified as a "best practice" or "evidence-based model" or a model validated by a review process such as the *What Works Clearinghouse* (www.whatworks.ed.gov).

To evaluate fidelity is to assess adherence to the core blueprint specifications of how a model program is supposed to be implemented. Models that aim at widespread dissemination strive for careful replication and the degree to which that replication is attained is a primary implementation evaluation question (e.g., Backer 2002). It is a question made all the more important by the substantial evidence that it is very difficult to maintain fidelity of widely disseminated program. Adoption of a model often becomes adaptation of the model. In such cases, how much adaptation is appropriate and what gets adapted are significant evaluation questions.

Evaluation Fidelity

No, evaluation fidelity isn't about whether married evaluators are having adulterous affairs. It concerns fidelity in implementing a particular evaluation model. Just as fidelity is a central issue in efforts to replicate effective programs to new localities (Are the replications faithful to the original model on which they are based?), *evaluation fidelity* concerns whether an evaluator following a particular model is faithful in implementing all the steps and processes of that model. Miller and Campbell (2006) reviewed 47 evaluations that called themselves "empowerment evaluations" and found wide variation in adherence to empowerment evaluation principles. Renger (2006) has described weak adherence to evaluation modeling prescriptions in U.S. federal government agencies. Stufflebeam (2001) examined the extent to which 22 different evaluation models manifested fidelity to the standards of evaluation. And I've seen a great many evaluations labeled *utilization-focused* that provided no evidence that primary intended users had been identified and worked with to focus the evaluation on those users' priorities. No fidelity there.

Model adaptation often takes shape slowly in response to emergent challenges and early trial-run experiences. In a classic study, Jerome Murphy (1976:96) found, in studying implementation of Title V of the Elementary and Secondary Education Act, that states exhibited great variation in implementation. He found no basis for what was then a widespread assumption that competently led bureaucracies should prescribe goal-directed, procedure-mandated, top-down, command-and-control (military-like) operations. Instead, implementers at the field level did what made sense to them rather than simply follow mandates from higher up. Moreover, the processes of implementation often became political as competing interests struggled to control what was done. For example, when a nationally acclaimed jobs training program was introduced into one new city, the local mayor and Chamber of Commerce became embroiled in controversy over who would control recruitment and job placements, and the compromise changed the model at both the front-end (recruitment and admission) and back-end (job placement and support on-the-job). Those changes affected the "middle" of the program (what participants did and what they were being prepared for).

For a half century, sociologists who study formal organizations, social change, and diffusion of innovations have documented the substantial slippage in organizations between plans and actual operations, especially under dynamic environmental conditions and where a number of locations are involved (Greenwood

2007; Hunt 2007; Westley, Zimmerman, and Patton 2006; Hage and Meeus 2006; Hage 1999; Kanter 1983; Hage and Aiken 1970). Original ideas are changed in the face of what's actually possible and how different sites adapt to innovation. Even where planning includes a trial and learning period, what finally gets adopted typically varies from what was tried out in the pilot effort (Rogers 2003; Rogers and Shoemaker 1971). Social scientists who study change and innovation emphasize two points: (1) routinization or final acceptance is never certain at the beginning and (2) the implementation process typically contains unknowns that change the ideal so that it looks different when and if it actually becomes operational.

In a renowned large-scale study of innovation, the Rand Corporation, under contract to the U.S. Office of Education, studied 293 federal programs supporting educational change—one of the most comprehensive studies of educational innovation ever conducted. The study concluded that implementation "dominates the innovative process and its outcomes":

> In short, where implementation was successful, and where significant change in participant attitudes, skills, and behavior occurred, implementation was characterized by a process of mutual adaptation in which project goals and methods were modified to suit the needs and interests of the local staff and in which the staff changed to meet the requirements of the project. This finding was true even for highly technological and initially well-specified projects; unless adaptations were made in the original plans or technologies, implementation tended to be superficial or symbolic, and significant change in participants did not occur. (McLaughlin 1976:169)

The Change Agent Study found that the usual emphasis on fidelity in dissemination of models was inappropriate. McLaughlin (1976) concluded,

> An important lesson that can be derived from the Change Agent Study is that unless the developmental needs of the users are addressed, and unless projects are modified to suit the needs of the user and the institutional setting, the promise of new technologies is likely to be unfulfilled. (P. 180)

The emphasis on the "user" in the Rand study brings us back to the importance of the personal factor and attention to primary intended users in evaluation of implementation processes. Formative, improvement-oriented evaluations can help users make the kinds of program adaptations to local conditions that Rand found so effective—*or* it can be used to maintain the fidelity of a model if it begins to depart from the prescribed blueprint. These are two fundamentally different purposes for and uses of formative evaluation. And they lead to two fundamentally different summative criteria: (1) successful adaptation of a model to local conditions *versus* (2) successful replication of a model that carefully follows prescribed processes.

In either of these contrasting utilization scenarios, evaluation can be a powerful tool for guiding program development during implementation; it can facilitate formative midcourse corrections as well as summative judgments about the connections between program activities and outcomes. But each specific implementation evaluation must also be focused on the criteria of primary intended users if the process and results are to be relevant, meaningful, and useful. Utilization-focused criteria for evaluating implementation must be developed through interaction with primary intended users. Evaluation facilitators will have to be active-reactive-interactive-adaptive in framing evaluation questions in the context of program implementation.

Program Implementation as Incremental Adaptation

There is a large body of literature to show that a centrally developed program undergoes changes when implemented at the local level. . . . Most programs and those implementing them undergo a process of mutual adaptation during implementation. That is, the implementor alters his or her action towards those specified by the program, but may not implement the program faithfully. The nature of the adaptation depends on local conditions and on the degree of support given by the developers for the change. Those programs are often not implemented in the rational fashion of adopting a set of means to achieve a predetermined end. From an incrementalist point of view, a program takes shape slowly as decision-makers react to the realities of the context, with its emerging complexities. Those concerned with program design must be aware that final acceptance is never certain at the beginning, and that things change from the plan to the operation.

This has implications for assessing the extent of implementation of a program. To understand how and why programs are implemented differently in different locations, there is an argument for implementation evaluation to document variations in use and factors which lead to patterns of use at each location or site. Evaluation methods thus need to be more flexible than those used in a fidelity approach. (Owen and Rogers 1999:272)

Variations and Options for Implementation Evaluation

In working with intended users to focus evaluation questions, several alternative purposes of implementation evaluation can be considered based on different intended uses. Let's consider an evaluation of emergency health services at a hospital. Implementation evaluation for *accountability* would focus on the extent to which the program is complying with mandated specifications. In the emergency room, this could involve a standard that all incoming patients with problems that are not life-threatening are examined by a qualified medical person within one half-hour. To what extent is that standard being met? Implementation evaluation for *program improvement* focuses on identifying a program's strengths and weaknesses so that problems can be solved and staff can build on what's working well while correcting deficiencies. In the emergency room example, this could involve getting feedback from incoming patients and those who brought them to the emergency room about how they were treated. *Summative*

implementation evaluation determines the core characteristics of a program to inform a decision about continuing, expanding, reducing, terminating, or disseminating the program model. There are competing models of how to run an emergency unit, for example, what tests are routinely administered for what conditions. A summative evaluation would make a judgment about the relative merit and worth of those competing models. *Developmental evaluation* would document ongoing processes of adaptation and innovation to increase the capacity to do rapid and accurate environmental sensing and provide quick feedback for development. Implementation evaluation for *lessons learned* aims to extract practice wisdom from staff to inform future implementation endeavors. In the emergency room, this could involve experienced staff members from several emergency units comparing their practice wisdom about how they managed triage during community-wide emergencies such as Hurricane Katrina, a major fire, or a terrorist attack. Menu 9.1 presents different evaluation questions for these distinctive purposes.

MENU 9.1

Implementation Questions for Different Evaluation Purposes

Accountability and Compliance Issues

1. What was originally proposed and intended for implementation? How important is *fidelity to the original design* as a criterion for judging the program?

2. How does the program as *actually implemented* compare with the original design? How significant are any departures from the original implementation blueprint? What explains these departures?

3. Who, if anyone, has a stake in the program being implemented as originally proposed and designed?

4. If program *fidelity* to a model is important, who has been responsible for implementation fidelity? How has implementation compliance been monitored by the program? What implementation benchmarks were established? To what extent have those benchmarks been met?

5. If implementation adaptation was expected (as opposed to fidelity), what has been adapted and why? What are the implications of those adaptations for accountability?

5. What resources were anticipated for full implementation? Were those resources available as needed?

6. What staff competencies and roles were anticipated? Do program staff members have those competencies? Are they playing anticipated roles?

7. What are the characteristics of program participants and how do those compare with the intended target population for the program?

8. What were the original intended timelines for implementation and to what extent have those been met? What are the reasons for and implications of departures from original timelines?

9. What aspects of implementation, if any, involve meeting legal mandates?

10. What potential threats to implementation were anticipated during design? To what extent have those potential problems surfaced and been dealt with?

11. Has implementation proved *feasible*? What aspects or components of the proved have raised concerns about feasibility?

Formative Evaluation Questions

1. What are the program's key characteristics as perceived by various stakeholders: participants, staff, administrators, funders? How similar or different are those perceptions? What's the basis for and implications of different perceptions?

2. What is participant and staff feedback about program processes: What's working well and not working so well from their perspectives?

3. What challenges and barriers have emerged as the program has been implemented? How has staff responded to these challenges and barriers? What "bugs" need to be worked out?

4. What original assumptions have proved true? What assumptions appear problematic? How accurate has the original needs assessment proved to be? To what extent, if at all, are participants' actual needs different from what was planned for?

6. What do participants actually do in the program? What are their primary activities (in detail)? What do they experience? To what extent are those experiences yielding the desired immediate results (short-term outcomes)? Why or why not? In essence, does the model appear to be working?

7. What do participants like and dislike? Do they know what they're supposed to accomplish as participants? Do they "buy into" the program's goals and intended outcomes?

8. How well are staff functioning together? Do they know and agree about what outcomes they're aiming for? To what extent do they "buy into" the program's goals and intended outcomes? What are their perceptions of participants? Of administrators? Of their own roles and effectiveness?

9. What has changed from the original design and why? On what basis are adaptations from the original design being made? Who needs to "approve" such changes? How are these changes being documented and reflect on, if at all?

10. What monitoring system has been established to assess implementation on an ongoing basis and how is it being used?

Developmental Evaluation Implementation Questions

1. What are the key factors and variables in the program's environment that need to be tracked so the program can adapt to emergent conditions? How are these variables interpreted and fed back to the program to support ongoing adaptation?

2. For each new development, what progress markers provide feedback on how that development is working out?

(Continued)

MENU 9.1 (Continued)

3. When have incremental changes accumulated to the point of constituting a new intervention (innovation)?

4. What values, vision, and principles undergird the emergent developments being tracked? Is the program (innovation) manifesting those values, visions, and principles as it unfolds and develops? Have those values, visions, and principles changed? If so, how and why, and with what implications?

Summative Implementation Questions

1. As the program has been implemented, what model has emerged? That is, to what extent can the program be modeled as a coherent, high-fidelity intervention or treatment with clear connections between inputs, activities, and outcomes? To what extent has implementation been routinized and implementation steps identified and documented?

2. To what extent and in what ways was the original implementation design feasible? What was not feasible? Why? Were deviations from the original design great enough that what was actually implemented constitutes a different model, treatment, or intervention from what was originally proposed? In other words, have the feasibility and viability of the original design actually been tested in practice, or was something else implemented?

3. How stable and standardized has the implementation become both over time and, if applicable, across different sites?

4. To what extent is the program amenable to implementation elsewhere? What aspects of implementation were likely situational? What aspects are likely generalizable?

5. What are the start-up and continuing costs of implementation?

6. Has implementation proved sufficiently effective and consistent that the program merits continuation or expansion?

Lessons Learned Implementation Questions

1. What has been learned about implementation of this specific program that might inform similar efforts elsewhere?

2. What has been learned about implementation in general that would contribute to scholarly and policy research on implementation?

NOTE: For a larger menu of more than 300 implementation evaluation questions, see King et al. (1987:129–41).

Different purposes, as reviewed above, render varying implementation evaluation questions. Cutting across these variations are options for focusing an implementation review. These options involve specific types of implementation evaluation. Over time, a comprehensive evaluation might include all five types of implementation evaluation considered below.

Always Look at Implementation

It is hard to imagine an evaluation study today that should not include some aspect of implementation evaluation. Implementation evaluation serves many useful purposes. It enhances program accountability by documenting program activities and efforts, provides objective evidence that the program is being delivered as planned, and helps senior managers and policy analysts make informed decisions about program design and policy direction (Love 2004:96).

Effort, Input, and Access Evaluation

Effort and input evaluations focus on documenting the quantity and quality of activity that takes place and the resources available for program activities. Effort evaluation moves up a step from asking if the program exists to asking how active the program is and at what level it is being or has been implemented. If relatively inactive, it is unlikely to be very effective; if inputs don't materialize in a timely way, the program will get off to a slow start.

Effort questions include the following: Have sufficient staff members been hired with the proper qualifications? Are staff-client ratios at desired levels? How many clients with what characteristics are being served by the program? Are necessary materials available? Is needed technology in place and operational? An effort evaluation

involves making *an inventory of program operations.* Such questions are especially important at initiation of a program when evaluation questions focus on getting services started. Later, questions concerning the appropriateness, quantity, and quality of services become more important. Continuing with the example of emergency hospital services, an effort and input evaluation would inventory whether staffing levels were adequate for patient loads, whether there are enough examination rooms with access to needed equipment, and how long waits are for getting initial care and then getting transferred to a regular hospital room, if needed.

Access evaluation focuses on whether those targeted for a program by policymakers actually receive services. For example, addressing health care disparities has become a major focus of health policy and program implementation (Hargreaves 2006). There are often disparities and discrepancies between the ideal of open access and actual recruitment practices creating *an implementation gap.* Ridde (2007a, 2007b) evaluated this implementation gap in health policies in the West African country of Burkina Faso. He found that during implementation of a major health reform initiative, efficient delivery of health services took precedent over and led to neglect of access and equity goals. For example, the evaluation results showed that the equity aspect of health policies was omitted during training on how to use revenues from drug sales and user fees. Donor agencies and nongovernmental agencies were preoccupied with efficiency rather than equity, thereby failing to ensure that indigents had free access to health care. Indeed, what constituted "access" and "equity" was perceived differently by different actors, often in ways inconsistent with official policies. Ridde identified three explanations for why equity was neglected. First, opportunities for achieving equity goals were not seized because of the focus on efficiency. Second, the implementation process did not connect problem streams with solutions streams, which is necessary for a successful implementation. Third, the relatively powerless situation of the indigents did not position them to demand access.

Monitoring Programs: Routine Management Information

Monitoring program implementation is typically an internal management function. An important way of monitoring implementation is to establish a management information system (MIS) that provides routine data on client intake, participation levels, program completion rates, caseloads, client characteristics, and program costs. Benchmarks provide a way of tracking the progress of implementation. The hardware and software decisions for a management information system have long-term repercussions, so the development of such an ongoing data collection system must be approached with special attention to questions of use and problems of managing the system (Patton 1982b). Establishing and using an MIS are often primary responsibilities of internal evaluators. External evaluators then audit and draw on the internal data to render independent judgments about how well implementation has unfolded. In the emergency room example, monitoring data involve routine medical records. If the accountability (quality control) standard is examining incoming patients within a half-hour (if their problem is not life-threatening), the MIS needs to track the time between when the patient enters the emergency facility and is actually examined. Think about what is involved in establishing and maintaining such a system, aggregating the data on some regular basis, reporting it (to

whom?), interpreting the results, and acting on the findings. Establishing a *useful* monitoring system presents some complicated challenges—and cannot be left to software experts. The software design should be driven by how the data will be used.

Process Evaluation

Process evaluation focuses on the internal dynamics and actual operations of a program in an attempt to understand its strengths and weaknesses. Process evaluations ask the following questions: What's happening and why? How do the parts of the program fit together? How do participants experience and perceive the program? This approach takes its name from an emphasis on looking at *how* a product or outcome is produced rather than looking at the product itself; that is, it is an analysis of the processes whereby a program produces the results it does. A process evaluation of an emergency room would map what happens to a patient from the moment the emergency call is placed to the discharge of the patient. How are the emergency calls handled? What happens on arrival at the emergency room? How does treatment unfold? How are discharges handled? What's the experience of family, friends, or coworkers accompanying the patient? How do patients experience and describe their treatment? What's the perspective of nurses? Of doctors? Of security personnel? Of administrators?

Examining Program or Policy Processes

When we evaluate the "process" of a program or policy, we are talking about taking a critical look at the quality or value of everything about the program (what it is and does) *except* outcomes and costs (Davidson 2005:56).

Process evaluations search for explanations of the successes, failures, and changes in a program. Under field conditions in the real world, people and unforeseen circumstances shape programs and modify initial plans in ways that are rarely trivial. The process evaluator sets out to understand and document the day-to-day reality of the setting or settings under study. This means unraveling what is actually happening in a program by searching for the major patterns and important nuances that give the program its character. A process evaluation requires sensitivity to both qualitative and quantitative changes in programs throughout their development; it means becoming intimately acquainted with the details of the program. Process evaluations not only look at formal activities and anticipated outcomes but also investigate informal patterns and unanticipated consequences in the full context of program implementation and development.

Finally, process evaluations usually include perceptions of people close to the program about how things are going. A variety of perspectives may be sought from people inside and outside the program. For example, process data for a classroom can be collected from students, teachers, parents, staff specialists, and administrators. These differing perspectives can provide unique insights into program processes as experienced and understood by different people.

A process evaluation can provide useful feedback during the developmental phase of a program as well as later, in providing details for diffusion and dissemination of an effective program. One evaluator in our utilization of federal health evaluations reported that process information had been particularly useful to federal officials in expanding a program nationwide. Process data from early pilot efforts were used to inform the designs of subsequent centers as the program expanded.

The Office on Smoking and Health (2007) at the Centers for Disease Control has published a number of examples of how process evaluation has been useful in programs aimed at tobacco use prevention and control. They found again and again that to make sense of and learn from outcomes data (reduced smoking by target populations such as high school students) they needed in-depth process evaluation.

Hoag and Wooldridge (2007) evaluated how Medicaid and State Children's Health Insurance Program (SCHIP) agencies used process evaluation to improve their enrollment and retention processes. Working together in "process improvement collaboratives," they identified practices that participants considered most effective at reducing barriers to enrollment in public health insurance programs. They found that

streamlining and enhancing the effectiveness of administrative procedures and processes can help state programs do more with less and can ease the burden on individuals who apply to these programs by clarifying instructions or allowing phone or Internet applications or renewals. In short, everyone could benefit from improved procedures. (P. 1)

This study is an exemplar of process evaluation.

Process Evaluation in the CIPP Model

Process evaluation is one of the four major components of the CIPP (context, input, process, product) model of evaluation (Stufflebeam 2002). Process evaluation involves (1) gathering data to detect or predict defects in the procedural design or its implementation during the implementation stages, (2) providing information for program decision, and (3) establishing a record of program development as it occurs. www.wmich.edu/evalctr/checklists/checklist menu.htm#models

Component Evaluation

The component approach to implementation involves a formal assessment of the distinct parts of a program. Programs can be conceptualized as consisting of separate operational efforts that may be the focus of a self-contained implementation evaluation. For example, the Hazelden Foundation Chemical Dependency Program typically includes the following components: detoxification, intake, group treatment, lectures, individual counseling, family events, release, and outpatient services. While these components make up a comprehensive chemical dependency treatment program that can be and is evaluated on the outcome of continued sobriety over time (Laundergan 1983; Patton 1980), there are important questions about the operation of any particular component that can be the focus of evaluation, either for improvement or to decide if that component merits continuation. In addition, linkages between one or more components may be evaluated.

Bickman (1985) has argued that one particularly attractive feature of the component approach is the potential for greater generalizability of findings and more appropriate cross-program comparisons:

> The component approach's major contribution to generalizability is its shift from the program as the unit of analysis to the component. By reducing the unit of analysis to a component instead of a program, it is more likely that the component as contrasted to entire programs can be generalized to other sites and other providers. . . .
>
> An example of this process might clarify the point. Any two early childhood programs may consist of a variety of components implemented in several different ways. Knowledge of the success of one program would not tell us a great deal about the success of the other unless they were structurally similar. However, given the diversity of programs, it is unlikely that they would have the same type and number of components. In contrast, if both had an intake component, it would be possible to compare them just on that component. A service provider in one part of the state can examine the effectiveness of a particular component in an otherwise different program in a different part of the state and see its relevance to the program he or she was directing. (P. 199)

Treatment Specification

Treatment specification involves identifying and measuring precisely what it is about a program that is supposed to have an effect. It means conceptualizing the program as a carefully defined intervention or treatment—or at least finding out if there's enough consistency in implementation to permit such a conceptualization. This requires elucidation of the program's *theory:* what precise mechanisms are hypothesized to produce desired results. Twelve-step programs to treat alcoholism are based on a series of propositions about what happens at each step and how one step leads to the next. In technical terms, treatment specification means identifying independent variables (the intervention dimensions) that are expected to lead to outcomes (the dependent variables). Treatment specification reveals the causal assumptions undergirding program activity.

> Any new program or project may be thought of as representing a theory or hypothesis in that—to use experimental terminology—the decision maker wants to put in place a treatment expected to *cause* certain predicted effects or outcomes. (Williams and Elmore 1976:274)

Measuring the degree to which conceptualized treatments actually occur can be a tricky and difficult task laden with methodological and conceptual pitfalls because programs are typically complex undertakings. A social program is more complex and multifaceted than a new strain of wheat or new drug. Testing agricultural and pharmaceutical innovations involve standardized and fixed entities that can be produced and tested again and again, with results replicated by other researchers under the same or different conditions. Social programs are not nearly so bounded and standardized. They vary in elements, styles, people, and procedures.

One approach to implementation evaluation is to attempt to identify and operationalize the program treatment. This is sometimes referred to as getting inside and opening up the *black box*, where "black box evaluation refers to those evaluations that examine the outputs of a program without examining its internal operations and processes" (Muñoz 2005:34–35). One form of black box evaluation in experimental designs involves the trap of relying on labels or program titles to distinguish different treatments. Because this practice yields data that may distort or misrepresent the treatments being compared, it's worth examining the problem in greater depth.

Opening the Black Box

Black-box outcome studies are no longer acceptable

(Mowbray et al. 2003:315)

The past decade has seen increasing recognition in prevention science of the need to move away from a black box approach to intervention evaluation and toward an approach that can elaborate on the mechanisms through which changes in the outcomes operate. An approach that examines issues of program implementation is particularly critical in the design of efficacy studies of school-based preventive interventions. Numerous preventive intervention strategies are now delivered within the schools, often by regular classroom teachers. The extent to which teachers faithfully deliver a particular curriculum or incorporate instructional strategies emphasized by an intervention is a critical question for the overall project evaluation.

SOURCE: From "Opening the Black Box: Using Process Evaluation Measures to Assess Implementation and Theory Building" (Karachi et al. 1999:711).

The Challenge of Accuracy-in-Labeling

Warning: This section sermonizes on the Pandorian folly attendant on those who believe program titles and names. What a program calls its intervention is no substitute for gathering actual data on program implementation. Labels are not treatments.

I suspect that overreliance on program labels is a major source of null findings in evaluation research. Aggregating results under a label can lead to mixing effective with ineffective programs that have nothing in common except their name. An evaluation of Residential Community Corrections Programs in Minnesota offers a case in point. The report, prepared by the Evaluation Unit of the Governor's

Commission on Crime Prevention and Control (GCCPC), compared recidivism rates for three "types" of programs: (1) halfway houses, (2) PORT (Probationed Offenders Rehabilitation and Training) projects, and (3) juvenile residences. The term *halfway house* referred to a "residential facility designed to facilitate the transition of paroled adult ex-offenders returning to society from institutional confinement." This distinguished halfway houses from juvenile residences, which served only juveniles. Offenders on probation were the target of the PORT projects (GCCPC 1976:8). What we have, then, are three different target groups, not three different treatments.

The report presented aggregated outcome data for each type of community corrections program, thereby combining the results for projects about which they had no systematic implementation data. In effect, they compared the outcomes of three labels: halfway houses, PORT projects, and juvenile residences. Nowhere in the several hundred pages of the report was there any systematic data about what juveniles experienced in these programs. Data on the juveniles were collected when they went in and when they completed time in the program; what happened in between was ignored by the evaluators.

The evaluation concluded that "the evidence presented in this report indicates that residential community corrections programs have had little, if any, impact on the recidivism of program clients" (GCCPC 1976:289). These preliminary findings resulted in a moratorium on funding of new residential community corrections, and the final report recommended maintaining that moratorium. With no attention to the meaningfulness of their analytical labels, and with no treatment specifications, the evaluators passed judgment on the effectiveness of an $11 million program.

The aggregated comparisons were essentially meaningless. When I interviewed staff in a few of these community corrections projects, it became clear that halfway houses varied tremendously in treatment modality, clientele, and stage of implementation. The report's comparisons were based on averages within the three types of programs, but the averages disguised important variations within each type. No "average" project existed; yet the different programs of like name were combined for comparative purposes. Within types, the report obscured individual sites that were doing excellent work as well as some of dubious quality.

One has only to read the journals that publish evaluation findings to find similar studies. In education, comparisons are made between "open" schools and "traditional" schools that present no data on actual dimensions of *openness*. In psychology, individual therapy is sometimes compared with group therapy with no attention to the homogeneity within either category of treatment.

A favorite cartoon shows several bureaucrats assembled around a table in a conference room. The chair of the group says, "Of course the welfare program has a few obvious flaws . . . but if we can just think of a catchy enough name for it, it just might work!" (Dunagin 1977). A common government fiction is that because money associated with an administrative label (e.g., Head Start) has been spent at many places and over a period of time, the entities spending the money are comparable from time to time and from place to place. Such assumptions can easily lead to misinterpretation of findings.

> A rose is a rose is a rose is a rose.
>
> —Gertrude Stein, *Sacred Emily* (1913)
>
> And a colonoscopy is a colonoscopy is a colonoscopy. Or is it? Are there variations? Does it matter how the process is done?
>
> A colonoscopy is an examination of the colon with a flexible scope, called an endoscope, to find and cut out any polyps that might cause colon cancer. A study of 12 highly experienced board-certified gastroenterologists in private practice found that some were 10 times better than others at finding adenomas, the polyps that can turn into cancer. One factor distinguishing the more effective from less effective colonoscopies was the amount of time the physician spent examining the colon (which involves an effort evaluation). Those who slowed down and took more time found more polyps. Some completed the procedure in less than 5 minutes; others spent 20 minutes or more. Insurers pay doctors the same no matter how much time they spend. But the stakes are high for patients. More than 4 million Americans a year have colonoscopies, hoping to protect themselves from colon cancer. The cancer, which kills about 55,000 Americans a year, is the second-leading cause of cancer death in the United States (Kolata, 2006b). So is it true that a colonoscopy is a colonoscopy is a colonoscopy?

Treatment Specification as an Alternative to Simplistic Labeling

Treatment specification means getting behind labels to identify what is expected to happen in the program that is hypothesized to make a difference. For example, one theory undergirding community corrections has been that integration of criminal offenders into local communities is the best way to rehabilitate those offenders and thereby reduce recidivism. It is therefore important to gather data about *the degree to which each project actually integrates offenders into the community.* Halfway houses and juvenile residences can be run like small-scale prisons, completely isolated from the surrounding community. Treatment specification tells us what to look for in each project to find out if the program's causal theory is actually being put to the test. (At this point, we are not dealing with the question of how to measure the relevant independent variables in a program theory, but only attempting to specify the intended treatment in nominal terms.)

Here's an example of how treatment specification can be useful. A county Community Corrections Department in Minnesota wanted to evaluate its foster group-home program for juvenile offenders. The primary intended users lacked systematic data about what the country's foster group homes were actually like. The theory undergirding the program was that juvenile offenders would be more likely to be rehabilitated if they were placed in warm, supportive, and nonauthoritarian environments where they were valued by others, could therefore learn to value themselves, and were provided caring guidance about how to make responsible decisions. The goals of the program included helping juveniles feel good about themselves and become capable of exercising independent judgment, thereby reducing subsequent criminal actions (recidivism).

The evaluation measured both outcomes and implementation with special attention to treatment environment. What kind of treatment is a youth exposed to in a group home? What are the variations in group homes? Do certain types of foster group homes attain better results, both providing positive experiences for youth and reducing recidivism?

The findings revealed that the environments of the sample of 50 group homes could be placed along a continuum from highly supportive and participatory home environments to nonsupportive and authoritarian ones. Homes were about evenly distributed along the continua of support versus nonsupport and participatory versus authoritarian patterns; that is, the juveniles experienced homes with measurably different climates. Juveniles from supportive-participatory group homes showed significantly lower recidivism rates than juveniles from nonsupportive-authoritarian ones ($r = .33$, $p < .01$). Variations in type of group-home environment were also correlated significantly with other outcome variables (Patton et al. 1977).

In terms of treatment specification, these data demonstrated two things: (1) in about half of the county's group homes, juveniles were not experiencing the kind of treatment that the program design called for and (2) outcomes varied directly with the degree to which program implementation involved the desired mechanisms hypothesized to produce desired outcomes. Clearly, it would make no sense to conceptualize these 50 group homes as a homogeneous treatment under the label "group home." We found homes that were run like prisons and homes in which juveniles were physically abused. We also found homes where young offenders were loved and treated as members of the family. Aggregating recidivism data from all 50 homes into a single average rate would disguise important variations. By specifying the desired treatment and measuring

implementation compliance, the program's theory could be examined in terms of both feasibility and effectiveness. (For an in-depth discussion of how to measure treatment environments for different kinds of programs—mental health institutions, prisons, family environments, military units, classrooms, businesses, schools, hospitals, and factories see Moos 1997, 1985; Ilgen, McKellar, and Moos 2007.)

Connecting Goals and Implementation

Causal processes that mediate treatment effects should be an important part of evaluation studies (Bishop and Vingilis 2006:140).

In complex programs with multiple goals, it can be useful to engage staff members in an exercise that concretely and specifically links activities to outcomes through specific measures for each. Exhibit 9.1 offers a matrix to guide this exercise. Once completed, the matrix can be used to focus the evaluation and decide what information would be most useful for program improvement and decision making.

Implementation Overview

This chapter has highlighted the importance of evaluating program implementation and reviewed various options, including (1) effort evaluation, (2) ongoing program monitoring, (3) process evaluation, (4) component evaluation, and (5) treatment specification. Depending on the nature of the issues involved and the information needed, any one, two, or all five approaches might be employed. The approach used will depend on the purpose of the evaluation. But the essential bottom-line point is that without information about actual program operations and causal

EXHIBIT 9.1

Format for Connecting Goals with Implementation Plans and Measurement

Goals: Expected Client Outcomes	Indicators: Outcome Data/Measurement Criteria	How Goals Will Be Attained (Implementation Mechanisms)	Data on Implementation Progress: Benchmarks
1.			
2.			
3.			
4.			

mechanisms, decision makers are limited in interpreting performance data for either program improvement or summative judgment. These different evaluations answer different questions and focus on different aspects of program implementation. The key is to match the type(s) of evaluation to the information needs of specific stakeholders and primary intended users. One of the decision makers we interviewed in our utilization study was emphatic on this point:

> Different types of evaluations are appropriate and useful at different times. . . . We tend to talk about evaluation as if it's a single thing. The word evaluation should not be used generically. It's harmful. We ought to stop talking about evaluation as if it's a single homogenous thing. [DM111:29]

When working with intended users to focus the evaluation, implementation options should be reviewed. Evaluators have a responsibility in their active-reactive-interactive-adaptive interactions with intended users to explore and explain options with intended users in order to decide jointly what will be most useful in the particular circumstances at hand. Sometimes, however, what primary users need and want varies from the evaluator's initial expectations.

Former Ambassador to China, The Honorable Winston Lord, was once driving in the Chinese countryside with his wife. They stopped at an ancient Buddhist temple, where the senior monk greeted them enthusiastically. "Would you do this temple a great honor and favor for our future visitors, to guide and instruct them? Would you write something for us in English?"

Ambassador Lord felt quite flattered because he knew that, traditionally, only emperors and great poets were invited to write for the temple. The monk returned shortly carrying two wooden plaques and said: "To guide and instruct future English visitors, would you write on this plaque the word 'Ladies' and on this plaque the word 'Gentlemen'?"

May the writings of evaluators be as useful.

Follow-Up Exercises

1. Identify a program. Describe the program and its purpose. For this program identify (a) an effort/input evaluation question or issue; (b) key process evaluation issues; and (c) other important implementation issues or questions. For each, describe why it is significant and how data from an evaluation could be used.

2. Identify a program with multiple components. Identify and discuss the different implementation issues for these different components.

3. Select a well-known or popular program approach whose title is widely recognized, like Head Start, community policing, a stop-smoking campaign, sex offender registration program, a welfare-to-work program, affirmative action, microcredit, or AIDS prevention. Discuss (a) the treatment specification issues that this approach involves and (b) key fidelity issues for the replication of this approach, i.e., fidelity versus adaptation.

4. In an evaluation workshop in South Africa, participants in small groups engaged in the following exercise: "A rural prenatal clinic for pregnant women is having trouble getting women to come for regular prenatal exams and classes. What are some possible (hypothetical) reasons that women might not be coming to the clinic?" In just 5 minutes of brainstorming, 8 groups of 10 people each identified 87 *possible* reasons. Identify at least 20 yourself. What does this exercise have to do with implementation evaluation? What value might this exercise have if done with primary intended users as part of a utilization-focused evaluation?

5. You are an evaluation consultant. You get this request (an actual request posted on the AEA listserv EvalTalk in 2007).

I have been asked to look into a problem with the implementation of a program within a number of reserves in Canada. The program in question was developed with the direct and active participation of the First Nations communities that were to use it. The program was seen as an effective response to a documented and recognized problem involving youths. Since the program was developed and ready for implementation there has been considerable difficulty in implementing it in the participating reserves. All parties still recognize the potential value and need for the program, but at least 4 (of 7) communities involved have not, after almost 2 years, adopted the program.

Through a preliminary conversation with program staff and administration of the agency offering the program, I have been told that the main reason for not implementing the program is partly community politics (new Chief and administration not seeing the program as a priority), partly personality conflicts (e.g., we're not going to implement this because so-and-so was involved), and partly the initiative being seen as an outsiders' (i.e., nonnative) initiative, despite the past and continuing local representation. I should add that the program costs the community virtually nothing. It is an e-learning complement to existing one-on-one counseling initiative.

The temptation is to say, "Well, they simply don't want the program," but when faced with the possibility of its being scrapped the communities protest. The main organization directly responsible for facilitating implementation on reserves is a First Nations agency.

How would you, as an evaluation consultant, advise approaching this in a meaningful way to generate useful information to help resolve the implementation problems?

10

Conceptualizing the Intervention

Alternatives for Evaluating Theories of Change

All the World's a Stage for Theory

In Tony Kushner's Pulitzer Prize–winning play, *Angels in America*, Part Two opens in the Hall of Deputies, the Kremlin, where Aleksii Antedilluvianovich Prelapsarianov, the World's oldest living Bolshevik, speaks with sudden, violent passion, grieving a world without theory:

How are we to proceed without Theory? What System of Thought have these Reformers to present to this mad swirling planetary disorganization, to the Inevident Welter of fact, event, phenomenon, calamity? Do they have, as we did, a beautiful Theory, as bold, as Grand, as comprehensive a construct . . . ? You can't imagine, when we first read the Classic Texts, when in the dark vexed night of our ignorance and terror the seed-words sprouted and shoved incomprehension aside, when the incredible bloody vegetable struggled up and through into Red Blooming gave us Praxis, True Praxis, True Theory married to Actual Life. . . . You who live in this Sour Little Age cannot imagine the grandeur of the prospect we gazed upon: like standing atop the highest peak in the mighty Caucasus, and viewing in one all-knowing glance the mountainous, granite order of creation. You cannot imagine it. I weep for you.

And what have you to offer now, children of this Theory? What have you to offer in its place? Market Incentives? American Cheeseburgers? Watered-down Bukharinite stopgap makeshift Capitalism? NEPmen! Pygmy children of a gigantic race!

Change? Yes, we must change, only show me the Theory, and I will be at the barricades, show me the book of the next Beautiful Theory, and I promise you these blind eyes will see again, just to read it, to devour that text. Show me the words that will reorder the world, or else keep silent.[1]

—Kushner 1994:13–14

Evaluation and Program Theory

Evaluability Assessment

The idea that evaluation should include conceptualizing and testing a program's theory of change emerged in the 1970s as part of a more general concern about assessing a program's *readiness for evaluation*. The notion was basically this: Before undertaking an evaluation, the program should be clearly conceptualized as some identifiable set of activities that are expected to lead to some identifiable outcomes. The linkage between those activities and outcomes should be both logical and testable. "Evaluability assessment is a systematic process for describing the structure of a program and for analyzing the plausibility and feasibility of achieving objectives; their suitability for in-depth evaluation; and their acceptance to program managers, policymakers, and program operators" (Smith 2005a:136; see also Smith 1989).

One primary outcome of an evaluability assessment is definition of a program's theory. This means specifying the underlying logic (cause and effect relationships) of the program, including what resources and activities are expected to produce what results. An evaluability assessment is also expected to gather various stakeholders' perspectives on the program theory and assess their interest in evaluation. Also assessed are the program's capacity to undertake an evaluation and its readiness for rigorous evaluation (e.g., whether the program's theory is sufficiently well conceptualized and measures of outcomes adequately validated to permit a meaningful summative evaluation).

Evaluability assessment was the evaluator's version of foreplay: getting the program ready for the act itself, the act being evaluation—leading to the climax of producing findings. Or if you find sexual innuendo distracting

or inappropriate, consider an agricultural analogy. Evaluability assessment involved tilling the soil before planting the seeds (evaluation questions) that, if properly nourished, would produce an abundant yield (useful findings).

In effect, evaluability assessment puts evaluators in the business of facilitating design of the program in order for it to be evaluated. For already existing programs, this means redesigning the program because the original program model was insufficiently specified to be evaluated. Intended outcomes are often vague or unmeasurable (as discussed in Chapter 7), and how desired outcomes will actually result from the program's activities is often far from clear. As evaluators became involved in working with program people to more clearly specify the program's model (or theory), it became increasingly clear that evaluation was an *up-front activity* not just a back-end activity. That is, traditional planning models laid out some series of steps in which planning comes first, then implementation of the program, and then evaluation, making evaluation a back-end, last-thing-done activity. But to get a program plan or design that could actually be evaluated meant involving evaluators—and evaluative thinking—from the beginning.

Evaluative thinking, then, becomes part of the program design process, including, especially, conceptualizing the program's theory of change: How will what the program does lead to the desired results? Engaging in this work is an example of *process use* (Chapter 5) in which the evaluation has an impact on the program quite apart from producing findings about program effectiveness. The very process of conceptualizing the program's theory of change can have an impact on how the program is implemented, understood, talked about, and improved. The evaluative thinking process has these impacts.

Process Use and Theory of Change

Assisting primary intended users to conceptualize the program's theory of change can have an impact on the program before any evaluative data are gathered about whether the program's theory works. This is an example of the *process use* of evaluation (as opposed to findings use). The very process of conceptualizing the program's theory of change can affect how the program is implemented, understood, talked about, and improved.

This has huge implications for evaluators. It means that evaluators have to be (1) astute at conceptualizing program and policy theories of change and (2) skilled at working with program people, policymakers, and funders to facilitate their articulation of their implicit theories of change. Given the importance of these tasks, it matters a great deal what theory of change frameworks the evaluator can offer. Options for doing theory of change work as part of a utilization-focused evaluation is the subject of this chapter.

Mountaintop Inferences

That evil is half-cured whose cause we know.

—Shakespeare

Causal inferences flash as lightning bolts in stormy controversies. While philosophers of science serve as meteorologists for such storms—describing, categorizing, predicting, and warning, policymakers seek to navigate away from the storms to safe harbors of reasonableness. When studying causality as a graduate student, I marveled at the multitude of mathematical and logical proofs necessary to demonstrate that the world is a complex place (e.g., Nagel 1961; Bunge 1959). In lieu of rhetoric on

the topic, I offer a simple Sufi story to introduce this chapter's discussion of the relationship between means and ends, informed and undergirded by theory.

The incomparable Mulla Nasrudin was visited by a would-be disciple. The man, after many vicissitudes, arrived at the hut on the mountain where the Mulla (teacher) was sitting. Knowing that every single action of the illuminated Sufi was meaningful, the newcomer asked Nasrudin why he was blowing on his hands. "To warm myself in the cold, of course," Nasrudin replied.

Shortly afterward, Nasrudin poured out two bowls of soup, and blew on his own. "Why are you doing that, Master?" asked the disciple. "To cool it, of course," said the teacher.

At that point, the disciple left Nasrudin, unable to trust any longer a man who used the same process to cause different effects—heat and cold.

—Adapted from Shah 1964:79–80

Conceptualizing Interventions

At the simplest level, we can model what the disciple observed as follows:

Hot soup → Blow on hot soup → Cooler soup

Cold hands → Blow on cold hands → Warmer hands

So, what's going on in these two sequences? What's the intervention? The intervention is Nasrudin's breath. The baselines are (1) hot soup and (2) cold hands. The results are (1) cooler soup and (2) warmer hands. We assume Nasrudin's breath temperature to be about the same temperature in each case. Puzzling this out, we can posit the following *intervention theory*: If the object being blown on is warmer than one's breath, then the object will be cooled by the blowing; if the object being blown on is cooler than one's breath, then the object will be warmed. That's a simple intervention theory. An intervention theory is basically an *if/then* assertion or hypothesis: If we do *x*, then *y* will result.

Now, using this simple sequential logic, let's turn to a program intervention.

Person lacks training needed to get a good job → Provide appropriate training → Trained person gets a good job

This is a simple (and common) program theory. If we train people, then they will get good jobs. It focuses on a single problem: lack of training. It provides a focused intervention: job training. It has a straightforward, measurable outcome: a good job. That's a starting place—and it's the starting place for many policymakers and program designers who want to help poor people get better jobs. Then we start asking deeper questions and surfacing assumptions. Does "training" mean just skill training (how to do keyboarding and data entry), or does it also include "soft skills" (how to get along in the workplace)? What is "appropriate" training? What is a "good" job? At this stage, these aren't measurement questions. We're not asking how we would measure whether or not a person got a good job. We're asking conceptual and values-based questions: Will the kind of training provided lead to the kind of job desired? Is it enough to give the person keyboarding skills? What if the person is a recent immigrant and speaks English poorly? Does the program intervention need to include language training? What if the trainee uses drugs? Does the program need to include drug treatment? What if the poor person is a single mother with young children? Does the program intervention need to include child care? How will the poor person get to training? Will the program intervention have to include transportation support to be effective? Is it enough to provide training, or will there need to be job placement services? And what about the workplace? If the poor

person being training is African American and the job opportunities are in companies with mostly white employees, will some kind of support be needed in the workplace to create an environment in which this newly trained person can succeed? As the questioning proceeds, the simple intervention above may morph into the more complicated program intervention as depicted in Exhibit 10.1, which presents the program theory of a real program.

The Jargon Challenge: What Are We Talking About?

A proliferation of terms has come into use describing how program activities lead to program outcomes. Some of the language emphasizes elucidating the logic of what the program does, so we have logic models, logical frameworks, and intervention logic. Some focus on theory: program theory, theory-based evaluation, theory-driven evaluation, theory of change, theory of action, and intervention theory. Some approaches emphasize linkages: chain of objectives, outcomes mapping, and impact pathway analysis. Three important distinctions are embedded in these different terms.

(1) *Logic modeling versus theory of change.* Does the model simply describe a logical sequence or does it also provide *an explanation* of why that sequence operates as it does? *Specifying the causal mechanisms transforms a logic model into a theory of change.*

A logic model only has to be logical and sequential. The logic of a logic model is partially temporal: It is impossible for an effect or outcome to precede its cause. A logic model expresses a sequence in the sense that one thing leads to another. You crawl before you walk before you run is a descriptive logic model. Crawling precedes walking, which precedes running. It becomes a theory

EXHIBIT 10.1

Theory of Change for an Employment Training Program

TWIN CITIES RISE!

Program Structure
- Highly structured program that supports participant progress
- Consistent expectations, follow-through and consequences based on market expectations

Training
- Training in empowerment skills
- Training in soft skills (time management, goal setting, others)
- Training in hard skills (basic skills, keyboarding, computers)
- Training in job skills (job search skills, other job skills)

Empowerment Helps Participants
- Reconnect with their core value
- Prioritize self-interest
- Regulate emotions
- Take responsibility for self
- Look within for solutions
- Manage core hurts

Participants Learn To
- Develop new soft and hard skills
- Develop new habits
- Set boundaries with family/friends
- Separate from unproductive relationships
- Maintain or develop healthy relationships
- Manage stability issues and crises

Coaching
- One-on-one weekly coaching, encouragement, and support
- Assistance with goal setting and planning
- Manage and reframe participant expectations
- Serve as a role model for the skills being taught
- Reinforce/support the application of empowerment skills

Program Culture
- Safe, respectful learning environment where participants feel comfortable making mistakes, learning new skills, and developing new relationships
- Reinforcement of empowerment skills and principles throughout the entire program
- Program culture that models expectations in the workplace

New Skills Lead to Living Wage Jobs
- Meet employer expectations for hard and soft skills
- Manage stability issues and crises that can affect job performance
- Internalize empowerment skills and use them daily
- Prioritize self-interest and set boundaries with friends and family
- Engage in a healthier lifestyle (exercise, nutrition, health insurance)
- Retain living wage employment
- Achieve self-sufficiency
- Participate in the broader community

Participant Experience

337

of change when you explicitly add the change mechanism. You crawl, and crawling develops the gross-motor skills and body control capabilities that make it possible to walk; you walk, and walking develops the balance, further gross-motor skills, and body control needed to run. *Adding the causal mechanism moves the model from program logic to program theory.*

(2) A second critical distinction involves the source of the model. The terms *program logic* or *program theory* imply that what is being depicted is what people who run the program believe is going on. It is the theory articulated by the program staff, administrators, and funders. In contrast, *theory-driven evaluation* or *theory-based evaluation* typically refers to the program as a test of some larger social science theory. Staff in a faith-based initiative may explain a program by saying it puts participants in touch with their inherent spiritual nature; this would be the program's theory. A social science researcher might look at the same program through the lens of a sociological theory that explains how cohesive groups function to create shared beliefs and norms that determine behavior; that approach would be theory driven. *Theory of change* can be a hybrid of both program theory and social science theory, and often is, as the idea of theory-based evaluation has evolved over the years (Mason and Barnes 2007; Rogers 2007; Weiss 2007) and come to include both "small theories" that are program specific (Leviton 2007; Lipsey 2007c; Layzer 1996) and the larger theories of which a specific program theory is but one manifestation.

(3) A third distinction concerns the *unit of analysis*—or we might say, the *unit of logic*, or the *boundaries of the theory of change*. In elucidating a program model, the term *program* is sometimes a discrete local effort, like a local employment training program. That local program has its own logic model and/or program theory that constitutes a specific intervention. But in large organizations like international development agencies or philanthropic foundations, a program can refer to a collection of interventions made up of several projects and grants. For example, The Atlantic Philanthropies as a philanthropic foundation has a Reconciliation and Human Rights strategic focus that consists of three program areas each with several distinct projects, grants, and intervention strategies, some of which fit together into a cluster. The cluster has its own theory of change distinct from but based on the logic models of individual grants. In such settings, one has to be careful to specify the unit of analysis for the theory of change. The language of intervention logic or intervention theory avoids confusion about what the word "program" means by focusing on a specific intervention which might be one strategy within an umbrella program (that has several interventions) or a strategy that cuts across a number of programs (where the overall intervention is a comprehensive, multifaceted, integrated, and omnibus development strategy). A policy or advocacy process can also be the unit of analysis for which one is developing a logic model (Coffman 2007a; Gardner and Geierstanger 2007; Hendricks-Smith 2007; Kay 2007).

The *theory of action* language comes from action research and organizational development traditions where the focus is typically on some specific solution to a specific problem (the "action"); that action may not be a full-scale intervention, program, policy, or theory—but an action taken within some concrete time period for some specific purpose. Doing something to reduce the dropout problem in a program would involve some theory of action. The theory of action tradition places particular emphasis on distinguishing "espoused theory" (how practitioners explain what they are attempting to do) from "theory-in-use" (what their

Program Theory and Logic Model Babel

Confusion reigns in the language describing how program activities lead to program outcomes:

* logic model * logical framework * program logic * program model * intervention logic * intervention model * chain of objectives * outcomes map * impact pathway analysis * program theory * theory-based evaluation * theory-driven evaluation * theory of change * theory of action * intervention theory *

Which term is best? That best designation is the one that makes the most sense to primary intended uses—the term they resonate to and has meaning within their context given the intended uses of the evaluation.

behavior reveals about what actually guides what they do). The major evaluative thrust of the theory of action framework is helping practitioners examine, reflect on, and deal with the discrepancies between their espoused theory and their theory-in-use (Argyris 1993, 1974; Schön 1987, 1983; Argyris and Schön 1978, 1974). "People do not always behave congruently with their beliefs, values, and attitudes (all part of espoused theories). . . . Although people do not behave congruently with their espoused theories, they do behave congruently with their theories-in-use" (Argyris 1982:85).

In this conundrum of dissonance between stated belief and actual practice lies a golden opportunity for reality testing: the heart of evaluation. Sociologist W. I. Thomas posited in what has become known as *Thomas' Theorem* that *what is perceived as real is real in its consequences.* Espoused theories are what practitioners perceive to be real. Those espoused theories, often implicit and only espoused when asked for and coached into the open, have real consequences for what practitioners do. Elucidating the theory of change held by primary users can help them be more deliberative about what they do and

more willing to put their beliefs and assumptions to an empirical test through evaluation. In short, the user-focused approach challenges decision makers, program staff, funders, and other users to engage in reality testing, that is, to test whether what they believe to be true (their espoused theory of action) is what actually occurs (theory-in-use).

Which Term Is Best?

Given all this diversity of and confusion in language, which term is best? Logic model? Theory of change? Intervention model? From a utilization-focused evaluation perspective, *that label is best that makes the most sense to primary intended uses*—the term they resonate to and has meaning within their context. Here are some examples of how contexts vary.

In international settings, logical frameworks or "Logframes" have a long history of use by government aid agencies (Norwegian Agency for Development Cooperation 1999). United Way of America has promoted logic models as a way for nonprofit agencies to present funding proposals (United Way 1996). Large-scale community development initiatives have adopted the "theory of change" language due in large part to an influential article by Carol Weiss (1995) widely disseminated by The Aspen Institute (Connell et al. 1995). *Program theory* has been a target for "advancement" among evaluators for more than two decades (Bickman 1994, 1990). *Program logic* and *program theory* are familiar terms in Australia and New Zealand due to the influential works of Bryan Lenne (1987), Sue Funnell (2005, 2000, 1997), and Patricia Rogers (2008, 2005b, 2005c, 2003, 2000a, 2000b). Theory-driven evaluation has been widely promoted by Huey-Tsyh Chen (2005a, 2005b, 2004, 1990) and, like its cousin, theory-based evaluation (Weiss 2007, 2000, 1997; Birckmayer and Weiss 2000) is a label that plays well in academic settings, theory being much revered in universities. Stewart Donaldson (2007), Director of the Institute of Organizational and Program Evaluation Research at Claremont Graduate University, argues that systematic attention to program theory in evaluation elevates evaluation to the status and prestige of *science*, what he calls *Program Theory-Driven Evaluation Science*. From a utilization-focused perspective, the choice of label depends on the purpose of the conceptual work and the preferences of primary intended users. As Rogers (2005c) has observed,

> Program logic is sometimes used interchangeably with program theory. . . . In many cases, the choice of term is based on local responses to the words *theory* and *logic* (each of which can be seen as unpalatable) and on the terms used in the specific texts used by the evaluators. (P. 339)

The challenge, then, is to use terms that have meaning within a particular context and tradition. We'll now look at some of these approaches more closely.

The Logic Model
Option in Evaluation: Constructing a Means-Ends Hierarchy

> *Causation. The relation between mosquitos and mosquito bites.*
>
> —Michael Scriven (1991b:77)

A theory links means and ends. The construction of a means-ends hierarchy for a program constitutes a comprehensive description of the program's model. For example, in his classic work on evaluation, Suchman (1967) recommended building a *chain of objectives* by trichotomizing objectives into immediate, intermediate, and ultimate goals. The linkages between these levels make up a continuous series of actions

wherein immediate objectives (focused on implementation) logically precede intermediate goals (short-term outcomes) and therefore must be accomplished before higher-level goals (long-term impacts). Any given objective in the chain is the outcome of the successful attainment of the preceding objective and, in turn, is a precondition to attainment of the next higher objective.

> Immediate goals refer to the results of the specific act with which one is momentarily concerned, such as the formation of an obesity club; the intermediate goals push ahead toward the accomplishment of the specific act, such as the actual reduction in weight of club members; the ultimate goal then examines the effect of achieving the intermediate goal upon the health status of the members, such as reduction in the incidence of heart disease. (Suchman 1967:51–52)

The means-ends hierarchy for a program often has many more than three links. In Chapter 7, I presented the mission statement, goals, and objectives of the Minnesota Comprehensive Epilepsy Program. One of the goals was to conduct high-quality research on epilepsy. Exhibit 10.2 presents the chain of objectives for that goal.

The full chain of objectives that links inputs to activities, activities to immediate outputs, immediate outputs to intermediate outcomes, and intermediate outcomes to ultimate goals constitutes a program's logical model. Any particular paired linkage in the theory displays an action and reaction: a hypothesized cause and effect. As one constructs a hierarchical/sequential model, it becomes clear that there is only a relative distinction between ends and means: "Any end or goal can be seen as a means to another goal, [and] one is free to enter the 'hierarchy of means and ends' at any point" (Perrow 1968:307). *In utilization-focused evaluation, the decision about where to enter the means-ends hierarchy for a particular evaluation is made on the basis of what information would be most*

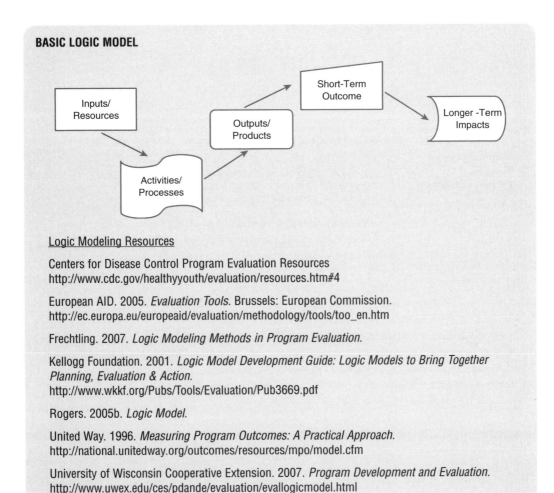

BASIC LOGIC MODEL

Logic Modeling Resources

Centers for Disease Control Program Evaluation Resources
http://www.cdc.gov/healthyyouth/evaluation/resources.htm#4

European AID. 2005. *Evaluation Tools.* Brussels: European Commission.
http://ec.europa.eu/europeaid/evaluation/methodology/tools/too_en.htm

Frechtling. 2007. *Logic Modeling Methods in Program Evaluation.*

Kellogg Foundation. 2001. *Logic Model Development Guide: Logic Models to Bring Together Planning, Evaluation & Action.*
http://www.wkkf.org/Pubs/Tools/Evaluation/Pub3669.pdf

Rogers. 2005b. *Logic Model.*

United Way. 1996. *Measuring Program Outcomes: A Practical Approach.*
http://national.unitedway.org/outcomes/resources/mpo/model.cfm

University of Wisconsin Cooperative Extension. 2007. *Program Development and Evaluation.*
http://www.uwex.edu/ces/pdande/evaluation/evallogicmodel.html

useful to the primary intended evaluation users. In other words, a formative evaluation might focus on the connection between inputs and activities (an implementation evaluation) and not devote resources to measuring outcomes higher up in the hierarchy until implementation was ensured. Elucidating the entire hierarchy does not incur an obligation to evaluate every linkage in the hierarchy. The means-ends hierarchy displays a series of choices for more focused evaluations while also establishing a context for such narrow efforts. Suchman (1967:55) used the example of a health education campaign to show how a means-ends hierarchy can be stated in terms of a series of measures or evaluation findings. See Exhibit 10.3.

Testing a Logic Model: A Policy Implementation Example

Let me offer a simple example of testing a logic model. A State Department of Energy allocated conservation funds through 10 regional districts. An evaluation was commissioned by the department to assess the impact of local involvement in priority setting. State and regional officials articulated the following *fair and equitable logic model* of decision making:

1. State officials establish funding targets for energy proposals from districts and rules for submitting proposals.

EXHIBIT 10.2

Epilepsy Program Logic Model

Mission and Goals of the Epilepsy Program

Program Mission   To improve the lives of people with epilepsy through research
Program Goal   To publish high-quality, scholarly research on epilepsy
Program Objective   To conduct research on neurological, pharmacological, epidemiological, and social psychological aspects of epilepsy

Epilepsy Research Goal Chain of Objectives

1. People with epilepsy lead healthy, productive lives
2. Provide better medical treatment for people with epilepsy
3. Increase physician's knowledge of better medical treatment for epileptics
4. Disseminate findings to medical practitioners
5. Publish findings in scholarly journals
6. Produce high-quality research findings on epilepsy
7. Establish a program of high-quality research on epilepsy
8. Assemble necessary resources (personnel, finances, facilities) to establish a research program
9. Identify and generate research designs to close knowledge gaps
10. Identify major gaps in knowledge concerning causes and treatment of epilepsy

2. District advisory groups assess each district's energy needs with broad citizen input and involvement.

3. District advisory groups develop funding proposals, based on the needs assessments that meet their district's state target and follow the state's rules.

4. The state approves the budgets based on the merit of the proposals within the guidelines, rules, and targets provided.

5. Expected results: (a) Approved funds equal original targets and (b) everyone perceives the funding as fair and equitable.

In short, the espoused logic model was that decisions would be made fairly based on explicit and transparent procedures, guidelines, and rules. The data showed this to be the case in only 6 of the 10 districts. In the other 4 districts, proposals from the districts exceeded the

assigned target amounts by 30 percent to 55 percent; for example, one district, assigned a target of $100 million by the state, submitted a proposal for $140 million (despite a "rule" that said proposals could not exceed targets). Moreover, the final, approved budgets exceeded the original targets by 20 percent to 40 percent. The district with a target of $100 million and a proposal for $140 million received $120 million. Four of the districts, then, were not engaged in a by-the-book equitable process; rather, their process was negotiated, personal, and political—and subsequently perceived as unfair. Needless to say, when these data were presented, the six districts that followed the guidelines and played the funding game by what they thought were uniform rules—the districts whose proposals equaled their assigned targets—were outraged. Testing the espoused theory of fairness and uniform

EXHIBIT 10.3

Logic Model Hierarchy of Evaluation Measures for a Health Education Campaign

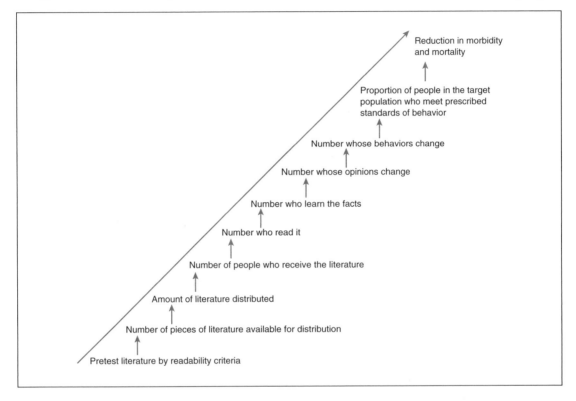

SOURCE: Adapted from Suchman 1967:55.

rules revealed that the reality (theory-in-use) in four districts did not match the espoused ideal in ways that had significant consequences for all concerned.

This is a simple, commonsense example of testing a logic model at the policy level. Nothing elegant. No academic trappings. The espoused model is a straightforward articulation of what all agreed was supposed to happen in the process to achieve desired outcomes. The linkages between processes and outcomes are made explicit. Evaluative data then revealed what actually happened—and where what actually happened departed from what was supposed to happen and the consequences of that discrepancy. At the district level, each district would have its own model of how funds were to be used and what those funds were supposed to accomplish.

Three Approaches to Program Theory

A logic model only has to be logical and sequential. Adding specification of the causal mechanism moves the model from program

The Logical Framework Matrix

A logical framework (Logframe) is a matrix that specifies each step in the chain of objectives and requires for each step that a target result be specified, that the data source be specified for measuring the result, and that any critical assumptions be stated. The *Logical Framework Approach* (IFAD 2002; NORAD 1999; Sartorius 1996, 1991) offers a format for connecting levels of impact with evidence. Used widely by international development agencies as a comprehensive map in designing projects, the framework begins by requiring specification of the overall goal and purposes of the project. Short-term outputs are linked logically to those purposes, and activities are identified that are expected to produce the outputs. Careful attention must be paid to the language of this model because what the logical framework calls a goal is what other models more commonly call mission; and "purposes" in this approach are similar to objectives or outcomes; outputs are short-term, end-of-project deliverables. For every goal, purpose, output, and activity, the framework requires specification of objectively verifiable indicators, means of verification (types of data), and important assumptions about the linkage between activities and outputs, outputs to purposes, and purposes to goals. In their very practical book on *RealWorld Evaluation*, Bamberger, Rugh, and Mabry (2006) discuss how to integrate logical framework and program theory approaches with excellent examples from their international development experiences.

logic to program theory. In this section, we will look at three major approaches to developing program theory for evaluation use:

1. *The deductive approach*—drawing on scholarly theories from the academic literature

2. *The inductive approach*—doing fieldwork on a program to generate grounded theory, for example, as part of an evaluability assessment process

3. *The user-focused approach*—working with intended users to extract and make explicit their implicit theory of action

The deductive approach draws on dominant theoretical traditions in specific scholarly disciplines to construct models of the relationship between program treatments and outcomes. For example, an evaluation of whether a graduate school teaches students to think critically could be based on the theoretical perspective of *a phenomenography of adult critical reflection*, as articulated by the Distinguished Professor of Education Stephen Brookfield (1994), an approach that emphasizes the visceral and emotional dimensions of critical thought as opposed to purely intellectual,

cognitive, and skills emphases. Illustrations of the deductive approach to evaluation are chronicled in Chen (2004), Rossi and Freeman (1993), Lipsey and Pollard (1989), and Chen and Rossi (1989, 1987). Testing social science theories may be a by-product of an evaluation in which the primary purpose is knowledge generation (see Chapter 4). However, the temptation in the deductive approach is to make the study more research than evaluation, that is, to let the scholarly contribution and theory testing take over the evaluation, making it useful academically but not necessarily useful to practitioners and policymakers.

The inductive approach involves the evaluator in doing fieldwork to generate program theory. Staying with the example of evaluating whether graduate students learn to think critically, the inductive approach would involve assessing student work, observing students in class, and interviewing students and professors to determine what model of education undergirds efforts to impart critical thinking skills. Such an effort could be done as an evaluation study unto itself, for example, as part of an early evaluability assessment process, or it could be done in conjunction with a deductive effort based on a literature review. The product of the inductive approach, and therefore a major product of the evaluation, would be an empirically derived theoretical model of the relationship between program activities and outcomes framed in terms of important contextual factors.

User-Focused Theory of Change Approach

In neither the deductive nor inductive approach to program theory does the evaluator have to engage with key stakeholders. That changes in *the user-focused approach* in which the evaluator's task is to facilitate intended users, especially program personnel, to articulate their operating theory. Continuing with the critical thinking example, this would mean bringing together students and professors to make explicit their educational assumptions and generate a program theory model that could then be tested as part of the evaluation.

Facilitating the program theory articulation process involves working with those who are knowledgeable about the program to construct a flowchart of what happens from the time a person enters a program to the time they leave. How are people recruited or selected into the program? What's their baseline situation when they enter? How are they oriented to the program once they enter? What are the early activities they engage in? How much are they expected to participate? What are they supposed to be doing, learning, acquiring, or changing during those early activities? During later activities? What's the sequence or stages of participants' experiences? What happens as the program approaches the end? What changes should have occurred in participants by the time they reach the end of the program? What mechanisms explain why these changes take place? To what extent are these changes

expected to be sustained? What additional outcomes are expected to occur after leaving the program (e.g., keeping a job or staying off of drugs).

The primary focus of utilization-focused evaluation is testing practitioner theories about why they do what they do and what they think results from what they do. Utilization-focused evaluation involves primary intended users in specifying the program's theory and in deciding how much attention to give to testing the theory generated, including how much to draw on social science theory as a framework for the evaluation (Patton 1989).

A Menu of Theory-Based Approaches

Each of the three approaches to program theory—deductive, inductive, and user-focused—has advantages and disadvantages. These are reviewed in Menu 10.1. The strategic calculations a utilization-focused evaluator must make include determining how useful it will be to spend time and effort elucidating a theory of change (or more than one where different perspectives exist, which is common); how to keep theory generation from becoming esoteric and overly academic; how formal to be in the process; and what combinations of the three approaches, or relative emphasis, should be attempted. Factors to consider in making these calculations will be clearer after some more examples, which follow.

Theory of Change and Evaluation: Getting at Causal Mechanisms and Assumptions

The purpose of thoroughly delineating a program's theory of change is to assist practitioners in making explicit their assumptions about the linkages between inputs, activities, immediate outputs,

MENU 10.1

Approaches to Generating Program Theory

Approach	Potential Advantages	Potential Disadvantages	Pitfalls to Avoid
User-focused approach: working with intended users to extract and specify their implicit theory of action to make it explicit action	Intended users understand the theory of action Intended users own the theory of action	As users struggle to articulate their theory, they may be defensive Formal explicit model may not reflect program realties	Don't oversimplify to the point of esoteric meaninglessness in an effort to manage conflict or varying perceptions Don't force articulation of a single theory. Different users may well have different theories of action
Inductive approach: doing fieldwork on a program to generate grounded theory	Theory grounded in real-world practice High relevance because theory is generated from actual program activities and observed outcomes Can focus an evaluability assessment effort	Fieldwork takes time and resources for evaluation and program Likely that different program people operate with different theories in large, multilevel, or complex programs	Don't force a single theory or model on the program where multiple theories of action are operating Don't let generating theory take on a life of its own and become a higher priority than generating useful results
Deductive approach: drawing on scholarly theories from the academic literature	Draws on existing knowledge and literature High academic credibility Connects to larger issues	May not be relevant to specific program May feel esoteric to practitioners Literature search takes time and resources	Don't force program into a theory pigeonhole Don't let theory testing become higher priority than generating useful results
Combining approaches	Uses strengths of each approach Provides diverse perspectives	Costly, time-consuming May lead to conflicting results	Don't let one approach trump another; treat each on its merits, fairly and in balance

Expert Advice from Carol Weiss on Theory-Based Evaluation

- When social science provides theory and concepts that ground and support local formulations, it can be of great evaluative value. The evaluator should bring her knowledge of the social science literature to bear on the evaluation at hand.
- When a number of different assumptions are jostling for priority, a theory-based evaluation is wise to include multiple theories. . . . . But the more theories that are tracked, the more complex and expensive evaluation. Choices have to be made.
- Select theories to test on the following criteria:
    o The first criterion is the beliefs of the people associated with the program, primarily the designers and developers who planned the program, the administrators who manage it, and the practitioners who carry it out on a daily basis. Also important may be the beliefs of the sponsors whose money funds the program and the clients who receive the services of the program. What do these groups assume are the pathways to good outcomes?
    o A second criterion is plausibility. . . . Can the program actually do the things the theory assumes, and will the clients be likely to respond in the expected fashion?
    o A third criterion is lack of knowledge in the program field. This allows the evaluation to contribute knowledge to the field.
    o A final criterion for choosing which theories to examine in a theory-based evaluation is the centrality of the theory to the program. Some theories are so essential to the operation of the program that no matter what else happens, the program's success hinges on the viability of this particular theory.

SOURCE: Weiss (2000:38–41).

intermediate outcomes, and ultimate goals. Suchman (1967) called beliefs about cause-effect relationships the program's *validity assumptions*. For example, many education programs are built on the validity assumptions that (1) new information leads to attitude change and (2) attitude change affects behavior. These assumptions are testable. Does new knowledge change attitudes? Do changed attitudes lead to changed behaviors? Carol Weiss (2000) has commented on the widespread nature of these assumptions:

> Many programs seem to assume that providing information to program participants will lead to a change in their knowledge, and increased knowledge will lead to positive change in behavior. This theory is the basis for a wide range of programs, including those that aim to reduce the use of drugs, prevent unwanted pregnancies, improve patients' adherence to medical regimens, and so forth. Program people assume that if you tell participants about the evil effects of illegal drugs, the difficult long-term consequences of unwed pregnancies, and the benefits of complying with physician orders, they will become more conscious of consequences, think more carefully before embarking on dangerous courses of action, and eventually behave in more socially acceptable ways.
>
> The theory seems commonsensical. Social scientists—and many program people—know that it is too simplistic. Much research and evaluation has cast doubt on its universal applicability. . . . So much effort is expended in providing information in an attempt to change behavior that careful investigation of this theory is warranted. (Pp. 40–41)

Knowing this, when an evaluator encounters a program theory that posits that information will produce knowledge change, and knowledge change will produce behavior change, it is appropriate to bring to the attention of those involved the substantial evidence that this model doesn't work. In being active-reactive-interactive-adaptive when working with primary intended users, the evaluator can and should bring social science and evaluation knowledge to the attention of those with whom they're working.

Consider this example. The World Bank provided major funding for a program in Bangladesh aimed at improving maternal and child health and nutrition. The theory of change was the classic one we are reviewing here: Information leads to knowledge change, knowledge change leads to practice change. It didn't work. Women in extreme poverty did not have the resources to follow the desired behaviors, even if they were inclined to do so (in other words, they could not afford the recommended foods). Moreover, they live in a social system where what they eat is heavily influenced, even determined, by their mothers-in-law and husbands. The World Bank commissioned an impact evaluation of the project which documented this substantial "knowledge-practice gap" and found that the program was ineffective in closing the gap. "All forms of knowledge transmitted by the project suffer from a knowledge-practice gap, so attention needs to be paid to both the resource constraints that create this gap and transmitting knowledge to other key actors: mothers-in-law and husbands" (World Bank 2005:43).

The larger question is, "Why are those designing interventions aimed at women in extreme poverty still operating on a theory of change that has been discredited time and time again?" We will return to this question later in this chapter, when we discuss bringing systems thinking to bear on program theory. For the moment, I want to use this example to introduce the critical role evaluators play in helping surface and then test a program's causal assumptions.

Identifying Critical Assumptions

Validity assumptions are the presumed causal mechanisms that connect steps in a logic model turning it into a theory of change. The proposition that gaining knowledge will lead to behavior change is undergirded by a validity assumption, namely, that the reason people aren't behaving in the desired manner is because they lack knowledge about what to do. Poor women in Bangladesh don't eat the right foods when they are pregnant because they don't know enough about proper nutrition. Teach them about proper nutrition and they will eat the right foods. It turned out that they gained the knowledge but didn't change their behavior. The validity assumption proved false, or at least insufficient. Knowledge of nutrition may be *a necessary but not sufficient condition* for proper eating.

As validity assumptions are articulated in a means-ends hierarchy, the evaluator can work with intended users to focus the evaluation on those critical linkages where information is most needed at that particular point in the life of the program. It is seldom possible or useful to test all the validity assumptions or evaluate all the means-ends linkages in a program's theory of action. The focus should be on testing the validity of critical assumptions. *In a utilization-focused evaluation, the evaluator works with the primary intended users to identify the critical validity assumptions where reduction of uncertainty about causal linkages could make the most difference.*

While the evaluators can and should bring their own knowledge of social science to bear in interactions with primary intended users, the evaluator's beliefs about critical assumptions is ultimately less important than what staff and decision makers believe. An evaluator can often have greater impact by helping program staff and decision makers empirically test their own causal hypotheses than by telling

Theory of Change

A Theory of Change defines all building blocks required to bring about a given long-term goal. This set of connected building blocks—interchangeably referred to as outcomes, results, accomplishments, or preconditions—is depicted on a map known as a pathway of change/change framework, which is a graphic representation of the change process.

Built around the pathway of change, a Theory of Change describes the types of interventions (a single program or a comprehensive community initiative) that bring about the outcomes depicted in the pathway of a change map. Each outcome in the pathway of change is tied to an intervention, revealing the often complex web of activity that is required to bring about change.

A Theory of Change would not be complete without an articulation of the assumptions that stakeholders use to explain the change process represented by the change framework. Assumptions explain both the connections between early, intermediate, and long-term outcomes and the expectations about how and why proposed interventions will bring them about. Often, assumptions are supported by research, strengthening the case to be made about the plausibility of theory and the likelihood that stated goals will be accomplished.

Stakeholders value theories of change as part of program planning and evaluation because they create a commonly understood vision of the long-term goals, how they will be reached, and what will be used to measure progress along the way.

SOURCE: *ActKnowledge* and the Aspen Institute Roundtable on Community Change (2007) www.theoryofchange.org.

See also Anderson (2005).

them such causal hypotheses are nonsense. This means working with them where they are. So despite my conviction that knowledge change alone seldom produces behavior change, I still find myself helping young program staff rediscover that lesson for themselves. Not only does the wheel have to be re-created from time to time, its efficacy has to be restudied and reevaluated. The evaluator's *certain belief* that square wheels are less efficacious than round ones may have little impact on those who believe that square wheels are effective. The evaluator's task is to delineate the belief in the square wheel, share other research on square wheels when available, and if they remain committed to a square wheel design, assist the true believers in designing an evaluation that will permit them to *test for themselves* how well it works.

I hasten to add that this does not mean that the evaluator is passive. In the active-reactive-interactive-adaptive process of negotiating the evaluation's focus and design, the evaluation facilitator can suggest alternative assumptions and theories to test, but first priority goes to evaluation of validity assumptions held by primary intended users.

Filling in the Conceptual Gaps and Testing the Reasonableness of Program Theories

Helping stakeholders examine conceptual gaps in their theory of change is another task in building program theory and making it evaluable. In critiquing a famous prison reform experiment, Rutman (1977) has argued that the idea of using prison guards as counselors to inmates ought never have been evaluated (Ward, Kassebaum, and Wilner 1971) because, *on the face of it, the idea is nonsense.* Why would anyone ever believe that prison guards could also be inmate counselors? But clearly, whether they should have or not, some people did believe that the program would work. Without reaching an evaluation conclusion prior to gathering data, the evaluator can begin by filling in the conceptual gaps in this program theory so that critical validity assumptions can be identified and examined. For example, is some kind of screening and selection part of the design so that the refined theory is that only certain kinds of guards with certain characteristics and in certain roles can serve as counselors to particular kinds of inmates? And what kind of training program for guards is planned? In what ways are guards supposed to be changed during such training? How will changed guard behavior be monitored and rewarded? The first critical assumptions to be evaluated may be whether prison guards can be recruited and trained to exhibit desired counselor attitudes and behaviors. Whether prison guards can learn and practice human relations skills can be evaluated without ever implementing a full-blown program.

Filling in the gaps in the program's theory of change goes to the heart of the implementation question: What series of activities must take place before there is reason even to hope that the desired outcomes will result? I once reviewed a logic model for an after-school program that would provide crafts, arts, and sports activities for middle-school students once a week for 2 hours for one semester—a total of 30 contact hours. The expected outcome was "increased self-esteem." On the face of it, is this a reasonable outcome? What are the causal mechanisms that link 30 hours of after-school group activities to increased self-esteem. Or consider a "dress-for-success" program that provided appropriate dress clothes for poor people to wear to job interviews. The program's stated outcome was the rather modest goal that the appearance of job applicants would make a positive impression. To justify funding the program, the funder wanted the program to change the outcome

to getting a job. Now the clothes might help in that regard, but would, at best, be a minor factor. The "dress-for-success" program appropriately resisted being evaluated on the criterion of whether those to whom they provided clothes got a job.

The logic of a chain of objectives is that if activities and objectives lower in the means-ends hierarchy will not be achieved or cannot be implemented, then evaluation of ultimate outcomes is problematic.

> There are only two ways one can move up the scale of objectives in an evaluation: (a) by proving the intervening assumptions through research, that is, changing an assumption to a fact, or (b) by assuming their validity without full research proof. When the former is possible, we can then interpret our success in meeting a lower-level objective as automatic progress toward a higher one. (Suchman 1967:57)

This has important implications for what kind of follow-up is needed in an evaluation to determine impact. Research shows that children immunized against polio do not get polio. The causal connection between the immunization and immunity against polio is established. Therefore, the evaluation can stop at determining that children have been immunized and confidently calculate how many cases of polio have been prevented based on epidemiological research. The evaluation design does not have to include follow-up to determine whether immunized children get polio. That question has been settled by research.

One important reason for testing critical validity assumptions is that some findings are counterintuitive. The Bangladesh maternal and child nutrition program provides an excellent example of the interface between research and evaluation. The program theory posited that proper nutrition for women during pregnancy would reduce the incidence of low birth weight babies. It seems commonsensical that the proper focus for maternal health would be on nutrition *during the pregnancy*. The evaluation findings questioned this assumption and added to the interpretation results from research showing that the pregnant women's *pre-pregnancy weight* was more predictive of babies' birth weight than weight gain during pregnancy. The evaluation concluded,

> Supplementary feeding for pregnant women appears to be a flawed approach on two grounds: (1) the pregnancy weight gain achieved is mostly too small to have a noticeable impact on birth weight; and (2) it is pre-pregnancy weight that evidence suggests to be the most important determinant of birth weight. . . . The fact that it is pre-pregnancy weight that matters suggests that a different approach altogether ought perhaps be considered, such as school feeding programs or targeting adolescent females in poorer areas. (World Bank 2005:43)

However, this evaluation finding appears to come with its own assumption, namely, that there are not sufficient resources to provide needed food and nutritional supplements to impoverished women *both before and during pregnancy*. By framing the evaluation conclusion as a choice between providing nutrition before pregnancy *or* during pregnancy, the evaluator has limited the policy and programming options. This illustrates how evaluators' own theories of change and assumptions come into play and need to be made explicit and questioned.

Using the Theory of Change to Focus the Evaluation: The New School Case

Once an espoused theory of change is delineated, the issue of evaluation focus remains. This involves more than mechanically evaluating lower-order validity assumptions and then moving up the hierarchy. Not all linkages in the hierarchy are amenable to

testing; different causal linkages require different resources for evaluation; data-gathering strategies vary for different objectives. In a summative evaluation, the focus will be on outcomes attainment and causal attribution. For formative evaluation, the most important factor is determining what information would be most useful at a particular point in time. This means identifying those targets of opportunity where additional information could make a difference to the direction of incremental, problem-oriented, program decision making. Having information about and answers to those select questions can make a difference in what is done in the program. Here's an example.

The New School of Behavioral Studies in Education, University of North Dakota, was established to support educational innovations that emphasized individualized instruction, better teacher-pupil relationships, and an interdisciplinary curriculum. The New School established a master's degree, teaching-intern program in which interns replaced teachers without degrees so that the latter could return to the university to complete their baccalaureates. The cooperating school districts released those teachers without degrees who volunteered to return to college and accepted the master's degree interns in their place. Over 4 years, the New School placed 293 interns in 48 school districts and 75 elementary schools, both public and parochial. The school districts that cooperated with the New School in the intern program contained nearly one third of the state's elementary school children.

The Dean of the New School formed a task force of teachers, professors, students, parents, and administrators to evaluate the program. We constructed the theory of change shown in Exhibit 10.4. The objectives stated in the first column are a far cry from being clear, specific, and measurable, but they were quite adequate for discussions aimed at focusing the evaluation question. The second

EXHIBIT 10.4

The New School Theory of Action: A Hierarchy of Objectives, Validity Assumption Linkages, and Evaluation Criteria

Hierarchy of Objectives	Causal Assumption Linkages	Evaluative Criteria
I. Ultimate Objectives 1. Prepare children to live full, rich, satisfying lives as adults. 2. Meet the affective and cognitive needs of individual children in North Dakota and the United States. 3. Facilitate and legitimize the establishment and maintenance of a larger number of more open classrooms in North Dakota and the United States. **II. Intermediate Objectives** 4. Provide parents and administrators in North Dakota with a firsthand demonstration of the advantages of open education.	Children whose affective and cognitive needs are met will lead fuller, richer, more satisfying lives as adults. More open classrooms will better meet the affective and cognitive needs of individual children. Parents and administrators will favor and expand open education once they have experienced it firsthand.	1. Longitudinal measures of child and adult satisfaction, happiness, and success. 2. Measures of student affective and cognitive growth in open and traditional schools. 3. Measures of increases in the number of open classrooms in North Dakota and the United States over time and measures of the influence of the New School on the number of open classrooms. 4. Measures of parent and administrator attitudes toward New School classrooms and open education, and measures and analysis of the factors affecting their attitudes.

Hierarchy of Objectives	Causal Assumption Linkages	Evaluative Criteria
5. Provide teachers and teachers-in-training with a one-year classroom experience in conducting an open classroom.	Teachers who have experienced the New School summer program can and will conduct open classrooms during the following intern year that are visible to local parents and administrators.	5. Measures of the degree of openness of New School teaching intern classrooms and the factors affecting the degree of openness of these classrooms.
III. Immediate Objectives		
6. Provides teachers and teachers-in-training with a summer program in how to conduct open classrooms.	Teachers who have experienced the summer program can and will conduct open classrooms.	6. Measures of teacher attitudes, teacher understanding, and teacher competency before and after the New School Program.
7. Provide teachers and teachers-in-training with a personalized and individualized learning experience in an open learning environment.	To learn about open education, it is best to experience it. Teachers teach the way they are taught.	7. Measures of the degree to which the New School training program is individualized and personalized, and measures of the cognitive and affective growth of teachers in the New School Program.

NOTE: The validity assumptions (middle column) link objectives (left column). Arrows indicate to which objectives the assumptions apply.

column lists validity assumptions underlying each linkage in the theory of action. The third column shows the measures that could be used to evaluate objectives at any level in the hierarchy. When the Evaluation Task Force discussed the program theory, members decided they already had sufficient contact with the summer program to assess the degree to which immediate objectives were being met. With regard to the ultimate objectives, the task force members thought it was premature to evaluate the ultimate outcomes of open education (Objectives 1 and 2), nor could they do much with information about the growth of the open education movement (Objective 3). However, a number of critical uncertainties surfaced at the level of intermediate objectives. Once students left the summer program for the 1-year internships, program staff members were unable to carefully and regularly monitor intern classrooms. They didn't know what variations existed in the openness of the classrooms, nor did they have reliable information about how local parents and administrators were reacting to intern classrooms. Those objectives were prime targets for formative evaluation focusing on three questions: (1) To what extent are summer trainees conducting open classrooms during the regular year? (2) What factors are related to variations in classroom "openness"? (3) What is the relationship between variations in classroom openness and parent/administrator reactions to intern classrooms?

At the onset, nothing precluded evaluation at any of the seven levels in the hierarchy of objectives. There was serious discussion of all levels and alternative foci. In terms of the educational literature, the issue of the outcomes of open education could be considered most important; in terms of university operations, the summer program would have been the appropriate focus; but in terms of the information needs of the primary decision makers and primary intended users on the task force, evaluation of the intermediate objectives had the highest potential for generating useful, formative information.

Theory Informing Practice, Practice Informing Theory

Comparing Program Theories

Much evaluation involves comparing different programs to determine which is more effective or efficient. Evaluations can be designed to compare the effectiveness of two or more programs with the same goal, but if those goals do not bear the same importance in the two programs' theories, the comparisons may be misleading. As part of undertaking a comparative evaluation, it is useful to compare program theories in order to understand the extent to which apparently identical or similarly labeled programs are in fact comparable.

Programs with different intended outcomes cannot be fairly compared to each other on a same outcomes basis. Teacher centers established to support staff development and resource support for school teachers provide an example. The U.S. Office of Education proposed that teacher centers be evaluated according to a single set of universal outcomes. But the evaluation found that teacher centers throughout the country varied substantially in both program activities *and* goals. Exhibit 10.5 describes three types of teacher centers, behavioral, humanistic, and developmental, and summarizes the variations among these types of centers.

Different teacher centers were trying to accomplish different outcomes, so to determine which one was *most effective* became problematic because they were trying to do different things. Evaluation could help determine the extent to which outcomes have been attained for each specific program, but empirical data could not determine which outcome was most desirable. *That is a values question.* An evaluation facilitator can help users clarify their value premises, but because the three teacher-center models were different, evaluation criteria for effectiveness varied for each type. In effect, three quite different theories of teacher development were operating in quite different educational environments. Attention to divergent theories of action helped avoid inappropriate comparisons and reframed the evaluation question from *Which model is best?* to *What are the strengths and weaknesses of each approach, and which approach is most effective for what kinds of educational environments?* Very different evaluation questions!

Matching a Theory of Change with Levels of Evidence

Claude Bennett (1982, 1979) conceptualized a relationship between the "chain of events" in a program and the "levels of evidence" needed for evaluation that became widely used and, in his honor, is known as "Bennett's Hierarchy." Although his work was originally aimed at evaluation of cooperative extension programs (agriculture, home economics, and 4-H/youth programs), his ideas are generally applicable to any education-oriented intervention. Exhibit 10.6 depicts Bennett's model.

The model presents a typical chain of program events.

1. Inputs (resources) must be assembled to get the program started.

2. Activities are undertaken with available resources.

3. Program participants (clients, students, beneficiaries) engage in program activities.

4. Participants react to what they experience.

5. As a result of what they experience, changes in knowledge, attitudes, and skills occur (if the program is effective).

EXHIBIT 10.5

Variations in Types of Teacher Centers

Type of Center	Primary Processes For Working with Teachers	Primary Outcomes of the Process
1. Behavioral centers	Curriculum specialists directly and formally instruct administrators and teachers.	Adoption of standardized curriculum systems, methods, and packages by teachers.
2. Humanistic centers	Informal, nondirected teacher exploration; "teachers select their own treatment."	Teachers feel supported and important; pick up concrete and practical ideas and materials for immediate use in their classroom.
3. Developmental centers	Advisers establish warm, interpersonal, and directive relationship with teachers working with them over time.	Teachers' thinking about what they do and why they do it is changed over time; individualized teacher personal development.

SOURCE: Adapted from Feiman (1977).

Theory-Practice Connection

Nothing as practical as a good theory.

Carol Weiss (1995:1)

It is sometimes said that there are two kinds of people in the world: thinkers and doers. And, of course, the third type: those who neither think nor do, but we won't worry about them just now. Thinkers are the world's theoreticians. They love ideas, many of which have yet to be tested and may prove quite impractical. Doers, on the other hand, are too busy doing to worry about theory. But ultimately, theory and practice ought to connect. Practice is the test of theory. Theory is the explanation of practice.

The evaluator's job is to challenge both practitioners and theoreticians. With the latter we ask, "So, it works in theory, but does it work in practice?" And with practitioners we ask, smiling diabolically, "Yes, it works in practice, but does it work in theory?"

6. Behavior and practice changes follow knowledge and attitude change.

7. Overall community impacts result as individual changes accumulate and aggregate—both intended and unintended impacts.

Bennett's Hierarchy is a values hierarchy because the model explicitly places higher value on higher-level results. The hierarchy places the highest value on attaining ultimate social and economic goals (e.g., increased agricultural production, increased health, or a higher quality of community life). Actual adoption of recommended practices and specific changes in client behaviors are necessary to achieve ultimate goals and are valued over knowledge, attitude, and skill changes. People may learn about some new agricultural technique (knowledge change), believe it's a good idea (attitude change), and know how to apply it (skill change)—but the higher-level criterion is whether they actually begin using the new technique (i.e., change their agricultural practices). Participant reactions (satisfaction, likes, and dislikes) are lower on the hierarchy. All these are outcomes, but they are not equally valued outcomes. The bottom part of the hierarchy

identifies the means necessary for accomplishing higher-level ends; namely, in descending order, (3) getting people to participate, (2) providing program activities, and (1) organizing basic resources and inputs to get started.

Evaluation Use Theory of Change

Interestingly, this same hierarchy can be applied to evaluating evaluations. Exhibit 10.7 shows a hierarchy of evaluation accountability. In utilization-focused evaluation, the ultimate purpose of evaluation is to improve programs and increase the quality of decisions made.

To accomplish this ultimate end, a chain of events must unfold.

1. Resources must be devoted to the evaluation, including stakeholder time and financial inputs.

2. Working with intended users, important evaluation issues are identified and questions focused; based on those issues and questions, the evaluation is designed and data are collected.

EXHIBIT 10.6

Theory-Evidence Hierarchy

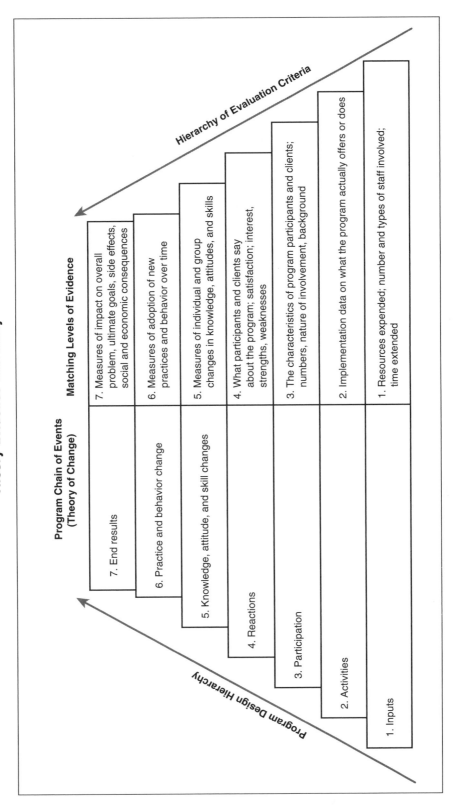

3. Key stakeholders and primary users are involved throughout the process.

4. Intended users react to their involvement (ideally in positive ways).

5. The evaluation process and findings provide knowledge and new understandings.

6. Intended users interpret results, generate and adopt recommendations, and use evaluation results.

7. The program improves, and wise decisions are made.

Each step in this chain can be evaluated. Exhibit 10.7 shows the evaluation question that corresponds to each level in the evaluation use logic model.

Cautions against Theory of Change Work

Eminent evaluation theorist Michael Scriven warns evaluators against thinking that logic modeling and theory testing are central to the work of evaluation. He wants evaluators to stay focused on the job of judging a program's merit or worth. From his perspective, rather than being essential, elucidating program theory is "a luxury for the evaluator." He considers it "a gross though frequent blunder to suppose that one needs a theory of learning to evaluate teaching" (1991b:360). One does not need to know anything at all about electronics, he observes, to evaluate computers. He also cautions that considerable time and expense can be involved in doing a good job of developing and testing a program theory. Because program theory development is really program development work rather than evaluation work, he would prefer to separate the cost of such work from the evaluation budget and scope of work. In commenting on the American Evaluation

Association (AEA) listserv, *Evaltalk,* Scriven, with his renowned wit, offered this advice to evaluators:

> First, there's no law or ethical reason why evaluators with the appropriate training can't do other things for their clients besides evaluation, e.g., market surveys or statistical analyses or logic models. The law and ethics only require that they not argue that these are an essential part of evaluation. . . . There are many cases where it is beyond the boundaries of scientific knowledge to provide the logic model, and in many others it's a huge task that risks jeopardizing the primary task of evaluation.
>
> Second, this isn't ALWAYS so, and when it can be done without undue cost, helping the program managers improve their logic models—which THEY certainly need—is a Good Thing to do. Prudence requires you to keep in mind that doing this will, on some occasions (if it is possible at all), completely antagonize the clients, since they are wedded to a type of logic model that evidence does not support; prayer is one such case, but there are many, many more where the model is essentially "their thing," into which their ego is woven. So this unnecessary extra task CAN cost you the contract, or the rehire; think twice before doing it IN PUBLIC. (Scriven 2006a)

Theory-driven evaluations can also seduce evaluators away from answering straightforward formative questions or making summative judgments into the ethereal world of academic theorizing. While theory construction is a mechanism by which evaluators can link program evaluation findings to larger social scientific issues for the purpose of contributing to scientific knowledge, when conducting a utilization-focused evaluation the initial theoretical formulations originate with primary stakeholders and intended users; scholarly interests are adapted to the evaluation

EXHIBIT 10.7

Evaluating Evaluation: Logic Model of Use

Hierarchy of Utilization Questions →

Evaluation Action Hierarchy →

Evaluation Action Hierarchy	Hierarchy of Utilization Questions
7. Program and decision impacts	7. To what extent and in what ways was the program improved? To what extent were informed, high-quality decisions made?
6. Practice and program change	6. To what extent did intended use occur? Were recommendations implemented?
5. Stakeholders knowledge and attitude changes	5. What did intended users learn? How were users' attitudes and ideas affected?
4. Reactions of primary intended users	4. What do intended users think about the evaluation? What's the evaluation's credibility? Believability? Relevance? Accuracy? Potential utility?
3. Stakeholder participation	3. Who was involved? To what extent were key stakeholders and primary decision makers involved throughout?
2. Evaluation activities	2. What data were gathered? What was the focus, the design, the analysis? What happened in the evaluation?
1. Inputs	1. To what extent were resources for the evaluation sufficient and well managed? Was time sufficient?

359

needs of relevant decision makers, not vice versa. Attention to theoretical issues can provide useful information to stakeholders when *their* theories are formulated and reality-tested through the evaluation process. As always, the decision about whether and how much to focus the evaluation on testing the program's theory is driven by the question of utility: Will helping primary intended users elucidate and test their theory of change lead to program improvements and better decisions. And as Scriven adjures, ask the cost-benefit question: Will the program theory work yield sufficient benefits to justify the likely added costs involved in such work?

As advocates of theory-driven evaluation assert, a better understood program theory can be the key that unlocks the door to effective action. But how much to engage stakeholders and intended users in articulating their theories of change is a matter for negotiation. Helping practitioners test their espoused theories and discover real theories-in-use can be a powerful learning experience, both individually and organizationally. The delineation of assumed causal relationships in a chain of hierarchical objectives can be a useful exercise in the process of focusing an evaluation. It is not appropriate to construct a detailed program theory for every evaluation situation, but it is important to consider the option. Therefore, the skills of a utilization-focused evaluation facilitator include being able to help intended users construct a means-ends hierarchy, specify validity assumptions, link means to ends, and lay out the temporal sequence of a hierarchy of objectives.

But that's not all. In the last decade, the options for conceptualizing and mapping program theories have expanded and now include bringing systems perspectives into evaluation. The remainder of this chapter presents, illustrates, and discusses what it means to bring systems thinking to bear in evaluating theories of change.

Systems Theory and Evaluation

All models are wrong, but some are useful.

—George Box
(quoted by Berk 2007:204)

Let's look at how modeling a program using systems thinking changes a program theory. We'll use as an example a program for pregnant teenagers. The purpose of the program is to teach pregnant teenagers how to take care of themselves so that they have healthy babies. Exhibit 10.8 shows a classic linear logic model for such a program. The teenager learns proper prenatal nutrition and self-care (increased knowledge), which increases the teenager's commitment to taking care of herself and her baby (attitude change), which leads to changed behavior (no smoking drinking, or drug use; eating properly and attending the prenatal clinic regularly). This is a linear model because *a* leads to *b* leads to *c*, et cetera: Program participation leads to knowledge change, which leads to attitude change, which leads to behavior change, which produces the desired outcome (a healthy baby). This is a linear cause-effect sequence as depicted in Exhibit 10.8. This is the traditional, widespread approach to logic modeling.

Now, let's ask some systems questions. What various influences actually affect a pregnant teenager's attitudes and behaviors? The narrowly focused, linear model in Exhibit 10.8 focuses entirely on the program's effects and ignores the rest of the teenager's world. When we ask about that world, we are inquiring into the multitude of relationships and connections that may

EXHIBIT 10.8

Linear Program Logic Model for Teenage Pregnancy Program

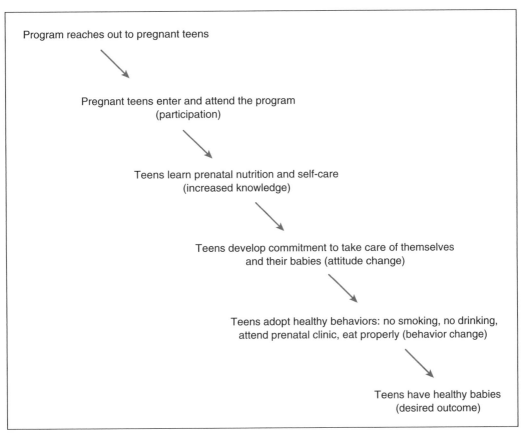

Program reaches out to pregnant teens

Pregnant teens enter and attend the program
(participation)

Teens learn prenatal nutrition and self-care
(increased knowledge)

Teens develop commitment to take care of themselves
and their babies (attitude change)

Teens adopt healthy behaviors: no smoking, no drinking,
attend prenatal clinic, eat properly (behavior change)

Teens have healthy babies
(desired outcome)

influence what the pregnant teenager does. Exhibit 10.9 is a rough sketch of possible system connections and influences. We know, for example, that teenagers are heavily influenced by their peer group. The linear, narrowly focused logic model, targets the individual teenager. A systems perspective that considered the influence of a pregnant teenager's peer group might ask how to influence the knowledge, attitudes, and behaviors of the entire peer group. This would involve changing the subsystem (the peer group) of which the individual pregnant teenager is a part. Likewise, the system's web of potential influences in Exhibit 10.9 invites us to ask about the relative influence of the teenager's parents and other family members, the pregnant teenager's boyfriend (the child's father), or teachers and other adults, as well as the relationship to the staff of the prenatal program. In effect, this systems perspective reminds us that the behavior of the pregnant teenager and the health of her baby will be affected by a number of relationships and not just participation in the prenatal program. In working with such a model with program staff, the conceptual elaboration of the theory of change includes specifying which direction arrows run (one way or both ways, showing mutual influence), which influences are strong (heavy solid lines) versus weak (dotted lines), and which influences are more dominant (larger circles versus smaller circles).

Exhibit 10.10 changes the conceptualization of the change process from a simple linear model of cause-effect to a systems dynamics model of reinforcing actions that depicts the change process as cumulative. When the pregnant teenager adopts healthy behaviors, she feels better; if and when she gets positive reinforcement from clinics nurses, family, and friends, her healthy behaviors are affirmed and reinforced, and she is more likely to continue them. The causal mechanism for sustained change in Exhibit 10.10 is ongoing positive

EXHIBIT 10.9

Systems Web Showing Possible Influence Linkages to a Pregnant Teenager

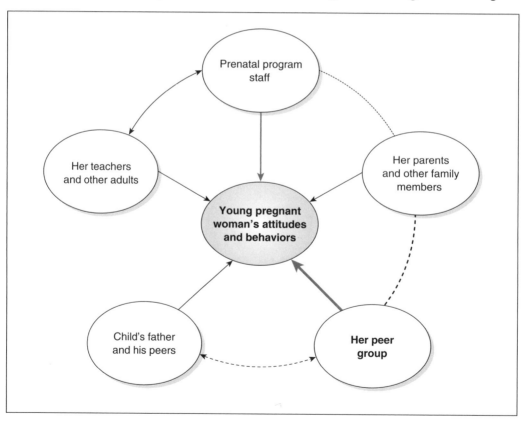

EXHIBIT 10.10

Sustainable Change: Systems Dynamic Reinforcing Feedback Loops

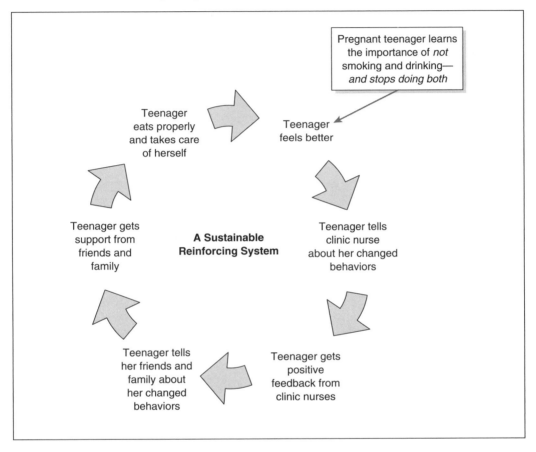

reinforcement from people who are important to the pregnant teenager, which is a different program theory from the linear model of knowledge alone leading to behavior change. Exhibit 10.10 guides the evaluator to ask not just how to produce the desire behavior—but how to sustain it. *How change is sustained is a systems question.*

Exhibit 10.11 presents yet another systems perspective depicting possible institutional influences affecting pregnant teenagers' attitudes and behaviors. The narrowly focused, linear logic model in Exhibit 10.8 treats the program's impact in isolation from other institutional and societal factors. In contrast, the systems web in Exhibit 10.11 shows the prenatal program as one potentially strong influence on pregnant teenagers but also takes into account the important influences of the youth culture, the school system, other community-based youth programs, the local clinic and hospital, and possibly the local church. Moreover, during her pregnancy the teenager may be affected by other systems: the welfare system (eligibility for financial support and food stamps), the legal system (laws governing the degree to which the teenager can make independent decisions or live on her own), nutrition programs that might collaborate with the prenatal program, the transportation system (which affects how the teenager gets to clinic visits and the program), and the pervasive influences of the media (television, movies, music) that affect teenager attitudes and behaviors. The systems diagram in Exhibit 10.11 also includes larger contextual factors such as the political environment; economic incentives that can affect a teenager's ability to live independently, get child care, continue to attend school, or get a job; and social norms and larger cultural influences that affect how society responds to a teenager's pregnancy.

EXHIBIT 10.11

Program Systems Web Showing Possible Institutional Influences Affecting Pregnant Teenagers' Attitudes and Behavior

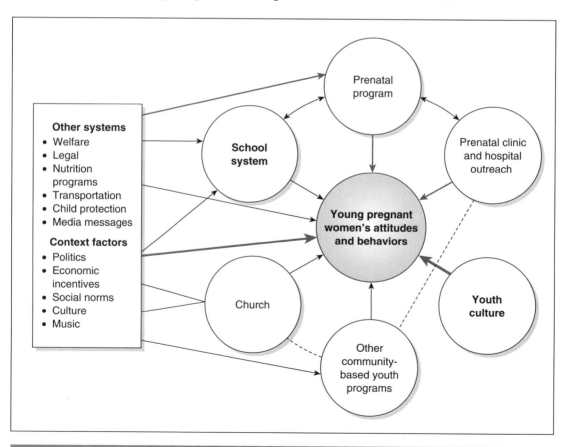

Constructing such a systems map with a prenatal program may lead the program to consider a more collaborative effort in which various institutional partners come together to work toward the desired outcome of a healthy pregnant teenager who delivers a healthy baby. The system diagrams suggest that the prenatal program by itself, focusing only on the teenager and only on its own delivery of knowledge to the teenager, is less likely to achieve the desired outcome than a model which takes into account the influences of other people in the teenager's system (the teenager's world) and collaborates with other institutions that can have an effect on the attainment of desired outcomes.

Systems Framework Premises

Looking at a program from a systems perspective is one way to deepen our understanding of the program and its outcomes. A systems framework is built on some fundamental relationships premises. We'll examine those premises using the program for pregnant teenagers to illustrate each one.

1. *The whole is greater than the sum of the parts.* If you look at Exhibit 10.9, you see interconnected parts—the pregnant teenager, her peer group, her family, her boyfriend, teachers and other adults who interact with her, and program staff. This *whole web of relationships* will be a unique constellation of interactions for each pregnant teenager. The *whole* may include consistent or contradictory messages about the teenager and her pregnancy. Moreover, that web of relationships isn't just built around her pregnancy. Messages about school, family, life, work, and love are all part of the mix. The systems picture reminds us that the teenager's life consists of a number of relationships and issues that extend well beyond her experience in the prenatal

program. The program is but *one influence in her whole life.* Linear program theories tend to be conceptualized as if the program is the only thing going on in the participant's life. Looking at a program as but one part of a participant's whole life is what Saville Kushner (2000) has described as "personalizing evaluation."

> I will be arguing for evaluators approaching programs through the experience of individuals rather than through the rhetoric of program sponsors and managers. I want to emphasize what we can learn about programs from Lucy and Ann. . . . So my arguments will robustly assert the need to address "the person" in the program. (Pp. 9–10)

Exhibit 10.9 is an abstract conceptualization of a set of relationships. If we put Lucy in the circle depicting the pregnant teenager and capture her story as a case study, we get a more holistic understanding of Lucy's life and where the program fits in Lucy's life. We then do the same thing for Ann. Each of those stories is its own whole, and the combination of stories of teenagers in the program gives us a sense of the program whole. But that program whole cannot be reduced to the individual stories (the parts) any more than Lucy's life can be reduced to the set of relationships in Exhibit 10.9. The whole is greater than the sum of parts. Moreover, Exhibit 10.11 reminds us that the program cannot be understood as a free-standing, isolated entity. The program as a whole includes relationships with other entities—schools, community organizations, churches—and larger societal influences. A systems framework invites us to understand the program in relation to other programs and as part of a larger web of institutions.

2. *Parts are interdependent such that a change in one part has implications for all*

parts and their interrelationships. Imagine that when Lucy becomes pregnant and enters the prenatal program, she has a close relationship with her boyfriend (the child's father) and her family, is doing well in school, and is active in church. The stress of the pregnancy leads Lucy and her boyfriend to break up. Things become tense in her family as everyone wants to give her advice. Her school attendance becomes irregular and she stops going to church. Without her boyfriend and with increased family tension, a small number of female peers become increasingly central to Lucy's life. What we begin to understand is that Lucy's *system of relationships* existed before she became pregnant. Her pregnancy affects all her relationships and those changes in relationships affect each other, ebbing and flowing. The pregnancy can't really be said to "cause" these changes. What happens between Lucy and her boyfriend when she becomes pregnant is a function of their whole relationship and their relationships with others. The program is part of that mix—but only a part. And how Lucy experiences the program will be affected by the other relationships in her life.

3. *The focus is on interconnected relationships.* The change in perspective that comes with systems thinking focuses our attention on how the web of relationships function together rather than as a linear chain of causes and effects. It is different to ask how things are connected than to ask does *a* cause *b*. It's not that one inquiry is right and the other is wrong. The point is that different questions and different frameworks provide different insights. Consider the example of your reading this book. We can ask, "To what extent does reading this book increase your knowledge of evaluation?" That's a fairly straightforward linear evaluation question. Now we

ask, "How does reading this book *relate to* the other things going on in your life?" That's a simple systems question. Each question has value, but the answers tell us very different things.

4. *Systems are made up of subsystems and function within larger systems.* Exhibit 10.9 shows a pregnant teenager's relationships with other people. Exhibit 10.11 shows the program's relationships with other institutions and how these, in combination, influence the teenager's attitudes and behavior. The "subsystems" are the various circles in these two exhibits. These subsystems—family, school, church, community, peer group—function within larger systems such as society, the legal system, the welfare system, culture, and the economy. How subsystems function within larger systems and how larger systems connect to and are influenced by subsystems can be part of a systems inquiry into understanding a program and its effects. Both the content and processes of a prenatal program for pregnant teenagers will be affected by larger societal norms. That's why programs in rural Mississippi, inner city Chicago, East Los Angeles, southern France, northern Brazil, and Burkina Faso would be different—*even if they supposedly were based on the same model.* The societal and cultural contexts would inevitably affect how the programs functioned.

5. *Systems boundaries are necessary and inevitably arbitrary.* Systems are social constructions (as are linear models). Systems maps are devices we construct to make sense of things. It is common in hiking to remind people in the wilderness that "the map is not the territory." The map is an abstract guide. Look around at the territory. What to include in a systems diagram and where to draw the boundaries are matters of utility. Including too much

makes the system overwhelming. Including too little risks missing important elements that affect program processes and outcomes. Given the purpose of evaluation, to inform judgment and action, the solution is to be practical. If we are mapping the relationships that affect a teenager's health during her pregnancy (Exhibit 10.9), we ask, "What are the primary relationships that will affect what the teenager does?" List those and map them in relationship to each other. Don't try to include every single relationship (a distant cousin in another city with whom she seldom interacts), but include all that are important—including that distant cousin if she is a teenager who has recently been through a pregnancy, which might be represented by a circle designating "other teenagers who have been or are pregnant who this teenager knows." The systems map of a program is a guide, a way to ask questions and understand the dynamics of what occurs. The systems map is not, however, the program.

A first step in moving beyond simple linear logic models is to add feedback loops to the model. Once a program is in operation,

---

Systems Framework Premises

A systems framework is built on some fundamental relationships premises.

- The whole is greater than the sum of the parts.
- Parts are interdependent such that a change in one part has implications for all parts and their interrelationships.
- Systems are made up of subsystems and function within larger systems.
- The focus is on interconnected relationships among parts, and between parts and the whole.
- Systems boundaries are necessary and inevitably arbitrary.

---

the relationships between links in the causal hierarchy are likely to be recursive rather than unidirectional. Instead of *a* causes *b*, the model becomes *a* causes *b*, and achieving *b* stimulates more of *a*. Take dieting and exercising to lose weight. Eating less and exercising leads to weight loss; losing weight leads to looking and feeling better. That's the simple linear chain. But looking and feeling better reinforces eating better and continuing to exercise. See Exhibit 10.12.

Recognizing such recursive feedback effects changes the model. For example, high-achieving schools affect the opinions and actions of parents, but parent reactions also affect the degree to which schools are committed to high achievement. The influence doesn't flow just one way. Classroom climate and school curriculum affect student achievement, but variations in student achievement also affect school climate and curriculum. From a systems perspective, a simple linear means-ends hierarchy without feedback loops or interdependencies is likely to be oversimplified, but there is no avoiding some simplification, even with systems maps. The basic dilemma is how much to simplify reality. *The challenge is to construct simplifications that pass the dual tests of usefulness and accuracy.*

The Increasing Importance of Systems Thinking in Evaluation

The preceding has provided only a brief introduction to the possibilities for

EXHIBIT 10.12
Converting a Linear Model to a Simple Feedback Model

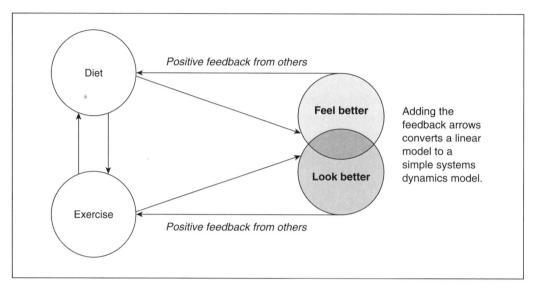

incorporating systems perspectives in evaluation. At the 2002 national conference of the AEA, president Molly Engle made systems the focus of the meeting. The keynote address by noted systems thinker John Sterman was titled "No Learning Without Feedback: The Vital Partnership of Evaluation and Systems Thinking." Shortly thereafter a Topical Interest group focused on Systems was formed within AEA and every national conference since has had a full strand of sessions devoted to systems approaches to evaluation. In 2006, AEA published its first-ever monograph, an expert anthology on *Systems Concepts in Evaluation* edited by Bob Williams and Iraj Iman. That monograph provides a wide range of systems approaches and demonstrates the diversity of approaches that congregate under the systems umbrella.

In commenting on this diversity the editors wrote,

For those of you looking for coherence about what we consider to be relevant systems concepts for evaluation, our advice when reading this publication is to look for patterns rather than definitions. For us, three patterns stand out:

1. *Perspectives.* Using systems concepts assumes that people will benefit from looking at their world differently. For systems practitioners, this motivation is explicit, deliberate, and is fundamental to their approach. However, just looking at the "bigger picture," or exploring interconnections does not make an inquiry "systemic." What makes it systemic is how you look at the picture, big or small, and explore interconnections. A "system" is as much an

"idea" about the real world as a physical description of it.

2. *Boundaries.* Boundaries drive how we "see" systems. Boundaries define who or what lies inside and what lies outside of a particular inquiry. Boundaries delineate or identify important differences (i.e., what is "in" and what is "out"). Boundaries determine who or what will benefit from a particular inquiry and who or what might suffer. Boundaries are fundamentally about values–they are judgements about worth. Defining boundaries is an essential part of systems work/inquiry/thinking.

3. *Entangled systems.* One can observe and perceive systems within systems, systems overlapping other systems, and systems tangled up in other systems. Thus it is unwise to focus on one view or definition of a system without examining its relationship with another system. Where does one system begin and the other end? Is there overlap? Who is best situated to experience or be affected by that overlap? What systems exist within systems and where do they lead? A systems thinker always looks inside, outside, beside, and between the readily identified systems boundary. He or she then critiques and if necessary changes that initial choice of boundary. (Williams and Iman 2006:6)

Part of the challenge of incorporating systems thinking in evaluation is that there are so many different systems meanings, models, approaches, and methods, including system dynamics, soft systems methodology, cultural-historical activity theory, and critical systemic thinking, each of which has specific implications for evaluation (Williams 2005b). More generally, critical systemic thinking can be considered as one element of *evaluative thinking* (see Chapter 5). Werner Ulrich (2000, 1998) has advocated that although not everyone should become a systems scholar, systems thinking involves new reflective skills that are essential in modern society for both professional competence and effective citizenship.

Evaluating Systems Reform

Systems thinking is pushing evaluators to conceptualize what we do in new ways and offers new frameworks for use in working with primary intended users to think about what they do and how they do it. This is especially the case where the targeted unit of change is, itself, *a system.* Thus, while much program evaluation has traditionally focused on the outcomes of programs aimed at individuals—students, farmers, chemically dependent people, parents, children, professionals, some initiatives target systems for reform and change. Policy initiatives can be aimed at reforming systems: the health care system, the educational system, the judicial system, the farming system, et cetera. Evaluating advocacy initiatives and policy change campaigns changes the unit of analysis (the *evaluand*) from the program level to the policy or systems level (Patton 2008, Coffman 2007a, b). While systems thinking is an option in looking at program outcomes for individuals, it is essential for evaluating system reform initiatives. And that provides a segue to one particularly challenging systems evaluation problem: How to evaluate emergent processes in complex nonlinear systems.

Evaluation in Complex Adaptive Systems

A Complex Adaptive System is a dynamic network of many interacting parts, continuously acting and reacting. The results of these interactions are dynamic, emergent, uncertain, and unpredictable. Examples are weather systems, stock markets, ecosystems, and anthills. One of the characteristics of complex adaptive systems is that small effects can have large consequences as

expressed by the butterfly effect metaphor, which suggests that a butterfly flapping its wings today in China may lead to a typhoon forming in the Pacific Ocean months later. This is represented in our everyday experience by the story of a chance, brief encounter that changes your life, or a phrase offered at an opportune moment that turns you in a new direction and alters forever your path. Since the 2000 presidential election, the butterfly effect has an additional meaning. Election officials in Palm Beach, Florida, experimented with a new format and procedure for voting called the "butterfly ballot." This resulted in voter confusion in a tight election, propelled the election results into the judicial system where the Supreme Court refused to allow a recount giving Florida to George Bush, which gave the presidency to George Bush, which led to the Iraq invasion, which led to global events and processes still unfolding.

Small actions (a changed ballot in one county) can have huge repercussions as that action reverberates through a complex adaptive system.

Sometimes complex effects take years. In 1933, the Belgians who controlled Rwanda as a colony issued identity cards classifying every Rwandan as Tutsi, Hutu, or Twa (a very minor category). In 1994, as part of the tragic genocide in Rwanda, those cards were used by Hutu to identify hundreds of thousands of Tutsi and kill them (Kinzer 2007:24). How does one portray such a connection? Certainly, not simple cause and effect. And somehow more than merely unintended consequences. A complex nonlinear system unfolded in an unpredictable fashion.

Complexity science is being used to understand phenomena in the biological world, policy analysis, ecosystems, economic systems, and in organizations (Fritjof et al. 2007; Dennard, Richardson, and Morcol 2005;

Richardson et al. 2005; Gribben 2004; Westley and Miller 2003; Gunderson and Holling 2002; Johnson 2001; Lewin 2001; Zimmerman, Lindbery, and Plsek 2001; Eoyang 1996; Waldrop 1992). *But what does this have to do with evaluation?* The answer lies in situational responsiveness and problem definition, which affect how we conceptualize and design evaluations.

Three Kinds of Problems: Simple, Complicated, Complex

> *To pursue greatness is to pursue Maybe.*
>
> —John Bare (2007), Vice President
> The Arthur M. Blank
> Family Foundation
> Atlanta, Georgia

In studying social innovations, we were impressed by the uncertainty and unpredictability of the innovative process, even looking back from a mountaintop of success, which is why we called the book *Getting to Maybe* (Westley, Zimmerman, and Patton 2006). Evaluating social innovations is a complex problem, as opposed to evaluating simple and complicated problems. A *simple* problem is how to bake a cake following a recipe. A recipe has clear cause-and-effect relationships and can be mastered through repetition and developing basic skills. There is a chance to standardize the process and to write the recipe with sufficient detail that even someone who has never baked has a high probability of success. Best practices for programs are like recipes in that they provide clear and high fidelity directions since the processes that have worked to produce desired outcomes in the past are highly likely to work again in the future. Assembly lines in factories have a "recipe" quality as do standardized school curricula.

Part of the attraction of the 12-Step program of Alcoholics Anonymous is its simple formulation.

A *complicated* problem is more like sending a rocket to the moon. Expertise is needed. Specialists are required and coordination of the experts is another area of expertise itself. Formulae and the latest scientific evidence are used to predict the trajectory and path of the rocket. Calculations are required to ensure sufficient fuel based on current conditions. If all the "homework" is completed, and if the coordination and communication systems are sophisticated enough to access the expertise, there is a high degree of certainty of the outcome. It is *complicated*, with many separate parts that need coordination, but it can be controlled by knowledgeable leaders and there is a high degree of predictability about the outcomes. Cause-and-effect relationships are still very clear, although not as straightforward as with simple problems. Coordinating large-scale programs with many local sites throughout a country or region is a complicated problem.

Parenting is *complex*. Unlike the recipe and rocket examples, there are no clear books or rules to follow to guarantee success. Clearly, there are many experts in parenting and many expert books available to parents. But none can be treated like a cookbook for a cake, or a set of formulae to send a rocket to the moon. In the case of the cake and the rocket, for the most part, we were intervening with inanimate objects. The flour does not suddenly decide to change its mind, and gravity can be counted on to be consistent too. On the other hand, children, as we all know, have minds of their own. Hence our interventions are always in relationship with them. There are very few stand-alone parenting tasks. Almost always, the parents and child interact to create outcomes. *Any highly individualized program has elements of complexity.* The outcomes will vary for different participants based on their differing needs, experiences, situations, and desires.

Exhibit 10.13 highlights the distinctions between the three kinds of problems. In all three cases, we tend to be optimistic that positive outcomes can be achieved. However, the way we intervene in each of these contexts is qualitatively different, as is how we

design an evaluation (Rogers 2008; Westley et al. 2006:8–10).

Simple formulations invite linear logic models that link inputs to activities to outputs to outcomes like a formula or recipe. Complicated situations invite system diagrams and maps that depict the relationships among the parts. Complex problems and situations are especially appropriate for *developmental evaluation* in which the

EXHIBIT 10.13

Simple, Complicated, and Complex Lenses

Simple	Complicated	Complex
Following a recipe	*Sending a rocket to the moon*	*Raising a child*
The recipe is essential.	Right protocols or formulae are critical and necessary.	Rigid protocols have a limited application or are counter-productive.
Recipes are tested to assure easy replication.	Sending one rocket to the moon increases assurance that the next will be also be a success.	Raising one child provides experience but is no guarantee of success with the next.
No particular expertise is required but cooking expertise increases success rate.	High levels of expertise and training in a variety of fields are necessary for success.	Expertise helps but only when balanced with responsiveness to the particular child.
A good recipe produces nearly the same cake every time.	Key elements of each rocket MUST be the same to succeed.	Every child is unique and must be understood as an individual.
The best recipes give good results every time.	There is a high degree of certainty of outcome.	Uncertainty of outcome remains.
A good recipe specifies the quantity and nature of the "parts" needed and the order in which to combine them, but there is room for experimentation.	Success depends on a blueprint that directs both the development of separate parts and specifies the exact relationship in which to assemble them.	Can't separate the parts from the whole; essence exists in the relationship between different people, different experiences, different moments in time.

SOURCE: Westley et al. (2006:9).

evaluation design is flexible, emergent, and dynamic, mirroring the emergent, dynamic, and uncertain nature of the intervention or innovation being evaluated. Tracking, monitoring, and evaluating complex policies requires continuous "streams of knowledge" rather than discrete and bounded studies (Stame 2006a, b). Evaluating in the face of the uncertainties of complexity requires anticipation and agility to improve evaluation quality, responsiveness, and real-time relevance (Morrell forthcoming, 2005).

Complexity scientist Ralph Stacey (2007, 1996, 1992) has offered a matrix of two dimensions that helps distinguish simple, complicated, and complex situations. One dimension scales the degree of certainty in the cause-effect relationship. Programs and interventions are close to certainty when cause and effect linkages in the logic model are highly predictable, as in the relationship between immunization and preventing disease. At the other end of the certainty continuum are innovative programs where the outcomes are highly unpredictable; a community development initiative would typically involve considerable uncertainty. Extrapolating from past experience is problematic because, like rearing a child, each community is unique. The vertical axis of the matrix captures the degree of agreement among various stakeholders about a program's needed inputs, goals, processes, outcomes measures, and likely long-term impacts. High levels of agreement make situations fairly simple; high degrees of values conflict foment complexity. Exhibit 10.14 shows where on this matrix the zones defining simple, complicated, and complex problems can be expected.

- Simple interventions are defined by high agreement and high causal certainty; immunization to prevent disease fits this zone on the matrix.

- Socially complicated situations are defined by fairly high predictability of outcomes, but great values conflict among stakeholders; abortion is an example.
- Technically complicated situations are defined by high agreement among stakeholders but low causal certainty; everyone wants children to learn to read but there are ferocious disagreements about which reading approach produces the best result (Schemo 2007).
- Complex situations are characterized by high values conflict and high uncertainty; what to do about global warming would fall in the complexity zone of the matrix.

Let me now explain and illustrate the evaluation implications of these different ways of understanding a program or intervention.

An Evaluation Example Illustrating Simple, Complicated, and Complex Designs

Consider a nationwide leadership development program that aims to infuse energy and vitality into a moribund nonprofit sector (a judgment based on funder assessment). The intensive 18-month program includes

(1) *skill development* (e.g., communications training, conflict resolution, needs assessment, strategic planning, appreciative inquiry methods) and knowledge acquisition (e.g., introduction to various theories of change, systems thinking, complexity science),

(2) *an organizational change project* in participants' own organizations, and

(3) *networking* with other participants around nonprofit sector issues of common interest and concern.

Skill development and knowledge acquisition can be modeled and evaluated

EXHIBIT 10.14

Matrix Depicting Simple to Complex

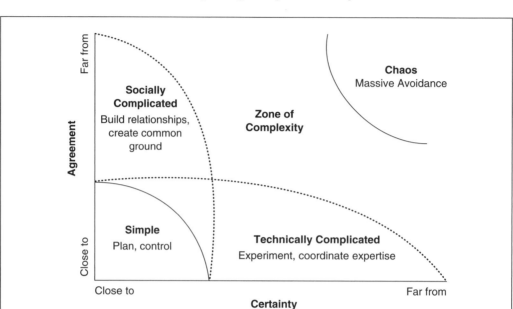

SOURCE: Adapted from Stacey (2007); Zimmerman, Lindbery and Plsek (2001:136–141).

with a linear framework. The desired outcomes are specifiable, concrete, and measurable, and the outcomes are connected directly to the curriculum and training in a short, observable time frame. Participants demonstrate their skills and knowledge by writing papers, carrying out assignments, and doing team projects. A linear logic model can appropriately capture and depict the hypothesized connections between inputs, activities, outputs, and outcomes as a framework for evaluation.

The second program component—carrying out organizational change projects in their own organizations—is congruent with relationship-focused systems modeling and systems change evaluation. The operations, culture, and constellation of units

within each participant's organization constitute a baseline organizational system at the time each participant enters the leadership development program. Each organization functions within some context and environment. As part of the leadership development experience, participants undertake some self-selected change effort, e.g., board development, strategic planning, staff development, reorganization, or evaluation, among many possibilities. These are efforts aimed at increasing the effectiveness of the participating organizations and can be modeled and evaluated as systems change initiatives. Evaluative case studies would capture the changed relationships within the organizations, both changed relationships among internal elements (e.g., between board and staff, or between technology support units and line management units) as well as changed relationships with organizations in the environment (e.g., collaborations, new or changed partnerships, new suppliers, changed community or funder relationships). The focus on changed relationships, linkages, and connections makes systems change evaluation an especially appropriate framework for this aspect of the program.

The third overall thrust of the program involves supporting self-organizing networks among participants to infuse new energies and synergies into the nonprofit sector. This constitutes a vision rather than a measurable goal. It's not at all clear what may emerge from such networking (no clear causal model), and the value of such networking is hard to measure. Indeed, there's no particular plan to support such networking other than bringing these leaders together and have them interact for intense periods of time. Beyond the networking, it's both impossible to predetermine what might occur as a result of the infusion of new leadership into the nonprofit sector and it would be politically inappropriate for the philanthropic funder to make such a determination because it would be controversial. Indeed, part of the intervention is support for the nonprofit and voluntary sector leaders to engage in dialogue around what actions and initiatives would revitalize the sector. The outcomes in this case will be entirely emergent. The evaluation would involve real-time monitoring of emergent initiatives watching for what the self-organizing networking yields. Indeed, in a real case where this form of emergent evaluation was actually undertaken, the results turned up conferences organized, regional institutes established, lobbying efforts coordinated, collaborations created, new partnerships, and shared development of materials. *None of these efforts were predictable in*

advance. They *emerged* from the process and were captured through developmental evaluation, specifically, periodically e-mailing participants to inquire about how they were working with others and, when something turned up, interviewing them about the details. Exhibit 10.15 summarizes and compares how these three evaluation approaches, representing different theories of change, can be combined in a single comprehensive evaluation of the leadership development program.

Matching the Evaluation Framework to the Nature of the Intervention

The principle illustrated by the preceding leadership development program is that the modeling framework and evaluation approach should be congruent with the nature of a program intervention. Understanding an intervention as simple, complicated, or complex can significantly affect how an evaluation is conducted (Rogers 2008; Martin and Sturmberg 2005).

When the intervention is readily understood as fitting traditional linear logic modeling, then the evaluation would document the program's inputs, processes, outputs, outcomes, and impacts, including viable and documentable linkages connecting the elements of the model. This is the traditional and dominant approach to program theory modeling and evaluation. In most cases, the outcomes for a linear logic model will be changes at the individual level among intended beneficiaries, e.g., changes in attitudes, knowledge, behavior, and status (well-being, health, employment, etc.). In other words, the unit of analysis for the evaluation is typically individuals and individual-level change.

Systems mapping offers an approach for evaluating systems change efforts. In many cases, the object of an intervention is

EXHIBIT 10.15

Evaluation Design for a Leadership Development Program: Different Components Manifest Different Theories of Change

Program component	*Leadership development.* Increased knowledge and skills, and use of those skills in their work.	*Organizational change.* Each participant carries out a project of his or her own choosing to develop the organization.	*Networking and leadership within the national nonprofit sector.* Vision of new energy and vitality.
Problem framing	Simple/Complex	Complicated/Complex	Complex
Type of theory of change	*Linear logic model.* Program training increases knowledge and skills. *Complex.* Additional unique, unanticipated, and emergent outcomes likely with such a high-powered group.	*Systems change.* Participants' organizational systems are changed through projects. Projects vary greatly and are chosen by participants and their organizations. *Complex.* Each is unique.	*Complex adaptive self-organizing network.* Informal groups emerge and decide to collaborate around shared interests.
Degree of certainty about how to achieve desired outcomes. (Horizontal axis on the Stacey Matrix)	*High certainty.* many leadership programs have produced changes in skills & knowledge. There is substantial knowledge about how to support professional development. Highly experienced instructors.	*Moderate to low certainty.* Degree to which organizations change dependent on a large number of factors, many of which are outside the leaders' control.	*Very low certainty.* Outcomes are unclear and unspecified; not even possible to specify all the variables that come into play; high likelihood that chance encounters will play a part.
Degree of agreement about the desired outcomes (Vertical axis on the Stacey Matrix)	High agreement that nonprofit leaders should have leadership skills and professional development opportunities.	Varied agreement about the need for organizational change among participants' organizations; some are open, some resistant; most uncertain about what is involved.	Low agreement about how these leaders should engage together in the larger nonprofit sector; vague vision of engagement, but the specifics will be emergent and opportunistic.
Evaluation questions	Are the desired outcomes achieved? Can these outcomes be attributed to the program? Do the trained leaders use their new skills in their work?	What projects do participants do in their organizations? How are their organizations changed? How are relationships altered? How are the organizations' relationships with external institutions affected?	What informal groups of participants self-organize? What do these emergent subgroups do together? What impacts flow from their emergent activities? What developments occur over time?
Evaluation design	Pre-post assessment of changed knowledge and skills. Follow-up to assess application of new skills.	Case studies of participants' projects focusing on how their organizations are changed.	Developmental evaluation follow-ups to track what emerges and develops over time.

a change in a system, for example, developing an organization (an organizational system change effort) or creating collaborative relationships among organizations, or connecting organizations and communities in some new ways. The unit of analysis is the system, and the focus is on changed relationships and interconnections, which are the defining elements of how the system functions. For example, philanthropic funders or government grants often seek to create genuinely collaborative relationships among organizations operating independently of each other (often referred to at the baseline as operating in "silos" or "elevator shafts"). An evaluation looking at the effectiveness and results of such a systems change initiative would map changes in relationships. Network analysis and mapping (McCarty et al. 2007; Durland and Fredericks 2005; Bryson et al. 2004) are powerful tools for capturing and depicting such dynamic and evolving system relationships (or absence of same when the change process fails to work).

Outcome mapping (International Development Research Centre 2007) is an approach that recognizes the complex nature of international development initiatives, especially those that involve multiple partners collaborating together, where each is contributing in some way to changes in the behaviors, relationships, activities, or actions of the people, groups, and organizations with whom a program works directly. *Outcome mapping* incorporates aspects of linear logic modeling by having a program map the behavior changes it can affect within its direct sphere of influence; it incorporates systems thinking by mapping relationships with partners and recognizing the impossibility of drawing simple causal attribution conclusions where many factors affect change and cooperating partners each make *contributions* to

change; and it brings an appreciation of complex adaptive processes to bear by treating an outcome map as emergent and dynamic, a map that can be and should be revisited and revised as conditions change (as they surely will) and as new understandings emerge (which is surely to be hoped for and encouraged).

This last point deserves emphasis. Logic models and program theories can change and evolve over the life of a program. Nick Tilley (2004) has described how the Crime Reduction Programme in the United Kingdom metamorphosed over its 3-year life, including changing theories of the program and changing forms of evaluation. The more volatile the environment of a program, the more likely it is that the program theory will be affected by that volatility—and by learning from what actually unfolds.

Developmental Evaluation for Complex Adaptive Systems

Developmental Evaluation is especially appropriate for situations with a high degree of uncertainty and unpredictability where the purpose of the evaluation is to support development, adaptation, and innovation in a complex adaptive environment characterized by rapid change and dynamic system relationships among important influences and actors. (See Chapter 8, pages 277–290, for an in-depth discussion of *Developmental Evaluation*.)

Developmental Evaluation

Developmental evaluation is especially appropriate for situations with a high degree of uncertainty and unpredictability where an innovator or funder wants to "put things in motion and see what happens." Using the example of the leadership development program, infusing a hundred highly trained and supported national leaders into the nonprofit sector fits these parameters. All kinds of things can happen; many unexpected results may emerge (and did in the actual initiative on which this example is based). Some form of real-time, open-ended tracking is needed to capture what emerges. This is especially appropriate for venture capital and highly entrepreneurial, seed money efforts where the strategy is to infuse people and resources to shake up a system, increase the rate and intensity of interactions among system elements and actors, and see what happens. As things start to happen, additional resources can be infused to support further development. The very act of capturing what emerges and feeding information back into the evolving system makes this form of developmental evaluation part of the intervention (a form of process use). In such developmental evaluation, there is not and cannot be a classic separation between the measurement process and what is being observed (Gamble 2007). The observations affect the emergent self-organizing by injecting new information into the dynamic and emergent system. For example, following up with the trained leaders to find out who they are networking with and what is emerging can stimulate them to network. Even the unit of analysis can change in emergent, developmental evaluation as the evaluator tracks whatever emerges; that is, the very definition of units of analysis is emergent as the evaluator follows the complex nonlinear dynamics of the connections and linkages among those exchanging information and engaged in some forms of self-organized collective action.

Attention to complex adaptive systems provides a framework for understanding such common evaluation issues as unintended consequences, irreproducible effects, lack of program fidelity in implementation, multiple paths to the same outcomes, "slippery" program requirements, and difficulty in specifying treatments (Morell 2005:72). Glenda Eoyang (2006a) has described how a complexity-based approach to evaluation was used in a large social services department with 3,000 employees at the county level to help integrate services and functions. The evaluation elucidated emergent "networks of meaning," supported new approaches to alignment in looking at how different units connected to each other, and tracked the evolution of language about what was happening, which shaped emergent meanings. Eoyang and Berkas (1998) have examined and generalized the particular contributions that the lens of complex adaptive systems can bring to evaluation. They concluded,

> The system-wide behaviors of a Complex Adaptive System (CAS) emerge over time. For this reason, the evaluation system should focus on developmental and emergent patterns of behavior that:
>
> Match the developmental stage of the system. . . . Consider the dynamical pattern that the system exhibits over time to design an evaluation program to capture the "differences that make a difference."
>
> Track patterns and pattern changes over time, rather than focusing exclusively on behaviors of specific individuals or groups. While it may be unreasonable to expect a particular path of development or a predetermined outcome from a CAS, emergent patterns of behavior can be expected outcomes. An effective evaluation system must be able to capture and report on these evolving patterns. (Eoyang and Berkas 1998: www.chaos-limited.com/CAS.htm; see also Eoyang 2007)

The Challenges of Establishing Causality

Theories of change are important in evaluation because causality is a central issue in making judgments about a program's merit, worth, or significance. The classic causal question, in all its simple brilliance, is: Did the program produce the desired and intended results? Or, to what extent can the observed outcomes be attributed to the program's intervention? Establishing causality becomes more complicated over longer periods of time, when there are multiple interventions occurring at the same time, influences flow in both directions because of feedback loops, and interdependent relationships in a dynamic system means that all kinds of interconnected elements can change at the same time. The notion of cause and effect can lose all meaning in highly dynamic and complex adaptive systems characterized by nonlinear patterns of interaction, where small actions can connect with other smaller and larger forces and factors that wander hither and yon, but then suddenly emerge, like a hurricane, as major change at some unpredicted and unpredictable tipping point. Evaluation methods, designs, and tools for measuring predetermined outcomes and attributing causes for simple interventions that can be depicted as linear logic models are of little use in tracking the effects of interventions in complex adaptive systems. Indeed, the imposition of such linear designs and simple measures can do harm by trying to control and thereby stifling the very innovative process being tracked. Different kinds of theories of change, then demand different evaluation approaches to conceptualizing and assessing causality (Rogers forthcoming), including the importance of developmental evaluation for use in complex adaptive systems. The challenge is to match the evaluation approach to the nature of the situation, the theory of change at work, and the information needs of primary intended users.

In all this, it is important to interpret results about causal linkages with prudence and care. In that regard, consider the wisdom of this Buddhist story.

One day an old man approached Zen Master Hyakujo. The old man said, "I am not a human being. In ancient times I lived on this mountain. A student of the Way asked me if the enlightened were still affected by causality. I replied saying that they were not affected. Because of that, I was degraded to lead the life of a wild fox for five hundred years. I now request you to answer one thing for me. Are the enlightened still affected by causality?

Master Hyakujo replied, "They are not deluded by causality." At that the old man was enlightened.

—Adapted from Hoffman 1975:138

Causal evaluation questions can be enlightening; they can also lead to delusions. Unfortunately, there is no clear way of telling the difference. So among the many perils evaluators face, we can add that of being turned into a wild fox for 500 years!

Follow-Up Exercises

1a. Identify a program that has identifiable and measurable outcomes for individual participants in the program and where the length of the program is less than one year. Examples would be programs that treat alcohol and drug abuse, parent education classes, an agricultural extension program for farmers, a job training program, and so on. Based on the written materials available on that program, construct a linear logic model and explain the steps in the model.

1b. Develop a logic model with the staff in an actual program. Describe how staff reacted to the process of developing the logic model.

2. Take a logic model and convert it to a theory of change by explicitly identifying the causal mechanisms and/or assumptions that explain why each step in the model should occur. For example, a simple logic model would specify that increased knowledge about the health risks of smoking would lead to reduced smoking (Exhibit 10.3). What predictive theory undergirds and explains the causal connection between knowledge and behavior change in this example? Pick your own logic model example and add the causal linkage explanations and/or validity assumptions that convert it to a theory of change.

3. Pick a highly visible political issue and depict it as a logic model. For example, what is the "logic model" that explains why torture is used to extract information from presumed terrorists (e.g., the Abu Ghraib torture controversy in the Iraq War)? Construct the logic model for some matter of visible public policy and then analyze and comment on the assumptions of advocates. Examples of topics: solutions to global warming; relief of Third World debt; more gender equity by educating girls in developing countries; banning gay marriage; stopping family violence; ending child prostitution; building a high wall between the United States and Mexico to stop illegal immigration; teaching young people to abstain from sex until marriage; cutting down old growth forests for timber; drilling for oil in the Alaska wilderness; or any current public policy controversy. Portray the proposed intervention

and alleged solution or desired result as a logic model. Discuss and explain the "logic" of the model you construct.

4. Exhibits 10.8, 10.9, 10.10, and 10.11 portray different ways of looking at a prenatal program for pregnant teenagers. Reconstruct those exhibits as a postnatal program. The intended and desired outcome of a prenatal program is a healthy baby and healthy mother when the baby is born. The intended outcome of a postnatal program is a healthy mother and child 2 years after the baby is born. Reconfigure those four models for a postnatal program. Discuss and explain the changes.

5. Pick an intervention of some kind, for example, a program aimed at stopping people from talking on cell phones (mobile phones) while driving. Pick your own example. Using the distinctions between simple, complicated, and complex (Exhibits 10.13, 10.14, and 10.15), present and analyze that intervention from the perspectives of (a) a simple problem that can be solved through a linear model; (b) a complicated problem that requires understanding and changing system relationships; and (c) a complex problem that is best portrayed as emergent and uncertain and requires developmental evaluation. In essence, look at the sample issue or intervention through these three different lenses. Compare and contrast what each illuminates and makes possible—and the evaluation implications of each perspective.

Note

1. Reprinted from *Angels in America, Part Two: Perestroika* by Tony Kushner. Copyright 1992 and 1994 by the author. Published by Theatre Communications Group. Used by permission.

PART 3

Appropriate Methods

Blowhard Evaluation

This is the story of three little pigs who built three little houses for protection from the BIG BAD WOLF.

The first pig worked without a plan, building the simplest and easiest structure possible with whatever materials happened to be laying around, mostly straw and sticks.

When the BIG BAD WOLF appeared, he had scarcely to huff and puff to blow the house down, whereupon the first pig ran for shelter and protection to the second pig's house.

The second pig's house was prefabricated in a most rigorous fashion with highly reliable materials. Architects and engineers had applied the latest techniques and most valid methods to the design and construction of these standardized, prefabricated models. The second pig felt quite confident that his house could withstand any attack.

The BIG BAD WOLF followed the first pig to the house of the second pig and commanded, "Come out! Come out! Or by the hair on my chinny-chin-chin, I'll huff and I'll puff and I'll blow your house down."

The second pig laughed a scornful reply: "Huff and puff all you want. You'll find no weaknesses in this house, for it was designed by experts using the latest and best scientific methods guaranteed not to fall apart under the most strenuous huffing and puffing."

So the BIG BAD WOLF huffed and puffed, and he huffed and puffed some more, but the structure was solid, and gave not an inch.

In catching his breath for a final huffing and puffing, the BIG BAD WOLF noticed that the house, although strong and well built, was simply sitting on top of the ground. It had been purchased and set down on the local site with no attention to establishing a firm connecting foundation that would anchor the house in its setting. Different settings require very different site preparation with appropriately matched foundations, but the prefabricated kit came with no instructions about how to prepare a local foundation.

Understanding all this in an instant, the sly wolf ceased his huffing and puffing. Instead, he simply reached down, got a strong hold on the underside of the house, lifted, and tipped it over. The second pig was shocked to find himself uncovered and vulnerable. He would have been easy prey for the BIG BAD WOLF had not the first pig, being more wary and therefore more alert, dashed out from under the house, pulling his flabbergasted brother with him. Together they sprinted to the house of the third pig, crying "wee wee wee" all the way there.

The house of the third pig was the source of some controversy in the local pig community. Unlike any other house, it was constructed of a hodgepodge of local materials and a few things borrowed from elsewhere. It incorporated some of the ideas seen in the prefabricated houses designed by experts, but those ideas had been altered to fit local conditions and the special interests and needs of the third pig. The house was built on a strong foundation, well anchored in its setting and carefully adapted to the specific conditions of the spot on which the house was built. Although the house was sometimes the object of ridicule because it was unique and different, it was also the object of envy and praise, for it was evident to all that it fit quite beautifully and remarkably in that precise location.

The BIG BAD WOLF approached the house of the third pig confidently. He huffed and puffed his best huffs and puffs. The house gave a little under these strenuous forces, but it did not break. Flexibility was part of its design, so it could sway and give under adverse and changed conditions without breaking and falling apart. Being firmly anchored in a solid foundation, it would not tip over. The BIG BAD WOLF soon knew he would have no pork chops for dinner that night.

Following the defeat of the BIG BAD WOLF, the third pig found his two brother pigs suddenly very interested in how to build houses uniquely adapted to and firmly grounded in a specific location with a structure able to withstand the onslaughts of the most persistent blowhards. They opened a consulting firm to help other pigs. The firm was called "Wee wee wee, all the way home."

—From Halcolm's *Evaluation Fairy Tales*

11

Evaluations Worth Using
Utilization-Focused Methods Decisions

*T*hey say there was method to his madness. Perhaps so. It is easier to select a method for madness than a single best method for evaluation, though attempting the latter is an excellent way of achieving the former.

—Halcolm

The three pigs story that precedes this chapter and introduces this part of the book on Appropriate Methods offers an evaluation parable. The first pig built a house that was the equivalent of what is disparagingly called a "quick and dirty evaluation." They are low-budget efforts that give the outward appearance of evaluation, but their value and utility are fleeting. They simply do not stand up under scrutiny. The second pig replicated a high-quality design that met uniform standards of excellence as specified by distant experts. Textbook designs have the advantage of elegance and sophistication, but they don't travel well. As the old proverb

cautions, when all you have is a hammer, everything looks like a nail. Prefabricated structures brought in from far away are vulnerable to unanticipated local conditions. Beware the evaluator who offers essentially the same design for every situation.

The third pig, then, exemplifies the utilization-focused evaluator, one who designs an evaluation to fit a specific set of circumstances, needs, and interests. The third pig demonstrated situational adaptability and responsiveness, a strategic stance introduced in Chapter 6. In this chapter, we'll examine how situational responsiveness affects methods decisions.

Methods to Support Intended Uses, Chosen by Intended Users

Methods decisions, like decisions about focus and priority issues, are guided and informed by our evaluation goal: *intended use by intended users*. Attaining this goal is enhanced by having intended users actively involving in methods decisions, an assertion I shall substantiate in depth throughout this chapter. It remains, however, a controversial assertion, evidence about its desirability and effectiveness notwithstanding. The source of the controversy, I'm convinced, is territorial.

For the most part, evaluation professionals have come to accept that use can be enhanced by actively involving intended users in decisions about the evaluation's purpose, scope, and focus to ensure relevance and buy-in. In other words, they can accept playing a consultative and collaborative role during the conceptual phase of the evaluation. Where I often part company with my colleagues is in the role to be played by intended users in making measurement and design decisions. "The evaluator is nothing," they argue, "if not an expert in methods and statistics. Clearly social scientists ought to be left with full responsibility for operationalizing program goals and determining data collection procedures." Edwards and Guttentag (1975) articulated the classic position, one that I find still holds sway today: "The decision makers' values determine on what variables data should be gathered. The researcher then decides how to collect the data" (p. 456).

Utilization-focused evaluation takes a different path.

Beyond Technical Expertise

The common perception of methods decisions among nonresearchers is that such decisions are primarily technical in nature. Sample size, for example, is determined by a mathematical formula. The evaluation methodologist enters the values of certain variables, makes calculations, and out pops the right sample size to achieve the desired level of statistical robustness, significance, power, validity, reliability, generalizability, and so on—all technical terms that dazzle, impress, and intimidate practitioners and nonresearchers. Evaluation researchers have a vested interest in maintaining this technical image of scientific expertise, for it gives us prestige, inspires respect, and, not incidentally, it leads nonresearchers to defer to us, essentially giving us the power to make crucial methods decisions and then interpret the meaning of the resulting data. It is not in our interest, from the perspective of maintaining prestige and power, to reveal to intended users that methods decisions are far from purely technical. But, contrary to public perception, evaluators know that methods decisions are never purely technical. Never. Ways of measuring complex phenomena involve simplifications that are inherently somewhat arbitrary, are always constrained by limited resources and time, inevitably involve competing and conflicting priorities, and rest on a foundation of values preferences that are typically resolved by pragmatic considerations, disciplinary biases, and measurement traditions.

The reason to debunk the myth that methods and measurement decisions are primarily technical is to enhance use. For we know that use is enhanced when practitioners, decision makers, and other users fully understand the strengths and weaknesses of evaluation data, and that such understanding is increased by being involved in making methods decisions. We know that use is enhanced when intended users participate in making sure that, when trade-offs are considered, as they inevitably are because of limited resources and time, the path chosen is informed by relevance. We know that use is enhanced when users buy into the design and find it credible and valid within the scope of its intended purposes as determined by them. And we know that when evaluation findings are presented, the substance is less likely to be undercut by debates about methods if users have been involved in those debates prior to data collection.

As in all other aspects of the evaluation, then, the utilization-focused evaluator advises intended users about options; points out the consequences of various choices; offers creative possibilities; engages with users actively, reactively, interactively, and adaptively to consider alternatives; and facilitates *their* methods decision. At the stage of choosing methods, the evaluator remains a technical adviser, consultant, teacher, and advocate for quality. The primary intended users remain decision makers about the evaluation. Exhibit 11.1 summarizes reasons why primary intended users should be involved in methods decisions. In the pages that follow, I'll elaborate on these rationales, explore the implications of this approach, and provide examples. Let's begin with an example.

EXHIBIT 11.1

Reasons Primary Users Should Be Involved in Methods Decisions

1. Intended use affects methods choices. Intended users can and should judge the utility of various design options and kinds of data.

2. Limited time and resources necessitate trade-offs: more of this, less of that. Primary users have the greatest stake in such decisions since findings are affected.

3. Methods decisions are never purely technical. Practical considerations constrain technical alternatives. Everything from how to classify participants to how to aggregate data has utility implications that deserve users' consideration.

4. No design is perfect. Intended users need to know the strengths and weaknesses of an evaluation to exercise informed judgment.

5. Different users may have different criteria for judging methodological quality. These should be made explicit and negotiated during methods discussions.

6. Credibility of the evidence and the perceived validity of the overall evaluation are key factors affecting use. These are matters of subjective user judgment that should inform methods decisions.

7. Intended users learn about and become more knowledgeable and sophisticated about methods and using data by being involved in methods decisions. This benefits both the current and future evaluations.

8. Methods debates should take place before data collection, as much as possible, so that findings are not undercut by bringing up concerns that should have been addressed during design. Methods debates among intended users after findings are reported distract from using evaluation results.

The Million Man March

On October 16, 1995, some number of African American men marched on Washington, D.C., as a call to action. The number of men in the march mattered a great deal to both its organizers and critics. Disputes about the number subsequently led to major lawsuits against the National Park Service, which provided the government's official estimates of demonstrations on the Capitol Mall. For weeks after the march, newspaper commentators, television journalists, policymakers, activists, academics, and pundits debated the number. The size of the march overshadowed its substance and intended message. Varying estimates of the number of marchers led to charges and countercharges of racism and bigotry.

Could this controversy have been anticipated, avoided, or at least tempered? Let's consider how the evaluation was conducted and then how a utilization-focused approach would have been different.

First, let's examine what made this march a focus for evaluation. The organizer of the march, Nation of Islam leader Louis Farrakhan, was a controversial figure often accused of being anti-Semitic and fomenting hatred against whites. Some black Congressman and the leadership of the National Association for the Advancement of Colored People refused to join the march. Many other black leaders worked to make it a success. From the moment the march was announced, through the months leading up to it, debate about the legitimacy and purpose of the march received high-visibility media coverage. As the day of the march approached, the central question became: How many will show up?

Why was the number so important? Because the target number became the name of the march: *The Million Man March.* The goal was unusually clear, specific, and measurable. The march's leaders staked their prestige on attaining *that* number. The march's detractors hoped for failure. The number came to symbolize the unity and political mobilization of African American men.

In time for the evening news on the day of the march, the National Park Service released its estimate: 400,000. This ranked the march as one of the largest in the history of the United States, but the number was far short of the 1 million goal. March advocates reacted with disbelief and anger. March critics gloated at Farrakhan's "failure." Who made the estimate? A white man, a career technician, in the National Park Service. He used the method he always used, a sample count from photographs. Leaders of the march immediately denounced the official number as racist. The debate was on. A week later, independent researchers at Boston University, using different counting methods, estimated the number at more than 800,000—double the National Park Service estimate. The leaders of the march continued to insist that more than a million participated. The significance of this historically important event remains clouded by rancorous debate over the seemingly simplest of all evaluation questions: How many people participated in the "program"? (Janofsky 1995).

Suppose, now, for the sake of illustration, that the responsible National Park official—a white male, remember—had taken a utilization-focused approach. In the time leading up the march, as its visibility and potential historical significance became apparent, he could have identified and convened a group of primary stakeholders: one or more representatives of the march's organizers, representatives of the other national black organizations, academics with expertise in crowd estimates, and perhaps police officials from other cities who had experience

Crowd Counting Is an Inexact Science

In estimating the size of the 1995 Million Man March, the Park Service used the same methods it had always used. Officials take pictures from a helicopter that flies along the sides of the Mall and then, using a grid, take into account the number of people per square foot. They also monitor the volume of passengers using local buses and subways. The Park Service said that its standards and methods of crowd measurement were prescribed by Congressional legislation. Farouk el-Baz, director of the Boston University Center for Remote Sensing, said the angle of the Park Service pictures had failed to capture many of those attending. But the center acknowledged that its own estimate of 870,000 people had a 25 percent margin of error, meaning the crowd could have been as small as 655,000 or as large as 1.1 million.

Samuel E. Jordan, acting director of the city's Office for Emergency Preparedness, who served as the city's liaison with march organizers, said that both the Park Service and the Boston estimates had failed to account for the density of people at the march, people standing under trees and those standing on side streets, well within view of giant screens on which the program was televised. "You can go up in a helicopter all you want, but you have to do it right," Mr. Jordan said. "You have to take it all into account." His estimate of one million, he said, had a margin of error of 20 percent.

SOURCE: Janofsky (1995).

estimating the size of large crowds. A couple of respected newsprint and television journalists could have been added to the group. Indeed, and this is surely a radical proposal, a professional evaluator might have been asked to facilitate the group's work.

Once such group was assembled, consider the challenging nontechnical decisions that have to be made to figure out the size of the march. These questions are in addition to technical questions of aerial photography sampling and computer programs designed to count heads in a crowd. To answer these questions requires some combination of common sense, political savvy, appreciation of different perspectives, and pragmatism. Here, then, are some questions that would occur to me if I had been asked to facilitate such a discussion:

1. Who gets counted? It's the million man march aimed at black men. Do women count? Do children count? Do whites count?

2. Do spectators and onlookers get counted as well as "marchers"?

3. When during the daylong event will counts be made? Is there a particular time that counts the most; for example, during Farrakhan's speech? (His speech was 3 hours long, so when or how often during his speech?)

4. Should the final number account for people who came and went over the course of the day or only people present at some single point in time?

5. What geographical boundary gets included in the count? What are the boundaries of the Capitol Mall for purposes of sampling?

6. Sympathy and support marches are scheduled to take place in other cities. Do their numbers count in the 1 million total?

7. Should we report a single number, such as 1 million, or communicate the variability of any such count by reporting a range, for example, 900,000 to 1.1 million?

8. Who are the most credible people to actually engage in or supervise the final analysis?

9. What reviews should the analysis undergo, by whom, before being released officially?

10. Who do we say determined the counting methods and under whose name, or combination of named sponsors, should the results be publicized?

I certainly don't assert that convening a group of primary stakeholders to negotiate answers to these questions would have ended all controversy, but I do believe it could have tempered the rancorous tone of the debate, diffused the racial overtones of the counting process, and permitted more focus on the substantive societal issues raised by the march—issues about family values, community involvement, social responsibility, economic opportunity, and justice. The evaluation task force, once convened to decide how to count from 1 to 1 million, might even have decided to prepare methods of following up the march to determine its longer-term impacts on black men, families, and communities—evaluation questions overshadowed by the controversy about the number of participants.

Parallel Evaluation Decisions

I like the Million Man March example because it shows how a seemingly simple question like "how many" can become quite complicated both technically and politically. Parallel challenges can be found in any program evaluation. For example, in most programs the dropout rate is an important indicator of how participants are reacting to a program. But when has someone dropped out? This typically turns out to involve some arbitrary cutoff. School districts vary widely in how they define, count, and report dropouts, as do chemical dependency, adult literacy, parent education, and all kinds of other programs.

No less vague and difficult are concepts such as *in the program* and *finished the program.* Many programs lack clear beginning and ending points. For example, a job-training program aimed at chronically unemployed minority men has a month-long assessment process, including testing for drug use and observing a potential participant's persistence in staying with the process. During this time, the participant, with staff support and coaching, develops a plan. The participant is on probation until he or she completes enough of the program to show seriousness and commitment, but the program is highly individualized so different people are involved in the early assessment and probation processes over very different time periods. There is no clear criterion for when a person has begun probation or completed probation and officially *entered* the program. Yet the decision, in aggregate, will determine the denominator for dropout and completion rates and will be the numerator for the program's "acceptance" rate. Making sure that such categories are meaningful and valid, so that the numbers are credible and useful, involves far more than statistics. Careful thought must be given, with primary intended users, to how the numbers and reported rates will be calculated and used, including whether they can be used for comparisons with similar programs.

Nor are these kinds of categorical decisions only a problem when measuring human behavior. The Minnesota Department of Transportation has categorized road projects as *preservation, replacement,* and *new or expansion.* How these categories are used to allocate funding to regions throughout the state has enormous implications. Now, consider the Lake Street Bridge that connects Minneapolis and Saint Paul. Old and in danger of being condemned, the bridge was torn down and a new one built. The old bridge had only two lanes and no decorative flourishes. The new bridge has four lanes and attractive design features.

Should this project be categorized as replacement or expansion? (In a time of economic optimism and expanding resources, such as the 1960s, new and expansion projects were favored. In a time of downsizing and reduced resources, like the 1990s, replacement projects are more politically viable.) Perhaps, you might argue, the Lake Street Bridge illustrates the need for a new category: part replacement/part expansion. But no replacements are pure replacements when new materials are used and updated codes or standards are followed. And few expansions are done without replacing something. How much mix, then, would have to occur for a project to fall into the new, combined part replacement/part expansion category? A doctoral degree in research and statistics provides no more guidance in answering this question than thoughtful consideration of how the data will be used, grounded in common sense and pragmatism—a decision that should be made by intended users with intended uses in mind. Such inherently arbitrary measurement decisions determine what data will emerge in findings.

Methods and Measurement Options

There cannot be acting or doing of any kind, till it be recognized that there is a thing to be done; the thing once recognized, doing in a thousand shapes becomes possible.

—Thomas Carlyle, philosopher and historian (1795–1881)

Mail questionnaires, telephone interviews, or personal face-to-face interviews? Individual interviews or focus groups? Even-numbered or odd-numbered scales on survey items? Opinion, knowledge, and/or behavioral questions? All closed questions or some open-ended? If some open-ended, how many? Norm-referenced or criterion-referenced tests? Develop our own instruments or adopt measures already available? Experimental design, quasi-experimental design, or case studies? Participant observation or spectator observation? A few in-depth observations or many shorter observations? Single or multiple observers? Standardized or individualized protocols? Fixed or emergent design? Follow up after 2 weeks, 3 months, 6 months, or a year? Follow up everyone or a sample? What kind of sample: simple random, stratified, and/or purposeful? What size sample? Should interviewers have the same characteristics as program participants: gender, age, race? What comparisons to make: past performance, intended goals, hoped-for goals, other programs? I won't list a thousand such options à la Thomas Carlyle, but I've no doubt it could be done. I would certainly never try the patience of primary stakeholders with a thousand options, but I do expect to work with them to consider the strengths and weaknesses of major design and measurement possibilities.

Christie (2007) found that decision makers could distinguish among the merits and uses of different kinds of designs. Using a set of scenarios derived from actual evaluation studies, she conducted a simulation to examine what decision makers' reported as evaluation design preferences and likely influences. Each scenario described a setting where results from one of three types of evaluation designs would be available: large-scale study data, case study data, or anecdotal accounts. The simulation then specified a particular decision that needed to be made. Decision makers were asked to indicate which type of design would influence their decision making. Results from 131 participants indicated that participants were influenced by all types of information, yet large-scale and case study data were more influential relative to anecdotal accounts; certain types of evaluation data were more influential among certain groups of decision makers; and choosing to use one type of evaluation data over the other two depended on the independent influence of other types of evaluation data on the decision maker, as well as prior beliefs about program efficacy. In essence, these decision makers had varying design preferences and were quite capable of distinguishing the credibility and utility of various types of evaluation studies—or measurement options. Let me illustrate with a common issue that arises in survey design.

The Odd-Even Question

Should response scales be even numbered (e.g., four or six response choices) or odd numbered (e.g., three or five choices)? It doesn't seem like such a big deal actually, but I've seen evaluators on both sides of the question go at each other with the vehemence of Marxists versus capitalists, osteopaths versus chiropractors, or cat lovers versus dog lovers. What's all the ruckus about? It's about the value and validity of a midpoint on questionnaire items. In conducting workshops on evaluation, one of the most common questions I get is "Should we give people a midpoint?"

An even-numbered scale has no midpoint.

Should the workshop be expanded from 1 day to 2 days?			
Strongly Agree	Agree	Disagree	Strongly Disagree

An odd-numbered scale has a midpoint.

Should the workshop be expanded from 1 day to 2 days?				
Strongly Agree	Agree	No Opinion	Disagree	Strongly Disagree

Even-numbered scales force respondents to lean in one direction or the other (although a few will circle the two middle responses creating their own midpoint if not provided one on the survey). Even-numbered scales allow the respondent to hedge, to be undecided, or, in less kind terms, to cop out of making a decision one way or the other, or yet again, to be genuinely in the middle.

One thing about surveys is clear: If given a midpoint, many respondents will use it.

Not given a midpoint, most respondents will answer leaning one way or the other.

Which one is best? Should respondents be given a midpoint? Having carefully considered the arguments on both sides of the issue, having analyzed a large number of questionnaires with both kinds of items, and having meditated on the problem at great length, I find that I'm forced to come down firmly and unwaveringly right smack in the middle. *It depends.* Sometimes odd-numbered scales are best and sometimes even-numbered scales are best. How to decide?

The issue is really not technical, statistical, or methodological. The issue is one of utility. What do intended users want to find out? Will the findings be more useful if respondents are forced to lean in one direction or the other? Or is it more useful to find out what proportion of people are undecided, or "don't know." The evaluator helps the primary intended users determine the value and implications of offering a midpoint. Do they believe that "down deep inside" everyone really leans one way or the other on the issue, or do they believe that some people are genuinely in the middle on the issue and they want to know how many have no opinion?

Not only can nonresearchers make this choice, but they also often enjoy doing so, and engaging them in thinking about such alternatives and their implications teaches evaluative thinking.

Ensuring Methodological Quality and Excellence

I am easily satisfied with the very best.

—Winston Churchill (1874–1965)
British Prime Minister
during World War II

One of the myths believed by nonresearchers is that researchers have agreed among themselves about what constitutes methodological quality and excellence. This belief can make practitioners and other nonacademic stakeholders understandably reluctant to engage in methods discussions. In fact, as the next chapter discusses in depth, researchers disagree with each other vehemently about what constitutes good research and, with a little

training and help, I find that nonresearchers can grasp the basic issues involved and make informed choices.

To increase the confidence of nonresearchers that they can and should contribute to methods discussions—for example, to consider the merits of telephone interviews versus face-to-face interviews or mail questionnaires—I'll often share the perspective of journal editors. Eva Baker, Director of the UCLA Center for the Study of Evaluation and former editor of *Educational Evaluation and Policy Analysis (EEPA)*, established a strong system of peer review for *EEPA*, requiring three independent reviewers for every article. Eva has told me that in several years as editor, *she never published an article on which all three reviewers agreed the article was good!* I edited the peer-reviewed *Journal of Extension* for 3 years and had the same experience. Robert Donmoyer (1996), features editor of *Educational Researcher,* reported that "peer reviewers' recommendations often conflict and their advice is frequently contradictory. . . . There is little consensus about what research and scholarship are and what research reporting and scholarly discourse should look like" (p. 19).

This kind of inside look at the world of research, like an inside look at how the Supreme Court makes decisions (Waldron 2007), can be shocking to people who think that there surely must be consensus regarding what constitutes "good" research or good jurisprudence. The real picture is more chaotic and warlike, what Donmoyer (1996) portrays as "a diverse array of voices speaking from quite different, often contradictory perspectives and value commitments" (p. 19). Perspectives and value commitments? Not just rules and formulas? Perspectives and value commitments imply stakes, which leads to stakeholders, which leads to involving stakeholders to represent their stakes,

---

Is There Agreement About What Constitutes Quality?

Robin Lin Miller became the distinguished editor of the *American Journal of Evaluation* in 2005, the profession's premier peer-reviewed scholarly journal. After three years experience editing *AJE,* I asked her how much consistency she found among reviewers.

> In most cases, by which I mean 75 to 80% of papers submitted, reviewers' judgments follow one of two patterns. In the first, the plurality agrees that a paper requires extensive rewriting to make a contribution of any sort, though the reviewers may not agree on *why* the paper is flawed and how it might be improved to make a contribution. In the second, opinions on the merit of the paper diverge widely, with opinions about it scattered along a continuum; where one reviewer sees novelty and a significant advance another sees flaws that are beyond tolerance or repair. It is only in a minority of cases that consensus does emerge. When it does, it tends to favor the view that the paper makes little in the way of a contribution. Agreement that a paper is good occurs rarely.

—Robin Lin Miller, Editor, *American Journal of Evaluation*

SOURCE: Reprinted with permission of Robin Miller.

---

even in methods decisions, or should we say, *especially* in methods decisions, since those decisions determine what findings will be available for interpretation and use.

The evidence of disagreements about research standards and criteria for judging quality will not surprise those inside science who understand that a major thrust of methodological training in graduate school is learning how to pick apart and attack any study. There are no perfect studies. And there cannot be, for there is no agreement on what constitutes perfection.

This has important implications for methods decisions in evaluation. There are no universal and absolute standards for judging methods. The consensus that has emerged within evaluation, as articulated by the Omnibus Metaevaluation Checklist (Stufflebeam 2007), the Joint Committee on Standards (1994), and the American Evaluation Association's Guiding Principles (Shadish et al. 1995) is that evaluations are to be judged on the basis of appropriateness, utility, practicality, accuracy, propriety, probity, credibility, and relevance. These criteria are necessarily situational and context bound. One cannot judge the adequacy of methods used in a specific evaluation without knowing the purpose of the evaluation, the intended uses of the findings, the resources available, and the trade-offs negotiated. Judgments about validity and reliability, for example, are necessarily and appropriately relative rather than absolute in that the rigor and quality of an evaluation's design and measurement depend on the purpose and *intended use* of the evaluation (Trochim 2006c). The Accuracy Standards of the Joint Committee on Standards (1994) make it clear that validity and reliability of an evaluation depend on the intended use(s) of the evaluation.

Valid Information: The information-gathering procedures should be chosen or developed and then implemented so that they will assure that the interpretation arrived at is valid *for the intended use* [italics added]. (P. A5)

Reliable Information: The information-gathering procedures should be chosen or developed and then implemented so that they will assure that the information obtained is sufficiently reliable *for the intended use* [italics added]. (P. A6)

The Art of Making Methods Decisions

Lee J. Cronbach (1982), an evaluation pioneer and author of several major books on measurement and evaluation, observed that designing an evaluation is as much art as science: "Developing an evaluation is an exercise of the dramatic imagination" (p. 239). This perspective can help free practitioners and other primary users who are nonresearchers to feel they have something important to contribute. It may also open the evaluator to valuing their contributions and facilitating their "dramatic imaginations." The art of evaluation involves creating a design that is appropriate for a specific situation and particular action or policy-making context. In art there is no single, ideal standard. Beauty is in the eye of the beholder, and the evaluation beholders include decision makers, policymakers, program managers, practitioners, participants, and the general public. Thus, any given design is necessarily an interplay of resources, possibilities, creativity, and personal judgments by the people involved.

No Perfect Design

"There is no single best plan for an evaluation, not even for an inquiry into a particular program, at a particular time, with a particular budget."

Lee J. Cronbach (1982:231), *Designing Evaluations of Educational and Social Programs.* Cronbach directed the Stanford Evaluation Consortium and was President of the American Educational Research Association, the American Psychological Association, and the Psychometric Society. He was also a member of the National Academy of Sciences and the American Academy of Arts and Sciences.

Instead of one massive experiment or quasi-experiment (the "horse race" model of evaluation), said Cronbach, he favored an eclectic, broad-based, open methodological approach to evaluation; a fleet of smaller studies, each pursuing an important case or component of the policy or program under study. Cronbach encouraged evaluators to design evaluations to understand in some depth the nature of each context and the quality of the intervention in that context. Over time, then, with many such studies, the policy-shaping community could learn in some depth about the social problem and how best to address it. In addition, Cronbach encouraged evaluators to involve members of the setting in the evaluation study and to provide feedback throughout the course of the study (for program improvement purposes) rather than just at the end.

SOURCE: *Encyclopedia of Evaluation* (2005:95).

Still, for nonresearchers, being expected to participate in design decisions can be intimidating. Evaluators reinforce and deepen any nascent inclination toward feeling intimidated by beginning with an emphasis on the importance of establishing "a theoretically sound conceptual framework" for the evaluation design. A theoretically sound conceptual framework sounds like something *The Music Man* would sell to the good people of River City to keep their children out of pool halls.

Conceptualizing an evaluation framework doesn't require some grandiose and theoretical posture or a voluminous and vortiginous vocabulary. That grand old evaluation savant Rudyard Kipling has offered all the conceptual framework one needs

I keep six honest serving men

They taught me all I knew:

Their names are What and Why and When

And How and Where and Who.

I find that the people with whom I'm working warm quickly to the task of designing the evaluation when I recall for them Kipling's "conceptual framework."

What? What do we want to find out?

Why? Why do we want to find that out?

When? When do we need the information?

How? How can we get the information we need?

Where? Where should we gather information?

Who? Who is the information for and from whom should we collect the information we need?

These questions guide the primary focus in making evaluation measurement and methods decisions—getting the best possible data to adequately answer primary users' evaluation questions given available resources and time. The emphasis is on *appropriateness and credibility*—measures, samples, and comparisons that are appropriate and credible to address key evaluation issues. Supplementing Kipling's framework, Exhibit 11.2 presents guidance on the scope and selection of information for an evaluation from Dan Stufflebeam's (2007) very useful *Omnibus Metaevaluation Checklist.*

Hard versus Soft Data

The next chapter will explore in depth the "paradigms debate" involving quantitative/ experimental methods versus qualitative/ naturalistic approaches. This is sometimes framed as "hard data" versus "soft data" or numbers versus narrative. At this point, it suffices to say that the issue is not hard versus soft but relevant and appropriate versus irrelevant and inappropriate. Participants in the Stanford Evaluation Consortium

---

EXHIBIT 11.2

Information Scope and Selection

Select and collect a range of information that is sufficient to judge the program's merit, worth, significance, and probity and address key questions of interest to clients and specified stakeholders.

- Determine and document the client's most important evaluation requirements.
- Interview stakeholders to determine their different perspectives on the program.
- Effect evaluator and client agreements on the evaluation's questions and required information.
- Assign priorities to the evaluation's questions and associated information requirements.
- Allocate the evaluation effort in accordance with the priorities assigned to the needed information.
- Allow flexibility for adding questions during the evaluation.
- Obtain sufficient information to address the stakeholders' most important evaluation questions, as appropriate.

SOURCE: Stufflebeam (2007:U3).

(Cronbach et al. 1980) observed that "merit lies not in form of inquiry but in relevance of information" (p. 7). My experience with stakeholders suggests that they would rather have "soft data" about an important question than "hard data" about an issue of less relevance.

Obviously, the ideal is hard data about important questions, *whatever hard data may mean in a particular context*. But in the real world of trade-offs and negotiations, the evaluator too often determines what is evaluated according to his or her own expertise or preference in what to measure, rather than by deciding first what intended users determine is worth evaluating and then doing the best he or she can with methods. Methods are employed in the service of relevance and use, not as their master. Exhibit 11.3 contrasts three pragmatic versus ideal design trade-offs.

EXHIBIT 11.3
Pragmatic Design Principles

Principles offer directional guidelines. They are not recipes, laws, or concrete, absolute prescriptions. Principles help in dealing with trade-offs in the less than perfect real world of evaluation design. Below are three ideals contrasted with three pragmatic options when the ideals cannot be achieved because of real-world constraints. These can be used to generate discussion and get people thinking about which way to lean when faced with tough choices.

Evaluation Ideal	Pragmatic Principle
1. Get the best possible data to affect decisions.	1. Less-than-perfect data *available in time to affect decisions* are better than more-perfect data available *after* decisions have been taken.
2. "Hard" data on all questions.	2. Softer data on important questions are better than harder data on less important questions (whatever "softer" and "harder" may mean in a particular context).
3. More and better data	3. To avoid information overload, *less can be more* when data are appropriately focused on priority questions and uses.

One implication of this perspective— that quality and excellence are situational, that design combines the scientific and artistic—is that it is futile to attempt to design studies that are immune from methodological criticism. There simply is no such immunity. Intended users who participate in making methods decisions should be prepared to be criticized regardless of what choices they make. Especially futile is the desire, often articulated by non-researchers, to conduct an evaluation that will be accepted by and respected within the academic community. As we demonstrated above in discussing peer-review research, the academic community does not speak with one voice. Any particular academics whose blessings are particularly important for evaluation use should be invited to participate in the evaluation design task force and become, explicitly, intended users. Making no pretense of pleasing the entire scientific community (an impossibility), utilization-focused evaluation strives to attain the more modest and attainable goal of pleasing primary intended users. This does not mean that utilization-focused evaluations are less rigorous. It means the criteria for judging rigor must be articulated for each evaluation.

Credibility and Use

Credibility affects use. Credibility includes the perceived accuracy, fairness, and believability of the evaluation *and* the evaluator. In the Joint Committee's (1994) standard on Evaluator Credibility, evaluators are admonished to be "both trustworthy and competent" so that findings achieve "maximum credibility and acceptance" (p. U2). Report clarity, full and frank disclosure of data strengths and weaknesses, balanced reporting, defensible information sources, valid and reliable measurement, justified conclusions, and impartial reporting are all specific standards aimed at credibility as a foundation for use.

For information to be useful and to merit use, it should be as accurate and believable as possible. Limitations on the degree of accuracy should be stated clearly. Decision makers want highly accurate and trustworthy data. This means they want data that are valid and reliable. But in the politically charged environment of evaluation, these traditional scientific concepts have taken on some new and broader meanings.

Overall Evaluation Validity

The government ministries are very keen on amassing statistics. They collect them, raise them to the nth power, take the cube root, and prepare wonderful diagrams. But you must never forget that every one of these figures comes in the first place from the village watchman, who just puts down what he damn well pleases.

—Sir Josiah Stamp, 1911,
English economist (1880–1941)

House (1980:249) has suggested that validity means "worthiness of being recognized": For the typical evaluation, this means being "true, credible, and right" (p. 250). Different approaches to evaluation establish validity in different ways. House applies the notion of validity to *the entire evaluation*, not just the data. An *evaluation* is perceived as valid in a global sense that includes the overall approach used, the stance of the evaluator, the nature of the process, the design, data gathering, and the way in which results are reported. Both the evaluation *and* the evaluator must be perceived as trustworthy for the evaluation to have high validity.

Alkin et al. (1979) studied use and found that "for evaluation to have impact, users must believe what evaluators have to say" (p. 245). The believability of an evaluation depends on much more than the perceived scientific validity of the data and findings. Believability depends on the users' perceptions of and experiences with the program being evaluated, users' prior knowledge and prejudices, the perceived adequacy of evaluation procedures, and the users' trust in the evaluator (Alkin et al. 1979:245–47). Trust, believability, and credibility are the underpinnings of *overall* evaluation validity.

Evaluation Design Checklist

Dan Stufflebeam (2004a) has developed a design checklist that is a generic guide to decisions one typically needs to consider when planning and conducting an evaluation. The checklist presents the logical structure of evaluation design and includes elements that commonly apply to a wide range of evaluation assignments and alternative evaluation approaches. The checklist is intended for use across a broad range of evaluation assignments—both small and large—and for use with a number of different approaches to evaluation. His introduction to the checklist describes the typically iterative and cycling nature of the design process as the evaluation is brought into focus and later adapted to changed understandings and emergent conditions.

When the contemplated evaluation is small in scope and will have only a modest budget, evaluators and their clients can find it useful to consider the full range of evaluation design issues before setting aside those that are not feasible, not particularly relevant to the situation, or especially important. . . . The user will need to exercise good judgment and discretion in determining and applying the most applicable parts of the checklist pursuant to the needs of particular evaluations. This checklist is intended both as an advance organizer and as a reminder of key matters to be considered before and during an evaluation. An ordered list of elements commonly included in evaluation designs is included but these elements are not necessarily intended to be treated in a strict linear sequence. Often, one cycles through the elements repeatedly while planning for and negotiating an evaluation and also during the course of the evaluation. In each such cycle, some elements are addressed, while others typically are set aside for attention later or abandoned because they don't apply to the particular situation. Evaluation design is as much process as product. In using this checklist the objective should be, over time, to evolve an evaluation plan to undergird a sound, responsive, and effective evaluation.

It is emphasized that evaluators and their clients are wise to revisit evaluation design decisions throughout the evaluation, especially as new questions and circumstances emerge. The following, then, is an ordered set of issues to consider when planning, conducting, and reporting an evaluation.

- Focusing the evaluation
- Collecting information
- Organizing information
- Analyzing information
- Reporting information
- Administering the evaluation

SOURCE: Stufflebeam (2004a).

It is important to understand how overall evaluation validity differs from the usual, more narrow conception of validity in scientific research. Validity is usually focused entirely on data collection procedures, design, and technical analysis, that is, whether measures were valid or whether the design allows drawing inferences about causality (internal design validity).

A measure is scientifically valid to the extent that it captures or measures the concept it is intended to measure. For example, asking if an IQ test really measures native intelligence (rather than education and socioeconomic advantage) is a validity question. Validity is often difficult to establish, particularly for new instruments. Over time, scientists develop some consensus about the relative validity of oft-used instruments, such as major norm-referenced standardized educational tests. Rossi, Freeman, and Wright (1979) posited three common criteria for validity of quantitative instruments.

1. *Consistency with Usage:* A valid measurement of a concept must be consistent with past work that used that concept. Hence, a measure of adoption must not be in contradiction to the usual ways in which that term had been used in previous evaluations of interventions.

2. *Consistency with Alternative Measures:* A valid measure must be consistent with alternative measures that have been used effectively by other evaluators. Thus, a measure must produce roughly the same results as other measures that have been proposed, or, if different, have sound conceptual reasons for being different.

3. *Internal Consistency:* A valid measure must be internally consistent. That is, if several questions are used to measure adoption, the answers to those questions should be related to each other as if they were alternative measures of the same thing (pp. 170–71).

Qualitative methods (e.g., such techniques as participant observation and in-depth, open-ended interviewing) pose different validity challenges. In qualitative methods, validity hinges to a greater extent on the skill, competence, and rigor of the researcher because *the observer or interviewer is the instrument.*

> Since as often as not the naturalistic inquirer is himself the instrument, changes resulting from fatigue, shifts in knowledge, and cooptation, as well as variations resulting from differences in training, skill, and experience among different "instruments," easily occur. But this loss in rigor is more than offset by the flexibility, insight, and ability to build on tacit knowledge that is the peculiar province of the human instrument. (Guba and Lincoln 1981:113)

Validity concerns also arise in using official statistics such as health or crime statistics. Joe Hudson (1977) has cautioned about the care that must be taken in using crime statistics because of validity problems:

> First, officially collected information used as measures of program outcomes are, by their very nature, indirect measures of behavior. For example, we have no practical or direct way of measuring the actual extent to which graduates of correctional programs commit new crimes. Second, the measurements provided are commonly open to serious problems. For example, the number of crimes known to authorities in most situations is only a fraction of the number of crimes committed, although that fraction varies from crime to crime. . . . The growing willingness of victims of sexual assault to report their crimes to the police and actively cooperate in prosecution is an example of the manner in which public attitudes can affect officially recorded rates of crime.
>
> Of the various criteria used to measure recidivism, that of arrest appears to be especially problematic. Recidivism rates based on arrest do not tell us whether those arrested have, in fact, returned to criminal behavior but only that they are presumed to have done so. . . . The widespread discretion exercised by the police to arrest is a further source of invalidity. For example, it is probably reasonable to expect that the number of individuals arrested for a particular type of crime within a jurisdiction is to some extent a direct reflection of changing police policies and not totally the function of changing patterns of law-violating behavior. In addition to the power of deciding when to arrest, police also have discretionary authority to determine which of a number of crimes an individual will be arrested for in a particular situation. Thus, if policy

emphasis is placed upon combating burglary, this may affect decisions as to whether
an arrestee is to be arrested for burglary,
simple larceny, or criminal damage to prop-
erty. In short, the discretion of the police to
control both the number and types of arrests
raises serious validity problems in evaluations which attempt to use this measure of
program outcome. (Pp. 88–89)

In summary, then, validity problems,
along with the trustworthiness of the evaluator, affect the overall credibility of the
evaluation, and this is true for all kinds of
data collection—quantitative measures,
questionnaires, qualitative observations,
government statistics, and social indicators.
The precise nature of the validity problem
varies from situation to situation, but evaluators must always be concerned about the
extent to which the data collected are credible and actually measure what is supposed
to be measured; they must also make sure
that intended users understand validity
issues. In addition, a validity issue of
special, though not unique, concern to
utilization-focused evaluators is *face validity*.

Face Validity in Utilization-Focused Measurement

Face validity concerns the extent to which
an instrument *looks* as if it measures what it
is intended to measure (Trochim 2006a). An
instrument has face validity if stakeholders
can look at the items and understand what is
being measured. From a utilization-focused
perspective, it is perfectly reasonable for
decision makers to want to understand and
believe in data they are expected to use. Face
validity, however, is generally held in low
regard by measurement experts. Predictive
validity, concurrent validity, and construct
validity—these technical approaches are
much preferred by psychometricians.
Nunnally (1970), in his classic work on psy-
chometrics, considered face validity to have
some possible value when data are gathered
for the general public, but he concluded,
"Although one could make a case for the
involvement of face validity in the measurement of constructs, to do so would probably
serve only to confuse the issues" (p. 150). To
deepen our understanding of the issue, consider the following case.

Face Validity

In face validity, you look at the operationalization and see whether "on its face" it seems like a good translation of the construct. This is probably the weakest way to try to demonstrate construct validity. For instance, you might look at a measure of math ability, read through the questions, and decide that yep, it seems like this is a good measure of math ability (i.e., the label "math ability" seems appropriate for this measure). Or, you might observe a teenage pregnancy prevention program and conclude, "Yep, this is indeed a teenage pregnancy prevention program." Of course, if this is all you do to assess face validity, it would clearly be weak evidence because it is essentially a subjective judgment call. (Note that just because it is weak evidence doesn't mean that it is wrong. We need to rely on our subjective judgment throughout the research process. It's just that this form of judgment won't be very convincing to others.) We can improve the quality of face validity assessment considerably by making it more systematic. For instance, if you are trying to assess the face validity of a math ability measure, it would be more convincing if you sent the test to a carefully selected sample of experts on math ability testing, and they all reported back with the judgment that your measure appears to be a good measure of math ability.

SOURCE: Trochim (2006a).

The board of directors of a major industrial firm decided to decentralize organizational decision making in hopes of raising worker morale. The president of the company hired an organizational consultant to monitor and evaluate the decentralization program and its effects. From the literature on the sociology of organizations, the evaluator selected a set of research instruments designed to measure decentralization, worker autonomy, communication patterns, and worker satisfaction. The scales had been used by sociologists to measure organizational change in a number of different settings, and the factorial composition of the scales had been validated. The instruments had high predictive and construct validity, but low face validity—that is, a nonresearcher could not look at the items and tell what they were measuring; interpretation depended on understanding factor analysis.

The evaluator found no statistically significant changes between pre- and posttest, so when he met with the board of directors, he dutifully reported that the decentralization program had failed and that worker morale remained low. The president of the company had a considerable stake in the success of the program; he did not have a stake in the evaluation data. He did what decision makers frequently do in such cases—he attacked the data.

President: How can you be so sure that the program failed?

Evaluator: We collected data using the best instruments available. I won't go into all the technical details of factor analysis and Cronbach's alpha. Let me just say that these scales have been shown to be highly valid and reliable. Take this 10-item scale on *individual autonomy*. The best predictor item in this particular scale asks respondents (a) "Do you take coffee breaks on a fixed schedule?" or (b) "Do you go to get coffee whenever you want to?"

President: [visibly reddening and speaking in an angry tone] Am I to understand that your entire evaluation is based on some kind of questionnaire that asks people how often they get coffee, that you never personally talked to any workers or managers, that you never even visited our operations? Am I to understand that we paid you $20,000 to find out how people get their coffee?

Evaluator: Well, there's a lot more to it than that, you see . . .

President: That's it! We don't have time for this nonsense. Our lawyers will be in touch with you about whether we want to press fraud and malpractice charges!

Clearly, the President was predisposed to dismiss any negative findings. But suppose the evaluator had reviewed the instrument and survey design with the president before gathering data. Suppose he had explained what the items were supposed to indicate and then asked,

Now, if we survey employees with these items measuring these factors, will they tell you what you want to know? Does this make sense to you? Are you prepared to act on this kind of data? Would you believe the results if they came out negative?

Such an exchange might not have made a difference. It's not easy to get busy executives to look carefully at instruments in advance, nor do evaluators want to waste time explaining their trade. Many decision makers are just as happy not being bothered with technical decisions. After all, that's why they hired an evaluator in the first place, to design and conduct the evaluation! But the costs of such attitudes to use can be high. Utilization-focused evaluators check out the face validity of instruments before data are collected. Subsequent data analysis, interpretation, and use are all facilitated by attention to face validity—making sure users understand and believe in the data.

Useful Designs

Face validity criteria can also be applied to design questions. Do intended users understand the design? Does it make sense to them? Do they appreciate the implications of comparing Program A with Program B? Do they know why the design includes, or does not include, a control group? Is the sample size sufficiently large to be believable? You can be sure that decision makers will have opinions about these issues when results are presented, particularly if findings turn out negative. By asking these questions before data collection, potential credibility problems can be identified and dealt with, and users' insights can help shape the design to increase its relevance. Consider the following case from an evaluation workshop I conducted.

The marketing director for a major retail merchandising company attended to find out how to get more mileage out of his marketing research department. He explained that 2 years earlier he had spent a considerable sum researching the potential for new products for his company's local retail distribution chain. A carefully selected representative sample of 285 respondents had been interviewed in the Minneapolis-Saint Paul greater metropolitan area. The results indicated one promising

new line of products for which there appeared to be growing demand. He took this finding to the board of directors with a recommendation that the company make a major capital investment in the new product line. The board, controlled by the views of its aging chairman, vetoed the recommendation. The reason: "If you had presented us with opinions from at least a thousand people, we might be able to move on this item. But we can't make a major capital commitment on the basis of a couple of hundred interviews."

The marketing director tactfully tried to explain that increased sample size would have made only a marginal reduction in possible sampling error. The chairperson remained unconvinced, the findings of an expensive research project were ignored, and the company missed out on a major opportunity. A year later, the item they rejected had become a fast-selling new product for a rival company.

It is easy to laugh at the board's mistake, but the marketing director was not laughing. He wanted to know what to do. I suggested that next time, he check out the research design with the board before collecting data, going to them and saying,

> Our statistical analysis shows that a sample of 285 respondents in the Twin Cities area will give us an accurate picture of market potential. Here are the reasons they recommend this sample size. . . . Does that make sense to you? If we come in with a new product recommendation based on 285 respondents, will you believe the data?

If the board responds positively, the potential for use will have been enhanced, though not guaranteed. If the board says the sample is too small, then the survey might as well include more respondents—or be canceled. There is little point in implementing a design that is known in advance to lack credibility.

Reliability and Error

Reliability has to do with consistency. A measure is reliable to the extent that essentially the same results can be reproduced repeatedly, as long as the situation does not change. For example, in measuring the height of an adult, one should get the same results from one month to the next. Measuring attitudes and behavior is more complex because one must determine whether measured change means the attitude has changed or the data collection is unreliable. Exhibit 11.4 presents the relationship between reliability and validity.

EXHIBIT 11.4
Reliability and Validity

Bill Trochim, 2008 President of the American Evaluation Association, has a favorite metaphor he uses to explain the relationship between reliability and validity. He begins by comparing the center of a target with the concept the evaluator is trying to measure. "Imagine that for each person you are measuring, you are taking a shot at the target. If you measure the concept perfectly for a person, you are hitting the center of the target. If you don't, you are missing the center. The more you are off for that person, the further you are from the center."

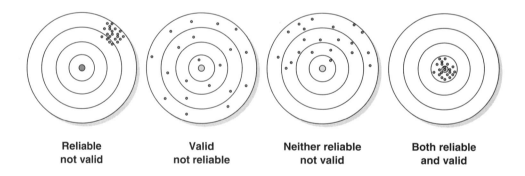

| Reliable | Valid | Neither reliable | Both reliable |
| not valid | not reliable | not valid | and valid |

The figures above show four possible situations. In the first one, the evaluator hits the target consistently, but misses the center of the target—consistently and systematically measuring the wrong value for all respondents. Such a measure is reliable, but not valid (that is, it's consistent but wrong). On the second target, the evaluator measurement efforts are randomly spread across the target, seldom hitting the center of the target but, on average, getting the right answer for the group (though not very accurate for individuals). The result is a valid, but inconsistent group estimate. The third target shows hits spread across the target and consistently missing the center. This measure is neither reliable nor valid. The final target displays what Trochim calls the "Robin Hood" scenario after the infamous medieval archer—the evaluator consistently hits the center of the target making the measure both reliable and valid.

SOURCE: Trochim (2006b). Reprinted with permission of William M. Trochim.

Inconsistent data collection procedures, for example, asking interview questions in different sequence to different respondents, can change results and introduce errors. Nonresearchers will often have unrealistic expectations about evaluation instruments, expecting no errors. For many reasons, all data collection is subject to some measurement error. Henry Dyer, a former president of the highly respected Educational Testing Service, tells of trying to explain to a government official that test scores, even on the most reliable tests, have enough measurement error that they must be used with understanding of their limitations. The high-ranking official responded that test makers should "get on the ball" and start producing tests that "are 100% reliable under all conditions."

Dyer's (1973) reflections on this conversation are relevant to an understanding of error in all kinds of measures. He asked,

> How does one get across the shocking truth that 100% reliability in a test is a fiction that, in the nature of the case, is unrealizable? How does one convey the notion that the test-reliability problem is not one of reducing measurement error to absolute zero, but of minimizing it as far as practicable and doing one's best to estimate whatever amount of error remains, so that one may act cautiously and wisely in a world where all knowledge is approximate and not even death and taxes are any longer certain? (P. 87)

Sources of error are many. For example, consider sources of error in an individual test score. Poor health on the day of the test can affect the score. Whether the student had breakfast can make a difference. Noise in the classroom, a sudden fire drill, whether or not the teacher or a stranger gives the test, a broken pencil, and any number of similar disturbances can change a test score. The mental state of the child—depression, boredom, elation, a conflict at home, a fight with another student, anxiety about the test, low self-confidence—can affect how well the student performs. Simple mechanical errors such as marking the wrong box on the test sheet by accident, inadvertently skipping a question, or missing a word while reading are common problems for all of us. Students who have trouble reading will perform poorly on reading tests, but they are also likely to perform poorly on social studies, science, and math tests.

Some children perform better on tests because they have been taught how to take written tests. Some children are simply better test takers than other children because of their background or personality or because of how seriously they treat the idea of the test. Some schools make children sit all day taking test after test, sometimes for an entire week. Other schools give the test for only a half-day or 2 hours at a time to minimize fatigue and boredom. Some children like to take tests; some don't. Some teachers help children with difficult words, or even read the tests along with the children; others don't. Some schools devote their curriculum to teaching students what is on the tests. Others place little emphasis on test taking and paper-and-pencil skills, thus giving students less experience in the rigor and tricks of test taking.

All these sources of error—and I have scarcely scratched the surface of possibilities—can seriously affect an individual score. Moreover, they have virtually nothing to do with how good the test is, how carefully it was prepared, or how valid its content is for a given child or group. Intrinsic to the nature of testing, these errors are always present to some extent and are largely uncontrollable. These are the reasons why statisticians can never develop a test that is 100 percent reliable.

The errors are more or less serious depending on how a test is used. When looking at test scores for large groups, we can expect that, because of such errors, some students will perform above their true level and other students will perform below their true score. For most groups, statisticians believe that these errors cancel each other. The larger the group tested, the more likely this is to be true.

Different evaluation instruments are subject to different kinds of errors. Whether the evaluation includes data from tests, questionnaires, management information systems, government statistics, or whatever—the analysis should include attention to potential sources of error, and, where possible, calculate and report the degree of error. The point is that evaluators need not be defensive about errors. Rather, they need to explain the nature of errors, help intended users decide what level of precision is needed, consider the costs and benefits of undertaking procedures to reduce error (for instance, a larger sample size), and help users to understand the implications for interpreting findings. Primary intended users can be helpful in identifying potential sources of error. In my experience, their overall confidence in their ability to correctly and appropriately use evaluation data is increased when there has been a frank and full discussion of *both* the data's strengths and weaknesses. In this way, evaluators help make evaluation clients more knowledgeable so they will understand what Dyer's government official did not: The challenge is not reducing measurement error to absolute zero, but rather minimizing it as far as practicable and doing one's best to estimate whatever amount of error remains, so that one may act cautiously and wisely in a world where all knowledge is approximate and not even death and taxes are any longer certain.

Trade-Offs

Different evaluation purposes affect how much error can be tolerated. A summative evaluation to inform a major decision that will affect the future of a program, perhaps touching the lives of thousands of people and involving allocations of millions of dollars, will necessarily and appropriately involve considerable attention to and resources for minimizing error. In contrast, a small-scale, fairly informal, formative evaluation aimed at stimulating staff to think about what they're doing will raise fewer concerns about error. There is a lot of territory between these extremes. How precise and robust findings need to be, given available resources, are matters for discussion and negotiation. The next two sections look at additional concerns that commonly involve negotiation and trade-offs: (1) breadth versus depth and (2) the relative generalizability of findings.

Breadth versus Depth

Deciding how much data to gather involves trade-offs between depth and breadth. Getting more data usually takes longer and costs more, but getting less data usually reduces confidence in the findings. Studying a narrow question or very specific problem in great depth may produce clear results but leave other important issues and problems unexamined. On the other hand, gathering information on a large variety of issues and problems may leave the evaluation unfocused and result in knowing a little about a lot of things, but not knowing a lot about anything.

During methods deliberations, some boundaries must be set on data collection. Should all parts of the program be studied or only certain parts? Should all participants be studied or only some subset of clients? Should the evaluator aim at describing all program processes and outcomes or only certain priority areas?

In my experience, determining priorities is challenging. Once a group of primary stakeholders gets turned on to learning from evaluative information, they want to know everything. The evaluator's role is to help them move from a rather extensive list of potential questions to a much shorter list of realistic questions and finally to a focused list of essential and necessary questions. This process moves from divergence to convergence, from generating many possibilities (divergence) to focusing on a few worthwhile priorities (convergence).

This applies to framing overall evaluation questions as well as to narrowing items in a particular instrument, such as a survey or interview. Many questions are interesting, but which are crucial? These end up being choices not between good and bad, but among alternatives, all of which have merit.

Internal and External Validity in Design

Trade-offs between internal and external validity have become a matter of debate in evaluation since Campbell and Stanley (1963) asserted that "internal validity is the sine qua non" (p. 175). Internal validity in its narrowest sense refers to certainty about cause and effect. Did X cause Y? Did the program intervention cause the observed outcomes? In a broader sense, it refers to the "trust-worthiness of an inference" (Cronbach 1982:106). External validity, on the other hand, refers to the degree of confidence one has in generalizing findings beyond the situation studied.

Internal validity is increased by exercising rigorous control over a limited set of carefully defined variables. However, such rigorous controls create artificialities that limit generalizability. The highly controlled situation is less likely to be relevant to a greater variety of more naturally occurring, less controlled situations. In the narrowest sense, this is the problem of going from the laboratory into the real world. In contrast, increasing variability and sampling a greater range of experiences or situations typically reduces control and precision, thereby reducing internal validity. The ideal is high-internal validity and high-external validity. In reality, there are typically trade-offs involved in the relative emphasis placed on one or the other.

Cronbach's (1982) discussion of these issues for evaluation is quite comprehensive and insightful. He emphasized that "both external validity and internal validity are natters of degree and external validity does not depend directly on internal validity" (p. 170). Being able to apply findings to future decisions and new settings is often more important than establishing rigorous causal relations under rigid experimental conditions. He introduced the idea of *extrapolation* rather than generalization. Extrapolation involves logically and creatively thinking about what specific findings mean for other situations, rather than the statistical process of generalizing from a sample to a larger population. He advocated that findings be interpreted in light of stakeholders' and evaluators' experiences and knowledge, and then applied or extrapolated using all available insights, including understanding about quite different situations. This focuses interpretation away from trying to determine truth in some absolute sense (a goal of basic research) to a concern with conclusions that are reasonable, justifiable, plausible, warranted, and useful.

The contrasting perspectives of Campbell (emphasis on internal validity) and Cronbach (emphasis on external validity) have elucidated the trade-offs between designs that give first priority to certainty about causal inference versus those that better support extrapolations to new settings. These evaluation pioneers formulated fundamentally different theories of practice (Shadish et al. 1991). In working with primary stakeholders to design evaluations that are credible, the evaluator will need to consider the degree to which internal and external validity are of concern, and to emphasize each in accordance with stakeholder priorities. Choices are necessitated by the fact that no single design is likely to attain internal and external validity in equal degrees.

Demand Validity and Consequential Validity

A quite different perspective on validity is "demand validity," a validity that comes from participants and people in communities affirming the value of a program and "demanding" continuation (or expansion). Lois-ellen Datta, one of evaluation's distinguished pioneers and former president of the Evaluation Research Society, originated this concept to describe the Head Start Program when it began in the 1960s: "The program obviously had face validity and demand validity" (Datta 2004:246). By this she meant that in her evaluation fieldwork, she had come to place emphasis on what parents and children reported, tending to "factor in a bit of self-interest when paid staff testify."

> When parents tell me of sitting for the first time "at the table," when they speak of how Head Start brought them pride and dignity, as well as hope for their children, when I see (as I did in 1968) a child so handicapped, he was drawn about in a little old red wagon yet integrated joyously into these simple programs—these to me are like a Seurat painting in contrast to the Sherlockian, subtractive approach. The concept perhaps gains a bit of strength because, in my experience, parent/participant stories are not always sunshine and roses. I will hear about

the problems, limitations, what should be happening but isn't. (Datta, L. 2007, personal communication)

Consequential validity as a criterion for judging an evaluation design or instrument makes the social consequences of its use a value basis for assessing its credibility and utility. Thus, standardized achievement tests are criticized because of the discriminatory consequences for minority groups of educational decisions made with "culturally biased" tests. Consequential validity asks for assessments of who benefits and who is harmed by an inquiry, measurement, or method (Thomas 2005). Exhibit 11.6 at the end of this chapter presents a discussion about the validity and consequences of various ways from around the world of gathering data on the racial and ethnic backgrounds of program participants.

Truth and Utility

Stakeholders want accurate information; they apply "truth tests" (Weiss and Bucuvalas 1980) in deciding how seriously to pay attention to an evaluation. They also want useful and relevant information. The ideal, then, is both truth and utility. In the real world, however, there are often choices to be made between the extent to which one maximizes truth and the degree to which data are relevant. The simplest example of such a choice is time. The timelines for evaluation are often ridiculously short. A decision maker may need whatever information can be obtained in 3 months, even though researchers insist that a year is necessary to get data of reasonable quality and accuracy. This involves a trade-off between truth and utility. Highly accurate data in a year are less useful to this decision maker than data of less precision and validity obtained in 3 months.

Decision makers regularly face the need to take action with limited and imperfect information. They prefer more accurate information to less accurate information, but they also prefer some information to no information. This is why research quality and rigor are "much less important to utilization than the literature might suggest" (Alkin et al. 1979:24).

The effects of methodological quality on use must be understood in the full context of a study, its political environment, the degree of uncertainty with which the decision maker is faced, and thus his or her relative need for any and all clarifying information. If information is scarce, then new information, even of less-than-ideal quality, may be somewhat helpful.

The scope and importance of an evaluation greatly affect the emphasis that will be placed on technical quality. Eleanor Chelimsky (2006a, 2006b, 1987a, 1987b), former president of the American Evaluation Association and founding Director of the Program Evaluation and Methodology Division of the U.S. Government Accountability Office, has insisted that technical quality is paramount in policy evaluations to Congress. The technical quality of national policy research matters, not only in the short term, when findings first come out, but over the long term as policy battles unfold and evaluators are called on to explain and defend important findings (Chelimsky 1995a).

On the other hand, debates about technical quality are likely to be much more center stage in national policy evaluations than in local efforts to improve programs at the street level, where the policy rubber hits the day-to-day programming road. One evaluator in our study of the use of federal health studies linked the issue of technical quality to the nature of uncertainty in organizational decision making. He acknowledged inadequacies in the data he had collected, but he had still worked with his primary users to apply the findings, fully recognizing their problematic nature:

> You have to make the leap from very limited data. I mean, that's what a decision's like. You make it from a limited data base; and, damn it, when you're trying to use quantitative data and it's inadequate, you supposedly can't make a decision. Only you're not troubled by that. You can use impressionistic stuff. Yeah, your intuition is a lot better. I get a gestalt out of this thing on every program.
>
> This may come as a great shock to you, but that is what you use to make decisions. In Chester Barnard's definition, for example, the function of the executive is to make a decision in the absence of adequate information. [EV148:11]

He went on to express some pride in the cost-benefit ratio of this evaluation, despite admitted methods inadequacies:

> It was a pretty small investment on the part of the government—$47,000 bucks. In the evaluation business that's not a pile of money. The questions I had to ask were pretty narrow and the answers were equally narrow and relatively decisive, and the findings were put to use immediately and in the long term. So, can you beat that? [EV148:8]

Another evaluator expressed similar sentiments about a study that had to be completed in only 3 months.

> There are a million things I'd do differently. We needed more time. . . . At the time, it was probably the best study we could do. . . . I'm satisfied in the sense that some people found it useful. It wasn't just kept on a shelf. People paid attention to that study and it had an impact. Now, I've done other studies that I thought were methodologically really much more elegant that were kind of ignored, just sitting on somebody's shelf.
>
> My opinion is that this really modest study probably has had impact all out of proportion to the quality of the research. It happened to

be at a certain place at a certain time, where it at least talked about some of the things that people were interested in talking about, so it got some attention. And many other studies that I know of that have been done, that I would consider of higher quality, haven't really gotten used. [EV145:34]

Technical quality (truth tests) may get less attention than researchers desire because many stakeholders are not very sophisticated about methods. Yet they know (almost intuitively) that the methods and measurements used in any study are open to question and attack, a point emphasized earlier in this chapter. They know that experts often disagree among themselves. As a result, experienced decision makers often apply less rigorous standards than academics and, as long as they find the evaluation effort credible and serious, they're more interested in discussing the substance of findings than in debating methods. Credibility involves more than technical quality, though that is an important contributing factor. Credibility, and therefore utility, are affected by "the steps we take to make and explain our evaluative decisions, [and] also intellectually, in the effort we put forth to look at all sides and all stakeholders of an evaluation" (Chelimsky 1995a:219). The perception of impartiality is at least as important as methodological rigor in highly political environments.

Another factor that can reduce the weight decision makers give to technical quality is skepticism about the return on investment of large-scale, elaborately designed, carefully controlled, and expensive studies. Cohen and Weiss (1977) reviewed 20 years of policy research on race and schools, finding progressive improvement in research methods (i.e., increasingly rigorous designs and ever more sophisticated analytical techniques). Sample sizes increased, multiple regression

and path analytic techniques were employed, and more valid and reliable data-gathering instruments were developed. After reviewing the findings of studies produced with these more rigorous methods, as well as the uses made of their findings, they concluded that "these changes have led to more studies that disagree, to more qualified conclusions, more arguments, and more arcane reports and unintelligible results" (Cohen and Weiss 1977:78). In light of this finding, simple, understandable, and focused evaluations have great appeal to practitioners and action-oriented evaluation users.

In utilization-focused evaluation, attention to technical quality is tied to and balanced by concern for relevance and timeliness. As one decision maker in our federal health evaluation study put it

You can get so busy protecting yourself against criticism that you develop such an elaborate methodology that by the time your findings come out, who cares? So, I mean, you get a balance—the validity of the data against its relevance. And that's pretty tough stuff. I mean, that's hard business. [DM111:26]

As no study is ever methodologically perfect, it is important for primary stakeholders to know firsthand what imperfections exist—and to be included in deciding which imperfections they are willing to live with in making the inevitable leaps from limited data to incremental action.

The Dynamics of Measurement and Design Decisions

Research quality and relevance are not set in stone once an evaluation proposal has been accepted. A variety of factors emerge throughout the life of an evaluation that require new decisions about methods.

Case Example of a Flexible Design

In 2006, *Innovation Network* faced the challenge of evaluating an immigration advocacy campaign mounted by the Coalition for Comprehensive Immigration Reform (CCIR). The political environment was especially volatile following May Day marches in cities around the country. The original evaluation design proposed a variety of methods, both quantitative and qualitative, to answer key evaluation questions. The mixed methods design included interviewing key informants, conducting surveys, reviewing documents, and documenting meetings on core strategies. Given the intensity of the immigration campaign, the evaluators needed to be especially sensitive to minimizing the data collection burden for CCIR leadership and coalition members. The design included tracking media coverage, legislation, field activities, and polling studies that did not require primary data collection from campaign staff. As both the campaign and evaluation unfolded, the design changed:

The fast pace of events, and the Coalition's rapid response to them, soon necessitated a greater amount of real-time data collection. The evaluation team began conducting more frequent observation and monitoring of the coalition dynamics that played out in meetings and conference calls. Other challenges inherent to collecting real-time data included massive amounts of data generated through numerous e-mail lists, documents, and field reports.

Two factors were particularly important in convincing the evaluators that they could not rely solely on traditional data collection and needed to redesign the evaluation:

- A legislative policy campaign, like advocacy work generally, involves faster cycles of evolving strategies out of the necessity to react to opportunity windows and respond to external factors.
- The complex interactions among myriad players and stakeholder audiences—who are located along a continuum of connections to and engagement with policymakers—present greater challenges in capturing multiple stories and angles that oftentimes occur simultaneously.

During the most intense periods of the campaign, the evaluators found that "it was unthinkable to conduct interviews with coalition leaders, which resulted in gaps in the data." But, following such intense periods, "there was tangible burnout among everyone in the campaign."

During high-intensity periods, the evaluators continued to monitor numerous meetings, conference calls, and hundreds of e-mails and documents.

The existing methods were not effective in fully capturing the multiple perspectives and many different stories of what happened, especially accounts of interactions with policymakers and their staff. In recognition of the context within which the evaluation was occurring, the evaluation team designed a "Debrief Interview Protocol" specifically for intense periods of advocacy. The intent of this protocol was to engage key players in a focus group shortly after a policy window or intense period occurred, to capture the following information:

- The public mood and political context of the opportunity window
- What happened and how the campaign members responded to events
- What strategies they followed
- Their perspective on the outcome(s) of the period
- How they would change their strategies going forward based on what they learned during that period

(Continued)

(Continued)

By focusing on a specific moment in the campaign and conducting it in a timely manner, this method gathered in-depth and real-time information, while keeping the interaction targeted, practical, and relevant. The idea of the debrief grew out of the need to have a forum that encouraged participation from key groups and individuals engaged in different layers or "spheres of influence" surrounding decision makers.

This emergent design approach proved particularly useful for those involved in the inner workings of the campaign to tell the story of what happened behind the scenes.

The novel aspects of the debrief lie in its systematic application to follow the peaks and valleys of the policy advocacy cycle. It also allows for continued tailoring of the selection of participants and, to some degree, the questions asked based on the nature of the intense period, the parties involved, and the activities that occur.

SOURCE: Stuart (2007:10–11).

Actively involving intended users in making methods decisions about these issues means more than a one-point-in-time acquiescence to a research design.

In every one of the 20 federal health studies we investigated, significant methods revisions and redesigns had to be done after data collection began. While little attention has been devoted in the evaluation literature to the phenomenon of slippage between the original design and methods as actually implemented, the problem is similar to that of program implementation, where original specifications typically differ greatly from what finally gets delivered (see Chapter 9).

In a groundbreaking study, McTavish et al. (1975) studied implementation of 126 research projects funded across seven federal agencies. All 126 projects were rated by independent judges along seven descriptive methodological scales. Both original proposals and final reports were rated; the results showed substantial instability between the two. The researchers concluded,

Our primary conclusion from the Predictability Study is that the quality of final report methodology is essentially not predictable from proposal or interim report documentation. This appears to be due to a number of factors. First, research is characterized by significant change as it develops over time. Second, unanticipated events force shifts in direction. Third, the character and quality of information available early in a piece of research makes assessment of some features of methodology difficult or impossible. (Pp. 62–63)

Earlier in the report, they had pointed out that

among the more salient reasons for the low predictability from early to late documentation is the basic change which occurs during the course of most research. It is, after all, a risky pursuit rather than a pre-programmed product. Initial plans usually have to be altered once the realities of data or opportunities and limitations become known. Typically, detailed plans for analysis and reporting are postponed and revised. External events also seem to have taken an unexpected toll in the studies we examined. . . . Both the context of research and the phenomena being researched are typically subject to great change. (P. 56)

If intended users are involved only at the stage of approving study proposals, they are likely to be surprised when they see a final report. Even interim reports bear only moderate resemblance to final reports. Thus, making decisions about methods is a continuous process that involves checking out changes with intended users as they are made. While it is impractical to have evaluator-stakeholder discussions about every minor change in methods, utilization-focused evaluators prefer to err in the direction of consultative rather than unilateral decision making, when there is a choice. Stakeholders also carry a responsibility to make sure they remain committed to the evaluation. One internal evaluator interviewed in our federal utilization study, still smarting from critiques of his evaluation as methodologically weak, offered the following advice to decision makers who commission evaluations:

> Very, very often those of us who are doing evaluation studies are criticized for poor methodology, and the people who levy the criticism sometimes are the people who pay for the study. Of course, they do this more often when the study is either late or it doesn't come up with the answers that they were looking for. But I think that a large share of the blame or responsibility belongs to the project monitor, sponsor, or funder for not maintaining enough control, direct hands-on contact with the evaluation as it's going on.
>
> We let contracts out and we keep our hands on these contractors all the time. And when we see them going down a road that we don't think is right, we pull them back and we say, "Hey, you know, we disagree." We don't let them go down the road all the way and then say, "Hey fella, you went down the wrong road." [EV32:15]

I have found this a useful quote to share with primary stakeholders who have expressed reluctance to stay involved with the evaluation as it unfolds. *Caveat emptor.*

Threats to Data Quality

Evaluators have an obligation to think about, anticipate, and provide guidance about how threats to data quality will affect interpreting and using results. Threats to internal validity, for example, affect any conclusion that a program produced an observed outcome. The observed effect could be due to larger societal changes, as when generally increased societal awareness of the need for exercise and proper nutrition contaminates the effects of specific programs aimed at encouraging exercise and proper nutrition. Maturation is a threat to validity when it is difficult to separate the effects of a program from the effects of growing older; this is a common problem in juvenile delinquency programs, as delinquency has been shown to decline naturally with age. Reactions to gathering data can affect outcomes independent of program effects, as when students perform better on a posttest simply because they are more familiar with the test the second time; or there can be interactions between the pretest and the program when the experience of having taken a pretest increases participants' sensitivity to key aspects of a program. Losing people from a program (experimental mortality) can affect findings since those who drop out, and therefore fail to take a posttest, are likely to be different in important ways from those who stay to the end.

However, it is impossible to anticipate all potential threats to data quality. Even when faced with the reality of particular circumstances and specific evaluation problems, it is impossible to know in advance precisely how a creative design or measurement approach will affect results. For example, having program staff do client interviews in an outcomes evaluation could (1) seriously reduce the validity and reliability of the data, (2) substantially increase the validity and reliability of the data, or (3) have no measurable effect on data quality. The nature and degree of effect would depend on staff relationships with clients, how staff were assigned to clients for interviewing, the kinds of questions being asked, the training of the staff interviewers, attitudes of clients toward the program, and so on. Program staff might make better or worse interviewers than external evaluation researchers, depending on these and other factors.

An evaluator must grapple with these kinds of data quality questions for all designs. No automatic rules apply. There is no substitute for thoughtful analysis based on the specific circumstances and information needs of a particular evaluation, both initially and as the evaluation unfolds.

Threats to Utility

Whereas traditional evaluation methods texts focus primarily on threats to validity, this chapter has focused primarily on threats to utility. Exhibit 11.5 summarizes

---

EXHIBIT 11.5
Threats to Utility

- Failure to focus on intended use by intended users
- Failure to design the evaluation to fit the context and situation
- Inadequate involvement of primary intended users in making methods decisions
- Focusing on unimportant issues—low relevance
- Inappropriate methods and measures given stakeholders questions and information needs
- Poor stakeholder understanding of the evaluation generally and findings specifically
- Low user belief and trust in the evaluation process and findings
- Low face validity
- Unbalanced data collection and reporting
- Perceptions that the evaluation is unfair or that the evaluator is biased or less than impartial
- Low evaluator credibility
- Political naïveté
- Failure to keep stakeholders adequately informed and involved along the way as design alterations are necessary

---

common threats to utility. We now have substantial evidence that paying attention to and working to counter these threats to utility will lead to evaluations that are worth using—and are actually used.

Designing Evaluations Worth Using: Reflections on the State of the Art

This chapter has described the challenges evaluators face in working with intended users to design evaluations worth using. My consulting brings me into contact with hundreds of evaluation colleagues and users. I know from direct observation that many evaluators are meeting these challenges with great skill, dedication, competence, and effectiveness. Much important and creative work is being done by evaluators in all kinds of difficult and demanding situations as they fulfill their commitment to do the most and best they can with the resources available, the short deadlines they face, and the intense political pressures they feel. They share a belief that doing something is better than doing nothing, so long as one is realistic and honest in assessing and presenting the limitations of what is done.

This last caveat is important. I have not attempted to delineate all possible threats to validity, reliability, and utility. This is not a design and measurement text. My purpose has been to stimulate thinking about how attention to intended use for intended users affect all aspects of evaluation practice, including methods decisions.

Pragmatism undergirds the utilitarian emphasis of utilization-focused evaluation. In designing evaluations, it is worth keeping in mind World War II General George S. Patton's Law: *A good plan today is better than a perfect plan tomorrow.*

Then, there is Halcolm's evaluation corollary to Patton's law: *Perfect designs aren't.*

Follow-Up Exercises

1. The chapter opens by asserting that involving primary intended users in making methods decisions is controversial and resisted by many evaluators. What is the controversy? What is the basis for the resistance? Present the essence of the argument against involving nonresearchers in methods decisions. Then, present the essence of the argument in favor of involvement. Finally, present your own philosophy and preference on this issue.

2. Using Rudyard Kipling's poem (below), present the primary design features of an evaluation for an actual program. Describe the program and then describe the evaluation specifying What, Why, When, How, Where, Who.

*I keep six honest serving men
They taught me all I knew:
Their names are What and Why and When
And How and Where and Who.*

3. Select an evaluation design or measurement issue and write a script for how you would present and explain the primary options available to nonresearchers who are primary intended users for the evaluation. Include in your explanation the likely consequences for credibility and utility of the results. An example in this chapter is the choice between odd-numbered and even-numbered response options in surveys. Another example would be telephone interviews versus face-to-face interviews. Select your own example and present the options in lay terms.

4. Locate an actual evaluation report for a completed evaluation. Examine the design and methods used in the evaluation. Summarize these design elements on the left-hand side of a page. Next to each design element, on the right side of the page, present two alternatives: (a) an option that would be significantly more expensive and (2) an option that would be significantly less expensive. (You will have to speculate on the level of expense associated with the evaluation's actual design.)

5. Using the views and options presented in Exhibit 11.6, identify at least three options for asking program participants about their race or ethnicity, then discuss the likely consequential validity of those options.

6. Explain *demand validity* and discuss the pros and cons of including this concept in an evaluation. Under what evaluation situation would it be appropriate and useful? Under what situation would it possibly reduce the evaluator's credibility. Why?

EXHIBIT 11.6

Gathering Background Data:
Race, Ethnicity, and Other Demographics

In March 2007, an extensive thread developed on EvalTalk, the American Evaluation Association listserv, concerning the validity and utility of collecting background data on program participants. Below are 20 comments (some edited) to illustrate the diverse perspectives generated from evaluators in different political, cultural, and national contexts. I offer this diversity of views as a way of illustrating why it is important to involve primary intended users in such design and measurement decisions to determine what they consider valid and useful within a particular context for a specific evaluation purpose. How to gather background data is not primarily a technical decision. It is a decision that has significant political, social, cultural, practical, and utility consequences.

Original Questions

What's the best way to ask about a survey respondent's race/ethnicity? Furthermore, what are the correct and most politically sensitive response categories?

As far as evaluation practice is concerned, how often do evaluation consumers use race as a meaningful variable in making decisions? It seems like we always ask race as a standard demographic, and it makes for a great chart or table, but does it always have meaning?

Responses

1. Race is a social construct and the definition of the term has changed over time, and differs from country to country and region to region. For comparative purposes, in 1997 the Office of Budget and Management (OMB) revised the definitions of race for Federal agencies, including the U.S. Census Bureau: (1) American Indian or Alaska Native, (2) Black or African American, (3) Native Hawaiian or Pacific Islander, (4) White, and (5) Some other race. OMB guidelines allow an individual to select more than one race. Additionally, the Feds use two ethnic categories: *Hispanic origin* and *Not of Hispanic origin*. My take is that because we are such a pluralistic society, even these categories may not match an individual's perception of their racial and ethnic identity. As a result, people may increasingly mark the "Some other race" option if offered, making these designations less useful over time.

2. I work in Australia and tend to use a slightly different set of questions (which are based on work by our national bureau of statistics).

They & I have found that in our environment, where we have great diversity in people's countries of origin and languages spoken, asking for ethnicity/race didn't work particularly well. Instead, we ask the following questions:

What country were you born in?
• Australia
• Other (choose from drop-down list)

Does your family come from another country?
• Yes, choose from drop-down list
• No

What is the main language you speak at home?
- English
- Other (choose from drop-down list)

Are you of Aboriginal or Torres Strait Islander descent? (NB. These are our indigenous peoples)
- Yes
- No

This gives us practical information about languages to publish information in and information about cultural heritage. Would this approach work in the States?

3. Given the complexity of race/ethnicity, I have often made this an open-ended sort of question: With what race/ethnicity(ies) do you most strongly identify? The drawback is that the responses don't necessarily align with U.S. Census categories—which can limit quantitative comparisons. The upside is that respondents can tell us as evaluators something about what matters—what has meaning—with regards to racial and ethnic identity.

4. A compromise I have used is to list the categories of the larger data set you intend to use for comparison, if there is one (e.g., federal categories), and a response option labeled "other," and give instructions: Please check all that apply. This allows for people of mixed race to respond with honesty, allows for self-definition of race or ethnicity, and is still more efficient to score than completely open-ended responses.

5. In the U.S., race/ethnicity is often used as a proxy for a host of social, psychological, and even biological variables. We need to focus our attention on measuring those variables directly in such situations, rather than relying on race/ethnicity.

6. I do use race in my evaluations. I use the data as a comparison with census bureau data. One of the issues in both these fields is race disproportionality and as such it's become a focal point in most things that I do. However, I must confess, that the only reason I use ethnicity data is because federal funders request this information. I'm not exactly sure how to use this otherwise.

7. One of the consequences (intended or not?) with the U.S. Government's recent switch to differentiating "Hispanic" ethnicity from racial categories is a blurring of data and obscuring of disparities. For example, I now run across government reports that combine "Hispanic whites" and "non-Hispanic whites" into "white/caucasians." This has the effect of lowering the appearance of racial/ethnic disparities in some reports. For example, while prior reports show a large disparity on some variables between African Americans and non-Hispanic Whites, with Hispanic Whites somewhere in between, the new reports now show a much smaller disparity between African Americans and Whites (Hispanic and non-Hispanic).

8. If your research is focusing on the impact of race and culture on some factor, one should "truly know" the target population(s) and the community of interest. Thus, if you are working in Florida or perhaps New York, it may be very important to allow respondents to share their national origin with you as well as their race, given immigration patterns from the Caribbean. This is particularly true for Hispanics/Latinos but also increasingly for Americans who are of African, Arab, and Asian descent, since they may come from a wide variety of countries, including those of Europe. To illustrate, if you are interacting with Hispanics in the Southwest, you may want to offer a wider variety of choices for respondents:

   Hispanic, Latino, Hispano, Spanish-speaking origin, Latin American,

   Mexican American, Puerto Rican, El Salvadorean, etc.

The same might be wise if the instrument will go to a variety of "Native Americans," who come from different tribes. Responses can also be influenced by the age and perhaps ideology of individuals. Thus, for some groups, often including Hispanics/Latinos, it may be critical to know whether respondents' families have lived in the United States for several generations or they are recent arrivals. The most effective practice, however, is to dialogue with representatives of the target population(s) you are particularly interested in encouraging to respond—and to learn from them what different groups within their community call themselves.

(Continued)

(Continued)

9. What we have here is a failure of communication. It is a clash with Anglo-Saxon/Northwestern European racial categorizations and Hispanic and Semitic ethnic categorizations. In the United States, what chiefly matters is whether you are dark skinned or not, and status and opportunities are accorded on that distinction. In Western Hemispheric Hispanic cultures, what chiefly matters is whether you are an Indian or not. The very concept "race" is defined differently. In the United States, race refers only to biological attributes of a person. In Hispanic culture, "la Raza" refers to which ethnicity one is. So your Raza may be Chicana, but your skin color may be dark or light. Members of this country are struggling with the reconciliation of Mexican American self-identity and traditional American self-identity. I am not contending that that is easy. For my part, I always pick "Other."

10. Here in Florida, we ran into the issue of respondents being offended that they had to select a race after being identified as Hispanic/Latino. That does reraise the question of whether or not Latino is a race as well as ethnicity, but the federal guidelines are pretty explicit:

   —When the survey is being completed by someone other than the respondent, you can use combined (race/ethnicity) categories;

   —When the survey is being completed by respondents themselves, race and ethnicity must be split and the only ethnic options are Hispanic/Latino or Not Hispanic/Latino.

We also ran into an issue where Arab Americans were extremely offended by these categories. It was said to me that Arab is an ethnicity and that they should be able to select a "race" given the various regions from which Arabs may hail. I also began trying to tackle this issue at a local Historically Black College & University. While the majority of the students are black, this particular institution has a strong Caribbean population. The administration pointed out that the services required by Caribbean black students were quite different from African Americans. They felt that, given the definition of ethnicity, they should be able to identify other ethnicities, even when the students are black.

11. I have to agree with those who say that race is an artificial social construct. However, I also have to agree that it is inarguably important in and of itself (aside from the correlations) because white people (primarily) treat others on the basis of their perceived race. Information about race is therefore used by the white-dominated society to treat others differently, and multiple data analyses prove that race is in fact a meaningful contributor to explaining differences in treatment. [On a major long term project] I contributed analyses of racial differences. Our studies showed that in many circumstances there is a separate and significant impact of race over and above the impact of the other variables mentioned. So IMHO race is both an artificial social category with little or no "reality" in biology or genetics AND a crucial piece of information used by individuals and institutions as a basis for classifying and behaving towards individuals.

12. Race will continue to matter in the U.S. until the subtle and overt conception of "American" is no longer "white." So until we address the myth of equality based on flimsy laws that do not account for "pure" and resultant "statistical" racism, race must stay in the picture, and we must work to close the gap between lofty ideas and lived reality by having open and honest discussions which force us all to look at how we maintain an investment in "whiteness."

13. Race comes into play when comparing work force with client population. There are varied opinions on the subject but generally when programs are accredited or funded by an external entity one of the areas that is looked at is the racial composition of staff to the client population. Generally, and this was a big argument a number of years ago in child welfare, the view is that the racial composition of staff should be in close proximity to the racial population of the client population. Some thought this important and believe it can have an effect on the quality of services offered to clients. In the end, there was a belief that staff who have similar backgrounds would be more sensitive to the needs of their client population and thereby provide better services. Thus, this is a reason for including race in an evaluation.

14. In Canada, we don't refer to our French population as another race, or for that matter a minority group. They are Canadians who speak French and possibly English as well. Black refers to a degree of skin pigment and other biological traits that only genetic testing could specify exactly, plus ethnic traits. Whites contain these traits to a degree as well. We wouldn't treat age as categorical—young vs. old. Why should we consider race/ethnicity as one or the other? Native Indian can mean a set of variables—biological, legal, ethnic, linguistic. "Metis" means mixed blood. . . but what percentage makes a person one or the other? There is no answer. Race is a useless variable. I prefer to dispense with the notion of race as antiquated, and I put ethnicity in the same category. Instead, we should measure the dimensions that they are supposed to represent: country of birth, legal status, first language, income, education, et cetera.

15. To be sensitive about how to present the categories on a form is important. We the evaluators have paid scant "professional" attention to recent advancements in human genomics. I got my genetic testing done and found out that I have more close relatives in my deep ancestry in West Asia and Europe than in my native India. In fact, in the current database I am more closely related to a Carter and a Campbell (we might have shared an ancestor as close as just a 100 generations ago) than a Srivastava (an Indian last name) in the same Y-Haplogroup. I faithfully and routinely note myself to be Asian on forms that follow the U.S. Census categories. The Africans have more genetic variations than all other types of humans combined! This is one of the pillars of our recent understanding of human origins in Africa. If you grow up in Asia, you learn that Syrians are Asians as are inhabitants of two-thirds of the Russia's. According to U.S. Census categories, if you are from Russia, you check white. If you are from Iran, you check white. If you are from anywhere in Asia East of Afghanistan, such as neighboring Pakistan, you check Asian. But wait, there's more—if you are from Siberia, which is way East of Afghanistan, you check white—Wow! So race is not only a social construct now, it is so because a particular branch of government told you so.

16. One will notice a significant difference in the race categories used by the National Center for Health Statistics (much finer grained) and those used by the U.S. Census (rather short on fine grains). Why? Because the purposes are different. The point is, one has to consider the purpose, why one is collecting this information. If your evaluation has implications for biologically based drug interventions, you may be better off collecting more genetically detailed categories as we do know genetics play a role in susceptibility to certain diseases and responses to medical interventions. If we are concerned purely about social interventions, we might as well get to the bottom of the socioeconomic construct that we intend to use the race category for.

17. I'm a little startled at the way "race" still appears to be treated as a neutral term by social scientists in government employ in the US. I'm quite sure any social scientist or government employee in Australia would recoil from the idea of using the word in any official document. Not simply that it's politically incorrect, more that it would be regarded as downright insulting—not to mention unscientific. Whatever else may have gone wrong over the last couple of decades, the message seems to have been successfully drummed into a couple of generations here that "There is no such thing as race." You could compare the way "aboriginal" is becoming correct usage to describe the original owners of Canada—and to a lesser extent, of North America generally—at exactly the same time as it seems to have been relegated to ideological unsoundness, in some quarters at least, when applied, as it has been for a couple of centuries, to the original owners of Australia.

18. Given the seemingly increasing complexity in measuring race, do we do more harm than good when we impose rigid categories on our participant subjects?

19. The best background form is one that is customized for the context of the program and the purpose of the evaluation. Off-the-shelf standardized forms (like census bureau categories) may help you in formulating possibilities, but content of any specific evaluation form should flow directly from the evaluation objectives and program's target population.

20. The essential question from a questionnaire construction standpoint is why do you need this information?

12

The Paradigms Debate and a Utilization-Focused Synthesis

*L*ady, *I do not make up things. That is lies. Lies is not true. But the truth could be made up if you know how. And that's the truth.*

— Lily Tomlin as character "Edith Ann,"
Rolling Stone, October 24, 1974

A former student sent me the following story, which she had received as an e-mail chain letter, a matter of interest only because it suggests widespread distribution.

Once upon a time, not so very long ago, a group of statisticians (hereafter known as quants) and a party of case study aficionados (quals) found themselves together on a train traveling to the same professional meeting. The quals, all of whom had tickets, observed that the quants had only one ticket for their whole group.

"How can you all travel on one ticket?" asked a qual.

"We have our methods," replied a quant.

Later, when the conductor came to punch tickets, all the quants slipped quickly behind the door of the toilet. When the conductor knocked on the door, the head quant slipped their one ticket under the door, thoroughly fooling the conductor.

On their return from the conference, the two groups again found themselves on the same train. The qualitative researchers, having learned from the quants, had schemed to share a single ticket. They were chagrined, therefore, to learn that, this time, the statisticians had boarded with no tickets.

419

"We know how you traveled together with one ticket," revealed a qual, "but how can you possibly get away with no tickets?"

"We have ever more sophisticated methods," replied a quant.

Later, when the conductor approached, all the quals crowded into the toilet. The head statistician followed them and knocked authoritatively on the toilet door. The quals slipped their one and only ticket under the door. The head quant took the ticket and joined the other quants in a different toilet. The quals were subsequently discovered without tickets, publicly humiliated, and tossed off the train at its next stop.

Quants and Quals

Who are *quants*? They're numbers people who, in rabid mode, believe that if you can't measure something, it doesn't exist. They live by Galileo's admonition, "Measure what is measurable, and make measurable what is not so." Their mantra is "What gets measured gets done." And *quals*? They quote management expert W. Edwards Deming: "The most important things cannot be measured." *Quals* find meaning in words and stories, and are ever ready to recite Albert Einstein's observation that "Everything that can be counted does not necessarily count; everything that counts cannot necessarily be counted." Relatively speaking, of course.

Quants demand "hard" data: statistics, equations, charts, and formulae. *Quals,* in contrast, are "softies," enamored with narrative and case studies. *Quants* love experimental designs and believe that the only way to prove that an intervention caused an outcome is with a randomized control trial (RCT). *Quants* are control freaks, say the *quals;* simplistic, even simpleminded, in their naive belief that the world can be reduced to independent and dependent variables. The *qual's* world is complex, dynamic, interdependent, textured, nuanced, unpredictable, and understood through stories, and more stories, and still more stories. *Quals* connect the causal dots through the unfolding patterns that emerge within and across these many stories and case studies. *Quants* aspire to operationalize key predictor variables and generalize across time and space—the holy grail of truth: if x, then y, and the more of x, the more of y. *Quals* distrust generalizations and are most comfortable immersed in the details of a specific time and place, understanding a story in the richness of context and the fullness of thick description. For *quals*, patterns they extrapolate from cross-case analyses are possible principles to think about in new situations but are not the generalized, formulaic prescriptions that *quants* admire and aspire to. *Quants* produce *best practices* that assert, "Do this because it's been proven to work in rigorous studies." *Quals* produce themes and suggest, "Think about this and what it might mean in your own context and situation."

Do opposites attract? Indeed, they do. They attract debate, derision, and dialectical differentiation—otherwise known as *the paradigms war*. The story of the *quals* and *quants* offers a window into how the paradigms debate has ebbed and flowed.

This debate about the relative merits of quantitative/experimental methods versus qualitative/case study methods has periodically run out of intellectual steam, but as this edition is being revised, the debate is once again ascendant, this time focused on whether randomized controlled experiments are *the gold standard* for impact evaluations. This chapter will examine the debate and offer a utilization-focused synthesis.

Methodological Debate

The debate has taken different forms over time, including periods of intense rancor as well as times of rapprochement. Thomas D. Cook, one of evaluation's luminaries—the Cook of Shadish, Cook, and Campbell (2001), *Experimental and Quasi-Experimental Designs for Generalized Causal Inference,* the bible of research design—pronounced in his keynote address to the 1995 International Evaluation Conference in Vancouver, "Qualitative researchers have won the qualitative-quantitative debate."

Won in what sense?

Won acceptance. Cook supports use of multiple methods in evaluation and has made it clear that qualitative approaches can be quite valuable for describing what happens in a classroom or program, how the program is implemented, and for deepening our understanding of what outcomes may mean. But to produce strong evidence about causality, he remains convinced of the superiority of experimental designs:

> Since the theoretical warrant for the experimental result is more compelling than the warrant for the non-experimental result, the presumption is that non-experiments are often biased and that, even if they are not, there would be no way to know this in particular instances unless a randomized experiment were also done. . . . The experiment is to be preferred over other potentially bias-free methods because it enjoys greater statistical power and its assumptions are more transparent and better understood when compared to other forms of causal research. (Cook 2006:2, 4)

The validity of experimental methods and quantitative measurement, appropriately used, has never been in doubt. By the 1990s, qualitative methods, appropriately used, had ascended to a level of comfortable respectability, at least as an adjunct to quantitative methods in mixed-methods evaluations. Along the path to valuing mixed methods, evaluation methodologists have engaged in sometimes acrimonious debate, as when Lee Sechrest, American Evaluation Association (AEA) president in 1991, devoted his presidential address to alternatively defending quantitative methods and ridiculing qualitative approaches. He lamented what he perceived as a decline in the training of evaluators, especially in conducting rigorous quantitative studies. He linked this to a more general "decline of numeracy" and increase in "mathematical illiteracy" in the nation. "My opinion," he stated, "is that qualitative evaluation is proving so attractive because it is, superficially, so easy" (Sechrest 1992:4). Partly tongue in cheek, he cited as evidence of qualitative evaluators' mathematical ineptitude a proposal he had reviewed from a qualitative researcher that contained a misplaced decimal point and, as another piece of evidence, an invitation to a meeting of "qualitative research types" that asked for a February 30 reply (p. 5). He concluded,

If we want to have the maximum likelihood of our results being accepted and used, we will do well to ground them, not in theory and hermeneutics, but in the dependable rigor afforded by our best science and accompanying quantitative analyses. (P. 3)

Beyond the rancor, however, Sechrest joined other eminent researchers in acknowledging a role for qualitative methods, especially in combination with quantitative approaches. He was preceded in this regard by distinguished methodological scholars such as Donald Campbell and Lee J. Cronbach. Ernest House (1977), describing the role of qualitative argument in evaluation, observed that "when two of the leading scholars of measurement and experimental design, Cronbach and Campbell, strongly support qualitative studies, that is strong endorsement indeed" (p. 18). In my own work, I have found increased interest in and acceptance of qualitative methods and, in particular, mixed methods (both quantitative and qualitative in combination).

While a consensus has emerged in the profession that evaluators need to know and use a variety of methods in order to be responsive to the nuances of particular evaluation questions and the idiosyncrasies of specific stakeholder needs, the question of what constitutes *the methodological gold standard* remains hotly contested. There is some contradiction in the assertion that (1) the issue is the appropriateness of methods for a specific evaluation purpose and question, and that where possible, using multiple methods—both quantitative and qualitative—can be valuable, BUT (2) one question is more important than others (the causal attribution question) and one method (RCTs) is superior to all other methods in answering that question. This is what is known colloquially as

talking out of both sides of your mouth. Thus, we have a problem. The ideal of evaluators being situationally responsive, methodologically flexible, and sophisticated in using a variety of methods runs headlong into the conflicting ideal that experiments are *the* gold standard and all other methods are, by comparison, inferior, what Scriven (2006b) has called "RCT imperialism" (p. 8). These conflicting ideals play out amidst the realities of limited evaluation resources, political considerations of expediency, and the narrowness of disciplinary training available to most evaluators—training that imbues them with varying degrees of methodological prejudice. Nor is the debate just among evaluation methodologists. Evaluation practitioners are deeply affected, as are users of evaluation—policymakers, program staff, managers, and funders. All can become mired in the debate about whether statistical results from experiments ("hard" data) are more scientific and valid than quasi-experiments and qualitative case studies ("softer" data). Who wants to conduct (or fund) a second-rate evaluation if there is an agreed-on gold standard? What really are the strengths and weaknesses of various methods, including experiments (which, it turns out, also have weaknesses)? What does it mean to match the method to the question?

If evaluators are to involve intended users in methods decisions, as utilization-focused evaluation advocates, evaluators and intended users need to understand the paradigms debate and evaluators need to be able to facilitate choices that are appropriate to a particular evaluation's purpose. This means educating primary stakeholders about the legitimate options available, the potential advantages of multiple methods, and the strengths and weaknesses of various approaches.

The Gold Standard Question

What does it mean for something to be the GOLD STANDARD?

The gold standard is a monetary system in which the standard economic unit of account is a fixed weight of gold. When several nations are using such a fixed unit of account, the rates of exchange among national currencies effectively become fixed to the value of gold. The United States stopped issuing promises to redeem dollars for gold in 1933—part of a policy change for dealing with the Great Depression. As World War II was ending, the international 1944 Bretton Woods system created an obligation for each country to maintain the exchange rate of its currency in terms of gold. The system collapsed in 1971 following the United States's suspension of convertibility from dollars to gold. The system failed, in part, because of its rigidity.

The gold standard question in evaluation is whether one particular method—*randomized control experiments*—should be held up as the best design for conducting impact evaluations and, by being best, should be the standard of excellence toward which evaluators should aspire and against which the quality of evaluation methods is judged. Do randomized control experiments merit the Olympic gold medal for evaluation? That is at the center of the methodological paradigms debate today.

Beyond Methods: The Paradigms Debate

A paradigm is a worldview built on implicit assumptions, accepted definitions, comfortable habits, values defended as truths, and beliefs projected as reality. As such, paradigms are deeply embedded in the socialization of adherents and practitioners: Paradigms tell them what is important, legitimate, and reasonable. Paradigms are also normative, telling the practitioner what to do without the necessity of long existential or epistemological consideration. But it is this aspect of paradigms that constitutes both their strength and their weakness—their strength in that it makes action possible, their weakness in that the very reason for action is hidden in the unquestioned assumptions of the paradigm. In his influential classic, *The Structure of Scientific Revolutions,* Thomas Kuhn (1970) explained how paradigms work.

> Scientists work from models acquired through education and subsequent exposure to the literature, often without quite knowing or needing to know what characteristics have given these models the status of community paradigms. . . . That scientists do not usually ask or debate what makes a particular problem or solution legitimate tempts us to suppose that, at least intuitively, they know the answer. But it may only indicate that neither the question nor the answer is felt to be relevant to their research. Paradigms may be prior to, more binding, and more complete than any set of rules for research that could be unequivocally abstracted from them. (P. 46)

Evaluation was initially dominated by the natural science paradigm of hypothetico-deductive methodology, which values quantitative measures, experimental design, and statistical analysis as the epitome of "good" science. Influenced by philosophical tenets of logical positivism, this model for evaluation came from the tradition of experimentation in agriculture, the archetype of applied research.

> The most common form of agricultural-botany type evaluation is presented as an assessment of the effectiveness of an innovation by examining whether or not it has reached

Paradigm Wars in Other Fields

Particle Physics Experimentalists versus Theorists. "Particle physicists come in two distinct varieties, which, like matter and antimatter, are very much intertwined and, at the same time, agonistic. Experimentalists build machines. Theorists sit around and think" (Kolbert 2007:74). "I am happy to eat Chinese dinners with theorists," the Nobel Prize-winning experimentalist Samuel C. C. Ting once reportedly said. "But to spend your life doing what they tell you to do is a waste of time."

"If I occasionally neglect to cite a theorist, it's not because I've forgotten. It's probably because I hate him," wrote Leon Lederman, another Nobel prize-winning experimentalist.

Arkani-Hamed, a theorist, counters, "It's a general fact about physics that the people you tend to remember are the theorists. At least in the mythology, experiment plays a less central role. And there's a natural reason for that, because the ultimate goal isn't to observe things about nature; the ultimate goal is to understand and explain things about nature. So, for that reason, it's a chicken-and-egg problem. But definitely you want to be a chicken" (Kolbert 2007:74-75).

Financial Analysis Fundamentalists versus Technicians. Technical analysts recommend stocks based entirely on statistical patterns, prediction equations, charts, various benchmarks (e.g., price-earnings ratios, 90-day moving averages, historical support levels, head and shoulder formations, etc.).

Pure technicians don't need to know what the company is or what business it's in; they just need to know the numbers. Fundamentalists, in contrast, visit companies, meet with management, get to know the CEO, examine business strategy, study detailed financial statements and annual reports—and make qualitative judgments about the quality of the company. Fundamentalists call technicians "elves" because they treat their numbers as magic formulae. Technicians accuse fundamental analysts of being soft in the head and numerically impaired.

Religion Literalists versus Interpretativists. Literalists of any religion view their holy scripture as the direct word of their god that must be taken literally: the world was created in 7 days; a virgin birth means a virgin birth; resurrection from the dead means just that; reincarnation means reincarnation; heaven and hell are real places; a ban against eating pork is absolute. Interpretativists view such stories and rules as symbolic and instructive, sources of moral guidance, but not literally true or absolute.

How widespread is this gap? A Gallup poll in 2006 found that nearly half of Americans believe that humans did not evolve over millions of years but were created by God in their present form within the last 10,000 years (Reuters 2007).

Jurisprudence Originalists versus Relativists. U.S. Supreme Court justices who are originalists seek to interpret the Constitution in terms of the original intent of its authors and signers.

Relativists view the Constitution as a living document that must be interpreted in light of changing times, conditions, and understandings.

required standards on prespecified criteria. Students—rather like plant crops—are given pretests (the seedlings are weighed or measured) and then submitted to different experiments (treatment conditions). Subsequently, after a period of time, their attainment (growth or yield) is measured to indicate the relative efficiency of the methods (fertilizer) used. Studies of this kind are designed to yield data of one particular type, i.e., "objective" numerical data that permit statistical analyses. (Parlett and Hamilton 1976:142)

By way of contrast, the alternative to the dominant quantitative/experimental paradigm was derived from the tradition of anthropological field studies and undergirded by the philosophical tenets of phenomenology and constructivism. Using in-depth, open-ended interviewing and direct observation, the alternative paradigm relies on qualitative data, naturalistic inquiry, and detailed description derived from close contact with people in the setting under study.

In utilization-focused evaluation, neither of these paradigms is intrinsically better than the other. They represent alternatives from which the utilization-focused evaluator can choose; both contain options for primary stakeholders and information users. *Issues of methodology are issues of strategy, not of morals.* Yet it is not easy to approach the selection of evaluation methods in this adaptive fashion. The paradigmatic biases in each approach are quite fundamental. Great passions have been aroused by advocates on each side. Kuhn (1970) has pointed out that this is the nature of paradigm debates:

> To the extent that two scientific schools disagree about what is a problem and what is a solution, they will inevitably talk through each other when debating the relative merits of their respective paradigms. In the partially circular arguments that regularly result, each paradigm will be shown to satisfy more or less the criteria that it dictates for itself and to fall short of a few of those dictated by its opponent. . . . Since no paradigm ever solves all problems it defines, and since no two paradigms leave all the same problems unanswered, paradigm debates always involve the question: Which problem is it more significant to have solved? (Pp. 109–10)

The contrary positions that sparked the debate in evaluation remain relevant because much social science training is still quite narrow. Evaluators and those who commission or use evaluation will naturally be most comfortable with those methods in which they have been trained and to which they have most often been exposed. A particular way of viewing the world, based on disciplinary training and specialization, becomes so second-nature that it takes on the characteristics of a paradigm. *When all you have is a hammer, everything looks like a nail.* When you are taught that experiments are the gold standard, every evaluation will look like it is an opportunity to conduct an experiment. When all you know is survey research, every evaluation will scream the need for a survey. When all you know is case studies, every evaluation becomes one.

The quantitative-qualitative paradigms debate has been a prominent and persistent topic in evaluation and has generated a substantial literature, only a sample of which is referenced here (Julnes and Rog 2007; Cook 2006; Davidson 2006a; Mark and Henry 2006; Scriven 2006a; Donaldson and Christie 2005; Greene and Henry 2005; Tashakkori and Teddlie 2003; Schwandt 2002; Denzin and Lincoln 2000; Patton 2000, 1978, 1975a; Donmoyer 1996; Cook 1995; Denzin and Lincoln 1994; Guba and Lincoln 1994, 1989, 1981; Eisner 1991; House 1991; Rizo 1991; Cochran-Smith and Lytle 1990; Guba 1990; Owen and Rogers 1999:86–104; Howe 1988; Lincoln and Guba 1985; Cronbach 1982, 1975; Heilman 1980; Reichardt and Cook 1979; Rist 1977; Guttentag and Struening 1975a). Paradigm discussions and debates have also been a regular feature at meetings of professional evaluators worldwide. So let's take a closer look at the two primary paradigm perspectives.

The Quantitative/ Experimental Paradigm

Evidence of the early dominance of the quantitative/experimental (hypotheti-co-deductive) paradigm as the method of choice in evaluation research can be found in the metaevaluation work of Bernstein and Freeman (1975). The purpose of their study was to assess the quality of evaluative research at the time. What is of interest to us here is the way Bernstein and Freeman defined quality. Exhibit 12.1 shows how they coded their major indicators of quality; a higher number represents higher-quality research. The highest quality rating was reserved for completely quantitative data obtained through an experimental design and analyzed with sophisticated statistical techniques. Bernstein and Freeman did not concern themselves with whether the evaluation findings were important or used, or even whether the methods and measures were appropriate to the problem under study. They judged the quality of evaluation research entirely by its conformance with the dominant quantitative/experimental paradigm. That was the unquestioned gold standard. Such rankings of methods continue today (Schwandt 2007b:119; Petticrew and Roberts 2003).

EXHIBIT 12.1

Experimental Gold Standard Paradigm:
Operational Definition of Evaluation Quality

Dimension of Evaluation Quality	Coding Scheme (Higher Number = Higher Quality)
Sampling	1 = Systematic random 0 = Nonrandom, cluster, or nonsystematic
Data analysis	2 = Quantitative 1 = Qualitative and quantitative 0 = Qualitative
Statistical procedures	4 = Multivariate 3 = Descriptive 2 = Ratings from qualitative data 1 = Narrative data only 0 = No systematic material
Impact procedures design	3 = Experimental or quasi-experimental randomization and control groups 2 = Experimental or quasi-experimental without both randomization and control groups 1 = Longitudinal or cross-sectional without control or comparison groups 0 = Descriptive, narrative

SOURCE: Bernstein and Freeman (1975).

Documenting the consensus that existed for how they defined evaluation quality, Bernstein and Freeman cited major evaluation texts of the time (Reicken and Boruch 1974; Rossi and Williams 1972; Caro 1971; Suchman 1967). Representative of the dominant perspective was that of Wholey et al. (1970), "Federal money generally should not be spent on evaluation of individual local projects unless they have been developed as field experiments, with equivalent treatment and control groups" (p. 93). In their widely used methodological primer, Campbell and Stanley (1963) called this paradigm "the only available route to cumulative progress" (p. 3). It was this belief in and commitment to the natural science model on the part of the most prominent academic researchers that made experimental designs and statistical measures dominant. As Kuhn (1970) has explained, "A paradigm governs, in the first instance, not a subject matter but rather a group of practitioners" (p. 80). Those most committed to the dominant paradigm were found in universities, where they employed the scientific method in their own evaluation research and socialized students into the dominant paradigm.

In our mid-1970s study of how federal health evaluations were used, every respondent answered methodological questions with reference to the dominant paradigm. If a particular evaluation being reviewed had departed from what were implicitly understood to be the ideals of "good science," long explanations about practical constraints were offered, usually defensively, under the assumption that since we were from a university, we would be critical of such departures. Studies were described as hard or soft along a continuum in which harder was clearly better and didn't even need explicit definition.

Advocacy of the quantitative/experimental paradigm as the gold standard continues today supported by many examples of the important results yielded by experiments (Boruch 2007). François Bourguignon, Chief Economist of the World Bank, was using randomized control trials as the gold standard when he asserted that only 2 percent of World Bank programs had been "properly evaluated" (Dugger 2004:A4), ignoring the great variety of World Bank programs and the vast amount of other kinds of excellent evaluation done by scores of World Bank evaluators and contractors (IEG 2006, 2007). The influential and prestigious Poverty Action Lab at the Massachusetts Institute of Technology has been a strong advocate of randomized control trials as evaluation's methodological gold standard (www.povertyactionlab.com). A widely circulated and influential report from the Center for Global Development entitled *When Will We Ever Learn?* advocates experimental designs as the best way to evaluate impact of international development aid (Evaluation Gap Working Group 2006).

The *What Works Clearinghouse* (WWC) was established in 2002 by the U.S. Department of Education's Institute of Education Sciences to provide educators, policymakers, researchers, and the public with a central and trusted source of scientific evidence of what works in education—and quickly adopted randomized controlled experimentation as its gold standard (Lawrenz and Huffman 2006). WWC (2006) has established standards of evidence for reviewing studies:

> In order for a study to be rated as meeting evidence standards (with or without reservations), it must employ one of the following types of research designs: a randomized controlled trial or a quasi-experiment (including quasi-experiments with regression discontinuity designs).

The only evaluations that fully meet the evidence standard, then, are randomized controlled trials (RCTs) or regression discontinuity designs that do not have problems with randomization, attrition, or disruption. What does this mean in practice? Let's use the *What Works Clearinghouse* review of the Middle School *Connected Mathematics Project* as an example. The methods of 22 studies of this curriculum were reviewed. Three met the methodological standard. Those three rigorous evaluations led to the not-very-helpful conclusion that "the curriculum had mixed effects on math achievement." The 19 excluded studies, many published in peer-reviewed journals, represented a variety of other methods but were not reviewed for patterns, learnings, trends, hypotheses, insights, or tendencies that might deepen understanding of the mixed findings. Because those studies did not meet the gold standard, they were dismissed out of hand. That is the epitome of applying paradigm blinders.

In reacting to the Institute of Education's advocacy of experimentation as the gold standard, distinguished evaluation leader Eleanor Chelimsky (2007) welcomed the commitment to more rigorous evaluations then added an illuminative analogy:

> It is as if the Department of Defense were to choose a weapon system without regard for the kind of war being fought; the character, history, and technological advancement of the enemy; or the strategic and tactical givens of the military campaign. (P. 14)

When the U.S. Department of Education's Institute of Education Sciences first published their criteria, the AEA took the unprecedented step of submitting a formal statement of concern opposing such a narrow and rigid view of how to engage in evaluation. The elected leadership of AEA adopted and submitted the position reproduced in Exhibit 12.2. That statement essentially opposes crowning RCTs as the methodological gold standard.

Not all AEA members supported the statement. Intense debate ensued, evoking strong emotions and reactions. For example, distinguished sociologist Peter Rossi, one of the founders of the field of evaluation research, one of the profession's most important textbook authors, and an original member of both the Evaluation Research Society and the AEA, terminated his membership in AEA saying, "Why be a member of the flat earth society?" (Quoted by Lipsey 2007b:202). Mark Lipsey, coauthor with Rossi of the widely used textbook *Evaluation: A Systematic Approach Evaluation* (Rossi, Lipsey, and Freeman 2003) also dropped out of AEA and has refused to attend subsequent national AEA conferences. Lipsey, a strong advocate of RCTs as the best way to conduct impact evaluations, has been active in debating the issues (Lipsey 2007b; Donaldson and Christie 2005), including twice with me at The Evaluators Institute. For the record, I support the AEA position against crowning any single method as the gold standard, though I was not involved in drafting the statement. It is important to understand that this position is not hostile to experiments and supports their use when appropriate and feasible; it is hostile to treating any method as inherently superior to others without regard to context, appropriateness, and feasibility.

This point is well-illustrated by the commentary of one of the evaluation profession's luminaries, Lois-ellin Datta, about the problem of mandating experimental designs. She has provided as powerful an example as I have seen illustrating the importance of taking context into account in deciding whether to conduct an experiment. Yielding to political pressure from advocates of RCTs, the U.S. Congress

EXHIBIT 12.2

American Evaluation Association Position on "Scientifically Based Evaluation Methods"

Response to the U.S. Department of Education's Institute of Education Sciences proposal, subsequently adopted, to make randomized control experiments the gold standard for evidence in evaluating educational curricula and programs

The American Evaluation Association applauds the effort to promote high quality in the U.S. Secretary of Education's proposed priority for evaluating educational programs using scientifically based methods. We, too, have worked to encourage competent practice through our Guiding Principles for Evaluators, Standards for Program Evaluation, professional training, and annual conferences. However, we believe the proposed priority manifests fundamental misunderstandings about (1) the types of studies capable of determining causality, (2) the methods capable of achieving scientific rigor, and (3) the types of studies that support policy and program decisions. We would like to help avoid the political, ethical, and financial disaster that could well attend implementation of the proposed priority.

1. *Studies Capable of Determining Causality.* Randomized control group trials (RCTs) are not the only studies capable of generating understandings of causality. In medicine, causality has been conclusively shown in some instances without RCTs, for example, in linking smoking to lung cancer and infested rats to bubonic plague. The secretary's proposal would elevate experimental over quasi-experimental, observational, single-subject, and other designs, which are sometimes more feasible and equally valid.

RCTs are not always best for determining causality and can be misleading. RCTs examine a limited number of isolated factors that are neither limited nor isolated in natural settings. The complex nature of causality and the multitude of actual influences on outcomes render RCTs less capable of discovering causality than designs sensitive to local culture and conditions and open to unanticipated causal factors.

RCTs should sometimes be ruled out for reasons of ethics. For example, assigning experimental subjects to educationally inferior or medically unproven treatments, or denying control group subjects access to important instructional opportunities or critical medical intervention, is not ethically acceptable even when RCT results might be enlightening. Such studies would not be approved by Institutional Review Boards overseeing the protection of human subjects in accordance with federal statute.

In some cases, data sources are insufficient for RCTs. Pilot, experimental, and exploratory education, health, and social programs are often small enough in scale to preclude use of RCTs as an evaluation methodology, however important it may be to examine causality prior to wider implementation.

2. *Methods Capable of Demonstrating Scientific Rigor.* For at least a decade, evaluators publicly debated whether newer inquiry methods were sufficiently rigorous. This issue was settled long ago. Actual practice and many published examples demonstrate that alternative and mixed methods are rigorous and scientific. To discourage a repertoire of methods would force evaluators backward. We strongly disagree that the methodological "benefits of the proposed priority justify the costs."

3. *Studies Capable of Supporting Appropriate Policy and Program Decisions.* We also strongly disagree that "this regulatory action does not unduly interfere with state, local, and tribal governments in the exercise of their governmental functions." As provision and support of programs are governmental functions so, too, is determining program effectiveness. Sound policy decisions benefit from data illustrating not only causality but also conditionality. Fettering evaluators with unnecessary and unreasonable constraints would deny information needed by policymakers.

While we agree with the intent of ensuring that federally sponsored programs be "evaluated using scientifically based research . . . to determine the effectiveness of a project intervention," we do not agree that "evaluation methods using an experimental design are best for determining project effectiveness." We believe that the constraints in the proposed priority would deny use of other needed, proven, and scientifically credible evaluation methods, resulting in fruitless expenditures on some large contracts while leaving other public programs unevaluated entirely.

SOURCE: American Evaluation Association (AEA) (2003). http://www.eval.org/doestatement.htm

mandated a randomized experimental evaluation to test the effectiveness of the Head Start program. When Head Start began in 1965, early childhood education for low-income families was rare. By the year 2000, the widespread availability of preschool programs made getting a genuine control group impossible. Still an RCT was mandated. Datta (2007b) commented,

> [T]his mandated randomized test is a horrific example of the inappropriate use of what can be, in appropriate circumstances, an excellent design for estimating the value-added of a program and helping establish attribution. . . . [T]he children who are randomly selected not to attend Head Start are unlikely to be sitting at home. Also, some of the children may be younger siblings of children who attended early childhood programs, with benefits to the siblings . . . , reducing the power of the design to detect between-group differences. . . . [T]he real world [is] a different planet than the "other-things-being-equal" assumption of the randomized experimental test. (Pp. 49–50)

The problem of inappropriately mandated experimental designs is by no means limited to the United States. The gold standard debate has global significance. In December 2007, the European Evaluation Society (EES) adopted a statement on "the importance of a methodologically diverse approach to impact evaluation—specifically with respect to development aid and development interventions." As context, the EES noted that

> this statement was prepared in response to strong pressure from some interests advocating for "scientific" and "rigorous" impact of development aid, where this is defined as primarily involving RCTs. This debate has the potential to influence the future direction of evaluation—not only with respect to development but potentially in other areas as well.

> EES however deplores one perspective currently being strongly advocated: that the best or only rigorous and scientific way of doing so is through randomised controlled trials (RCTs). In contrast, the EES supports multi-method approaches to IE [impact evaluation] and does not consider any single method such as RCTs as first choice or as the "gold standard." (EES 2007:1)

In 2007, *Network of Networks on Impact Evaluation* (NONIE) was established by international evaluation offices representing more than 100 United Nations, World Bank, and other development organizations, plus representatives from developing countries and various regional and global organizations. That group drafted a document providing guidance for conducting impact evaluations in developing countries. As this book was going to press, NONIE's draft statement had not yet been officially adopted and published, but the near-final draft being circulated for comment emphasized the importance of methodological diversity and appropriateness in support of rigor, and warned against designating any single design as a gold standard. The literature cited in support of this position and the EES statement includes a number of prominent evaluation theorists and methodologists (Scriven 2008; Bamberger and White 2007; Carden 2007; Chatterji 2007; Julnes and Rog 2007; Picciotto 2007; Pawson 2002a, 2000b; Weiss 2002).

The gold standard debate revolves around "diverse visions for evaluation in the new millennium" (Donaldson and Scriven 2003). In the pages that follow, I will unpack the issues in the debate as I see them, trying to do justice to the competing perspectives while acknowledging that as a utilization-focused evaluator I advocate methodological eclecticism and adapting evaluation methods to the nature of the evaluation question and the information needs of primary intended users. *Methodological appropriateness is the utilization-focused gold standard.*

In a nutshell, the problem from a utilization-focused perspective is that the very dominance of the quantitative/experimental paradigm has cut off serious consideration of alternative methods and channels millions of dollars of evaluation funds into support for a method that not only has strengths but also has significant weaknesses. The gold standard accolade means that funders and evaluators begin by asking "How can we do an experimental design" rather than asking "Given the evaluation situation and the information needed, what is the appropriate evaluation design?" The prestige of the method determines the evaluation question and design rather than considerations of utility, feasibility, propriety, and accuracy. Under the gold standard label, high-quality impact evaluation is *defined* as testing hypotheses, formulated deductively, through random assignment of program participants to treatment and control groups, and measuring outcomes quantitatively. No other options are worthy of serious consideration—*by definition.*

Yet alternatives exist, as the AEA and EES statements posit. There are ways other than experiments of assessing program processes, outcomes, *and* impacts. In the last quarter century, these alternatives have been used by evaluators and practitioners who found that the dominant paradigm failed to answer—or even ask—their questions. The importance of having an alternative is captured powerfully by the distinguished adult educator Malcolm Knowles (1989) who, in his autobiography, *The Making of an Adult Educator,* listed discovery of an alternative way of evaluating adult learning as one of the eight most important episodes of his life,

right there alongside his marriage. Let's find out what he found so illuminating.

The Qualitative/Naturalistic Paradigm

The alternative qualitative/naturalistic methods paradigm was derived most directly from anthropological field methods and more generally from qualitative sociology, phenomenology, and constructionism. It was undergirded by the doctrine of *Verstehen* (understanding):

> Advocates of some version of the *Verstehen* doctrine will claim that human beings can be understood in a manner that other objects of study cannot. Humans have purposes and emotions, they make plans, construct cultures, and hold certain values, and their behavior is influenced by such values, plans, and purposes. In short, a human being lives in a world which has "meaning" to him, and, because his behavior has meaning, human actions are intelligible in ways that the behavior of nonhuman objects is not. (Strike 1972:28)

In essence, the *Verstehen* doctrine asserts that applied social sciences need methods different from those used in agriculture and pharmacology because human beings are different from plants and medicines. The alternative paradigm emphasizes attention to the meaning of human behavior, the context of social interaction, and the connections between subjective states and behavior. The tradition of *Verstehen* places emphasis on the human capacity to know and understand others through empathic introspection and reflection based on detailed description gathered through direct observation, in-depth, open-ended interviewing, and case studies. Evaluation came to have advocates for and users of alternative methods. Robert Stake's (1975) responsive approach was one such early alternative.

Responsive evaluation is an alternative, an old alternative, based on what people do naturally to evaluate things; they observe and react. The approach is not new. But this alternative has been avoided in district, state, and federal planning documents and regulations because it is subjective and poorly suited to formal contracts. It is also capable of raising embarrassing questions. (P. 14)

Stake recommended responsive evaluation because "it is an approach that trades off some measurement precision in order to increase the usefulness of the findings to persons in and around the program" (p. 14). Stake influenced a new generation of evaluators to think about the connection between methods and use, and his books on *The Art of Case Research* (1995) and *Multiple Case Study Analysis* (2005) have extended that influence.

I became engaged in the paradigms debate when, after being thoroughly indoctrinated into the dominant paradigm in graduate school as a quantitative sociologist, I became involved in evaluating an open education program whose practitioners objected to the narrow and standardized outcomes measured by standardized tests. Because they advocated an educational approach that they considered individualized, personal, humanistic, and nurturing, they wanted evaluation methods with those same characteristics. In attempting to be responsive to my intended users (open educators) and do an evaluation that was credible and useful to them, I discovered qualitative methods. That led me to write a monograph comparing alternative paradigms (Patton 1975a), reactions to which embroiled me directly and personally in the passions and flames of the great paradigms debate. At the time it was exhilarating. Looking back from today's vantage point of methodological eclecticism, the barbs traded by opposing camps would appear silly but

for the fact that, in circles not yet touched by the light that eventually emerged from the debate, friction and its attendant heat still burn evaluators who encounter true believers in the old orthodoxies. It is to prepare for such encounters, and be able to rise gently above the acrimony they can inspire, that students of evaluation need to understand the dimensions and passions of the debate.

Dimensions of the Competing Paradigms

By the end of the 1970s, the evaluation profession had before it the broad outlines of two competing research paradigms. Exhibit 12.3 displays the contrasting emphases of the two methodological paradigms. Beyond differences in basic philosophical assumptions about the nature of reality (ontological differences), in its details the paradigms debate included a number of contrasting dimensions, like the relative merits of being close to versus distant from program participants during an evaluation. While reviewing these dimensions will illuminate the nature of the paradigms debate, they also can be thought of as options that might be offered to intended users during methods deliberations and negotiations. We'll begin with the debate about the relative merits of numbers versus narrative—and the mixed-methods approach of valuing both.

Quantitative and Qualitative Data: Different Perspectives on the World

> *In God we trust. All others must have data.*
>
> —W. Edwards Deming

Both *quals* and *quants* agree with Deming. What they disagree about is what constitutes good data.

EXHIBIT 12.3

Primary Dimensions of the Contrasting Methodological Paradigms

Qualitative/Naturalistic Paradigm	Quantitative/Experimental Paradigm
Qualitative data (narratives, description, quotations)	Quantitative data (numbers, statistics)
Naturalistic inquiry (openness)	Experimental designs (control)
In-depth case studies	Treatment and control groups
Inductive analysis	Deductive hypothesis testing
Subjective perspective valued	Objectivity
Close and direct observation of the program	Distant from and independent of the program
Holistic contextual portrayal	Independent and dependent variables
Systems perspective focused on interdependencies	Linear, sequential modeling
Dynamic, continuous view of change	Pre- and postmeasurement of change
Purposeful sampling of relevant cases	Probabilistic, random sampling
Focus on uniqueness and diversity	Standardized, uniform procedures
Emergent, flexible designs	Fixed, controlled design protocols
Thematic content analysis	Statistical analysis
Value uniqueness, particularity	Replication
Extrapolations (lessons and principles)	Generalizations (empirically based external validity)

Quantitative measures strive for precision by focusing on things that can be counted. Quantitative data come from questionnaires, tests, standardized observation instruments, information systems, official indicators, and program records. Gathering numerical data requires conceptualizing categories that can be treated as ordinal or interval data and subjected to statistical analysis. The experiences of people in programs and the important variables that describe program outcomes are fit into these standardized categories to which numerical values are attached. The following opinion item is a common example:

How would you rate the quality of course instruction?

| 1. Excellent | 2. Good | 3. Fair | 4. Poor |

In contrast, the evaluator using a qualitative approach seeks to capture what a program experience means to participants *in their own words,* through interviews or open-ended questionnaire items, and in day-to-day program settings, through observation. An open-ended course evaluation question would ask

In your own words, how would you describe the quality of the instruction in this course?

Exhibit 12.4 contrasts other examples of quantitative and qualitative questions.

Qualitative data consist of words and narratives: quotations from open-ended questionnaires; detailed descriptions of situations, events, people, interactions, and observed behaviors; interview responses from people about their experiences, attitudes, beliefs, and thoughts; and excerpts or entire passages from documents, correspondence, records, and case histories. The data are collected as open-ended narrative without predetermined, standardized categories such as the response choices that make up typical questionnaires or tests. The evaluation findings are presented as case studies and analysis of patterns across cases (Patton 2002a; Yin 2002).

EXHIBIT 12.4

Quantitative and Qualitative Questions: Examples from Evaluation Questionnaires

Standardized, Quantitative Items	*Qualitative, Open-Ended Items*
A. The program's goals were clearly communicated to us? 　1. strongly agree 　2. agree 　3. disagree 　4. strongly disagree	A. From your perspective, and in your own words, what are the primary goals of this program?
B. How relevant was this training to your job? 　1. very relevant 　2. somewhat relevant 　3. a little relevant 　4. not at all relevant	B. How, if at all, does this training relate to your job? *Please be as specific as possible.*
C. How much did you learn from this program? 　*I learned* 　1. a great deal 　2. a fair amount 　3. a little bit 　4. nothing at all	C. What are the most important things you learned from your participation in this program?

Numbers are parsimonious and precise; words provide individualized meanings and nuance. Each way of turning the complexities of the world into data has strengths and weaknesses. Qualitative data capture personal meaning and portray the diversity of ways people express themselves; quantitative data facilitate comparisons because all program participants respond to the same questions on standardized scales within predetermined response categories. Standardized tests and surveys measure the reactions of many respondents in a way that statistical aggregation and analysis are relatively straightforward, following established rules and procedures. In contrast, qualitative methods typically produce a wealth of detailed data about a much smaller number of people and cases; finding patterns and themes in the diverse narratives can be painstaking, time-consuming, and uncertain. But qualitative data in program evaluation is aimed at letting people in programs express their reactions in their own terms rather than impose on them a preconceived set of limited response categories.

So what is there to debate about quantitative versus qualitative when each can contribute in important ways to our understanding of program? And why not just use both approaches, what is called a *mixed-methods design?* Mixed methods are often used, but one kind of data is often valued over the other. The debate about the relative merits of quantitative versus qualitative data stems from underlying assumptions and deeply held values. "If you can't measure it, if you can't quantify it, it doesn't exist," is a refrain many program staff have heard from evaluators insisting on "clear, specific, and measurable goals" (see Chapter 7 on the goals clarification game). Statistics, because they are concrete and precise, seem more factual—and "getting the facts right" is at the heart of good evaluation (Berk 2007). "What gets measured gets done," the mantra of management by objectives and performance measurement, communicates that only what can be quantified is important. Statistical presentations tend to have more credibility, to seem more like "science," whereas qualitative narratives tend to be associated with "mere" journalism. A certain assertiveness, even machismo, often accompanies the demand that outcomes be quantified: hard data connote virility; soft data are flaccid. (Sexual innuendo works in science no less than in advertising, or so it would seem.) But qualitative advocates have their own favorite quotations, among them the famous assertion of nineteenth-century British Prime Minister Benjamin Disraeli "There are three kinds of lies: lies, damned lies, and statistics." Disraeli also observed, "As a general rule the most successful man in life is the man who has the best information." The quantitative-qualitative debate is about what constitutes the "best information."

Kuhn (1970), a philosopher and historian of science, observed that the values scientists hold "most deeply" concern predictions: "quantitative predictions are preferable to qualitative ones" (pp. 184–85). It's a short distance from a preference for quantitative data to the virtual exclusion of other types of data. Bernstein and Freeman (1975) even ranked evaluations that gathered both quantitative and qualitative data as lower in methodological quality than those that gathered only quantitative data (see Exhibit 12.1). The *What Works Clearinghouse* only uses quantitative findings and ignores qualitative data, even in mixed-methods studies. These are examples of what distinguished sociologist C. Wright Mills (1961) classically labeled "abstracted empiricism" (p. 50).

If the problems upon which one is at work are readily amenable to statistical procedures, one should always try them first. . . . No one, however, need accept such procedures, when generalized, as the only procedures available. Certainly no one need accept this model as a total canon. It is not the only empirical manner.

It is a choice made according to the requirements of our problems, not a "necessity" that follows from an epistemological dogma. (Pp. 73–74)

Valuing quantitative measures to the exclusion of other data limits not only what one can find out but also what one is even willing to ask. It is appropriate and easy to count the words a child spells correctly, but what about that same child's ability to use those words in a meaningful way? It is appropriate to measure a student's reading level, but what does reading *mean* to that student? Different kinds of problems require different types of data. If we only want to know the frequency of interactions between children of different races in desegregated schools, then statistics are appropriate. However, if we want to understand the *meanings of interracial interactions,* open-ended, in-depth interviewing will be more appropriate.

One evaluator in our federal utilization study told of struggling with this issue. He was evaluating community mental health programs and reported that statistical measures frequently failed to capture real differences among programs. For example, he found a case in which community mental health staff cooperated closely with the state hospital. On one occasion, he observed a therapist from the community mental health center accompany a seriously disturbed client on the "traumatic, fearful, anxiety-ridden trip to the state hospital." The therapist had been working with the client on an outpatient basis. After commitment to the state facility, the therapist continued to see the client weekly and

assisted that person in planning toward and getting out of the state institution and back into the larger community as soon as possible. The evaluator found it very difficult to measure this aspect of the program quantitatively.

This actually becomes a qualitative aspect of how they were carrying out the mental health program, but there's a problem of measuring the impact of that qualitative change from when the sheriff used to transport the patients from that county in a locked car with a stranger in charge and the paraphernalia of the sheriff's personality and office. The qualitative difference is obvious in the possible effect on a disturbed patient, but the problem of measurement is very, very difficult. So what we get here in the report is a portrayal of some of the qualitative differences and a very limited capacity of the field to measure those qualitative differences. We could describe some of them better than we could measure them. [EV5:3]

A more extended example will help illustrate the importance of seeking congruence between the phenomenon studied and the data gathered for an evaluation. In a seminal study, Edna Shapiro (1973) found no achievement test differences between (1) children in an enriched Follow Through (FT) program modeled along the lines of open education and (2) children in comparison schools not involved in FT or other enrichment programs. When the children's test scores were compared, no differences of any consequence were found. However, when she observed children in their classrooms, she could see striking differences between the FT and comparison classes. First, the environments were observably different (implementation evaluation). She characterized the FT classrooms as "lively, vibrant, with a diversity of curricular projects and children's products, and an atmosphere of friendly, cooperative endeavor." In contrast, she described the non-FT classrooms as "relatively uneventful, with a narrow range of curriculum, uniform activity, a great deal of seat work, and less equipment; teachers as well as children were quieter and more concerned with maintaining or submitting to discipline" (Shapiro 1973:529).

Her observations also revealed that the children performed differently in the two environments on important dimensions that standardized achievement tests failed to detect. Shapiro concluded that the narrow nature of the questions asked on standardized tests predetermined nonsignificant statistical results.

> "I assumed," she reflected, "that the internalized effects of different kinds of school experience could be observed and inferred only from responses in test situations, and that the observation of teaching and learning in the classroom should be considered auxiliary information, useful chiefly to document the differences in the children's group learning experiences." (Shapiro 1973:532)

But then she thought about how tests were administered. To assure consistency, each child was removed from the classroom and given the same exact instructions so that differences in scores would show what has been learned that survived outside the familiarity of the classroom. But she came to worry that this imposed an artificiality in the evaluation that actually disguised significant differences in what children had learned and could do.

She observed such marked disparities between children's classroom responses and test responses that she reevaluated the role of classroom data, individual test situation data, and the relation between them. If we minimize the importance of the child's behavior in the classroom, she

asked, do we not have to apply the same logic to the child's responses in the test situation, which is also influenced by situational variables? The quantitative test scores provided one, but only one, form of evaluation of what children had learned. Qualitatively observing them answer questions and do school work in their classrooms provided very different findings about what children knew. These intriguing and important differences in learning outcomes under different conditions led her to believe that *both kinds of data should be valued and used*. Fast forward a quarter of a century to the fixation on standardized test scores in federal *No Child Left Behind* accountability standards and it is clear that Shapiro's insights have not been incorporated in any significant way in educational evaluation. Test scores trump all other kinds of data.

It is worth remembering in this regard that one of the functions of scientific paradigms is to provide criteria for choosing problems that can be assumed to have solutions: "Changes in the standards governing permissible problems, concepts, and explanations can transform a science" (Kuhn 1970:106). The problem in education has been defined as raising test scores and reducing disparities in scores. A particular way of measuring learning has come to define the very nature of the problem. Asking a broader question leads to different kinds of evaluation data: What are ways in which children can demonstrate what they have learned? The answer can include test scores, to be sure, but can also include examining the work children do in the classroom, their performance on teacher-made tests, portfolios of students' work, examples of their homework, and their performance on integrated projects where they use what they know. If the educational problem and corresponding evaluation question is defined at the outset as how to increase test scores, then the curriculum becomes based on that intended outcome (teach to the tests because what gets measured gets done) and the definition of learning becomes entirely quantitative and standardized. Those who value qualitative evaluation data tend to emphasize individualized learning, diverse ways of capturing what students know, and placing what children can do in the context of what opportunities they have to demonstrate what they know. Thus, the methods debate in educational evaluations is integrally interconnected to competing educational paradigms about how children learn and what is important to learn.

Mixed-Methods Designs: Combining Qualitative and Quantitative Data

From a utilization-focused evaluation perspective, both qualitative and quantitative data can contribute to all aspects of evaluative inquiries. In its simplest form in college exams, mixed methods means asking both multiple-choice questions and open-ended essay questions. In evaluations it can mean collecting data with both fixed-choice surveys and using statistical indicators of outcomes as well as conducting open-ended interviews and case studies. Evaluators should be able to use a variety of tools if they are to be sophisticated and flexible in matching research methods to the nuances of particular evaluation questions and the idiosyncrasies of specific decision-maker needs. In *Qualitative Research and Evaluation Methods* (Patton 2002a), I have elaborated the conditions under which qualitative methods are particularly appropriate in evaluation research, for example, when program outcomes are highly individualized so case studies are essential to capture

variations in outcomes. Sometimes quantitative methods alone are most appropriate as in counting how many graduates of an employment program get and keep jobs. But in many cases, *both qualitative and quantitative methods should be used together* and there are no logical reasons why both kinds of data cannot be used together (Patton 1982a). Mixed methods have been of interest in evaluation for some time, including *Advances in Mixed-Method Evaluation: The Challenges and Benefits of Integrating Diverse Paradigms* (Greene and Caracelli 1997). As interest and practice have grown, mixed-methods designs are receiving more attention than ever, including a new *Journal of Mixed Methods Research* hailing the "New Era of Mixed Methods" (Tashakkori and Creswell 2007), Jennifer Greene's important book on *Mixing Methods in Social Inquiry* (2007) with its emphasis on *meaningful engagement with difference,* and publication of the *Handbook of Mixed Methods in Social and Behavioral Research* (Tashakkori and Teddlie 2003). A special issue of the journal *Research in the Schools* was devoted to "New Directions in Mixed Methods Research" (Johnson 2006).

All mixed-methods designs combine qualitative and quantitative data in some way. Some mixed designs are primarily quantitative, with qualitative data as supplementary; others are primarily qualitative with quantitative data as ancillary, as when using ethnography in conjunction with statistical data in a mixed-method strategy (Caracelli 2006). "Pure mixed methods designs" give "equal status" to quantitative and qualitative data (Johnson, Onwuegbuzie, and Turner 2007). In whatever combinations multiple methods are used, the contributions of each kind of data should be fairly assessed. In many cases, this means that evaluators working

Mixed and Emergent Methods:
Adapting Both Program and Evaluation to Changing Conditions

In the fall of 2005, a program I run called the National College Choreography Initiative announced a grant to Tulane University to bring two choreographers, Sara Pearson and Patrik Widrig, to its New Orleans campus. Based on 2 years of research and over a decade of visits to New Orleans, they would work with students to create a dance about the environment, in collaboration with the university's Center for Bioenvironmental Research, to be performed on the Mississippi River.

Then Hurricane Katrina hit, the levees broke, and that didn't happen.

On the spur of the moment, with the help of faculty members at the University of Texas at Austin, students were transported to Texas to attend classes there. The choreographers could have abandoned the project, but instead reenvisioned it as *Katrina, Katrina: Love Letters to New Orleans*. Through their art, they expressed their great love for the Big Easy, and students were led through a process that helped them cope with being torn from their homes, friends, and college.

Dancers were costumed with remnants of emergency blue tarps and carried water bottles. Audiences were enthusiastic and others in the arts world took notice. The Kennedy Center booked it twice for its free performance series and then made it part of the center's national outreach program. It then toured the country.

But a logic model would probably have shown the project as an utter failure. After all, the environmental project never happened, the goal changed, most of the original partners didn't participate, and the stated results weren't achieved. Instead, the innovation on the part of artists and faculty members led to a transformative experience: They took stock of the situation and created an experience that would be meaningful to people during a time of dire concern about a national disaster.

Had Dance/USA, the organization that distributed the money, or the National Endowment for the Arts, which provided the funds, insisted on rigid accountability, the grant would not have been made, but Dance/USA released the funds and trusted the faculty members and artists. As stakeholders, they understood the context in which the grantee was operating and honored their extraordinary efforts to fulfill the project in a manner that served the colleges.

How should we evaluate this project? Would its impact be captured by saying that 350 people attended and that the budget balanced? Or should we design a longitudinal study to find out how many kids returned to New Orleans? Or finished college?

When we evaluated the National College Choreography Initiative program—including the Katrina project by Ms. Pearson and Mr. Widrig—we gathered statistics from all 34 projects. We learned that more than 10,000 students participated, 60,000 people attended 174 performances and 226 outreach activities, and more than $665,000 was raised to match the $272,000 in money that was initially provided.

But the numbers don't tell the whole story.

We systematically reviewed the stories that came from faculty members at all 34 colleges. From them, we identified more than 30 indicators of what had changed since the grants were made. Using content analysis, we developed a coding system for areas such as outreach beyond campus, professional networking, new jobs, in-state touring, collaborations with other colleges, and other indicators. We know, for example, that two of the grants led to professional opportunities for students, including a job with a ballet company, and eight involved opportunities for a program to spread beyond the campus grounds, such as the creation of dance curricula for elementary and secondary schools.

Each year, Dance/USA creates a publication that documents not just the statistics, but also the stories showing the successes of each project. And, the National Endowment for the Arts knows of the impact of its grant, and what was to be a one-time effort has now received four rounds of financial support.

SOURCE: Callahan (2007).

Suzanne Callahan is founder of Callahan Consulting for the Arts and the Laboratory for Arts Evaluation. Her book, *Singing Our Praises: Case Studies in the Art of Evaluation*, was awarded Outstanding Publication of the Year from the American Evaluation Association in 2005.

in teams will need to work hard to overcome their tendency to dismiss certain kinds of data without first considering seriously and fairly the merits of those data (Guest and MacQueen 2007). Exhibit 12.5 presents the evaluation standards for including and appropriately analyzing both quantitative and qualitative data in evaluations, giving equal weight to each.

The Gold Standard Debate

While it's not so hard to combine numbers with narratives to create mixed-methods evaluations, it is not so easy to combine experimental designs with naturalistic inquiry designs. The rigor and validity of experiments depend on controlling, standardizing, and precisely measuring the intervention and its effects. Naturalistic inquiry designs eschew control and observe the program as it unfolds naturally including the emergent and diverse effects on participants.

In considering the relative virtues of experimental versus naturalistic designs, the paradigms debate centers on the importance of causal questions in evaluation and how best to conduct impact evaluations. Those evaluation researchers who believe that the most important and central function of evaluation is to measure the effects of programs on participants to make valid causal inferences are strong advocates of randomized experiments as "the standard against which other designs for impact evaluation are judged" (Boruch and Rindskopf 1984:121). This is *the gold standard position* discussed earlier in this chapter. In advocating experimental designs as the gold standard, evaluation researchers such as Boruch (2007); Cook (2006); Rosen, Manor, Engelhard, and Zucker (2006); Lipsey (2007a, 2005, 1990); Schatschneider (2003); Shadish, Cook, and Campbell (2001); and Campbell and Boruch (1975) have demonstrated the power and feasibility of randomized experiments for a variety of programs and interventions. The concerns

---

EXHIBIT 12.5

Evaluation Standards for Quantitative and Qualitative Data

The evaluation standards give equal attention, weight, and credence to qualitative and quantitative data.

Program Outcomes—Document the full range of program outcomes, so that interested parties can assess the program's success against goals and assessed needs of intended beneficiaries and also assess its positive and negative side effects.

Document the qualitative and quantitative indicators that were employed to assess goal achievement. (S5)

Analysis of Quantitative Information—Appropriately and systematically analyze the evaluation's quantitative information, so that evaluation questions are effectively answered. (A7)

Analysis of Qualitative Information—Appropriately and systematically analyze the evaluation's qualitative information, so that evaluation questions are effectively answered. (A8)

SOURCE: The Omnibus Metaevaluation Checklist (Stufflebeam 2007).

that permeate these writings are concerns about increased rigor, well-controlled interventions, reducing threats to internal validity, precise estimates of program effects, and statistical power—which in combination increase confidence in attributing an outcome to an intervention.

Naturalistic inquiry, in contrast, involves observing ongoing programs as they unfold without attempting to control or manipulate the setting, situation, people, or data. Naturalistic inquiry evaluations look at programs within and in relation to their naturally occurring context. Instead of random assignment, for example, which controls who gets the treatment (program), naturalistic inquiry looks at how staff select participants or how they self-select into a program.

Randomized Control Trials: Heaven or Gold Standard

Randomized controlled trials (RCTs) are positioned as *the methodological gold standard* among advocates of experimental designs (Dugger 2004). Professor David Storey (2006) of Warwick Business School, University of Warwick, has offered a competing metaphor. He has posited "six steps to heaven" in conducting evaluations, where heaven is a randomized experiment. So materially oriented and worldly evaluators are admonished to aspire to the gold standard, while the more spiritually inclined can aspire to follow the path to heaven, where heaven is an RCT.

The metaphors of naturalistic inquiry are more along the lines of *staying grounded*, looking at *the real world* as it unfolds, *going with the flow*, *being adaptable*, and *seeing what emerges*.

Guba and Lincoln (1981) identified two dimensions along which types of scientific inquiry can be described: the extent to which the scientist manipulates some phenomenon in advance in order to study it, and the extent to which constraints are placed on output measures; that is, the extent to which predetermined categories or variables are used to describe the phenomenon under study. They then defined naturalistic inquiry as a "discovery-oriented" approach that minimizes investigator manipulation of the study setting and places no prior constraints on what the outcomes of the research will be. Naturalistic inquiry is thus contrasted to experimental research, in which, ideally, the investigator controls external influences and measures only hypothesized outcome variables.

Debate about whether experimental designs constitute the methodological gold standard revolves, in part, around what level and kind of evidence is needed to determine that an intervention is effective. Consider the challenge of eradicating intestinal worms in children, a widespread problem in developing countries (Bundy and Drake 2004; Drake and Bundy 2001; Brooker et al. 2000; Dickson et al. 2000; Albonico et al. 1997). Suppose we want to evaluate an intervention in which school-age children with diarrhea are given anti-worm medicine to increase their school attendance and performance. To attribute the intervention to the desired outcome, advocates of randomized controlled trials (RCTs) would insist on an evaluation design in which students suffering from diarrhea are randomly divided into a treatment group (those who receive worm medicine) and a control group (those who do not receive the medicine). The school attendance and test performance of the two groups would then be compared. If, after a month on the medicine, those receiving the intervention show higher attendance and school performance at a statistically significant level compared with the control group (the counterfactual), then the increased outcomes can be attributed to the intervention (the worm medicine).

Advocates of qualitative inquiry question the value of the control group in this case. Suppose that students, parents, teachers, and local health professionals are interviewed about the reasons students miss school and perform poorly on tests. Independently, each of these groups assert that diarrhea is a major cause of the poor school attendance and performance. Gathering data separately from different informant groups (students, parents, teachers, heath professionals) is called *triangulation,* a way of checking the consistency of findings from different data sources. Following the baseline interviews, students are given a regimen of worm medicine. Those taking the medicine show increased school attendance and performance, and in follow-up interviews, the students, parents, teachers, and health professionals independently affirm their belief that the changes can be attributed to taking the worm medicine and being relieved of the symptoms of diarrhea. Is this credible, convincing evidence?

Those who find such a design sufficient argue that the results are both reasonable and empirical, and that the high cost of adding a control group is not needed to establish causality. Nor, they would assert, is it ethical to withhold medicine from students with diarrhea when relieving their symptoms has merit in and of itself. The advocates of RCTs respond that without the control group, other unknown factors may have intervened to affect the outcomes and that *only the existence of a counterfactual* (control group) will establish with certainty the impact of the intervention.

As this example illustrates, those evaluators and methodologists on opposite sides of this debate have different worldviews about what constitutes sufficient evidence for attribution and action in the real world. This is not simply an academic debate. Millions of dollars of evaluation funds are at stake and the results of these evaluations around the world will affect billions of dollars of international development assistance.

Consider as another example RCTs evaluating microfinance loans being supported by the International Finance Corporation (IFC) of The World Bank. Microfinance programs give very small loans to people in extreme poverty without any collateral for the loans. With as little as $100, a group of women are able to purchase a sewing machine and make clothes for sale, or a group of men may purchase tools to set up a bicycle repair business. Microfinance loans provide capital to people in poverty when commercial banks are unwilling to take the risk of such loans or when those in poverty are subject to the extremely high interest rates of loan sharks. The differences in income can be quite small because the income levels and loan amounts are quite small. For example, in such a program in Pakistan, the Kashf Foundation reported that 90 percent of its clients were living on less than $1 a day and that, over time, those who had received loans reported 51 percent higher income than new clients applying for loans (Arjumand and Associates 2004).

IFC is funding evaluation of such microfinance programs with RCTs, randomly assigning loan applicants to those who receive the loans and a control group of people who do not receive loans. The financial status of people in both groups are compared over time, sometimes adding additional measures of health, social mobility, nutrition, and children's education. Differences on these indicators, if any, between the treatment and control group, can confidently be attributed to the loans. One such study conducted by researchers from MIT's Poverty Action Lab, which specializes in conducting randomized experiments in developing countries, found that "those offered credit were more likely to retain wage employment, less likely to experience severe hunger in their households, and less likely to be impoverished" (Karlan and Zinman 2006:1).

In questioning the cost-benefit of such rigorous evaluation designs, advocates of naturalistic inquiry question the added value and expense of the control groups. In contrast to the randomized control group design, the naturalistic inquiry narrative would gather case data on the financial status and lives of people in poverty before they receive the loans. Their longtime history of poverty and lack of access to capital would be documented. Once they receive the loans, they would be periodically interviewed and observed to determine how they had used the loans and what differences the loans have made in their lives as reported by them and by others who know them (triangulation of sources). When the results show that they have used the loans to engage in economic activity that has increased their income and that the increased income has increased their quality of life, these narrative results would support a conclusion that the changes in their lives can reasonably be attributed to the loans. The connection between receiving the loans and enhanced lives is directly observable and measurable, and the attribution reasonable, without the need for a control group. Advocates of RCTs worry that other unknown factors may be at work and that the only way to establish attribution with confidence is to compare the intervention to a counterfactual (control group). The advocates of naturalistic inquiry find no added value in the

control group and believe that the costs of monitoring the control group are unjustified and possibly unethical, especially in those designs where randomly denying people small loans puts them at risk of being perceived as being bad credit risks because they have, in fact, been turned down for a loan.

In a utilization-focused evaluation design process, these alternative design scenarios can be presented to primary intended users to help them determine what level of evidence is needed and appropriate given the purposes of and intended audiences for the evaluation. The MIT Poverty Action Lab is conducting a number of such experiments around the world for the IFC and other international donors. My experience with IFC decision makers is that they are treating RCTs as the gold standard because they want to be credible with academics and the Ph.D. economists of The World Bank. Politically, RCTs are the safe way to go to achieve academic respectability.

At a practical policy level, people in the field who implement these programs ask what burning evaluation question about the value of microfinance loans justifies continuing to fund RCTs. Muhammad Yunus won the 2006 Nobel Peace Prize for his work on microfinance that led to his founding the Grameen Bank, which has helped hundreds of thousands of people and has been disseminated as a model throughout the world, although adapted to local cultures and economies as it has been implemented. Yunus did not conduct RCTs to determine the value of small loans to impoverished women and men, but based his judgments on practical observations of the effects on thousands of people's lives. The Grameen Bank is considered a world-changing success story (Westley, Zimmerman, and Patton 2006). What, then, are the RCTs on

microfinance trying to prove? What is the policy question that justifies the large expense of RCT designs to evaluate microfinance programs?

Answering these questions involves decisions about what level of evidence is needed to establish the value of something and the cost-benefit of gathering such evidence. Those convinced by naturalistic inquiry narratives argue that the cause-effect linkage in microfinance is fairly direct and observable. For the cost of administering a control group design, a large number of additional microfinance loans could be given. Control group designs are expensive. The practical question, then, is the following: Given the nature of evidence that can be gathered by following up recipients of small loans to document the effects of those loans on the recipients' lives, what is the added value of a control group? Is the cost of such a control group (and the evidence it would yield) more valuable than making a larger

number of loans and following up the effects of those additional loans, thereby substantially increasing the sample size for directly studying the intervention itself. This cost-benefit methodological decision also introduces *ethical considerations* into the trade-off between gathering data from a control group versus giving loans to more people.

There is also the practical question of using results from randomized experiments. One of the field-level development workers I met at an IFC conference on evaluation told me of the difficulties she experienced in administering the microfinance program because of the design rigidities of the experimental design. She was having trouble understanding and explaining the value of randomization beyond its status among academic researchers. She asked, "Can you imagine an agency, government, or bank running a microfinance program based on randomization? What of any practical significance do you learn from randomization? We have limited resources," she went on. "We have to make selections. Even if randomization was more fair and equitable, giving loans randomly to applicants is not a viable political option. Indeed, the critical questions about microfinance are about how people become eligible, how they are selected to receive a loan, and how the decision is made about how much to give them. *Administering loans randomly is just not a viable policy option*," she emphasized, shaking her head in frustration.

The randomization process, she felt, made the evaluation results less useful because the design was rigid and artificial. This, she had concluded, was a primary reason why no major businesses conduct such RCTs for their services. North American, European, and Australasian banks do not roll out new services with RCTs. They do, however, engage in thorough and rigorous evaluation. They try out pilot programs before going to scale. They seek customer feedback. They observe carefully what customers respond to and how they behave. They compare one delivery approach with another different delivery approach, with real customers in the real world, and they adjust their services accordingly. Likewise, Microsoft does not introduce and study new software through RCTs. They have a large group of pilot testers (as many as 750,000 worldwide) who provide real-time feedback from real-world uses of their software. One would think that if RCTs were so valuable in determining the effectiveness of services, this field worker speculated, businesses would use them routinely to boost profits. In point of fact, businesses engage in continuous improvement evaluation based on feedback and observing the reactions and behaviors of real customers as well as soliciting feedback from noncustomers. RCTs

are more often an academic laboratory-like enterprise for research, not a real-world evaluation exercise to figure out how things work under real-world conditions. Or so goes the critique—and the debate.

Advocates of RCTs respond that you cannot really attribute the increased income and business activity of the loan recipients without a control group of people who did not receive the loans. For certain academics, using RCTs as *the only way* to establish causality is a matter of strong belief. To get results published in many of the most prestigious academic journals, a researcher needs to have conducted an RCT. *But what level of evidence does a typical policymaker need?* If small loans are given to very poor people with a history of poverty and an evaluator documents that they use those loans for businesses and make a small profit, which they use to improve their lives, is that sufficient evidence of the value of such a program? From a policy perspective, the "control condition" is not a viable policy option because *doing nothing is seldom an option.* International agencies and governments are not considering NOT doing microfinance programs. In an RCT design, then, a great deal of money is spent comparing doing something (a treatment) with not doing something (control), when the control condition is not really a policy option. In contrast to the "doing nothing" control condition, policymakers are interested in evaluating different ways of delivering microfinance loans. A comparison design that examines delivering microfinance in different ways, with alternative selection criteria, with alternative support mechanisms, and with alternative sizes of loans, would provide important policy results. An RCT answers one and only one question: Did this one particular approach produce this one particular outcome in this one particular situation compared with a control group? That question tends to be of much less policy relevance and interest than the question, "What are the costs, benefits, and effects of delivering the intervention in different ways?"

Remember, at the root of paradigm debates are different formulations of the problem, different evaluation questions, and different beliefs about what level of evidence is needed to take action. Exhibit 12.6 provides a summary overview of the logic of experimental designs and 10 common critiques of such designs.

Credibility Issues

From Objectivity versus Subjectivity to Fairness and Balance

Qualitative evaluators are accused frequently of *subjectivity*—a term with the power of an epithet in that it connotes the very antithesis of scientific inquiry. Objectivity has been considered the sine qua non of the scientific method. To be subjective has meant to be biased, unreliable, and nonrational. Subjectivity implies opinion rather than fact, intuition rather than logic, and impression rather than rigor. Evaluators are advised to avoid subjectivity and make their work "objective and value free."

In the paradigms debate, the means advocated by scientists for controlling subjectivity through the scientific method were the techniques of the dominant quantitative/experimental paradigm. Yet quantitative and experimental methods can work in practice to limit and even bias the kinds of questions that are asked and the nature of admissible solutions. Michael Scriven (1972a), evaluation's long-time resident philosopher, has insisted that quantitative

methods are no more synonymous with objectivity than qualitative methods are synonymous with subjectivity:

> Errors like this are too simple to be explicit. They are inferred confusions in the ideological foundations of research, its interpretations, its application. . . . It is increasingly clear that the influence of ideology on methodology and of the latter on the training and behavior of researchers and on the identification and disbursement of support is staggeringly powerful. Ideology is to research what Marx suggested the economic factor was to politics and what Freud took sex to be for psychology. (P. 94)

The possibility that "ideological" preconceptions can lead to dual perspectives about a single phenomenon goes to the very heart of the contrasts between paradigms. Two scientists may look at the same thing, but because of different theoretical perspectives, assumptions, or ideology-based methodologies, they may literally not see the same thing (Petrie 1972:48). Indeed, Kuhn (1970) has pointed out,

> Something like a paradigm is prerequisite to perception itself. What a man sees depends both upon what he looks at and also upon what his previous visual-conceptual experience has taught him to see. In the absence of such training there can only be, in William James's phrase, "a bloomin' buzzin' confusion." (P. 113)

A child's parable, the story of Han and the Dragon, illustrates this point at another level of simplicity. Han, a small boy, lived in a city threatened by wild horsemen from the North. The Mandarin ruler and his advisers decided that only the Great Cloud Dragon could save the city, so they prayed for the Dragon's intervention. As he prayed, the Mandarin envisioned a dragon that looked like a proud lord—a Mandarin. The captain

EXHIBIT 12.6

The Logic of Experimental Designs and 10 Common Criticisms

When experiments are advocated as the gold standard in evaluations it is because of how they assess *cause* and *effect* relationships. Experimental designs are viewed as the ideal because they control the hypothesized cause (the intervention or program) to ensure that the cause precedes the effect, that the cause is related to the effect, and that extraneous factors that could produce the effect can be ruled out. One of the few ways of establishing and validating causality a priori is to carefully design the experiment to test an explicit hypothesis, namely, *this* intervention will produce *this* outcome. Hypothesis testing avoids the problems and weaknesses of post hoc, after-the-fact, retrospective speculations on causality. As historian Lee Simonson observed, "Any event, once it has occurred, can be made to appear inevitable by a competent historian" (Forbes 2007:196).

Random Assignment and the Hypothetical Counterfactual

The ideal way to control extraneous influences is to randomly assign people (or other units of analysis, e.g., classrooms, programs, communities) to two groups: those that experience the hypothesized cause (the intervention) and a control group that does not receive the intervention. Random assignment controls selection bias and creates a *hypothetical counterfactual* that represents what would have happened to the treatment group had they not received the treatment. By statistically comparing the outcomes of the control group (hypothetical counterfactual) with the treatment group, the evaluator can assess the extent to which the outcomes can be attributed to the treatment (in other words, to judge whether the intervention caused the outcomes). Random assignment distributes potential extraneous or unknown causes across both groups so that the only difference between the two groups is the intervention. This increases confidence in determining causality because any other influence on the observed outcome would only occur by chance.

Replicability

Well-designed experiments allow for replication and contribute to meta-analyses. Two carefully conducted randomized experiments undertaken with subjects from the same population and using the same protocols should arrive at essentially the same results. The possibility of replication increases the credibility of any particular findings and meta-analyses of results from multiple experiments generate especially rigorous results (Lipsey and Wilson 2000).

Ten Common Criticisms of Experimental Designs for Evaluation

1. *Experiments Have Limited Applicability.* Experiments work for only quite specific, standardized, highly controlled and high-fidelity interventions, like an immunization or a standardized curriculum. A good example is an evaluation in 178 Kenyan schools conducted by researchers at MIT's Poverty Action Lab. Large, poster-sized flip charts were provided to one-half of the schools in classrooms covering science, mathematics, geography, and health. With 2 years of follow-up data, the evaluation concluded that the impact of flip charts on student test scores was nearly zero and statistically insignificant (Glewwe, Kremer, Moulin, and Zitzewitz 2004). Those skeptical of such narrow studies wonder why one would even conduct such a large-scale, expensive study to test the hypothesis that flip charts, by themselves, would raise test scores.

In the real world, program interventions are seldom as controlled and standardized as flip charts because staff adapts what they do to the needs of particular participants and changing circumstances, using multiple interventions together. Complex community interventions and programs that unfold over longer periods of time are especially hard to control and standardize during the experimental period. The simple, linear cause-effect models on which experimental designs are based cannot capture the complexities of complex, dynamic, nonlinear systems (see Chapter 10).

(Continued)

(Continued)

What if interventions that change only one thing at a time fail . . . *because* they change only one thing at a time? Then, the evaluators have defined out of evaluation consideration precisely the interventions most likely to have an impact. The multipronged, interactive, custom-tailored, evolving interventions that draw on many disciplines and systems to impact not only individuals but also neighborhoods, institutions, and systems are anathema to the traditional evaluator (Schorr 1998:144).

2. *Experiments Interfere with Adaptive Management and Continuous Improvement.* The requirement for standardization and control of the intervention can actually interfere with the program and reduce effectiveness because staff are constrained from adapting the intervention and individualizing the treatment. A rigorous experiment requires ensuring that the intervention has high fidelity (is rigorously implemented in a standardized manner), but this reduces flexibility and prohibits ongoing improvements in the program.

3. *The Black Box Critique.* RCTs may establish that an intervention caused an outcome but not *why* it did so. Moreover, unless there is very good implementation data about the intervention, the classic pre-post RCT may not be able to report details about what the intervention actually was, which severely limits interpreting the results. To understand how an intervention works, like, for example, international aid, evaluators have to "open the black box" (Bourguignon and Sundberg 2007).

4. *Failing to Learn from Natural Variation.* Within an intervention (or program), some people gain a lot, some a little, and some nothing. Because the primary (and often only) comparison is between the aggregate treatment group outcomes and the aggregate control group outcomes, significant within-group variation is not sufficiently analyzed and understood. What factors contribute to within-group variations? RCTs don't answer this question. Indeed, most experimental designs yield findings of no significant difference between the treatment and control, what Peter Rossi called "the iron law of evaluation" (Chen 2007; Rossi 1987). RCTs, by their very design, may fail to capture and understand important differences within the treatment group itself. With limited time and resources, as is always the case, which question would produce more useful results for policymaking and program improvement: (a) the RCT question that asks *how does the average outcome in the treatment group compare with the average outcome in the control group*, versus (b) the natural variation question that asks *what factors explain different levels of outcomes within the program and what are the implications of those different levels of outcome for setting policy and improving the program.*

5. *The Control Condition Is an Irrelevant Policy Option.* Comparing the costs and benefits of alternative interventions is typically more important to policymakers than a standard RCT design that compares a single intervention to a control group (no intervention). Doing nothing is seldom a policy option. Policymakers want data to choose among competing interventions or to establish the level at which an intervention must be implemented to achieve desired outcomes. Pragmatically, comparison of a treatment with a control is less interesting and meaningful because not doing anything is seldom the realistic policy alternative. This distinguishes the comparative method in program evaluation from RCTs (Scriven 1991b:112).

Moreover, finding meaningful control conditions for national programs such as Head Start can be especially problematic. One of evaluation's pioneers, Lois-ellin Datta, has thoughtfully reviewed the mandate by Congress to conduct a RCT of Head Start. Bringing her considerable experience and expertise to bear on this mandate, she concluded, "The randomized control design has no stronger proponent than me when the circumstances are appropriate. A primary reason that the design is inappropriate in the Head Start circumstance is that the control condition for the test is likely to be anything but that . . . For such situations, one perhaps thinks more of evaluation designs derived from sytems and complexity theories" (Datta 2007b:49–50).

6. *Limited Generalizability of Experimental Results.* RCTs aim for high "internal validity," that is, confidence that the outcome can be attributed to the intervention. To achieve this, RCTs control variation and extraneous factors. Controls are necessary to achieve a confident level of attribution and thereby make the specific results of a single RCT valid for that situation. *But those very same controls reduce the generalizability of the results.* The distinguished psychometrician and evaluation pioneer Lee J. Cronbach (1982) wrote an extensive treatise on the trade-offs between internal validity and external validity (generalizability) and concluded that policymakers are more often interested in extrapolating findings to other places than in ensuring the cause-effect relationship in one highly controlled setting. High internal validity typically reduces external validity, while designs that look at patterns across a number of variations can increase the likelihood of finding meaningful extrapolations. RCTs tend to pay little or no attention to contextual factors such as culture, societal context, and politics. Indeed, RCTs attempt to control for such factors through random assignment. But contextual factors are enormously important for understanding generalizability. Suppose one tests an HIV/AIDS education effort in one part of South Africa using an RCT. Would you have confidence that those results could be generalized to Niger? to Mexico? to China? Even to other parts of South Africa? Cronbach emphasized the importance of cumulative learning about the effectiveness of interventions as we go from one situation to the next, "refining our understanding as we go, as well as extrapolating what is learned in one setting to others."

Cronbach argued against using evaluation simply to answer the question, "Did this program cause the desired outcomes in participants?" both because the question is very difficult to answer in the diverse settings of the real world and because the question misses the point. The point being that because the program will look somewhat different in each context, evaluation should endeavor to understand in rich detail the challenges and the potentialities of a given social or educational intervention in this context and in that one and in that one over there, toward important insights into how to best address our persistent social problems" (Greene 2004:175).

7. *Randomization Is Artificial.* In the real world, people don't get into programs randomly. Self-selection, staff selection, and active recruitment, the bane of experimentalists, are the way participants get into real programs. Randomization reduces generalizability to real-world conditions. People tend to come to programs in social groups or to be selected through staff assessments that involve some degree of judgment. It is more useful to evaluate programs as they occur in the real world rather than under the artificial, nongeneralizable, and nonsustainable conditions of randomization. A related critique is that the behavior of participants in the treatment group may be affected by the experiment (Hawthorne effect) since double-blind experiments typically are not possible in program evaluation. It is also often quite difficult to keep people in the control and treatment groups from having contact. These issues don't mean that experiments can't be done, but they are not easy to administer, and the more controls introduced to make sure the experiment is well implemented, the more artificial the results may become.

8. *High Costs of Control Group Designs.* Designs involve cost-benefit calculations: What is the value of likely findings given the costs of getting those findings? For the high cost of getting data from a control group (which as Item 5 asserts is typically not a viable policy option, and as the previous item asserts, has limited generalizability), an evaluator could gather more in-depth data comparing implementation factors, contextual variables, variations in outcomes, and comparing various real intervention alternatives.

(Continued)

(Continued)

9. *Ethical Concerns.* Control groups involve withholding an intervention from those in need. This is usually justified because there aren't enough resources to serve all those in need and/or because the intervention is unproven so it's by no means certain that something of value is being withheld. Many creative solutions to ethical concerns have been developed, but ethical gray areas remain and it can be politically difficult to explain why a group of people in need is being randomly denied a service.

10. *The Experimental Goal Standard Creates Distorted Incentives in Making Methods Decisions.* The most basic wisdom in research and evaluation is that you begin by assessing the situation, figure out what information is needed, and determine the appropriate and relevant questions. The methods are then selected to answer those questions. However, when RCTs are treated as the *gold standard*, evaluators begin by asking, "How do I do an RCT?" This puts the method before the question. It also creates perverse incentives. For example, in some agencies, project managers are getting positive performance reviews and even bonuses for supporting and conducting RCTs. Under such incentive conditions, project managers will seek to do RCTs whether they are appropriate or not. No one wants to do a second-rate evaluation, but if RCTs are really the gold standard, anything else is second-rate. As distinguished evaluator Nick Smith (2007) has asked

When the federal government anoints a particular method as the gold standard for conducting evaluation, is it not likely that many other groups . . . may infer that alternative methods are thus inferior? Might this not result in the overgeneralization and inappropriate use of the gold standard method and diminished use of alternative approaches that may be more effective in those contexts? (p. 120).

This also leads to rushing into RCT designs before the program is ready. For example, a widely circulated and influential report from the Center for Global Development advocates RCTs for impact evaluation of international development aid. The report posits that RCTs "must be considered from the start—the design phase—rather than after the program has been operating for many years, when stakeholders may ask, "So what is the program really accomplishing?" (Evaluation Gap Working Group 2006:13). That sounds reasonable, but for an RCT to work, an intervention (a program) must be clearly identified, standardized, and carefully controlled. This means you would never begin a new effort, program, or innovation with an RCT. The most well substantiated finding in a quarter century of evaluation may be that new efforts need a period of time to work out bugs, overcome initial implementation problems, and stabilize the intervention. Not even drug studies begin with RCTs. They begin with basic efficacy studies and dosage studies to find out if there is initial evidence that the drug produces the desired outcome without unacceptable side effects. Only then are RCTs undertaken. Beginning new projects with RTC designs shows a fundamental lack of understanding about how programs unfold in the real world. It fails to understand the role of formative evaluation in getting ready for summative evaluation. It also increases the likelihood of finding no impact because the intervention wasn't yet ready for summative RCT testing.

Nor do RCTs work well for complex interventions, like comprehensive, multifaceted community initiatives. Carol Weiss (2002) has observed: "Random assignment has a spare beauty all its own, but the sprawling changeable world of community programs is inhospitable to it" (p. 222). In explaining why an alternative was needed to RCTs for such initiatives, Lisbeth Schorr (1998) wrote

The new approaches to the evaluation of complex interventions share at least four attributes: They are built on a strong theoretical and conceptual base, emphasize shared interests rather than adversarial relationships between evaluators and program people, employ multiple methods and perspectives, and offer both rigor and relevance. (P. 147) of the army imagined and prayed to a dragon that looked like a warrior. The merchant thought that a dragon would appear rich and splendid, as he was. The chief workman was convinced that a dragon would be tough and strong. The wise man conceived of the dragon as "the wisest of all creatures," which meant it must look like a wise man. In the midst of the crisis, a small fat man with long beard and bald head arrived and announced that he was the Great Cloud Dragon. The Mandarin and his advisers ridiculed the old man and dismissed him rudely. Only because of Han's kindness did the old man save the city, transforming himself into a magnificent dragon the color of sunset shining through rain, scales scattering the light, claws and teeth glittering like diamonds, beautiful and frightening at the same time, and most important, beyond any possibility of preconception because the dragon was beyond prior human experience. But only Han saw the dragon, because only he was open to seeing it (Williams 1976).

Qualitative researchers prefer to describe themselves as open rather than subjective. They enter a setting without prejudgment, including no preconceived hypotheses to test. Scriven (1991b) has defined objectivity as being "unbiased or unprejudiced," literally, not having "prejudged." This definition

> misleads people into thinking that anyone who comes into a discussion with strong views about an issue can't be unprejudiced. The key question is whether the views are justified. The fact that we all have strong views about the sexual abuse of small children and the importance of education does not show prejudice, only rationality. (P. 248)

The debate about objectivity versus subjectivity includes different assumptions about whether it is possible for us to view the complexities of the real world without

somehow filtering and simplifying those complexities. The qualitative assumption is that, at even the most basic level of sensory data, we are always dealing with perceptions, not "facts" in some absolute sense. "The very categories of things which comprise the 'facts' are theory dependent" (Petrie 1972:49) or, in this case, paradigm dependent. It was this recognition that led the distinguished qualitative sociologist Howard Becker (1970) to argue that "the question is not whether we should take sides, since we inevitably will, but rather whose side we are on" (p. 15).

Distinguished evaluation theorist and methodologist Robert Stake (2004) answered this question in an important article on advocacies in evaluation (see sidebar). He began by noting that we often care about the thing being evaluated—*and should care.* We don't have to pretend neutrality about the problems programs are attacking to do fair, balanced, and neutral evaluations of those programs. Who wants an uncaring evaluator who professes neutrality about homelessness, hunger, child abuse, community violence, or HIV/AIDS? My younger brother died of AIDS early in the epidemic. My entire family has been involved actively in AIDS Walks and other activities. When I am engaged with HIV/AIDS monitoring and evaluation systems (Patton 2004), I do not pretend neutrality. I want to see prevention programs work. That means I am motivated to hold staff feet to the fire of evaluation to assure that the program works—because I know from personal experience that lives are at risk.

As a utilization-focused evaluator, I find it helpful to replace the traditional scientific search for objective truth with a search for useful and balanced information. For the classic mandate to be objective, I substitute the mandate to be fair and conscientious in taking account of multiple perspectives,

Beyond Neutrality: What Evaluators Care About

1. We often care about the thing being evaluated.

2. We, as evaluation professionals, care about evaluation.

3. We advocate rationality.

4. We care to be heard. We are troubled if our studies are not used.

5. We are distressed by underprivilege. We see gaps among privileged patrons and managers and staff and underprivileged participants and communities.

6. We are advocates of a democratic society.

SOURCE: Robert Stake (2004:103–107).

multiple interests, and multiple realities. The Program Evaluation Standards reflect this change in emphasis:

Propriety Standard on Complete and Fair Assessment: The evaluation should be complete and fair in its examination and recording of strengths and weaknesses of the program being evaluated, so that strengths can be built on and problem areas addressed (Joint Committee 1994:P5).

Accuracy Standard on Impartial Reporting: Reporting procedures should guard against distortion caused by personal feelings and biases for any party to the evaluation, so that evaluation reports fairly reflect the evaluation findings (Joint Committee 1994:A11).

Words such as fairness, neutrality, and impartiality carry less baggage than objectivity and subjectivity. To stay out of arguments about objectivity, I talk with intended users about balance, fairness, and being explicit about what perspectives, values, and priorities have shaped the evaluation, both the design and findings. Others choose to use the term *objective* because of its political power. At the national policy level, former AEA President Eleanor Chelimsky recommended

Although all of us realize that we can never be entirely objective, that is hardly an excuse for skewed samples, or grandiloquent conclusions or generalizations that go beyond the evaluator's data, or for any of 101 indications to a careful reader that a particular result is more desired than documented.

There are, in fact, a great many things that we can do to foster objectivity and its appearance, not just technically, in the steps we take to make and explain our evaluative decisions, but also intellectually, in the effort we put forth to look at all sides and all stakeholders of an evaluations. (1995a:219)

The Continuum of Distance from versus Closeness to the Program

Here are the opposing paradigm positions: Too much closeness may compromise objectivity. Too much distance may diminish insight and understanding.

Quantitative researchers depend on distance to guarantee neutrality and academic integrity. Scholarly comportment connotes calm and detached analysis without personal involvement or emotion. The qualitative paradigm, in contrast, assumes that without empathy and sympathetic introspection derived from direct experience, one cannot fully understand a program. Understanding comes from trying to put oneself in the other person's shoes, thereby discerning how others think, act, and feel. Methodologically, this means getting close to the action, observing people in the realities of program life, and attending to detail by observing program participants over time.

Qualitative evaluators strive to capture participants' experiences in their own terms, learn how they think about and experience the program. In the Shapiro study of FT open classrooms, her presence in classrooms over an extended period of time and her closeness to the children allowed her to see things that were not captured by standardized tests. She could see what they were learning. She could feel their tension in the testing situation and their spontaneity in the more natural classroom setting. Had she worked solely with data collected by others or only at a distance, she would never have discovered the crucial differences she uncovered between FT and non-FT classrooms—differences that allowed her to evaluate the innovative program in a meaningful and relevant way.

In a similar vein, one evaluator in our utilization of federal health evaluations expressed frustration at trying to make sense out of data from more than 80 projects when site visit funds were cut out of the evaluation: "There's no way to understand something that's just data, you know. You have to go look" [EV111:3]. Qualitative methodologist John Lofland (1971) concluded likewise,

> In everyday life, statistical sociologists, like everyone else, assume that they do not know or understand very well people they do not see or associate with very much. They assume that knowing and understanding other people require that one see them reasonably often and in a variety of situations relative to a variety of issues. Moreover, statistical sociologists, like other people, assume that in order to know or understand

others, one is well-advised to give some conscious attention to that effort in face-to-face contacts. They assume, too, that the internal world of sociology—or any other social world—is not understandable unless one has been part of it in a face-to-face fashion for quite a period of time. How utterly paradoxical, then, for these same persons to turn around and make, by implication, precisely the opposite claim about people they have never encountered face-to-face—those people appearing as numbers in their tables and as correlations in their matrices! (P. 3)

It is instructive to remember that many major contributions to our understanding of the world have come from scientists' personal experiences—Piaget's closeness to his children, Freud's proximity to and empathy with his patients, Darwin's closeness to nature, and even Newton's intimate encounter with an apple.

On the other hand, closeness is not the only way to understand human behavior. For certain questions and for situations involving large groups, distance is inevitable. But, where possible, face-to-face interaction can deepen insight, especially in program evaluation. This returns us to the recurrent themes of using mixed methods and matching evaluation methods to intended use by intended users.

The issue of distance from versus closeness to the program supersedes methods in that it concerns the basic relationship between evaluators and those being evaluated, which affects how evaluations are used. VanLandingham (2007) has contended that, in the U.S. federal government, too much independence "can restrict evaluators' role to that of a voice crying in the wilderness rather than speaking truth to power" (p. 25). In a similar vein, experienced auditors Perry, Thomas, DuBois, and McGowan (2007) presented a case study involving county jails in which they concluded that "the traditional focus on ensuring independence has led agencies conducting legislative audits to avoid utilization-focused strategies and overlook the benefits of engaging stakeholders" (p. 69). They found that they could conduct a utilization-focused evaluation that

> not only provided independently verified information and analysis of current jail operations and costs, but also developed objective tools that proved useful for prospective analysis by stakeholders. . . . Working closely with agency management and developing tools and methodologies for their future use did not compromise the independence of the auditing function. (P. 76)

Of Variables and Wholes

The quantitative/experimental paradigm operationalizes independent and dependent variables, then measures their relationships statistically. Outcomes must be identified and measured as specific variables. Treatments and programs must also be conceptualized as discrete, independent variables. Program participants are also described along standardized, quantified dimensions. Sometimes a program's goals are measured directly, for example, student achievement test scores, recidivism statistics for a group of juvenile delinquents, or sobriety rates for participants in chemical dependency treatment programs. Evaluation measures can also be indicators of a larger construct, for example, "community well-being" as a general construct measured by indicators such as crime rates, fetal deaths, divorce, unemployment, suicide, and poverty.

Adherents of the qualitative paradigm argue that the variables-based approach (1) oversimplifies the interconnected complexities of real-world experiences, (2) misses major factors of importance that are not easily quantified, and (3) fails to capture a sense of the program and its impacts as a "whole." The qualitative/naturalistic paradigm strives to be holistic in orientation. It assumes that the whole is greater than the sum of its parts; that the parts cannot be understood without a sense of the whole; and that a description and understanding of a program's context is essential to an understanding of program processes and outcomes. This, of course, follows the wisdom of the fable about the blind children and the elephant. As long as each felt only a part— a fanlike ear, the ropelike tail, a treelike leg, the snakelike trunk—they could not make sense of the whole elephant. The qualitative, systems-oriented paradigm goes even further. Unless they could see the elephant at home in the African wilderness, they would not understand the elephant's ears, legs, trunk, and skin in relation to how the elephant has evolved in the context of its ecological niche.

Philosopher and educator John Dewey (1956) advocated a holistic approach to both teaching and research, if one was to reach into and understand the world of the child.

> The child's life is an integral, a total one. He passes quickly and readily from one topic to another, as from one spot to another, but is not conscious of transition or break. There is no conscious isolation, hardly conscious distinction. The things that occupy him are held together by the unity of the personal and social interests which his life carries along. . . . [His] universe is fluid and fluent; its contents dissolve and re-form with amazing rapidity. But after all, it is the child's own world. It has the unity and completeness of his own life. (Pp. 5–6)

Again, Shapiro's (1973) work in evaluating innovative FT classrooms is instructive. She found that test results could not be interpreted without understanding the larger cultural and institutional context in which the individual child was situated. Nor is this only true for children. Beyer and Gillmore (2007) have made the case for more holistic, longitudinal, and multi-dimensional assessment of student learning in higher education because "simplistic measures aren't enough" (p. 43). Years ago Deutscher (1970) cautioned that despite our personal experience as living, working human beings, we have focused in our research on parts to the virtual exclusion of wholes:

> We knew that human behavior was rarely if ever directly influenced or explained by an isolated variable; we knew that it was impossible to assume that any set of such variables was additive (with or without weighting); we knew that the complex mathematics of the interaction among any set of variables was incomprehensible to us. In effect, although we knew they did not exist, we defined them into being. (P. 33)

Although most scientists would view this radical critique of variable analysis as too extreme, I find that teachers and practitioners often voice the same criticisms. Innovative teachers complain that experimental results lack relevance for them because they have to deal with the whole in their classrooms; they can't manipulate just a couple of factors in isolation from everything else going on. The reaction of many program staff to scientific research is like the reaction of Copernicus to the astronomers of his day: "With them," he observed,

> it is as though an artist were to gather the hands, feet, head, and other members for his images from diverse models, each part excellently drawn, but not related to a single body, and since they in no way match each other, the results would be monster rather than man. (Quoted in Kuhn 1970:83)

How many program staff have complained of the evaluation research monster?

Yet it is no simple task to undertake holistic evaluation, to search for the gestalt in programs. The challenge for the participant observer is "to seek the essence of the life of the observed, to sum up, to find a central unifying principle" (Bruyn 1966:316).

The advantages of using variables and indicators are parsimony, precision, and ease of analysis. Where key program elements can be quantified with validity, reliability, and credibility (with appropriate statistical analysis and independence of measurement), statistical portrayals can be quite powerful and succinct. The advantage of in-depth case studies and qualitative portrayals of holistic settings and impacts is that attention can be given to nuance, setting, interdependencies, complexities, idiosyncrasies, and context. In combination, the two approaches can be powerful and comprehensive; they can also be contradictory and divisive.

Two Views of Change

The paradigms debate is in part about how best to understand and study change. The quantitative/experimental paradigm typically involves gathering data at two points in time, pretest and posttest, then comparing the treatment group with the control group statistically. Ideally, participants are assigned to treatment and control groups randomly, or, less ideally, are matched on critical background variables. Such designs assume an identifiable, coherent, and consistent treatment. Moreover, they assume that, once introduced, the treatment remains relatively constant and unchanging. In some designs, time series data are gathered at several predetermined points rather than just at pretest and posttest. The purpose of these designs is to determine the extent to which the program (treatment) accounts for measurable changes in participants to make a summative decision about the value and effectiveness of the program in producing desired change (Lipsey 1990; Boruch and Rindskopf 1984; Mark and Cook 1984).

In contrast, the qualitative/naturalistic paradigm conceives programs as dynamic and ever developing, with "treatments" changing in subtle but important ways as staff members learn, as clients move in and out, and as conditions of delivery are altered. Qualitative/naturalistic evaluators seek to describe these dynamic program processes and understand their holistic effects on participants. Thus, part of the paradigms debate has been about the relative utility, desirability, and possibility of understanding programs from these quite different perspectives for different purposes.

The quantitative/experimental/summative approach is most relevant for fairly established programs with stable, consistent, and identifiable treatments and clearly quantifiable outcomes, in which a major decision is to be made about the effectiveness of one treatment in comparison with another (or no) treatment.

The qualitative/naturalistic/formative approach is especially appropriate for developing, innovating, or changing programs in which the focus is improving the program, facilitating more effective implementation, and exploring a variety of effects on participants. This can be particularly important early in the life of a program or at major points of transition. As an innovation or program change is implemented, it frequently unfolds in a manner quite different from what was planned or conceptualized in a proposal. Once in operation, innovative programs are often changed as practitioners learn what works and what does not, and as

they experiment, grow, and change their priorities. Developmental evaluation, which tracks incremental changes and forks-in-the-road over time, takes a dynamic view of programs.

Changing developmental programs can frustrate evaluators whose design approach depends on specifiable unchanging treatments to relate to specifiable predetermined outcomes. Evaluators have been known to do everything in their power to stop program adaptation and improvement so as to maintain the rigor of their research design. The deleterious effect this may have on the program itself, discouraging as it does new developments and redefinitions in midstream, is considered a small sacrifice made in pursuit of higher-level scientific knowledge. But there is a distinct possibility that such artificial evaluation constraints will contaminate the program treatment by affecting staff morale and participant response.

Were some science of planning and policy or program development so highly evolved that initial proposals were perfect, one might be able to sympathize with these evaluators' desire to keep the initial program implementation intact. In the real world, however, people and unforeseen circumstances shape programs, and initial implementations are modified in ways that are rarely trivial.

Under conditions in which programs are subject to change and redirection, the naturalistic evaluation paradigm replaces the static underpinnings of the experimental paradigm with a dynamic orientation. A dynamic evaluation is not tied to a single treatment or to predetermined outcomes but rather focuses on the actual operations of a program over a period of time, taking as given the complexity of a changing reality and variations in participants' experiences over the course of program participation.

Again, the issue is one of matching the evaluation design to the program, of meshing evaluation methods with decision-maker information needs. The point of contrasting fixed experimental designs with dynamic process designs in the paradigms debate is to release evaluators "from unwitting captivity to a format of inquiry that is taken for granted as the naturally proper way in which to conduct scientific inquiry" (Blumer 1969:47).

Nowhere is this unwitting captivity better illustrated than in those agencies that insist, in the name of science, that all evaluations must employ experimental designs. Two examples will illustrate this problem. In Minnesota, the Governor's Commission on Crime Prevention and Control required experimental evaluation designs of all funded projects. A small Native American alternative school was granted funds to run an innovative crime prevention project with parents and students. The program was highly flexible; participation was irregular and based on self-selection. The program was designed to be sensitive to Native American culture and values. It would have been a perfect situation for formative responsive evaluation. Instead, program staff was forced to create the illusion of an experimental pretest and posttest design. The evaluation design interfered with the program, alienated staff, wasted resources, and collected worthless information, unrelated to evolving program operations, under the guise of maintaining scientific consistency. The evaluators refused to alter or adapt the design and data collection in the face of a program dramatically different from the preconceptions on which they had based the design.

The second example is quite similar but concerns the Minnesota Department of Education. The state monitor for an innovative arts program in a free school for at-risk students insisted on quantitative, standardized test measures collected in pretest and posttest situations; a control group was also required. The arts program was being tried out in a free school as an attempt to integrate art and basic skills. Students were self-selected and participation was irregular; the program had multiple goals, all of them vague; even the target population was fuzzy; and the treatment depended on who was in attendance on a given day. The free school was a highly fluid environment for which nothing close to a reasonable control or comparison group existed. The teaching approach was highly individualized, with students designing much of their program of study. Both staff and students resented the imposition of rigid, standardized criteria that gave the appearance of a structure that was not there. Yet the Department of Education insisted on a static, hypothetico-deductive evaluation approach because "it's departmental evaluation policy."

On the other hand, the direction of the design error is not always the imposition of overly rigid experimental formats. Boruch (2007), Cook (2006), and Campbell and Boruch (1975) have shown that many evaluations suffer from an underutilization of experimental designs, which may do a disservice to a program by underestimating outcomes and removing uncertainty about attribution. Eminent evaluation methodologist Peter Rossi emphasized that rigorous experimental designs increased credibility by permitting replication; because statistical tools can be implemented in systematic ways, it is

> both possible and desirable for any quantitative analysis to be replicated. Two randomized experiments undertaken with subjects from the same population and using the same protocols should arrive at the same results, save for a bit of noise. If

one program evaluator analyzed the data set, it should be possible for another program evaluator to retrace the steps undertaken and arrive at the same results. The threat of replication helped keep all parties honest and, when results were reproduced, helped bolster the credibility of any findings. (Berk 2007:204)

Matching methods to programs and decision-maker needs is a creative process that emerges from a thorough knowledge of the organizational dynamics and information uncertainties of a particular context. Regulations to the effect that all evaluations must be of a certain type serve neither the cause of increased scientific knowledge nor that of greater program effectiveness, which was the central message of the AEA statement on experimental designs discussed earlier in this chapter (see Exhibit 12.2). Julnes and Rog (2007) edited an important volume of *New Directions for Evaluation* on "Informing Federal Policies on Evaluation Methodology: Building the Evidence Base for Method Choice in Government Sponsored Evaluation." It provides important insights into how the paradigms debate translates into practical issues of "actionable evidence" (pp. 4–5).

Alternative Sampling Logics

The quantitative paradigm employs random samples sufficient in size to permit valid generalizations and appropriate tests of statistical significance. Qualitative inquiry involves small "purposeful samples" of information-rich cases (Patton 2002a:230–47). Differences in logic, assumptions, and purposes distinguish these sampling strategies. When the evaluation is aimed at generalization, some form of random probabilistic sampling is the design of choice. A needs assessment, for example, aimed at determining how many residents in a county have some particular problem would be strongest if based on a random sample of county residents.

Case studies, on the other hand, become particularly useful when intended users need to understand a problem, situation, or program in great depth, and they can identify cases rich in needed information—"rich" in the sense that a great deal can be learned from a few exemplars of the phenomenon of interest. For example, much can be learned about how to improve a program by studying dropouts or successes *within the context* of a particular program. Case studies are context specific.

But what about generalizations? Paradigm differences emerge in the relative value attached to generalizing.

Cronbach (1975) observed that generalizations decay over time; that is, they have a half-life much like radioactive materials. Guba and Lincoln (1981) were particularly critical of the dependence on generalizations in quantitative methods because, they asked, "What can a generalization be except an assertion that is context free? . . . [Yet] *it is virtually impossible to imagine any human behavior that is not heavily mediated by the context in which it occurs*" (p. 62).

Cronbach and colleagues in the Stanford Evaluation Consortium (1980) offered a middle ground in the paradigms debate with regard to the problem of generalizability and the relevance of evaluations. They criticized experimental designs that were so focused on controlling cause and effect that the results were largely irrelevant beyond the experimental situation. On the other hand, they were equally concerned that entirely idiosyncratic case studies yield little of use beyond the case study setting. They suggested, instead, that designs balance depth and breadth, realism and control, so as to permit reasonable *extrapolation* (pp. 231–35).

Unlike the usual meaning of the term *generalization,* an *extrapolation* connotes that one has gone beyond the narrow confines of the data to think about other applications of the findings. Extrapolations are modest speculations on the likely applicability of findings to other situations under similar, but not identical, conditions. Extrapolations are logical, thoughtful, and problem oriented rather than purely empirical, statistical, and probabilistic. Evaluation users often expect evaluators to thoughtfully extrapolate from their findings in the sense of pointing out lessons learned and potential applications to future efforts.

Designs that combine probabilistic and purposeful sampling (mixed methods designs) have the advantage of extrapolations supported by quantitative and qualitative data. Larger samples of statistically meaningful data can address questions of incidence and prevalence (generalizations to a known population), while case studies add depth and detail to make interpretations more meaningful and grounded. Such designs can also introduce a balance between concerns about individualization and standardization, the distinction in the next section.

Standardization or Diversity: Different Emphases

The quantitative paradigm requires the variety of human experience to be captured along standardized scales. Individuals and groups are described as exhibiting more or less of some trait (self-esteem, satisfaction, competence, knowledge), but everyone is rated or ranked on a limited set of predetermined dimensions. Statistical analyses of these dimensions present central tendencies (averages and deviations from those averages). Critics of standardized instrumentation and measurement are concerned that such an approach only captures quantitative

differences thereby missing significant qualitative differences and important idiosyncrasies. Critics of statistics are fond of telling about the person who drowned in a creek with an average depth of 6 inches; what was needed was some in-depth information about the 6-foot pool in the middle of the creek.

The qualitative paradigm pays particular attention to uniqueness, whether this be an individual's uniqueness or the uniqueness of a program, community, home, or other unit of analysis. When comparing programs, the qualitative evaluator begins by trying to capture the unique, holistic character of each program with special attention to context and setting. Patterns across individuals or programs are sought only after the uniqueness of each case has been described.

For program staff in innovative programs aimed at individualizing treatments, the central issue is how to identify and deal with individual differences among participants. Where the emphasis is on individualization of teaching or on meeting the needs of individual clients in social action programs, an evaluation strategy of case studies is needed that focuses on the individual, one that is sensitive both to unique characteristics in people and programs and to similarities among people and commonalities across treatments. Case studies can and do accumulate. Anthropologists have built up an invaluable wealth of case study data that includes both idiosyncratic information and patterns of culture (Human Relations Area Files 2007).

Using both quantitative and qualitative approaches can permit the evaluator to address questions about quantitative differences on standardized variables and qualitative differences reflecting individuals and program uniquenesses. The more a program aims at individualized outcomes, the greater the appropriateness of qualitative methods. The more a program emphasizes common outcomes for all participants, the greater the appropriateness of standardized measures of performance and change.

Whither the Evaluation Methods Paradigms Debate?

Evaluation is much too important to be left to the methodologists.

—Halcolm

Early in the development of evaluation, the paradigms debate became characterized and labeled as the *qualitative-quantitative debate*. Overall, in the last quarter century, evaluation has become more methodologically eclectic with an increased emphasis on methodological appropriateness—matching the data collection and design to the nature of the evaluation situation and questions, and the information priorities of primary stakeholders. This makes *methodological pluralism and appropriateness the new gold standard* (e.g., Lawrenz and Huffman 2006). This is even true of advocates of experimental designs, who focus their advocacy primarily on summative evaluations for attributing impact, recognizing that other kinds of evaluation (e.g., formative and developmental) benefit from other methods. Many evaluation theorists and methodologists have worked to resolve conflict as an artist might, creating swirls and strokes to connect ideas and approaches where there was once the void of misunderstanding and mistrust. Eight trends support and illuminate this movement toward methodological appropriateness as the true gold standard for evaluation as posited in Exhibit 12.7.

EXHIBIT 12.7

Gold Standard Question Revisited: Methodological Appropriateness Trumps Experimental Design Orthodoxy

This chapter opened by observing that the *gold standard question in evaluation* is whether one particular method—*randomized control experiments*—should be held up as the best design for conducting impact evaluations and, by being best, should be the standard of excellence toward which evaluators should aspire and against which the quality of evaluation methods are judged. Do randomized control experiments merit the Olympic gold medal for evaluation? That is at the center of the methodological paradigms debate today.

The Utilization-Focused Evaluation Gold Standard Is *Methodological Appropriateness*

Methodological appropriateness means matching the evaluation design to the evaluation situation taking into account the priority questions and intended uses of primary intended users, the costs and benefits of alternative designs, the decisions that are to be made, the level of evidence necessary to support those decisions, ethical considerations, and utility. No design should be lauded as a gold standard without regard to context and situation. To do so is to create incentives to do randomized control experiments regardless of their appropriateness or meaningfulness.

1. *Evaluation has matured as a genuinely interdisciplinary and multimethod field of professional practice.* A balanced approach to methods has become commonplace with increasing emphasis on using mixed methods whenever possible to overcome the inherent and inevitable weaknesses and limitations of any single method. Methodological tolerance, flexibility, and concern for appropriateness rather than orthodoxy now characterize the practice, literature, and discussions of evaluation as evidenced by the AEA statement in Exhibit 12.1. The sense of tolerance and emphasis on appropriateness are nicely captured in the title of the volume of *New Directions for Evaluation* edited by Julnes and Rog (2007): "Informing Federal Policies on Evaluation Methodology: Building the Evidence Base for Method Choice in Government Sponsored Evaluation." Note the emphasis on *choice*. In their introduction, they emphasize that different kinds of evidence can inform different kinds of actions.

2. *Increasing attention to evaluation use has contributed to this methodological diversity.* When the utilization crisis emerged in the 1960s, two major recommendations for solving the problem were offered. The first focused on upgrading methodological rigor to increase the accuracy, reliability, and validity of evaluation data, and thereby increasing use. The second set of recommendations focused on evaluation processes: increasing attention to stakeholder needs, acting with greater political savvy, championing findings among intended users, and matching methods to questions. Methodological rigor alone has not proven an effective strategy for increasing use. Direct attention to issues of use, as in utilization-focused evaluation, has proven effective. High-quality evaluations manifest both technical adequacy and utility.

3. *Professional standards adopted by evaluation associations around the world have emphasized methodological appropriateness rather than paradigm orthodoxy.* These standards (e.g., Stufflebeam 2007) provide criteria in addition to methodological quality for judging the excellence of evaluations. This has made it possible to employ a variety of methods and still do an evaluation judged of high quality.

4. *Attention to general evaluation competencies and the accumulation of practical evaluation experience during the last two decades has reduced paradigms polarization.* The practical experience of evaluators working to improve program effectiveness has led them to become pragmatic in their approaches to methods issues. In that *pragmatism* (Morgan 2007) has emerged a commitment to do what works rather than a commitment to methodological rigor as an end in itself. This also means having more than methodological competence. The important and influential work of King et al. (2001) on a "Taxonomy of Essential Program Evaluator Competencies" shows that professional evaluators not only need "Systematic Inquiry" skills (which include knowledge of quantitative, qualitative, and mixed methods) but also skills in Professional Practice, Situational Analysis, Project Management, Reflective Practice, and Interpersonal Competence (e.g., communication skills).

5. *The strengths and weaknesses of both quantitative/experimental methods and qualitative/naturalistic methods are now better understood.* In the original debate, quantitative methodologists tended to attack some of the worst examples of qualitative evaluations while the qualitative evaluators tended to hold up for critique the worst examples of quantitative/experimental

approaches. With exemplars of both qualitative and quantitative evaluations, analyses of the strengths and weaknesses of each, and experience in how to combine methods, the meaning and utility of methodological appropriateness has become clearer.

6. *Advances in methodological sophistication and diversity within both paradigms, and in mixed methods, have strengthened diverse applications to evaluation problems.* The proliferation of books and journals in evaluation, including but not limited to methods contributions, has converted the field into a rich mosaic that cannot be reduced to quantitative versus qualitative in primary orientation. This is especially true of qualitative methods, which had more catching up to do, in which a great deal of important work has been published addressing questions of validity, reliability, and systematic analysis (Stake 2005; Patton 2002a; Yin 2002; Denzin and Lincoln 2000). The paradigms debate, in part, increased the amount of qualitative and mixed methods work being done, created additional opportunities for training in qualitative methods, and brought attention by methodologists to problems of increasing the quality of qualitative data and mixed methods designs. As the quality of qualitative methods has increased and the utility of qualitative approaches has been demonstrated, the attacks on qualitative methods have become both less strident and less common. The same can be said of developments in quantitative/experimental methods, as methodologists have focused on fine-tuning and adapting social science methods to a variety of evaluation and public policy situations (Patton 2008; Scriven 2008; Julnes and Rog 2007; Mohan and Sullivan 2007; Hudley and Parker 2006; Durland and Fredericks 2005; Braverman et al. 2004; Greene and Caracelli 1997; Sechrest and

Scott 1993; Smith 1992; Lipsey 1990; and Trochim 1986). Lipsey (1988), whose quantitative/experimental credentials are impeccable, epitomized the emergent commitment to matching methods to problems and situations when he concluded

Much less evaluation research in the quantitative-comparative mode should be done. Though it is difficult to ignore the attractiveness of assessing treatment effects via formal measurement and controlled design, it is increasingly clear that doing research of this sort well is quite difficult and should be undertaken only under methodologically favorable circumstances, and only then with extensive prior pilot-testing regarding measures, treatment theory, and so forth. The field of evaluation research and the individual treatments evaluated would generally be better served by a thorough descriptive, perhaps qualitative, study as a basis for forming better concepts about treatment, or a good management information system that provides feedback for program improvement, or a variety of other approaches rather than by a superficially impressive but largely invalid experimental study. (Pp. 22–23)

7. *Support for methodological eclecticism from major figures and institutions in evaluation has increased methodological tolerance.* Early in this chapter, I noted that when eminent measurement and methods scholars such as Donald Campbell and Lee J. Cronbach, their commitment to rigor never being in doubt, began publicly recognizing the contributions that qualitative methods could make, the acceptability of qualitative/naturalistic approaches was greatly enhanced. Another important endorsement of multiple methods came from the Program Evaluation and Methodology Division of the United States General Accounting Office (GAO), which arguably did the most important and influential evaluation work at the national level (until it was disbanded in 1996). Under the

leadership of Assistant Comptroller General and Former AEA President (1995) Eleanor Chelimsky, GAO published a series of methods manuals, including *Quantitative Data Analysis* (GAO 1992d), *Case Study Evaluations* (GAO 1990a), *Prospective Evaluation Methods* (GAO 1990b), and *The Evaluation Synthesis* (GAO 1992c). The GAO manual on *Designing Evaluations* (1991) puts the paradigms debate to rest as it describes what constitutes a strong evaluation. Strength is not judged by adherence to a particular paradigm. It is determined by use and technical adequacy, whatever the method, within the context of purpose, time, and resources.

Strong Evaluations

Strong evaluations employ methods of analysis that are appropriate to the question; support the answer with evidence; document the assumptions, procedures, and modes of analysis; and rule out the competing evidence. Strong studies pose questions clearly, address them appropriately, and draw inferences commensurate with the power of the design and the availability, validity, and reliability of the data. Strength should not be equated with complexity. Nor should strength be equated with the degree of statistical manipulation of data. Neither infatuation with complexity nor statistical incantation makes an evaluation stronger.

The strength of an evaluation is not defined by a particular method. Longitudinal, experimental, quasi-experimental, before-and-after, and case study evaluations can be either strong or weak. . . . That is, the strength of an evaluation has to be judged within the context of the question, the time and cost constraints, the design, the technical adequacy of the data collection and analysis, and the presentation of the findings. A strong study is technically adequate and useful—in short, it is high in quality.

SOURCE: From *Designing Evaluations*, Government Accountability Office (1991:15–16).

---

8. *Evaluation professional societies have supported exchanges of views and high-quality professional practice in an environment of tolerance and eclecticism.* The evaluation professional societies and journals serve a variety of people from different disciplines who operate in different kinds of organizations at different levels, in and out of the public sector, and in and out of universities. This diversity, and opportunities to exchange views and perspectives, has contributed to the emergent pragmatism, eclecticism, and tolerance in the field. A good example is the volume of New Directions for Program Evaluation on "The Qualitative-Quantitative Debate: New Perspectives" (Reichardt and Rallis 1994a). The tone of the eight distinguished contributions in that volume is captured by phrases such as "peaceful coexistence," "each tradition can learn from the other," "compromise solution," "important shared characteristics," and "a call for a new partnership" (Datta 1994; Reichardt and Rallis 1994b, 1994c; Rossi 1994; Yin 1994). That volume also emphasized mixed methods and included these themes: "blended approaches," "integrating the qualitative and quantitative," "possibilities for integration," "qualitative plus quantitative," and "working together" (Datta 1994; Hedrick 1994; House 1994; Reichardt and Rallis 1994c; Smith 1994; see also Mark and Shotland 1987).

Pragmatism Ascendant

Over the years of the debate, the philosophical paradigms debate that focuses on fundamental differences in epistemology and ontology has been distinguished from the more narrow methodological paradigms debate. For example, Guba and Lincoln (1981) have argued that the experimentalist (scientific) and naturalistic paradigms contain incompatible assumptions about the inquirer/subject relationship and the nature of truth. The experimental/scientific paradigm assumes that reality is "singular, convergent, and fragmentable," while the naturalistic paradigm holds a view of reality that is "multiple, divergent, and inter-related" (Guba and Lincoln 1981:57). These opposite assumptions are not about methods alternatives; they are fundamental assumptions about the nature of reality. Pragmatically, an evaluator can conduct interviews and observations under either set of assumptions—and the data will stand on their own. Let me illustrate.

An evaluator is working with a group of educators, some of whom are "progressive, open education" adherents and some of whom are "back-to-basics" fundamentalists. The open education group wants to frame the evaluation of a particular program within a qualitative/naturalistic framework. The basic skills people want a rigorous, quantitative/experimental approach. Must the evaluator make an either/or choice to frame the evaluation within either one or the other paradigm? Must an either/or choice be made about the kind of data to be collected? Are the views of each group so incompatible that each must have its own evaluation?

I've been in precisely this situation a number of times. I do not try to resolve their paradigms debate but, rather, to inform their dialogue. I try to establish an environment of tolerance and respect for different, competing viewpoints, and then focus the discussion on the actual information that is needed by each group: Test scores? Interviews? Observations? The design and measures must be negotiated. Multiple methods and multiple measures will give each group some of what they want. The naturalistic paradigm educators will want to be sure that test scores are interpreted within a larger context of classroom activities, observations, and outcomes. The quantitative paradigm educators will likely use interview and observational data as background to explain and justify test score interpretations. My experience suggests that both groups can agree on an evaluation design that includes multiple types of data and that each group will ultimately pay attention to and use "the other group's data." In short, a particular group of people can arrive at agreement on an evaluation design that includes both qualitative and quantitative data without resolving ultimate paradigmatic issues (e.g., whether reality is absolute or socially constructed). Such agreement is not likely, however, if the evaluator begins with the premise that the paradigms are incompatible and that the evaluation must be conducted within the framework of either one or the other.

Perhaps an analogy will help here. A sensitive, practical evaluator can work with a group to design a meaningful evaluation that integrates concerns from both paradigms in the same way that a skillful teacher can work with a group of Buddhists, Christians, Jews, and Muslims on issues of common empirical concern without resolving which religion has the "correct" worldview.

Another example is an agricultural project in the Caribbean that included social scientists and government officials of varying political persuasions. Despite their fundamental policy and philosophical differences,

the Marxist and Keynesian economists and sociologists had little difficulty agreeing on what data were needed to understand agricultural extension needs in each country. Their interpretations of those data also differed less than I expected.

Thus, the point I'm making about the paradigms debate extends beyond methodological issues to embrace a host of potential theoretical, philosophical, religious, and political perspectives that can separate the participants in an evaluation process. I am arguing that, from a practical perspective, the evaluator need not even attempt to resolve such differences. By focusing on and negotiating data collection alternatives in an atmosphere of respect and tolerance, the participants can come together around a commitment to an empirical perspective, that is, bringing data to bear on important program issues. As long as the empirical commitment is there, the other differences can be negotiated in most instances. This is what David Morgan (2007) has called "Paradigms Lost and Pragmatism Regained."

Debating paradigms with one's clients, and taking sides in that debate, is different from debating one's colleagues about the nature of reality. I doubt that evaluators will ever reach consensus on the ultimate nature of reality. But the methodological paradigms debate can go on among evaluators without paralyzing the practice of practical evaluators who are trying to work responsively with primary stakeholders to get answers to relevant empirical questions. The belief that evaluators must be true to only one paradigm in any given situation underestimates the human capacity for handling ambiguity and duality, shifting flexibly between perspectives. In short, I'm suggesting that evaluators would do better to worry about understanding and being sensitive to the worldviews and evaluation needs of their clients than to maintain allegiance to or work within only one perspective.

Beyond Paradigm Orthodoxies: A Paradigm of Choices

The paradigms debate elucidates the complexity of choices available in evaluation. It also demonstrates the difficulty of moving beyond narrow disciplinary training to make decisions based on utility. It is premature to characterize the practice of evaluation as completely flexible and focused on methodological appropriateness rather than disciplinary orthodoxy, but it is fair to say that the goals have shifted dramatically in that direction. The debate over which paradigm was the right path to truth has been replaced, at the level of methods, by *a paradigm of choices.*

Exhibit 12.8 summarizes the contrasting themes of the paradigms debate and describes the synthesis that is emerging with the shift in emphasis from methodological orthodoxy to methodological appropriateness and utility. *Utilization-focused evaluation offers a paradigm of choices.* Today's evaluator must be sophisticated about matching research methods to the nuances of particular evaluation questions and the idiosyncrasies of specific decision-maker needs. The evaluator must have a large repertoire of research methods and techniques available to use on a variety of problems.

The utilization-focused evaluator works with intended users to include any and all data that will help shed light on evaluation questions, given constraints of resources and time. Such an evaluator is committed to research designs that are relevant, rigorous, understandable, and able to produce useful results that are valid, reliable, and believable. The *paradigm of choices* recognizes

that different methods are appropriate for different situations and purposes.

What Are Appropriate Standards of Evidence? Different Methods Yield Different Findings

It would be easy to conclude from this review of the paradigms debate that mixed methods are the solution. But the fact is that different methods often yield conflicting results. When that happens, which findings take priority? Which pass muster? Relaxing the gold standard on the front-end of design by incorporating mixed methods may just mean that it reappears on the back end when divergent and conflicting results have to be interpreted. Consider this cautionary tale.

For over a decade, the David and Lucile Packard Foundation made grants to test the effectiveness of a home visitation approach to parents with young children. Educators and health professionals visited parents in their homes to educate them about appropriately interacting with their children to enhance learning. While in the home they did developmental screening for children to look for problems that might need attention. Home visitation is an early intervention program to prevent child abuse or neglect, identify potential developmental needs of children in high-risk groups, and enhance school readiness. The Foundation's Center for the Future of

EXHIBIT 12.8

The Evaluation Methods Paradigms Debate
Summary of Emphases: Thesis, Antithesis, Synthesis

	Thesis: Originally Dominant Social Science Research Paradigm	*Antithesis: Original Alternative Paradigm*	*Synthesis: Utilization-Focused Evaluation Paradigm of Choices*
Purpose	Summative	Formative	Intended use by intended users
Measurement	Quantitative data	Qualitative data	Appropriate, credible, useful data
Design	Experimental designs	Naturalistic inquiry	Creative, practical, situationally responsive designs, mixed methods
Researcher stance	Objectivity	Subjectivity	Fairness and balance
Conceptualization	Independent and dependent variables	Holistic interdependent system	Stakeholder questions and issues
Relationships	Distance, detachment	Closeness, engagement	Collaboration, consultative
Approach to study of change	Pre-post measures, time series, static portrayals at discrete points in time	Process-oriented, evolving, capturing ongoing dynamism	Developmental, action oriented. What needs to be known to get program from where it is to where it wants to be?
Relationship to prior knowledge	Confirmatory, hypothesis testing	Exploratory, hypothesis generating	Either or both
Sampling	Random, probabilistic	Purposeful, key informants	Combinations, depending on what information is needed
Primary approach to variations	Quantitative differences on uniform, standardized variables	Qualitative differences, uniquenesses	Flexible: focus on comparison most relevant to intended users and evaluation questions
Analysis	Descriptive and inferential statistics	Case studies, content and pattern analysis	Answer to stakeholders' questions
Types of statements	Generalizations	Context bound	Extrapolations, lessons learned
Contribution to theory	Validating theoretical propositions from scientific literature	Grounded theory derived from the situation	Describing, exploring, and testing stakeholders' and program's theory of action
Goals	Truth, scientific acceptance	Understanding, perspective	Utility, relevance: meaningful and useful to intended users

Children publishes a journal called *The Future of Children* with a distribution of 40,000 to 50,000 copies and a $1 million cost per issue. It can take 18 months to develop a single issue. The journal has become prestigious as a credible source of information (Sherwood 2005).

In 1999 a special issue of *The Future of Children* was planned entitled "Home Visiting: Recent Program Evaluations." Both the Packard Foundation's evaluations using randomized trials and evaluations of others were screened for inclusion. As findings from several home visiting experiments were reported from 1996 to 1998, a pattern of mixed or no significant effects became evident. The Foundation brought together a group of evaluators, program directors, and independent experts to review findings for the special publication. Controversy centered on what kind of evidence would be reported since there were evaluation examples that employed experimental designs, quasi-experimental designs, mixed methods, and qualitative methods—and *evaluations with different methods were yielding different results*. What were appropriate standards of evidence?

The view of the Foundation staff was that *only* the main effects of randomized trials should qualify for publication. Those findings were largely negative, showing no or very small effects. Analysis of effects for subgroups was more positive, as was qualitative evidence, case studies, and some quasi-experimental evaluations. Indeed, the results from the randomized trials were consistently less positive than the results from the quasi-experimental studies (e.g., matched samples instead of random samples).

The implications of these findings would be far-reaching. Considerable contentiousness developed. Should *only* the results of randomized controlled experiments be considered credible and published? Should a variety of evaluations be published showing mixed and conflicting results? How should such different findings from varying methods be interpreted? After much debate, the journal published results from a range of research designs, including findings from experimental evaluations and patterns from the non-experimental research. The overall conclusion was that the results were mixed because of variations in program delivery, quality of service, and implementation. But the fact remained: different methods yielded different findings, a common occurrence in mixed methods evaluations.

Live by the Evidence, Die by the Evidence

As you ponder the challenges of methods choices, let me close this chapter with one more cautionary tale, a true story. A major philanthropic foundation invited a distinguished and well-known evaluation methodologist to conduct a day of training on methods. He was a powerful and insistent advocate of randomized controlled experiments as the only evidence worth having if the Foundation was going to have an impact on policy, which was its aspiration. He emphasized that only the findings from experiments were sufficiently credible to be useful and technically respectable.

The day after the training, the staff gathered to debrief what they had learned. The senior staff member who had arranged the training opened by apologizing. This surprised the group.

"Well, he was not the greatest presenter, it's true," replied a junior staff member, "but he's an academic. At least he knew his stuff."

"But he doesn't live by his own advice. As far as I'm concerned, he had no credibility after the first break, and it got worse throughout the day."

The whole group looked at her in stunned silence, completely surprised by this strong reaction. Finally someone asked, "What'd he say that so turned you off?"

"It wasn't what he said. It's what he did. On every break he dashed outside to smoke a couple of cigarettes. Live by the evidence, die by the evidence. We won't be having him back again."

Follow-Up Exercises

1. Locate a Web site for an organization that funds evaluations. This can be an international agency, federal or state government, philanthropic foundation, or independent research institution. Find where it discusses its approach to evaluation. Use the paradigm dimensions discussed in this chapter to characterize the evaluation methods being advocated. What is the paradigm perspective, either explicit or implicit, in this approach? Give concrete examples to support your judgment.

2. Locate an evaluation that used mixed methods, both quantitative and qualitative data. To what extent and in what ways were the data synthesized and integrated, or did they involve separate and distinct evaluation questions? Discuss the differences and complementarities of the two kinds of data.

3. What is your opinion about the methodological gold standard issue? Should there be a methodological gold standard? If so, what—and why? If not, why not? What is illuminating and what is distorting about the "gold standard" metaphor applied to evaluation methods?

4. Identify a program and one or more evaluation questions for that program. Provide an overview of a design that is (a) entirely quantitative/experimental, (b) entirely qualitative/naturalistic, and (c) mixed methods. Offer these three alternatives in the form of a memo written to primary intended users of the proposed evaluation. Identify strengths and weaknesses of each approach.

5. Assess your own methodological strengths and weaknesses. What methods are you most knowledgeable about and comfortable with? Why? In what evaluation methods do you lack training and expertise? Discuss how your competences and training affect your capability to match methods to the nature of the evaluation questions. To what extent can you be methodologically flexible and eclectic? Do a capacity assessment. For assistance, see "A Professional Development Unit for Reflecting on Program Evaluation Competencies" (Ghere et al. 2006).

13

The Meanings and Reporting of Evaluation Findings

Analysis, Interpretation, Judgment, and Recommendations

*W*hat is the sound of one hand clapping?

—Hakuin

This question was first posed by the Japanese Zen master Hakuin (1686–1769) as a means of facilitating enlightenment. "The disciple, given a Koan [riddle] to see through, was encouraged to put his whole strength into the singleminded search for its solution, to be 'like a thirsty rat seeking for water . . . ,' to carry the problem with him everywhere, until suddenly, if he were successful, the solution came" (Hoffman 1975:22). The koan is a technique originated by the Zen masters to shake their students out of routine ways of thinking and

acting, open up new possibilities, and help individual students realize their full potential. An effective evaluator can facilitate these same processes. Utilization-focused evaluation helps decision makers and intended users stand outside the program and look at what is happening; evaluations can help shake staff out of routine ways of doing things, open up new possibilities, and help programs realize their full potential.

The Zen search through koans consists of three basic parts: a question, an answer, and interpretation/assimilation of the answer in terms of the student's own life; evaluation involves a question, an empirical answer, and interpretation/utilization of the answer in the context of the program's own dynamics. A fundamental tenet of the koanic method is that the question is as important as the answer; the same principle applies to utilization-focused evaluation. The Zen master carefully matches the koan to the student; the responsive evaluator focuses on questions that are relevant to specific intended users. Finally, the Zen student must struggle to make sense out of the answer to the koanic riddle; in evaluation, the meaning of empirical data emerges from interpretation, dialogue, and situational application. Consider the following koanic exchange, titled "A Flower in Bloom."

A monk asked Master Ummon, "What is the pure body of truth?"
Master Ummon said, "A flower in bloom."
Monk: "'A flower in bloom'—what's it mean?"
Master: "Maggot in the shit hole, pus of leprosy, scab over a boil"

—Hoffman 1975:119

"What's it mean?" may be a philosophical, religious, or epistemological question. It can also be the very concrete, practical question of program staff laboring over statistical tables. For any given set of data, meaning depends on who is interpreting the data. Some people see flowers; others see maggots.

Evaluators and decision makers can deceive themselves into believing that once data have been collected it will be clear whether or not the program works. But data have to be interpreted. In utilization-focused evaluation, interpretation involves the active participation of primary users because, in the end, they are the ones who must translate data into decisions and action, and evidence into conclusions.

Setting the Stage for Use

Simulated Data Interpretation Scenarios

The stage can be set for analysis, interpretation, and use *before* data are ever

---

Evidence

What is the meaning of the word evidence?

When it comes to evidence, what is believable to one analyst is incredible to another. Evidence may be hard or soft, conflicting or incontrovertible, it may be unpersuasive or convincing, exculpatory or damning, but with whatever qualifier it is presented, the noun evidence is neutral: it means "a means of determining whether an assertion is truthful or an allegation is a fact. (Safire 2006:18)

The first analytical task in evaluation is assembling and organizing the evidence to answer priority evaluation questions. Once presented, evidence can then be interpreted and a judgment rendered.

---

collected. Once instruments have been designed—but before data collection—I like to conduct a simulated use session. This involves fabricating possible results and interpreting the action implications of the made-up data.

The evaluator prepares some possible "positive" and "negative" findings on the most important issues. For example, suppose primary users have chosen the job placement rate as the priority outcome variable for a vocational training program. The evaluator might construct data showing a placement rate of 40 percent for black participants and 75 percent for white participants. The evaluator facilitates analysis by asking such questions as the following: "What do these results mean? What actions would you take based on these results? How would you use these data?"

Such a discussion accomplishes four things:

1. The simulated analysis is a check on the design to make sure that all the relevant data for interpretation and use are going to be collected. (Remember this session occurs before actually gathering data.) All too often, at the analysis stage, after data collection, evaluators and stakeholders realize that they forgot to ask an important question.

2. The simulated use session trains and prepares stakeholders for the real analysis later. They learn how to interpret data and apply results.

3. Working through a use scenario prior to data collection helps set realistic expectations about what the results will look like. Strengths and limitations of the design emerge. Methodological and measurement issues can be discussed. This helps prepare users for the necessity of interpreting findings in relation to possible actions and likely ambiguities.

4. Use scenarios help build the commitment to use—or reveal the lack of such commitment. When intended users are unable to deal with how they would use findings prior to data collection, a warning flag goes up that they may be unable, or unwilling, to use findings after data collection. The commitment to use can be cultivated by helping intended users think realistically and concretely about how findings might be applied before data collection gets under way. The relatively safe, even fun, exercise of analyzing simulated data can help strengthen the resolve to use before being confronted with real findings and decisions. This can help overcome resistance to evaluation and remove any remaining barriers to implementing the evaluation data collection (Taut and Alkin 2003; Taut and Brauns 2003).

Quantitative data are fairly easy to fabricate once instruments have been developed. With qualitative data, it's necessary to construct imagined quotations and case examples. This extra work can pay large dividends as decision makers develop a utilization-focused mindset based on an actual experience struggling with data. Athletes, performing artists, astronauts, fire fighters, and entertainers spend hundreds of hours preparing for events that take only a few hours. Is it too much to ask intended users to spend a couple of hours practicing to get mentally and analytically ready for the climax of an evaluation?

Standards of Desirability

A simulated use session also offers a prime opportunity to think about and formalize criteria for making judgments—*before data collection*. With quantitative data this can be done quite precisely by establishing standards of desirability. I like to have users set at least three levels of attainment:

1. level at which the program is considered highly effective,

The Power of Interpretative Frameworks: Positive, Negative, Balanced? Expected, Unexpected?

How should an evaluator facilitate stakeholders' thinking about findings? One way to begin the process and set the stage for interpretation is to have primary intended users spend a few minutes thinking about their interpretive tendencies. Do they tend to see the glass as half-full, half empty, or simply descriptively: The 8 ounce glass has 4 ounces of water.

For more than a half-century, "The Power of Positive Thinking" (Peale 1952) has been a dominant mind set in Western culture. Reflecting on this perspective, Harvard medical School Surgeon Atul Gawande (2007) counters that, to increase effectiveness, the key is "negative thinking: looking for, and sometimes expecting, failure" (p. A23).

Gawande tells of visiting the Walter Reed military hospital early in the Iraq war. He participated in a session interpreting eye-injury statistics. The doctors were having considerable success saving some soldiers from blindness, a positive outcome. But digging deeper, the doctors asked why so many severe eye injuries were occurring. Interviewing their patients, they learned that the young soldiers weren't wearing their protective goggles because they were considered too ugly and uncool. They recommended that the military switch to "cooler-looking Wiley X ballistic eyewear. The soldiers wore their eyegear more consistently, and the eye-injury rate dropped immediately" (p. A23). By "negative thinking," Gawande means not just looking for what's going well but asking hard questions about and digging deeply into problems.

Evaluators typically seek to facilitate balance between the positive and negative. The point of introducing the discussion with stakeholders is to get them thinking about what lens they typically bring to interpreting findings.

Another framework involves distinguishing confirming from disconfirming findings. People tend to like to have their opinions confirmed and may view findings from that perspective. In contrast, organizational development researchers Weick and Sutcliffe (2001) found that high performance organizations are always on the lookout for the unexpected. Helping intended users identify their interpretive tendencies can increase their willingness to engage evaluation findings openly.

2. level at which the program is considered adequate, and

3. level at which the program is considered inadequate.

Such standards can be established for implementation targets (e.g., program participation and completion rates) as well as outcomes (data on how participants have changed). Suppose one is collecting satisfaction data on a workshop. At what level of satisfaction is the workshop a success? At what level is it merely adequate? At what level of participant satisfaction is the workshop to be judged ineffective? It's better to establish these kinds of standards

of desirability in a calm and deliberative manner *before* actual results are presented. This exercise, done before data collection, may also reveal that satisfaction data alone are an inadequate indicator of effectiveness while there's still time to measure additional outcomes.

The process of specifying objectives sometimes involves setting performance targets: for example, "75% of workshop participants will be satisfied." However, this doesn't tell us what constitutes an outstanding accomplishment; it doesn't distinguish adequacy from excellence. Nor does it make it clear whether 65 percent satisfaction is inadequate or merely "lower than we hoped for but acceptable."

Moreover, objectives are often set a long time before the program is under way or well before an actual evaluation has been designed. Reviewing objectives and establishing precise standards of desirability just before data collection increases the likelihood that judgment criteria will be up to date, realistic, and meaningful.

During the early conceptual stage of an evaluation, questions of use are fairly general and responses may be vague. The evaluator asks, "What would you do if you had an answer to your evaluation question? How would you use evaluation findings?" These general questions help focus the evaluation, but once the context has been delineated, the priority questions focused, and methods selected, the evaluator can pose much more specific use questions based on what results might actually look like.

For example, if recidivism in a community corrections program is 55 percent, is that high or low? Does it mean the program was effective or ineffective? The program had some impact, but what level of impact is desirable? What level spells trouble?

Consider the evaluation of a teacher resource center. One of the implementation issues concerned the extent to which teachers used the center intensively (three or more times) versus superficially (once or twice). Actual baseline data from such a study are shown in Exhibit 13.1 with three categories for primary intended users to set future standards of desirability for the next period of implementation.

Now, suppose the staff assembles in six months to discuss the actual results *without* having set standards of desirability or performance targets.

First staff member:	Those results are about what I anticipated.
Second staff member:	Plus, remember, the data don't include teachers in our workshops and special classes.
Third staff member:	I think the time was really too short to conclude anything. We're still getting established.
First staff member:	I agree. And winter is bad. You know, everyone is depressed with winter, and . . .

Soon it becomes apparent that either the findings don't tell staff much about teacher engagement, at least not without other data, or staff members are not prepared to deal with what the data do show. Such resistance and defensiveness are not unusual when staff first interpret evaluation data.

Now, let's try a different scenario. At the outset of evaluation, the program staff discuss their notions of what their task is and how teacher change occurs. They decide that the kind of impact they want cannot occur in one or two visits to the teacher center. "If teachers don't return after one or two visits, we must be doing something

wrong." The period of time in question is a full 12-month period. Before the data are collected, the staff fill in the table establishing standards of desirability as shown in Exhibit 13.1.

A record-keeping system of teacher visits must be established that staff believes has credibility. The data will provide clear feedback about the effectiveness of the program's outreach and implementation in attempting to engage teachers on a multiple-contact basis. The key point is that if staff members are unwilling or unable to set expectancy levels *before data collection,* there is no reason to believe they can do so afterward. In

EXHIBIT 13.1

Intensity of Teachers' Use of a Teacher Center: Baseline Data and Standards of Desirability

Category of Visits by a Teacher in a Month	Baseline Number of Visits per Month	Percentage of Total Teacher Visits
1 or 2	185	80.4
3 or more	45	19.6

Given the baseline data (above), what are the Teacher Center *Standards of Desirability* for the next year?

Judgment	Percentage and Number of Teachers Who Use the Center Three or More Times
We're doing an outstanding job of engaging teachers at this level	
We're doing an adequate job of engaging teachers at this level	
We're doing a poor job of engaging teachers at this level	

addition, going through this process ahead of time alerts participants to any additional data they will need to make sense of and act on the results; clearly, measuring the frequency of visits is only a starting place.

Many of the most serious conflicts in evaluation are rooted in the failure to clearly specify standards of desirability ahead of data collection. This can lead both to collection of the wrong data and to intense disagreement about criteria for judging effectiveness. Without explicit criteria, data can be interpreted to mean almost anything about a program—or to mean nothing at all.

Preparing for Use

Another way of setting the stage for analysis and use is having stakeholders speculate about results prior to seeing the real data. This can be done prior to data collection or after data collection but prior to actual presentation of findings. Stakeholders are given an analysis table with all the appropriate categories but no actual data (a dummy table). They then fill in the missing data with their guesses of what the results will be.

This kind of speculation prepares users for how the results will be formatted and

The Importance of Interpretive Frameworks

Management scholars Kathleen Sutcliffe and Klaus Weber (2003) examined the performance of business organizations in relation to the amount and accuracy of information used by senior executives as well as the "interpretive frameworks" they used to make sense of information. They concluded that *the way senior executives interpret their business environment is more important for performance than the accuracy of data they have about their environment.* That is, they concluded that there was less value in spending a lot of money increasing the marginal accuracy of data available to senior executives compared with the value of enhancing *their capacity to interpret* whatever data they have. Executives were more limited by a lack of capacity to make sense of data than by inadequate or inaccurate data. In essence, they found that interpretive capacity, or "mind-sets," distinguish high performance more than data quality and accuracy.

Enhancing the quality and accuracy of our evaluation data through better methods and measures will add little value unless those using the data have the capacity to think evaluatively, think critically, and be able to appropriately interpret findings to reach reasonable and supportable conclusions.

increases interest by building a sense of anticipation. I've even had stakeholders establish a betting pool on the results. Each person puts in a dollar, and the person closest to the actual results on the major outcome wins the pot. That creates interest! And the winner must be present at the unveiling of the findings to win. Strange how attendance at the presentation of findings is increased under these conditions!

A second and more important function of having stakeholders write down their guesses is to provide a concrete basis for determining the extent to which actual results come close to expectations. Program staff members, for example, sometimes argue that they don't need formal evaluations because they know their clients, students, or program participants so well that evaluation findings would just confirm what they already know. I've found that when staff members commit their guesses to paper ahead of seeing actual results, the subsequent comparison often calls into question just how well some staff members know what is happening in the program. At least with written guesses on paper, program staff and other stakeholders can't just

say, "That's what I expected." A baseline (in the form of their guesses) exists to document how much something new has been learned.

You can combine establishing standards of desirability and speculating on results. Give stakeholders a page with two columns. The first column asks them to specify what outcomes they consider desirable, and the second column asks them to guess what results they believe will be obtained. Having specified a standard of desirability and guessed at actual results, users have a greater stake in and a framework for looking at the actual findings. When real results are presented, the evaluator facilitates a discussion on the implications of the data falling below, at, or above the desired response, and why the actual findings were different from or the same as what they guessed. In facilitating this exercise, the outcomes data presented must be highly focused and limited to major issues. In my experience, animated interactions among users follow as they fully engage and interpret the results.

I find that, given the time and encouragement, stakeholders with virtually no methods or statistics training can readily identify the strengths, weaknesses, and implications of the findings. The trick is to move people from passive reception—from audience status—to active involvement and participation.

A Framework for Engaging Findings

Four distinct processes are involved in making sense out of evaluation findings: (1) *analysis,* which involves organizing raw data into an understandable form that reveals basic patterns and constitutes the evaluation's empirical findings; (2) *interpretation,* which involves determining the significance of and explanations for the findings; (3) *judgment,* which brings values to bear to determine merit or worth and decide whether the results are positive or negative; and (4) *recommendations,* which involve determining the action implications of the findings. Primary intended users should be actively involved in all four of these processes so that they fully understand the findings and their implications. Facilitating these processes, especially helping stakeholders understand these four fundamental distinctions, requires skills that go well beyond what is taught in statistics courses. Working with stakeholders to analyze and interpret findings is quite different from doing it on one's own as a researcher. Exhibit 13.2 summarizes this framework. We'll now consider each of these processes in greater depth.

Arranging Data for Ease of Interpretation: Focusing the Analysis

> *Unless one is a genius, it is best to aim at being intelligible.*
>
> —Sir Anthony Hope (1863–1933)

EXHIBIT 13.2

A Utilization-Focused Framework for Engaging Findings

Four distinct processes are involved in helping primary intended users make sense out of evaluation findings.

1. *Basic Findings, Description and Analysis*: Organize raw data, both quantitative and qualitative, into a form that reveals basic patterns so that primary intended users can understand the results.

2. *Interpretation*: Engage the findings with primary intended users. Help them ask: What do the results mean? What's the significance of the findings? Why did the findings turn out this way? What are possible explanations of the results? Interpretations *go beyond the data* to add context, determine meaning, and tease out substantive significance.

3. *Judgment*: Values are added to analysis and interpretations to make judgments. Determining merit or worth means determining the extent to which results are positive or negative, what is good or bad, desirable or undesirable, in the outcomes, and to what extent standards of desirability have been met. Help primary intended users make judgments.

4. *Recommendations*: The final step (if agreed to be undertaken) adds action to analysis, interpretation, and judgment. What should be done? What are the action implications of the findings? Only recommendations that follow from and are grounded in the data ought to be formulated.

In working with primary intended users, aim for the simplest presentation that will handle the facts. Evaluators may need and use sophisticated statistical techniques to enhance analytic power or uncover nuances in data, but understandable presentations are needed to give decision makers who are not researchers access to evaluation findings. Certainly, an evaluator can use sophisticated techniques to confirm the strength and meaningfulness of discovered patterns, but the next step is to think creatively about how to organize those findings into a straightforward and understandable format. This means, for example, that the results of a regression analysis might be reduced to nothing more complex than a chi-square table or a set of descriptive statistics (percentages and means). This need not distort the presentation. Quite the contrary, it will usually focus and highlight the most important findings while allowing the evaluator to explain in a footnote or appendix the more sophisticated techniques that were used to confirm the findings.

Our presentations must be like the skilled acrobat who makes the most dazzling moves look easy, the audience being unaware of the long hours of practice and the sophisticated calculations involved in what appear to be simple movements. Likewise, skilled evaluators craft and polish their presentations so that those participating will quickly understand the results, unaware of the long hours of arduous work involved in sifting through the data, organizing it, arranging it, testing relationships, taking the data apart, and creatively putting them back together to arrive at that moment of public unveiling.

Simplicity as a virtue means that we are rewarded not for how much we complicate the analysis or impress with our expertise but for how much we enlighten. It means

that we make users feel they can master what is before them, rather than intimidate them with our own knowledge and sophistication. It means distinguishing the complexity of analysis from the clarity of presentation and using the former to inform and guide the latter. Simplicity as a virtue is not simple. It often involves more work and creativity to simplify than to rest content with a presentation of complicated statistics as they originally emerged from analysis.

The first step is realizing that providing descriptive statistics in a report means more than simply reproducing the results in raw form. Data need to be arranged, ordered, and organized in some reasonable format that permits decision makers to detect patterns. Consider the three presentations of data shown in Exhibit 13.3. Each presents data from the same survey items, but the focus and degree of complexity are different in each case.

The first presentation reports items in the order in which they appeared on the survey with percentages for every category of response. It is difficult to detect patterns with 40 numbers to examine, so primary intended users will be overwhelmed by the first presentation. The second presentation simplifies the results by dividing the scale at the midpoint and reducing the four categories to two. Sometimes, such an analysis would be very revealing, but, in this case, no priorities emerge. Since *determining priorities was the purpose of the survey,* decision makers would conclude from the second presentation that the survey had not been useful.

The third presentation arranges the data so that decision makers can immediately see respondents' priorities. Support for employment programs now ranks first as a great need (58 percent) in contrast to social programs (11 percent), rated lowest in priority. Users can go down the list and decide where

EXHIBIT 13.3

Three Presentations of the Same Data

Presentation 1: Raw results presented in the same order as items appeared in the survey				
Expressed Needs of 478 Physically Disabled People	*Great Need for This (Percent)*	*Much Need (Percent)*	*Some Need (Percent)*	*Little Need (Percent)*
Transportation	35	36	13	16
Housing	33	38	19	10
Educational opportunities	42	28	9	21
Medical care	26	45	25	4
Employment opportunities	58	13	6	23
Public understanding	47	22	15	16
Architectural changes	33	38	10	19
Direct financial aid	40	31	12	17
Changes in insurance regulations	29	39	16	16
Social opportunities	11	58	17	14

Presentation 2: Results combined into two categories. No priorities emerge.		
	Great or Much Need (Percent)	*Some or Little Need (Percent)*
Transportation	71	29
Housing	71	29
Educational opportunities	70	30
Medical care	71	29
Employment opportunities	71	29
Public understanding	69	31
Architectural changes in buildings	71	29
Direct financial assistance	71	29
Changes in insurance regulations	68	32
Social opportunities	69	31

Presentation 3: Utilization-focused results arranged in rank order by "Great Need" to highlight priorities	
Rank Order	*Great Need for This (Percent)*
Employment opportunities	58
Public understanding	47
Educational opportunities	42
Direct financial assistance	40
Transportation	35
Housing	33
Architectural changes in buildings	33
Changes in insurance regulations	29
Medical care	26
Social opportunities	11

to draw the line on priorities, perhaps after "direct financial assistance" (40 percent). Failure to arrange the data as displayed in the third presentation places decision makers at an analytical disadvantage. This presentation is utilization-focused because it facilitates quick understanding of and engagement with the results for their intended purpose: setting priorities for programs supporting people with disabilities.

Balance

The counterpoint to valuing simplicity is that evaluation findings are seldom really simple. In striving for simplicity, one must be careful to avoid simplemindedness. This happens most often in evaluation when results are boiled down, in the name of simplicity, to some single number—a single percentage, a single cost-benefit ratio, or a

single proportion of the variance explained. Striving for simplicity means making the data understandable, but balance and fairness need not be sacrificed in the name of simplicity. Achieving balance may mean that multiple findings have to be represented through several different numbers, all of them presented in an understandable fashion. Much advertising is based on the deception of picking the one number that puts a product in the best light, e.g., gas mileage instead of price. Politicians often do likewise, picking the statistic that favors their predetermined analysis. For example, Exhibit 13.4 shows how seemingly contradictory statements can both be true: "In the last four years, median incomes for African Americans have risen faster than white incomes" and "after the last years, African Americans are worse off than whites in terms of income." The data in Exhibit 13.4 show that both statements can be true.

Each statement represents only part of the picture. To understand what is happening in the relationship between black and white incomes, one needs to know, at a minimum, *both* absolute income levels and percentage changes. When a report gives only one figure or the other (i.e., only absolute changes or only percentage changes), the reader has cause to suspect that the full picture has not been presented.

EXHIBIT 13.4

Different Data Tell Different Stories:
Illustrative Data (Constructed)

	Beginning Level	Absolute Level 4 Years Later	Amount of Change	Percentage Increase
Median white income	$20,100	$21,205	$1,105	5.5
Median African American income	$10,400	$11,336	$936	9.0

These data support seemingly contradictory conclusions, each of which is true: "In the last four years, median income for African Americans has risen faster than white incomes" (9% versus 5.5%) *and* "in the last years, African Americans are worse off than whites in terms of income" (the absolute gap in median incomes has increased in this illustration).

Another example comes from a study of Internal Revenue Service (IRS) audits conducted by the U.S. Government Accountability Office (GAO). The cover page of the report carried the sensational headline that IRS audits in five selected districts missed $1 million in errors in four months. The IRS response to the GAO report pointed out that the same audit cases with $1 million in errors had uncovered over $26 million in errors that led to adjustments in tax. Thus, the $1 million represented only about 4 percent of the total amount of money involved. Moreover, the IRS disputed the GAO's $1 million error figure because the GAO included all potential audit items, whereas the IRS ignored differences of $100 or less. In the data presented by the GAO, it is impossible to tell what proportion of the $1 million involved errors of under $100, which are routinely ignored by the IRS as not worth the costs of pursuing. Finally, the $1 million error involves cases of two types: instances in which additional tax would be due to the IRS and instances in which a refund would be due to the taxpayer from the IRS. In point of fact, the $1 million error would result in virtually no additional revenue to the government had all the errors been detected and followed up.

The gross simplification of the evaluation findings and the headlining of the $1 million error represent considerable distortion of the full picture. *Simplicity at the expense of accuracy is no virtue; complexity in the service of accuracy is no vice.* The point is to make complex matters understandable without distortion. The omitted information from the GAO report could not be justified on the basis of simplification. The omissions constituted distortions rather than simplification.

Striving for balance means thinking about how to present the full picture without getting bogged down in trivia or extraneous details. It can mean providing both absolute changes and percentage changes; reporting the mean, median, and mode to fully represent the distribution of data; providing multiple measures of an attitude or behavior; categorizing data more than one way to see what differences those categorical distributions make; providing information about mean, range, and standard deviations (represented as straightforward and understandable confidence limits); presenting both positive and negative quotes from interviewees; and finding ways to show the same thing in more than one way to increase understanding.

Be Clear about Definitions

Confusion or uncertainty about what was actually measured can lead to misinterpretations. In workshops on data analysis, I give the participants statistics on farmers, on families, and on recidivism. In small groups, the participants interpret the data. Almost invariably they jump right into analysis without asking how *farmer* was defined, how *family* was defined, or what *recidivism* actually meant in the data at hand. A simple term such as *farmer* turns out to be enormously variable in its use and definition. When does the weekend gardener become a farmer, and when does the large commercial farmer become an "agribusinessperson?" A whole division of the Census Bureau wrestles with these problems.

Defining *family* is no less complex. There was a time, not so long ago, when Americans

may have shared a common definition of *family*. Now there is a real question about who has to be together under what arrangement before we call them a family. Single-parent families, foster families, same-sex "marriages," and extended families are just a few of the possible complications. Before interpreting any statistics on families it would be critical to know how *family* was defined.

Measuring recidivism is common in evaluation, but the term offers a variety of different definitions and measures. *Recidivism* may mean (1) a new arrest, (2) a new appearance in court, (3) a new conviction, (4) a new sentence, (5) or actually committing a new crime regardless of whether the offender is apprehended. The statistics will vary considerably depending on which definition of recidivism is used.

A magazine cartoon I like shows a group of researchers studying cartoon violence. As they watch a television cartoon, one asks: "When the coyote bounces after falling off the cliff, does the second time he hits the ground count as a second incidence of violence?" Of such decisions are statistics made.

During the 2000 presidential campaign of George W. Bush, Houston School Superintendent Rod Paige was given credit for "The Texas Miracle," reducing the school system's once-high dropout rate to just 2 percent. Once elected, President Bush named Paige to be Secretary of Education and the Houston's reforms became the basis for the President's "No Child Left Behind" education reform act. It turned out, however, that the celebrated reduction in school dropouts was achieved by redefining what a dropout was and coding dropouts as leaving for acceptable reasons, for example, going on to other things or moving to another school. Independent and external calculations put Houston's true dropout rate somewhere between 25 and 50 percent

---

Defining and Measuring "Abnormal Sex"

Definitions matter. They determine results. A study published by the National Federation of Decency measured the decadent content of a daytime television "talk show." One of the categories of analysis included programs that encouraged "abnormal sex." The author of the report later acknowledged that it was probably a bit excessive of the federation to have included breast feeding in this category (Boulder *Daily Camera*, September 30, 1981:2). But, then, definitions of abnormal sex do seem to vary somewhat. Any reader of a research report on the subject would be well advised to look with care at the definition used by the researcher. Of course, any savvy evaluator involved in such a study would be careful to make sure that his or her own sexual practices were categorized as normal!

(still quite an error range), never anywhere near 2 percent (CBS 2004).

Such examples are not meant to make people cynical about statistics. Many distortions of this kind are inadvertent, due to sloppiness of thinking, unexamined assumptions, or hurrying to complete a final report. Sometimes, of course, they're the result of incompetence or unscrupulousness as asserted in the old adage that "figures lie, and liars figure." Widespread skepticism about statistics is all the more reason for evaluators to exercise care in making sure that data are useful, accurate, and understandable. Clear definitions provide the foundation for utility, accuracy, and understandability. A Sufi story reinforces the importance of being clear about definitions before drawing conclusions.

The wise fool Mulla Nasrudin and a friend went to the circus together. They were dazzled by the tightrope walker. Afterwards, Nasrudin's friend kept raving about the performance of the tightrope walker. Nasrudin tired of the conversation, but his companion resisted all attempts to change the subject. Finally, in frustration, Nasrudin asserted, "It wasn't really such a great feat as all that. I myself can walk a tightrope."

Angry at Nasrudin's boasting, the friend challenged him with a substantial wager. They set a time for the attempt in the town center so that all the villagers could be

witness. At the appointed hour Mulla Nasrudin appeared with the rope, stretched it out on the ground, walked along it, and demanded his money.

"But the tightrope must be in the air for you to win the wager!" exclaimed the companion.

"I wagered that I could walk a tightrope," replied Nasrudin. "As everyone can see, I have walked the tightrope."

The village judicial officer ruled in Nasrudin's favor. "Definitions," he explained to the assembled villagers, "are what make laws."

They also make evaluations.

Make Comparisons Carefully and Appropriately

Noncomparative evaluations are comparatively useless.

—Michael Scriven (1993:58)

Virtually all evaluative analysis ends up in some way being comparative. Numbers in isolation, standing alone without a frame of reference or basis of comparison, seldom make much sense. A recidivism rate of 40 percent is a meaningless statistic. Is that high or low? Does that represent improvement or deterioration? An error of $1 million in tax audits is a meaningless number. Some basis of comparison or standard of judgment is needed in order to interpret such statistics. The challenge lies in selecting the appropriate basis of comparison. In the earlier example of the IRS audit, the U.S. GAO believed that the appropriate comparison was an error of zero dollars—absolute perfection in auditing. The IRS considered such a standard unrealistic and suggested, instead, comparing errors against the total amount of corrections made in all audits.

Skepticism can undermine evaluation when the basis for the comparison appears arbitrary or contrived. Working with users to select appropriate comparisons involves considering a number of options. Menu 13.1 presents 10 possibilities plus combinations. Evaluators should work with stakeholders to decide which comparisons are appropriate and relevant to give a full and balanced view of what is happening in the program.

Consider the new jogger or running enthusiast. At the beginning, runners are likely to use as a basis for comparison their previously sedentary lifestyle. By that standard, the initial half-mile run appears pretty good. Then the runner discovers that there are a lot of other people running, many of them covering 3 miles, 4 miles, 5 miles, or

MENU 13.1

Menu of Program Comparisons

The outcomes of a program can be compared with

1. The outcomes of selected "similar" programs

2. The outcomes of the same program the previous year (or any other trend period, e.g., quarterly reports)

3. The outcomes of a representative or random sample of programs in the field

4. The outcomes of special programs of interest, e.g., those known to be exemplary models (a purposeful sample comparison, Patton 2002a:230–34)

5. The stated goals of the program

6. Participants' goals for themselves

7. External standards of desirability as developed by the profession

8. Standards of minimum acceptability, e.g., basic licensing or accreditation standards

9. Ideals of program performance

10. Guesses made by staff or other decision makers about what the outcomes would be.

Combinations of these comparisons are also possible and usually desirable.

10 miles a week. Compared with seasoned joggers, the runner's half-mile doesn't look so good. On days when new runners want to feel particularly good, they may compare themselves with all the people who don't run at all. On days when they need some incentive to push harder, they may compare themselves with people who run twice as far as they do. Some adopt medical standards for basic conditioning, something of the order of 30 minutes of sustained and intense exercise a least three times a week. Some measure their progress in miles, others in minutes and hours. Some compare themselves with friends; others get involved in official competitions and races. All these comparisons are valid, but each yields a different conclusion because the basis of comparison is different in each case.

In politics, it is said that conservatives compare the present with the past and see all the things that have been lost, while liberals compare the present with what could be in the future and see all the things yet to be attained. Each basis of comparison provides a different perspective. A fascination with comparisons undergirds sports, politics, advertising, management, and, certainly, evaluation.

Interpretations

Sometimes something historical gives you a better perspective. You can see the latest dumbness as just the end of a long line of dumbnesses that have been taking place for thousands of years.

—Cartoonist J. B. Handelsman (quoted by Franklin 2007:27)

We have been discussing how to analyze and organize data so that primary intended users can engage the evaluation findings. The discussion has included focusing the analysis, clarity of presentation, striving for balance, being clear about definitions, and making comparisons carefully and appropriately. These are all elements of providing intended users with understandable and credible findings that can be interpreted. *Interpretation involves deciding what the findings mean.* How significant are the findings? What explains the results? Even when those receiving evaluation findings agree on the facts and findings, they can disagree vociferously about what the findings *mean*.

In resisting the temptation to bear alone the burden of interpretation, the utilization-focused evaluator views the interpretive process as a training opportunity through which users can become more sophisticated about data-based decision making. Science fiction author and futurist H. G. Wells anticipated the importance of making statistical thinking accessible to nonstatisticians when he observed, "Statistical thinking will one day be as necessary for efficient citizenship as the ability to read and write." For evaluation users, that day is now. Incorporating a training perspective into evaluation (process use) will mean being prepared to help users with statistical reasoning. The logic of inductive qualitative analysis also needs to be made accessible to stakeholders.

Researchers have internalized the differences between analysis and interpretation, but that distinction will need reinforcement for nonresearchers. In working with stakeholders to understand interpretation, four themes deserve special attention.

1. *Numbers and qualitative data must be interpreted to have meaning.* Numbers are neither bad nor good, they're just numbers. Interpretation means thinking about what the data mean and how they ought to be applied. No magic formulas, not even those for statistical significance, can infuse meaning into data. Only thinking humans can do that. Interpretation is a

human process, not a computer process. Statisticians have no corner on the ability to think and reason. The best guideline may be Einstein's dictum that "the important thing is to keep on questioning."

2. *Data are imperfect indicators or representations of what the world is like.* Just as a map is not the territory it describes, the statistical tables describing a program are not the program. That's why they have to be interpreted.

3. *Statistics and qualitative data contain errors.* Research offers probabilities, not absolutes. The switch from absolute assertions (things either are or are not) to probabilistic thinking (things are more or less likely) is fundamental to empirical reasoning and careful interpretations.

4. *Look for interocular significance.* Fred Mosteller, the great applied statistician, was fond of saying that he did not care much for statistically significant differences. He was more interested in interocular differences, *the differences that hit us between the eyes* (Scriven 1993:71).

Different stakeholders will bring varying perspectives to the evaluation. Those perspectives will affect their interpretations. The first task is get agreement on the basic findings—the "facts." As Daniel Patrick Moynihan, a former United States Senator and distinguished social scientist, was fond of saying, "Everyone is entitled to his own opinion, but not his own facts." Once there is understanding of the findings, the evaluator facilitates interpretation by having participants in the process elaborate possibilities and options. Then follows the work of seeking convergence—aiming to reach consensus, if possible, on the most reasonable and useful interpretations supported by the data. Where different perspectives prevail, those varying interpretations

should be reported and their implications explored. Judgments (discussed later in this chapter) follow analysis and interpretations.

> Everyone is entitled to his own opinion, but not his own facts.
>
> —Daniel Patrick Moynihan (1927–2003)
> U.S. Senator and
> distinguished social scientist

While this kind of facilitation usually occurs with a small number of primary users, the process can be facilitated for very large groups. The following example involved more than 200 people in a half-day process of analysis, interpretation, judgment, and generating recommendations—moving back and forth between small groups and full session reporting and adopting conclusions.

A Utilization-Focused Data-Based Deliberation with Stakeholders

In an evaluation of foster group homes for juvenile offenders, we collected data from natural parents, foster parents, juveniles, and community corrections staff. The primary intended users, the Community Corrections Advisory Board, agreed to a findings review process that involved a large number of stakeholders from both the field and policy levels. We had worked closely with the board in problem identification, research design, and instrumentation. Once the data were collected, we employed a variety of statistical techniques, including alpha factor analysis and stepwise forward regression analysis. We then reduced these findings to a few pages in a simplified form and readable format for use at a half-day meeting with community corrections staff, welfare department staff, court services staff, and members of the county board. That meeting included some 40 of the most powerful elected and appointed officials in the county as well as another 160 field professionals.

A major purpose of the evaluation was to describe and conceptualize effective foster group homes for juvenile delinquents so that future selection of homes and training of foster parents could be improved. The evaluation was also intended to provide guidance about how to achieve better matches between juvenile offenders and foster parents. We had data on how variations in recidivism, runaway rates, and juvenile attitudes varied with different kinds of group home environments. We had measured variations in homes with a 56-item instrument. Factor analysis of 56 items uncovered a single major factor that explained 54 percent of the variance in recidivism, with 19 items loading above .45 on that factor. *The critical task in data interpretation was to label that*

factor in such a way that its relationship to dependent variables would represent something meaningful to identified information users. We focused the half-day work session on this issue.

The session began with a brief description of the evaluation's methods, and then the results were distributed. In randomly assigned groups of four, these diverse stakeholders were asked to look at the items in Exhibit 13.5 and *label the factor or theme represented by those items in their own words.* After the groups reported their labels, discussions followed. A consensus emerged around the terms *participation and support* as representing one end of the continuum and *authoritarian and nonsupportive* for the other end. We also asked the groups to describe the salient elements in the factor. These descriptions were combined with the labels chosen by the group. The resulting conceptualization—as it appeared in the final evaluation report—is shown in Exhibit 13.6.

EXHIBIT 13.5

Composition of the Group Home Treatment Environment Scale

The items that follow are juvenile interview items that are highly interrelated statistically in such a way that they can be assumed to measure the same environmental factor. The items are listed in rank order by factor loading (from .76 to .56 for a six-factor alpha solution). This means that when the scales were combined to create a single numerical scale the items higher on the list received more weight in the scale (based on factor score coefficients).

From your perspective, what underlying factor or theme is represented by the combination of these questions? What do these different items have in common?

1. The [group home parent's names] went out of their way to help us.
almost always	30.9%	
a lot of times	10.9%	
just sometimes	34.5%	
almost never	23.6%	*Factor loading = .76*

2. At the foster group home, personal problems were openly talked about.
   almost always   20.0%
   a lot of times   9.1%
   just sometimes   32.7%
   almost never   38.2%   *Factor loading = .76*

3. Did you feel like the group home parents tried to help you understand yourself?
   almost always   23.6%
   a lot of times   29.1%
   just sometimes   23.6%
   almost never   23.6%   *Factor loading = .74*

4. How often did your foster parents take time to encourage you in what you did?
   almost always   27.3%
   a lot of times   20.0%
   just sometimes   30.9%
   almost never   21.8%   *Factor loading = .73*

5. At the foster home, how much were you each encouraged to make your own decisions about things? Would you say that you were . . .
   almost always   18.9%
   a lot of times   30.2%
   just sometimes   30.2%
   almost never   20.8%   *Factor loading = .68*

6. How often did the foster parents let you take responsibility for making your own decisions?
   almost always   23.6%
   a lot of times   20.0%
   just sometimes   25.5%
   almost never   30.9%   *Factor loading = .67*

7. We really got along well with each other at the foster home.
   almost always   23.6%
   a lot of times   29.1%
   just sometimes   32.7%
   almost never   14.5%   *Factor loading = .66*

8. Would the group home parents tell you when you were doing well?
   almost always   30.9%
   a lot of times   10.9%
   just sometimes   29.1%
   almost never   9.1%   *Factor loading = .64*

9. How often were you allowed to openly criticize the group home parents?
   almost always   14.8%
   a lot of times   7.4%
   just sometimes   24.1%
   almost never   53.7%   *Factor loading = .59*

(Continued)

(Continued)

10. How much of the time would you say there was a feeling of "togetherness" at the foster home?
    almost always   27.3%
    a lot of times   23.6%
    just sometimes   32.7%
    almost never   16.4%   *Factor loading = .59*

11. How much did the foster parents help you make plans for leaving the group home and returning to your real home?
    almost always   9.1%
    a lot of times   21.8%
    just sometimes   21.8%
    almost never   47.3%   *Factor loading = .58*

12. How often would the foster parents talk with you about what you'd be doing after you left the group home?
    almost always   7.3%
    a lot of times   18.2%
    just sometimes   36.4%
    almost never   38.2%   *Factor loading = .58*

13. How much of the time did the kids have a say about what went on at the foster home?
    almost always   13.0%
    a lot of times   29.6%
    just sometimes   27.8%
    almost never   29.6%   *Factor loading = .56*

14. How much were decisions about what you all had to do at the group home made only by the foster parents without involving the rest of you?
    almost always   30.9%
    a lot of times   18.2%
    just sometimes   32.7%
    almost never   18.2%   *Factor loading = .56*

15. How much of the time were discussions at the foster home aimed at helping you understand your personal problems?
    almost always   23.6%
    a lot of times   23.6%
    just sometimes   18.2%
    almost never   34.5%   *Factor loading = .56*

EXHIBIT 13.6

Group Home Treatment Environment Continuum: Description of Group Home Ideal Types

Supportive-Participatory Foster Homes	*Nonsupportive-Authoritarian Foster Homes*
In group homes nearer this end of the continuum, juveniles perceive group home parents as helpful, caring, and interested in them. Juveniles are encouraged and receive positive reinforcement. Juveniles are involved in decisions about what goes on in the home. Kids are encouraged to make their own decisions about the things they do personally. There is a feeling of togetherness, of being interested in each other, of caring about what happens now and in the future. Group home parents discuss the future with the kids and help them plan. There is a feeling of mutual support, and kids feel that they can openly express their feelings, thoughts, problems, and concerns.	In group homes nearer this end of the continuum, juveniles report that group home parents are less helpful, less open with them, and less interested in them personally. Juveniles are seldom encouraged to make their own decisions, and the foster parents tend to make decisions without asking their opinions about things. There isn't much planning things together or talking about the future. Kids are careful about what they say, are guarded about expressing their thoughts and feelings. Kids get little positive reinforcement. There is not much feeling of togetherness, support, and mutual caring; group home parents keep things well under control.

NOTE: *The descriptions presented here are based on stakeholders' interpretations of the factor analysis in Exhibit 13.5.*

EXHIBIT 13.7

Relationship between Different Home Environments and Recidivism

	No Recidivism	*Recidivism*	*Total*
Supportive-participatory homes	76% ($N = 19$)	24% ($N = 6$)	100% ($N = 25$)
Nonsupportive-authoritarian homes	44% ($N = 11$)	56% ($N = 14$)	100% ($N = 25$)

Primary intended users were asked to interpret what this table meant. This table was used in conjunction with Exhibits 13.5 and 13.6.

NOTE: Correlation $r = .33$; significant at .009 level.

The groups then studied accompanying tables showing the relationships between this treatment environment factor and program outcome variables (see Exhibit 13.7). The relationships were statistically significant and quite transparent. Juveniles who reported experiencing more supportive-participatory corrections environments had lower recidivism rates, lower runaway rates, and more positive attitudes. Having established the direction of the data, we discussed the limitations of the findings, the methodological weaknesses, and the impossibility of making firm causal inferences. Key decision makers were already well aware of these problems. Then, given those constraints, the group was asked for recommendations. The basic thrust of the discussion concerned ways to increase the supportive-participatory experiences of juvenile offenders. The people carrying on that discussion were the people who fund, set policy for, operate, and control juvenile offender programs. The final written evaluation report included the recommendations that emerged from that meeting as well as our own independent conclusions and recommendations as evaluators. But the final written report took another four weeks to prepare and print; the use process was already well under way as the meeting ended (both *findings use* and *process use*).

Four main points are illustrated here about a utilization-focused approach to findings. First, nonresearchers can understand and interpret data when presented with clear, readable, and simplified statistical tables. Second, as experienced data analysts know, the only way to really understand a data set is to spend some time getting inside it; busy decision makers are unwilling and unable to spend days at such a task, but a couple of hours of structured time spent in facilitated analysis and interpretation can pay off in a greater understanding of and commitment to

using results. Third, evaluators can learn a great deal from stakeholders' interpretations of data if they are open and listen to what people knowledgeable about the program have to say. Just as decision makers do not spend as much time in data analysis as do evaluators, so do evaluators not spend as much time in program analysis, operations, and planning as do decision makers. Each can learn from the other in the overall effort to make sense out of the data and provide a future direction for the program. Fourth, the transition from analysis to action is facilitated by having key actors involved in analysis. Use does not then depend on or have to wait for a written report.

Making Causal Inferences: Attribution and Contribution

Water floats a ship; water sinks a ship.

—Chinese proverb
Causal attribution lifts an evaluation; causal attribution sinks an evaluation.

—Halcolm

Using social science findings generally and evaluation findings specifically means interpreting the significance and relevance of findings—and this typically includes some inference about causality. The extent to which an intervention can be said to have caused observed outcomes is one of the crucial interpretation issues in evaluation. "If an 'outcome' is not caused by a program, it is not an outcome at all; it's a coincidence. Coincidences cannot legitimately be documented as though they are outcomes; some evidence of a causal link is essential" (Davidson 2006b:1).

Chapter 12, on alternative paradigms, explored the debate about whether experimental designs with randomized control groups as counterfactuals are the gold standard for establishing causality (see especially Exhibit 12.6). Since the conditions for implementing high-quality experimental designs limit their applicability in evaluation, we need other ways of dealing with attribution. As we do so, a central question is *what level of evidence is needed.* Evaluation is meant to inform action and decision making. What degree of certainty is needed by primary intended users to use the evaluation findings? Research aims to prove. Definitive proof being elusive under the real-world time and resource constraints of decision making, evaluation more often aims to improve and inform.

An example from Chapter 12 is relevant here. Suppose decision makers need to determine whether to give worm medicine to school-age children with diarrhea to increase their school attendance and performance. First, some context: 600 million people have hookworms. In Congo, one study found that 82 percent of children have worms, making 70 percent anemic and affecting school attendance. Worms, elephantiasis, and trachoma kill 500,000 people annually; ordinary worms kill 130,000 people a year, through anemia and intestinal obstruction. Citing these statistics, advocates argue. "The cheapest way to increase school attendance in poor countries isn't to build more schools, but to deworm children. Yet almost no government aid goes to deworming. In Africa, you can deworm a child for 50 cents" (Kristof 2007:A19). So what kind of evaluation evidence is needed to take action? Does one need a randomized controlled experiment to establish the linkage between deworming and school attendance—and the cost-benefit of spending 50 cents per child per year? Or, if students, parents, teachers, and health professionals all affirm in interviews that diarrhea is a major cause of the poor school attendance and performance, and

we follow up those given a regimen of worm medicine, can we infer causation at a reasonable enough level to recommend action? If those taking the medicine show increased school attendance and performance, and in follow-up interviews, the students, parents, teachers, and health professionals independently affirm their belief that the changes can be attributed to taking the worm medicine and being relieved of the symptoms of diarrhea, is this credible, convincing evidence? Is such evidence sufficient to inform decision making? *Primary intended users must ultimately answer these questions.* The evaluator facilitates this deliberative process by illuminating the strengths, weaknesses, and implications of data and design options. Attention to degrees of evidence in relation to the stakes involved for decision makers further informs these deliberations and negotiations (Chatterji 2007).

Direct inquiry into the relationship between worm medicine and school attendance involves tracing the causal chain and looking for reasonable evidence of linkages along the causal chain. This is how coroners determine cause of death, how arson investigators determine the cause of a fire, and how accident investigators determine the cause of an airplane crash. Epidemiologists follow backward the chain of events and contacts to establish the source of a disease or explain the outbreak of an epidemic. In all these cases, those carrying out the investigation examine the evidence and determine *the most probable cause.* Often they apply the principle of Occam's Razor in choosing among alternative explanations:

All things being equal, the simplest solution tends to be the best one.

Michael Scriven has called a related form of causal tracing the *modus operandi method.* This language comes from detective

---

Occam's Razor: Valuing Straightforward Explanations

In the 14th century, an English logician, William of Ockham, postulated the principle that the explanation of any phenomenon should make as few assumptions as possible—eliminating or "shaving off" unnecessary complications. The simplest explanation *compatible with the data* is most valued. This principle, sometimes called the "law of parsimony," is popularly known as *Occam's Razor*.

All things being equal, the simplest solution tends to be the best one.

Occam's Razor is a heuristic guide to interpretation that emphasizes economy, parsimony, and simplicity—useful attributes for evaluators to aspire to in working with primary intended users.

---

work in which a criminal's MO (modus operandi or method of operating) is established as a *signature trace* that connects the same criminal to different crimes. "The modus operandi method works best for evaluands that have highly distinctive patterns of effects" (Davidson 2005:75). I evaluated an employment training program aimed at chronically unemployed, poorly educated men of color. Prior to the program they blamed society for their problems and expressed overt anger. After the program, which included an intense empowerment component, they described themselves as taking control of their lives, abandoning anger, no longer indulging in a "victim mentality," and of taking responsibility for their actions and the consequences of those actions. This language was the "signature" of the program. When graduates who had attained jobs attributed their success to being "empowered" and continued to express themselves in this way a year after leaving the program, it seemed reasonable to attribute this change in outlook to the program. Connecting the dots along the causal chain means looking at the participants' baseline attitudes and behaviors, looking at what they experienced in the program, and examining their subsequent attitudes, behaviors, and job status. The connections in this case were direct and reasonable.

Direct observation and logic are a powerful source of attribution. We don't need a randomized controlled trial to understand why parachutes work as they do (see sidebar). Engineers design machines, bridges, and buildings based on meeting specific criteria about what works. You don't need a counterfactual to determine if a bridge will get people across a river—or if using solar cookers in Africa reduces wood use (and deforestation). The evidence is direct and observable.

In working with primary intended users, it can be quite useful to distinguish between attribution analysis and contribution analysis. John Mayne (2007b) distinguishes attribution questions from contribution questions as follows:

Traditional causality questions (attribution)

- Has the program caused the outcome?
- To what extent has the program caused the outcome?
- How much of the outcome is caused by the program?

Contribution questions
- Has the program made a difference? That is, has the program made an important contribution to the observed result? Has the program influenced the observed result?

A study in the *British Medical Journal* by Smith and Pell (2003) found that

No randomized control trials of parachute use have been undertaken.

As with many interventions intended to prevent ill health, the effectiveness of parachutes has not been subjected to rigorous evaluation by using randomized controlled trials. Advocates of evidence based medicine have criticized the adoption of interventions evaluated by using only observational data.
We think that everyone might benefit if the most radical protagonists of evidence-based medicine organized and participated in a double blind, randomized, placebo-controlled, crossover trial of the parachute.

SO

Only two options exist. The first is that we accept that, under exceptional circumstances, commonsense might be applied when considering the potential risks and benefits of intervention.

OR

Those who criticize interventions that lack an evidence base will not hesitate to demonstrate their commitment by volunteering for a double blind, randomized, placebo-controlled, crossover trial.

SOURCE: http://bmj.bmjjournals.com/cgi/content/full/327/7429/1459?ck=nck

- How much of a difference has the program made? How much of a contribution?

Contribution analysis is especially appropriate where there are multiple projects and partners working toward the same outcomes, and where the ultimate impacts occur over long time periods influenced by several cumulative outputs and outcomes over time. Outcome Mapping (IDRC 2007) provides a conceptual framework for mapping contributions in complex and dynamic environments with collaborating partners where simple notions of linear attribution are neither meaningful nor accurate (Iverson 2003). Exhibit 13.8 elaborates contribution analysis.

Program Theory and Realist Evaluation Explanations

Program theory can and should play a central role when interpreting evaluation findings. The program's theory of change should specify the expected attribution chain from activities to outcomes and impacts. A map of the anticipated contributions of collaborating programs to desired outcomes also constitutes a theory of change for multidimensional interventions in complex environments. A well-conceived program theory (see Chapter 10) provides a solid basis for interpreting evaluation findings and assessing causal claims (Rogers forthcoming, 2008, 2007, 2005c, 2003, 2000a, 2000b; Davidson 2000). Indeed, program theory is indispensable for testing and interpreting causality. Moreover, and this is quite important, a revised program theory is often a primary product of a theory-based evaluation thus fulfilling a knowledge-building purpose (Mason and Barnes 2007). This theory-testing and knowledge-building function can support and enhance both formative and summative evaluation purposes but should be understood as distinct from them as we "unbundle" and focus intended evaluation uses (Alkin and Taut 2003). Different approaches to theory-building, theory-testing, and explanation make quite a difference in how evaluations are designed and how findings are interpreted (Blamey and Mackenzie 2007). Experimental and quasi-experimental designs frame the explanatory issue as determining whether the program produced the observed outcomes controlling

EXHIBIT 13.8
Contribution Analysis

Contribution analysis (Mayne 2007b, 2001) examines a postulated theory of change against logic and evidence to test the theory of change including examining other potentially influencing factors that could explain observed results. The overall aim is to reduce uncertainty about the contribution the program is making to the observed results.

The result of a contribution analysis is not definitive proof that the program has made an important contribution but rather evidence and argumentation from which it is reasonable to draw conclusions about the degree and importance of the contribution, within some level of confidence. The aim is to get *plausible association* based on a preponderance of evidence, as in the judicial tradition. The question is whether a reasonable person would agree from the evidence and argument that the program has made an important contribution to the observed result. In utilization-focused evaluation, the "reasonable" persons making this assessment are the primary intended users.

A contribution analysis produces a *contribution story* that presents the evidence and other influences on program outcomes. A major part of that story may tell about behavioral changes that intended beneficiaries have made as a result of the intervention as emphasized in Outcome Mapping (IDRC 2007), which also uses the language of contribution rather than attribution in looking at what various collaborating partners contribute to outcomes.

Attributes of a credible contribution story
A credible statement of contribution would entail:

- a well-articulated context of the program, discussing other influencing factors,
- a plausible theory of change (no obvious flaws) that is not disproven,
- a description of implemented activities and resulting outputs of the program,
- a description of the observed results,
- the results of contribution analysis,
- the evidence in support of the assumptions behind the key links in the theory of change,
- a discussion of the roles of other influencing factors, and
- a discussion of the quality of the evidence provided, noting weaknesses.

for context. In contrast, *realist evaluation* makes understanding context a primary basis for explaining variations in outcomes. *Realist evaluation* begins with skepticism about the generalizability of intervention effects across participants and contexts and seeks, instead, to understand and explain *what works for whom in what ways through what mechanisms in what contexts*. This is, fundamentally, a different question than whether aggregate outcomes can be attributed to the program without regard to variations in participants and contexts. *Realist evaluations* view programs as theories that, once actually implemented, are embedded in open social systems and must be understood in interaction with and in the context of the systems within which they operate. *Realist evaluation* doesn't treat the overall program as the intervention to be tested but rather looks for the actual *mechanisms* that elucidate and explain what it is about programs and interventions that produce observed outcomes. In this way, *realist evaluation* is attentive to both intended and unintended outcomes, and seeks to test a "context-mechanism-outcome pattern configuration" (Pawson and Tilley 2005:365). *Realist evaluation* critiques experimental designs as overly simplistic and overgeneralized, seeking instead more nuanced and context-specific explanations (Blamey and Mackenzie 2007; Greenhalgh, Kristjansson, and Robinson 2007; Pawson and Tilley 2005, 1997; Pawson 2002a, 2002b; Mark, Henry, and Julnes 2000).

To Explain or Not to Explain?

Both attribution analysis and contribution analysis involve explaining the findings. Each attempts to interpret and explain the relationship between the program intervention and observed outcomes. Theory of change approaches make explaining causality a primary evaluation function and responsibility. Scriven (2006a) cautions that offering such explanations may exceed the evaluator's responsibility and, more importantly, the evaluator's competence. He argues that the purpose of program evaluation is to determine the effects of the program, if any, and judge the program's merit, worth, or significance. It is *not* the task of the evaluator to *explain* these effects, he insists, other than by showing that there *are* effects of the program. Whatever effects are documented may lead to questions about why those effects occurred (or why desired effects did not occur), and the evaluator may or may not be able to help with this task, but it's a completely different task, a task of explaining a phenomenon, not of evaluating it. Scriven argues that explaining causation requires the specialized substantive knowledge of people who are professionally expert in the program's arena of focus. The evaluator is not likely to be one of these, he suggests, and does not acquire that expertise by evaluating one or several programs in that field, any more than a radiologist who is an expert at telling whether the patient has or has not got cancer becomes an expert about what causes cancer as a result of acquiring radiology skills. Scriven acknowledges the allure of offering explanations but thinks this temptation is due to confusion between the role of the scientist and the role of the evaluator. Scientists explain how the world works. Evaluators judge whether a program works. The reason why this is not just a semantic quibble, he insists, is that since trying to find out why a program works is sometimes more than *anyone* has so far been able to do, even scientists expert in the field, for evaluators to think they can do it will sidetrack the often vital task of finding out *whether* the program works, which, he emphasizes, is the primary obligation—and vital service—of the evaluator.

A utilization-focused evaluator can solve this problem, at least in part, by supporting and facilitating primary intended users, including program staff and substantive experts, to engage in the process of interpreting the data in search of explanations. Since the question of "why did these results occur" will inevitably arise, the evaluator can help primary intended users anticipate what level of evidence they will need to credibly answer that question to their own satisfaction, including understanding the challenges of establishing causality, and what expertise will be needed to generate explanations if doing so is deemed important.

Making Claims

The level of evidence needed in an evaluation challenges the evaluator to determine

EXHIBIT 13.9

Important and Rigorous Claims

	Importance of Claims	
	Major	*Minor*
Strong		
Weak		

Rigor of claims

GOAL: Strong claims of major importance.

The most powerful, useful, and credible claims are those that are of major importance and have strong empirical support.

Characteristics of a Claim of MAJOR IMPORTANCE

- Involves making a difference, having an impact, or achieving desirable outcomes
- Deals with a problem of great societal concern
- Affects large numbers of people
- Provides a sustainable solution (claim deals with something that lasts over time)
- Saves money
- Saves time, that is, accomplishes something in less time than is usually the case (an efficiency claim)
- Enhances quality
- Claims to be "new" or innovative
- Shows that something can actually be done about a problem, that is, claims the problem is malleable
- Involves a model or approach that could be used by others (meaning the model or approach is clearly specified and adaptable to other situations)

Characteristics of a STRONG CLAIM

- Valid, believable evidence to support the claim
- Follow-up data over time (longer periods of follow up provide stronger evidence than shorter periods, and any follow up is stronger than just end-of-program results)
- The claim is about a clear intervention (model or approach) with solid implementation
- Documentation
- The claim is about clearly specified outcomes and impacts:
    Behavior outcomes are stronger than opinions, feelings, and knowledge.
- The evidence for claims includes comparisons:
    To program goals
    Over time (pre-, post-, follow-up)
    With other groups
    With general trends or norms

- The evidence for claims includes replications:
  Done at more than one site
  More than one staff person attained outcomes
  Different cohort groups of participants attained comparable outcomes over time
  Different programs attained comparable results using comparable approaches
- Claims are based on more than one kind of evidence or data (i.e., triangulation of data):
  Quantitative and qualitative data
  Multiple sources (e.g., kids, parents, teachers, and staff corroborate results)
- There are clear logical and/or empirical linkages between the intervention and the claimed outcomes.
- The evaluators are independent of the staff (or where internal evaluation data are used, an independent, credible person reviews the results and certifies the results).
- Claims are based on systematic data collection over time.

CAVEAT: Importance and rigor are not absolute criteria. Different stakeholders, decision makers, and claims makers will have different definitions of what is important and rigorous. What staff deem to be of major importance may not be so to outside observers. What is deemed important and rigorous changes over time and across contexts. Making public claims is a political action. Importance and rigor are, to some extent, politically defined and dependent on the values of specific stakeholders.

Related Distinctions

1. Program *premises* are different from but related to and dependent on program *claims.*

Premises are the basic assumptions on which a program is based, for example, that effective, attentive parenting is desirable and more likely to produce well-functioning children who become well-functioning adults. This premise is based on research. The program cannot "prove" the premise (though supporting research can and should be provided). The program's claims are about the program's actual implementation and concrete outcomes, for example, that the program yielded more effective parents who are more attentive to their children. The program does not have to follow the children to adulthood before claims can be made.

2. Evidence is different from claims—but claims depend on evidence.

    Claim: This program trains welfare recipients for jobs and places them in jobs, and, as a result, they become self-sufficient and leave the welfare rolls.

    Evidence: Numbers and types of job placements over time; pre-, post-, and follow-up data on welfare status; participant interview data about program effects; employer interview data about placements; and so on.

just what kinds of claims are appropriate and what level of certainty is required to make findings useful (Davidson 2000; Smith 1987, 1982, 1981). One way of meeting this challenge is to engage with primary stakeholders, especially program administrators and staff, about *making claims*. I ask: "Having reviewed the data, what can you claim about the program?" I then ask them to list possible claims: (1) participants like the program, (2) participants get jobs as a result of the program, (3) the dropout rate is low, (4) changes in participants last over the long term, (5) the program is cost-effective, (6) the program does not work well with people of color, etc. Having generated a list of possible claims, I then have them sort the claims into the categories (or cells) shown in Exhibit 13.9. This matrix distinguishes claims by their importance and rigor. Important claims speak to major issues of societal concern. Participants getting and keeping jobs as a result of a training program is a more important claim than that they're satisfied. Rigor concerns the amount and quality of evidence to support claims. The program might have very strong evidence of participant satisfaction but very weak follow-up data about job retention. The most powerful, useful, and credible claims are those of major importance that have strong empirical support.

This claims framework can also be useful in the design phase to help intended users focus on gathering rigorous data about important issues so that, at the end, the evaluation will be able to report important and strong claims.

Rendering Judgment

The four-part framework of this chapter on elucidating the meanings of evaluation findings consists of (1) analyzing and organizing the data so that primary intended users can understand and engage the findings, (2) facilitating interpretation, (3) facilitating judgment, and (4) generating recommendations. Having covered the first two, we arrive at the third, *the essence of the evaluative function*. At the center of the word *evaluation* is *valu*[*e*]. Rendering a judgment involves applying values to the data and interpretation of the findings. Data are data. Findings alone do not determine whether a result is good or bad. Values and standards are needed for that determination. Data may show that gender equity or racial integration has increased as a result of a project intervention. Whether that increase is "good" depends on what values inform that judgment. If one supports gender equity or racial integration, it is good. If one opposes gender equity or racial integration, the findings are bad. Regardless, the findings remain the findings. It is the judgment that varies depending on the values brought to bear.

Who makes this judgment? One perspective is that the evaluator must independently render judgment (Scriven 1994, 1991a, 1967). Others have argued that the evaluator's job can be limited to supplying the data and that the stakeholders alone make the final judgment (e.g., Stake 1996). Utilization-focused evaluation treats these opposing views as options to be negotiated with primary users. The evaluator's job can include offering interpretations, making judgments, and generating recommendations if, as is typical, that is what the evaluation users want. Even so, to facilitate direct engagement and increase users' ownership, prior to offering *my* interpretations, judgments, and recommendations, I first give decision makers and intended users an opportunity to arrive at their own conclusions unencumbered by my perspective but facilitated by me. That puts me in the role of *evaluation facilitator*—facilitating others' interpretation, judgments, and recommendations. In doing so, I find that I have to keep returning, sensitively and diplomatically, to the distinctions among analysis, interpretation, judgment, and recommendations. Having facilitated the engagement of primary intended users, I can also render my own interpretations and judgments, either separately or as part of our interactive process. At that point I am playing the role of *evaluator*. In the active-reactive-interactive-adaptive role of a utilization-focused evaluation (Chapter 6), I can move back and forth between the roles of evaluation facilitator and evaluator. In doing so, I am alternating between the tasks of facilitating others' judgments and rendering my own. Some are skeptical that these dual roles of evaluation facilitator and independent judge can both be played without confusion about roles or contamination of independence. Poorly executed, those are real dangers. But I find that primary intended users easily understand and value both roles.

I liken this process to that of skilled teachers who engage in both asking students questions (facilitating their critical thinking) and, alternatively, direct instruction (giving them answers and telling them what they need to know).

In facilitating judgments, I typically begin by offering three caveats:

- The quality of your judgment depends on the quality of the findings and thinking that informs it, thus the hand-in-glove link between findings and judgment.
- Don't condemn the judgment of another because it differs from your own. You may both be wrong.
- Forget "judge not that ye be not judged." The evaluator's mantra: Judge often and well so that you get better at it.

> **Practice Judging**
>
> Forget "judge not that ye be not judged."
>
> The evaluator's mantra: *Judge often and well so that you get better at it.*
>
> —Halcolm

Recommendations

Student: What is the major source of problems in the world?

Sage: Solutions

Student: How can one recognize a problem in advance?

Sage: Look for a recommendation about to be implemented.

Student: What does this mean?

Sage: Evaluators who make recommendations are assuring future work for evaluators.

—Halcolm

Recommendations are often the most visible part of an evaluation report. Well-written, carefully derived recommendations and conclusions can be the magnet that pulls all the other elements of an evaluation together into a meaningful whole. Done poorly, recommendations can become a lightning rod for attack, discrediting what was otherwise a professional job because of hurried and sloppy work on last-minute recommendations. I suspect that one of the most common reasons evaluators get into trouble when writing recommendations is that they haven't allowed enough time to really think through the possibilities and discuss them with people who have a stake in the evaluation. I've known cases in which, after working months on a project, the evaluators generated recommendations just hours before a final reporting session, under enormous time pressure. In our follow-up study of federal health evaluations, we asked 20 decision makers about the usefulness of the recommendations they had received. The following reactions provide a flavor of typical reactions to recommendations:

- I don't remember the specific recommendations.
- The recommendations weren't anything we could do much with.
- It was the overall process that was useful, not the recommendations.
- I remember reading them, that's about all.
- The recommendations looked like they'd been added as an afterthought. Not impressive.

Useful and Practical Recommendations: Ten Guidelines

Recommendations, when they are included in a report, draw readers' attention like bees to a flower's nectar. Many report readers will turn to recommendations before anything else. Some never read beyond the recommendations. Given their importance, then, let me offer 10 guidelines for evaluation recommendations.

1. *The focus of recommendations should be negotiated and clarified with stakeholders and evaluation funders as part of the design.* Not all evaluation reports include recommendations. The kinds of recommendations to be included in a report, if any, are a matter for negotiation. For example, are recommendations expected about program improvements? About future funding? About program expansion? About sustainability? Asking questions about what recommendations are expected can clarify the focus and purpose of an evaluation *before data collection.*

2. *Recommendations should clearly follow from and be supported by the evaluation findings.* The processes of analysis, interpretation, and judgment should lead logically to recommendations.

3. *Distinguish different kinds of recommendations.* Recommendations that deal directly with central questions or issues should be highlighted and separated from recommendations about secondary or minor issues. Distinctions should be made between summative and formative recommendations. It may be helpful and important to distinguish between recommendations that can be implemented immediately, those that can be implemented in the short term (within 6 months to a year), and those aimed at the long-term development of the program. In still other cases, it may be appropriate to orient recommendations toward certain groups of people: one set of recommendations for funders and policymakers; others for program administrators; still others for program staff or program participants.

Another way of differentiating recommendations is to distinguish those that are strongly supported from those that are less so. Strong support may mean the findings directly lead to the recommendations or that the evaluation task force had strong agreement about the recommendation; other recommendations may be less directly supported by the data or there may be dissension among members of the task force. In similar fashion, it is important to distinguish between recommendations that involve a firm belief that some action should be taken and recommendations that are meant merely to stimulate discussion or suggestions that might become part of an agenda for future consideration and action.

The basic point here is that long, indiscriminate lists of recommendations at the end of an evaluation report diffuse the focus and diminish the power of central recommendations. By making explicit the different amounts of emphasis that the evaluator intends to place on different recommendations, and by organizing recommendations so as to differentiate among different kinds of recommendations, the evaluator increases the usefulness of the recommendations as well as the likelihood of the implementation of at least some of them.

4. *Some decision makers prefer to receive multiple options rather than recommendations that advocate only one course of action.* This approach may begin with a full slate of possible recommendations: terminate the program; reduce funding for the program; maintain program funding at its current level; increase program funding slightly; and increase program funding substantially. The evaluator then lists pros and cons for each of these recommendations, showing which findings, assumptions, interpretations, and judgments support each option.

5. *Discuss the costs, benefits, and challenges of implementing recommendations.* When making major recommendations that involve substantial changes in program operations or policies, evaluators should study, specify, and include in their reports some consideration of the benefits and costs of making the suggested changes, including the costs and risks of not making them.

6. *Focus on actions within the control of intended users.* A major source of

frustration for many decision makers is that the recommendations in evaluation reports relate mainly to things over which they have no control. For example, a school desegregation study that focuses virtually all its recommendations on needed changes in housing patterns is not very useful to school officials, even though they may agree that housing changes are needed. Is the implication of such a recommendation that the schools can do nothing? Is the implication that anything the school does will be limited in impact to the extent that housing patterns remain unchanged? Or, again, are there major changes a school could make to further the aims of desegregation, with the evaluator getting sidetracked on the issue of housing patterns and never getting back to concrete recommendations for the school? Of course, the best way to end up with recommendations that focus on manipulable variables is to make sure that, in conceptualizing the evaluation, the focus was on the manipulability of the problem.

7. *Exercise political sensitivity in writing recommendations.* Ask yourself these questions: If I were in their place with their responsibilities, their political liabilities, their personal perspectives, how would I react to this recommendation stated in this way? What arguments would I raise to counter the recommendations? Work with stakeholders to analyze the political implications of recommendations. This doesn't mean recommendations should be weak but, rather, that evaluators should be astute. Controversy may or may not serve the cause of getting findings used. But, at the very least, controversies should be anticipated.

8. *Be thoughtful and deliberate in wording evaluations.* Important recommendations can be lost in vague and obtuse language. Powerful recommendations can be

diluted by an overly meek style, while particularly sensitive recommendations may be dismissed by an overly assertive style. Avoid words that confuse or distract from the central message. Here are examples.

Obtuse and meek recommendation: Consider whether current staffing competencies meet program needs and professional standards in light of changing knowledge and skill expectations.

Straightforward recommendation: Increase the amount and quality of staff development to meet accreditation standards.

9. *Allow time to do a good job on recommendations,* time to develop recommendations collaboratively with stakeholders, and time to pilot-test recommendations for clarity, understandability, practicality, utility, and meaningfulness.

10. *Develop strategies for getting recommendations taken seriously.* Simply listing recommendations at the end of a report may mean they get token attention. Think about how to facilitate serious consideration of recommendations. Help decision makers make decisions on recommendations, including facilitating a working session that includes clear assignment of responsibility for follow-up action and timelines for implementation.

Controversy about Recommendations

An evaluation without a recommendation is like a fish without a bicycle.

—Michael Scriven (1993:53)

While evaluators such as Mike Hendricks and Elizabeth Handley (1990) have argued that "evaluators should almost always offer recommendations" (p. 110), Michael Scriven has disagreed. Earlier I noted Scriven's insistence on distinguishing rendering judgments from offering explanations (only the former being a core evaluative responsibility). In a similar vein, he has been vociferous in warning evaluators against the "logical fallacy" of thinking that judging the merit or worth of something leads directly to recommendations. He considers it one of the "hard-won lessons in program evaluation" that evaluators seldom have the expertise to make recommendations and that they are generally well advised to stop at what they are qualified to do: render judgment.

It is widely thought that program evaluations should always conclude with a recommendations section, but this view is based on a misunderstanding of the logic of evaluation, and the misunderstanding has seriously unfortunate effects. The conclusion of an evaluation is normally a statement or set of statements about the merit, worth, or value of something, probably with several qualifications (for example, These materials on planetary astronomy are probably the best available, for middle-school students with well-developed vocabularies). There is a considerable step from the conclusion to the recommendations (for example, You should buy these materials for this school), and it is a step that evaluators are often not well-qualified to make. For example, in teacher evaluation, an evaluator, or, for that matter, a student, may be able to identify a bad teacher conclusively. But it does not follow that the teacher should be fired or remediated or even told about the result of the evaluation (which may be informal). In making one of those recommendations, the evaluator must have highly specific local knowledge (for example, about the terms of the teacher's contract, the possibility of early retirement, and temporary traumas in the teacher's home life) and special expertise (for example, about the situation), both of which go a long way beyond the skills necessary for evaluation. If the evaluator is looking at recommendations aimed not at actions but at improvement (for example, suggested changes in the way in which the teacher organizes the lesson and changes in the frequency of question-asking), then he or she moves into an area requiring still further dimensions of expertise. (Scriven 1993:53)

While Scriven's counsel to avoid making recommendations if one lacks expertise in remediation or design is wise as far as it goes, he fails to take the added step of making it part of the evaluator's responsibility to seek such expertise and facilitate experts' engagement with the data. Utilization-focused evaluation does offer a way of taking that extra step by actively involving primary intended users in the process of generating recommendations based on their knowledge of the situation and their shared expertise. Utilization-focused recommendations are not the evaluator's alone; they result from a collaborative process that seeks and incorporates the very expertise Scriven says is necessary for informed action.

Moreover, in recent years, in response to engagement with clients and what they want, Scriven (2007) has had a change of heart. He has acknowledged that clients want recommendations and he recommends doing a simulation to show they are realistic. He also recommends following up on what has happened to evaluations in long-term relationships.

> We're finishing our third year of doing an impact evaluation of the overseas efforts of a large international aid charity. Each year we've made recommendations. In the plans for the fourth year, it seems to me we really should include a minor study of the impact of our prior recommendations. . . . Moreover, I think this should be standard operating practice for all continuing evaluation relationships. I also think this will have considerable impact, so you should be careful about doing it. Some organizations will be very nervous about having anyone check on whether they

actually use the evaluations/recommendations they commission and some evaluators will not be too keen to have past recommendations dragged back into the light of day, since some of them will look less plausible now than they did at the time, and others will look even more vacuous than they did then (both possibilities strike me as good reasons for doing this, so that you can refine them and admit errors). (Scriven 2007:1)

A Futures Perspective on Recommendations

Show the future implications of recommendations.

—Hendricks and Handley (1990:114)

Recommendations have long struck me as the weakest part of evaluation. We have made enormous progress in ways of studying programs, in methodological diversity, and in a variety of data-collection techniques and designs. The payoff from those advances often culminates in recommendations, but we have made comparatively less progress in how to construct useful recommendations. I have found that teaching students how to go from data, interpretation, and judgment to recommendations is often the most challenging part of teaching evaluation. It's not a simple, linear process. A common complaint of readers of evaluation reports is that they cannot tell how the evaluators arrived at their recommendations. Recommendations can become lengthy laundry lists of undifferentiated proposals. They're alternatively broad and vague or pointed and controversial. But what recommendations always include, usually implicitly, are assumptions about the future.

The field of futures studies includes a broad range of people who use a wide variety of techniques to make inquiries about the nature of the future. Futurists study the future in order to alter perceptions and actions in the present. Evaluators, on the other hand, study the past (what programs have already done) in order to alter perceptions and actions in the present. In this sense, then, both futurists and evaluators are interested in altering perceptions and actions in the present, the impact of which will be a changed future. Evaluators do so by looking at what has already occurred; futurists do so by forecasting what may occur.

In effect, *at the point where evaluators make recommendations, we become futurists*. Recommendations constitute a forecast of what will happen if certain actions are taken. These forecasts are based on our analysis of what has occurred in the past. The accuracy of such forecasts, as with any predictions about the future, is subject to error due to changed conditions and the validity of assumptions that are necessarily made. Futurists have developed approaches for dealing with the uncertainties of their forecasts. Some of these approaches, I think, hold promise for evaluation. For example, futurists have developed techniques for constructing alternative scenarios that permit decision makers to consider the consequences of different assumptions and trends. These are variations on "if → then . . ." constructions. There are often "three to four different scenarios constructed: a pessimistic scenario, an optimistic scenario, and one or two middle-of-the-road or most likely-case scenarios.

The very presentation of scenarios communicates that the future is uncertain and that the way one best prepares for the future is by preparing for a variety of possibilities. General Robert E. Lee is reputed to have said, "I am often surprised, but I am never taken by surprise." That is the essence of a futures perspective—to be prepared for whatever occurs by having reflected on different possibilities, even those that are unlikely.

The advantage of scenarios in evaluation presentations is threefold. First, they permit us to communicate that recommendations are based on assumptions and thus, should those assumptions prove unwarranted, the recommendations may need to be altered accordingly. Second, the presentation of scenarios directs attention to those trends and factors that should be monitored so that as future conditions become known, program actions can be altered in accordance with the way the world actually unfolds (rather than simply on the basis of how we thought the world would unfold). Third, they remind us, inherently, of our limitations, for the "results of a program evaluation are so dependent on the setting that replication is only a figure of speech; the evaluator is essentially an historian" (Cronbach et al. 1980:7).

Communicating Evaluation

Communication is part of all program evaluation activities. Indeed, it is probably not an exaggeration to say that evaluation without communication would not be possible.

The very conduct of an evaluation is, itself, communication.

The evaluator needs to draw on all the resources available to him or her to consider the context of the program, to encourage processes that will animate reporting (that is, that make the results come alive), and to consider alternative forms of communication, appreciating the fact that multiple forms of presentation may increase the likelihood that a larger audience will be reached, realizing that what clicks with one stakeholder may not click with another.

—Marv Alkin, Tina Christie, and Mike Rose
(2006:384, 401–402).

Putting It All Together: Analysis, Interpretation, Judgment, and Recommendations

This chapter has reviewed and discussed the four elements in a comprehensive framework for engaging findings: analysis, interpretation, judgment, and recommendations. A useful report brings these elements together in a coherent manner and relates them together so that analysis informs interpretations; analysis and interpretations, together, are the basis for judgments; and analysis, interpretations, and judgments lead to and are the explicit basis for recommendations. Exhibit 13.10 shows the outline for an evaluation summary that brings together and reports in sequence the data analysis findings, interpretations, judgments, and recommendation options for an employment training program targeted at high school dropouts. With this integrating framework in mind, the concluding sections of this chapter discuss additional factors that can increase the utility of evaluation reporting.

Utilization-Focused Reporting

In utilization-focused evaluation, use does not center on the final report. Traditionally, evaluators and users have viewed the final written report as the climax—the end of the evaluation—and the key mechanism for use. From an academic perspective, use is achieved through dissemination of a published report. Moreover, use often doesn't emerge as an issue until there is something concrete (a report) to use. In contrast, *utilization-focused evaluation is concerned with use from the beginning, and a final written report is only one of many mechanisms for facilitating use.*

The Minnesota Group Home Evaluation reviewed earlier illustrates this point. Major use was under way well before the report was written, as a result of the half-day work session devoted to analyzing the results with major stakeholders. The final report was almost an anticlimax, and appropriately so.

The data from our study of federal health evaluations revealed that much important reporting is interpersonal and informal. In hallway conversations, over coffee, before and after meetings, over the telephone, and though informal networks, the word gets passed along when something useful and important has been found. Knowing this, evaluators can strategize about how to inject findings into important informal networks. This is not to diminish the importance of formal oral briefings, which, presented with thoughtful preparation and skill, can have an immediate and dramatic impact.

In all cases, reporting is driven by the intended evaluation purpose and the information needs of primary intended users. Formative reporting is different from a summative report. A lessons learned report is distinct from an accountability report. Where a single report serves multiple purposes (and audiences), clear distinctions should be made between sections of the report. Bottom line: *Communicating and reporting should be strategic* (Torres, Preskill, and Piontek 1996), which means honed and adapted to achieving use by targeted users.

Report Menu

As with other stages in utilization-focused evaluation, the reporting stage offers a smorgasbord of options. Menu 13.2 displays alternatives for reporting format and style, content, contributors, and perspectives. As just noted, selecting from

EXHIBIT 13.10

Putting It All Together:
Analysis, Interpretation, Judgment, and Reporting

Evaluation of employment training program for high school drop-outs
This shows the outline for an evaluation summary that brings together and reports in sequence the data analysis findings, interpretations, judgments, and recommendation options.

Findings from data analysis:
All participants admitted to the program met the selection criteria of being high school drop-outs who were chronically unemployed

- 47% dropped out during the first 6 months this year (45 of 95) compared with a 57% dropout rate in the same period the previous year.
- The dropout rate for comparable programs that target a similar population is above 50%.
- Of those who completed the program in the past year (35), 86% got a job and kept it for a year making at least $12 an hour with benefits. The goal was 70%.

Interpretation: The program is serving its target population and exceeding its goal with those who complete the program. The dropout rate is in line with other programs. The program attained these results at a time when the economy was sluggish and unemployment was somewhat higher than the historical average for this reason. No one has solved the drop-out problem. This is a tough target population and difficult problem. The problem remains significant. The program has learned important lessons about how to retain and graduate participants (lessons reported separately).

Judgment: These are positive results. This is a fairly good program addressing an important societal issue. There is room for improvement, and the program shows promise for improvement based on results to date and lessons learned.

Recommendation options:

1. Renew funding at the current level for two more years to give the program more time to prove itself.

2. Increase funding to expand the program by 50% to test the program's capacity to increase its impact and go to scale.

---

the menu is affected by the purpose of the evaluation (see Chapter 4). A summative report will highlight an overall judgment of merit or worth with supporting data. A knowledge-generating report aimed at policy enlightenment may follow a traditional academic format. A formative report may take the form of an internal memorandum with circulation limited to staff. I am often asked by students to show them the standard or best format for an evaluation report. The point of Menu 13.2 is that there can be no standard report format, *and the best format is the one that fulfills the purposes of the evaluation and meets the needs of specific intended users in a specific situation.* In many cases, multiple reporting strategies can be pursued to reach different intended users and dissemination audiences. For a comprehensive discussion of evaluation strategies for communicating and reporting aimed at "enhancing learning in organizations," see Torres, Preskill, and Piontek (2004).

Utilization-Focused Reporting Principles

I've found the following principles helpful in thinking about how to make reporting useful:

1. Be intentional about reporting, that is, know the purpose of a report and stay true to that purpose.

2. Stay user-focused: Focus the report on the priorities of primary intended users.

3. Organize and present findings to facilitate understanding and interpretation.

4. Avoid surprising primary stakeholders.

5. Prepare users to engage with and learn from "negative" findings.

6. Distinguish dissemination from use.

Let me elaborate each of these principles.

Be Intentional and Purposeful about Reporting

Being intentional means negotiating a shared understanding of what it's going to mean to close-out the evaluation, that is, to achieve use. Use of the evaluation findings and processes is the desired outcome, not producing a report. A report is a means to an end—use. You need to communicate at every step in the evaluation your commitment to utility. One way to emphasize this point during early negotiations is to ask if a final report is expected. This question commands attention. "Will you want a final report?" I ask.

They look at me and they say, "Come again?"

I repeat, "Will you want a final report?"

They respond, "Of course. That's why we're doing this, to get a report."

And I respond. "I see it a little differently. I think we've agreed that we're doing this evaluation to get useful information to improve your programming and decision making. A final written report is one way of communicating findings, but there's substantial evidence now that it's not always the most effective way. Full evaluation reports don't seem to get read much and it's very costly to write final reports. A third or more of the budget of an evaluation can be consumed by report writing. Let's talk about how to get the evaluation used, then we can see if a full written report is the most cost-effective way to do that." Then I share Menu 13.2 and we start talking reporting options.

Often, I find that, with this kind of interaction, my primary intended users really start to understand what utilization-focused evaluation means. They start to comprehend that evaluation doesn't have to mean producing a thick report that they can file under "has been evaluated." They start to think about use. Caveat: Whatever is agreed on, especially if there's agreement not to produce a traditional academic

MENU 13.2

Evaluation Reporting Menu

Style and Format Options: Written Report

Traditional academic research monograph
Executive summary followed by a full report
Executive summary followed by a few key tables, graphs, and data summaries
Executive summary only (data available to those interested)
Different reports (or formats) for different targeted users
Newsletter article for dissemination
Press release
Brochure (well crafted, professionally done)
No written report; only oral presentations

Style and Format Options: Oral and Creative

Oral briefing with charts
Short summary followed by questions (e.g., at a board meeting or legislative hearing)
Discussion groups based on prepared handouts that focus issues for interpretation and judgment based on data
Half-day or full-day retreat-like work session with primary intended users
Videotape or audiotape presentation
Dramatic, creative presentation (e.g., role-playing perspectives)
Involvement of select primary users in reporting and facilitating any of the above
Advocacy-adversary debate or court for and against certain conclusions and judgments
Written and oral combinations

Content Options

Major findings only; focus on data, patterns, themes, and results
Findings and interpretations with judgments of merit or worth (no recommendations)
   a. Summative judgment about overall program
   b. Judgments about program components
Recommendations backed up by judgments, findings, and interpretations
   a. Single, best-option recommendations
   b. Multiple options with analysis of strengths, weaknesses, costs, and benefits of each
   c. Options based on future scenarios with monitoring and contingency suggestions
   d. Different recommendations for different intended users

Authors of and Contributors to the Report

Evaluator's report; evaluator as sole and independent author

Collaborative report coauthored by evaluator with others involved in the process

Report from primary users, written on their behalf by the evaluator as facilitator and adviser, but ownership of the report residing with others

Combinations:

a. Evaluator generates findings; collaborators generate judgments and recommendations

b. Evaluator generates findings and makes judgments; primary users generate recommendations

c. Separate conclusions, judgments, and recommendations by the evaluator and others in the same report

Perspectives Included

Evaluator's perspective as independent and neutral judge

Primary intended users only

Effort to represent all major stakeholder perspectives (may or may not be the same as primary intended users)

Program staff or administrators respond formally to the evaluation findings (written independently by the evaluator); GAO approach

Review of the evaluation by an external panel—*metaevaluation*: "Formatively and summatively evaluate the evaluation against . . . pertinent standards, so that its conduct is appropriately guided and, on completion, stakeholders can closely examine its strengths and weaknesses" (Stufflebeam 2007:A11).

monograph, get the agreement in writing and remind them of it often. A commitment to alternative reporting approaches may need reinforcement, especially among stakeholders used to traditional formats.

Focus Reports on Primary Intended Users

A dominant theme running throughout this book is that use is integrally intertwined with users. That's the thrust of the personal factor (Chapter 3). The style, format, content, and process of reporting should all be geared toward *intended use by intended users*. For example, we've learned, in general, that busy, big-picture policymakers and funders are more likely to read concise executive summaries than full reports, but detail-oriented users want—what else?—details. Some users prefer recommendations right up front at the beginning of the report; others want them at the end; and I had one group of users who wanted the recommendations in a separate document so that readers of the report had to reach their own conclusions without interpreting everything in terms of recommendations. Methods sections may be put in the body of the report, put in an appendix, or omitted and shared only with the methodologically interested. Sometimes users can't articulate what they want until they see a draft. Then they know what they don't want, and the responsive evaluator will have to do some rewriting. Consider this story from an evaluator in our federal use study.

> Let me tell you the essence of the thing. I had almost no direction from the government [about the final report] except that the project officer kept saying, "Point 8 is really important. You've got to do point 8 on the contract."
>
> So, when I turned in the draft of the report, I put points 1 through 9, without 8, in the first part of the report. Then I essentially wrote another report after that just on point 8 and made that the last half of the report. It was a detailed description of the activities of the program that came to very specific conclusions. It wasn't what had been asked for in the proposal I responded to, but it was what they needed to answer their questions. The project officer read it, and the comment back was, "It's a good report except for all that crap in the front."
>
> OK, so I turned it around in the final version, and moved all that "crap" in the front into an appendix. If you look at the report, it has several big appendices. All of that, if you compare it carefully to the contract, all that "crap" in the appendix is what I was asked to do in the original request and contract. All the stuff that constitutes the body of the report was above and beyond the call, but that's what he wanted and that's what got used. [EV367:12]

Organize and Present Findings to Facilitate Understanding and Interpretation

I emphasized this point earlier in this chapter (e.g., Exhibit 13.3), but it's worth repeating and re-emphasizing with another example. Michael Hendricks (1994, 1984, 1982) has studied effective techniques for executive summaries and oral briefings. The key, he has found, is good charts and graphics to capture attention and communicate quickly. A trend line, for example, can be portrayed more powerfully in graphic form than in a table, as Exhibit 13.11 shows. Mike Hendricks regularly trains evaluators on reporting, and he asserts emphatically: "Evaluators have got to learn graphics. I'm amazed at how bad the charts and graphics are that I see in reports. You can't emphasize it too much. Reporting means GRAPHICS! GRAPHICS! GRAPHICS!" This involves "visible thinking," which includes causal mapping and other data displays (Bryson et al. 2004).

Avoid Surprising Stakeholders: Share Findings First in Draft Form

The story just told emphasizes the importance of sharing draft reports with primary users in time to let them shape the format of the final report. This doesn't mean fudging the results to make evaluation clients happy. It means focusing so that priority information needs get priority. Collaborating with primary users means that evaluators cannot wait until they have a highly polished final report prepared to share major findings. Evaluators who prefer to work diligently in the solitude of their offices until they can spring a final report on a waiting world may find that the world has passed them by. Formative feedback, in particular, is most useful as part of a process of thinking about a program rather than as a one-shot information dump. In the more formal environment of a major summative evaluation, surprises born of the public release of a final report are not going to be well received by important stakeholders caught unawares.

EXHIBIT 13.11

The Power of Graphics Data in a Table

2001	43 graduates
2002	49
2003	56
2004	46
2005	85
2006	98
2007	115
2008	138

The same data in graphic form

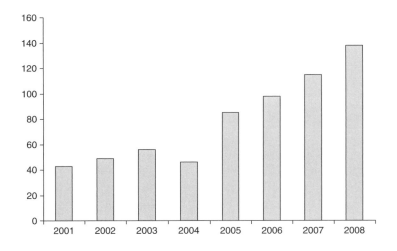

In our study of the use of federal health evaluations, we asked the following question:

Some suggest that the degree to which the findings of a study were expected can affect the study's impact. Arguments go both ways. Some say that surprise findings have the greatest impact because they bring to light new information and garner special attention. Others say that surprises will usually be rejected because they don't fit in with general expectations. What's your experience and opinion?

We found that minor surprises on peripheral questions created only minor problems, but major surprises on central questions were unwelcome. One decision maker we interviewed made the point that a "good" evaluation process should build in feedback mechanisms to primary users that guarantee the relative predictability of the content of the final report.

Evaluation isn't a birthday party, so people aren't looking for surprises. If you're coming up with data that are different than the conventional wisdom, a good evaluation effort, I would suggest, would get those ideas floated during the evaluation process so that when the final report comes out, they aren't a surprise.

Now, you could come up with findings contrary to the conventional wisdom, but you ought to be sharing those ideas with the people being evaluated during the evaluation process and working on acceptance. If you present a surprise, it will tend to get rejected.

See, we don't want surprises. We don't like surprises around here. [DM346:30–31]

The evaluator for this project expressed the same opinion: "Good managers are rarely surprised by the findings. If there's a surprising finding it should be rare. I mean, everybody's missed this insight except this great evaluator? Nonsense!" [EV364:13]. Surprise attacks may make for good war strategy, but in evaluation, the surprise attack does little to add credence to a study.

Prepare Users to Engage with and Learn from "Negative" Findings—and Think Positive about Negatives

John Sununu: (while Governor of New Hampshire in 1988, discussing the economy and upcoming presidential election): "You're telling us that the reason things are so bad is that they are so good, and they will get better as soon as they get worse?"

James A. Baker: (then President Reagan's Secretary of the Treasury): "You got it."

The program staff's fear of negative results can undermine an evaluation. On the other hand, the absence of negative findings can call into question the evaluator's independence, integrity, and credibility. Here, then, is where evaluation use can take a back seat to other agendas. Staff will resist being made to look bad and will often treat the mildest suggestions for improvements as deep criticisms. Evaluators, worried about accusations that they've lost their independence, emphasize negative findings. In the next chapter, on politics and ethics, we'll revisit this confrontation of perspectives. In this section, I want to make two points: (1) one person's negative is another person's positive; and (2) evaluators can do much to increase staff receptivity by shifting the focus of reporting to learning and use rather than simply being judged as good or bad.

The context for these two points is a general belief that most evaluations have negative findings. Howard Freeman (1977), an evaluation pioneer, expressed the opinion that the preponderance of negative findings diminished use. He recommended, somewhat tongue-in-cheek, that "in view of the experience of the failure of most evaluations to come up with positive impact findings, evaluation researchers probably would do well to encourage the 'biasing' of evaluations in the direction of obtaining positive results" (p. 30). He went on to add that evaluators ought to play a more active role in helping design programs that have some hope of demonstrating positive impact, based on treatments that are highly specific and carefully targeted.

Freeman's colleague Peter Rossi, coauthor of one of the most widely used evaluation texts (Rossi and Freeman 1993), shared the view that most evaluations show zero impacts on targeted clients and problems. He asserted, also tongue-in-cheek, that "only those programs likely to fail are evaluated." This led him to formulate Rossi's Plutonium Law of Evaluation: "Program operators will explode when exposed to typical evaluation research findings" (quoted in Shadish et al. 1991:386–87).

On the other hand, Michael Scriven (1991b) has observed presumably the same scene and concluded that evaluations display a "General Positive Bias" such that there is a "strong tendency to turn in more favorable results than are justified" (p. 175).

The problems I have with either stereotype, that most evaluations are negative or most are positive, is, first, they are impressions, not the result of any systematic analysis, and, second, they impose a dichotomous win/lose, pass/fail, success/failure, and positive/negative construct on evaluation results that, in my experience, actually display considerable diversity and balance. This tendency to label evaluation findings as either positive or negative seems born of a tendency I find common among evaluators and decision makers: to think of evaluation findings in monolithic, absolute, and purely summative terms. This becomes especially true when evaluation findings get into the media—which tends to exaggerate the negative because negative findings make more compelling and attention-grabbing headlines. In my experience, evaluation findings are seldom either completely positive or completely negative. Furthermore, whether findings are interpreted as positive or negative depends on who is using and interpreting the findings. As the old adage observes, *Whether the glass is half empty or half full depends on whether you're drinking or pouring.*

Consider these data. In our 20 federal health evaluation case studies, respondents described findings as follows:

Evaluator and decision maker independently agreed that the findings were:

Basically positive	5
Basically negative	2
Mixed positive-negative	7
Evaluator and decision maker disagreed in characterizing the findings	6

Our sample was not random, but it was as systematic and representative of federal evaluations as we could make it given the difficulty of identifying a "universe" of evaluations. Only 2 of 20 were basically negative; the most common pattern was a mix of positive and negative; and in 6 of 20 cases, the evaluator and primary decision maker disagreed about the nature of the judgment rendered. Moreover, in only one case did any of our respondents feel that the positive or negative nature of findings explained much about use. Because we encountered few summative decisions, the overall positive or negative nature of the evaluation was less important than how the findings could be used to improve programs. In addition, the positive or negative findings of a particular study constituted only one piece of information that fed into a larger process of deliberation and was interpreted in the larger context of other available information. Absolute judgments of a positive or negative nature were less useful than specific, detailed statements about levels of impact, the nature of relationships, and variations in implementation and effectiveness. This shifts the focus from whether findings are negative or positive to whether the evaluation results contain useful information that can provide direction for programmatic action.

Evaluators can shape the environment and context in which findings are reviewed so that the focus is on learning and improvement rather than absolute judgment (see Torres et al. 2004). Placing emphasis on organizational learning, action research, participatory evaluation, collaborative approaches, developmental evaluation, and empowerment evaluation—approaches discussed in Chapter 5—can defuse fear of and resistance to negative judgment.

As this discussion illustrates, when striving to get evaluations used, we often focus on overcoming resistance to findings, especially negative findings. The opposite problem, less often discussed, is overcoming apathy—or boredom. In Exhibit 13.12, experienced internal evaluator Gene Lyle offers advice about overcoming boredom when presenting routine performance data to the same intended users on a regular basis (e.g., annual reports).

Finally, it's worth remembering, philosophically, that the positive or negative nature of evaluation findings can never be established with any absolute certainty. As Sufi wise-fool Mulla Nasrudin once advised, a heavy dose of humility should accompany judgments about what is good or bad. Nasrudin had the opportunity to render this caution at a teahouse. A monk entered and said:

"My Master taught me to spread the word that mankind will never be fulfilled until the man who has not been wronged is as indignant about a wrong as the man who actually has been wronged."
The assembly was momentarily impressed. Then Nasrudin spoke: "My Master taught me that nobody at all should become indignant about anything until he is sure that what he thinks is a wrong is in fact a wrong—and not a blessing in disguise."

—Shah 1964:58–59

Distinguish Dissemination from Use

Dissemination of findings to audiences beyond intended users is distinct from the kind of use that has been the focus of this book. Studies can have an impact on all kinds of audiences in all kinds of ways. As a social scientist, I value and want to encourage the full and free dissemination of evaluation findings. Each of us ought to be permitted to indulge in the fantasy that our evaluation reports will have an impact across the land and through the years. But only a handful of studies will ever enjoy (or suffer) such widespread dissemination.

Dissemination takes us beyond intended use by intended users into the broader concept of evaluation influence, both intended and unintended (e.g., Kirkhart 2000). This includes instances where planned dissemination *hopes for* broader influence but can't be sure if or where this will occur. Exhibit 13.13 reminds us of the boundaries between intended use of both evaluation findings and processes and unintended influences that can accompany dissemination. In between is a gray area of hope and possibility that is less than fully intentional and more than laissez-faire unintentional use.

Dissemination efforts will vary greatly from study to study. The nature of dissemination, like everything else, is a matter for negotiation between evaluators and decision makers. In such negotiations, dissemination costs and benefits should be estimated. The questions addressed in an evaluation will have different meanings for people not directly involved in the painstaking process of focusing the evaluation.

Studying Use

We have very good methods for gathering social science knowledge but considerably less good advice about how to put it to use. What we most need to study is not how to do social science *but how to use it.*

—Michael Scriven (2005e:78).

EXHIBIT 13.12

Overcoming the Boredom of Repeat Presentations

As I was writing this chapter, Gene Lyle retired from a long and distinguished career as an internal evaluator in Ramsey County Community Human Services Department in Minnesota. The American Evaluation Association recognized Gene for his work by awarding him the Alva and Gunnar Myrdal Government Award in 2000. I asked Gene if, as an internal evaluator having presented findings many, many times over the years, there was some special evaluation reporting issue that he had never seen addressed in the literature. He quickly responded: "Boredom." I asked him to elaborate. Here, then, is the wisdom of experience speaking on the challenge of making evaluation presentations interesting.

On Boredom

Since internal evaluation often involves the management of systems that generate routine reports over time—performance measurement being an example—the evaluator often must present essentially the same data sets over and over again, often with little variation in outcomes. This can lead to a dulling of interest. Therein lies one of the skeletons in the internal evaluator's closet: boredom!

When data from a reporting system are first presented—we're pretty much talking formative evaluations here—there is usually curiosity, questioning, high interest, and motivation to explore the data. Let's say we're looking at data about the effectiveness of social work and foster care in returning children to their parental homes, and this information is being presented once every three months. The first two or three times people will be eager to see the results, study them, ask for more information than what may already be in the evaluation, and maybe even make decisions based upon the findings. But if the results do not change significantly over time, if they remain static (even if that's a good thing), they may become fainter and fainter blips on the intended users' radar screens.

How to deal with this eventuality? Here are some suggestions.

- Pre-review the results before meeting with reviewers. Anticipate questions they may ask based on the data and results.
- Present results in person if at all possible. Also, if possible, review results with the people who are actually and directly providing the service.
- Encourage dialog about the results.
- Do not overinterpret. Encourage the reviewers to interpret for themselves.
- When the review is finished, take time on your own to reflect on what you heard and saw. You may later recall suggestions or concerns that were overlooked in the review itself.
- Follow up on any recommendations for change to the evaluation itself. Negotiate with the reviewers to incorporate their suggestions.
- At the very least, do an annual review of the evaluation with the stakeholders to determine where it meets, and doesn't meet, their needs. For example, are the measures still appropriate? Do we need different data from different sources? Are the programs we're evaluating operating any differently now compared with when the evaluation was established? (But don't wait until an annual review to ask these questions and make changes if they are necessary.)

In the real world evaluations can only be sustained for a limited time in the format in which they were first developed. They will inevitably need to be changed within a year or two of their initiation. Within five years they will either be totally different or will have disappeared altogether. There are too many forces operating against static evaluations. Boredom is one of the indicators that the wise evaluator will use to monitor the need for change.

SOURCE: Printed with permission of Gene Lyle.

Different individuals and audiences will be interested in a given evaluation for reasons not always possible to anticipate. Effective dissemination involves skills in extrapolating the evaluation specifics of a particular study for use by readers in a different setting (raising issues of external validity and generalizability).

The problematic utility of trying to design an evaluation relevant to multiple audiences, each conceptualized in vague and general terms, was what led to the emphasis in utilization-focused evaluation on identification and organization of primary intended users. Dissemination can broaden and enlarge the impact of a study in important ways, but the nature of those long-term impacts is largely beyond the control of the evaluator. What the evaluator can control is the degree to which findings address the concerns of specific intended users. That is the use for which I take responsibility: intended use by intended users. Dissemination is not use, though it can be useful.

Use Is a Process, Not a Report

Analyzing and interpreting results can be exciting processes. Many nights have turned into morning before evaluators have finished trying new computer runs to tease out the nuances in some data set. The work of months, sometimes years, finally comes to fruition as data are analyzed and interpreted, conclusions drawn, and recommendations considered. Great relief comes in finishing an evaluation report, so much relief that it can seem like the report was the purpose. But use is the purpose, and, as this

EXHIBIT 13.13

Matrix of Intentionality and Use/Influence

	Findings Use/Influence	Process Uses/Influences
Intended	Intended use by intended users	Includes explicit, planned evaluation capacity building as well as other process uses
Intended/unintended—gray area	Intentionality focused on primary intended users, but planned dissemination *hopes for* broader influence (though can't be sure if or where this will occur).	Evaluator facilitates the evaluation process to build capacity, but this is implicit and those stakeholders who are involved are motivated by and focused on findings use.
Unintended	Unplanned influence of findings beyond primary intended users—and even beyond original dissemination	Evaluation capacity building is implicit (an artifact of participation in the evaluation)

book has emphasized throughout, use is a process, not a report or single event. This chapter has emphasized that the challenges and excitement of analysis, interpretation, and judgment ought not be the sole prerogative of evaluators. Stakeholders can become involved in struggling with data, too, increasing both their commitment to and understanding of the findings.

I remember fondly the final days of an evaluation when my co-evaluators and I were on the phone with program staff two or three times a day as we analyzed data on an educational project to inform a major decision about whether it met criteria as a valid model for federal dissemination funding. Program staff shared with us the process of watching the findings take final shape. Preliminary analyses appeared negative; as the sample became more complete, the findings looked more positive to staff; finally, a mixed picture of positive and negative conclusions emerged. Because the primary users had been intimately involved in designing the evaluation, we encountered no last-minute attacks on methods to explain away negative findings. The program staff understood the data, from whence it came, what it revealed, and how it could be used for program development. They didn't get the dissemination grant that year, but they got direction about how to implement the program more consistently and increase its impact. Two years later, with new findings, they did win recognition as a "best practices" exemplar, an award that came with a dissemination grant.

Figuring out what findings mean and how to apply them engages us in that most human of processes: making sense of the world. Utilization-focused evaluators invite users along on the whole journey, alternatively exciting and treacherous, from determining what's worth knowing to interpreting the results and following through with action. In that spirit, Marvin Alkin (1990:148) suggested a tee shirt that user-oriented evaluators could give to intended users:

COME ON INTO THE DATA POOL

Follow-Up Exercises

1. Locate an evaluation report. Identify the major findings. Now imagine that you were working with primary intended users for the evaluation *before* the data were collected. (a) Fabricate simulated findings that could be used to prepare intended users for subsequent data engagement, for example, findings that are better and worse than those actually attained. Format the simulated data for presentation to intended users. What facilitation questions would you ask to help the intended users engage with the simulated data? (b) Construct standards of desirability that would guide intended users in interpreting the findings. What facilitation questions would you have asked to help the intended users of this evaluation generate standards of desirability before data collection?

2. Locate an evaluation report on some program of interest to you. Examine how the report handles the distinctions between analysis, interpretation, judgment, and recommendations (see Exhibit 13.2 and Exhibit 13.10). Give examples of these distinctions from the report. Comment on and critique the extent to which these distinctions are adhered to in the evaluation. Based on your reading and review of this report, how important do you believe it is to adhere to these distinctions? What are the challenges of adherence?

3. Identify a commonly used and widely cited statistic like the crime rate, inflation rate, unemployment rate, poverty rate, dropout rate, HIV infection rate, or divorce rate. Locate at least three media reports where this statistic is used. Find out how it is defined. Identify alternative definitions, meanings, and uses. What issues would you raise about this statistic if primary intended users wanted to include it in an evaluation as a basis of comparison for a program outcome? Discuss how you would use such statistics in an evaluation and how you would discuss their use with primary intended users.

4. Locate an evaluation report that includes recommendations. Convert those recommendations into (a) at least three options for each recommendation (as if you were presenting primary intended users with choices) and (b) three *futures-oriented*

scenarios, one based on optimistic assumptions, one based on pessimistic assumptions, and one that assumes that the future will be much like the recent past. (Note: Items a and b are separate tasks.)

5. Using Menu 13.1 (Menu of Program Comparisons), use the actual outcome for a real program from that program's evaluation and discuss what comparisons were made. Construct comparisons using all the alternatives in Menu 13.1. (You may have to make up data for some comparisons.)

6. Using Menu 13.2, discuss the reporting situation that would be appropriate for each of the Style and Format Options (both Written and Oral). Show that you can match the reporting option to a situation for which that option is a good match. Make it clear how the situation you describe lends itself to each reporting option.

PART 4

Realities and Practicalities of Utilization-Focused Evaluation

In Search of Universal Evaluation Questions

A long time ago, a young evaluator set out on a quest to discover the perfect evaluation instrument, one that would be completely valid, always reliable, and universally applicable. His search led to Halcolm, known far and wide for his wisdom.

Young Evaluator:	Great Master Halcolm, forgive this intrusion, but I am on a quest for the perfect evaluation instrument.
Halcolm:	Tell me about this perfect instrument.
Young Evaluator:	I seek an instrument that is valid and reliable in all evaluation situations that can be used to evaluate all projects, all programs, all impacts, all benefits, and all people. . . . I am seeking an evaluation tool that anyone can use to evaluate anything.
Halcolm:	What would be the value of such an instrument?
Young Evaluator:	Free of any errors, it would rid evaluation of politics and make evaluation truly scientific. It would save money, time, and frustration. We'd finally be able to get at the truth about programs.
Halcolm:	Where would you use such an instrument?
Young Evaluator:	Everywhere!

Halcolm:	With whom would you use it?
Young Evaluator:	Everyone!
Halcolm:	What, then, would become of the process of designing situationally specific evaluations?
Young Evaluator:	Who needs it?
Halcolm:	[Silence]
Young Evaluator:	Am I on the right path, asking the most important questions?
Halcolm:	[Silence]
Young Evaluator:	What do I need to do to get an answer?
Halcolm:	[Silence]
Young Evaluator:	What methods can I use to find out what I want to know?
Halcolm:	[Silence]
Young Evaluator:	(In obvious frustration), Oh, what's the use?
Halcolm:	(Smiling wisely) You already have what you seek. Your last five questions are the answer.

14

Power, Politics, and Ethics

 theory of evaluation must be as much a theory of political interaction as it is a theory of how to determine facts.

—Lee J. Cronbach and Associates (1980:3)

Politics and Evaluation:
A Case Example

During the mid-1970s, the Kalamazoo Education Association (KEA) in Michigan was locked in battle with the local school administration over the Kalamazoo Schools Accountability System. The accountability system consisted of 13 components, including teacher and principal performance; fall and spring standardized testing; teacher-constructed criterion-referenced tests in high school; teacher peer evaluations; and parent, student, and principal evaluations of teachers. The system had received considerable national attention, as when *The American School Board Journal* (in April 1974) editorialized that Kalamazoo Schools had designed

"one of the most comprehensive computerized systems of personnel evaluation and accountability yet devised" (p. 40).

Yet conflict enveloped the system as charges and countercharges were exchanged. The KEA, for example, charged that teachers were being demoralized; the superintendent responded that teachers didn't want to be accountable. The KEA claimed widespread teacher dissatisfaction; the superintendent countered that the hostility to the system came largely from a vocal minority of malcontent unionists. The newspapers hinted that the administration might be so alienating teachers that the system could not operate effectively. School board members, facing reelection, were nervous.

Ordinarily, a situation of this kind would continue to be one of charge and countercharge based entirely on selective perception, with no underlying data to clarify and test the reality of the opposing positions. But the KEA sought outside assistance from Vito Perrone, Dean of the Center for Teaching and Learning, University of North Dakota, who had a reputation for fairness and integrity. The KEA proposed that Dean Perrone conduct public hearings at which interested parties could testify on and be questioned about the operations and consequences of the Kalamazoo Accountability System. Perrone suggested that such a public forum might become a political circus; moreover, he was concerned that a fair and representative picture of the system could not be developed in such an openly polemical and adversarial forum. He suggested instead that a survey of teachers be conducted to describe their experiences with the accountability system and to collect a representative overview of teacher opinions about their experiences.

Perrone attempted to negotiate the nature of the accountability review with the superintendent of schools, but the administration refused to cooperate, arguing that the survey should be postponed until after the school board election when everyone could reflect more calmly on the situation. Perrone decided to go forward, believing that the issues were already politicized and that data were needed to inform public debate. The evaluation was limited to providing a review of the accountability program *from the perspective of teachers* based on a mail survey conducted independently by the Minnesota Center for Social Research (which is how I became involved, as its Director). The evaluation staff of the school system previewed the survey instrument and contributed wording changes.

The results revealed intense teacher hostility toward and fear of the accountability system. Of the respondents, 93 percent

believed that "accountability as practiced in Kalamazoo creates an undesirable atmosphere of anxiety among teachers," 90 percent asserted that "the accountability system is mostly a public relations effort," and 83 percent rated the "overall accountability system in Kalamazoo" either "poor" or "totally inadequate."

The full analysis of the data, including teachers' open-ended comments, suggested that the underlying problem was a hostile teacher-administration relationship created by the way in which the accountability system was developed (without teacher input) and implemented (forced on teachers from above). The data also documented serious misuse of standardized tests in Kalamazoo. The school board, initially skeptical of the survey, devoted a full meeting to discussion of the report.

The subsequent election eroded the school administration's support and the superintendent resigned. The new superintendent and school board used the survey results as a basis for starting fresh with teachers. A year later, the KEA officials reported a new environment of teacher-administration cooperation in developing a mutually acceptable accountability system.

The evaluation report was only one of many factors that came into play in Kalamazoo at that time, but the results answered questions about the scope and nature of teachers' perspectives. Candidates for the position of superintendent called Dean Perrone to discuss the report. It became part of the political context within which administration-teacher relations developed throughout the following school year—information that had to be taken into account. The evaluation findings were used by teacher association officials to enhance their political position and increase their input into the accountability system.

The Political Nature of Evaluation

Scientists become uneasy when one group pushes a set of findings to further its own political purposes, as happened in Kalamazoo. They much prefer that the data serve all parties equally in a civilized search for the best answer. Research and experience suggest, however, that the Kalamazoo case, in which use was conditioned by political considerations, is quite common. In our study of how federal health evaluations were used, we found that use was affected by intra- and inter-agency rivalries, budgetary fights with the Office of Management and Budget and Congress, power struggles between Washington administrators and local program personnel, and internal debates about the purposes or accomplishments of pet programs. Budgetary battles seemed to be the most political, followed by turf battles over who had the power to act, but *political considerations intruded in some way into every evaluation we examined.*

Political considerations include ideology. Former U.S. Surgeon General Richard H. Carmona testified before the U. S. Congress that from 2002 to 2006, senior White House officials repeatedly tried to weaken or suppress important public health reports because of ideological considerations. For example, he testified, officials delayed for years and tried to "water down" landmark research on secondhand smoke that concluded that even brief exposure to cigarette smoke could cause immediate harm (Harris 2007). The administration of President George W. Bush spent hundreds of millions of dollars on abstinence programs long after evaluations showed that such programs were largely ineffective. Investigative journalist Michael Specter (2006) interviewed a former senior official at the prestigious Centers for Disease Control who described systematic distortions and misrepresentations of evaluation findings about the effectiveness of sex education programs, the use of condoms to prevent disease, and the ineffectiveness of abstinence-only approaches with teenagers. "They were the most horrific examples of manipulating science I have ever seen. Abstinence is the only thing that matters to this crowd" (p. 60). Specter cites a long list of health policy decisions in which evaluation and research findings reviewed and supported by science advisory committees internal to the U.S. federal government were ignored by political appointees who took actions directly contrary to those recommended by the scientists.

One can find such examples in every political administration, whether in the United States or around the world (e.g., Flyvjerg 2001). What varies is the degree, breadth, and insidiousness of such political intrusions. Nor are attempts to suppress evaluation findings for political reasons new. Shortly after the end of World War II, distinguished Keynesian economist John Kenneth Galbraith (before he became famous) was asked to conduct a study of the effectiveness of America's bombing in undermining German economic production. He reviewed captured documents and interviewed former senior German military personnel. His team found that only 5 percent of German production capacity had actually been destroyed by the extensive Allied bombing. The Army Air Force disliked and disputed Galbraith's findings, first suppressing them, then delaying them, and eventually burying them in a much larger report (Parker 2006). Such examples abound.

Eleanor Chelimsky, former Director of the Evaluation Institute at the Government Accountability Office (GAO), in her 2006 plenary address at the American Evaluation Association (AEA) annual conference

regaled the audience with stories of dealing with political machinations in getting the U.S. Congress to pay attention to important evaluation findings. She titled her presentation: "A Clash of Cultures: Improving the Fit Between Evaluative Independence and the Political Requirements of a Democratic Society"—and that nicely captures the challenge. In his plenary presentation at the same conference the next day, distinguished evaluation theorist Ernie House described in detail how political considerations, power dynamics, and money corrupt pharmaceutical research and the supposedly independent regulatory processes of approving drugs.

The Program Evaluation Standards acknowledge the political nature of evaluation and offer guidance for making evaluations politically viable:

The evaluation should be planned and conducted with anticipation of the different positions of various interest groups, so that their cooperation may be obtained, and so that possible attempts by any of these groups to curtail evaluation operations or to bias or misapply the results can be averted or counteracted. (Joint Committee 1994:F2)

A political perspective also informs the Guiding Principles of the American Evaluation Association (AEA Task Force 1995) as they address the "Responsibilities for General and Public Welfare: Evaluators should articulate and take into account the diversity of interests and values that may be related to the general and public welfare" (p. 20). This principle mandates a political responsibility that goes well beyond just collecting and reporting data.

Meeting the standard on political viability and the principle of general responsibility will necessitate some way of astutely identifying various stakeholders and their interests. *Stakeholder mapping* (Crosby and Bryson 2005) can be helpful in this regard.

Anticipating Political Reactions to Evaluation

Eleanor Chelimsky, as Assistant Comptroller General for Program Evaluation and Methodology at the Government Accountability Office (formerly the General Accounting Office) (GAO), directed scores of evaluations in the highly political environment of the U.S. federal government, goring the oxen of both the executive and legislative branches, as well as lobbyists and advocates on all sides. She has reflected extensively and insightfully about the importance of *anticipating political reactions to evaluation* as an added incentive to be hypervigilant about an evaluation's credibility. Ensuring an evaluation's credibility, she has insisted, "remains a critical weapon in the political battles that evaluation faces" (2007:28).

> Fortunately, the need to be methodologically credible is part and parcel of the evaluator's armamentarium. It is ingrained, a product of our training and our awareness that the ultimate audience for our work will be other evaluators (p. 28).

We can use anticipation of how other evaluators will judge our work, Chelimsky argues, to counter various political pressures that might undermine our credibility. Understanding that we are part of a profession with standards and principles, and asserting our professional responsibility to conduct credible evaluations that are useful—and actually used—does not mean avoiding political perspectives but, rather, anticipating them and thereby being prepared to address them. She reflects that at GAO the evaluation staff had

> so many experiences in which our own need for credibility succeeded in countering the various pressures brought by congressional or agency stakeholders that after a while, we developed all our evaluation designs with an eye toward defending them and especially, our methods and analysis choices. Also, because all of our work often depended heavily on its methodological quality . . . , there was a utilization-focused component, along with self-defense and survivability, inherent in our efforts. (2007:28)

Chelimsky includes among the things that must be anticipated, attempts by those in power to hide needed data from evaluators, and therefore the public. Or to suppress government evaluation findings by classifying reports as *top secret*. So she warns,

> evaluators will have to learn to deal with secrecy even as it expands to grotesque levels and even, as happened to us, they are faced with the bizarre situation in which their report is classified so high that they, the evaluators who wrote it, are no longer allowed to read it. (p. 25).

SOURCE: Eleanor Chelimsky (2007).

Exhibit 14.1 offers one kind of matrix for use in mapping stakeholders according to their initial inclination toward the program being evaluated (support, opposition, or neutrality) and how much they have at stake in the evaluation's outcome (a high state, a moderate stake, or little stake).

Evaluation's Coming of Age: Beyond Political Innocence and Naivete

The article most often credited with raising evaluators' consciousness about the politics of evaluation was Carol Weiss's 1973 analysis of "Where Politics and Evaluation Research Meet." Reprinted 20 years later in *Evaluation Practice,* in recognition of its status as a classic, the article identified three major ways in which politics intrude in evaluation: (1) programs and policies are "creatures of political decisions" so evaluations implicitly judge those decisions; (2) evaluations feed political decision making and compete with other perspectives in the political process; and (3) evaluation is inherently political by its

EXHIBIT 14.1

Mapping Stakeholders' Stakes

	Estimate of Various Stakeholders' Initial Inclination Toward the Program		
How high are the stakes for various primary stakeholders?	Favorable	Neutral or Unknown	Antagonistic
High			
Moderate			
Low			

very nature because of the issues it addresses and the conclusions it reaches. Weiss ([1973] 1993) concluded,

> Knowing that political constraints and resistances exist is not a reason for abandoning evaluation research; rather it is a precondition for useable evaluation research. Only when the evaluator has insight into the interests and motivations of other actors in the system, into the roles that he himself is consciously or inadvertently playing, the obstacles and opportunities that impinge upon the evaluative effort, and the limitations and possibilities for putting the results to work—only with sensitivity to the politics of evaluation research—can the evaluator be as creative and strategically useful as he should be. (P. 94)

Weiss showed that politics and use are joined at the hip. In this classic analysis, she made use directly contingent on the political sophistication of evaluators. How, then, can utilization-focused evaluators become politically sophisticated? The first step comes with being able to recognize what is political.

Often, in our interviews with evaluators about how federal health evaluations had been used, we found them uneasy about discussing the tensions between their research and politics; they were hesitant to acknowledge the ways in which the evaluation was affected by political considerations. We found that many evaluators disassociated themselves from the political side of evaluation, despite evidence throughout their interviews that they were enmeshed in politics. One interviewee, a research scientist with 12 years experience doing federal evaluations, described pressure from Congress to accelerate the evaluation, then added, "We really had no knowledge or feeling about political relationships. We are quite innocent on such matters. We may not have recognized [political factors]. We're researchers" [EV5:7].

In another case, the decision maker stated that the evaluation was never used because program funding had already been terminated before the evaluation was completed. When asked about this in a later interview the evaluator replied, "I wasn't aware that the program was under any serious threat. Political matters related to the evaluation did not come up with us. It was not discussed to my recollection before, during, or after the study" [EV97:12–13].

Part of evaluator's innocence or ignorance about political processes stemmed from a definition of politics that included only happenings of momentous consequence. Evaluators frequently answered our questions about political considerations only in terms of the overall climate of presidential or congressional politics and campaigns. They didn't define the day-to-day negotiations out of which programs and studies evolve as politics. One evaluator explained that no political considerations affected the study because "this was not a global kind of issue. There were vested interests all right, but it was not what would be considered a hot issue. Nobody was going to resign over whether there was this program or not" [EV145:12].

Failing to recognize that an issue involves power and politics reduces an evaluator's strategic options and increases the likelihood that the evaluator will be used unwittingly as some stakeholder's political puppet. It is instructive to look at cases in which the evaluators we interviewed described their work as nonpolitical. Consider, for example, the responses of an academic researcher who studied citizen boards of community mental health programs. At various points in the interview, he objected to the term *evaluation* and explained that he had conducted "basic research," not an evaluation, thus the nonpolitical nature of his work; this despite the fact that the study was classified by the funding agency as an evaluation and was used to make policy decisions about the processes studied. He was adamant throughout the interview that no political considerations or factors affected the study or its use in any way. He explained that he

had demanded and received absolute autonomy so that no external political pressures could be brought to bear. In his mind, his work exemplified nonpolitical academic research. Consider, then, responses he gave to other questions.

Item: When asked how the study began, the evaluator admitted using personal connections to get funding for the project:

We got in touch with some people [at the agency] and they were rather intrigued by this.... It came at year's end and, as usual, they had some funds left over.... I'm pretty certain we were not competing with other groups; they felt a sole bid kind of thing wasn't going to get other people angry. [EV4:1, 5–6]

Item: The purpose of the study?

We were wondering about conflict patterns in citizen boards. At that time, the funding agency was concerned because many of their centers were in high-density ghetto areas, not only cutting across the black population, but with Mexican Americans or Puerto Ricans thrown in. Up until the time of the study, many agencies' boards were pretty middle-class. Now, you can put in "poor people" and minorities—how is that going to work? Is that going to disturb the system as far as the middle-class people were concerned? Of course, some of them were pretty conservative, and they were afraid that we were rocking the boat by looking at this. [EV4:4]

Item: The study presented recommendations about how citizen boards should be organized and better integrated into programs, matters of considerable controversy.

Item: The results were used to formulate agency policy and, eventually, Congressional legislation.

We kept people talking about citizen participation—What does it truly mean? You see, that generated a lot of thinking. [EV4:14]

Item: How did the results get disseminated?

We released the results in a report. Now, the fascinating thing, like throwing a pebble in a pond, [was that] Psychology Today picked up this report and wrote a glowing little review . . . ; then they made some nasty comments about the cost of government research. [EV4:10–11]

Item: The researcher recounted a lengthy story about how a member of nationally visible consumer advocate Ralph Nader's staff got hold of the study, figured out the identity of local centers in the study's sample, and wrote a separate report. The researcher and his colleagues engaged lawyers but were unable to stop Nader's staff from using and abusing their data and sources, some of whom were identified incorrectly.

We just didn't have the money to fight them, so we were furious. We thought that we would go to our lawyer friends and see if they couldn't do something, but they all came back with pretty much the same kind of negative response. What finally happened was that when [Nader's] big report came out, using our stuff, they gave it to the New York Times and various newspapers. [EV4:11–12]

Item: After the study, the researchers were involved in several regional and national meetings about their findings.

We go to an enormous number of meetings. And so we talked . . . and we've become known in a limited circle as "the experts in this sort of thing." [EV4:20]

At one such meeting, the researcher became involved in an argument with local medical staff.

The doctors and more middle-class people in mental health work said we were just making too much of a fuss, that things were really going along pretty well. And I remember distinctly in that room, which must have had 200 people that day, the blacks and

some of the—you might call them militant liberals—were whispering to each other and I began to feel the tension and bickerings that were going on. [EV4:19]

Politics by Any Other Name

The researcher who conducted this study—a study of class and race conflict on mental health citizen boards that *judged the effectiveness of such boards and included recommendations* for improving their functioning—insisted that his work was nonpolitical academic research, not an evaluation. Yet his own interview responses reveal that personal influence was used to get funding. The research question was conceived in highly value-laden terms: *middle-class boards* versus *poor people's boards.* Concerns emerged about "rocking the boat." The study's controversial findings and recommendations were cited in national publications and used in policy formulation. The researchers became expert advocates for a certain view of citizen participation. *Personal contacts, value-laden definitions, rocking the boat, controversial recommendations, taking sides, defending positions—of such things are politics made.* These political influences on the evaluation were not direct, heavy-handed intrusions, or formal and official political action, what is sometimes called "big 'P' Politics." Rather, these are exemplars of "*small 'p' politics*"—in-the-trenches, day-to-day, cumulative political forces at work in evaluation. To ignore *small "p" politics* is to risk making an evaluation a *phantasmagorical political farce.*

Sources of Evaluation's Political Inherency

The political nature of evaluation stems from several factors:

1. The fact that people are involved in evaluation means that the values,

perceptions, and politics of everyone involved (scientists, decision makers, funders, program staff) impinge on the process from start to finish.

2. The fact that evaluation requires classifying and categorizing makes it political. Categories inevitably filter the data collected. One of the more politically sophisticated evaluators we interviewed described the politics of categories:

> Our decision to compare urban and rural reflected the politics of the time—concerns that city problems are different from rural problems. Since this was a national program, we couldn't concentrate solely on problems in the city and not pay any attention to rural areas. That wouldn't have been politically smart.
>
> And then our decision to report the percent nonwhite mental illness, that certainly reflects attention to the whole political and socioeconomic distribution of the population. In that we used factors important in the politics of the nation, to that extent we were very much influenced by political considerations. We tried to reflect the political, social, and economic problems we thought were important at that time. [EV12:7–8]

3. The fact that empirical data undergird evaluation makes it political because data always require interpretation. Interpretation is only partly logical and deductive; it's also value laden and perspective dependent.

4. The fact that actions and decisions follow from evaluation makes it political. Decisions affect allocation of resources and distribution of power. To the extent that information is an instrument, basis, or reason for making decisions within or among institutions, evaluation is a political activity.

5. The fact that programs and organizations are involved makes evaluation political. Organizations allocate power, status, and resources. Evaluation affects those allocation processes.

One of the weapons employed in organizational conflicts is evaluative information and judgments.

6. The fact that information is involved in evaluation makes it political. Information leads to knowledge; knowledge reduces uncertainty; reduction of uncertainty facilitates action; and action is necessary to the accumulation of power.

The "Is" and the "Ought" of Evaluation Politics

We have not been discussing if evaluation should be political. The evidence indicates that whether researchers like it or not, evaluation will be influenced by political factors. The degree of politicalization varies, but it is never entirely absent. One astute decision maker we interviewed had made his peace with the inevitability of politics in evaluation as follows:

> [Government decision making] is not rational in the sense that a good scientific study would allow you to sit down and plan everybody's life. And I'm glad it's not because I would get very tired, very early, of something that ran only by the numbers. Somebody'd forget part of the numbers. So, I'm not fighting the system. But you do have to be careful what you expect from a rational study when you insert it into the system. It can have tremendous impact, but it's a political, not a rational process. . . . Life is not a very simple thing. [DM328:18–19]

In our interviews, evaluators tended to portray their findings as rational and objective while other inputs into the decision-making process were subjective and political. One evaluator lamented that his study wasn't used because "politics outweighed our results" [EV131:8]. Such a dichotomy between evaluation and politics fails to recognize the political and power-laden nature of evaluative information.

The Power of Evaluation

Power corrupts.
PowerPoint corrupts absolutely.

—Bob Williams

Connecting evaluation use to a theory of power has helped me explain to intended users how and why their involvement in a utilization-focused evaluation is in their own best interest. It provides a basis for understanding how knowledge is power. In essence, use of evaluation will occur in direct proportion to its power-enhancing capability. Power-enhancing capability is determined as follows: *The power of evaluation varies directly with the degree to which the findings reduce the uncertainty of action for specific stakeholders.*

This view of the relationship between evaluation and power is derived from the classic organizational theories of Michael Crozier (1964) and James Thompson (1967). Crozier studied and compared a French clerical agency and a tobacco factory. He found that power relationships developed around uncertainties. Every group tried to limit its dependence on others and, correspondingly, enlarge its own areas of discretion. They did this by making their own behavior unpredictable in relation to other groups. Interpreting what he found, Crozier drew on Robert Dahl's (1957) definition of power: "The power of a person A over a person B is the ability of A to obtain that B do something he would not otherwise have done." Systems attempt to limit conflicts over power through rationally designed and highly routinized structures, norms, and

tasks. Crozier (1964) found, however, that even in a highly centralized, routinized, and bureaucratic organization, it was impossible to eliminate uncertainties.

> In such a context, the power of A over B depends on A's ability to predict B's behavior and on the uncertainty of B about A's behavior. As long as the requirements of action created situations of uncertainty, the individuals who have to face them have power over those who are affected by the results of their choice. (P. 158)

Crozier found that supervisors in the clerical agency had no interest in passing information on to their superiors, the section chiefs. Section chiefs, in turn, competed with one another for attention from their superior—the division head. Section chiefs distorted the information they passed up to the division head to enhance their own positions. Section chiefs could get away with distortions because the lower-level supervisors, who knew the truth, were interested in keeping what they knew to themselves. The division head, on the other hand, used the information he received to schedule production and assign work. Knowing that he was dependent on information from others, and not being able to fully trust that information, his decisions were carefully conservative in the sense that he aimed only at safe, minimal levels of achievement because he knew he lacked sufficient information to narrow risks.

> The power of prediction stems to a major extent from the way information is distributed. The whole system of roles is so arranged that people are given information, the possibility of prediction and therefore control, precisely because of their position within the hierarchical pattern. (P. 158)

Whereas Crozier's analysis centered on power relationships and uncertainties between individuals and among groups within organizations, James Thompson (1967) found that a similar set of concepts could be applied to understand relationships between whole organizations. He argued that organizations are open systems that need resources and materials from outside and that "with this conception the central problem for complex organizations is one of coping with uncertainty" (p. 13). He found that assessment and evaluation are used by organizations as mechanisms for reducing uncertainty and enhancing their control over the multitude of contingencies with which they are faced. They evaluate themselves to assess their fitness for the future, and they evaluate the effectiveness of other organizations to increase their control over the maintenance of crucial exchange relationships. Information for prediction is information for control: thus the power of evaluation.

The Kalamazoo Schools Accountability System case example with which this chapter opened offers a good illustration of evaluation's role in reducing uncertainty and, thereby, enhancing power. The accountability system was initiated, in part, to control teachers. Teachers' hostility to the system led to uncertainty concerning the superintendent's ability to manage. The superintendent tried to stop the study that would establish the degree to which teacher opposition was widespread and crystallized. The board members let the study proceed because, as politicians, they deplored uncertainty. Once the study confirmed widespread teacher opposition, union officials used the results to force the superintendent's resignation, mobilize public opinion, and gain influence in the new administration. In particular, teachers won the right to participate with administration in developing the system that would be used to evaluate them, thereby enhancing their power and reducing their uncertainty.

The Kalamazoo case and cumulative results from studies of evaluation use illustrate a second theory of power that informs utilization-focused evaluation, the theory that decision making now takes place in a "shared-power" world, one in which no one is "in charge" so no single person, position, organization, or authority has the legitimacy or intelligence to act alone on important matters that affect many people (Crosby and Bryson 2005). A "shared-power" world is one in which coalitions and collaborations are needed to shape and inform action. Effective leaders throughout the world are having to adapt to sharing power (Crosby 1999), whether in policy development, strategic planning (Bryson 2004a) or evaluation. Sharing power means providing a process for diverse stakeholders to hear each other, build consensus, generate collective wisdom, and agree on a direction for action. Such a process, well-facilitated, grounds policy and interventions in sufficient credibility to make change viable and sustainable. *Utilization-focused evaluation*, with its sensitivity to diverse stakeholder interests and perspectives, and its emphasis on a negotiated approach to evaluation questions, design, and use, offers a strategy and process for making evaluation meaningful and useful in a *shared-power world*.

Transparency

Transparency concerns public access to evaluation data and findings and openness about methodological decisions and interpretations of conclusions. As Midge Smith, founder of The Evaluators Institute, observed in commentary about the future of the evaluation profession, "The increased prominence of politics in evaluation brings heightened expectations for transparency in our methods, procedures, and outcomes" (2003:384). Transparency is an issue in managing evaluations generally (Walker and

Wiseman 2006:374) and, especially, in government-sponsored evaluations (Davies, Newcomer, and Soydan 2006:174).

> Transparency in the activities of government and public service agencies has become a democratic *sine qua non*, legislated by access to information laws in many countries . . . . [However], it is clear that the present methods (principally legal ones) obliging organizations to practise greater transparency cannot fully achieve their purposes in the absence of a profound cultural change in favour of the said transparency. (Pasquie and Villeneuve 2007:147)

Evaluation associations worldwide have been working in support of this cultural shift by strongly advocating for transparency of government decision making and public access to data in a timely fashion. The European Evaluation Society (EES) has exercised particular leadership in this regard as shown in conference themes and presentations that have linked transparency to the larger issues of democracy and governance in civil society:

- "Taking Evaluation to the People," 2000, Lausanne
- "Governance, Democracy and Evaluation," 2004, Berlin
- "Evaluation in Society: Critical Connections," 2006, London
- "Evaluation in the Knowledge Society," 2007, Odense
- "Evaluation in Governance, Development and Progress," 2008, Lisbon

Distinguished evaluation scholar Ernest House, in his 2004 EES keynote speech, highlighted "control of information that threatens evaluation—and perhaps democracy" (House 2006:119). The litany of mechanisms used to control information includes suppressing evaluation reports, bureaucratic delays in finalizing publication of reports that amount to suppression, using national security concerns and fears to justify withholding information from the public, systematically distorting scientific information to support official policy positions, omitting from reports data that do not conform to ideological preferences, expunging information on government Web sites that contradict preferred policies, and even changing the findings of scientific reports.

Transparency is an antidote to the poison of secrecy among the powerful and privileged. But, as I noted in my 2000 EES keynote,

> It is worth remembering the long-standing and fundamental distinction between dissemination and utilization of evaluations. Transparency will mean the most when evaluation reports are presented in ways that are understandable, relevant and usable, characteristics that are often lacking in published evaluation reports. Innovative and creative forms of reporting that include actively engaging primary intended users in thinking about findings and their implications will extend and deepen the impacts of increased transparency. (Patton 2002c:130)

Transparency must be coupled with increasing the public's capacity for evaluative thinking if it is to translate into more deliberative and democratic civil societies.

Limits on Knowledge as Power

There is nothing a government hates more than to be well-informed; for it makes the process of arriving at decisions more complicated and difficult.

—British economist John Maynard Keynes (1883–1946); quoted in Sharpe (1977:44)

Knowledge is not always powerful. In pondering how social scientists came to

Evaluation in a "Shared-Power" World

A "shared-power" world is one in which no one is "in charge" (Crosby and Bryson 2005). It is a world in which no single person, position, organization, or authority has the legitimacy or intelligence to act alone on important matters that affect many people. A "shared-power" world is one in which coalitions and collaborations are needed to shape and inform action. Sharing power means providing a process for diverse stakeholders to hear each other, build consensus, generate collective wisdom, and agree on a direction for action. Such a process, well-facilitated, grounds policy and interventions in sufficient credibility to make change viable and sustainable. *Utilization-focused evaluation*, with its sensitivity to diverse stakeholder interests and perspectives, and its emphasis on a negotiated approach to evaluation questions, design, and use, offers a strategy and process for making evaluation meaningful and useful in a *shared-power world*.

overestimate their potential influence on government decision making, L. J. Sharpe (1977) concluded that

> one important cause of this overoptimism is the widespread assumption that governments are always in need of, or actively seek, information. But it seems doubtful whether this is the case. It is more likely that government has too much information, not too little—too much, that is, by its own estimation. (P. 44)

Having information, Sharpe argued, delays and complicates government decision making. Politicians are quite comfortable letting their politics be the basis for their policy preferences. Cynics accuse politicians who resist research and evaluation findings as operating from a stance of: "Don't confuse me with the facts."

Certainly, there are limitations to the maxim that knowledge is power. Four qualifiers on this maxim derive from the premises of utilization-focused evaluation.

Political Maxims for Utilization-Focused Evaluators

1. *Not All Information Is Useful*

To be power laden, information must be relevant and in a form that is understandable to users. Crozier (1964) recognized this qualifier in linking power to reduced uncertainty: "One should be precise and specify *relevant* uncertainty. . . . People and organizations will care only about what they can recognize as affecting them and, in turn, what is possibly within their control" (p. 158).

Government, in the abstract, may well have too much irrelevant, trivial, and useless information, but individual stakeholders, whether in government or other institutional settings, will tell you that they are always open to timely, relevant, and accurate information that can reduce uncertainty and increase their control.

2. *Not All People Are Information Users*

Individuals vary in their aptitude for handling uncertainty and their ability to exercise discretion. Differential socialization, education, and experience magnify such differences. In the political practice of evaluation, this means that information is power only in the hands (minds) of people who know how to use it and are open to using it. The challenge of use remains one of matching: *getting the right information to the right people*.

One evaluator in our use study insisted on this point. Drawing on 35 years in government, 20 of those years directly involved in research and evaluation, and several years as a private evaluation contractor on some 80 projects, he opined that good managers are anxious to get useful information.

In fact, they're hungry for it. The good manager "is interested in finding out what your views are, not defending his. . . . You know my sample is relatively small, but I'd say probably there are a quarter (25 percent) of what I'd call good managers" [EV346:15]. *These, he believed, were the people who use evaluation.*

What of people who are not inclined to use information—people who are intimidated by, indifferent to, or even hostile to evaluation? A utilization-focused evaluator looks for opportunities and strategies for creating and training information users. Thus, the challenge of increasing use consists of two parts: (1) finding and involving those who are, by inclination, information users and (2) training those not so inclined. Just as in cards you play the hand you're dealt, in evaluation, you sometimes have to play the stakeholders you're dealt.

It's helpful in this regard to consider the 20-50-30 rule proffered by organizational change specialist Price Pritchett (1996). He estimates that 20 percent of people are change friendly; another 50 percent are fence-sitters waiting to see which way the wind blows; and the remaining 30 percent are resisters. He counsels wooing the fence-sitters rather than the resisters while devoting generous attention to supporters of the process. "You must be willing to let squeaky wheels squeak. Save your grease for the quieter wheels that are carrying the load" (p. 4). Such political calculations undergird any change effort—and evaluation inherently holds the potential for change.

3. *Information Targeted at Use Is More Likely to Hit the Target*

It's difficult knowing in advance of a decision precisely what information will be most valuable. In the battle for control over uncertainty, one thing is certain—no one wants to be caught with less information than competitors for power. This fear leads to a lot of information being collected "just in case." One evaluator we interviewed explained the entire function of his office in these terms:

> I wouldn't want to be quoted by name, but there was a real question whether we were asked for these reports because they wanted them for decision making. We felt that the five-foot shelf we were turning out may have had no particular relevance to the real world. . . . But, this operation made it impossible for some Congressmen, or someone, to say that the issue had never been studied. Therefore, it would be a fairly standard administration ploy to study the issue so that it was not possible for somebody to insist you never even looked at the issue. [EV152:18]

Such a "just in case" approach to gathering data wastes scarce evaluation resources and fills shelves with neglected studies. It's impossible to study every possible future contingency. Utilization-focused evaluation requires a focus on real issues with real timelines aimed at real decisions—the opposite of "just in case" evaluation. In that way, utilization-focused evaluation aims at closing the gap between potential and actual use, between knowledge and action. Targeting an evaluation at intended use by intended users increases the odds of hitting the target.

4. *Only Credible Information Is Ultimately Powerful*

Eleanor Chelimsky, one of the profession's most experienced and successful evaluators in dealing with Congress, has reiterated at every opportunity that the foundation of evaluation use is credibility—not just information, but *credible* information. "Whether the issue is fairness, balance, methodological quality, or accuracy, no effort to establish credibility is ever wasted. The memory of poor quality lingers long" (Chelimsky 1987a:14).

Independent audits of evaluation quality offer one strategy for dealing with what Thomas Schwandt (1989a) called "the politics of verifying trustworthiness." The Program Evaluation Standards, in calling for *meta-evaluation* (Joint Committee 1994:A12; Schwandt and Halpern 1988) articulate an obligation to provide stakeholders with an independent assessment of an evaluation's strengths and weaknesses to guide stakeholders in judging an evaluation. Evaluation audits and meta-evaluation ensure evaluation credibility to users in the same way that independent financial audits ensure the credibility of profit reports to business investors. From a political perspective, however, not every evaluation effort merits the resources required for full meta-evaluation. I would propose the following practical guideline: *The higher the stakes for evaluation use (e.g., summative evaluations), the more politicized the context in* *which an evaluation is conducted, and the more visible an evaluation will be in that politicized environment, the more important to credibility will be an independent assessment of evaluation quality.* This amounts to a form of matching in which safeguards of evaluation credibility are designed to anticipate and counter specific political intrusions within particular political environments. Political sophistication requires situational responsiveness. For guidance on how to anticipate the possible intrusion of politics into evaluation, see Exhibit 14.2.

The Political Foundations of Organizing Primary Intended Users into an Evaluation Task Force

Where possible and practical, an evaluation task force can be organized to make major decisions about the focus, methods, and

EXHIBIT 14.2
When Is Evaluation Not Political?

In 1988, my duties as President of the American Evaluation Association included posing a "Presidential Problem" to the membership, a tradition begun by Michael Scriven. The theme of the annual national meeting that year was "The Politics of Evaluation." The problem I posed was: What is and is not politics in evaluation, and by what criteria does one judge the difference?

The winning entry from Robin Turpin (1989) asserted that "politics has a nasty habit of sneaking into all aspects of evaluation" (p. 55). All the other entries took essentially the same position; politics is omnipresent in evaluation.

This anonymous entry, my personal favorite, was unequivocal.

Evaluation is NOT political under the following conditions:

- No one cares about the program.
- No one knows about the program.
- No money is at stake.
- No power or authority is at stake.
- And, no one in the program, making decisions about the program, or otherwise involved in, knowledgeable about, or attached to the program, is sexually active.

purpose of the evaluation. The task force is a vehicle for actively involving key stakeholders in the evaluation. Moreover, the very processes involved in making decisions about an evaluation will typically increase stakeholders' commitment to use results while also increasing their knowledge about evaluation, their sophistication in conducting evaluations, and their ability to interpret findings. The task force allows the evaluator to share responsibility for and facilitate decision making about the evaluation by providing a forum for the political and practical perspectives that best come from those stakeholders who will ultimately be involved in using the evaluation.

Several things can be accomplished with a group or evaluation task force that are less likely to occur with individuals, assuming that participants are willing and the group is well facilitated.

1. *Transparency*. A process of transparency can be facilitated to reduce suspicions and fears about the evaluation. The key stakeholders who participate in the process know how decisions are made and who was involved in making them. This can reduce political paranoia.

2. *Sensitivity to Diverse Perspectives*. Participants in the process become sensitized to the multiple perspectives that exist around any program. Their views are broadened as they are exposed to the varying agendas of people with different concerns. This increases the possibility of conducting an evaluation that is respectful of and responsive to different interests and values.

3. *Spur Creativity*. New ideas often emerge out of the dynamics of group interaction.

4. *Ownership*. A sense of shared responsibility for the evaluation can be engendered that is often greater than the responsibility that would be felt by isolated individuals. Commitments made in groups, in front of others, are typically more lasting and serious than promises made to an evaluator in private.

5. *Openness*. An open forum composed of various stakeholders makes it difficult to suppress touchy questions or negative findings. Issues get raised and findings get publicized that otherwise might never see the light of day.

6. *Situation Assessment*. When facilitating a task force and being situationally responsive (*active-reactive-interactive-adaptive*), the evaluator has an opportunity to observe firsthand the relationships among various stakeholders and assess how this will affect use.

7. *Momentum*. To keep the evaluation moving forward, momentum can be built through group pressure that helps reduce delays or counter roadblocks resulting from the attitudes or actions of one person.

8. *United Front*. The evaluator(s) and stakeholders in a group process will often jell so that it's not the evaluator against the world. The task force can present a united front about critical issues and decisions.

9. *Follow Through*. The task force may continue to function after the evaluation is completed, for example, following through on recommendations. After all, in most cases the evaluator is present for only a limited period. Stakeholders stay with the program after the evaluation is over. A task force can become a repository for evaluation knowledge and carry forward an appreciation of evaluation processes (*process use*).

10. *Shared Power and Influence*. Groups, acting in concert, have more power and influence than individuals in a

"shared-power world" (Crosby and Bryson 2005).

Of course, all these positive outcomes of group dynamics assume an effective group process. Success depends on (1) who participates in that process, (2) the questions dealt with by the group, that is, the focus and quality of the process, and (3) the quality of facilitation. Any group rapidly becomes greater than the sum of its parts. Bringing together a group of incompetents seems to increase geometrically the capacity for incompetent and misguided action. On the other hand, a group of competent, politically sensitive, and thoughtful people can create something that is more useful than any of them individually might have created. Shared decision making may mean compromise; it can also mean powerful chain reactions leading to increased energy and commitment, especially commitment to use evaluation findings in which group members have increased their "stake" through involvement in the evaluation decision-making process.

Political Considerations in Forming an Evaluation Task Force

Several criteria are important in forming an evaluation task force. Not all of these criteria can be met to the same degree in every case, but it is helpful to have in mind a basic framework for the composition of the group.

1. *Representativeness.* The members of the task force should represent the various groups and constituencies that have an interest and stake in the evaluation findings and their use, including the interests of program participants.

2. *Influential People.* The task force members should either be people who have authority and power to use evaluation findings in decision making, or to influence others who do have such power and authority. Again, this includes representatives of the program's clients, who may be powerless as anonymous individuals but whose interests can be organized and taken into consideration for evaluation purposes.

3. *Shared Belief.* The task force members should believe that the evaluation is worth doing.

4. *Caring About Use.* The task force members should care how the results are used.

5. *Commitment.* The task force members should be willing to make a firm commitment of time, including a commitment to attend all the evaluation task force meetings. One of the common problems in working with an evaluation task force is having different people show up at different meetings. With inconsistent attendance, the process never really moves forward.

6. *Manageable Size.* The composition and size of a task force are limited for practical reasons. Not every stakeholder can or should participate, though an attempt should be made to represent all major stakeholder constituencies and points of view. The evaluator should be fair, but practical, in working with program administrators, funders, clients, program staff, and public officials to establish a task force (and imbue it with the necessary authority to make decisions).

Chairing the Task Force

I prefer to have one of the task force participants act as chair of the group. The chair's responsibility is to convene meetings, see that agendas for meeting are followed, and keep discussions on the topic at hand. Having a stakeholder chair the task force helps symbolize the responsibility and authority of the group. The evaluator is a consultant to the group and is paid to do the nitty-gritty staff work for the evaluation, but the task force should assume responsibility for the overall direction of the process. As facilitator, trainer, and collaborator, the evaluator will command a good deal of floor time in task force sessions. However, an effective evaluator can accomplish everything needed by working with the chair, rather than being the chair. On the other hand, I've experienced groups where the best way to maintain a balance of power and shared commitment about primary intended users was for me to act as both facilitator and chair. As with all other elements of situational responsive, who serves as chair (or whether there even is a chair) requires sensitive political strategizing.

Making the Process Work

Major stakeholders on an evaluation task force are likely to be busy people whose time constraints must be respected. The evaluator must be able to help focus the activities of the group so that time is used well, necessary decisions get made, and participants do not become frustrated with a meandering and ambiguous process. Minimize time spent on decisions about the group process and maximize the time spent on decisions about substantive evaluation issues. Exhibit 14.3 presents four essential decisions that must be made by a utilization-focused evaluation task force. These decisions can be made, at a minimum, in four 2-hour meetings with the task force.

The bare-bones scenario of four focused meetings with primary intended users in Exhibit 14.3 illustrates the minimum commitment (8 hours) one needs from busy

stakeholders. Large-scale, complex evaluations with many stakeholders may involve more face-to-face sessions and different kinds of interactions. Thus, the four-session outline is *not* a recipe, but rather a beginning framework for thinking politically and instrumentally about how to make the stakeholder involvement process meaningful, practical, and focused.

Rules of Engagement in Support of Use

The degree to which an evaluation becomes caught up in destructive power politics can be mitigated by savvy evaluators. By recognizing the inherently political nature of evaluation, evaluators can enter the political fray as power players in a game where the rules are subject to manipulation. The evaluator then works to negotiate rules in the power game that favor informed and intended use by intended users. Here are some rules of the power game that I find consistent with utilization-focused evaluation. These rules have been influenced by *Power: The Infinite Game* (Broom and Klein 1995) and adapted to fit evaluation.

1. *In working with stakeholders, seek to negotiate win/win scenarios.* For example, in an environment of controversy, with strong program advocates versus strong program adversaries, the evaluation question "Is the program effective?" frames a win/lose scenario. That is, the very way the question is posed—dichotomously—frames a win/lose answer (yes/effective, no/ineffective). In contrast, a strengths and weaknesses framing of the question focuses on learning and improvement rather than a good versus bad judgment: "For what kinds of participants, in

EXHIBIT 14.3

Priority Evaluation Task Force Agenda Items:
Four Meetings, Four Decisions

At a minimum, a utilization-focused evaluation task force needs to meet four times to accomplish four priority agenda items.

1. *Focus/Conceptualization Session.* The first task force decision is to determine the purpose and focus of the evaluation. The group considers alternative purposes, priorities, questions, issues, problems, and goals to decide the purpose and direction of evaluation. (See Menus 4.1 and 4.2 in Chapter 4, and Menu 5.1 in Chapter 5 for options.)

2. *Methods and Measurement Options.* The second task force decision involves determining how to conduct the evaluation, given the evaluation's focus (the preceding decision, Item 1). The evaluator presents various measurement approaches and different designs that might be used. Time considerations and intended uses are clarified so that methods can be selected that are manageable, credible, and politically sensitive. Issues of validity, reliability, generalizability, and appropriateness are also discussed in ways that are understandable and meaningful.

3. *Design and Instrument Review.* Between the second and third sessions, the evaluator will design the instruments to be used and write a concrete methods proposal specifying units of analysis, control or comparison groups to be studied, sampling approaches and sample size, and the overall data collection strategy. In reviewing the proposed design and instruments, the task force members should understand what will be done and what will not be done, what findings will and will not be generated, and what questions will and will not be asked. This third session will usually involve some changes in instrumentation—additions, deletions, revisions—and adjustments in the design. Basically, this meeting is aimed at providing final input into the research methods before data collection begins. The evaluator leaves the meeting with a clear mandate to begin data collection. This third meeting is also a good time to do a simulated use exercise in which task force members consider specifically how various kinds of findings might be used, given fabricated results. In presenting possible findings, the evaluator asks, "If we get these answers to this question, what would that mean? What would you do with these results?"

4. *Results Reporting and Interpretation Session.* The fourth and final agenda in this minimum scenario of evaluation task force decision making focuses on data analysis, interpretation, judgment, and recommendations (see Exhibit 13.2 in Chapter 13). The evaluator will have arranged the data so that the task force members can understand and interpret the results. Decisions about reporting will also be finalized (see Menu 13.2 in Chapter 13).

---

what ways, and under what conditions is the program most effective? And for whom is the program less effective?" Identifying strengths and acknowledging weaknesses is a win/win outcome. Forcing a judgment of effective/ineffective is a win/lose outcome.

2. *Help primary stakeholders avoid getting their egos attached to how the evaluation turns out.* When someone's ego or sense of esteem is at risk, the political stakes skyrocket. Emphasize the value of learning, regardless of what the results show, rather than being right or wrong.

Help users derive ego strength from being astute information users rather than whether their a priori position is affirmed.

3. *Helps users develop a long-term view of learning, improvement, and knowledge use.* Short-term "negative" results are less threatening when placed in a longer-term context of ongoing development. If a short-term result becomes associated in a user's mind with ultimate success or failure, the stakes skyrocket, and the power games become potentially nastier.

4. *Create an environment of interpretation that values diverse perspectives.* Everyone doesn't have to reach the same conclusion. Dialogue, discussion, and respect for differences enhance enlightenment. A focus on truth frames the results in a way that someone is right and someone else is wrong: again, win/lose instead of win/win.

5. *Seek to affirm and reaffirm that everyone is interested in what works best for intended beneficiaries.* Head off tendencies to lose sight of this high purpose when stakeholders are tempted to focus on power games such as who gains and loses resources or who gets credit or blame. Those issues are real and will need to be understood and negotiated, but within the context of a commitment to effectiveness. People do, in fact, respond to noble purposes—or can be forced to take such purposes into account even when pursing their own selfish interests.

6. *Avoid getting entangled in group process rules, such as like Robert's Rules, or stifling voting procedures.* Seek consensus shared ownership. Voting can lead to winners and losers. Consensus is inclusive of everyone. Of course, this isn't always possible. With large groups and cantankerous stakeholders, formal process rules and voting may become necessary, but I think it's worth striving for the ideal of operating by consensus.

7. *Diverge, then converge. Generate alternatives, then focus. Get diverse points of view, then prioritize.* Keep before the group the message that many possibilities exist. There's no single best approach or design. Utility and practicality are the order of the day, not rigid adherence to a preconceived notion of the best model. That's why this book has presented menus for the major decisions intended users must make.

8. *Keep in mind that what happens in a particular process aimed at making decisions for a specific evaluation has implications, not only for that evaluation, but for future evaluations.* Each evaluation process becomes part of one's evaluation legacy. Think long-term. The worst political abuses often occur in the name of short-term gain. Stay on the high road.

Overcoming Fears of Political Cooptation

I encounter a lot of concern that in facilitating utilization-focused evaluation, the evaluator may become coopted by stakeholders. How can evaluators maintain their integrity if they become involved in close, collaborative relationships with stakeholders? How does the evaluator take politics into account without becoming a political tool of only one partisan interest?

The nature of the relationship between evaluators and the people with whom they work can be complex. On the one hand, evaluators are urged to maintain a respectful distance from the people they study to safeguard objectivity and minimize personal and political bias. On the other hand, the human relations perspective emphasizes that close, interpersonal contact is a necessary condition for building mutual understanding. Evaluators thus find themselves on the proverbial horns of a dilemma: Getting too close to decision makers may jeopardize credibility; remaining distant may undermine use.

A program auditor at a workshop put the issue less delicately when he asked, "How can we get in bed with decision makers without losing our virginity?"

This is a fascinating and revealing metaphor, showing just how high the stakes can seem. The evaluator is portrayed as the innocent, the policymaker as the coopting tempter planning a seduction. I once reported this metaphor to a group of policymakers who immediately reframed the question: "How do we get in bed with evaluators without getting sadistically abused?" Different stakes, different fears.

One way to handle concerns about cooptation is to stay focused on evaluation's empirical foundation. In Chapter 2, I discussed the importance of and ways to engender a commitment to reality testing among intended users. The empirical basis of evaluation involves making assumptions and values explicit, testing the validity of assumptions, and carefully examining a program to find out what is actually occurring.

The integrity of an evaluation depends on its empirical orientation—that is, its commitment to systematic and credible data collection and reporting. Likewise, the integrity of an evaluation group process depends on helping participants adopt an empirical perspective. A commitment must be engendered to find out what is really happening, at least as nearly as one can, given the limitations of research methods and scarce resources. Engendering such commitment involves teaching and facilitating.

When stakeholders first begin discussing the purpose of an evaluation, they will often do so in nonempirical terms. "We want to *prove* the program's effectiveness." Proving effectiveness is a public relations job, not an evaluation task. This statement tells the evaluator about that person's attitude toward the program, and it indicates a need for diplomatically, sensitively, but determinedly, reorienting that stakeholder from a concern with public relations to a concern with learning about and documenting actual program activities and effects. Consider this dialogue.

Program Director:	We want to prove the program's effectiveness.
Evaluator:	What kind of information would do that?
Program Director:	Information about how much people like the program.
Evaluator:	Does everyone like the program?
Program Director:	I think most everyone does.
Evaluator:	Well, we could find out just how many do and how many don't. So there's a reasonable evaluation question: "What are participants' attitudes toward the program?" Later, we'll need to get more specific about how to measure their attitudes, but first let's consider some other things we could find out. Assuming that some people don't like the program, what could be learned from them?
Program Director:	I suppose we could find out what they don't like and why.
Evaluator:	Would that kind of information be helpful in looking at the program, to find out about its strengths and weaknesses so that

perhaps you could improve it in some ways? [This is a deliberately leading question, very hard to say "No" to.]

Program Director: Well, we know some of the reasons, but we can always learn more.

Evaluator: What other information would be helpful in studying the program to find out about its strengths and weaknesses? [Here the evaluator has carefully rephrased the original concern from "proving the program's effectiveness" to "finding out about the program's strengths and weaknesses."]

In this dialogue, the evaluator chips away at the program director's biased public relations perspective by carefully helping an empirical perspective emerge. At some point, the evaluator may want to, or need to, address the public relations concern with a bit of a speech (or sermonette).

I know you're concerned about proving the program's effectiveness. This is a natural concern. A major and common purpose of evaluation is to gather information so that judgments can be made about the value of a program. To what extent is it effective? To what extent is it worthwhile?

If we only gathered and presented positive information, it would lack credibility. If you read a report that only says good things about a program, you figure something's been left out. In my experience, an evaluation has more credibility if it's balanced. No program is perfect. I've yet to see a program in which everyone was happy and all goals were achieved. You may find that it's more politically astute to study and report both strengths and weaknesses, and then show that you're serious about improving the program by presenting a strategy for dealing with areas of ineffectiveness. By so doing, you establish your credibility as serious program developers who can deal openly and effectively with inevitable difficulties.

Sometimes the opposite bias is the problem. Someone is determined to kill a program—to present only negative findings and to "prove" that the program is ineffective. In such cases, the evaluator can emphasize what can be learned by finding out about the program's strengths. Few programs are complete disasters. An empirical approach means gathering data on actual program activities and effects and then presenting those data in a fair and balanced way so that information users and decision makers can make their own judgments about goodness or badness, effectiveness or ineffectiveness. Such judgments, however, are separate from the data. In my experience, evaluation task force members will readily move into this kind of empirical orientation as they come to understand its utility and fairness. It's the evaluator's job to help them adopt that perspective.

I don't want to imply that shifting to an empirical orientation occurs easily or as the result of a single interaction. Quite the contrary, the empirical orientation of evaluation requires ongoing reinforcement. Some stakeholders never make the shift. Others do so enthusiastically. The savvy evaluator will monitor the empirical orientation of intended users and, in an active-reactive-interactive-adaptive mode of situational responsiveness, take appropriate steps to keep the evaluation on an empirical and useful path.

Thus far in this chapter we've been considering the political nature of evaluation. We turn now to ethical issues, a natural segue, because *politics and ethics are interdependent* (Simons 2006).

Ethics of Being User Focused

It is truly unethical to leave ethics out of program evaluation.

—Michael Scriven (1993:30)

Building and sustaining appropriate relationships with intended users requires astute and vigilant attention to ethical boundaries and issues. Speaking truth to power, one of evaluation's functions, is risky—risky *business*. Not only is power involved, but money is involved. The Golden Rule of consulting is, "Know who has the gold." Evaluators work for paying clients. The jobs of internal evaluators depend on the pleasure of superiors, and future work for independent evaluators depends on client satisfaction. Thus, there's always the fear that "those who pay the piper call the tune"—not just determining the focus of the evaluation, but also prescribing the results. Evaluators can find themselves in conflict between their professional commitment to

honest reporting and their personal interest in monetary gain or having future work. This conflict is so pervasive that Scriven (1991b) believes evaluation suffers from "General Positive Bias—a tendency to turn in more favorable results than are justified" (p. 174).

The Program Evaluation Standards provide general ethical guidance: Evaluation agreements should be in writing; rights of human subjects should be protected; evaluators should respect human dignity; assessments should be complete and fair; findings should be openly and fully disclosed; conflicts of interests should be dealt with openly and honestly; and sound fiscal procedures should be followed. The Propriety Standards "are intended to ensure that an evaluation will be conducted legally, ethically, and with due regard for the welfare of those involved in the evaluation, as well as those affected by the results" (Joint Committee 1994:P1–P8). Likewise, the "Guiding Principles" of the American

Evaluation Association (AEA Task Force 1995) insist on integrity and honesty throughout the entire evaluation process, from initial negotiations with clients and stakeholders through reporting. Professional evaluation associations around the world have formulated and adopted codes of ethics. The American Journal of Evaluation has a feature section on "Ethical Challenges" in which evaluators offer guidance on common ethical challenges and scenarios (e.g., Cooksy 2007).

Ethicality

Ethicality requires studies to be morally upright, honest, fair, respectful, honorable, professionally responsible, and accountable; to be free of graft, fraud, and abuse; and to manifest due regard for the welfare of those involved in or affected by the evaluation (Stufflebeam 2007:2).

Newman and Brown (1996) have generated a framework for making ethical decisions in evaluation: (1) pay attention to one's intuition that something isn't quite right; (2) look for rules that provide guidance; (3) examine how the situation looks in terms of basic ethical principles: autonomy (rights involved), nonmaleficence (doing no harm), beneficence (doing good), justice (fairness), and fidelity (adhering to agreements); (4) examine your personal values—be in touch with your own beliefs and comfort levels; and (5) act, which can include consulting with colleagues, calculating trade-offs, and making and following a plan. They provide case problems, evaluation examples, and ethical challenges that illuminate how the framework can be applied in real situations. Exhibit 14.4 lists common ethical challenges evaluators face.

Ethical Concerns Specific to Utilization-Focused Evaluation

The Program Evaluation Standards, the Newman/Brown Framework for Making Ethical Decisions, and other ethical frameworks for evaluators (e.g., McDavid and Hawthorn 2006:393; Simons 2006; Morris 2005) provide general ethical guidance and make it clear that evaluators encounter all kinds of situations that require a strong grounding in ethics and may demand courage. Beyond general ethical sensitivity, however, the ethics of utilization-focused evaluators are most likely to be called into question around three essential aspects of utilization-focused evaluation: (1) limiting stakeholder involvement to primary intended users, (2) working closely with those users, and (3) judging an evaluation by the extent to which it achieves intended use by intended users. The ethics of limiting and focusing stakeholder involvement concern who has access to the power of evaluation knowledge. The ethics of building close relationships concerns the integrity, neutrality, and corruptibility of the evaluator. The ethics of focusing on intended use by intended users concerns the values that undergird evaluation practice. Each of these concerns center on the fundamental ethical question: *Who does an evaluation—and an evaluator—serve?*

Consider the following exchange I had with Carol Weiss, who was arguing that findings must stand on their own rather than depend on interpersonal relationships, and Ernest House, who believes that evaluators are ethically obligated to consider the interests of the poorly educated or less powerful in society who are not in a position to advocate on their own behalf.

Carol Weiss: I think we limit ourselves too much if we think of interpersonal interaction as the critical component in utilization.

Michael Patton: From my perspective, I feel a great responsibility to serve my clients.

Ernest House: How far would you pursue this orientation? Surely, you can't consider your only purpose to be meeting your client's interests?

Michael Patton: Tell me why I can't?

Ernest House: Why? It's an immoral position.

Michael Patton: I could argue. . . .

Ernest House: You can't. You can't. It would be a long argument which you'd lose.

Michael Patton: Let's go for it.

Ernest House: Who has the money to purchase evaluation? The most proper people in society. You would serve only the most proper people in society? You wouldn't condone that. . . . A doctor can't be concerned only with a particular patient and not concerned with the distribution of his or her services across society as a whole. . . . Medicine only for the richest? Surely you can't condone that kind of position. . . .

Michael Patton: What I am talking about is my responsibility to the specific set of people I work with, who will be different from case to case. What I take immediate responsibility for is what they do and the things that I do with them. I recognize that there's a broader set of things that are going to be of concern, but I can't take responsibility for all of what happens with that broader set of concerns.

Ernest House: Well, you must.

Michael Patton: But I can't.

Ernest House: Then you are immoral. Right? You'll back off that position. You cannot justify that position. You don't hold that position. I mean, you say it, but you can't hold it. . . . You have to have a concern that you're taking beyond the immediate welfare of the immediate client. I believe that you do that.

Michael Patton: I think I build that larger concern you're talking about into my interactions with that client. . . . There is a moral concern. There is a moral and value context that I bring to bear in that interaction with my clients.

Ernest House: You have to show concern for the rest of society. You can't just sell your services to whoever can purchase them. That would be an immoral position. . . . I say that you should be concerned about the interests of the less advantaged people in society. (Excerpted and edited from a transcription by Alkin 1990:101–105)

EXHIBIT 14.4

Common Ethical Challenges Evaluators Face

At the beginning of an evaluation

- A powerful person makes it clear what the evaluation is "expected" to find or otherwise tries to predetermine the evaluation's results and recommendations.
- A stakeholder asserts that certain questions are "off limits" or unnecessary, even though those questions are clearly germane, thereby trying to control what gets evaluated.
- The funder of the evaluator or some other powerful stakeholder tries to exclude the participation or perspectives of certain other legitimate stakeholders.
- The evaluator is denied access to key data sources or people.

Toward the end of an evaluation

- The evaluator is pressured to alter, suppress, de-emphasize, or leave out certain findings.
- The evaluator discovers that only positive (or only negative) findings are being disseminated by certain stakeholders.
- An evaluation report is subject to endless approval or final review delays that keep the findings from being reported in a timely way.
- The evaluator is pressured to violate confidentiality by revealing which interviewees said what.
- The evaluator is accused of bias or conflict of interest by those who don't like the findings and conclusions.

SOURCE: Morris (2005).

I've reproduced a portion of our discussion to offer a taste of its intensity. As the dialogue unfolded, three things were illuminated for me with regard to utilization-focused evaluation: (1) Evaluators need to be deliberative and intentional about their own moral groundings; (2) evaluators must exercise care, including ethical care, in selecting projects to work on and stakeholders to work with; and (3) evaluators must be clear about whose interests are more and less represented in an evaluation. Let me elaborate these points.

First, evaluators need to be deliberative and intentional about their own moral groundings. An evaluator, such as Ernest House, will and should bring moral concerns about social justice into negotiations over the design of an evaluation, including concerns about whose interests are represented in the questions asked and who will have access to the findings. The *active* part of being active-reactive-interactive-adaptive is bringing your own concerns, issues, and values to the table. The evaluator is also a stakeholder—not the primary stakeholder—but, *in every evaluation, an evaluator's reputation, credibility, integrity, and beliefs are on the line.* A utilization-focused evaluator is not passive in simply accepting and buying into whatever an intended user initially desires. The active-reactive-interactive-adaptive process includes an obligation on the part of the evaluator to represent the standards and principles of the profession as well as his or her own sense of morality and integrity, while also attending to and respecting the beliefs and concerns of other primary users.

A second important point reinforced by the debate was the importance of project and stakeholder selection. At one point in the debate, Ross Connor, a former president of the AEA, asked me, "You pick and choose clients, right?" I affirmed that I did. "My concern," he replied, "would be those who don't have the luxury of picking and choosing who they work with" (quoted in Alkin 1990:104). One way in which I take into account the importance of the personal factor is by careful attention to whom I work with. Whether one has much choice in that, or not, it will affect the way in which ethical issues are addressed, especially what kinds of ethical issues are likely to be of concern. In challenging what he has called "clientism"—"the claim that whatever the client wants . . . is ethically correct." House (1995) asked, "What if the client is Adolph Eichmann, and he wants the evaluator to increase the efficiency of his concentration camps?" (p. 29).

A third issue concerns how the interests of various stakeholder groups are represented in a utilization-focused process. Despite House's admonitions, I'm reluctant, as a white, middle-class male, to pretend to represent the interests of people of color or society's disadvantaged. My preferred solution is to work to get participants in affected groups representing themselves as part of the evaluation negotiating process. As discussed in Chapter 3, user-focused evaluation involves real people, not just attention to vague, abstract audiences. Thus, where the interests of disadvantaged people are at stake, ways of hearing from or involving them directly should be explored, rather than having them represented in a potentially patronizing manner by the

advantaged. Whether and how to do this may be part of what the evaluator attends to during active-reactive-interactive-adaptive interactions.

In the end, however, power and money can threaten evaluation integrity. Evaluators may find themselves alone in facing inappropriate and unethical demands from those with influence and resources. Exhibit 14.5 presents just such an example from the real world, in the trenches, and *"On the Ground."*

Guarding against Corruption of an Evaluation

Ethics is not something for a special occasion; it is a part of daily practice.

—Newman and Brown (1996:187)

While Ernie House has raised concerns about how working with a selective group of intended users can serve the powerful and ignore (or harm) the interests of the poor and less powerful, a different concern about utilization-focused evaluation is raised by Michael Scriven when he worries about undermining what he considers evaluation's central purpose—rendering independent judgments about merit or worth. If evaluators take on roles beyond judging merit or worth, such as creating learning organizations or empowering participants, or, alternatively, eschew rendering judgment to facilitate judgments of intended users, he believes that the opportunities for loss of independence become so pervasive as to be overwhelming.

For Scriven, evaluators don't serve specific people. They serve truth. Truth may be a victim when evaluators form close working relationships with program staff. Scriven (1991b:182) admonishes evaluators to

Evaluators' Experiences of Evaluation Misuse

In a 2006 online survey of members of the American Evaluation Association (Fleischer 2007), 991 evaluators responded to the following question:

In your experience, how often do you see a client do the following on a scale of 1 (not at all) to 4 (very often)?

Items Reported	Mean Results
Selectively report results	2.6
Dismiss undesirable results	2.3
Exaggerate results	2.3
Ignore results	2.3
Prematurely disseminate results	1.9
Attribute findings that deviate from actual results	1.8

guard their independence scrupulously. Involving intended users in evaluation design, interpretation, and judgment, he argues, risks weakening the hard-hitting judgments the evaluator must render. Evaluators, he has observed, must be able to deal with the loneliness that may accompany independence and guard against "going native," the tendency to be coopted by and become an advocate for the program being evaluated. Going native leads to "incestuous relations" in which the "evaluator is 'in bed' with the program being evaluated" (p. 192). Scriven (1991a) has condemned any failure to render independent judgment as "the abrogation of the professional responsibility of the evaluator" (p. 32). He has derided what he mockingly called "a kinder, gentler approach" to evaluation (p. 39). His concerns stem from what he has experienced as the resistance of evaluation clients to negative findings and the difficulty evaluators have—psychologically—providing negative feedback.

Thus, he has admonished evaluators to be uncompromising in reporting negative results. "The main reason that evaluators avoid negative conclusions is that they haven't the courage for it" (p. 42).

My experience has been different from Scriven's, so I reach different conclusions. Operating selectively, as I acknowledged earlier, I choose to work with clients who are hungry for quality information to improve programs. They are people of competence and integrity who are able to use and balance both positive and negative information to make informed decisions. I take it as part of my responsibility to work with them in ways that they can hear the results, both positive *and* negative, and use them for intended purposes. I don't find them resistant. I find them quite eager to get quality information that they can use to develop the programs to which they have dedicated their energies. I try to render judgments, when we have negotiated my taking that role, in ways that can be understood,

EXHIBIT 14.5

Ethical Choices *on the Ground*

By Donna Podems

Executive Director

OtherWISE: Research and Evaluation

Cape Town, South Africa

An international organization hired me to do an evaluation on the socioeconomic impacts of landmines in Somaliland. This experience caused me to reflect on the reality of how Western evaluation methods are used in international development and relief work. This poem represents a dialogue between the donor and me.

On the Ground

We want a survey.

But it's an oral society.

Do a survey and get the answers.

But they have been surveyed to death; they know what answers to give.

We want statistics.

But there is no census.

Get statistics and analyze the differences among the groups.

But they all say they are the same group; it is only the foreigner who differentiates.

We want our literature reviewed.

But the literature is not correct.

Use our literature and summarize it.

But the local people say it is not true; it is only you the funder who believes what you write.

We want you to rewrite your report.

But it is based on solid research findings.

Leave in the positive and take out your criticism of the methodology and its findings.

But it is what I found; I have presented my findings based on my data, my experience.

Rewrite the report.

No.

Rewrite the report, or you will not be paid.

My graduate school fees are due.

SOURCE: Reprinted with permission of Donna Podems.

valued, and heard, and I work with intended users to facilitate their arriving at their own conclusions. They are often harsher on themselves than I would be.

In my experience, it doesn't so much require courage to provide negative feedback as it requires skill. Nor do evaluation clients have to be unusually enlightened for negative feedback to be heard and used if, through skilled facilitation, the evaluator has built a foundation for such feedback so that it is welcomed for long-term effectiveness. Dedicated program staff don't want to waste their time doing things that don't work.

I have followed in the tracks of, and cleaned up the messes left by, evaluators who took pride in their courageous, hard-hitting, negative feedback. They patted themselves on the back for their virtues and went away complaining about program resistance and hostility. I watched them in action. They were arrogant, insensitive, and utterly unskilled in facilitating feedback as a learning experience. They congratulated themselves on their independence of judgment and commitment to "telling it like it is" and ignored their largely alienating and useless practices. They were closed to feedback about the ineffectiveness of their feedback.

It's from these kinds of experiences that I have developed a preference for constructive and utilization-focused feedback. In any form of feedback, it's hard to hear the substance when the tone is highly judgmental and demeaning. This applies to interactions between parents and children (in either direction), between lovers and spouses, among colleagues, and, most decidedly, between evaluators and intended users. Being kinder and gentler in an effort to be heard need not indicate cowardice or a loss of virtue. In this world of ever-greater diversity, sensitivity and respect are not only virtues, they're more effective and, in evaluation, more likely to lead to results being used.

Moral Discourse

Another concern about utilization-focused evaluation is that it pays insufficient attention to moral discourse. Thomas Schwandt (1989b), in a provocative article, set out to "recapture the moral discourse in evaluation." He challenged the "bifurcation of value and fact"; he questioned assertions that the integrity of an evaluation rests on its empirical orientation; and he expressed doubts about "the instrumental use of reason." He called for a rethinking of what it means to evaluate and invited us "to imagine what it would be like to practice evaluation without an instrumentalist conception of evaluation theory and practice" (p. 14). In contrast to an instrumental and utilitarian approach, he advocated raising fundamental questions about the morality of programs, that is, not just asking if programs are doing things right, but *are they doing right (moral) things?* He argued for inquiry into the morals and values that undergird programs, not just whether programs work, but what their workings reveal about quality of life and the nature of society.

Such questions and such a focus for inquiry are compatible with a utilization focus so long as intended users choose such an inquiry. The option to do so ought to be part of the menu of choices offered to primary stakeholders—and has been in this book. The process uses of evaluation discussed in Chapter 5 include participatory, collaborative, empowering, and social justice approaches, which emphasize the learning and development that derive from evaluative inquiry as an end in itself quite apart from the use of findings. Examining fundamental values, instrumental assumptions, and societal context are typically part of such processes. In Schwandt's vision (2002), the principal focus of the evaluator's work becomes helping practitioners acquire the ability to deliberate well—to assist them in developing their own wise practice. In brief, it would mean helping them to cultivate and bring to the level of reflective awareness a sophisticated set of interpretive skills. . . . It may also mean assisting them in developing critical (versus operational) intelligence—a capacity to question and debate the value of various ends of a given practice. (P. 57)

In this regard, Schwandt's perspective follows in the tradition of philosopher Hannah Arendt who believed that people need to *practice thinking* if democratic societies are to avoid totalitarianism. Toward that end she developed "six exercises in political thought" (Arendt 1963). As discussed in chapter 5, from this point of view, every evaluation might be considered an opportunity for those involved to practice critical thinking.

Social Betterment

Lawyers are disbarred.
Clergy are defrocked.
Musicians are denoted.
Evaluators are devalued.

—Halcolm

Mark, Henry, and Julnes (2000:22) deny that direct utilization should be a criterion for judging the worth of evaluation. Instead, they call for evaluations to be judged by their contribution to *social betterment:* "the reduction of social problems and increased meeting of human needs" (p. 24).

Without the possibility of social betterment, evaluation would be at worst an empty exercise, at best a fulfillment of curiosity. That the possibility of social betterment exists is both a personal motivation for evaluators and a critical part of the rationale for the field. (P. 24)

To determine the connection to and path toward social betterment in any specific evaluation, they would involve stakeholders in a formal *values inquiry,* making sure that such an inquiry is not merely an ancillary process use but, in fact, generates findings on values as part of the evaluation.

Gary Henry (2000) worries that "the goal of utilization traps evaluators" because of "the *paradox of persuasion.* . . . If one begins an evaluation with the *goal* of persuasion, then the evaluation loses the credibility necessary to persuade" (p. 86). Henry also worries that making use a priority leads to an overemphasis on evaluation for program improvement and insufficient attention to other evaluation purposes such as oversight and compliance, assessing merit or worth, and knowledge generation (p. 96). Henry and Mark (2003) have been part of shifting the focus from use to influence, and examining the "Consequences of Evaluation," the theme Mel Mark, as President of the American Evaluation Association (AEA), chose as the theme for the 2006 AEA national conference. Focusing on consequences explicitly treats evaluation as an intervention and inquires into its outcomes and impacts, especially whether it contributes, from a values perspective, to social betterment.

My interpretation of this emphasis on judging an evaluation by its contribution to social betterment is a reminder that use is not an end in itself, inherently good, but must ultimately be judged by its larger contribution to a better world. Social betterment extends the logic model of evaluation beyond short-term and immediate uses to longer-term impacts on society. This recalls Ernie House's question cited earlier in this chapter asking what ethics would guide an evaluator's response to a request to increase the efficiency of gas chambers in a concentration camp. Or make apartheid work better.

Attention to social betterment provides a larger context for considering, reflecting on, and assessing evaluation use. But it is hard to see how it replaces or supersedes utilization as a criterion for evaluating evaluations. How can an evaluation contribute to social betterment unless it is used? And social betterment involves a very long time frame. In the short-term, evaluators will still be accountable for intended use by intended users. In so doing, making explicit the assumptions and values that connect intended use by intended users to social betterment is a worthy endeavor.

Unscrupulous Evaluators

Not all ethical challenges related to evaluation involve evaluators faced with

pressure from funders, powerful political figures, fearful program staff, or conniving program participants. Sometimes, unfortunately, the evaluator is the problem. Alexey Kuzmin did his doctoral dissertation on evaluation capacity-building in Russia. In the course of his fieldwork, he turned up a number of instances of unscrupulous evaluators engaged in unethical practices, which he reported at the International Evaluation Conference in Toronto in 2005. In one case, an American site visitor to a small program arrived late one day, left early the next, never visited the program, and refused to take the documents offered by the program. Sometime later, the program director received an urgent demand from the funder for required documentation (the very documentation that the evaluator was supposed

Site Visit Ethics

Near the end of World War II, rumors began to circulate about the Nazi extermination of Jews. The Nazis wanted to refute those rumors, so they took one camp, called Theresienstadt, in what was then Czechoslovakia, and turned it, if ever so briefly, into a model town. They shot a movie there to prove how well they treated the Jews and invited the Red Cross to inspect it. This was 1944. In preparation for the Red Cross inspection (aka evaluation), a beautification plan was implemented. They painted buildings, planted flowers, opened stores, and put up a bandstand in the town square. They built a kindergarten in a small park, near a children's home. They opened a coffee shop. They turned the concentration camp into a pleasant little town. And they made it a lot less crowded. Just before the Red Cross delegation arrived, the Nazis shipped 7,500 people off to the Auschwitz death camp, reducing crowding and creating more open spaces.

On June 23, 1944, the Red Cross delegates came for a one-day inspection. The Red Cross delegates went exactly where the Nazis took them—and only where they took them. They didn't question a single prisoner. The Swiss head of the delegation took pictures showing how happy the children looked—and included them in his report.

The final report of the Red Cross delegation reported that Theresienstadt looked like a normal provincial town where the "elegantly dressed women all had silk stockings scarves and stylish handbags." The delegates also wrote that Theresienstadt was a final destination camp and that people who come there were not sent elsewhere—because that's what the inspection team was told. In fact, by the time of the visit, some 68,000 people had already been shipped from there to the death camps (CBS News 2007) (www.cbsnews.com/stories/2007/02/23/60minutes/main2508458_page2.shtml).

to have taken, analyzed, and presented to the funder), which it took considerable expense to get to the funder; subsequently, the program was denied additional funding for lack of an evaluation having been completed.

In another instance, again in Russia, an external evaluator arrived, one without any substantive expertise in the program's area of focus. He spent a couple of days with the program, then disappeared leaving an unpaid hotel bill and expenses that the program had to cover because it had made arrangements for his visit. A couple of months later, the program director received a draft evaluation report for her comments, but the deadline for sending comments had already passed. The evaluation contained numerous errors and biased conclusions based on the evaluators' own prejudices. The program director spent a considerable amount of time writing a response to the evaluation, but the evaluation, with its errors and negative judgments, had already been posted on a prominent Web site. The program had to resort to expensive legal action to have the evaluation removed.

The third example concerns a very affable evaluator of a program in Siberia undergoing an external midterm review. The American evaluation team leader was a charming man who gave a great deal of attention to the program director. In a private conversation with her, he talked in-depth about an organizational development model he had recently implemented in another country in Central Europe. It gradually became clear that the evaluator was offering positive evaluation findings if the director hired him as a consultant to return and implement his model in her agency. He said, "I really want to say good things about your program. I want to

Are Evaluation Competence and Ethics an Issue?

I recently had a lengthy exchange with an evaluator who was disturbed by having just come from a mid-term site visit of a large and important but controversial project funded by an international agency in a developing country. All sites visited were selected by the host government. Only project participants selected by the host government were interviewed and always with project and/or government people present. Most requested documents and data were "not available." The team had to produce and hand in their report in the country before they departed. It is not clear what happened to the report. On the mid-term review team of several people, only one person had any evaluation background, knowledge, or training—the person who was telling me about the experience—and that person was the only one who saw any problem with the way the review was organized and the only one who complained, to no avail. I can't reveal details of the project without breaking confidentiality, but I can tell you that the project involved issues of life and death for the intended beneficiaries and huge potential embarrassment to the host country.

Mid-term and end-of-project visiting review/inspection/evaluation teams may well be the most common form of formal evaluation activity in the world. There are thousands of such reviews commissioned by scores of international agencies every year. A session at the joint AEA/CES International Evaluation Conference in Toronto featured many horror stories about such reviews documenting that external site visit evaluators hired by international donors often lack minimum evaluation competencies and expertise to carry out their assignments.

support it, but I need to hear some things from you before I do that." The program director, feeling quite vulnerable, contacted a lawyer for advice about how to protect herself and her agency, advice she heeded, but found the whole experience traumatic.

Age-Old Evaluation Questions

Standards and principles provide guidance for dealing with politics and ethics, but there are no absolute rules. These arenas of existential action are replete with dilemmas, conundrums, paradoxes, perplexities, quandaries, temptations, and competing goods. Utilization-focused evaluation may well exacerbate such challenges, so warnings about potential political corruption, ethical entrapments, and moral turpitude direct us to keep asking fundamental questions: What does it mean to be useful? Useful to whom? Who benefits? Who is hurt? Who decides? What values inform the selection of intended users and intended users? Why? These are the age-old evaluation questions. We never outgrow them.

Follow-Up Exercises

1. Search the news over the last year for an example of controversial evaluation findings that got significant public attention. Use Exhibit 14.1 to estimate and map various stakeholders' stakes. Discuss how their stakes and perspectives affected their reaction to the evaluation findings. If this had been your evaluation report, how would you have handled the reactions to the evaluation?

2. Identify a program that you have or might evaluate. Analyze the political issues that surround that program. Write a script for what you would say to the

members of a diverse Evaluation Task Force at the first meeting regarding the evaluation's political context. In your script, acknowledge the political context and explain how the evaluation can and will take into account that political context without being coopted by any one political perspective. In essence, make the case for how you will conduct the evaluation to assure both its political relevance and political independence to assure the evaluation's credibility.

3. The *American Journal of Evaluation* (AJE) has a regular feature section on "Ethical Challenges" in which evaluators offer guidance on common ethical challenges and scenarios. Find an issue of AJE that presents an ethical challenge. After reviewing the suggestions made by the evaluators invited to offer commentary, analyze the basis for their agreements and disagreements, and present how you would handle that ethical challenge. Justify your ethical stance.

4. Politics and ethics are deeply affected by cultural context. The Diversity Committee of the American Evaluation Association (2004) has undertaken *A Cultural Reading of the Program Evaluation Standards*. Review and discuss how the propriety standards are affected by cultural issues. (www.eval.org/aea05.culturalreading/aea05.cr.Propriety.pdf)

From your own experience and background, identify a specific cultural characteristic or issue that would affect ethical or political guidance for an evaluation. Explain the cultural context and how it would specifically affect interpretation and application of one of the propriety standards within that cultural context.

5. Both the Canadian Evaluation Society (CES) and the Australasian Evaluation Society (AES) have developed codes of ethics for evaluators. Compare and contrast these codes of ethics.

Canadian code of ethics: www.evaluation canada.ca/site.cgi?s=5&ss=4&_lang=en

Australasian code of ethics: www.aes .asn.au/about

Alternatively, select the standards of two international organizations to compare and contrast. www.europeanevaluation .org/?page=761942

(NOTE: Web site addresses may change. Go to the Web home pages of CES and AES to locate their current codes of ethics. Go to the Web home page of the European Evaluation Society to find linkages to standards for international organizations or go to the home pages of the evaluation units of those international agencies.)

15

Utilization-Focused Evaluation

Processes and Premises

*A**sking questions about impact—that's evaluation.*
        Gathering data—that's evaluation.
Making judgments—that's evaluation.
Facilitating use—that's evaluation.
Putting all those pieces together in a meaningful whole that tells people something they want to know and can use about a matter of importance. Now that's really evaluation!

—Halcolm

A User's Perspective

This final chapter will provide a summary overview of utilization-focused evaluation. I want to set the stage by presenting the perspective of a very thoughtful evaluation user, distinguished educator Dr. Wayne Jennings. At the time of the following interview, he was actively reflecting on the role of evaluation in schools as principal of the innovative Saint Paul Open School, which had just been externally evaluated. Concerns such as those he expresses helped inspire utilization-focused evaluation.

Patton: You recently participated in a federal evaluation of your school. Why was it undertaken?

Jennings: It was mandated as part of federal funds we received. We hoped there would be some benefit to the school, that school staff would learn things to improve our program. We were interested in an evaluation that would address basic issues of education. Our school operates on the assumption that students learn from experience, and the more varied experiences they have, the more they learn. So we hoped to learn what parts of the program made a contribution to and what parts maybe detracted from learning.

We hoped also to learn whether the program affected different groups of students differently, for instance, whether the program was more effective for younger children or older children. We wanted to know how well it worked for kids who have a lot of initiative and drive and are self-motivated learners versus the experiences and learnings of those who don't have that kind of attitude. And we were interested in determining what we should concentrate on more— as well as continue or discontinue. But we didn't get information to make those kinds of basic decisions.

We asked the research firm for an evaluation that would help us with those kinds of questions. They came up with a design that seemed far off target— not at all what we had asked for. It takes a little imagination to do an evaluation that fits an innovative program. We got a standard recipe approach. I'm convinced that if we'd asked totally different questions, we'd have gotten the same design. It's as though they had a cookie cutter, and whether they were evaluating us or evaluating vocational education or anything—a hospital or a prison—it would have been the same design.

Patton: So why did you accept the design? Why participate in an evaluation you thought would be useless educationally?

Jennings: That's a good question. It happened like this. The first year, we worked with an out-of-state firm that had won the federal contract. The president came for the initial discussion in September, when school was getting started. He said he'd like to look around. Ten minutes later, I found him sitting in the front hall in state of what appeared to be absolute shock. He was not prepared for our program, not in the least. He came and found kids running around. Students were noisy. They weren't seated in straight rows. We didn't resemble his conception of a school in any way, apparently. He just wasn't prepared for open education—for an alternative approach. That was the last we saw of him. He sent out a new researcher who didn't walk around the school. We simply met in the office and hashed out what data were required by funders. These people were not prepared to analyze a nonstandard school operation or adapt their design to our situation.

I think schools have operated pretty much in the same way for so long that all of us have a mind-set of what school is. So to see something different can shock—culture shock. We've seen that in the eyes of several evaluators we've had in here. Now, I don't know how to prepare a standard educational evaluator to be open to an open school. Maybe we needed more of a participant observer, an anthropological type, someone who would come in and live here for a while and find out what the hell's going on.

Patton: You couldn't find that kind of evaluator?

Jennings: We did have, somewhere along the line, a proposal from a firm that had experience with our kind of schools. They were going to give us the kind of evaluation we were very much interested in, the kind we could learn from. We wanted to pursue that design, but State Department of Education officials said, "No, that won't provide us with concrete, comparable data for accountability."

Patton: The design approved by the State Department of Education, did that provide some "concrete, comparable data for accountability"? What were the findings?

Jennings: We knew politically that we had to achieve certain degree of respectability with regard to standardized testing, so we looked at test results, reading scores, and all that sort of thing, and they seemed satisfactory. We didn't discover anything particularly startling to cause any serious problems with our Board of Education or the State Department of Education.

Patton: In what form did you receive the findings?

Jennings: In a report: I think it would have been helpful for the evaluators to meet with our staff and talk us through the report, elaborate a little on it, but that didn't happen—partly because the report came either during the summer or the following fall.

Patton: So of what use was the evaluation?

Jennings: It served to legitimize us. Our local Board of Education, the district administration, and the State Department of Education were all interested in seeing an evaluation undertaken, but I don't think a single member of the board or administration read it. They may have glanced at the summary, and the summary said that the school was OK. That was it.

Patton: Any uses besides legitimization? Anything you learned?

Jennings: I supposed you could say we learned how difficult it is to get helpful evaluations.

Patton: What was staff reaction to the report?

Jennings: I doubt many bothered to read it. They were looking for something worthwhile and helpful, but it just wasn't there. Staff were interested in thinking through a good evaluation, but that would have required the evaluators to become thoroughly backgrounded in order to help us think it through and provide a proper evaluation. As it turned out, I think the staff has acquired a negative attitude about evaluation. I mean, they are interested in evaluation, but then the reports seem to lack anything that would help us with day-to-day decision making or give us a good mirror image of what's going on in the school, from an outsider's point of view, in terms of the growth and development of kids in all dimensions.

Patton: Let me broaden the question about use. Sometimes evaluations have an impact on things that go beyond immediate program improvements—things like general thinking on issues that arise from the study, or board policies, or legislation. Did the evaluation have an impact in any broader ways?

Jennings: I'm glad you're getting into that area, because that's of major interest to me. I had hoped that as the school got under way, it would become fairly clear, or would be evident to those interested in finding out, that this was a highly effective educational program that was making a considerable difference in the lives of most children. Well, the study didn't address that; the study simply said, "The program's OK." That's all it said. *Given the limited resources and imagination that were put into the evaluation, I'm not convinced they had enough knowledge to say even that—to say anything about the effectiveness of the program!*

Our major job is to educate 500 students, but we're engaged in a much larger struggle, at least I am, and that is to show that a less formal approach based on experiential education can be highly effective, including bringing students to the same level of achievement in a shorter time. We're concerned about achievement, but also about producing genuinely humane people for a complex, changing world.

Now, to be fair, the evaluation did something useful. When parents or other educators ask if the program has been evaluated and what the findings were, we say, "Yes, the evaluation shows the program is effective." On the other hand, anyone worth their salt, I suspect, if they read the evaluation carefully, would decide that it doesn't show much of anything, really, when you come right down to it. *We're left where we began, but we have the illusion of at least having been evaluated.*

Patton: I pulled some of the recommendations out of the study, and I'd just like to have you react to how those were received and used in any way by the school. The first one that's listed in the report is that objectives as they are related to the goals of the Open School should be written in performance-specific language. What was the reaction to that recommendation?

Jennings: I know that's the current popular view in education today, but I'm not sure it could be done. It would require an enormous amount of energy. Many of our objectives are not very specific subject-matter kinds of objectives. The general goals of the school are more philosophical in tone, and I guess we're just not willing to invest the time and energy to reduce those to the kinds of performance objectives they're speaking of, and I don't know if the end results would be particularly helpful.

Patton: Did it seem to you that that recommendation followed from the findings of the study?

Jennings: When I read that one, I thought—Where did that come from? You know, how did they arrive at that? Is that just some conventional wisdom in education today that can be plugged into any set recommendations?

Patton: What, then, was your overall reaction to the recommendations?

Jennings: Each was simpleminded. They showed that the evaluators lacked depth of understanding of what the program was trying to accomplish. Each recommendation could have been a report in itself rather than some surface scratching and coming up with some conclusions that just weren't helpful.

Patton: Bottom line—what'd the evaluation accomplish?

Jennings: Legitimation. Just by existing, it served that function. With an impressive cover, even if it was filled with Chinese or some other language, as long as it was thick and had a lot of figures in it and people thought it was an evaluation and somewhere near the end it said that the school seemed to be doing a reasonably good job, that would be satisfactory for most people.

Patton: What about the evaluation supported the legitimation function?

Jennings: Its thickness. The fact that it's got numbers and statistics in it. It's authored by some Ph.D.s. It was done by an outside firm. Those things all lend credibility.

Patton: What would it have taken to make it more useful?

Jennings: I would say that to do the job right, we'd have to have people on our own staff who were free from most other responsibilities so that they could deal with designing the evaluation and work with the evaluators. Then, I think that as the evaluation proceeded, there should probably have been regular interactions to adjust the evaluation—keep it relevant.

Patton: There's a side effect of evaluation studies that affects the way people like yourself, who are administrators and work in government and agencies and schools, feel about evaluation. How would you describe your general opinion of evaluation? Positive? Negative? Favorable? Unfavorable?

Jennings: We want careful evaluation. We want to know what we're doing well and not so well. We want data that will help us improve the program. We want that. We want the best that's available, and we want it to be accurate and we want the conclusions to be justified, and so on. *We just desperately want and need that information, to know if we're on the right track.* But we haven't gotten that so, by and large, my opinion of evaluation is not very good. Most reports look like they were written the last week before they're published, with hastily drawn conclusions and sometimes data that's manipulated for a preconceived conclusion fitting the evaluators' or funders' biases.

Patton: Have you given up on evaluation?

Jennings: I guess the reason hope springs eternal is that I have read carefully done evaluations that have informed my thinking about education and brought me to my present beliefs. I'd guess that 99 percent of evaluation is done on a model of education that I consider obsolete, like a factory trying to perfect its way of making wagon wheels. We need more relevant and useful approaches, something beyond wagon wheels evaluations.

I also interviewed the evaluators of the Open School, but when they read Jennings's comments, they asked that their interview not be used and that they not be named because their business might be hurt. The thrust of their comments was that they had viewed the state and federal education agencies as their primary audiences. They did what they were contracted to do. Once they submitted their reports, they had no further contacts with the funders of the evaluation and did not know how or if the reports had been useful. Federal and state officials we contacted said that they received hundreds of such evaluations and could not comment on specific case examples among the many they monitor.

What Utilization-Focused Evaluation Offers

Shortly after my interview with Jennings, he formed an evaluation task force made up of teachers, parents, students, community people, and graduate students trained in utilization-focused evaluation. With very limited resources, they designed an intensive study of Saint Paul Open School processes and outcomes using a variety of methods, both quantitative and qualitative. That evaluation provided useful information for incremental program development. Exhibit 15.1 contrasts their internal Open School Task Force evaluation with the earlier, mandated external evaluation. These contrasts highlight the critical elements of utilization-focused evaluation.

The 3 years of external, federally mandated evaluation at the Saint Paul Open School cost about $40,000—not a great deal of money as research goes. Yet, in the aggregate, evaluations on hundreds of programs like this cost millions of dollars. They constitute the major proportion of all evaluations conducted in the country. The

benefit of those dollars is problematic. The internal, utilization-focused evaluation cost less than $1,000 in hard cash because the labor was all volunteer and release time. Due to the success of the internal task-force effort, the school continued the utilization-focused approach shown in Exhibit 15.1. Staff supported the evaluation with their own school resources because they found the process and results useful.

The Flow of a Utilization-Focused Evaluation Process

Exhibit 15.2 presents a flowchart of utilization-focused evaluation. First, intended users of the evaluation are identified (Chapter 3). These intended users are brought together or organized in some fashion, if possible (e.g., an evaluation task force of primary stakeholders), to work with the evaluator and share in making major decisions about the evaluation.

Second, the evaluator and intended users commit to the intended uses of the evaluation (Chapters 4 and 5) and determine the focus of the evaluation (Chapters 2 and 8). This can include considering the relative importance of focusing on attainment of goals (Chapter 7), program implementation (Chapter 9), and/or the program's theory of action (Chapter 10). The menu of evaluation possibilities is vast, so many different types of evaluations may need to be discussed. (See Menu 8.1 at the end of Chapter 8 for a suggestive list of different evaluation questions and types.) The evaluator works with intended users to determine priority uses with attention to political and ethical considerations (Chapter 14). In a style that is active-reactive-interactive-adaptive and situationally responsive (Chapter 6), the evaluator helps intended users answer these questions: Given expected uses, is the

EXHIBIT 15.1

Contrasting Evaluation Approaches

Open School Utilization-Focused Evaluation	*Original External Mandated Evaluation*
1. Task force of primary intended users representing various and diverse stakeholder interests was formed to focus evaluation questions.	1. The evaluation was aimed vaguely at multiple audiences: federal funders, the school board, State Department of Education staff, the general public, and Open School staff.
2. The Evaluation Task Force group worked together to determine what information would be useful for program improvement and public accountability. The first priority was formative evaluation.	2. The evaluators unilaterally determined the evolution focus based on what they thought their audiences would want. Evaluators had minimal interactions with those audiences.
3. The evaluation included both implementation (process) data and outcomes data (achievement data and follow-up of Open School graduates).	3. The evaluation was a pure outcomes study. Evaluators collected data on presumed operational goals (i.e., scores on standardized achievement tests) based on a model that fit the evaluators' but not the program's assumptions.
4. The task force based their evaluation on an explicit statement of educational philosophy (a theory of action).	4. Evaluators ignored the program's philosophy and conceptualized the evaluation in terms of their own implicit educational theory of action.
5. A variety of methods were used to investigate a variety of questions. Methods were selected jointly by evaluators and intended users using multiple criteria: methodological appropriateness, face validity of instrumentation, believability, credibility, and relevance of the design and measuring instruments to information users and decision makers; and available resources. The task force was involved on a continual basis in making methods and measurement decisions as circumstances changed.	5. Measurement relied on standardized tests that had low face validity, low credibility, and low relevance to program staff. Other audiences, especially federal funders and state agency staff, appeared to want such instruments, but it was unclear who the evaluation was supposed to serve. Methods were determined largely by evaluators, based on available resources, with only initial review by program staff and federal and state officials.
6. Task force members worked together to analyze and interpret data as they were gathered. Data were discussed in rough form over a period of time before the evaluators wrote the final report. Findings and conclusions were known and being used before the final report was ready for dissemination.	6. Evaluators analyzed and interpreted data by themselves. A final report was the only form in which findings were presented. No interpretation sessions with program staff or any audience were ever held. Recommendations appeared to be preconceived based on evaluators' prejudgments about what constitutes educational quality.
7. When the report was made public, the school principal and evaluators made presentations to parents, staff, and school officials.	7. The final report was mailed to funding agencies. No verbal presentations were made. No discussions of findings took place.
8. The evaluation was used by Open School staff for program development and shared with interested accountability audiences to show how the program was being improved.	8. No specific use was made of the evaluation though it may have helped legitimize the program by giving the "illusion" of outcomes evaluation.

evaluation worth doing? To what extent and in what ways are intended users committed to intended use?

The third part of the process as depicted in the flowchart involves methods, measurement, and design decisions (Chapters 11 and 12). A variety of options are considered: qualitative, quantitative, and mixed data; naturalistic, experimental, and quasi-experimental designs; purposeful and probabilistic sampling approaches; greater and lesser emphasis on generalizations; and alternative ways of dealing with potential threats to validity, reliability, and utility. More specifically, the discussion at this stage will include attention to issues of methodological appropriateness, believability of the data, understandability, accuracy, balance, practicality, propriety, and cost. As always, the overriding concern will be utility. *Will results obtained from these methods be useful—and actually used?*

Once data have been collected and organized for analysis, the fourth stage of the utilization-focused process begins. Intended users are actively and directly involved in interpreting findings, making judgments based on the data, and generating recommendations (Chapter 13). Specific strategies for use can then be formalized in light of actual findings, and the evaluator can facilitate following through on actual use.

Finally, decisions about dissemination of the evaluation report can be made beyond whatever initial commitments were made earlier in planning for intended use. This reinforces the distinction between intended use by intended users (planned utilization) and more general dissemination for broad public accountability (where both hoped for and unintended evaluation influences may occur).

While the flowchart in Exhibit 15.2 depicts a seemingly straightforward, one-step-at-a-time logic to the unfolding of a utilization-focused evaluation, in reality the process is seldom simple or linear. The flowchart attempts to capture the sometimes circular and iterative nature of the process by depicting loops at the points where intended users are identified and again where evaluation questions are focused. For the sake of diagrammatic simplicity, however, many potential loops are missing. The active-reactive-interactive-adaptive evaluator who is situationally responsive and politically sensitive may find that new stakeholders become more important or new questions emerge in the midst of methods decisions. Nor is there a clear and clean distinction between the processes of focusing evaluation questions and making methods decisions.

The real world of utilization-focused evaluation manifests considerably more complexity than a flowchart can possibly capture. The flowchart strives to outline the basic logic of the process, but applying that logic in any given situation requires flexibility and creativity. Exhibit 15.3, the utilization-focused evaluation checklist at the end of this chapter, provides an alternative way of capturing and representing the steps and decisions in this complex dance between evaluators and primary intended users.

The Achilles' Heel of Utilization-Focused Evaluation

Achilles' fame stemmed from his role as hero in Homer's classic, the *Iliad*. He was the Greeks' most illustrious warrior during the Trojan War, invulnerable because his mother had dipped him in the Styx, the river of the underworld across which Charon ferried the dead. His heel, where she held him in the river, was his sole point of vulnerability, and it was there that he was fatally wounded with an arrow shot by Paris.

The Achilles' heel of utilization-focused evaluation, its point of greatest vulnerability, is turnover of primary intended users. The process so depends on the active engagement of intended users that to lose users along the way to job transitions, reorganizations, reassignments, and elections can undermine eventual use. Replacement users who join the evaluation late in the process seldom come with the same agenda as those who were present at the beginning. The best antidote involves working with a task force of multiple intended users so that the departure of one or two is less critical. Still, when substantial turnover of primary intended users occurs, it may be necessary to reignite the process by renegotiating the design and use commitments with the new arrivals on the scene.

Previous chapters have discussed the challenges of selecting the right stakeholders, getting them to commit time and attention to the evaluation, dealing with political dynamics, building credibility, and conducting the evaluation in an ethical manner. All these challenges revolve around the relationship between the evaluator and intended users. When new intended users replace those who depart, new relationships must be built. That may mean delays in original time lines, but such delays pay off in eventual use by attending to the foundation of understanding and relationships on which utilization-focused evaluation is built.

Fundamental Premises of Utilization-Focused Evaluation

A society that aspires to greatness will ultimately be known by how it treats its evaluators.

—Halcolm

Evaluation Humor

A man in a hot air balloon realized he was lost. He reduced altitude and spotted a woman below. He descended a bit more and shouted, "Excuse me, can you help me? I promised a friend I would meet him an hour ago, but I don't know where I am."

The woman below replied, "You are in a hot air balloon hovering approximately 30 feet above the ground. You are between 40 and 41 degrees north latitude and between 59 and 60 degrees west longitude."

"You must be an evaluator," said the balloonist.

"I am," replied the woman, "How did you know?"

"Well," answered the balloonist, "everything you told me is technically correct, but I have no idea what to make of your information, and the fact is I am still lost. Frankly, you've not been much help so far."

The woman below responded, "You must be a manager."

"I am," replied the balloonist, "but how did you know?"

"Well," said the woman, "you don't know where you are or where you are going. You have risen to where you are due to a large quantity of hot air. You made a promise which you have no idea how to keep, and you expect me to solve your problem. The fact is you are in exactly the same position you were in before we met, but now, somehow, it's my fault."

SOURCE: Carol Sullins, quoted by Jane Davidson, *EvalTalk*, July 10, 2003.

EXHIBIT 15.2

Utilization-Focused Evaluation Flow Chart

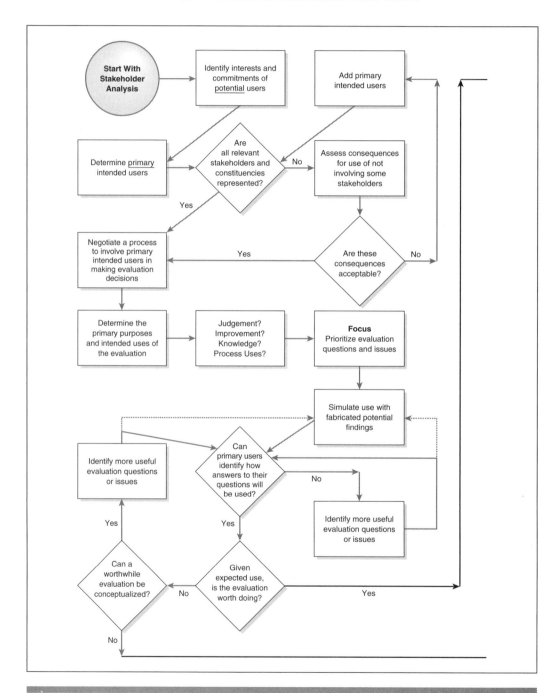

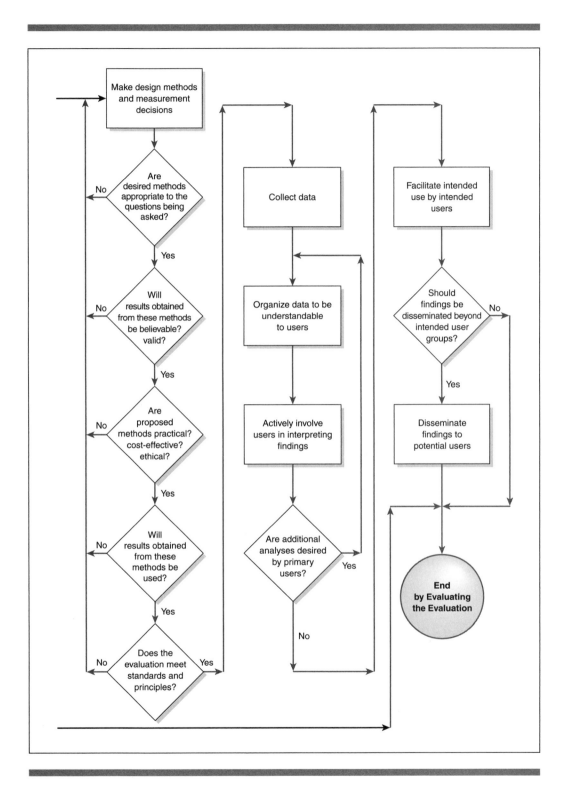

Chapter 9 discussed the importance of examining program implementation in evaluation and asking the following questions: To what extent was the program implemented as designed? What adaptations occurred during implementation and what are the implications of those adaptations for intended and unintended outcomes? *These same questions are crucial in evaluating evaluations.* There are many slips between cup and lip in evaluation. The evaluation standards call for *metaevaluation* of evaluations to examine adherence to the standards in practice not just in rhetoric (Joint Committee 1994:A12). Metaevaluation should include the degree to which an evaluation that purports to follow a particular approach or model actually adheres to that approach or model. Looking beyond the label and rhetoric attached to an evaluation to examine actual practice often reveals a gap between what was promised and what was, in fact, delivered (Donaldson 2007; Bastoe 2006; Miller and Campbell 2006). I see a lot of evaluations published that use the label "utilization-focused evaluation," but show no evidence of having focused on intended use by intender users and fail to adhere to the fundamental premises of utilization-focused evaluation. To conclude this book, then, let me review those fundamental premises.

First, a cautionary note and tale: Articulating fundamental premises requires making assumptions and values explicit. What seems obvious to one person may not be at all obvious to another. Consider, for example, the Sufi story about Mulla Nasrudin standing in the center of the marketplace while a compatriot stopped passersby, whispering to them how they could entertain themselves by showing Nasrudin to be an idiot.

When offered a choice between two coins of different value, Nasrudin always chose the one worth less.

One day, a kind man tried to enlighten the foolish Nasrudin. "You should take the coin of greater value," he urged, "then you'd have more money and people would no longer be able to make a fool of you."

"But," replied Nasrudin, "if I take the more valuable coin, people will stop offering me money to prove that I'm more idiotic than they are. Then I would have no money at all."

—Adapted from Shah (1973:52)

The premises of utilization-focused evaluation will seem obvious to some, of dubious merit to others, and controversial to a few. The rationales for and evidence supporting these various premises have been articulated throughout this book. Here, then, as a summary of what has gone before, I offer 15 fundamental premises of utilization-focused evaluation.

1. *Commitment to intended use by intended users should be the driving force in an evaluation.* At every decision point— whether the decision concerns purpose, focus, design, methods, measurement, analysis, or reporting—the evaluator asks intended users: How would that affect your use of this evaluation?

2. *Strategizing about use is ongoing and continuous from the very beginning of the evaluation.* Use isn't something one becomes interested in at the end of an evaluation. By the end of the evaluation, the potential for use has been largely determined. From the moment stakeholders and evaluators begin interacting and conceptualizing the evaluation, decisions are being made that will affect use in major ways. In Fleisher's 2006 survey of members of the American Evaluation Association,

the factor rated most influential in facilitating use was *planning for use at the beginning of the evaluation* (Fleisher 2007).

3. *The personal factor contributes significantly to use.* The personal factor refers to the research finding that the personal interests and commitments of those involved in an evaluation undergird use. Thus, evaluations should be *specifically* user oriented—aimed at the interests and information needs of specific, identifiable people, not vague, passive audiences.

4. *Careful and thoughtful stakeholder analysis should inform identification of primary intended users.* Identifying primary intended users involves taking into account the varied and multiple interests that surround any program, and therefore, any evaluation. Staff, program participants, directors, public officials, funders, and community leaders all have an interest in evaluation, but the degree and nature of their interests will vary. Political sensitivity and ethical judgments are involved in identifying primary intended users and users.

5. *Evaluations must be focused in some way; focusing on intended use by intended users is the most useful way.* Resource and time constraints will make it impossible for any single evaluation to answer everyone's questions or to give full attention to all possible issues. Because no evaluation can serve all potential stakeholders' interests equally well, stakeholders representing various constituencies should come together to negotiate what issues and questions deserve priority.

6. *Focusing on intended use requires making deliberate and thoughtful choices.* I've provided menus throughout the book to emphasize that utilization-focused evaluation requires thoughtful choices among alternative purposes and approaches.

Menu 4.1 in Chapter 4 identified six primary uses of findings: (1) judging overall merit or worth (e.g., summative evaluation); (2) improving programs (learning-oriented evaluation); (3) accountability; (4) monitoring (routine reporting and ongoing program management); (5) development (adapting to changing conditions); and (6) generating knowledge (generating lessons).

Menu 5.1 in Chapter 5 presented six kinds of process use: (1) infusing evaluative thinking into the organizational culture, (2) enhancing shared understandings among those involved in a program, (3) supporting and reinforcing the program interventions, (4) instrumentation effects and reactivity (what gets measured gets done), (5) supporting participant engagement, and (6) developing programs and organizations.

No single evaluation can or should undertake all six findings uses and process uses. Choices must be made about focus. However, uses can change and evolve over time as a program matures and evolves.

7. *Useful evaluations must be designed and adapted situationally.* Standardized recipe approaches won't work. The relative value of a particular utilization focus (Premises 5 and 6) can only be judged in the context of a specific program and the interests of intended users. Situational factors affect use. As Exhibit 6.1 in Chapter 6 showed, these factors include community variables, organizational characteristics, nature of the evaluation, evaluator credibility, political considerations, and resource constraints. In conducting a utilization-focused evaluation, the active-reactive-interactive-adaptive evaluator works with intended users to assess how various factors and conditions may affect the potential for use.

8. *Intended users' commitment to use can be nurtured and enhanced by actively involving them in making significant*

Evaluators' Ratings of Top Factors That Influence Use

In a 2006 online survey of members of the American Evaluation Association (Fleischer 2007), 991 respondents rated which factors were most influential in facilitating use from 1 (not at all influential) to 5 (extremely influential). The three factors rated most influential in facilitating use were

1. Planning for use at the beginning of the evaluation (mean = 4.5)

2. Identifying and prioritizing intended uses of the evaluation (mean = 4.3)

3. Developing a communicating and reporting plan (mean = 4.3)

decisions about the evaluation. Involvement increases relevance, understanding, and ownership of the evaluation, all of which facilitate informed and appropriate use.

9. *High-quality participation is the goal, not high-quantity participation.* The quantity of group interaction time can be inversely related to the quality of the process. Evaluators conducting utilization-focused evaluation must be skilled group facilitators.

10. *High-quality involvement of intended users will result in high-quality evaluations.* Many researchers worry that methodological rigor may be sacrificed if nonscientists collaborate in making methods decisions. But decision makers want data that are useful *and* accurate. Validity and utility are interdependent. Threats to utility are as important to counter as threats to validity. Skilled evaluation facilitators can help nonscientists understand methodological issues so that they can judge for themselves the trade-offs involved in choosing among the strengths and weaknesses of design options and methods alternatives.

11. *Evaluators have a rightful stake in an evaluation in that their credibility and integrity are always at risk, thus the mandate for evaluators to be active-reactive-interactive-adaptive.* Evaluators are active in presenting to intended users their own best judgments about appropriate evaluation

focus and methods; they are reactive in listening attentively and respectful to others' concerns; they are interactive in the give-and-take of negotiating all aspects of the evaluation; and they are adaptive in finding ways to design evaluations that incorporate diverse interests, including their own, while meeting high standards of professional practice. Evaluators' credibility and integrity are factors affecting use as well as the foundation of the profession. In this regard, evaluators should be guided by the profession's standards and principles (see Exhibits 1.3 and 1.4 in Chapter 1).

12. *Evaluators committed to enhancing use have both an opportunity and a responsibility* to *train users* in evaluation processes and the uses of information. Every utilization-focused evaluation is an opportunity not only to generate useful findings for a particular purpose and situation but also to build evaluation capacity, enhance evaluative thinking, reinforce evaluation as a high-level, transdisciplinary "cognitive process" (Scriven 2007, 2003), and deepen the commitment of those involved for the future. Training stakeholders in evaluation methods and processes attends to both short-term and long-term evaluation uses. Making decision makers more sophisticated about evaluation can contribute to greater use of evaluation over time. That increased

sophistication includes differentiating and valuing findings about both program strengths (the glass is half-full) and weaknesses (the glass is half-empty), a distinction that is insightfully highlighted in Patricia Rogers's (2001) hopeful vision for evaluation: "The whole world is evaluating. We are better at describing half-full glasses. And because of this we are making the world a better place" (p. 431).

13. *Use is different from reporting and dissemination.* Reporting and dissemination may be means to facilitate use, but they should not be confused with such intended uses as making decisions, improving programs, changing thinking, empowering participants, and generating knowledge (see Premise 6).

14. *Serious attention to use involves financial and time costs that are far from trivial.* The benefits of these costs are manifested in greater use. These costs should be made explicit in evaluation proposals and budgets so that utilization follow-through is not neglected for lack of resources. This means building into evaluation budgets time to work with intended users and time to facilitate use of findings *after* the report has been concluded. The evaluation is not over when a report is completed. Reports are a means to use, not the endpoint of use.

15. *Commitment to improving practice means following up evaluations to find out how they were used.* We should walk the talk of evaluation by evaluating our evaluations. How were findings and recommendations used, if at all? What was valuable about the evaluation processes and findings? What was not helpful? What can be learned from this particular evaluation to improve future practice? We need to become astute and rigorous evaluators of evaluations, or it will remain true, as Roger Miranda, Evaluation Officer at the United Nations Office on Drugs and Crime observed in correspondence with me:

Just as doctors are the worst patients, we evaluators are the worst users!

The Use of Uselessness

"You always speak of the use of uselessness," said Hueitse to Chuangtse.

"One must understand the use of uselessness before he can speak of the use of usefulness. Surely, the earth is vast and great, yet what man can put to use is only where his feet rest. However, when a man turns up his toe and his body is laid in the grave, can he still find the earth useful?"

"Then the earth is useless to him," replied Hueitse.

"Is it not clear, therefore, that the useless (grave) is useful (because of the hollow or the nonexistence of the earth)?"

A man walks on the ground by stepping on it, but it is only through the ground that he does not step upon (the distance between the steps) that he is able to reach a great distance.

—The Tao of Lao-Tse
Chinese Philosopher, sixth century BCE

The Vision of an Experimenting Society and Experimenting Evaluators

An experimenting society would vigorously try out possible solutions to recurrent problems and would make hard-headed, multidimensional evaluations of outcomes, and when the evaluation of one reform showed it to have been ineffective or harmful, would move on to try other alternatives.

—Donald T. Campbell (1988:291)

To be truly scientific we must be able to experiment. We must be able to advocate without that excess of commitment that blinds us to reality testing.

—Donald T. Campbell (1969:410)

Donald T. Campbell, one of the pioneers of scientific evaluation, died in 1996 after nearly four-score years, many of them working to realize his vision of an Experimenting Society. His vision lives on. Its realization will depend on a shared commitment to engage in active reality testing by all those involved in and touched by programs and policies, not just researchers and evaluators. But evaluators must point the way. Utilization-focused evaluation invites stakeholders to join with evaluators as informed citizens of an Experimenting Global Society.

Utilization-focused evaluation combines style and substance, activism and science, personal perspective and systematic information. I have tried to capture the complexity and potential of utilization-focused evaluation with scenarios, case examples, findings from our study of federal evaluation use, Sufi parables, and children's stories. In the end, this approach to evaluation must also be judged by its usefulness.

I have presented research and theories that support the premises of utilization-focused evaluation. Still, skeptics will be skeptical—some who don't want to take the time to work with stakeholders, others who don't want to give up control of the process, and still others who are convinced that it probably works for certain kinds of evaluators (the personable, the human-relations types, whatever . . .), but that it won't work for them.

Certainly, I can offer no guarantees that a utilization-focused approach will always work. Just as decision makers live in a world of uncertainty, so too evaluators are faced with the ever-present possibility that, despite their best efforts, their work will be ignored or, worse, misused. Producing good evaluation studies that actually are used constitutes an enormous challenge. In many ways, the odds are all against use, and it's quite possible to become cynical about the futility of trying to have an impact in a world in which situation after situation seems impervious to change. Utilization-focused evaluators may be told, or may sometimes feel, that they are wasting their time. A final Sufi story provides, perhaps, something for skeptics to ponder.

> Yogurt is made by adding a small quantity of old yogurt to a larger measure of milk. The action of the bacillus bulgaricus in the seeding portion of yogurt will in time convert the whole into a mass of new yogurt.
>
> One day some friends saw Nasrudin down on his knees beside a warm forest spring adding a mass of yogurt to the water. One of the passers-by asked, "What are you trying to do, Nasrudin?"
>
> "I'm trying to make yogurt."
>
> "But you can't make yogurt like that," he scoffed.
>
> "Perhaps not, but just supposing it works!"
>
> The next day Nasrudin invited the entire village to taste his concoction. It wasn't like the yogurt they were used to, but all agreed it was unique and delicious.

The following day Nasrudin returned to the warm spring to make another batch. The result this time tasted acrid and made many who tried it sick.

For weeks thereafter, Nasrudin returned to the spring, each day trying to make again his original tasty creation. But, having failed to carefully observe and write down what he had done and what conditions prevailed at the time, he never succeeded in reproducing the original. He did, however, produce other tasty delicacies, but the villagers were reluctant to try them since they never knew for sure whether they would be delighted or made sick. Eventually, Nasrudin gave up, since he could never predict with certainty what would result in the changing conditions of the forest spring.

—Adapted from Shah (1964:90)

Getting intended users to taste evaluation may, indeed, be a long shot in many situations. Many have been made "sick" by past concoctions called evaluation. The results of any particular effort cannot be guaranteed. Each evaluation being a blend of unique ingredients, no standardized recipe can ensure the outcome. We have only principles, premises, and utilization-focused processes to guide us, and we have much yet to learn. But the potential benefits merit the efforts and risks involved. At stake is improving the effectiveness of programs that express and embody the highest ideals of humankind. At stake is the vision of an Experimenting Society. It may be a long shot, "but just *supposing* it works!" And works for you. The only way to find out is to try it—and evaluate the results. Build the study of use into your evaluations and thereby help make not only programs, but also evaluations, accountable. Experiment with ways of making evaluation useful, for the vision of an Experimenting Society ultimately depends on experimenting and innovating evaluators and evaluation users working together.

And as you strive to make evaluations useful, pay attention to what works. The altogether avoidable aspect of Nasrudin's failure to reproduce his delicious concoction was that he neglected to carefully observe and write down what he had done and what conditions prevailed at the time. This book is a record of how useful evaluations can be produced, a record based on the observations and conclusions of those who have studied evaluation use, reflected on their evaluation practice, and paid attention to the factors and principles that support increased use. The cumulative evidence presented in this book provides guidance for how to create evaluation concoctions that will delight the palates of intended users and have them coming back for more.

Evaluation Checklists

The Evaluation Center at Western Michigan University has developed checklists to guide various aspects of evaluation. These checklists, available on the Evaluation Center Web site (www.wmich.edu/evalctr/checklists/index.html), provide evaluation specialists and users with refereed guidelines for designing, budgeting, contracting, staffing, managing, and assessing evaluations of programs, personnel, students, and other purposes; collecting, analyzing, and reporting evaluation information; and determining merit, worth, and significance. Each checklist has been created by an experienced evaluation professional to offer a distillation of valuable lessons learned from practice. Exhibit 15.3, beginning on the next page, presents an updated Utilization-Focused Evaluation Checklist.

EXHIBIT 15.3

Utilization-Focused Evaluation (U-FE) Checklist

The 12 parts of the checklist are divided into 2 columns. Primary U-FE tasks are identified in the columns on the left. Because of the emphasis on facilitation in U-FE, particular facilitation challenges are identified in the columns on the right. Underlying premises are made explicit for each step in the U-FE process.

1. *Program/Organizational Readiness Assessment*	
Premise: Key people who want the evaluation conducted need to understand and be interested in a utilization-focused evaluation (U-FE).	*Premise: U-FE requires active and skilled guidance from and facilitation by an evaluation facilitator.*
Primary Tasks:	*Evaluation Facilitation Challenges:*
Assess primary evaluation clients' commitment to doing useful evaluation based on an explanation of U-FE.	Explaining U-FE and enhancing readiness for evaluation generally and U-FE specifically.
Assess if the program is ready to spend time and resources on evaluation.	Communicating the value and requirements of U-FE, assessing commitment, and building commitment as needed.
Determine if primary evaluation clients are ready to assess various stakeholder constituencies to select primary intended users of the evaluation.	Explaining and facilitating stakeholder assessment; distinguishing between stakeholders in general and primary intended users in particular.
Assess what needs to be done and can be done to enhance readiness.	Planning, negotiating, and facilitating increased readiness with evaluation clients as needed.
2. *Evaluator Readiness and Capability Assessment*	
Premise: Facilitating and conducting a utilization-focused evaluation requires a particular philosophy and special skills.	*Premise: Evaluation facilitators need to know their strengths and limitations and develop the skills needed to facilitate utilization-focused evaluations.*
Primary Tasks:	*Evaluation Facilitation Challenges:*
Assess the match between the *evaluator's knowledge* and what will be needed in the evaluation.	Getting a good match between the evaluator's knowledge and what will be needed in the evaluation.
Assess the match between the *evaluator's commitment* and the likely challenges of the situation.	Maintaining focus on and commitment to intended use by intended users as the primary outcome of the evaluation.
Assess the match between the evaluator's skills and what will be needed in the evaluation.	Developing facilitation skills to fit the challenges of the specific people and situation.
Make sure the evaluators are prepared to have their effectiveness judged by the use of the evaluation by primary intended users.	Honest self-reflection by the evaluators.

3. *Identification of Primary Intended Users*	
Premise: Primary intended users are people who have a direct, identifiable stake in the evaluation and meet the criteria below to some extent. (Caveat: These judgments are necessarily subjective and negotiable.)	*Premise: The U-FE facilitator needs to both assess the characteristics of primary intended users and reinforce characteristics that will contribute to evaluation use.*
Primary Task:	*Evaluation Facilitation Challenges:*
Find and recruit people who are	
Interested	Determining real interest; building interest as needed; sustaining interest throughout the U-FE process.
Knowledgeable	Determining knowledge; increasing knowledge as needed.
Open	Facilitating an evaluation climate of openness.
Connected to an important stakeholder constituency	Working with primary intended users to examine stakeholder connections and their implications for use.
Credible	Building and sustaining credibility.
Teachable	Teaching evaluation and U-FE.
Available for interaction throughout the evaluation process	Outlining and facilitating a process that intended users want to be part of.
4. *Situational Analysis*	
Premises: Evaluation use is people- and context-dependent. Use is likely to be enhanced when the evaluation takes into account and is adapted to crucial situational factors such as those below.	*Premise: The evaluator has responsibility to identify, assess, understand, and act on situational factors that may affect use.*
Primary Tasks:	*Evaluation Facilitation Challenges:*
Examine program's prior experiences with evaluation.	Learning the extent to which past evaluations were useful.
Look for possible barriers or resistance to use.	Looking at typical barriers—people, resources, culture, turbulence—while also looking out for unusual or unexpected barriers.
Identify factors that may support and facilitate use.	Looking at typical supports—e.g., accountability demands—while also looking out for unusual or unexpected ones.
Get clear about resources available for evaluation.	Including in the budget resources beyond analysis and reporting to facilitate use.
Identify any upcoming decisions, deadlines, or timelines that the evaluation should meet to be useful.	Being realistic about timelines.

(Continued)

(Continued)

Assess the evaluation knowledge level and experiences of primary intended users.	Building into the evaluation process opportunities to increase the knowledge of primary intended users.
Understand the political context for the evaluation, and calculate how political factors may affect use.	Including attention to both potential uses and potential misuses.
Make sure that important constituencies and diverse stakeholder groups for the evaluation are represented among the primary intended users and assess the consequences of any omissions for use.	Staying focused on intended use by intended users while assuring that intended users represent important and legitimate interests of diverse stakeholders—done on an ongoing basis as new information surfaces throughout the evaluation.
5. *Identification of Primary Intended Uses*	
Premise: Intended use by primary intended users is the U-FE goal of the evaluation.	*Premise: The rich menu of evaluation options are reviewed, screened, and prioritized to focus the evaluation.*
Primary Tasks:	*Evaluation Facilitation Challenges:*
Consider how evaluation could contribute to program improvement.	Guiding primary intended users in reviewing formative evaluation options.
Consider how evaluation could contribute to making major decisions about the program.	Guiding primary intended users in reviewing summative and major decision-oriented evaluation options.
Consider accountability uses.	Guiding users in assessing oversight and compliance issues and the accountability context for the evaluation.
Consider monitoring uses.	Guiding users in examining the relationship between monitoring and evaluation.
Consider developmental uses.	Guiding users in distinguishing developmental evaluation from other uses, especially program improvement (i.e., the difference between improvement and *development*).
Consider how evaluation could contribute by generating knowledge.	Guiding primary intended users in considering the possibility of using evaluation to generate lessons learned and evidence-based practices that might apply beyond the program being evaluated.
Consider process uses of evaluation.	Infusing evaluative thinking into organizational culture; enhancing communications; reinforcing the program intervention; engaging participants; instrumentation effects (what gets measured gets done); and organizational development.
6. *Focusing the Evaluation*	
Premise: The focus derives from primary intended uses of the evaluation by primary intended users.	*Premise: Primary intended users will often need considerable assistance identifying and agreeing on priority evaluation uses and the major focus for the evaluation.*

Primary Tasks:	Evaluation Facilitation Challenges:
Make sure that all *high-priority* questions are addressed in the evaluation design—or be clear about why they aren't included.	Actively involving primary intended users in determining priorities; narrowing the options and determining what *specific* evaluation questions and issues will be addressed by the evaluation based on *priority intended uses.*
Make sure that the intended uses of answers to the specific evaluation questions are reasonably clear.	Actively involving primary intended users in determining the specific relevance of intended uses of findings.
7. Evaluation Design	
Premises: The evaluation should be designed to lead to useful findings. Methods should be selected and the evaluation designed to support and achieve intended use by primary intended users.	*Premise: Evaluators and users have varying responsibilities in the design decision-making process.*
Primary Tasks:	Evaluation Facilitation Challenges:
Select methods appropriate to the questions being asked.	Making sure that methods are selected jointly by primary intended users and the evaluator(s).
Assure that results obtained by the methods selected will be believable, credible, and valid to primary intended users.	Making sure that primary intended users play an active role in reviewing methods to examine their believability, credibility, and validity.
Assure that the proposed methods and measurements are	Making sure that methods and measures are reviewed jointly by primary intended users and the evaluator(s).
Practical	
Cost-effective	
Ethical	
Assure that the results obtained from these methods will be able to be used as intended.	Facilitating serious review of intended use by primary intended users.
Review the evaluation as designed in relation to professional standards and principles.	Taking professional standards and principles seriously— not just treating them as boilerplate or window dressing.
Consider seriously whether involving primary intended users or other stakeholders in actual data collection will enhance *process use.*	Seeking creative possibilities for enhancing process uses; examining potential trade-offs between utility (process uses specifically) and credibility.
8. Simulation of Use	
Premise: Before data are collected, a simulation of potential use can be done with fabricated findings in a real-enough way to provide a meaningful learning experience for primary intended users.	*Premise: It's important to move discussions of use from the abstract to the concrete, and a simulation of use based on fabricated data helps do that.*
Primary Tasks:	Evaluation Facilitation Challenges:

(Continued)

(Continued)

Fabricate findings based on the proposed design and measures.	Fabricating realistic findings that show varying results and offer good grist for simulated interaction among primary intended users.
Guide primary intended users in interpreting the potential (fabricated) findings.	Helping primary intended users take the simulation seriously so that they can use the experience to improve design and be better prepared for real use of findings.
Interpret the simulation experience to determine if any design changes or additions to the data collection would likely increase utility.	Taking time to do this final, critical check before data collection.
As a final step before data collection, have primary intended users make an explicit decision to proceed with the evaluation given likely costs and expected uses.	Helping primary intended users seriously ask: Given likely costs and expected uses, is the evaluation worth doing? Assuring that primary intended users feel ownership of the design and measures.
9. *Data Collection*	
Premise: Data collected should be managed with use in mind.	*Premise: It's important to keep primary intended users informed and involved throughout all stages of the process.*
Primary Tasks:	*Evaluator Facilitation Challenges:*
Keep primary intended users informed of progress.	Noting any problems or delays as soon as they are known.
Inform primary intended users of important interim findings to maintain interest in the evaluation.	Getting intended users to understand that preliminary findings are subject to revision.
If involving primary intended users or other stakeholders in actual data collection, manage this process carefully.	Offering opportunities to reflect on the process and learn from it; debriefing process learnings as they occur.
10. *Data Analysis*	
Premise: Analysis should be organized to facilitate use by primary intended users.	*Premise: Facilitating data interpretation among primary intended users increases their understanding of the findings, their sense of ownership of the evaluation, and their commitment to use the results.*
Primary Tasks:	*Evaluation Facilitation Challenges:*
Organize data to be understandable and relevant to primary intended users.	Basing organization of data on primary intended uses of the evaluation.
Actively involve users in interpreting findings and generating recommendations.	Helping users distinguish between findings, interpretations, judgments, and recommendations.
Examine the findings and their implications from various perspectives with focus on primary intended uses by primary intended users.	Offering opportunities to reflect on the analytical process and learn from it; helping users distinguish varying degrees of certainty in the findings; being open and explicit about data strengths, weaknesses, and limitations.

11. *Facilitation of Use*	
Premise: Use doesn't just happen naturally; it needs to be facilitated.	*Premise: Facilitating use is a central part of the evaluator's job.*
Primary Tasks:	*Evaluation Facilitation Challenges:*
Work with primary intended users to use the findings and *learnings from the process* in intended ways.	Actively facilitating the users' sense of ownership of the findings and their commitment to act on those findings.
Examine potential uses and users beyond those intended and originally targeted (dissemination).	Reviewing the larger, and possibly changed, stakeholder environment. (There may be a separate action group that the evaluation findings and recommendations would be passed on to for implementation.)
Decide on dissemination mechanisms and avenues consistent with intended uses and additional desired uses.	Reviewing the larger, and possibly changed, stakeholder environment and resources available to support dissemination; *clearly differentiating use from dissemination.*
Identify possible misuses, and plan action to assure appropriate uses.	Being clear about the ethical obligations of being an evaluator.
Stay involved beyond formal reporting, and engage in follow-up facilitation as needed to enhance use.	Building in from the beginning time and resources to facilitate use beyond just writing a report—additional resources may be needed if new uses or users are added.
12. *Meta-evaluation: Evaluating Use*	
Premise: Utilization-focused evaluations should be evaluated by whether primary intended users used the evaluation in intended ways.	*Premise: A U-FE facilitator can learn something from each evaluation.*
Primary Tasks:	*Evaluation Facilitation Challenges:*
After the evaluation is completed, follow-up to determine the extent to which intended use by intended users was achieved.	Taking the time for ongoing learning to achieve long-term, utilization-focused evaluation excellence.
Follow-up to determine the extent to which additional uses or users were served beyond those initially targeted.	Finding time and resources to do the necessary fieldwork.
Follow-up to determine and learn from any misuses or unintended consequences of the evaluation.	Helping primary intended users be open and reflective about their U-FE experience.

Follow-Up Exercises

1. Select one of the premises of Utilization-Focused Evaluation in this chapter and write a script for how you would explain that premise—its importance, relevance, and significance—to a specific, targeted group of primary intended users. Specify the stakeholders you are addressing and describe their evaluation situation. Given that specific context, explain how the premise you have selected would be relevant to (and possibly adapted to) that context and those specific stakeholders.

2. Review the checklists offered by The Evaluation Center (www.wmich .edu/evalctr/checklists/index.html). Select a checklist and (a) critically review it, (b) compare it with the utilization-focused evaluation checklist (Exhibit 15.3) in both content and format, and (c) discuss how you might use that checklist in conjunction with a utilization-focused evaluation.

3. In a 2006 on-line survey of members of the American Evaluation Association (Fleischer 2007), respondents were asked to rate which factors were most influential in facilitating use from 1 (not at all influential) to 5 (extremely influential). The three factors rated most influential in facilitating use were (1) planning for use at the beginning of the evaluation (mean = 4.5); (b) identifying and prioritizing intended uses of the evaluation (mean = 4.3); and (c) developing a communicating and reporting plan (mean = 4.3). The three factors rated least influential in facilitating use were (1) taking steps to prevent the misuse of evaluation findings (mean = 3.7); (2) demonstrating that the benefits of the evaluation will outweigh the costs (mean = 3.6); and (3) establishing a balance of power among stakeholders (mean = 3.3). Discuss and interpret these findings; relate the findings to each other and discuss their implications for utilization-focused evaluation.

4. Exhibit 15.2 presents Utilization-Focused Evaluation as a flowchart. Exhibit 15.3 presents Utilization-Focused Evaluation as a checklist. Compare and contrast these two different depictions of the steps and stages of Utilization-Focused Evaluation. How are they alike? How are they different? What is the significance of the differences? How might you use each one?

References

Abma, Tineke. 2006. "The Practice and Politics of Responsive Evaluation." *American Journal of Evaluation* 27(1):31–43.

Abramson, M. A. 1978. *The Funding of Social Knowledge Production and Application: A Survey of Federal Agencies.* Washington, DC: National Academy of Sciences.

African Evaluation Association (AfrEA). 2007. "African Evaluation Guidelines: Standards and Norms." Adopted at the AfrEA Conference, Niamey, Niger, January 12. http://www.afrea.org.

Albonico, M., H. M. Chwaya, A. Montresor, R. Stolfzus, J. Tielsch, K. Alawi, and L. Savioli. 1997. "Parasitic Infections in Pemba Island Schoolchildren." *East African Medical Journal* 75(5):294–98.

Alkin, Marvin C. 2005. "Utilization of Evaluation." Pp. 434–36 in *Encyclopedia of Evaluation*, edited by S. Mathison. Thousand Oaks, CA: Sage.

_____, ed. 2004. *Evaluation Roots: Tracing Theorists' Views and Influences.* Thousand Oaks, CA: Sage.

_____. 2003. "Evaluation Theory and Practice: Insights and New Directions." *The Practice-Theory Relationship in Evaluation. New Directions for Evaluation* 97:81–90.

_____. 1995. "Lessons Learned about Evaluation Use." Panel presentation at the International Evaluation Conference, American Evaluation Association, November 2, Vancouver, British Columbia.

_____, ed. 1990. *Debates on Evaluation.* Newbury Park, CA: Sage.

_____. 1985. *A Guide for Evaluation Decision Makers.* Beverly Hills, CA: Sage.

_____. 1975. "Evaluation: Who Needs It? Who Cares?" *Studies in Educational Evaluation* 1(3):201–12.

_____. 1972. "Wider Context Goals and Goal-Based Evaluators." *Evaluation Comment: The Journal of Educational Evaluation* (Center for the Study of Evaluation, UCLA) 3(4):10–11.

_____. 1970. "A Review of the Evaluation of the Follow through Program." Working Paper 10, Center for the Study of Evaluation. UCLA.

Alkin, Marvin, Christina Christie, and Mike Rose. 2006. "Communicating Evaluation." Pp. 384–403 in *Handbook of Evaluation: Policies, Programs and Practices,* edited by I. Shaw, J. Greene, and M. Mark. Thousand Oaks, CA: Sage.

Alkin, Marvin and Christina Christie. 2005. "Unraveling Theorists' Evaluation Reality." *Theorists' Models in Action. New Directions for Evaluation* 106:111–28.

Alkin, Marvin and Christina Christie. 2004. "An Evaluation Theory Tree." Pp. 12–65 in *Evaluation Roots: Tracing Theorists' Views and Influences,* edited by Marvin C. Alkin. Thousand Oaks, CA: Sage.

Alkin, Marvin C. and Sandy Taut. 2003. "Unbundling Evaluation Use." *Studies in Educational Evaluation* 29:1–12.

Alkin, Marvin and Karin Coyle. 1988. "Thoughts on Evaluation Misutilization." Presented at the Annual Meeting of the American Educational Research Association, April 5, New Orleans. See also, *Studies in Educational Evaluation* 14:331–40.

Alkin, Marvin C., Richard Daillak, and Peter White. 1979. *Using Evaluation:*

Does Evaluation Make a Difference? Beverly Hills, CA: Sage.

Alkin, M., C. Hofstetter, and X Ai. 1998. "Stakeholder Concepts." *Advances in Educational Productivity* 7:87–113.

Alkin, Marvin C., with P. Jacobson, J. Burry, P. White, and L. Kent. 1985. *Organizing for Evaluation Use. A Handbook for Administrators.* Los Angeles, CA: Center for the Study of Evaluation, UCLA.

Alkin, Marvin and Alex Law. 1980. "A Conversation on Evaluation Utilization." *Educational Evaluation and Policy Analysis* 2(3):73–79.

Allison, Graham T. 1971. *Essence of Decision: Explaining the Cuban Missile Crisis.* Boston, MA: Little, Brown.

Altschuld, James and David Kumar. 2005. "Needs Assessment." Pp. 276–77 in *Encyclopedia of Evaluation*, edited by S. Mathison. Thousand Oaks, CA: Sage.

American Council of Voluntary Agencies for Foreign Service (ACVAFS). 1983. *Evaluation Sourcebook.* New York: American Council of Voluntary Agencies for Foreign Service.

American Evaluation Association (AEA). 2004. *A Cultural Reading of The Program Evaluation Standards.* Diversity Committee of the American Evaluation Association. http://www.eval.org/aea05.culturalreading/aea05.cr.Propriety.pdf.

American Evaluation Association (AEA). 2003. "Scientifically Based Evaluation Methods." http://www.eval.org/doestatement.htm.

American Evaluation Association (AEA) Task Force on Guiding Principles for Evaluators. 1995. "Guiding Principles for Evaluators." *New Directions for Program Evaluation* 66:19–34.

American Heritage® Dictionary of the English Language, The. 2006. 4th ed. Boston, MA: Houghton Mifflin.

Amo, Courtney and J. Bradley Cousins. 2007. "Going through the Process: An Examination of the Operationalization of Process Use in Empirical Research on Evaluation." *New Directions for Evaluation* 116:5–26.

Anderson, Andrea. 2005. "An Introduction to Theory of Change." *The Evaluation Exchange* XI(2) Summer. Cambridge, MA:

HFRP. http://www.gse.harvard.edu/hfrp/eval/issue30/expert3.html.

Anderson, Barry F. 1980. *The Complete Thinker.* Englewood Cliffs, NJ: Prentice Hall.

Anderson, John R., Lynne M. Reder, and Herbert Simon. 1996. "Situated Learning and Education." *Educational Researcher* 25(4):5–21.

Anderson, Richard B. 1977. "The Effectiveness of Follow through: What Have We Learned?" Presented at the annual meeting of the American Educational Research Association, New York.

Angelica, Marion Peters. 1999. *Resolving Conflict in Nonprofit Organizations.* St. Paul, MN: Wilder Foundation.

Arendt, Hannah. 1963. *Between Past and Future: Six Exercises in Political Thought.* New Haven, CT: Meridian books.

Argyris, Chris. 1993. *Knowledge for Action: A Guide to Overcoming Barriers to Organizational Change.* San Francisco, CA: Jossey-Bass.

_____. 1982. *Reasoning, Learning, and Action.* San Francisco, CA: Jossey-Bass.

_____. 1974. *Theory in Practice: Increasing Professional Effectiveness.* San Francisco, CA: Jossey-Bass.

Argyris, Chris R. Putnam, and D. M. Smith. 1985. *Action Science.* San Francisco, CA: Jossey-Bass.

Argyris, Chris and Donald Schön. 1978. *Organizational Learning.* Reading, MA: Addison-Wesley.

_____. 1974. *Theory in Practice: Increasing Professional Effectiveness:* San Francisco, CA: Jossey-Bass.

Arjumand and Associates. 2004. *Impact Assessment of Kashf's Microfinance and Karvaan Enterprise Development Programme.* Final report submitted to DFID (the Department for International Development). Quest reference No. 593299. Karachi, Pakistan: Kashf Foundation.

Aubel, Judi. 1993. *Participatory Program Evaluation: A Manual for Involving Stakeholders in the Evaluation Process.* Dakar, Senegal: Catholic Relief Services under a U.S. AID grant.

Aucoin, Peter and Ralph Heinzman. 2000. "The Dialectics of Accountability for Performance in Public Management

Reform." *International Review of Administrative Sciences* 66(1):45–66.

Auditor General of Canada. 1993. *Program Evaluation.* Report to the House of Commons of the Auditor General of Canada.

Auspos, Patricia and Anne C. Kubisch. 2004. *Building Knowledge about Community Change: Moving Beyond Evaluations.* New York: Aspen Institute.

Australasian Evaluation Society (AES). 1995. "Evaluation! Are You Being Served? How Well Are Evaluation Practices Serving Customers, Clients, and Other Stakeholders." Presented at the 1995 Annual Conference, Sydney, Australia.

Azumi, Koya and Jerald Hage, eds. 1972. *Organizational Systems.* Lexington, MA: D. C. Heath.

Backer, Thomas E. 2002. *Finding the Balance: Program Fidelity and Adaptation in Substance Abuse Prevention: A State-of-the Art Review.* Rockville, MD: Substance Abuse and Mental Health Services Administration (SAMHSA), Center for Substance Abuse Prevention (CSAP).

Baizerman, Michael, Don Compton, and Stacey Stockdill. 2005. "Capacity Building." Pp. 38–39 in *Encyclopedia of Evaluation*, edited by S. Mathison. Thousand Oaks, CA: Sage.

Baker, Anita. 2008. *Building Evaluation Capacity Presentation Slides for Participatory Evaluation Essentials: A Guide for Non-Profit Organizations and Their Evaluation Partners.* Rochester, NY: Bruner Foundation. http://www.bruner foundation.org/ei.

Baker, Anita and Beth Bruner with Kim Sabo. 2006. *Evaluation Capacity & Evaluative Thinking in Organizations.* Cambridge, MA: Bruner Foundation. http://www .brunerfoundation.org/ei/sub_page.php? page=eti.

Baker, Anita and Kimberly Sabo. 2004. *Participatory Evaluation Essentials: A Guide for Non-Profit Organizations and Their Evaluation Partners.* Cambridge, MA: Bruner Foundation.

Bales, Robert F. 1951. *Interaction Process Analysis: A Method for the Study of Small Groups.* Reading, MA: Addison-Wesley.

Bamberger, Michael and Howard White. 2007. "Using Strong Evaluation Designs in

Developing Countries: Experience and Challenges." *Journal of MultiDisciplinary Evaluation* 4(8):58–73.

Bamberger, Michael and Donna Podems. 2002. "Feminist Evaluation in the International Development Context." *New Directions for Evaluation* 96:83–96.

Bamberger, Michael, Jim Rugh, and Linda Mabry. 2006. *RealWorld Evaluation: Working under Budget, Time, Data, and Political Constraints.* Thousand Oaks, CA: Sage.

Bare, John. 2002. "Risk." *The Evaluation Exchange* VIII(2, Fall). http://www.gse .harvard.edu/hfrp/eval/issue19/pp3.html.

Barkdoll, Gerald L. 1980. "Type III Evaluations: Consultation and Consensus." *Public Administration Review* March/April: 174–79.

Barley, Zoe A. and Mark Jenness. 1993. "Cluster Evaluation: A Method to Strengthen Evaluation in Smaller Programs with Similar Purposes." *Evaluation Practice* 14(2):141–47.

Barrett, Katherine and Richard Greene. 2006. "Big Dreams." The B & G Report, The Governing Management Letter." December, *Governing Magazine.* newsletter@gov-media.com.

Barringer, Felicity. 2005. "Predictions Vary for Refuge as Drilling Plan Develops." *New York Times*, March 20, p. 16.

Bastoe, Per Oyvind. 2006. "Implementing Results-Based Management." Pp. 97–110 in *From Studies to Streams: Managing Evaluative Systems*, edited by R. Rist and N. Stame. New Brunswick, NJ: Transaction Books.

Becker, Howard. 1970. "Whose Side Are We On?" Pp. 15–26 in *Qualitative Methodology*, edited by William J. Filstead. Chicago, IL: Markham.

Bedell, J. R., J. C. Ward, Jr., R. P. Archer, and M. K. Stokes. 1985. "An Empirical Evaluation of a Model of Knowledge Utilization." *Evaluation Review* 9(2):109–26.

Bellavita, C., J. S. Wholey, and M. A. Abramson. 1986. "Performance-Oriented Evaluation: Prospects for the Future." Pp. 286–92 in *Performance and Credibility: Developing Excellence in Public and Nonprofit Organizations*, edited by J. S. Wholey, M. A. Abramson, and C. Bellavita. Lexington, MA: Lexington.

Bemelmans-Videc, Marie-Louise, Jeremy Lonsdale, and Burt Perrin, eds. 2007. *Making Accountability Work: Dilemmas for Evaluation and for Audit*. London: Transaction Books.

Bennett, Claude F. 1982. *Reflective Appraisal of Programs*. Ithaca, NY: Cornell University Media Services.

_____. 1979. *Analyzing Impacts of Extension Programs*. Washington, DC: U.S. Department of Agriculture.

Berk, Richard A. 2007. "What Would Pete Say?" *American Journal of Evaluation* 28(2):203–206.

Bernstein, Ilene and Howard E. Freeman. 1975. *Academic and Entrepreneurial Research: Consequences of Diversity in Federal Evaluation Studies*. New York: Russell Sage.

Beyer, Catharine H. and Gerald Gillmore. 2007. "Longitudinal Assessment of Student Learning: Simplistic Measures Aren't Enough." *Change Magazine* 39(3), May/June:43–47.

Beyer, Janice M. and Harrison M. Trice. 1982. "The Utilization Process: A Conceptual Framework and Synthesis of Empirical Findings." *Administrative Science Quarterly* 27:592–622.

Bickman, Leonard. 2005. "Evaluation Research." P. 141 in *Encyclopedia of Evaluation*, edited by S. Mathison. Thousand Oaks, CA: Sage.

_____. 1994. "An Optimistic View of Evaluation." *Evaluation Practice* 15(3):255–59.

_____, ed. 1990. *Advances in Program Theory. New Directions for Program Evaluation*, No. 47.

_____. 1985. "Improving Established Statewide Programs: A Component Theory of Evaluation." *Evaluation Review* 9(2):189–208.

Birckmayer, Johanna and Carol H. Weiss. 2000. "Theory-Based Evaluation in Practice: What Do We Learn?" *Evaluation Review* 24(4):407–31.

Bishop, Joan and Evelyn Vingilis. 2006. "Development of a Framework for Comprehensive Evaluation of Client Outcomes in Community Mental Health Services." *Canadian Journal of Program Evaluation* 21(2):133–80.

Blamey, Avril and Mhairi Mackenzie. 2007. "Theories of Change and Realistic Evaluation: Peas in a Pod or Apples and Oranges?" *Evaluation* 13(4):439–55.

Blanchard, Ken. 1986. *Situational Leadership* (2 vols., 12-tape audiotape set). Escondido, CA: Blanchard Training and Development.

Blumer, Herbert. 1969. *Symbolic Interactionism*. Englewood Cliffs, NJ: Prentice Hall.

Bodley-Scott, Sam and Alan Brache. 2005. *Implementation: How to Transform Strategic Initiatives into Blockbuster Results*. New York: McGraw-Hill.

Boorstin, Daniel. 1958. "The Altruism of an Unheroic Age." *The Americans: The Colonial Experience*. New York: Vintage Books.

Boruch, Robert. 2007. "Encouraging the Flight of Error: Ethical Standards, Evidence Standards, and Randomized Trials." *Informing Federal Policies on Evaluation Methodology: Building the Evidence Base for Method Choice in Government Sponsored Evaluation. New Directions for Program Evaluation* 113:55–73.

Boruch, Robert and Anthony Petrosino. 2004. "Meta-Analysis, Systematic Reviews, and Research Syntheses." Pp. 176–203 in *Handbook of Practical Program Evaluation*, edited by Wholey, Hatry, and Newcomer. San Francisco, CA: Jossey-Bass.

Boruch, Robert and David Rindskopf. 1984. "Data Analysis." Pp. 121–58 in *Evaluation Research Methods*, edited by Leonard Rutman. Beverly Hills, CA: Sage.

Bossidy, Larry and Ram Charan. 2002. *Execution: The Discipline of Getting Things Done*. Largo, MD: Crown Business.

Bourguignon, François and Mark Sundberg. 2007. *Aid Effectiveness—Opening the Black Box*. http://siteresources.worldbank.org/DEC/Resources/Aid-Effectiveness-MS-FB.pdf.

Brandl, John. 1994. "Must Deal with the Bureaucracy—But Exactly How Is Harder to Say." *Minneapolis Star Tribune*, September 5, p. 13A.

Brandon, Paul R. 1998. "Stakeholder Participation for the Purpose of Helping Ensure Evaluation Validity: Bridging the Gap between Collaborative and Non-collaborative Evaluations." *American Journal of Evaluation* 19(3):325–38.

Braskamp, L. A. and R. D. Brown, eds. 1980. *Utilization of Evaluative Information*.

New Directions for Program Evaluation, No. 5.

Braverman, Marc T., Norman A. Constantine, and Jana Kay Slater, eds. 2004. *Foundations and Evaluation: Contexts and Practices for Effective Philanthropy.* San Francisco, CA: Jossey-Bass.

Breul, Jonathan P. 1994. "How the Government Performance and Results Act Borrows from the Experience of OECD Countries." Paper prepared for the Fullbright Symposium on Public Sector Reform, July 22–24, Brisbane, Australia.

Brinkerhoff, Robert. 2005. "Success Case Method." Pp. 401–402 in *Encyclopedia of Evaluation,* edited by S. Mathison. Thousand Oaks, CA: Sage.

_____. 2003. *The Success Case Method.* San Francisco, CA: Berrett Koehler.

Brooker, S., E. Miguel, S. Moulin, A. Luoba, D. Bundy, and M. Kremer. 2000. "Epidemiology of Single and Multiple Species of Helminth Infections among School Children in Busia District, Kenya." *East African Medical Journal* 77(3):157–61.

Brookfield, Stephen D. 1994. "Tales from the Dark Side: A Phenomenography of Adult Critical Reflection." *International Journal of Lifelong Learning* 13(3):203–16.

_____. 1990. *Understanding and Facilitating Adult Learning.* San Francisco, CA: Jossey-Bass.

Broom, Michael F. and Donald C. Klein. 1995. *Power: The Infinite Game.* Amherst, MA: HRD Press.

Brown, Kevin. 2007. "Tax News." *Tax Hotline,* 27(1, January):1.

Bruyn, Severyn. 1966. *The Human Perspective in Sociology: The Methodology of Participant Observation.* Englewood Cliffs, NJ: Prentice Hall.

Bryk, Anthony S., ed. 1983. *Stakeholder-Based Evaluation. New Directions for Program Evaluation,* No. 17.

Bryson, John. 2004a. *Strategic Planning for Public and Nonprofit Organizations: A Guide to Strengthening and Sustaining Organizational Achievement.* 3d ed. San Francisco, CA: Jossey-Bass.

_____. 2004b. "What to Do When Stakeholders Matter: Stakeholder Identification and Analysis Techniques." *Public Management Review* 6(1):21–53.

Bryson, John, Fran Ackermann, Colin Eden, and Charles Finn. 2004. *Visible Thinking: Unlocking Causal Mapping for Practical Business Results.* West Sussex, UK: John Wiley and Sons.

Bryson, John and John Cullen. 1984. "A Contingent Approach to Strategy and Tactics in Formative and Summative Evaluation." *Evaluation and Program Planning* 7:267–90.

Buck, Connie. 1995. "The World According to Soros." *The New Yorker,* January 23, pp. 54–78.

Bundy, D. A. P. and L. J. Drake. 2004. *Intestinal Helminths: The Burden of Disease.* 3d ed. Cambridge, UK: Cambridge University Press.

Bunge, Mario. 1959. *Causality.* Cambridge, MA: Harvard University Press.

Burry, James. 1984. *Synthesis of the Evaluation Use Literature,* NIE Grant Report. Los Angeles, CA: UCLA Center for the Study of Evaluation.

Cabaj, Mark. 2007. "The Land of Big Ideas." Waterloo, Canada: Tamarack Vital Communities. http://tamarackcommunity.ca/downloads/index/MC_Big_Ideas.pdf.

Caiden, Gerald E. 2006. "Improving Government Performance." *Public Administration Review* 66(1):139–42.

Callahan, Suzanne. 2007. "How to End the Evaluation Tug of War." *Chronicle of Philanthropy,* April 5, p. 45.

_____. 2005. *Singing Our Praises: Case Studies in the Art of Evaluation.* Washington, DC: Association of Performing Arts Presenters.

Campbell, Donald T. 1999. "The Experimenting Society." Pp. 9–45 in *Social Experimentation,* edited by Donald T. Campbell and M. Jean Russo. Thousand Oaks, CA: Sage.

_____. [1971] 1991. "Methods for the Experimenting Society." *Evaluation Practice* 12(3):223–60. Reprint. Presentation to the American Psychological Association.

_____. 1988. *Methodology and Epistemology for Social Science: Selected Papers,* edited by E. S. Overman. Chicago: University of Chicago Press.

_____. 1983. "Threats to Validity Added When Applied Social Research Is Packaged as 'Program Evaluation' in the Service of Administrative Decision Making." Presented at the Conference on Family Support

Programs: The State of the Art, Sponsored by the Bush Center in Child Development and Social Policy, Yale University, New Haven, CT.

_____. 1969. "Reforms as Experiments." *American Psychologist* 24:409–29.

Campbell, Donald T. and Robert F. Boruch. 1975. "Making the Case for Randomized Assignment to Treatments by Considering the Alternatives: Six Ways in Which Quasi-Experimental Evaluations in Compensatory Education Tend to Underestimate Effects." Pp. 195–296 in *Evaluation and Experiment*, edited by Carol A. Bennett and Arthur A. Lumsdaine. New York: Academic Press.

Campbell, Donald T. and Julian C. Stanley. 1963. *Experimental and Quasi-Experimental Designs for Research*. Chicago: Rand McNally.

Campbell, Jeanne L. 1983. "Factors and Conditions Influencing Usefulness of Planning, Evaluation, and Reporting in Schools." Ph.D. dissertation, University of Minnesota, MN.

Canadian Evaluation Society. 1982. *The Bottom Line: Utilization of What, by Whom?* Proceedings of the 3rd Annual Conference of the Canadian Evaluation Society. Toronto, ON, Canada: University of Toronto.

Caracelli, Valerie J. 2006. "Enhancing the Policy Process through the Use of Ethnography and Other Study Frameworks: A Mixed-Method Strategy." *Research in Schools* 13(1):84–92.

Caracelli, Valerie and Hallie Preskill, eds. 2000. *The Expanding Scope of Evaluation Use. New Directions for Evaluation*, No. 88.

_____. 1996. "Evaluation Use Survey." Evaluation Use Topical Interest Group, American Evaluation Association.

Carden, Fred. 2007. "The Real Evaluation Gap." *Alliance Magazine* 12(4):53–54.

Carden, Fred and Sarah Earl. 2007. "Infusing Evaluative Thinking as Process Use: The Case of the International Development Research Centre (IDRC)." *New Directions for Evaluation* 116:61–74.

Carlsson, J., M. Eriksson-Baaz, Ann Marie Fallenius, and Eva Lövgren. 1999. *Are Evaluations Useful: Cases from Swedish Development Co-operation*. Stockholm, Sweden: SIDA Department for Evaluation and Internal Audit.

Carnevale, David. 2002. *Organizational Development in the Public Sector*. Boulder, CO: Westview Press.

Caro, Francis G., ed. 1971. *Readings in Evaluation Research*. New York: Russell Sage.

Carroll, Lewis. 2006. *Alice in Wonderland*. Ann Arbor, MI: Ann Arbor Media.

Carver, John. 1997. *Boards That Make a Difference*. San Francisco, CA: Jossey-Bass.

CBS. 2004. "The 'Texas Miracle.'" *60 Minutes*, August 25. http://www.cbsnews.com/stories/2004/01/06/60II/main591676.shtml.

CBS News. 2007. "Brundibar: How The Nazis Conned The World." *60 Minutes*. February 25. http://www.cbsnews.com/stories/2007/02/23/60minutes/main2508458_page2.shtml.

Chatterji, Madhabi. 2007. "Grades of Evidence: Variability in Quality of Findings in Effectiveness Studies of Complex Field Interventions." *American Journal of Evaluation* 28(3):239–55.

Chelimsky, Eleanor. 2007. "Factors Influencing the Choice of Methods in Federal Evaluation Practice." *Informing Federal Policies on Evaluation Methodology: Building the Evidence Base for Method Choice in Government Sponsored Evaluation. New Directions for Program Evaluation* 113:13–33.

_____. 2006a. "The Purposes of Evaluation in a Democratic Society." Pp. 33–55 in *The Sage Handbook of Evaluation: Policies, Programs and Practices*, edited by Ian F. Shaw, Jennifer C. Greene, and Melvin M. Mark. Thousand Oaks, CA: Sage.

_____. 2006b. "A Clash of Culture: Improving the Fit between Evaluative Independence and the Political Requirements of a Democratic Society." Presidential Strand Plenary Keynote, American Evaluation Association National Conference, Portland, OR, November 3.

_____. 1997. "The Coming Transformations in Evaluation." In *Evaluation for the 21st Century*, edited by Eleanor Chelimsky and Will Shadish. Thousand Oaks, CA: Sage.

_____. 1995a. "The Political Environment of Evaluation and What It Means for the Development of the Field." Presented at the American Evaluation Association Presidential Address, November, Vancouver. Published in *Evaluation Practice* 16(3):215–25.

_____. 1995b. "Comments on the AEA Guiding Principles." *Guiding Principles for Evaluators. New Directions for Program Evaluation,* 66:53–54.

_____. 1992. "Expanding Evaluation Capabilities in the General Accounting Office." *Evaluation in the Federal Government: Changes, Trends, and Opportunities. New Directions for Program Evaluation,* 55:91–96.

_____. 1987a. "The Politics of Program Evaluation." *Evaluation Practice in Review. New Directions for Program Evaluation,* 34:5–22.

_____. 1987b. "What We Have Learned about the Politics of Program Evaluation." *Educational Evaluation and Policy Analysis* 9:199–213.

_____. 1983. "Improving the Cost Effectiveness of Evaluation." Pp. 149–70 in *The Costs of Evaluation,* edited by Marvin C. Alkin and Lewis C. Solomon. Beverly Hills, CA: Sage.

Chen, Huey T. 2007. "An Intimate Portrait of Evaluation Mentorship under Peter H. Rossi." *American Journal of Evaluation,* 28(2):207–10.

Chen, Huey-Tsyh. 2005a. "Program Theory." Pp. 340–42 in *Encyclopedia of Evaluation,* edited by S. Mathison. Thousand Oaks, CA: Sage.

_____. 2005b. "Theory-Driven Evaluation." Pp. 415–19 in *Encyclopedia of Evaluation,* edited by S. Mathison. Thousand Oaks, CA: Sage.

_____. 2004. *Practical Program Evaluation: Assessing and Improving Planning, Implementation, and Effectiveness.* Thousand Oaks, CA: Sage.

_____. 1990. *Theory-Driven Evaluations.* Newbury Park, CA: Sage.

_____, ed. 1989. "Special Issue: The Theory-Driven Perspective." *Evaluation and Program Planning* 12(4).

Chen, Huey-Tsyh and Peter Rossi. 1989. "Issues in the Theory-Driven Perspective." *Evaluation and Program Planning* 12(4):299–306.

_____. 1987. "The Theory-Driven Approach to Validity." *Evaluation and Program Planning* 10(1):95–103.

Christie, Christina. 2007. "Reported Influence of Evaluation Data on Decision Makers' Actions: An Empirical Examination."

American Journal of Evaluation 28(1):8–25.

_____. 2005. "A Conversation with Ross Connor." *American Journal of Evaluation* 26(3):369–77.

_____. 2003. "What Guides Evaluation? A Study of How Evaluation Practice Maps onto Evaluation Theory." *The Practice-Theory Relationship in Evaluation. New Directions for Evaluation* 97:7–36.

Christie, Christina and Marvin Alkin. 2003. "The User-Oriented Evaluator's Role in Formulating a Program Theory: Using a Theory-Driven Approach." *American Journal of Evaluation* 24(3):373–85.

_____. 1999. "Further Reflections on Evaluation Misutilization." *Studies in Educational Evaluation* 25:1–10.

Cicarelli, Victor, 1971. "The Impact of Head Start: Executive Summary." Pp. 397–401 in *Readings in Evaluation Research,* edited by Francis G. Caro. New York: Russell Sage.

Clarke, R. V. G. 1998. *Situational Crime Prevention: Successful Case Studies.* Monsey, NY: Criminal Justice Press.

Clayson, Zoe Cordoza, Xochitl Castaneda, Emma Sanchez, and Claire Brindis. 2002. Unequal Power—Changing Landscapes: Negotiations between Evaluation Stakeholders in Latino Communities. *American Journal of Evaluation* 23(1):33–44.

Clement, Jonathan. 2006. "Net Gains." *Wall Street Journal,* March 15, p. D1.

Cochran-Smith, Marilyn and Susan Lytle. 1990. "Research on Teaching and Teacher Research: The Issues That Divide." *Educational Researcher* 19(2):2–11.

Coffman, Julia. 2007a. "Evaluation Based on Theories of the Policy Process." *The Evaluation Exchange,* Harvard Family Research Project, Spring:6–7.

Coffman, Julia. 2007b. "What's Different about Evaluating Advocacy and Policy Change?" *The Evaluation Exchange* XIII:2–4.

Cohen, David K. and Janet A. Weiss. 1977. "Social Science and Social Policy: Schools and Race." Pp. 67–84 in *Using Social Research in Public Policy Making,* edited by Carol H. Weiss. Lexington, MA: D. C. Heath.

Cole, M. B. 1984. "User-Focused Evaluation of Training Programme Effectiveness in a

South African Industrial Company." Presented at the National Productivity Institute Conference, University of Witwatersrand, Johannesburg, South Africa.

Colton, Dave. 1997. "The Design of Evaluations for Continuous Quality Improvement." *Evaluation and the Health Professions* 20(3):265–85.

Columbia Accident Investigation Board. 2003. *Final Report*, Vols. I–VI. Washington, DC: Government Printing Office. See also http://caib.nasa.gov.

Combs, Arthur. 1972. *Educational Accountability: Beyond Behavioral Objectives.* Washington, DC: Association for Supervision and Curriculum Development.

Compton, Don, M. Baizerman, and S. Stockdill, eds. 2002. *The Art, Craft, and Science of Evaluation Capacity Building. New Directions for Evaluation, No. 93.*

Connell, J. P., A. C. Kubisch, L. B. Schorr, and C. H. Weiss, eds. 1995. *New Approaches to Evaluating Community Initiatives: Concepts, Methods, and Contexts.* Washington, DC: Aspen Institute. http:// www.aspeninstitute.org/site/c.huLWJeMR KpH/b.612045/k.4BA8/Roundtable_on_ Community_Change.htm.

Connor, Ross. 2005. "The Colorado Healthy Communities Initiative." *American Journal of Evaluation* 26(3):363–77.

_____. 2004. "Developing and Implementing Culturally Competent Evaluation: A Discussion of Multicultural Validity in Two HIV Prevention Programs for Latinos." *New Directions for Evaluation* 102:51–66.

_____. 1988. "Structuring Knowledge Production Activities to Facilitate Knowledge Utilization: Thoughts on Important Utilization Issues." *Studies in Educational Evaluation* 14:273–83.

Connor, Ross, Victor Kuo, Marli Melton, and Ricardo Millet. 2004. "Adapting Evaluation to Accommodate Foundation's Structural and Cultural Characteristics." Pp. 161–184 in *Foundations and Evaluation: Contexts and Practices for Effective Philanthropy*, edited by Marc Braverman, Norman Constantine, and Jana Kay Slater. San Francisco, CA: Jossey-Bass.

Conte, Christopher. 1996. "Workfare on Trial." *Governing*, April, pp. 19–23.

Cook, Thomas D. 2006. "Describing What Is Special about the Role of Experiments in Contemporary Educational Research: Putting the 'Gold Standard' Rhetoric into Perspective." *Journal of MultiDisciplinary Evaluation* 3(6):1–7. http://survey.ate .wmich.edu/jmde/index.php/jmde_1/issue/ view/22.

_____. 1995. "Evaluation Lessons Learned." Plenary keynote address at the International Evaluation Conference, Evaluation '95, November 4, Vancouver, BC, Canada.

Cooksy, Leslie. 2007. "Ethical Challenges." *American Journal of Evaluation* 28(1): 76–78.

Cooley, William W. and William E. Bickel. 1985. *Decision-Oriented Educational Research.* Boston, MA: Kluwer-Nijhoff.

Coryn, Chris L. and John Hattie. 2006. "The Transdisciplinary Model of Evaluation" *Journal of MultiDisciplinary Evaluation* 3(4):107–14. http://survey.ate.wmich.edu/ jmde/index.php/jmde_1/issue/view/16.

Council on Foundations. 1993. *Evaluation for Foundations: Concepts, Cases, Guidelines, and Resources.* San Francisco, CA: Jossey-Bass.

Cousins, J. Bradley, ed. 2007. *Process Use. New Directions for Evaluation*, No. 116.

_____. 2006a. *Evaluation Report: The International Program for Development Evaluation Training.* Ottawa, ON, Canada: J. B. Cousins Research Services for the Operations Evaluation Department, World Bank. http://www.ipdet.org.

_____. 2006b. "Data Use Leads to Data Valuing: An Evaluation Capacity Building Thesis." Invited address to the annual meeting of the American Evaluation Association, Portland, OR, November.

_____. 2004. "Crossing the Bridge: Toward Understanding Use Through Systematic Inquiry." Pp. 319–330 in *Evaluation Roots: Tracing Theorists' Views and Influences*, edited by M. C. Alkin. Thousand Oaks, CA: Sage.

_____. 2003. "Utilization Effects of Participatory Evaluation." Pp. 245–265 in *International Handbook of Education Evaluation*, edited by T. Kellaghan, D. L. Stufflebeam, and L. Wingate. Boston, MA: Kluwer.

_____. 2001. "Do Evaluator and Program Practitioner Perspectives Converge in

Collaborative Evaluation?" *Canadian Journal of Evaluation* 16(2):113–33.

Cousins, J. Bradley and Elizabeth Whitmore. 2007. "Framing Participatory Evaluation." *New Directions for Evaluation* 114:87–105.

Cousins, J. Bradley and Lyn M. Shulha. 2006. "A Comparative Analysis of Evaluation Utilization and Its Cognate Fields of Inquiry: Current Issues and Trends." Pp. 266–291 in *The Sage Handbook of Evaluation: Policies, Programs and Practices*, edited by Ian F. Shaw, Jennifer C. Greene, and Melvin M. Mark. Thousand Oaks, CA: Sage.

Cousins, Brad, Swee Goh, and Shannon Clark. 2006. "Data Use Leads to Data Valuing: Inquiry for School Decision Making." *Leadership and Policy in Schools* 5:155–76.

Cousins, Brad, S. Goh, S. Clark, and L. Lee. 2004. "Integrating Evaluative Inquiry into the Organizational Culture: A Review and Synthesis of the Knowledge Base." *Canadian Journal of Program Evaluation* 19(2):99–141.

Cousins, J. B., J. J. Donohue, and G. A. Bloom. 1996. "Collaborative Evaluation in North America: Evaluators' Self-reported Opinions, Practices and Consequences." *Evaluation Practice* 17(3):207–25.

Cousins, J. Bradley and Lorna M. Earl, eds. 1995. *Participatory Evaluation in Education: Studies in Evaluation Use and Organizational Learning*. London: Falmer.

Cousin, J. Bradley and Lorna M. Earl. 1992. "The case for Participatory Evaluation." *Educational Evaluation and Policy Analysis* 14:397–418.

Cousins, J. Bradley and K. A. Leithwood. 1986. "Current Empirical Research on Evaluation Utilization." *Review of Educational Research* 56(3):331–64.

Covey, Stephen R. and Jennifer Colosimo. 2004. *The Four Disciplines of Execution* [Audiotape]. West Valley City, UT: FranklinCovey.

Craig, Paul A. 2001. *Controlling Pilot Error: Situational Awareness*. New York: McGraw-Hill.

Cronbach, Lee J. 1982. *Designing Evaluations of Educational and Social Programs*. San Francisco, CA: Jossey-Bass.

_____. 1975. "Beyond the Two Disciplines of Scientific Psychology." *American Psychologist* 30:116–17.

Cronbach, Lee J. and Associates. 1980. *Toward Reform of Program Evaluation*. San Francisco, CA: Jossey-Bass.

Cronbach, Lee J. and P. Suppes, eds. 1969. *Research for Tomorrow's Schools: Disciplined Inquiry of Education*. New York: Macmillan.

Crosby, Barbara. 1999. *Leadership for Global Citizenship*. Thousand Oaks, CA: Sage.

Crosby, Barbara and John Bryson. 2005. *Leadership for the Common Good: Tackling Public Problems in a Shared-Power World*. 2d ed. San Francisco, CA: Jossey-Bass.

Crozier, Michel. 1964. *The Bureaucratic Phenomenon*. Chicago, IL: University of Chicago Press.

Cyert, Richard and James G. March. 1963. *A Behavioral Theory of the Firm*. Englewood Cliffs, NJ: Prentice Hall.

Dahl, Robert. 1957. "The Concept of Power." *Behavioral Science* 2(July):201–15.

Dallaire, Romeo A. and Brent Beardsley. 2004. *Shake Hands with the Devil: The Failure of Humanity in Rwanda*. Toronto, ON, Canada: Random House Canada.

Danida (Danish Development Assistance). 2006. *Evaluation Guidelines*. Copenhagen, Denmark: Ministry of Foreign Affairs of Denmark.

Danida, Evaluation Department, Ministry of Foreign Affairs. 2005. *Lessons from Rwanda: Lessons for Today*. Copenhagen, Denmark. http://www.um.dk/en/menu/DevelopmentPolicy/Evaluations/ReportsBy Year/2004/Lessons+from+Rwanda+-+ Lessons+for+Today.htm.

Daniel, Stacey, 1996. "Process or Outcomes? Different Approaches for Different Stages." *Foundation*, March/April, pp. 46–48.

Datta, Lois-ellin. 2007a. "A Short History of New Directions for Evaluation." *New Directions for Evaluation* 114:9–10.

_____. 2007b. "Looking at the Evidence: What Variations in Practice Might Indicate." *Informing Federal Policies on Evaluation Methodology: Building the Evidence Base for Method Choice in Government Sponsored Evaluation. New Directions for Program Evaluation* 113:35–54.

_____. 2005. "Judicial Model of Evaluation." Pp. 214–17 in *Encyclopedia of Evaluation*, edited by S. Mathison. Thousand Oaks, CA: Sage.

_____. 2004. "The Oral History Project Part II: The Professional Development of Lois-ellin Datta." Interview by Robin Miller and Valerie Caracelli. *American Journal of Evaluation* 25(2):243–53.

_____. 1994. "Paradigm Wars: A Basis for Peaceful Coexistence and Beyond." *The Qualitative-Quantitative Debate: New Perspectives. New Directions for Program Evaluation* 61:53–70.

Davidson, E. Jane. 2006a. "The RCTs-Only Doctrine: Brakes on the Acquisition of Knowledge?" *Journal of MultiDisciplinary Evaluation* 3 (6): ii–v. http://survey.ate.wmich.edu/jmde/index.php/jmde_1/issue/view/22.

_____. 2006b. "Causal Inference Nuts and Bolts." Presentation at the American Evaluation Association National Conference, Portland, OR, November 3.

_____. 2005. *Evaluation Methodology Basics: The Nuts and Bolts of Sound Evaluation.* Thousand Oaks, CA: Sage.

_____. 2003. "Evaluation Humor." *EvalTalk*, July 10.

_____. 2000. "Ascertaining Causality in Theory-Based Evaluation." *New Directions for Evaluation* 87:17–26.

Davies, Philip, Kathryn Newcomer, and Haluk Soydan. 2005. "Government as Structural Context for Evaluation." Pp. 163–183 in *The Sage Handbook of Evaluation: Policies, Programs and Practices*, edited by I. Shaw, J. Greene, and M. Mark. Thousand Oaks, CA: Sage..

Davis, Howard R. and Susan E. Salasin. 1975. "The Utilization of Evaluation." Pp. 621–66 in *Handbook of Evaluation Research*, Vol. 1, edited by Elmer L. Struening and Marcia Guttentag. Beverly Hills, CA: Sage.

Dawid, H., K. Doerner, G. Dorffner, T. Fent, M. Feurstein, R. Hartl, A. Mild, M. Natter, M. Reimann, and A. Taudes. 2002. *Quantitative Models of Learning Organizations.* New York: Springer.

Dawson, Gary. 1995. "Agency Evaluation Reports Disregarded by Legislators Who Had Requested Them." *Saint Paul Pioneer Press*, August 7, p. 4B.

Dawson, Judith A. and J. J. D'Amico. 1985. "Involving Program Staff in Evaluation Studies: A Strategy for Increasing Use and Enriching the Data Base." *Evaluation Review* 9(2):173–88.

Deitchman, Seymour. 1976. *The Best-Laid Schemes: A Tale of Social Research and Bureaucracy.* Cambridge: MIT Press.

Dennard, Linda, Kurt Richardson, and Goktug Morcol, eds. 2005. *E:CO Annual, Vol. 7(1). Complexity and Policy Analysis.* Mansfield, OH: ISCE Publishing.

Denzin, Norman and Yvonna S. Lincoln, eds. 2000. *Handbook of Qualitative Research.* 2d ed. Thousand Oaks, CA: Sage.

_____. 1994. *Handbook of Qualitative Research.* Thousand Oaks, CA: Sage.

Dessler, Gary. 2004. *Human Resource Management.* Upper Saddle River, NJ: Prentice Hall.

Deutscher, Irwin. 1970. "Words and Deeds: Social Science and Social Policy." Pp. 27–51 in *Qualitative Methodology*, edited by William J. Filstead. Chicago, IL: Markham.

Dewey, John. 1956. *The Child and the Curriculum.* Chicago, IL: University of Chicago Press.

Dial, Micah. 1994. "The Misuse of Evaluation in Educational Programs." *Preventing the Misuse of Evaluation. New Directions for Program Evaluation* 64:61–68.

Dick, Bob and Tim Dalmau. 1999. *Values in Action: Applying the Ideas of Argyris and Schön.* 2d ed. Chapel Hill, NC: Interchange.

Dickey, Barbara. 1981. "Utilization of Evaluation of Small-Scale Educational Projects." *Educational Evaluation and Policy Analysis* 2(6):65–77.

Dickey, Barbara and Eber Hampton. 1981. "Effective Problem-Solving for Evaluation Utilization." *Knowledge: Creation, Diffusion, Utilization* 2(3):361–74.

Dickson, Rumona, Shally Awasthi, Paula Williamson, Colin Demellweek, and Paul Garner. 2000. "Effects of Treatment for Intestinal Helminth Infection on Growth and Cognitive Performance in Children: Systematic Review of Randomised Trials." *British Medical Journal*, June 24. http://findarticles.com/p/articles/mi_m0999/is_7251_320/ai_63563313.

Diversity Committee of the American Evaluation Association. 2004. *A Cultural*

Reading of the Program Evaluation Standards. 2d ed. http://www.eval.org/aea05 .culturalreading/aea05.cr.Propriety.pdf.

Donaldson, Stewart I. 2007. *Program Theory-Driven Evaluation Science.* New York: Lawrence Erlbaum.

Donaldson, Stewart I. and Christina A. Christie. 2005. "The 2004 Claremont Debate: Lipsey vs. Scriven: Determining Causality in Program Evaluation and Applied Research: Should Experimental Evidence Be the Gold Standard?" *Journal of Multi-Disciplinary Evaluation* 2(3):60–77. http:// survey.ate.wmich.edu/jmde/index.php/ jmde_1/issue/view/21.

Donaldson, Stewart and Michael Scriven. 2003. "Diverse Visions for Evaluation in the New Millennium: Should We Integrate or Embrace Diversity?" Pp. 3–18 in *Evaluating Social Programs and Problems,* edited by S. Donaldson and M. Scriven. Mahwah, NJ: Lawrence Erlbaum.

Donaldson, Stewart, Laura Gooler, and Michael Scriven. 2002. "Strategies for Managing Evaluation Anxiety: Toward a Psychology of Program Evaluation." *American Journal of Evaluation* 23(3):261–73.

Donmoyer, Robert. 2005a. "Artistic Evaluation." Pp. 20–21 in *Encyclopedia of Evaluation,* edited by S. Mathison. Thousand Oaks, CA: Sage.

———. 2005b. "Connoisseurship." Pp. 76–80 in *Encyclopedia of Evaluation,* edited by S. Mathison. Thousand Oaks, CA: Sage.

———. 1996. "Educational Research in an Era of Paradigm Proliferation: What's a Journal Editor to Do?" *Educational Researcher* 25(2):19–25.

Drake, L. J. and D. Bundy. 2001. "Multiple Helminth Infections in Children: Impact and Control." *Parasitology* 122:S73–S81.

Drucker, Peter F. 2003. *The Essential Drucker: The Best of Sixty Years of Peter Drucker's Essential Writings on Management.* New York: HarperCollins.

———. 2000. *Wisdom from Peter Drucker: His Four Greatest Lessons.* Annual Conference of the Peter F. Drucker Foundation for Nonprofit Management, November 6, New York City. http://www.leadnet.org/ epubarchive.asp?id=41&db=archive_ explorer#wisdom.

———. 1993. *The Five Most Important Questions You Will Ever Ask about Your Nonprofit Organization.* San Francisco, CA: Jossey-Bass.

Duffy, Barbara Poitras. 1994. "Use and Abuse of Internal Evaluation." *Preventing the Misuse of Evaluation. New Directions for Program Evaluation* 64:25–32.

Dugan, Margaret. 1996. "Participatory and Empowerment Evaluation: Lessons Learned in Training and Technical Assistance." Pp. 277–303 in *Empowerment Evaluation: Knowledge and Tools for Self-Assessment and Accountability,* edited by D. M. Fetterman, A. J. Kaftarian, and A. Wandersman. Thousand Oaks, CA: Sage.

Dugger, Celia. 2004. "World Bank Challenged: Are the Poor Really Helped?" *New York Times,* July 28, pp. A4–A5.

Dunagin, Ralph. 1977. *Dunagin's People.* Sentinel Star, Field Newspaper Syndicate, August 30.

Dunning, David and Justin Kruger. 1999. "Unskilled and Unaware of It: How Difficulties in Recognizing One's Own Incompetence Lead to Inflated Self-Assessments." *Journal of Personality and Social Psychology* 77(6):1121–34.

Durland, Maryann and Kimberly Fredericks, eds. 2005. *Social Network Analysis in Program Evaluation. New Directions for Evaluation,* No. 107.

Dyer, Henry S. 1973. "Recycling the Problems in Testing." Assessment in Pluralistic Society: Proceedings of the 1972 Invitational Conference on Testing Problems, Educational Testing Service, Princeton, NJ.

Eden, C. and Ackermann, F. 1998. *Making Strategy: The Journey of Strategic Management.* London: Sage.

Edison, Thomas. 1983. *The Diary and Observations.* New York: Philosophical Library.

Edwards, Ward and Marcia Guttentag. 1975. "Experiments and Evaluation: A Reexamination." Pp. 409–63 in *Evaluation and Experiment: Some Critical Issues in Assessing Social Programs,* edited by Carl Bennet and Arthur Lumsdaine. New York: Academic Press.

Edwards, Ward, Marcia Guttentag, and Kurt Snapper. 1975. "A Decision-Theoretic Approach to Evaluation Research." Pp. 139–82 in *Handbook of Evaluation Research,* Vol. 1, edited by Elmer L. Struening and Marcia Guttentag. Beverly Hills, CA: Sage.

Eisner, Elliot. 1991. *The Enlightened Eye: Qualitative Inquiry and the Enhancement of Educational Practice.* New York: Macmillan.

Emery, F. W. and E. L. Trist. 1965. "The Causal Texture of Organizational Environment." *Human Relations* 18(February): 21–31.

Encyclopedia of Evaluation. 2005. Edited by S. Mathison. Thousand Oaks, CA: Sage.

Engel, Paul and Charlotte Carlsson. 2002. "Enhancing Learning through Evaluation: Approaches, Dilemmas and Some Possible Ways Forward." Paper presented at the European Evaluation Conference, Seville, October 10–12.

Eoyang, Glenda H. 2007. *Patterns of Performance: Human Systems Dynamics and High Performance Technology.* Minneapolis, MN: HSD Institute.

———. 2006a. "Human Systems Dynamics: Complexity-based Approach to a Complex Evaluation." Pp. 123–40 in *Systems Concepts in Evaluation: An Expert Anthology*, edited by Bob Williams and Iraj Iman. AEA Monograph. Point Reynes, CA: EdgePress.

———. 2006b. "What? So What? Now What?" *Attractors, Newsletter of the Human Systems Dynamics Institute*, Vol. 3, No. 1. Minneapolis, MN. http://www.hsdinstitute .org/about.asp.

———. 1996. *Coping with Chaos: Seven Simple Tools.* Minneapolis, MN: HSD Institute Press. http://www.odnetwork.org/resources/ HSD/products.php#chaos_ebook.

Eoyang, Glenda and Tom Berkas. 1998. "Evaluation in a Complex Adaptive System (CAS)." Pp. 313–335 in *Managing Complexity in Organizations*, edited by M. Lissack & H. Gunz. Westport, CT: Quorum Books. http://www.chaos-limited .com/CAS.htm.

European AID. 2005. *Evaluation Tools.* Brussels: European Commission. http://ec .europa.eu/europeaid/evaluation/methodo logy/tools/too_en.htm.

Evaluation Capacity Development Group (ECDG). 2006. *Evaluation Capacity Development Group Toolkit.* http://evaluation .freenet.uz/craig_russon.html.

European Evaluation Society (EES). 2007. *EES Statement on EES Statement: The Importance of a Methodologically Diverse Approach to Impact Evaluation.* http://www .europeanevaluation.org/news?newsId=196 9406.

Evaluation Gap Working Group. 2006. *When Will We Ever Learn? Improving Lives through Impact Evaluation.* Washington, DC: Center for Global Development. http://www.cgdev.org/section/initiatives/_ active/evalgap.

Evans, Gerry and Roger Blunden. 1984. "A Collaborative Approach to Evaluation." *Journal of Practical Approaches to Developmental Handicaps* 8(1):14–18.

Evans, John W. 1971. "Head Start: Comments on Criticisms." Pp. 401–407 in *Readings in Evaluation Research*, edited by Francis G. Caro. New York: Russell Sage.

Fadiman, Clifton and Andre Bernard. 2000. *Bartlett's Book of Anecdotes.* Boston, MA: Little, Brown.

Fawson, T. J., V. Moss-Summers, and S. M. May (2004). "'Somewhere Out There:' A Survey of the Lone Journey of Evaluators Working in Business and Industry Settings." *Evaluation and Program Planning* 27:335–40.

Feiman, Sharon. 1977. "Evaluation Teacher Centers." *Social Review* 8(May):395–411.

Feinstein, Osvaldo. 2002. "Use of Evaluations and Evaluation of Their Use." *Evaluation* 8(4):433–39.

Fetterman, David. 2005a. "A Window into the Heart and Soul of Empowerment Evaluation." Pp. 1–26 in *Empowerment Evaluation Principles in Practice*, edited by D. Fetterman and A. Wandersman. New York: Guilford Press.

———. 2005b. "Empowerment Evaluation: From the Digital Divide to Academoic Distress." Pp. 92–122 in *Empowerment Evaluation Principles in Practice*, D. Fetterman and A. Wandersman. New York: Guilford Press.

———. 2003. "A Process Use Distinction and a Theory." *The Practice-Theory Relationship in Evaluation. New Directions for Evaluation* 97:47–52.

———. 1995. "In Response to Dr. Dan Stufflebeam." *Evaluation Practice* 16(2): 179–99.

———. 1994a. "Empowerment Evaluation." American Evaluation Association

Presidential Address. *Evaluation Practice* 15(1):1–15.

———. 1994b. "Steps of Empowerment Evaluation: From California to Cape Town." *Evaluation and Program Planning* 17(3):305–13.

———. 1993. "Empowerment Evaluation: Theme for the 1993 Evaluation Meeting." *Evaluation Practice* 14(1):115–17.

Fetterman, D. M., A. J. Kaftarian, and A. Wandersman, eds. 1996. *Empowerment Evaluation: Knowledge and Tools for Self-Assessment and Accountability.* Thousand Oaks, CA: Sage.

Fetterman, David and Abraham Wandersman, eds. 2005. *Empowerment Evaluation Principles in Practice.* New York: Guilford Press.

Fisher, Deborah Pamela Imm, Matthew Chinman, and Abe Wandersman. 2006. *Getting to Outcomes with Developmental Assets: Ten Steps to Measuring Success in Youth Programs and Communities.* Minneapolis, MN: Search Institute.

Fitzpatrick, Jody. 2004. "Exemplars as Case Studies: Reflections on the Links between Theory, Practice, and Context." *American Journal of Evaluation* 25(4):541–59.

———. 2000. "Conversation with Gary Henry." *American Journal of Evaluation* 21(1):108–17.

Fleischer, D. 2007. *Evaluation Use: A Survey of U.S. American Evaluation Association Members.* Unpublished Master's Thesis, Claremont Graduate University, Claremont, CA.

Fletcher, Joseph. 1966. *Situation Ethics: The New Morality.* London: Westminster John Knox.

Flyvjerg, Bent, ed. 2001. *Making Social Science Matter.* Cambridge, UK: Cambridge University Press.

Forbes. 2007. *Thoughts on the Business of Life.* "Lee Simonson." May 21, p. 196.

Forss, Kim, Claus Rebien, and Jerker Carlsson. 2002. "Process Uses of Evaluations: Types of Use That Precede Lessons Learned and Feedback." *Evaluation* 8(1):29–45.

Foster, Deanne and Mary Keefe. 2004. "Hope Community: The Power of People and Place." *End of One Way.* Minneapolis, MN: McKnight Foundation.

Fournier, Deborah M. 2005a. "Evaluation." Pp. 139–40 in *Encyclopedia of Evaluation,* edited by S. Mathison. Thousand Oaks, CA: Sage.

———. 2005b. "Logic of Evaluation: Working Logic." Pp. 238–42 in *Encyclopedia of Evaluation,* edited by S. Mathison. Thousand Oaks, CA: Sage.

———, ed. 1995. *Reasoning in Evaluation: Inferential Links and Leaps. New Directions for Program Evaluation,* No. 68.

Franklin, Nancy. 2007. "The Cartoonist J. B. Handelsman." *The New Yorker,* July 2, p. 27.

Fraser, Sheila. 2006. "The Role of the Office of the Auditor-General in Canada and the Concept of Independence." *Canadian Journal of Program Evaluation* 21(1):1–10.

Frechtling, Joy. 2007. *Logic Modeling Methods in Program Evaluation.* San Francisco, CA: Jossey-Bass.

Freeman, Howard E. 1977. "The Present Status of Evaluation Research." Pp. 17–51 in *Evaluation Studies Review Annual,* Vol. 2, edited by Marcia Guttentag. Beverly Hills, CA: Sage.

Freeman, R. E. 1984. *Strategic Management: A Stakeholder Approach.* Boston, MA: Pitman.

Friedman, Victor, Jay Rothman, and Bill Withers. 2006. "The Power of Why: Engaging the Goal Paradox in Program Evaluation." *American Journal of Evaluation* 27(2):201–18.

Fritjof, Capra, Juarrero Alicia, Sotolongo Pedro, and Jacco van Uden, eds. 2007. *Reframing Complexity: Perspectives from the North and South.* Mansfield, OH: ISCE Publishing.

Fuchs, Stephan. 2007. "Agency (and Intention)." Pp. 60–61 in *The Blackwell Encyclopedia of Sociology,* edited by George Ritzer. Boston, MA: Blackwell.

Funnell, Sue. 2005. "Reflections on Evaluation Practice: Some Observations from a Grumpy Old Evaluator." Keynote address, Australasian Evaluation Society, Brisbane, Australia.

———. 2000. "Developing and Using a Program Theory Matrix for Program Evaluation and Performance Monitoring." *Program Theory in Evaluation: Challenges and Opportunities. New Directions for Evaluation* 87:91–101.

_____. 1997. "Program Logic: An Adaptable Tool for Designing and Evaluating Programs." *AES 'Evaluation News and Comment* 6(1):5–12.

Gamble, Jamie. 2007. *A Developmental Evaluation Primer.* Montreal, Canada: J. W. McConnell Family Foundation.

Gardiner, Peter C. and Ward Edwards. 1975. "Measurement for Social Decision Making." Pp. 1–38 in *Human Judgment and Decision Processes,* edited by Martin F. Kaplan and Steven Schwartz. New York: Academic Press.

Gardner, Annette and Sara Geierstanger. 2007. "Working with Logic Models to Evaluate a Policy and Advocacy Program." *The Evaluation Exchange,* Harvard Family Research Project, Spring:8–9.

Gawande, Atul. 2007. "The Power of Negative Thinking." *New York Times,* May 1, p. A23.

Ghere, Gail, Jean King, Laurie Stevahn, and Jane Minnema. 2006. "A Professional Development Unit for Reflecting on Program Evaluation Competencies." *American Journal of Evaluation* 27(1):108–23.

Gigerenzer, Gerd, Peter M. Todd, and the ABC Research Group. 1999. *Simple Heuristics That Make Us Smart.* New York: Oxford University Press.

Gill, Carol. 1999. "Invisible Ubiquity: The Surprising Relevance of Disability Issues in Evaluation." *American Journal of Evaluation* 20(2):279–88.

Gladwell, Malcolm. 2002. *The Tipping Point: How Little Things Can Make a Big Difference.* Boston, MA: Little, Brown.

Glaser, Edward M., Harold H. Abelson, and Kathalee N. Garrison, 1983. *Putting Knowledge to Use.* San Francisco, CA: Jossey-Bass.

Glewwe, Paul, Michael Kremer, Sylvie Moulin, and Eric Zitzewitz. 2004. *Retrospective vs. Prospective Analyses of School Inputs: The Case of Flip Charts in Kenya.* Cambridge, MA: MIT Poverty Action Lab. http://www.povertyactionlab.com/projects/project.php?pid=26.

Goodman, Ellen. 1995. "Patients, Doctors, Hospitals Must End Silence on Journey to Death." Syndicated column distributed by *Washington Post* Writers Group, appearing in the *Saint Paul Pioneer* Press, December 3, p. 17A.

Gordimer, Nadine. 1994. *None to Accompany Me.* New York: Penguin Books.

Government Accountability Office (GAO). 2006a. *GAO's High Risk Program.* GAO-GAO-06–184. GAO-05–207. Washington, DC: GAO.

_____. 2006b. *OMB's PART Reviews Increased Agencies' Attention to Improving Evidence of Program Results.* GAO-06–67. Washington, DC: GAO. http://www.gao.gov/cgi-bin/getrpt?GAO-06–67.

_____. 2006c. *Performance Budgeting: PART Focuses Attention on Program Performance, But More Can Be Done to Engage Congress.* GAO-06–28. Washington, DC: GAO. http://www.gao.gov/cgi-bin/getrpt?GAO-06–28.

_____. 2005. *High Risk Series: An Update.* GAO-05–207. Washington, DC: GAO. http://www.gao.gov/pas/2005.

_____. 2004. *Performance Budgeting: Observations on the Use of OMB's Program Assessment Rating Tool for the Fiscal Year 2004.* GAO-04–174. Washington, DC: GAO.

_____. 2003. *Youth Illicit Drug Use Prevention: DARE Long-Term Evaluations and Federal Efforts to Identify Effective Programs.* GAO-03–172R Youth Illicit Drug Use Prevention. Washington, DC: U.S. General Accounting Office.

_____. 1995. *Program Evaluation: Improving the Flow of Information to the Congress,* GAO/PEMPD-95–1. Washington, DC: GAO.

_____. 1992a. *Program Evaluation Issues.* GAO/OCG-93–6TR. Washington, DC: GAO.

_____. 1992b. *Adolescent Drug Use Prevention: Common Features of Promising Community Programs.* GAO/PEMD-92–2. Washington, DC: GAO.

_____. 1992c. *The Evaluation Synthesis.* GAO/PEMD-10.1.2. Washington, DC: GAO.

_____. 1992d. *Quantitative Data Analysis.* GAO/PEMD-10.1.11. Washington, DC: GAO.

_____. 1991. *Designing Evaluations.* GAO/PEMD-10.1.4. Washington, DC: GAO.

_____. 1990a. *Case Study Evaluations.* Transfer Paper 10.1.9. Washington, DC: GAO.

_____. 1990b. *Prospective Evaluation Methods: The Prospective Evaluation*

Synthesis. Transfer Paper 10.1.10. Washington, DC: GAO.

_____. 1987. *Federal Evaluation. Fewer Units, Reduced Resources.* GAO/PMED-87-9. Washington, DC: GAO.

_____. 1981. *Federal Evaluations:* Washington, DC: Government Printing Office.

Governor's Commission on Crime Prevention and Control (GCCPC). 1976. *Residential Community Corrections Program in Minnesota: An Evaluation Report.* Saint Paul, MN: State of Minnesota.

Graff, Fiona and Miranda Christou. 2001. "In Evidence Lies Change: The Research of Whiting Professor Carol Weiss." *Harvard Graduate School of Education News,* September 10. http://www.gse.harvard.edu/news/features/weiss09102001.html.

Grasso, Patrick. 2003. "What Makes an Evaluation Useful? Reflections from Experience in Large Organizations." *American Journal of Evaluation* 24(4): 507–14.

Greene, Jennifer. 2007. *Mixing Methods in Social Inquiry.* San Francisco, CA: Jossey-Bass.

_____. 2006. "Stakeholders." Pp. 397–8 in *Encyclopedia of Evaluation,* edited by S. Mathison. Thousand Oaks, CA: Sage.

_____. 2004. "The Educative Evaluator: An Interpretation of Lee J. Cronbach's Vision of Evaluation." Pp. 169–180 in *Evaluation Roots: Tracing Theorists' Views and Influences,* edited by M. C. Alkin. Thousand Oaks, CA: Sage.

_____. 2003. "Commentary: Margaret Mead, the Salzberg Seminar, and a Historic Evaluation report." *American Journal of Evaluation* 24(1):115–21.

_____. 1997. "Evaluation as Advocacy." *Evaluation Practice* 18(1):25–35.

_____. 1990. "Technical Quality versus User Responsiveness in Evaluation Practice." *Evaluation and Program Planning* 13(3):267–74.

_____. 1988a. "Communication of Results and Utilization in Participatory Program Evaluation." *Evaluation and Program Planning* 11:341–51.

_____. 1988b. "Stakeholder Participation and Utilization in Program Evaluation." *Evaluation Review* 12:91–116.

Greene, Jennifer and Gary Henry. 2005. "Qualitative-Quantitative Debate in Evaluation. Pp. 345–50 in *Encyclopedia of Evaluation,* edited by Sandra Mathison. Thousand Oaks, CA: Sage.

Greene, Jennifer and Valerie Caracelli, eds. 1997. Advances in Mixed-Method Evaluation: *The Challenges and Benefits of Integrating Diverse Paradigms. New Directions for Evaluation,* No. 74.

Greenhalgh, Trisha, Elizabeth Kristjansson, and Vivian Robinson. 2007. "Realist Review to Understand the Efficacy of School Feeding Programmes." *British Medical Journal* 335:858–86. http://www.bmj.com/cgi/content/full/335/7625/858.

Greenwood, Royston. 2007. "Organization Theory." Pp. 3281–85 in *The Blackwell Encyclopedia of Sociology,* edited by George Ritzer. Boston, MA: Blackwell.

Gribben, John. 2004. *Deep Simplicity: Bringing Order to Chaos and Complexity.* New York: Random House.

Grob, George. 2003. "A Truly Useful Bat is One Found in the Hands of a Slugger." *American Journal of Evaluation* 24(4):499–505.

Groopman, Jerome. 2007. "What's the Trouble? How Doctors Think." *The New Yorker,* January 29, pp. 36–41.

Guba, Egon G., ed. 1990. *The Paradigm Dialog.* Newbury Park, CA: Sage.

_____. 1977. "Overcoming Resistance to Evaluation." Presented at the Second Annual Conference on Evaluation, University of North Dakota.

Guba, Egon and Yvonna Lincoln, 1994. "Competing Paradigms in Qualitative Research." Pp. 105–17 in *Handbook of Qualitative Research,* edited by N. K. Denzin and Y. S. Lincoln. Thousand Oaks, CA: Sage.

_____. 1989. *Fourth Generation Evaluation.* Newbury Park, CA: Sage.

_____. 1981. *Effective Evaluation: Improving the Usefulness and Evaluation Results through Responsive and Naturalistic Approaches.* San Francisco, CA. Jossey-Bass.

Guest, Greg and Kate MacQueen, eds. 2007. *Handbook for Team-Based Qualitative Research.* New York: Altamira.

Gunderson, Lance and C. S. Holling. 2002. *Panarchy: Understanding Transformations in Human and Natural Systems.* Washington, DC: Island Press.

Guttentag, Marcia and Elmer L. Struening. 1975a. *Handbook of Evaluation Research,* Vols. 1 and 2. Beverly Hills, CA: Sage.

_____. 1975b. "The Handbook: Its Purpose and Organization." Pp. 3–10 in *Handbook of Evaluation Research,* Vol. 2, edited by Marcia Guttentag and Elmer D. Struening. Beverly Hills, CA: Sage.

Guttmann, David and Marvin B. Sussman, eds., 1995. "Exemplary Social Intervention Programs for Members and Their Families." Special issue of *Marriage and Family Review* 21(1, 2).

Hage, Jerald. 1999. *Organizational Innovation.* London: Ashgate.

Hage, Jerald and Marius Meeus, eds. 2006. *Innovation, Science, and Institutional Change: A Research Handbook.* New York: Oxford University Press.

Hage, Jerald and Michael Aiken. 1970. *Social Change in Complex Organizations.* New York: Random House.

Hall, Holly. 1992. "Assessing the Work of a Whole Foundation." *Chronicle of Philanthropy,* January 14, pp. 9–12.

Hamilton, Ralph, Prudence Brown, Robert Chaskin, Leila Fiester, Harold Richman, Aaron Sojourner, and Josh Weber. 2006. *Learning for Community Change: Core Components of Foundations that Learn.* Chicago, IL: Chapin Hall Publications, University of Chicago.

Hammond, Sue Annis and Andrea Mayfield. 2004. *Naming Elephants: How to Surface Undiscussables for Greater Organizational Success.* Bend, OR: Thin Book Publishing.

Hannum, Kelly, Jennifer Martineau, and Claie Reinelt, eds. 2007. *The Handbook of Leadership Development Evaluation.* Greensboro, NC: Center for Creative Leadership.

Hargreaves, Margaret. 2006. *Beyond Formal Plans: Using Complexity Theory to Address Minnesota's Health Care Disparities.* Unpublished doctoral dissertation, Union Institute and University, Cincinnati, OH.

Harnar, Michael and Hallie Preskill. 2007. "Evaluators' Descriptions of Process Use: An Exploratory Study." *New Directions for Evaluation* 116:27–44.

Harris, Gardiner. 2007. "Surgeon General Sees 4-Year Term as Compromised." *NY Times,* July 11, p. A1.

Harvard Family Research Project (HFRP). 1996a. *Noteworthy Results-Based Accountability Publications: An Annotated Bibliography.* Cambridge, MA: Harvard Family Research Project Publications.

_____. 1996b. *State Results-Based Accountability Efforts.* Cambridge, MA: Harvard Family Research Project Publications.

Hatry, Harry, Joseph Wholey, and Kathryn Newcomer. 2004. "Other Issues and Trends in Evaluation." Pp. 670–684 in *Handbook of Practical Program Evaluation,* edited by J. Wholey, H. Hatry, and K. Newcomer. San Francisco, CA: Jossey-Bass.

Havelock, Ronald G. 1980. "Forward." Pp. 11–14 in *Using Research in Organizations,* edited by Jack Rothman. Beverly Hills, CA: Sage.

Hedrick, Terry E. 1994. "The Quantitative-Qualitative Debate: Possibilities for Integration." *The Qualitative-Quantitative Debate: New Perspectives, New Directions for Program Evaluation* 61:45–52.

HHS. 1983. *Compendium of Health and Human Services.* Washington, DC: Department of Health and Human Services.

Heilman, John G. 1980. "Paradigmatic Choices in Evaluation Methodology." *Evaluation Review* 4(5):693–712.

Hendricks, M., M. F. Mangano, and W. C. Moran, eds. 1990. *Inspectors General: A New Force in Evaluation. New Directions for Program Evaluation,* No. 48.

Hendricks, Michael. 1994. "Making a Splash: Reporting Evaluation Results Effectively." Pp. 549–75 in *Handbook of Practical Program Evaluation,* edited by J. S. Wholey, H. P. Hatry, and K. E. Newcomer. San Francisco, CA: Jossey-Bass.

_____. 1984. "Preparing and Using Briefing Charts." *Evaluation News* 5(3):19–20.

_____. 1982. "Oral Policy Briefings." Pp. 249–58 in *Communication Strategies in Evaluation,* edited by Nick L. Smith. Beverly Hills, CA: Sage.

Hendricks, Michael and Elisabeth A. Handley. 1990. "Improving the Recommendations from Evaluation Studies." *Evaluation and Program Planning* 13:109–17.

Hendricks-Smith, Astrid. 2007. "Pioneers: The California Endowment Approach to Evaluating Advocacy." *The Evaluation Exchange,* Harvard Family Research Project, Spring:12–13.

Henry, Gary. 2003. "Influential Evaluations." *American Journal of Evaluation* 24(4): 515–24.

_____. 2002. "Choosing Criteria to Judge Program Success: A Values Inquiry." *Evaluation* 8(2):182–204.

_____. 2000. "Why not use?" *New Directions for Evaluation* 88:85–98.

Henry, G. T. and M. M. Mark. 2003. "Beyond Use: Understanding Evaluation's Influence on Attitudes and Actions." *American Journal of Evaluation* 24(3):293–314.

Herman, Joan L. and Edward H. Haertel. 2005. *Uses and Misuses of Data for Educational Accountability and Improvement.* The 104th Yearbook of the National Society for the Study of Education, Part 2. Malden, MA: Blackwell Publishing.

Hersey, Paul. 1985. *Situational Leader.* Charlotte, NC: Center for Leadership.

Hersh, Seymour M. 2003. "The Stovepipe: How Conflicts between the Bush Administration and the Intelligence Community Marred the Reporting on Iraq's Weapons." *The New Yorker*, October 27 (posted October 10, 2003). http://www.newyorker.com/fact/content/?031027fa_fact.

Herzog, Elizabeth. 1959. *Some Guidelines for Evaluative Research.* Washington, DC: U.S. Department of Health, Education, and Welfare.

Hevey, Denise. 1984. "An Exercise in Utilization-Focused Evaluation: The Under-Fives Coordinators." Preschool Evaluation Project, Bristol University, Bristol, UK. Unpublished manuscript.

Hinton, Barb. 1988. "Audit Tales: Kansas Intrigue." *Legislative Program Evaluation Society (LPES) Newsletter*, Spring, p. 3.

Hoag, Sheila and Judith Wooldridge. 2007. *Improving Processes and Increasing Efficiency: The Case for States Participating in a Process Improvement Collaborative.* Princeton, NJ: Mathematica Policy Research.

Hoffman, Yoel. 1975. *The Sound of One Hand.* New York: Basic Books.

Hofstetter, Carolyn Huie and Marvin Alkin. 2003. "Evaluation Use Revisited." Pp. 197–222 in *International Handbook of Education Evaluation*, edited by T. Kellaghan, D. L. Stufflebeam, and L. Wingate. Boston, MA: Kluwer.

Hood, Stafford L. 2005. "Culturally Responsive Evaluation." Pp. 96–100 in *Encyclopedia of Evaluation*, edited by S. Mathison. Thousand Oaks, CA: Sage.

_____. 2004. "A Journey to Understand the Role of Culture in Program Evaluation: Snapshots and Personal reflections of One African American Evaluator." *New Directions for Evaluation* 102:21–38.

Hopkins, J. Castell. 1898. *Canada. An Encyclopedia of the Country*, Vol. 1. Toronto, ON, Canada: Linscott.

Hopson, Rodney, ed. 2000. *How and Why Language Matters in Evaluation. New Directions for Evaluation*, No. 86.

_____. 1999. "Minority Issues in Evaluation Revisited." *American Journal of Evaluation* 20(3):433–37.

Horton, Douglas, Anastasia Alexaki, Samuel Bennett-Lartey, Kim Noële Brice, Dindo Campilan, Fred Carden, José de Souza Silva, Le Thanh Duong, Ibrahim Khadar, Albina Maestrey Boza, Imrul Kayes Muniruzzaman, Jocelyn Perez, Matilde Somarriba Chang, Ronnie Vernooy, and Jamie Watts. 2003. *Experiences from Research and Development Organizations around the World Evaluating Capacity Development.* The Hague, The Netherlands: International Service for National Agricultural Research (ISNAR).

Horton, Douglas and Ronald Mackay. 2003. "Using Evaluation to Enhance Institutional Learning and Change: Recent Experiences with Agricultural Research and Development." *Agricultural Systems* 78(2, November):127–42.

House, Ernest R. 2006. "Democracy and Evaluation." *Evaluation* 12(1):119–27.

House, Ernest R. 2005a. "Deliberative Democratic Evaluation." Pp. 104–108 in *Encyclopedia of Evaluation*, edited by S. Mathison. Thousand Oaks, CA: Sage.

_____. 2005b. "Social Justice." Pp. 393–96 in *Encyclopedia of Evaluation*, edited by S. Mathison. Thousand Oaks, CA: Sage.

_____. 2004. "Intellectual History in Evaluation." Pp. 218–24 in *Evaluation Roots: Tracing Theorists' Views and Influences*, edited by M. C. Alkin. Thousand Oaks, CA: Sage.

_____. 2003. "Stakeholder Bias." *The Practice-Theory Relationship in Evaluation. New Directions for Evaluation* 97:53–56.

_____. 1999. "Evaluation and People of Color." *American Journal of Evaluation* 20(3):433–37.

_____. 1995. "Principled Evaluation: A Critique of the AEA Guiding Principles." *Guiding Principles for Evaluators. New Directions for Program Evaluation* 66:27–34.

_____. 1994. "Integrating the Qualitative and Quantitative." *The Qualitative-Quantitative Debate: New Perspectives. New Directions for Program Evaluation* 61:13–22.

_____. 1993. *Professional Evaluation: Social Impact and Political Consequences.* Newbury Park, CA: Sage.

_____. 1991. "Realism in Research." *Educational Researcher* 20(6):2–9.

_____. 1990a. "Trends in Evaluation." *Educational Researcher* 19(3):24–28.

_____. 1990b. "Methodology and Justice." *Evaluation and Social Justice: Issues in Public Education. New Directions for Program Evaluation* 45:23–36.

_____. 1980. *Evaluating with Validity.* Beverly Hills, CA: Sage.

_____. 1977. "The Logic of Evaluative Argument." In *CSE Monograph Lines in Evaluation,* Vol. 7. Los Angeles: UCLA Center for the Study of Education.

_____. 1972. "The Conscience of Educational Evaluation." *Teachers College Record* 73(3):405–14.

House, Ernest R. and Kenneth Howe. 2000. "Deliberative Democratic Evaluation." *Evaluation as a Democratic Process. New Directions for Evaluation* 85:3–12.

_____. 1999. *Values in Evaluation and Social Research.* Thousand Oaks, CA: Sage.

Howe, K. 1988. "Against the Quantitative-Qualitative Incompatibility Thesis." *Educational Researcher* 17(8):10–16.

Huberman, Michael. 1995. "Research Utilization: The State of the Art." *Knowledge and Policy* 7(4):13–33.

Huberty, Carl J. 1988. "Another Perspective on the Role of an Internal Evaluator." *Evaluation Practice* 9(4):25–32.

Hudley, Cynthia and Robert Parker, eds. 2006. *Pitfalls and Pratfalls: Null and Negative Findings in Evaluating Interventions. New Directions for Evaluation,* No. 110.

Hudson, Joe. 1977. "Problems of Measurement in Criminal Justice." Pp. 73–100 in *Evaluation Research Methods,* edited by Leonard Rutman. Beverly Hills, CA: Sage.

Hudson, Joe, John Mayne, and R. Thomlison, eds. 1992. *Action-Oriented Evaluation in Organizations: Canadian Practices.* Toronto, ON, Canada: Wall and Emerson.

Hughes, Adam and J. Robert Shull. 2005. *PART Backgrounder.* Washington, DC: OMB Watch. http://www.ombwatch.org/article/articleview/2680/1/90?TopicID=1.

Hughes, Malcolm and Saville Kushner. 2005. "Accreditation." Pp. 4–7 in *Encyclopedia of Evaluation,* edited by S. Mathison. Thousand Oaks, CA: Sage.

Human Relations Area Files. 2007. "Cultures and Cultural Traits in HRAF." Bloomington, IN: Indiana University Wells Library. http://www.libraries.iub.edu/index.php?pageId=2261.

Hunt, Stephen. 2007. "Organizations." Pp. 3310–15 in *The Blackwell Encyclopedia of Sociology,* edited by George Ritzer. Boston, MA: Blackwell.

Hurty, Kathleen. 1976. "Report by the Women's Caucus." *Proceedings: Educational Evaluation and Public Policy, a Conference.* San Francisco, CA: Far West Regional Laboratory for Educational Research and Development.

Idarius, Jerri-Jo. 1998. "The Iroquois Confederacy." *Sojourn Magazine* Winter(707):964–1674.

Ilgen, Mark, John McKellar, and Rudolf Moos. 2007. Personal and Treatment-Related Predictors of Abstinence Self-Efficacy. *Journal of Studies on Alcohol* 68(1):126–27.

Inbar, Michael. 1979. *Routine Decision-Making.* Beverly Hills, CA: Sage.

Independent Evaluation Group (IEG). 2007. *IEG Annual Report on Operations Evaluation.* Washington, DC: The World Bank. http://www.worldbank.org/ieg.

_____. 2006. *Annual Review of Development Effectiveness 2006: Getting Results.* Washington, DC: The World Bank. http://www.worldbank.org/ieg/arde2006?intcmp=5321182.

Inter-American Development Bank. 2001. *Summary of Findings: Decentralization and Effective Citizen Participation: Six Cautionary Tales.* RE-250. Washington, DC: Office of Evaluation and Oversight, OVE, Inter-American Development Bank.

International Development Research Centre (IDRC). 2007. *Outcome Mapping.* Ottawa, Canada: IDRC. http://www.idrc.ca/en/ev-26586-201-1-DO_TOPIC.html.

_____. 2006. "About IDRC." http://www.idrc.ca/en/ev-8513-201-1-DO_TOPIC.html.

International Fund for Agricultural Development (IFAD). 2002. A Guide for Project M & E. Rome, Italy: IFAD.

International Herald Tribune. 2001. "China's Whopper of a Fish Tale." December, p. 1.

International Organization for Migration (IOM). 2006. *IOM Evaluation Guidelines.* Geneva, Switzerland: IOM Office of the Inspector General. http://www.old.iom.int/en/PDF_Files/evaluation/Evaluation_Guidelines_2006_1.pdf.

International Qualitative Research in Education Conference (IQREC). 1997. "Democratizing Inquiry through Qualitative Research." Presented at IQREC, University of Georgia, Athens, GA.

Iverson, Alex. 2003. *Attribution and Aid Evaluation in International Development: A Literature Review.* Ottawa, Canada: International Development Research Centre. http://www.idrc.ca/ev_en.php?ID=32055_201&ID2=DO_TOPIC.

Jackson, Edward T. 2005. "Participatory Monitoring and Evaluation." P. 296 in *Encyclopedia of Evaluation,* edited by S. Mathison. Thousand Oaks, CA: Sage.

Jacobs, Francine, H. 1988. "The Five-Tiered Approach to Evaluation." Pp. 37–68 in *Evaluating Family Programs,* edited by H. B. Weiss and F. Jacobs. Hawthorne, NY: Aldine.

James, William. 1950. "Discrimination and Comparison." *The Principles of Psychology,* Vol. 1, Chapter 13. Mineola, NY: Dover Publications.

Janofsky, Michael. 1995. "Federal Parks Chief Calls 'Million Man' Count Low." *New York Times,* October 21, p. A1.

Janowitz, Morris. 1979. "Where Is the Cutting Edge of Sociology?" *Midwest Sociological Quarterly* 20:591–93.

Johansen, Bruce, E. 1998. *Debating Democracy: Native American Legacy of Freedom.* Santa Fe, NM: Clear Light Books.

_____. 1987. *The Forgotten Founders: How the American Indian Shaped Democracy.* Cambridge, MA: Harvard Common Press.

Johnson, R. Burke, ed. 2006. "New Directions in Mixed Methods Research." *Research in the Schools,* 13(1).

_____. 1998. "Toward a Theoretical Model of Evaluation Utilization." *Evaluation and Program Planning* 21:93–110.

_____. 1995. "Estimating an Evaluation Utilization Model Using Conjoint Measurement and Analysis." *Evaluation Review* 19(3):313–38.

Johnson, R. Burke, Anthony Onwuegbuzie, and Lisa Turner. 2007. "Toward a Definition of Mixed Methods Research." *Journal of Mixed Methods Research* 1(2):112–33.

Johnson, Robert, Marjorie Willeke, and Deila Steiner. 1998. "Stakeholder Collaboration in the Design and Implementation of a Family Literacy Portfolio Assessment." *American Journal of Evaluation* 19(3):339–54.

Johnson, Steven. 2001. *Emergence: The Connected Lives of Ants, Brains, Cities, and Software.* New York: Scribner.

Joint Committee on Standards for Educational Evaluation. 1994. *The Program Evaluation Standards.* Thousand Oaks, CA: Sage. http://www.wmich.edu/evalctr/jc.

_____. 1981. *Standards for Evaluations of Educational Programs, Projects, and Materials.* New York: McGraw-Hill.

Jonas, R. Kirk, ed. 1999. *Legislative Program Evaluation: Utilization Driven Research for Decision Makers. New Directions for Evaluation,* No. 81.

Joyce, Phillip. 1997. "Using Performance Measures for Budgeting." *Using Performance Measurement to Improve Public and Nonprofit Programs. New Directions for Evaluation* 75:45–62.

Julnes, George and Debra Rog, eds. 2007. *Informing Federal Policies on Evaluation Methodology: Building the Evidence Base for Method Choice in Government Sponsored Evaluation. New Directions for Program Evaluation,* No. 113.

Kahneman, Daniel and Amos Tversky, eds. 2000a. *Choices, Values, and Frames.* Boston, MA: Cambridge University Press.

_____. 2000b. "Prospect Theory: An Analysis of Decision Under Risk." Pp. 17–43 in *Choices, Values, and Frames,* edited by Daniel Kahneman and Amos Tversky. Cambridge, UK: Cambridge University Press.

Kanter, Rosabeth Moss. 1983. *The Change Masters.* New York: Simon and Schuster.

Karachi, Tracy, Robert Abbott, Richard Catalano, Kevin Haggerty, and Charles

Fleming. 1999. "Opening the Black Box: Using Process Evaluation Measures to Assess Implementation and Theory Building." *American Journal of Community Psychology* 27(5):711–32.

Karlan, Dean and Jonathan Zinman. 2006. *Expanding Credit Access: Using Randomized Supply Decisions to Estimate the Impacts.* Cambridge: MIT Poverty Action Lab. http://www.povertyactionlab.com/projects/project.php?pid=62.

Karoly, Lynn, Rebecca Kilburn, and Jill Cannon. 2005. *Early Childhood Interventions: Proven Results, Future Promise.* Santa Monica, CA: Rand Corporation.

Kay, Jackie Williams. 2007. "Pioneers: The Atlantic Philanthropies Approach to Evaluating Advocacy." *The Evaluation Exchange,* Harvard Family Research Project, Spring:13–14.

Kearns, Kevin P. 1996. *Managing for Accountability.* San Francisco, CA: Jossey-Bass.

Kellogg Foundation. 2001. *Logic Model Development Guide: Logic Models to Bring Together Planning, Evaluation & Action.* Battle Creek, MI: W. K. Kellogg Foundation. http://www.wkkf.org/Pubs/Tools/Evaluation/Pub3669.pdf.

———. n.d. (circa 1995). *W. K. Kellogg Foundation Cluster Evaluation Model of Evolving Practices.* Battle Creek, MI: W. K. Kellogg Foundation.

Kennedy, M. M. 1983. "The Role of the In-House Evaluator." *Evaluation Review* 7(4):519–41.

Kennedy School of Government. 1995. "Innovations in America Government Awards Winners." *Governing,* November, pp. 27–42.

Kettl, Donald F., William Fanaras, Jennifer Lieb, and Elena Michaels. 2006. *Managing for Performance: A Report on Strategies for Improving the Results of Government.* Washington, DC: Brookings Institution Press.

King, Jean A. 2007a. "Developing Evaluation Capacity through Process Use." *New Directions for Evaluation* 116: 45–61.

———. 2007b. "Making Sense of Participatory Evaluation." *New Directions for Evaluation* 114:83–86.

———. 2005. "Participatory Evaluation." Pp. 291–94 in *Encyclopedia of Evaluation,* edited by S. Mathison. Thousand Oaks, CA: Sage.

———. 2003. "The Challenge of Studying Evaluation Theory." *The Practice-Theory Relationship in Evaluation. New Directions for Evaluation* 97:57–68.

———. 2002. "Building the Evaluation Capacity of a School District." *New Directions for Evaluation* 93:63–80.

———. 1995. "Involving Practitioners in Evaluation Studies: How Viable Is Collaborative Evaluation in Schools." Pp. 86–102 in *Participatory Evaluation in Education: Studies in Evaluation Use and Organizational Learning,* edited by J. Bradley Cousins and Lorna Earl. London: Falmer.

———. 1988. "Research on Evaluation Use and Its Implications for the Improvement of Evaluation Research and Practice." *Studies in Educational Evaluation* 14:285–99.

———. 1985. "Existing Research on Evaluation Use and Its Implications for the Improvement of Evaluation Research and Practice." Presented at invited conference on evaluation use, UCLA Center for the Study of Evaluation.

———. 1982. "Studying the Local Use of Evaluation: A Discussion of Theoretical Issues and an Empirical Study." *Studies in Educational Evaluation* 8:175–83.

King, Jean, Julie Nielsen, and Jeanette Colby. 2004. "Lessons for Culturally Competent Evaluation from the Study of a Multicultural Initiative." *New Directions for Evaluation* 102:67–80.

King, Jean, Laurie Stevahn, Gail Ghere, and Jane Minnema. 2001. "Toward a Taxonomy of Essential Program Evaluator Competencies." *American Journal of Evaluation* 22(2):229–47.

King, Jean A., Lynn Lyons Morris, and Carol T. Fitz-Gibbon. 1987. *How to Assess Program Implementation.* Newbury Park, CA: Sage.

King, Jean A. and Ellen Pechman. 1984. "Pinning a Wave to Shore: Conceptualizing School Evaluation Use." *Educational Evaluation and Policy Analysis* 6(3):241–51.

———. 1982. *Improving Evaluation Use in Local Schools.* Washington, DC: National Institute of Education.

King, Neil, Jr. and Jason Dean. 2005. "Untranslatable Word in U.S. Aide's Speech Leaves Beijing Baffled Zoellick

Challenges China to Become 'Stakeholder'; What Does That Mean?" *The Wall Street Journal,* December 7, p. A1.

Kinzer, Stephen. 2007. "Big Gamble in Rwanda." *The New York Review of Books,* LIV(5), March 29, pp. 23–26.

Kirkhart, Karen. 2005. "Through a Cultural Lens: Reflections on Validity and Theory in Evaluation." Pp. 21–29 in *The Role of Culture and Cultural Context: A Mandate for Inclusion, the Discovery of Truth, and Understanding in Evaluative Theory and Practice,* edited by S. Hood, R. K. Hopson, and H. T. Frierson. Greenwich, CT: Information Age Publishing.

_____. 2000. "Reconceptualizing Evaluation Use: An Integrated Theory of Influence." *The Expanding Scope of Evaluation Use. New Directions for Evaluation* 88:5–23.

_____. 1995. "Seeking Multicultural Validity: A Postcard from the Road." *Evaluation Practice* 16(1):1–12.

Klein, Gary. 1999. *Sources of Power: How People Make Decisions.* Cambridge, MA: MIT Press.

Knowledge Assessment Methodology (KAM). 2006. *Knowledge Assessment Methodology.* Washington, DC: World Bank Institute, Knowledge for Development, The World Bank Group. http://web.worldbank.org/WBSITE/EXTERNAL/WBI/WBIPROGRAMS/KFDLP/EXTUNIKAM/0,,menuPK:1414738~pagePK:64168427~piPK:64168435~theSitePK:1414721,00.html.

Knowles, Malcolm S. 1989. *The Making of an Adult Educator: An Autobiographical Journey.* San Francisco, CA: Jossey-Bass.

Knowles, Malcolm S. and Associates. 1985. *Andragogy in Action: Applying Modern Principles of Adult Learning.* San Francisco, CA: Jossey-Bass.

Knox, Alan B. 1987. *Helping Adults Learn.* San Francisco, CA: Jossey-Bass.

Kochen, Manfred. 1975. "Applications of Fuzzy Sets in Psychology." Pp. 395–407 in *Fuzzy Sets and Their Applications to Cognitive and Decision Processes,* edited by Lofti A. Zadeh, King-Sun Fu, Kokichi Tanaka, and Masamichi Shimura. New York: Academic Press.

Kolata, Gina. 2006a. "Race to the Swift? Not Necessarily." *New York Times,* July 18, Health and Fitness Section, p. 1. http://www.nytimes.com/2006/07/18/health/nutrition/18mara.html?ex=1161576000&en=e3459e26ae236e6d&ei=5070.

_____. 2006b. "Study Questions Colonoscopy Effectiveness." *New York Times,* December 14, p. A36.

Kolbert, Elizabeth. 2007. "Crash Course." *The New Yorker,* May 14, pp. 68–76.

Kourilsky, Marilyn. 1974. "An Adversary Model for Educational Evaluation." *Evaluation Comment* 4:2.

Kramer, Mark and William Bickel. 2004. "Foundations and Evaluation as Uneasy Partners in Learning." Pp. 51–75 in *Foundations and Evaluation: Contexts and Practices for Effective Philanthropy,* edited by Marc Braverman, Norman Constantine, and Jana Kay Slater. San Francisco, CA: Jossey-Bass.

Kristof, Nicolas. 2007. "Attack of the Worms." *New York Times,* July 2, p. A19.

Kuhn, Thomas. 1970. *The Structure of Scientific Revolutions.* Chicago, IL: University of Chicago Press.

Kusek, Jody Zall and Ray Rist. 2004. *Ten Steps to a Results-Based Monitoring and Evaluation System.* Washington, DC: The World Bank.

Kushner, Saville. 2005. "Personalizing Evaluation." P. 308 in *Encyclopedia of Evaluation,* edited by S. Mathison. Thousand Oaks, CA: Sage.

_____. 2000. *Personalizing Evaluation.* London: Sage.

Kushner, Tony. 1994. *Angels in America. Part Two: Perestroika.* New York: Theatre Communications Group.

Kuzmin, Alexey. 2005. "Exploration of Factors That Affect the Use of Evaluation Training in Evaluation Capacity Development." Ph.D. dissertation, Union Institute and University, Cincinnati, OH.

Lahr, John. 2006. "Pterified: The Horrors of Stagefright." *The New Yorker,* August 28, pp. 38–42.

Landry, Réjean, Moktar Lamari and Nabil Amara. 2003. "The Extent and Determinants of the Utilization of University Research in Government Agencies." *Public Administration Review,* 63(2):192–206.

Laperrière, Hélène N. 2006. "Taking Evaluation Contexts Seriously: A Cross-Cultural Evaluation in Extreme Unpredictability." *Journal of MultiDisciplinary Evaluation* 3(4):41–57. http://survey.ate.wmich.edu/jmde/index.php/jmde_1/issue/view/16.

Laundergan J. Clark. 1983. *Easy Does It*. Center City, MN: Hazelden Foundation.

Law, Nancy. 1996. "VP News." *Reality-Test*. The Division H Newsletter of the American Educational Research Association, January, p. 1.

Lawler, E. E., III, A. M. Mohrman, Jr., S. A. Mohrman, G. E. Ledford, Jr., T. G. Cummings, and Associates. 1985. *Doing Research That Is Useful for Theory and Practice*. San Francisco, CA: Jossey-Bass.

Lawrenz, Frances, Douglas Huffman, and J. Randy McGinnis. 2007. "Process Use in Multi-site Evaluation: Challenges, Dilemmas & Issues." *New Directions for Evaluation* 116:75–86.

Lawrenz, Frances and Douglas Huffman. 2006. "Methodological Pluralism: The Gold Standard of STEM Evaluation." *Critical Issues in STEM Evaluation. New Directions for Evaluation* 109:19–34.

Layzer, Jean I. 1996. "Building Theories of Change in Family Support Programs." *The Evaluation Exchange* 2(1):10–11.

Lee, Barbara. 1999. "The Implications of Diversity and Disability for Evaluation Practice." *American Journal of Evaluation* 20(2):289–94.

Leeuw, Frans. 2002. "Evaluation in Europe 2000: Challenges to a Growth Industry." *Evaluation* 8(1):5–12.

Leeuw, Frans, L. Ray, C. Rist, and Richard C. Sonnichsen, eds. 1999. *Can Governments Learn? Comparative Perspectives on Evaluation and Organizational Learning*. Somerset, NJ: Transaction Publishers.

———. 1993. *Comparative Perspectives on Evaluation and Organizational Learning*. New Brunswick, NJ: Transaction.

Le Guin, Ursula K. 1969. *The Left Hand of Darkness*. New York: Ace Books.

Lenne, Bryan. 1987. *Describing Program Logic*. Program Evaluation Bulletin. Sydney, Australia: New South Wales Public Service Board.

Leonard, Jennifer. 1996. "Process or Outcomes? Turn Outcome 'Sticks' Into Carrots." *Foundation*, March/April, pp. 46–48.

Lester, James P. and Leah J. Wilds. 1990. "The Utilization of Public Policy Analysis: A Conceptual Framework." *Evaluation and Program Planning* 13(3):313–19.

Levin, B. 1993. "Collaborative Research in and with Organizations." *Qualitative Studies in Education* 6(4):331–40.

Levin, Henry. 2005a. "Cost-Benefit Analysis." Pp. 86–90 in *Encyclopedia of Evaluation*, edited by S. Mathison. Thousand Oaks, CA: Sage.

———. 2005b. "Cost Effectiveness." P. 90 in *Encyclopedia of Evaluation*, edited by S. Mathison. Thousand Oaks, CA: Sage.

Leviton, Laura. 2007. "A Big Chapter about Small Theories." *New Directions for Evaluation* 114:27–29.

———. 2003. "Evaluation Use: Advances, Challenges and Applications." *American Journal of Evaluation* 24(4):525–35.

Leviton, Laura and Robert Boruch. 1984. "Why the Compensatory Education Evaluation Was Useful." *Journal of Policy Analysis and Management* 3:299–305.

Leviton, L. A. and E. F. X. Hughes. 1981. "Research on Utilization of Evaluations: A Review and Synthesis." *Evaluation Review* 5(4):525–48.

Lewin, Kurt. 1948. *Resolving Social Conflicts: Selected Papers on Group Dynamics*, edited by Gertrude W. Lewin. New York: Harper and Row.

Lewin, Roger. 2001. *Complexity*. Troy, MI: Phoenix Press.

Lewy, Arieh and Marvin Alkin. 1983. *The Impact of a Major National Evaluation Study: Israel's Van Leer Report*. Los Angeles, CA: UCLA Center for the Study of Evaluation.

Light, Paul C. 2006. "The Tides of Reform Revisited: Patterns in Making Government Work, 1945–2002." *Public Administration Review* 66(1):6–19.

Lincoln, Yvonna S. 1991. "The Arts and Sciences of Program Evaluation." *Evaluation Practice* 12(1):1–7.

Lincoln, Yvonna S. and Egon G. Guba. 1985. *Naturalistic Inquiry*. Beverly Hills, CA: Sage.

Lindblom, Charles E. 1965. *The Intelligence of Democracy*. New York: Free Press.

———. 1959. "The Science of Muddling Through Public Administration." *Public Administration Review* 19:79–99.

Lion, Cristina, Paola Martini, and Stefano Volpi. 2006. "Evaluating the Implementation Process: A Contribution within the Framework of the European Social Fund Programme." *Evaluation* 12(3):313–29.

Lipsey, Mark W. 2007a. "Peter H. Rossi: Formative for Program Evaluation." *American Journal of Evaluation* 28(2): 199–202.

_____. 2007b. "Method Choice for Government Evaluation: The Beam in Our Own Eye." *Informing Federal Policies on Evaluation Methodology: Building the Evidence Base for Method Choice in Government Sponsored Evaluation. New Directions for Program Evaluation* 113:113–15.

_____. 2007c. "Theory as Method: Small Theories of Treatments." *New Directions for Evaluation* 114:30–62.

_____. 2005. "The 2004 Claremont Debate: Lipsey vs. Scriven: Determining Causality in Program Evaluation and Applied Research: Should Experimental Evidence Be the Gold Standard?" Reported by Stewart I. Donaldson and Christina A. Christie, *Journal of MultiDisciplinary Evaluation*, 2(3):60–77 http://survey.ate.wmich.edu/jmde/index.php/jmde_1/issue/view/21.

_____. 1990. *Design Sensitivity: Statistical Power for Experimental Research*. Newbury Park, CA: Sage.

_____. 1988. "Practice and Malpractice in Evaluation Research." *Evaluation Practice* 9(4):5–24.

Lipsey, Mark and David B. Wilson. 2000. *Practical Meta-Analysis*. Thousand Oaks, CA: Sage.

Lipsey, Mark W. and John A. Pollard. 1989. "Driving toward Theory in Program Evaluation: More Models to Choose From." In "Special Issue: The Theory-Driven Perspective," edited by Huey-Tsyh Chen. *Evaluation and Program Planning* 12(4):317–28.

Lofland, John. 1971. *Analyzing Social Settings*. Belmont, CA: Wadsworth.

Love, Arnold. 2005. "Internal Evaluation." Pp. 206–207 in *Encyclopedia of Evaluation*, edited by S. Mathison. Thousand Oaks, CA: Sage.

_____. 2004. "Implementation Evaluation." Pp. 98–125 in *Handbook of Practical Program Evaluation*, edited by Wholey, Hatry, and Newcomer. San Francisco, CA: Jossey-Bass.

_____. 1991. *Internal Evaluation: Building Organizations from Within*. Newbury Park, CA: Sage.

_____, ed. 1983. *Developing Effective Internal Evaluation. New Directions for Program Evaluation*, No. 20.

Lowenstein, Roger. 2006. "When Business Has Questions, Drucker Still Has Answers." *New York Times*, January 22, Section3, p. 7.

Lunt, Neil, Carl Davidson, and Kate McKegg, eds. 2003. *Evaluating Policy and Practice: A New Zealand Reader*. Auckland, New Zealand: Pearson Prentice Hall.

Lynn, Joanne. 1995. "Patients, Doctors, Hospitals Must End Silence on Journey to Death." Ellen Goodman op-ed column, *Saint Paul Pioneer Press,* December 3, p. 17A.

Lynn, Lawrence E., Jr. 1980a. "Crafting Policy Analysis for Decision Makers." Interview conducted by Michael Kirst in *Educational Evaluation and Policy Analysis* 2:85–90.

_____. 1980b. *Designing Public Policies: A Casework on the Role of Policy Analysis*. Santa Monica, CA: Goodyear.

Lyon, Eleanor. 1989. "In-House Research: A Consideration of Roles and Advantages." *Evaluation and Program Planning* 12(3):241–48.

MacDonald, Barry and Saville Kushner. 2005. "Democratic Evaluation." Pp. 109–13 in *Encyclopedia of Evaluation*, edited by S. Mathison. Thousand Oaks, CA: Sage.

Machiavelli, Niccolo. 1513. *The Prince*.

MacKenzie, R. A. 1972. *The Time Trap*. New York: AMACOM.

Maclure, Richard. 2006. "Pragmatism or Transformation? Participatory Evaluation of a Humanitarian Education Project in Sierra Leone." *Canadian Journal of Evaluation* 21(1):107–29.

Madison, Anna. 2007. "Cultural Issues and Issues of Significance to Underrepresented Groups." *New Directions for Evaluation* 114:107–13.

Mark, Mel. 2007. "AEA and Evaluation: 2006 (and Beyond)." *New Directions for Evaluation* 114:115–20.

_____. 2006. "The Consequences of Evaluation: Theory, Research, and Practice." Plenary Presidential Address, Annual Conference of the American Evaluation Association, November 2, Portland, OR.

Mark, Melvin and Gary Henry. 2006. "Methods for Policy-Making and Knowledge Development Evaluations." Pp. 317–39 in *Handbook of Evaluation: Policies, Programs and Practices*, edited by I. Shaw, J. Greene, and M. Mark. Thousand Oaks, CA: Sage.

———. 2004. "The Mechanisms and Outcomes of Evaluation Influence." *Evaluation* 10(1):35–57.

Mark, Melvin M., Jennifer C. Greene, and Ian S. Shaw. 2006a. Pp. 1–30 in *Handbook of Evaluation: Policies, Programs and Practices*, edited by I. Shaw, J. Greene, and M. Mark. Thousand Oaks, CA: Sage.

Mark, Melvin, Gary Henry, and George Julnes. 2000. *Evaluation: An Integrated Framework for Understanding, Guiding, and Improving Public and Nonprofit Policies and Programs*. San Francisco, CA: Jossey-Bass.

Mark, Melvin M. and Lance Shotland, eds. 1987. *Multiple Methods in Program Evaluation. New Directions for Program Evaluation*, No. 35.

Mark, Melvin M. and Thomas D. Cook, 1984. "Design of Randomized Experiments and Quasi-Experiments." Pp. 65–120 in *Evaluation Research Methods*, edited by Leonard Rutman. Beverly Hills, CA: Sage.

Martin, C. M. and Sturmberg, J. P. 2005. "General Practice: Chaos, Complexity and Innovation." *Medical Journal of Australia* 183:106–109.

Mason, Paul and Marian Barnes. 2007. "Constructing Theories of Change: Methods and Sources." *Evaluation* 13(2):151–70.

Mathison, Sandra, ed. 2007. Enduring Issues in Evaluation: The 20th Anniversary of the Collaboration between NDE and AEA. *New Directions for Evaluation*, No. 114.

———, ed. 2005. *Encyclopedia of Evaluation*. Thousand Oaks, CA: Sage.

Mayer, Steven. 1993. "Common Barriers to Effectiveness in the Independent Sector," Pp. 7–11 in *A Vision of Evaluation*, edited by Sandra Trice Gray. Washington, DC: Independent Sector.

———. 1976. *Organizational Readiness to Accept Program Evaluation Questionnaire*. Minneapolis, MN: Program Evaluation Resource Center.

———. 1975. "Are You Ready to Accept Program Evaluation" and "Assess Your Program Readiness for Program Evaluation." *Program Evaluation Resource Center Newsletter* 6(1):1–5 and 6(3):4–5. Published by Program Evaluation Resource Center, Minneapolis, MN.

Mayne, John. 2007a. "Evaluation for Accountability: Myth or Reality?" Pp. 63–84 in *Making Accountability Work: Dilemmas for Evaluation and for Audit*, edited by Bemelmans-Videc, Marie-Louise, Jeremy Lonsdale, and Burt Perrin. London: Transaction Books.

Mayne, John. 2007b. "Exploring Cause-Effect Questions Using Contribution Analysis." In *Evaluation the Complex: Attribution, Contribution and Beyond*, edited by Robert Schwartz, Mitta Mara, and Kim Forss. New Brunswick, NJ: Transaction Books.

———. 2006. "Audit and Evaluation in Public Management: Challenges, Reforms, and Different Roles." *Canadian Journal of Program Evaluation* 21(1):11–46.

———. 2001. "Addressing Attribution through Contribution Analysis: Using Performance Measures Sensibly." *Canadian Journal of Program Evaluation* 16(1):1–24.

McCarty, Christopher, Jose Luis Molina, Claudia Aguilar, and Laura Rota. 2007. "A Comparison of Social Network Mapping and Personal Network Visualization." *Field Methods* 9(2):145–62.

McDavid, James and Laura Hawthorn. 2006. *Program Evaluation and Performance Measurement*. Thousand Oaks, CA: Sage.

McDonald, B., P. J. Rogers, and B. Kefford. 2003. "Teaching People to Fish? Building the Evaluation Capability of Public Sector Organizations." *Evaluation* 9(1):9–29.

McGarvey, Craig. 2007. *Participatory Action Research*. New York: GrantCraft, Ford Foundation.

———. 2006. *Making Measures Work for You: Outcomes and Evaluation*. New York: GrantCraft, Ford Foundation. http://www.grantcraft.org/index.cfm?fuseaction=Page.viewPage&pageID=835.

McIntosh, Winsome. 1996. "Process or Outcomes? Keep the Context Long-Term." *Foundation*, March/April, pp. 46–48.

McIntyre, Ken. 1976. "Evaluating Educational Programs." *Review* (University Council for Educational Administration) 18(1):39.

McKegg, Kate. 2003. "From Margins to Mainstream: The Importance of People and Context in Evaluation Utilisation." Pp. 214–34 in *Evaluating Policy and Practice: A New Zealand Reader*, edited by Neil Lunt, Carl Davidson, and Kate McKegg. Auckland, New Zealand: Pearson Prentice Hall.

McLaughlin, John A., Larry J. Weber, Robert W. Covert, and Robert B. Ingle, eds. 1988. *Evaluation Utilization. New Directions for Program Evaluation*, No. 39.

McLaughlin, Milbrey. 1976. "Implementation as Mutual Adaption." Pp. 167–80 in *Social Program Implementation*, edited by Walter Williams and Richard F. Elmore. New York: Academic Press.

McTavish, Donald, E. Brent, J. Cleary, and K. R. Knudsen. 1975. *The Systematic Assessment and Prediction of Research Methodology*, Vol. 1, Advisory Report. Final Report on Grant OEO 005-P-20–2–74, Minnesota Continuing Program for the Assessment and Improvement of Research. Minneapolis, MN: University of Minnesota.

Menand, Louis. 2006. "Breaking Away." *The New Yorker*, LXXXII, March 27, pp. 82–84.

Mendelow, Aubrey L. 1987. "Stakeholder Analysis for Strategic Planning and Implementation." Pp. 176–91 in *Strategic Planning and Management Handbook*, edited by W. R. King and D. I. Cleland. New York: Van Nostrand Reinhold.

Mertens, Donna M. 2007. *Transformative Research and Evaluation*. New York: Guilford Press.

_____. 2005. "Inclusive Evaluation." Pp. 195–98 in *Encyclopedia of Evaluation*, S. Mathison. Thousand Oaks, CA: Sage.

Meyers, William R. 1981. *The Evaluation Enterprise*. San Francisco, CA: Jossey-Bass.

Miall, Hugh, Oliver Ramsbotham, and Tom Woodhouse. 2005. *Contemporary Conflict Resolution: The Prevention, Management and Transformation of Deadly Conflicts*. Boston, MA: Blackwell.

Michalski and Cousins. 2001. "Multiple Perspectives on Training Evaluation: Probing Stakeholder Perceptions in a Global Network Development Firm." *American Journal of Evaluation* 22(1):37–54.

Mickwitz, Per. 2006. *Environmental Policy Evaluation: Concepts and Practice*. Helsinki, Finland: Finnish Society of Sciences and Letters.

Miller, D. E. 1981. *The Book of Jargon*. New York: Macmillan.

Miller, Katherine. 2005. *Organizational Communication: Approaches and Processes*. Belmont, CA: Wadsworth.

Miller, Robin Lin and Rebecca Campbell. 2006. "Taking Stock of Empowerment Evaluation: An Empirical Review." *American Journal of Evaluation* 27(3):296–319.

Millett, Ricardo A. 1996. "Empowerment Evaluation and the W. K. Kellogg Foundation." Pp. 65–76 in *Empowerment Evaluation: Knowledge and Tools for Self-Assessment and Accountability*, edited by D. M. Fetterman, A. J. Kaftarian, and A. Wandersman. Thousand Oaks, CA: Sage.

Mills, C. Wright. 1961. *The Sociological Imagination*. New York: Grove.

_____. 1959. *The Sociological Imagination*. New York: Oxford University Press.

Minnich, Elizabeth K. 1990. *Transforming Knowledge*. Philadelphia, PA: Temple University Press.

Minoff, Elisa. 2005. *The UK Commitment: Ending Child Poverty by 2020*. Washington, DC: Center for Economic and Social Policy. http://www.clasp.org/publications/uk_childpoverty.pdf.

Mintzberg, Henry. 2007. *Tracking Strategies*. New York: Oxford University Press.

_____. 1996. "Managing Government, Governing Management." *Harvard Business Review* 72(5):75–83.

Moe, Barbara L. 1993. "The Human Side of Evaluation: Using the Results." Pp. 19–31 in *A Vision of Evaluation*, edited by Sandra Trice Gray. Washington, DC: Independent Sector.

Mohan, Rakesh and Kathleen Sullivan, eds. 2007. *Promoting the Use of Government Evaluations in Policymaking. New Directions for Evaluation*, No. 113.

Mohan, Rakesh, Minakshi Tikoo, Stanley Capela, and David J. Bernstein. 2007. "Increasing Evaluation Use among Policymakers through Performance Measurement." *Promoting the Use of Government Evaluations in Policymaking. New Directions for Evaluation* 113:89–98.

Mohan, Rakesh, David J. Bernstein, and Maria D. Whitsett, eds. 2002. *Responding to Sponsors and Stakeholders in Complex Evaluation Environments. New Directions for Evaluation*, No. 95.

Moos, Rudolf H. 1997. *Evaluating Treatment Environments: The Quality of Psychiatric and Substance Abuse Programs*. 2d ed. Somerset, NJ: Transaction.

_____. 1985. *The Human Context: Environmental Determinants of Behavior.* Melbourne, FL: Krieger.

Morabito, Stephen M. 2002. "Evaluator Roles and Strategies for Expanding Evaluation Process Influence." *American Journal of Evaluation* 23(3):321–30.

Morgan, David. 2007. "Paradigms Lost and Pragmatism Regained: Methodological Implications of Combining Qualitative and Quantitative Methods." *Journal of Mixed Methods Research* 1(1):48–76.

Morell, Jonathan A. Forthcoming. *Evaluating in the Face of Uncertainty: Anticipation and Agility to Improve Evaluation Quality.* New York: Guilford Press.

_____. 2005. "Complex Adaptive Systems." Pp. 71–72 in *Encyclopedia of Evaluation,* edited by S. Mathison. Thousand Oaks, CA: Sage.

Morris, Daniel. 2002. "The Inclusion of Stakeholders in Evaluation: Benefits and Drawbacks." *The Canadian Journal of Evaluation* 17(2):49–58.

Morris, Lynn Lyons and Carol Taylor Fitz-Gibbon. 1978. *How to Deal with Goals and Objectives.* Beverly Hills, CA: Sage.

Morris, Michael. 2005. "Ethics." Pp. 131–34 in *Encyclopedia of Evaluation,* edited by S. Mathison. Thousand Oaks, CA: Sage.

Mowbray, Carol T. 1994. "The Gradual Extinction of Evaluation within a Government Agency." *Preventing the Misuse of Evaluation. New Directions for Program Evaluation* 64:33–48.

Mowbray, Carol, Mark Holter, Gregory Teague, and Deborah Bybee. 2003. "Fidelity Criteria: Development, Measurement, and Validation." *American Journal of Evaluation* 24(3):315–40.

Moynihan, Donald P. 2006. "Managing for Results in State Government: Evaluating a Decade of Reform. *Public Administration Review* 66(1):77–89.

Mueller, Marsha. 1996. *Immediate Outcomes of Lower-Income Participants in Minnesota's Universal Access Early Childhood Family Education Program.* Saint Paul, MN: Department of Children, Families and Learning.

Muñoz, Marco. 2005. *Black Box.* Pp. 34–35 in *Encyclopedia of Evaluation,* edited by S. Mathison. Thousand Oaks, CA: Sage.

Murphy, Jerome. 1976. "Title V of ESEA: The Impact of Discretionary Funds on State Education Bureaucracies." Pp. 77–100 in Walter Williams and Richard Elmore (eds.), *Social Program Implementation.* New York: Academic Press.

Nagao, Masafumi. 1995. "Evaluating Global Issues in a Community Setting." Keynote address, Evaluation '95, International Evaluation Conference, November 3, Vancouver, BC, Canada.

Nagel, Ernest. 1961. *The Structure of Science.* New York: Harcourt Brace Jovanovich.

Nance, Earthea. 2005. "Multistakeholder Evaluation of Condominial Sewer Services." *American Journal of Evaluation* 26(4):480–500.

National Academy of Sciences. 1968. *The Behavioral Sciences and the Federal Government.* Washington, DC: Government Printing Office.

Newcomer, Kathryn, ed. 1997. *Using Performance Measurement to Improve Public and Nonprofit Programs. New Directions for Evaluation,* No. 75.

Newcomer, Kathryn, Harry Hatry, and Joseph Wholey, eds. 2004. *Handbook of Practical Program Evaluation.* 2d ed. San Francisco, CA: Jossey-Bass.

Newman, Dianna and Robert Brown. 1996. *Applied Ethics for Program Evaluation.* Thousand Oaks, CA: Sage.

New York Times. 1996. "Educators Show How Not to Write English," Editorial distributed by *New York Times* News Service and published in the *Minneapolis Star Tribune,* March 24, p. A24.

Nicholson-Crotty, Sean, Nick A. Theobald, and Jill Nicholson-Crotty. 2006. "Disparate Measures: Public Managers and Performance-Measurement Strategies." *Public Administration Review* 66(1): 101–13.

Nickols, Fred. 2003. *The Goals Grid: A Tool for Clarifying Goals & Objectives: A Paper in the Solution Engineering Series.* Distance Consulting. http://home.att.net/~OPSINC/goals_grid.pdf.

Nolan, Marie and Victoria Mock. 2005. *Measuring Patient Outcomes.* Thousand Oaks, CA: Sage.

Northwest Regional Educational Laboratory (NWREL). 1977. *3-on-2 Evaluation Report,* 1976–1977, Vols. 1–3. Portland, OR: NWREL.

Norwegian Agency for Development Cooperation (NORAD). 1999. *Logical Framework Approach: Handbook for Objectives-Oriented Planning.* Oslo, Norway: NORAD. http://www.norad.no/default.asp?V_ITEM_ID=1069.

Nowakowski, Jeri, ed. 1987. *The Client Perspective on Evaluation. New Directions for Program Evaluation,* No. 36.

Nunnally, Jim C., Jr. 1970. *Introduction to Psychological Measurement.* New York: McGraw-Hill.

Nutt, Paul. 2002. *Why Decisions Fail: Avoiding the Blunders and Traps That Lead to Debacles.* San Francisco, CA: Berrett-Koehler.

Odiorne, George S. 1984. *Strategic Management of Human Resources.* San Francisco, CA: Jossey-Bass.

Office of Program Analysis, General Accounting Office (GAO). 1976. *Federal Program Evaluations: A Directory for the Congress.* Washington, DC: Government Printing Office.

Office on Smoking and Health. 2007. *Introduction to Process Evaluation in Tobacco Use Prevention and Control.* Atlanta, GA: Centers for Disease Control.

Organisation for Economic Co-operation and Development (OECD). 2006. *Guidance for Managing Joint Evaluations.* Paris: OECD. http://www.oecd.org/site/0,2865, en_21571361_34047972_1_1_1_1_1,00.html.

Orthner, Dennis, Patricia Cook, Yekutiel Sabah, and Jona Rosenfeld. 2006. "Organizational Learning: A Cross-national Pilot-test of Effectiveness in Children's Services. *Evaluation and Program Planning* 29:70–78.

Osborne, David and Ted Gaebler. 1992. *Reinventing Government: How the Entrepreneurial Spirit Is Transforming the Public Sector from Schoolhouse to Statehouse, City Hall to the Pentagon.* Reading, MA: Addison-Wesley.

Owen, John. 2007. "Making Public Interventions More Effective: The Case for Accountability Up and Accountability Down." Pp. 181–92 in *Making Accountability Work: Dilemmas for Evaluation and for Audit,* edited by Bemelmans-Videc, Marie-Louise, Jeremy Lonsdale, and Burt Perrin. London: Transaction Books.

Owen, John. 2005. "Learning Organization." Pp. 225–26 in *Encyclopedia of Evaluation,* edited by S. Mathison. Thousand Oaks, CA: Sage.

Owen, John with Patricia Rogers. 1999. *Program Evaluation: Forms and Approaches.* New South Wales, Australia: Allen and Unwin.

Owens, Thomas. 1973. "Education Evaluation by Adversary Proceeding." In *School Evaluation: The Politics and Process,* edited by Ernest R. House. Berkeley, CA: McCutchan.

PACT. 1986. *Participatory Evaluation: A User's Guide.* New York: Private Agencies Collaborating Together.

Pandolfini, Bruce. 1998. *The Winning Way: The How What and Why of Opening Strategems.* Palmer, AK: Fireside.

Parker, Glenn M., David Zielinski, and Jerry McAdams. 2000. *Rewarding Teams: Lessons from the Trenches.* San Francisco, CA: Jossey-Bass.

Parker, Richard. 2006. *John Kenneth Galbraith: His Life, His Politics, His Economics.* Chicago, IL: University of Chicago Press.

Parlett, Malcolm and David Hamilton. 1976. "Evaluation as Illumination: A New Approach to the Study of Innovatory Programs." Pp. 140–57 in *Evaluation Studies Review Annual,* Vol. 1, edited by Gene V. Glass. Beverly Hills, CA: Sage.

Pasquie, Martial and Jean-Patrick Villeneuve. 2007. "Organizational Barriers to Transparency: A Typology and Analysis of Organizational Behaviour Tending to Prevent or Restrict Access to Information." *International Review of Administrative Sciences* 73(1):147–62.

Patton, Michael Quinn. 2008. "Advocacy Impact Evaluation." *Journal of Multi-Disciplinary Evaluation* 5(9):1–10.

_____. 2007. "Process Use as a Usefulism." *New Directions for Evaluation* 116:99–112.

_____. 2006. "Too Much of a Good Thing: Overuse and Mechanical Use." Keynote address, Minnesota Evaluation Studies Institute, March 22, Minneapolis, MN.

_____. 2005a. "Developmental Evaluation." P. 116 in *Encyclopedia of Evaluation,* edited by S. Mathison. Thousand Oaks, CA: Sage.

_____. 2005b. "Misuse of Evaluations." Pp. 254–55 in *Encyclopedia of Evaluation*, edited by S. Mathison. Thousand Oaks, CA: Sage.

_____. 2004. "A Microcosm of the Global Challenges Facing the Field: Commentary on HIV/AIDS Monitoring & Evaluation." *HIV/AIDS Monitoring and Evaluation. New Directions for Evaluation* 103:163–71.

_____. 2003. "Distant Echoes of a Strong Voice: Reflections on Margaret Mead's Evaluation of the Salzberg Seminar in 1946." *American Journal of Evaluation* 24(1):123–31.

_____. 2002a. *Qualitative Research and Evaluation Methods*. 3d ed. Thousand Oaks, CA: Sage.

_____. 2002b. "Teaching and Training with Metaphors." *American Journal of Evaluation* 23(1):93–100.

_____. 2002c. "A Vision of Evaluation That Strengthens Democracy." *Evaluation* 8(1):125–39.

_____. 2001. "Evaluation, Knowledge Management, Best Practices, and High-Quality Lessons Learned." *American Journal of Evaluation* 22(3):329–36.

_____. 2000. "Language Matters." *How and Why language Matters in Evaluation. New Directions for Evaluation* 86:5–16.

_____. 1999a. *Grand Canyon Celebration: A Father-Son Journey of Discovery*. Amherst, NY: Prometheus Books.

_____. 1999b. "Organizational Development and Evaluation." *Canadian Journal of Program Evaluation*, Special Issue:93–113.

_____. 1999c. "Some Framing Questions about Racism and Evaluation." *American Journal of Evaluation* 20(3):437–44.

_____. 1998. "Discovering Process Use." *Evaluation* 4(2):225–33.

_____. 1996. "A World Larger Than Formative and Summative." *Evaluation Practice* 17(Spring-Summer):131–43.

_____. 1994a. "Developmental Evaluation." *Evaluation Practice* 15(3):311–20.

_____. 1994b. "The Program Evaluation Standards Reviewed." *Evaluation Practice* 15(2):193–99.

_____. 1989. "A Context and Boundaries for a Theory-Driven Approach to Validity." *Evaluation and Program Planning* 12(4):375–78.

_____. 1988a. "The Evaluator's Responsibility for Utilization." *Evaluation Practice* 9(1):5–24. Reprinted pp. 185–202 in *Debates on Evaluation*, edited by Marvin Alkin. Newbury Park, CA: Sage, 1990.

_____. 1988b. "Integrating Evaluation into a Program for Increased Utility and Cost-Effectiveness." *Evaluation Utilization. New Directions in Program Evaluation* 39:85–95.

_____. 1986. *Utilization-Focused Evaluation*. 2d ed. Beverly Hills, CA: Sage.

_____, ed. 1985. *Culture and Evaluation*. San Francisco, CA: Jossey-Bass.

_____. 1982a. *Practical Evaluation*. Beverly Hills, CA: Sage.

_____. 1982b. "Managing Management Information Systems." Pp. 227–39 in *Practical Evaluation*, edited by M. Q. Patton. Beverly Hills, CA: Sage.

_____. 1981. *Creative Evaluation*. Beverly Hills, CA: Sage.

_____. 1980. *The Process and Outcomes of Chemical Dependency*. Center City, MN: Hazelden Foundation.

_____. 1978. *Utilization-Focused Evaluation*. Beverly Hills, CA: Sage.

_____. 1975a. *Alternative Evaluation Research Paradigm*. Grand Forks, ND: University of North Dakota.

_____. 1975b. "Understanding the Gobbledy Gook: A People's Guide to Standardized Test Results and Statistics." Pp. 18–26 in *Testing and Evaluation: New Views*. Washington, DC: Association for Childhood Education International.

Patton, Michael Q., John Bare, and Deborah Bonnet. 2004. "Foundation-Grantee Relationships and the Role of Evaluation." Pp. 76–95 in *Foundations and Evaluation: Contexts and Practices for Effective Philanthropy*, edited by Marc Braverman, Norm Constantine, and Jana Kay Slater. San Francisco, CA: Jossey-Bass.

Patton, Michael Quinn and Masafumi Nagao. 2000. *Utilization-Focused Evaluation* (in Japanese). Tokyo, Japan: G.PAM Communication.

Patton, Michael Q. with M. Bringewatt, J. Campbell, T. Dewar, and M. Mueller. 1993. *The McKnight Foundation Aid to Families in Poverty Initiative: A Synthesis of Themes, Patterns, and Lessons*

Learned. Minneapolis, MN: McKnight Foundation.

Patton, Michael Q., Patricia S. Grimes, Kathryn M. Guthrie, Nancy J. Brennan, Barbara D. French, and Dale A. Blyth. 1977. "In Search of Impact: An Analysis of the Utilization of Federal Health Evaluation Research." Pp. 141–64 in *Using Social Research in Public Policy Making*, edited by Carol H. Weiss. Lexington, MA: D. C. Heath.

Patton, Michael Q., Kathy Guthrie, Steven Gray, Carl Hearle, Rich Wiseman, and Neala Yount. 1977. *Environments That Make a Difference: An Evaluation of Ramsey County Corrections Foster Group Homes.* Minneapolis: Minnesota Center for Social Research, University of Minnesota.

Pawson, Ray. 2002a. "Evidence-Based Policy: In Search of a Method." *Evaluation* 8(2):157–81.

_____. 2002b. "Evidence-Based policy: The Promise of 'Realist Synthesis'." *Evaluation* 8(3):340–58.

Pawson, Ray and Nick Tilley. 2005. "Realistic Evaluation." Pp. 362–67 in *Encyclopedia of Evaluation*, edited by S. Mathison. Thousand Oaks, CA: Sage.

_____. 1997. *Realistic Evaluation.* Thousand Oaks, CA: Sage.

Peale, Norman Vincent. 1952. *The Power of Positive Thinking.* Englewood Cliffs, NJ: Prentice Hall.

Peltz, Michael. 1999. "Winner's Choice." *WORTH*, February, 8(2):103–105.

Perlman, Ellen. 1996. "Sirens That Repel." *Governing*, April, pp. 37–42.

Perrin, Burt. 2007. "Towards a New View of Accountability." Pp. 41–62 in *Making Accountability Work: Dilemmas for Evaluation and for Audit*, edited by Bemelmans-Videc, Marie-Louise, Jeremy Lonsdale, and Burt Perrin. London: Transaction Books.

_____. 2002. "Towards a New View of Accountability." Paper presented to the European Evaluation Society annual conference, Seville, Spain, October 11.

_____. 1998. "Effective Use and Misuse of Performance Measurement." *American Journal of Evaluation* 19(3):367–79.

Perrone, Vito, Michael Q. Patton, and Barbara French. 1976. *Does Accountability Count without Teacher Support?* Minneapolis: Minnesota Center for Social Research, University of Minnesota.

Perrow, Charles. 1970. *Organizational Analysis: A Sociological View.* Belmont, CA: Wadsworth.

_____. 1968. "Organizational Goals." Pp. 305–11 in *International Encyclopedia of Social Sciences.* New York: Macmillan.

Perry, Ron, Bob Thomas, Elizabeth DuBois, and Rob McGowan. 2007. "A Utilization-Focused Approach to Evaluation by a Performance Audit Agency." *Promoting the Use of Government Evaluations in Policymaking. New Directions for Evaluation* 113:67–78.

Peters, Tom. 1996. *Liberation Management.* New York: Ballentine Books.

Petrie, Hugh G. 1972. "Theories Are Tested by Observing the Facts: Or Are They?" Pp. 47–73 in *Philosophical Redirection of Educational Research: The Seventy-First Yearbook of the National Society for the Study of Education*, edited by Lawrence G. Thomas. Chicago, IL: University of Chicago Press.

Petticrew, M. and H. Roberts. 2003. "Evidence, Hierarchies, and Typologies: Horses for Courses." *Journal of Epidemiology and Community Health* 57:527–29.

Peyser, Mark. 2006. "Truthiness." *Newsweek.* February 13. http://www.msnbc.msn.com/id/11182033/site/newsweek.

Picciotto, Robert. 2007. "The New Environment for Development." *American Journal of Evaluation* 28(4):509–21.

Plutarch. 2001. "Alexander." Pp. 139–198 in *Plutarch's Lives: The Lives of the Noble Grecians and Romans, Great Books of the Western World*, Vol. 2. New York: Modern Library.

Podems, Donna Rae. 2007. "Process Use: A Case Narrative from Southern Africa." *New Directions for Evaluation* 116:87–98.

_____. 2005. *Nonprofit Evaluation in South Africa: A Study of Relationships between the Donor and Nonprofit Organization in the Developing World.* Ph.D. dissertation, Union Institute & University, Cincinnati, OH.

Poister, Theodore. 2004. "Performance Monitoring." Pp. 98–125 in *Handbook of Practical Program Evaluation*, edited by Wholey, Hatry, and Newcomer. San Francisco, CA: Jossey-Bass.

Popham, James W. 1995. "An Extinction-Retardation Strategy for Educational Evaluators." *Evaluation Practice* 16(3):267–74.

Popham, James W. and Dale Carlson. 1977. "Deep Dark Deficits of the Adversary Evaluation Model." *Educational Researcher,* June, pp. 3–6.

Posavac, Emil. J. 1994. "Misusing Program Evaluation by Asking the Wrong Questions." *Preventing the Misuse of Evaluation. New Directions for Program Evaluation* 64:69–78.

Powell, Arthur B., Dawud A. Jeffries, and Aleshia E. Selby. 1989. "Participatory Research: Empowering Students and Teachers and Humanizing Mathematics." *Humanistic Mathematics Network Newsletter* 4:29–38.

Preskill, Hallie. 2007. "Evaluation's Second Act: A Spotlight on Learning." Presidential Address, 21st annual conference of the American Evaluation Association, Baltimore, MD, November 8, 2007.

———. 2005a. "Appreciative Inquiry." Pp. 18–19 in *Encyclopedia of Evaluation,* edited by S. Mathison. Thousand Oaks, CA: Sage.

———. 2005b. "Process Use." Pp. 327–28 in *Encyclopedia of Evaluation,* edited by S. Mathison. Thousand Oaks, CA: Sage.

Preskill, Hallie and Darlene Russ-Eft. 2005. *Building Evaluation Capacity: 72 Activities for Teaching and Training.* Thousand Oaks, CA: Sage

Preskill, Hallie, Barbra Zuckerman, and Bonya Matthews. 2003. "An Exploratory Study of Process Use: Findings and Implications for Future Research." *American Journal of Evaluation* 24(4):423–42.

Preskill, Hallie and Rosalie Torres. 1999. *Evaluative Inquiry for Learning in Organizations.* Thousand Oaks, CA: Sage.

Preskill, Hallie and Valerie Caracelli. 1997. "Current and Developing Conceptions of Use: Evaluation Use TIG Survey Results." *American Journal of Evaluation* 18(3):209–26.

Pressman, Jeffrey L. and Aaron Wildavsky. 1984. *Implementation.* Berkeley, CA: University of California Press.

Pritchett, Price. 1996. *Resistance: Moving Beyond the Barriers to Change.* Dallas, TX: Pritchett and Associates.

Programme for Strengthening the Regional Capacity for Monitoring & Evaluation of IFAD's Rural Poverty Alleviation Projects in Latin America and the Caribbean (PREVAL). 2006. *Participatory Process Facilitation.* Quarterly Electronic Bulletin, PREVAL, July-September Newsletter. http://www.preval.org/newsletter/index.php?boletin=82.

Provus, Malcolm. 1971. *Discrepancy Evaluation for Educational Program Improvement and Assessment.* Berkeley, CA: McCutchan.

Radin, Beryl. 2006. *Challenging the Performance Movement: Accountability, Complexity, and Democratic Values.* Washington, DC: Georgetown University Press.

Rafter, David O. 1984. "Three Approaches to Evaluation Research." *Knowledge: Creation, Diffusion, Utilization* 6(2):165–85.

Ragin, Charles. 2000. *Fuzzy-Set Social Science.* Chicago, IL: University of Chicago Press.

Reichardt, Charles S. and Thomas D. Cook. 1979. "Beyond Qualitative Versus Quantitative Methods." Pp. 7–32 in *Qualitative and Quantitative Methods,* edited by T. Cook and C. S. Reichardt. Beverly Hills, CA: Sage.

Reichardt, Charles S. and Sharon F. Rallis, eds. 1994a. *The Qualitative-Quantitative Debate: New Perspectives. New Directions for Program Evaluation,* No. 61.

———. 1994b. "The Relationship between the Qualitative and Quantitative Research Traditions." *The Qualitative-Quantitative Debate: New Perspectives. New Directions for Program Evaluation* 61:5–12.

———. 1994c. "Qualitative and Quantitative Inquiries Are Not Incompatible: A Call for a New Partnership." *The Qualitative-Quantitative Debate: New Perspectives. New Directions for Program Evaluation* 61:85–91.

Reicken, Henry W. and Robert F. Boruch. 1974. *Social Experimentation: A Method for Planning and Evaluating Social Intervention.* New York: Academic Press.

Renger, Ralph. 2006. "Consequences to Federal Programs When the Logic-Modeling Process Is Not Followed with

Fidelity." *American Journal of Evaluation* 27(4):452–63.

Resnick, Michael. 1984. "Teen Sex: How Girls Decide." *Update-Research Briefs* (University of Minnesota) 11(5):15.

Reuters News. 2007. *New Museum Says Dinosaurs Were on Noah's Ark.* May 26. http://uk.reuters.com/article/scienceNews/idUKN2621240720070526.

Richardson, Kurt, Jeffrey Goldstein, Peter Allen, and David Snowden, eds. 2005. *E:CO Annual, Vol. 6. Emergence, Complexity and Organization.* Mansfield, OH: ISCE Publishing.

Ridde, Valéry. 2007a. Equity and Health Policy Implementation in Burkina Faso. Paris, France: L'Harmattan.

————. 2007b. "The Equity and Health Policy Implementation Gap in Burkina Faso." *Social Science & Medicine* 20:1–11.

————. 2006. "Le Magicien Du Temps: Approche Participative Axée sur le Développement d'un Projet et L'utilisation des Résultats d'une Évaluation." *Canadian Journal of Program Evaluation* 21(3): 235–55.

————. 2005. "Evaluation Practice around the World: Afghanistan." Pp. 433–34 in *Encyclopedia of Evaluation*, edited by S. Mathison. Thousand Oaks, CA: Sage.

Ridde, Valéry and C. Dagenais, eds. 2007. *Théories et pratiques en évaluation de programme—Manuel d'enseignement.* Montreal, Canada: Les Presses de l'Université de Montréal.

Rippey, R. M. 1973. "The Nature of Transactional Evaluation." Pp. 1–16 in *Studies in Transactional Evaluation*, edited by R. M. Rippey. Berkeley, CA: McCutchan.

Rist, Ray C. 2006a. "The 'E' in Monitoring and Evaluation: Using Evaluative Knowledge to Support a Results-Based Management System." Pp. 3–22 in *From Studies to Streams: Managing Evaluative Systems*, edited by Ray C. Rist and Nicoletta Stame. New Brunswick, NJ: Transaction Books.

————. 2006b. "Conclusion: A Brief Critique." Pp. 283–86 in *From Studies to Streams: Managing Evaluative Systems*, edited by Ray C. Rist and Nicoletta Stame. New Brunswick, NJ: Transaction Books.

————. 1977. "On the Relations among Educational Research Paradigms: From Disdain to Detente." *Anthropology and Education* 8:42–49.

Rist, Ray C. and Nicoletta Stame, eds. 2006. *From Studies to Streams: Managing Evaluative Systems.* New Brunswick, NJ: Transaction Books.

Rizo, Felipe M. 1991. "The Controversy about Quantification in Social Research." *Educational Researcher* 20(9):9–12.

Rog, Debra J. 1985. "A Methodological Assessment of Evaluability Assessment." Ph.D. dissertation, Vanderbilt University, Nashville, TN.

Rogers, Everett. 2003. *Diffusion of Innovation.* 5th ed. New York: Free Press.

Rogers, Everett M. and Floyd F. Shoemaker. 1971. *Communication of Innovation.* New York: Free Press.

Rogers, Patricia J. Forthcoming. *Because: Evidence for Whether, How, and Why.*

————. 2008. "Using Programme Theory for Complicated and Complex Programmes." *Evaluation*, 14(1):29–48.

————. 2007. "Theory-Based Evaluation: Reflections Ten Years On." *New Directions for Evaluation* 114:63–67.

————. 2006. "Monitoring for Results-Based Management: Emergent Approach or Outdated Technology?" Paper presented with Jerome A. Winston at the joint conference of the European Evaluation Society and the United Kingdom Evaluation Society, October 2006, London.

————. 2005a. "Accountability." Pp. 2–4 in *Encyclopedia of Evaluation*, edited by S. Mathison. Thousand Oaks, CA: Sage.

————. 2005b. "Logic Model." Pp. 232–35 in *Encyclopedia of Evaluation*, edited by S. Mathison. Thousand Oaks, CA: Sage.

————. 2005c. "Program Logic." Pp. 339–40 in *Encyclopedia of Evaluation*, edited by S. Mathison. Thousand Oaks, CA: Sage.

————. 2003. "Reflections on Learning about Australasian Evaluation Theory and Practice." *Evaluation Journal of Australasia* 2(1):30–34.

————. 2001. "The Whole World Is Evaluating Half-Full Glasses." *American Journal of Evaluation* 22(3):431–35.

_____. 2000a. "Causal Models in Program Theory Evaluation: Challenges and Opportunities." *Program Theory in Evaluation: Challenges and Opportunities. New Directions for Evaluation* 87:47–55.

_____. 2000b. "Program Theory Evaluation: Not Whether Programs Work But How They Work. Pp. 209–32 in *Evaluation Models*, edited by G. Madaus, D. Stufflebeam, and T. Kellaghan. New York: Kluwer Press.

Rogers, Patricia and Bob Williams. 2006. "Evaluation for Practice Improvement and Organizational Learning." Pp. 76–97 in *Handbook of Evaluation*, edited by I. Shaw, J. Greene, and M. Mark. Thousand Oaks, CA: Sage.

Rogers, Patricia, Timothy Hacsi, Anthony Petrosino, and Tracy Huebner, eds. 2000. *Program Theory Evaluation: Challenges and Opportunities. New Directions in Evaluation*, No. 87.

Rosen, Laura, Orly Manor, Dan Engelhard, and David Zucker. 2006. "In Defense of the Randomized Controlled Trial for Health Promotion Research." *American Journal of Public Health* 96:1181–86. http://www.ajph.org/cgi/content/abstract/AJPH.2004.061713v1?papetoc.

Rosenström, Ulla, Per Mickwitz, and Matti Melanen. 2006. "Participation and Empowerment-Based Development of Socio-Cultural Indicators Supporting Regional Decision-Making for Eco-Efficiency." *Local Environment* 11(2):183–200.

Rossi, Peter. 2004. "My Views of Evaluation and Their Origins." Pp. 122–31 in *Evaluation Roots: Tracing Theorists' Views and Influences*, edited by M. Alkin. Thousand Oaks, CA: Sage.

_____. 1994. "The War between the Quals and the Quants: Is a Lasting Peace Possible?" *The Qualitative-Quantitative Debate: New Perspectives. New Directions for Program Evaluation* 61:23–36.

_____. 1987. "The Iron Law of Evaluation and Other Metallic Rules." *Research in Social Problems* 4:3–20.

_____. 1972. "Testing for Success and Failure in Social Action." Pp. 11–65 in *Evaluating Social Programs*, edited by Peter H. Rossi and Walter Williams. New York: Seminar Press.

Rossi, Peter, Mark Lipsey, and Howard Freeman. 2003. *Evaluation: A Systematic Approach*. 7th ed. Thousand Oaks, CA: Sage.

Rossi, Peter H. and H. E. Freeman. 1993. *Evaluation: A Systematic Approach*. 5th ed. Newbury Park, CA: Sage.

Rossi, Peter H., Howard E. Freeman, and Sonia R. Wright. 1979. *Evaluation: A Systematic Approach*. Beverly Hills, CA: Sage.

Rossi, Peter H. and Walter Williams, eds. 1972. *Evaluating Social Programs: Theory, Practice, and Politics*. New York: Seminar Press.

Rothschild, Steve. Forthcoming. *Principle-Driven Change*.

Rothwell, William J. and Roland Sullivan. 2005. *Practicing Organization Development: A Guide for Consultants*. Hoboken, NJ: Pfeiffer.

Royal Statistical Society Working Party on Performance Monitoring in the Public Services. 2003. *Performance Indicators: Good, Bad, and Ugly*. London: Royal Statistical Society. http://www.rss.org.uk/main.asp?page=1222.

Russ-Eft, Darlene. 2005. "Questions, Evaluation." P. 355 in *Encyclopedia of Evaluation*, edited by S. Mathison. Thousand Oaks, CA: Sage.

Russ-Eft, Darlene, Regina Atwood, and Tori Egherman. 2002. "Use and Non-Use of Evaluation Results: Case Study of Environmental Influences in the Private Sector." *American Journal of Evaluation* 23(1):19–31.

Russon, Craig. 2005. "Cluster Evaluation." Pp. 66–67 in *Encyclopedia of Evaluation*, edited by S. Mathison. Thousand Oaks, CA: Sage.

Russon, Craig and Gabrielle Russon, eds. 2004. *International Perspectives on Evaluation Standards. New Directions for Evaluation*, No. 104.

Russon, Craig and Timothy Ryback. 2003. "Margaret Mead's Evaluation of the First Salzberg Seminar." *American Journal of Evaluation* 24(1):97–114.

Rutman, Leonard. 1977. "Barriers to the Utilization of Evaluation Research." Presented at the 27th Annual Meeting of the Society for the Study of Social Problems, Chicago, IL.

Ryan, Katherine and Lizanne DeStefano, eds. 2000. *Evaluation as a Democratic Process: Promoting Inclusion, Dialogue, and Deliberation. New Directions for Evaluation*, No. 85.

Safire, William. 2007. "Halfway Humanity," On Language. *New York Times Sunday Magazine*, May 6. http://www.nytimes.com/2007/05/06/magazine/06wwln-safire-t.html.

_____. 2006. "On Language: Bridge to Nowhere." *New York Times Sunday Magazine*, October 8. http://www.nytimes.com/2006/10/08/magazine/08wwln_safire.html.

Salmen, Lawrence and Eileen Kane. 2006. *Bridging Diversity: Participatory Learning for Responsive Development*. Washington, DC: World Bank.

Sanders, James. 2007. "Evaluation." Pp. 1498–501 in *The Blackwell Encyclopedia of Sociology*, edited by George Ritzer. Boston, MA: Blackwell.

_____. 2002. "Presidential Address: On Mainstreaming Evaluation." *American Journal of Evaluation* 23(3):253–73.

_____. 1997. "Cluster Evaluation." Pp. 396–404 in *Evaluation for the 21st Century*, edited by Eleanor Chelimsky and Will Shadish. Thousand Oaks, CA: Sage.

Sartorius, Rolf H. 1996. "Third Generation Logical Framework." *European Journal of Agricultural Education and Extension*, March. Unpublished manuscript.

_____. 1991. "The Logical Framework Approach to Project Design and Management." *Evaluation Practice* 12(2):139–47.

Saxe, Leonard and Daniel Koretz, eds. 1982. *Making Evaluation Research Useful to Congress*. San Francisco, CA: Jossey-Bass.

Schatschneider, Christopher. 2003. *Research Designs That Assess Effectiveness*. Presentation at the preapplication meeting for the Interagency Education Research Initiative (IERI), Institute of Education Sciences, February 21. Washington, DC: U.S. Department of Education.

Schein, Edgar H. 1985. *Organizational Culture and Leadership*. San Francisco, CA: Jossey-Bass.

Schein, L. 1989. *A Manager's Guide to Corporate Culture*. New York: Conference Board.

Schemo, Diana Jean. 2007. "War over Teaching Reading." *New York Times*, March 9. http://www.nytimes.com/2007/03/09/education/09reading.html?ex=1174708800&en=2cbb6a85da135c47&ei=5070.

Schön, Donald A. 1987. *Educating the Reflective Practitioner*. San Francisco, CA: Jossey-Bass.

_____. 1983. *The Reflective Practitioner*. New York: Basic Books.

Schorr, Lisbeth. 1998. *Common Purpose: Strengthening Families and Neighborhoods to Rebuild America*. New York: Anchor Books.

_____. 1988. *Within Our Reach: Breaking the Cycle of Disadvantage*. New York: Doubleday.

Schwandt, Thomas A. 2008. *The Relevance of Practical Knowledge Traditions to Evaluation Practice*. Pp. 29–40 in *Fundamental Issues in Evaluation*, edited by N. L. Smith and P. R. Brandon. New York: Guilford Press.

_____. 2007a. "Judging Interpretations." *New Directions for Evaluation* 114:11–14.

_____. 2007b. "Thoughts on Using the Notion of Evidence in the Controversy over Methods Choices." *Informing Federal Policies on Evaluation Methodology: Building the Evidence Base for Method Choice in Government Sponsored Evaluation. New Directions for Program Evaluation* 113:115–23.

_____. 2002. *Evaluation Practice Reconsidered*. New York: Peter Lang.

_____. 1989a. "The Politics of Verifying Trustworthiness in Evaluation Auditing." *Evaluation Practice* 10(4):33–40.

_____. 1989b. "Recapturing Moral Discourse in Evaluation." *Educational Researcher* 19(8):11–16.

Schwandt, T. A. and E. S. Halpern. 1988. *Linking Auditing and Metaevaluation*. Newbury Park, CA: Sage.

Schwartz, Jeffrey and Sharon Begley. 2003. *The Mind and the Brain: Neuroplasticity and the Power of Mental Force*. New York: Regan Books, HarperCollins.

Schwartz, Robert and John Mayne, eds. 2004. *Quality Matters: Seeking Confidence in Evaluation, Auditing and Performance Reporting*. New Brunswick, NJ: Transaction Publishers.

Scriven, Michael. 2008. "A Summative Evaluation of RCT Methodology: And Some New Entries in the Gold Standards

Cup." *Journal of MultiDisciplinary Evaluation* 5(9):11–16.

_____. 2007a. "Activist Evaluation." *Journal of MultiDisciplinary Evaluation* 4(7). http://survey.ate.wmich.edu/jmde/index.php/jmde_1/article/view/25/5.

_____. 2007b. "Evaluation as a Cognitive Process." *Journal of MultiDisciplinary Evaluation* 4(8):74–75.

_____. 2006a. "Back to Logic Models: What Are They Good For, and Who Has Evidence?" *EvalTalk*, August 30. (Note: Entry edited for readability.)

_____. 2006b. "Converting Perspective to Practice." *Journal of MultiDisciplinary Evaluation* 3(6):8–9. http://survey.ate.wmich.edu/jmde/index.php/jmde_1/issue/view/22.

_____. 2005a. "Logic of Evaluation." Pp. 235–38 in *Encyclopedia of Evaluation*, edited by S. Mathison. Thousand Oaks, CA: Sage.

_____. 2005b. "Metaevaluation." Pp. 249–51 in *Encyclopedia of Evaluation*, Sandra Mathison. Thousand Oaks, CA: Sage.

_____. 2005c. "Transdiscipline." P. 422 in *Encyclopedia of Evaluation*, S. Mathison. Thousand Oaks, CA: Sage.

_____. 2005d. "Causal Claims: Warranting Them and Using Them." Paper for the National Research Council Conference on Evidence in the Social Sciences, March. Washington, DC: National Science Foundation.

_____. 2005e. "Warranting Causal Claims and Using Them." Paper presented at the National Research Council Conference on Evidence in the Social Sciences and for Social Policy, March, and the Nordic Social Science Conference on the Effects of Public Policy Interventions, August.

_____. 2004. "Reflections." Pp. 183–95 in *Evaluation Roots: Tracing Theorists' Views and Influences*, edited by M. Alkin. Thousand Oaks, CA: Sage.

_____. 2003. "Evaluation in the New Millennium: The Transdisciplinary Vision." Pp. 19–42 in *Evaluating Social Programs and Problems*, edited by S. Donaldson and M. Scriven. Mahwah, NJ: Lawrence Erlbaum.

_____. 1996. "Types of Evaluations and Types of Evaluators." *Evaluation Practice* 17(Spring-Summer):151–62.

_____. 1995. "The Logic of Evaluation and Evaluation Practice." *Reasoning in Evaluation: Inferential Links and Leaps. New Directions for Program Evaluation* 68:49–70.

_____. 1994. "The Final Synthesis." *Evaluation Practice* 15(3):367–82.

_____, 1993. *Hard-Won Lessons in Program Evaluation. New Directions for Program Evaluation*, No. 58.

_____. 1991a. "Beyond Formative and Summative Evaluation." Pp. 18–64 in *Evaluation and Education: At Quarter Century, 90th Yearbook of the National Society for the Study of Education*, edited by M. W. McLaughlin and D. C. Phillips. Chicago, IL: University of Chicago Press.

_____. 1991b. *Evaluation Thesaurus*. 4th ed. Newbury Park, CA: Sage.

_____. 1980. *The Logic of Evaluation*. Iverness, CA: Edgepress.

_____. 1972a. "Objectivity and Subjectivity in Educational Research." Pp. 94–142 in *Philosophical Redirection of Educational Research: The Seventy-First Yearbook of the National Society for the Study of Education*, edited by Lawrence G. Thomas. Chicago, IL: University of Chicago Press.

_____. 1972b. "Prose and Cons about Goal-Free Evaluation." *Evaluation Comment: The Journal of Educational Evaluation* 3(4):1–7.

_____. 1967. "The Methodology of Evaluation." Pp. 39–83 in *Perspective of Curriculum Evaluation*, edited by Ralph W. Tyler, Robert Gagne, and Michael Scriven, AERA Monograph Series on Curriculum Evaluation, Vol. 1. Chicago, IL: Rand McNally.

Sears, Robin. 2006. "The Old Accountability Shuffle." *Policy Options* 27(5):19–27.

Sechrest, Lee. 1992. "Roots: Back to Our First Generations." *Evaluation Practice* 13(1):1–7.

Sechrest, Lee B. and Anne G. Scott, eds. 1993. *Understanding Causes and Generalizing About Them. New Directions for Program Evaluation*, No. 57.

Seigart, Denise. 2005. "Feminist Evaluation." Pp. 154–57 in *Encyclopedia of Evaluation* edited by S. Mathison. Thousand Oaks, CA: Sage.

Seigart, Denise and Sharon Brisolara, eds. 2002. *Feminist Evaluation: Explorations and Experiences. New Directions for Evaluation*, No. 96.

Senge, Peter M. 2006. *The Fifth Discipline: The Art and Practice of the Learning Organization.* New York: Doubleday.

_____. 1999. *The Dance of Change: The Challenges to Sustaining Momentum in Learning Organizations: A Fifth Discipline Resource.* New York: Doubleday.

SenGupta, Saumitra, Rodney Hopson, and Melva Thompson-Robinson. 2004. "Cultural Competence in Evaluation: An Overview." *New Directions for Evaluation* 102:5–20.

Shadish, William R., Jr. 1987. "Program Micro- and Macrotheories: A Guide for Social Change." *Using Program Theory in Evaluation. New Directions for Program Evaluation* 33:93–110.

Shadish, William R., Thomas D. Cook, and Donald T. Campbell. 2001. *Experimental and Quasi-Experimental Designs for Generalized Causal Inference.* Boston, MA: Houghton Mifflin.

Shadish, William R., Jr., Thomas D. Cook, and Laura C. Leviton. 1991. *Foundations of Program Evaluation: Theories of Practice.* Newbury Park, CA: Sage.

Shadish, William R. and Jason Luellen. 2005. "History of Evaluation." Pp. 183–86 in *Encyclopedia of Evaluation*, S. Mathison. Thousand Oaks, CA: Sage.

Shadish, William R., Jr., Dianna L. Newman, Mary Ann Scheirer, and Christopher Wye, eds. 1995. *Guiding Principles for Evaluators. New Directions for Program Evaluation*, No. 66.

Shah, I. 1964. *The Sufis.* Garden City, NY: Doubleday.

Shah, Idries. 1973. *The Subtlties of the Inimitable Mulla Nasrudin.* New York: E. P. Dutton.

Shapiro, Edna. 1973. "Educational Evaluation: Rethinking the Criteria of Competence." *School Review,* November, pp. 523–49.

Sharpe, L. J. 1977. "The Social Scientist and Policymaking: Some Cautionary Thoughts and Transatlantic Reflections." Pp. 37–54 in *Using Social Research for Public Policy Making,* edited by Carol H. Weiss. Lexington, MA: D. C. Heath.

Shea, Michael. 1991. *Program Evaluation Utilization in Canada and Its Relationship to Evaluation Process, Evaluator and Decision Context Variables.* Ph.D. Dissertation. Windsor, University of Windsor, Ontario, Canada.

_____ and Arnold Love. 2007. *Self-Assessment of Stage of Internal Evaluation Organizational Capacity Development.* Toronto, Canada: Unpublished manuscript.

Sherwood, Kay. 2005. "Evaluating Home Visitation: A Case Study of Evaluation at the David and Lucile Packard Foundation." *Teaching Evaluation Using the Case Method. New Directions for Evaluation* 105:59–81.

Shipman, Stephanie. 2003. "Program Evaluation: Improving Performance and Accountability." *The Public Manager* 34(3):53–54.

Shirky, Clay. 2007. "In Defense of Ready, Fire, Aim." Breakthrough Ideas in *Harvard Business Review* 85(2):20–56.

Shreeve, James. 2006. "Human Journey." *National Geographic,* 209(3):60–73.

Shulha, Lynn and Brad Cousins. 1997. "Evaluation Use: Theory, Research, and Practice since 1986." *Evaluation Practice* 18(3):195–208.

Siegel, Karolynn and Peter Tuckel. 1985. "The Utilization of Evaluation Research: A Case Analysis." *Evaluation Review* 9(3):307–28.

Simon, Herbert. 1978. "On How We Decide What to Do." *Bell Journal of Economics* 9:494–507.

_____. 1957. *Administrative Behavior.* New York: Macmillan.

Simons, Helen. 2006. "Ethics in Evaluation." Pp. 243–65 in *Handbook of Evaluation: Policies, Programs and Practices*, edited by I. Shaw, M. Mark, and J. Greene. Thousand Oaks, CA: Sage.

Sirotnik, Kenneth A., eds. 1990. *Evaluation and Social Justice: Issues in Public Education. New Directions for Program Evaluation*, No. 45.

Smith, Doris Shackelford. 1992 "Academic and Staff Attitudes Towards Program Evaluation in Nonformal Educational Systems." Ph.D. dissertation, University of California, Berkeley, CA.

Smith, Gordon and Jill Pell. 2003. "Parachute Use to Prevent Death and Major Trauma Related to Gravitational Challenge:

Systematic Review of Randomised Controlled Trials." *British Medical Journal* 327(20 December):1459–61. http://bmj.bmjjournals.com/cgi/content/full/327/7429/1459?ck=nck.

Smith, Mary Lee. 1994. "Qualitative Plus/Versus Quantitative." *The Qualitative-Quantitative Debate: New Perspectives. New Directions for Program Evaluation* 61:37–44.

Smith, Midge F. 2005a. "Evaluability Assessment." Pp. 136–39 in *Encyclopedia of Evaluation*, edited by S. Mathison. Thousand Oaks, CA: Sage.

_____. 2005b. "Implementation." P. 195 in *Encyclopedia of Evaluation*, edited by S. Mathison. Thousand Oaks, CA: Sage.

_____. 2003. "The Future of the Evaluation Profession." Pp. 373–86 in *International Handbook of Education Evaluation*, edited by T. Kellaghan, D. L. Stufflebeam, and L. Wingate. Boston, MA: Kluwer.

_____. 1989. *Evaluability Assessment*. Boston, MA: Kluwer Academic.

_____. 1988. "Evaluation Utilization Revisited." *Evaluation Utilization. New Directions for Program Evaluation* 39:7–19.

Smith, Nick. 2007. "Judging Methods." *Informing Federal Policies on Evaluation Methodology: Building the Evidence Base for Method Choice in Government Sponsored Evaluation. New Directions for Program Evaluation* 113:119–23.

_____, ed. 1992. *Varieties of Investigative Evaluation. New Directions for Program Evaluation*, No. 56.

_____. 1987. "Toward the Justification of Claims in Evaluation Research." *Evaluation and Program Planning* 10:309–14.

_____. 1982. "Levels of Evidence and Degrees of Certainty in Evaluation." *Evaluation and Program Planning* 5:313–15.

_____, ed. 1981. *Metaphors for Evaluation: Sources of New Methods*. Beverly Hills, CA: Sage.

_____. 1980. "Studying Evaluation Assumptions." *Evaluation Network Newsletter*, Winter, pp. 39–40.

Social Science Research Council, National Academy of Sciences. 1969. *The Behavioral and Social Sciences: Outlook and Need*. Englewood Cliffs, NJ: Prentice Hall.

Sonnichsen, Richard C. 2000. *High Impact Internal Evaluation*. Thousand Oaks, CA: Sage.

_____. 1994. "Evaluators as Change Agents." Pp. 534–48 in *Handbook of Practical Program Evaluation*, edited by J. S. Wholey, H. P. Hatry, and K. E. Newcomer. San Francisco, CA: Jossey-Bass.

_____. 1993. "Can Governments Learn?" Pp. 97–118 in *Comparative Perspectives on Evaluation and Organizational Learning*, edited by F. Leeuw, R. Rist, and R. Sonnichsen. New Brunswick, NJ: Transaction Books.

_____. 1988. "Advocacy Evaluation: A Model for Internal Evaluation Offices." *Evaluation and Program Planning* 11(2):141–48.

_____. 1987. "An Internal Evaluator Responds to Ernest House's Views on Internal Evaluation." *Evaluation Practice* 8(4):34–36.

Special Commission on the Social Sciences, National Science Foundation. 1968. *Knowledge into Action: Improving the Nation's Use of the Social Sciences*. Washington, DC: Government Printing Office.

Specter, Michael. 2006. "Political Science: The Bush Administration's War on the Laboratory." *The New Yorker*, LXXXII(4), March 13:58–69.

"Speed." 1995. *The New Yorker*, March 27, p. 40.

Sridharan, Sanjeev, Bernadette Campbell, and Heidi Zinzow. 2006. "Developing a Stakeholder-Driven Anticipated Timeline of Impact for Evaluation of Social Programs." *American Journal of Evaluation* 27(2):148–62.

Stacey, Ralph D. 2007. *Strategic Management and Organizational Dynamics*. 5th ed. Upper Saddle River, NJ: Prentice Hall.

_____. 1996. *Complexity and Creativity in Organizations*. San Fransisco, CA: Berrett-Koehler.

_____. 1992. *Managing the Unknowable: Strategic Boundaries between Order and Chaos in Organizations*. San Francisco, CA: Jossey-Bass.

Stake, Robert. 2005. *Multiple Case Study Analysis*. New York: Guilford Press.

_____. 2004. "How Far Dare an Evaluator Go Toward Saving the World?" *American Journal of Evaluation* 25(1):103–107.

_____. 1996. "Beyond Responsive Evaluation: Developments in This Decade." Minnesota

Evaluation Studies Institute presentation, College of Education and Human Development, University of Minnesota, June 25, Minneapolis, MN.

_____. 1995. *The Art of Case Research.* Newbury Park, CA: Sage.

_____. 1981. "Case Study Methodology: An Epistemological Advocacy." Pp. 31–40 in *Case Study Methodology in Educational Evaluation,* edited by W. W. Welch. Minneapolis: Minnesota Research and Evaluation Center.

_____. 1975. *Evaluating the Arts in Education: A Responsive Approach.* Columbus, OH: Charles E. Merrill.

Stake, Robert and Tineke Abma. 2005. "Responsive Evaluation." Pp. 376–79 in *Encyclopedia of Evaluation,* edited by S. Mathison. Thousand Oaks, CA: Sage.

Stalford, Charles B. 1983. "School Board Use of Evaluation Information." Presented at the joint meeting of the Evaluation Network and the Evaluation Research Society, Chicago, IL.

Stame, Nicoletta, ed. 2007. *I Classici della Valutazione* (Reader on Program Evaluation). Milano, Italy: FrancoAngeli.

Stame, Nicoletta. 2006a. "Complex Policies and Evaluative Streams of Knowledge." Pp. 113–28 in *From Studies to Streams: Managing Evaluative Systems,* edited by R. Rist and N. Stame. New Brunswick, NJ: Transaction Books.

_____. 2006b. "Introduction: Streams of Evaluative Knowledge." Pp. vii–xxi in *From Studies to Streams: Managing Evaluative Systems,* edited by Ray C. Rist and Nicoletta Stame. New Brunswick, NJ: Transaction Books.

Stanfield, John H., II. 1999. "Slipping Through the Front Door: Relevant Social Scientific Evaluation in the People-of-Color Century." *American Journal of Evaluation* 20(3):415–32.

Stecher, Brian M. and W. Alan Davis. 1987. *How to Focus an Evaluation.* Newbury Park, CA: Sage.

Stehr, Nico. 1992. *Practical Knowledge.* Newbury Park, CA: Sage.

Stern, Elliot. 2004. "What Shapes European Evaluation? A Personal Reflection." *Evaluation* 10(1):7–15.

Stevahn, Laurie, Jean King, Gail Ghere, and Jane Minnema. 2006. "Evaluator Competencies in University-Based Evaluation Training Programs." *Canadian Journal of Program Evaluation* 20:101–23.

——2005. "Establishing Essential Program Evaluator Competencies." *American Journal of Evaluation* 26(1):43–59.

Stevens, Carla J. and Micah Dial, eds. 1994. *Preventing the Misuse of Evaluation. New Directions for Program Evaluation,* No. 64.

Stockdill, S. H., R. M. Duhon-Sells, R. A. Olson, and M. Q. Patton. 1992. "Voice in the Design and Evaluation of a Multicultural Education Program: A Developmental Approach." *Minority Issues in Program Evaluation, New Directions in Program Evaluation* 53:17–34.

Storey, David. 2006. "Evaluating Business Entrepreneurship Programs." Presentation at the International Finance Corporation (IFC) Technical Assistance Programs Monitoring and Evaluation Meeting, "Results Measurement for Technical Assistance." May 8. Washington, DC: IFC.

Stossel, John. 2006. *Myths, Lies, and Downright Stupidity: Get Out the Shovel—Why Everything You Know is Wrong.* New York: Hyperion Books.

Strike, Kenneth. 1972. "Explaining and Understanding the Impact of Science on Our Concept of Man." Pp. 26–46 in *Philosophical Redirection of Educational Research: The Seventy-First Yearbook of the National Society for the Study of Education,* edited by Lawrence G. Thomas. Chicago, IL: University of Chicago Press.

Stuart, Jennifer Bagnell. 2007. "Necessity Leads to Innovative Evaluation Approach and Practice." *Evaluation Exchange* XIII(1), Spring:10–11. Cambridge, MA: Harvard Family Research Project.

Studer, Sharon L. 1978. "A Validity Study of a Measure of 'Readiness to Accept Program Evaluation.'" Ph.D. dissertation. University of Minnesota, Minneapolis, MN.

Stufflebeam, Daniel L. 2007. *Omnibus Metaevaluation Checklist.* Kalamazoo, MI: Center for Evaluation, Western Michigan University. http://www.wmich.edu/evalctr/checklists.

_____. 2005. "CIPP Model." Pp. 60–65 in *Encyclopedia of Evaluation,* edited by S. Mathison. Thousand Oaks, CA: Sage.

_____. 2004a. *Evaluation Design Checklist.* Kalamazoo, MI: Center for Evaluation, Western Michigan University. http://www

.wmich.edu/evalctr/checklists/evaldesign .pdf.

_____. 2004b. "A Note on the Purposes, Development, and Applicability of the Joint Committee Evaluation Standards." *American Journal of Evaluation* 25(1): 99–102.

_____. 2002. *CIPP Evaluation Model Checklist*. Kalamazoo, MI: Evaluation Center, Western Michigan University. http://www.wmich.edu/evalctr/checklists/ checklistmenu.htm#models.

_____. 2001. *Evaluation Models. New Directions for Evaluation*. No. 89.

_____. 1994. "Empowerment Evaluation, Objectivist Evaluation, and Evaluation Standards: Where the Future of Evaluation Should Not Go and Where It Needs to Go." *Evaluation Practice* 15(3):321–38.

_____. 1980. "An Interview with Daniel L. Stufflebeam." *Educational Evaluation and Policy Analysis* 2(4):90–92.

Stufflebeam, Daniel and Anthony Shinkfield. 2007. *Evaluation Theory, Models, and Applications,* San Francisco, CA: Jossey-Bass.

Suchman, Edward A. 1967. *Evaluative Research: Principles and Practice in Public Service and Social Action Programs*. New York: Russell Sage.

Sutcliffe, Kathleen and Klaus Weber. 2003. "The High Cost of Accuracy." *Harvard Business Review,* 81(May):74–82.

Symonette, Hazel. 2007. "Making Evaluation Work for the Greater Good: Supporting Provocative Possibility and Responsive Praxis in Leadership Development." Chapter 4 in *The Handbook of Leadership Development Evaluation*, edited by K. Hannum, J. Martineau, and C. Reinelt. Greensboro, NC: Center for Creative Leadership.

_____. 2004. "Walking Pathways toward Becoming a Culturally Competent Evaluator: Boundaries, Borderlands, and Border Crossings." *New Directions for Evaluation* 102:95–110.

Tashakkori, Abbas and John Creswell. 2007. "The New Era of Mixed Methods." *Journal of Mixed Methods Research* 1(1):3–7.

Tashakkori, Abbas and Charles Teddlie, eds. 2003. *Handbook of Mixed Methods in Social and Behavioral Research*. Thousand Oaks, CA: Sage.

Taut, Sandy. 2007. "Studying Self-Evaluation Capacity Building in a Large International Development Organization." *American Journal of Evaluation* 28(1):45–59.

Taut, Sandy and Alkin, Marvin C. 2003. "Program Staff Perceptions of Barriers to Evaluation Implementation." *American Journal of Evaluation* 24(2):213–26.

Taut, Sandy and Brauns, Dieter. 2003. "Resistance to Evaluation: A Psychological Perspective." *Evaluation* 9(3):247–69.

Terry, Robert W. 2001. *Seven Zones of Leadership*. Mountain View, CA: Davies-Black.

_____. 1993. *Authentic Leadership*. San Francisco, CA: Jossey-Bass.

Thiele, Graham, Andre Devaux, Claudio Velasco, and Douglass Horton. 2007. "Horizontal Evaluation: Fostering Knowledge Sharing and Program Development Within a Network." *American Journal of Evaluation* 28(4):493–508.

Thomas, Charles. 2005. "Consequential Validity." P. 80 in *Encyclopedia of Evaluation*, edited by S. Mathison. Thousand Oaks, CA: Sage.

Thompson, James D. 1967. *Organizations in Action*. New York: McGraw-Hill.

Thompson, Mark. 1975. *Evaluation for Decision in Social Programmes*. Lexington, MA: D. C. Health.

Thoreau, Henry D. 1838. *Journal,* March 14.

Tilley, Nick. 2004. "Applying Theory-Driven Evaluation to the British Crime Reduction Programme. *Criminal Justice,* 4(3):255–76.

Toffler, Alvin. 1970. *Future Shock*. New York: Random House.

Torres, Rosalie, Hallie Preskill, and Mary Piontek. 2004. *Evaluation Strategies for Communicating and Reporting: Enhancing Learning in Organizations*. Thousand Oaks, CA: Sage.

Torres, Rosalie, Sharon Padilla Stone, Deborah Butkus, Barbara Hook, Jill Casey, and Sheila Arens. 2000. "Dialogue and Reflection in a Collaborative Evaluation: Stakeholder and Evaluator Voices." *Evaluation as a Democratic Process. New Directions for Evaluation* 85:27–38.

Torres, Rosalie, Hallie Preskill, and Mary Piontek. 1997. "Communicating and

Reporting: Practices and Concerns of Internal and External Evaluators." *Evaluation Practice* 18(2):105–26.

_____. 1996. *Evaluation Strategies for Communicating and Reporting: Enhancing Learning in Organizations.* Thousand Oaks, CA: Sage.

Treasury Board of Canada. 2002. *Case Studies on the Uses and Drivers of Effective Evaluations in the Government of Canada.* Ottawa, Canada: Treasury Board of Canada. http://www.tbs-sct.gc.ca/eval/tools_outils/impact/impact_e.asp#5.0.

Tripodi, Tony, Phillip Felin, and Irwin Epstein. 1971. *Social Program Evaluation Guidelines for Health, Education, and Welfare Administration.* Itasca, IL: Peacock.

Trochim, William. 2006a. "AEA and Expect More." *EvalTalk* listserv, April 24.

_____. 2006b. "Measurement Validity Types." *Research Methods Knowledge Base.* http://www.socialresearchmethods.net/kb/measval.php.

_____. 2006c. "Reliability & Validity Types." *Research Methods Knowledge Base.* http://www.socialresearchmethods.net/kb/relandval.php.

_____, ed. 1986. *Advances in Quasi-Experimental Design and Analysis. New Directions for Program Evaluation,* No. 31.

Tuan, Y-Fu. 2000. *Escapism.* Baltimore, MD: Johns Hopkins University Press.

Tucker, Eugene. 1977. "The Follow through Planned Variation Experiment: What Is the Pay-Off?" Presented at the annual meeting of the American Educational Research Association, April. New York.

Turner, Terilyn C. and Stacy H. Stockdill, eds. 1987. *The Technology for Literacy Project Evaluation.* St. Paul, MN: Saint Paul Foundation.

Turpin, Robin. 1989. "Winner of the President's Prize on the Problem of Evaluation Politics." *Evaluation Practice* 10(10):54–57.

Tversky, Amos and Craig Fox. 2000. "Weighing Risk and Uncertainty." Pp. 93–117 in *Choices, Values, and Frames,* edited by Daniel Kahneman and Amos Tversky. Boston, MA: Cambridge University Press.

Tversky, Amos and Daniel Kahneman. 2000. "Advances in Prospect Theory: Cumulative Representation of Uncertainty." Pp. 44–65 in *Choices, Values, and Frames,* edited by Daniel Kahneman and Amos Tversky. Cambridge, UK: Cambridge University Press.

_____. 1974. "Judgments under Uncertainty: Heuristics and Biases." *Science* 185:1124–25.

Ulrich, Werner. 2000. "Reflective Practice in the Civil Society: The Contribution of Critically Systemic Thinking." *Reflective Practice* 1(2):247–68.

_____. 1998. *Systems Thinking as if People Mattered: Critical Systems Thinking for Citizens and Managers.* Working Paper No. 23. Lincoln School of Management, University of Lincolnshire & Humberside, England.

United Nations. 1996. *The United Nations and Rwanda 1993–1996.* New York: United Nations.

United Nations Development Programme (UNDP). 2007. *Evaluation Guidance.* New York: UNDP. http://www.undp.org/eo.

United Nations Evaluation group (UNEG). 2007. *Considerations in Strengthening of UN System-wide Evaluation.* Rome, Italy: United Nations System Chief Executives Board for Coordination.

_____. 2005a. *Norms for Evaluation in the UN System.* New York: United Nations.

_____. 2005b. *Standards for Evaluation in the UN System.* New York: United Nations.

United Way. 1996. *Measuring Program Outcomes: A Practical Approach.* Alexandria, VA: United Way of America. http://national.unitedway.org/outcomes/resources/mpo/model.cfm.

University of Wisconsin Cooperative Extension. 2007. *Program Development and Evaluation.* Madison, WI: U.W. Cooperative Extension. http://www.uwex.edu/ces/pdande/progdev/index.html.

Uphoff, Norman. 1991. "A Field Methodology for Participatory Self-Evaluation." Special issue. Evaluation of Social Development Projects, in *Community Development Journal* 26(4):271–85.

U.S. Department of Health and Human Services. 1983. *Compendium of HHS Evaluation Studies.* Washington, DC: HHS Evaluation Documentation Center.

U.S. House of Representatives, Committee on Government Operations, Research and Technical Programs Subcommittee. 1967. *The Use of Social Research in Federal Domestic Programs*. Washington, DC: Government Printing Office.

U.S. Senate Select Committee on Intelligence. 2004. Report of the Select Committee on Intelligence on the U.S. Intelligence Community's Prewar Intelligence Assessments on Iraq. Washington, DC: U.S. Senate.

VanLandingham, Gary. 2007. "A Voice Crying in the Wilderness: Legislative Oversight Agencies' Efforts to Achieve Utilization." *Promoting the Use of Government Evaluations in Policymaking, New Directions for Evaluation* 113:25–40.

Vernooy, Ronnie, Sun Qui, and Xu Jianchu. 2003. "Voices for Change: Participatory Monitoring and Evaluation in China." Ottawa, ON, Canada: International development Research Centre.

von Oech, Roger. 1983. *A Whack on the Side of the Head: How to Unlock Your Mind for Innovation*. New York: Warner Books.

Vroom, Phyllis I., Marie Columbo, and Neva Nahan. 1994. "Confronting Ideology and Self-Interest: Avoiding Misuse of Evaluation." *Preventing the Misuse of Evaluation. New Directions for Program Evaluation* 64:61–68.

Wadsworth, Yoland. 1995. "'Building In Research and Evaluation to Human Services." Unpublished report to the Winston Churchill Memorial Trust of Australia, Melbourne, Australia.

_____. 1993. "What Is Participatory Action Research?" Melbourne, Australia: Action Research Issues Association.

_____. 1984. *Do It Yourself Social Research*. Melbourne, Australia: Victorian Council of Social Service and Melbourne Family Care Organisation in association with Allen and Unwin.

Wageningen International UR. 2006. *Participatory Planning, Monitoring and Evaluation*. Wageningen, The Netherlands: IAC. http://portals.wi.wur.nl/ppme/?Home.

Waldron, Jeremy. 2007. "Temperamental Justice." *The New York Review of Books* LIV(8), May 10:15–17.

Waldrop, M. Mitchell. 1992: *Complexity: The Emerging Science at the Edge of Order and Chaos*. New York: Touchstone.

Walker, Robert and Michael Wiseman. 2006. "Managing Evaluations." Pp. 360–83 in *The Sage Handbook of Evaluation: Policies, Programs and Practices*, edited by I. Shaw, J. Greene, and M. Mark. Thousand Oaks, CA: Sage.

Ward, David, Gene Kassebaum, and Daniel Wilner. 1971. *Prison Treatment and Parole Survival: An Empirical Assessment*. New York: John Wiley.

Wargo, Michael J. 1995. "The Impact of Federal Government Reinvention on Federal Evaluation Activity." *Evaluation Practice* 16(3):227–37.

_____. 1989. "Characteristics of Successful Program Evaluations." Pp. 71–82 in *Improving Government Performance: Evaluation Strategies for Strengthening Public Agencies and Programs,* edited by J. S. Wholey and K. E. Newcomer. San Francisco, CA: Jossey-Bass.

Weaver, Lynda and J. Bradley Cousins. 2004. "Unpacking the Participatory Process." *Journal of MultiDisciplinary Evaluation* 1(1):19–40. http://survey.ate.wmich.edu/jmde/index.php/jmde_1/issue/view/19.

Weber, Max. 1947. *The Theory of Social and Economic Organizations*. New York: Oxford University Press.

Weick, Karl and Kathleen Sutcliffe. 2001. *Managing the Unexpected: Assuring High Performance in an Age of Complexity*. San Francisco, CA: Jossey-Bass.

Weidman, Donald R., Pamela Horst, Grace Taher, and Joseph S. Wholey. 1973. *Design of an Evaluation System* for NIMH, Contract Report 962–7. Washington, DC: Urban Institute.

Weinberger, David. 2007. "The Folly of Accountabalism." Breakthrough Ideas in *Harvard Business Review* 85(2):20–56.

Weiss, Carol H. 2007. "Theory-Based Evaluation: Past, Present, and Future." *New Directions for Evaluation* 114:68–81.

_____. 2004. "Rooting for Evaluation: A Cliff Notes Version of My Work." Pp.153–68 in *Evaluation Roots: Tracing Theorists' Views and Influences*, edited by M. C. Alkin. Thousand Oaks, CA: Sage.

_____. 2002. "What to Do Until the Random Assigner Comes." Chapter 8 in *Evidence Matters: Randomized Trials in Education Research*, edited by Fred Mosteller and Robert Boruch. Washington, DC: Brookings Institution Press.

_____. 2000. "Which Links in Which Theories Shall We Evaluate?" *Program Theory in Evaluation: Challenges and Opportunities. New Directions for Evaluation* 87:35–45.

_____. 1998a. *Evaluation Research.* 2d ed. Upper Saddle River, NJ: Prentice Hall.

_____. 1998b. "Have We Learned Anything New about the Use of Evaluation?" *American Journal of Evaluation* 19(1):21–33.

_____. 1997. "How Can Theory-Based Evaluation Make Greater Headway?" *Evaluation Review* 21(4):501–24.

_____. 1995. "Nothing as Practical as Good Theory: Exploring Theory-Based Evaluation for Comprehensive Community Initiatives for Children and Families." Pp.1–16 in *New Approaches to Evaluating Community Initiatives. Vol. 1: Concepts, Methods, and Contexts*, edited by J. P. Connell, A. C. Kubish, L. B. Schoor, and C. H. Weiss. Washington, DC: Aspen Institute.

_____. 1993. "Where Politics and Evaluation Research Meet." *Evaluation Practice* 14(1):93–106. (Original work published 1973)

_____. [1988] 1990. "Evaluation for Decisions: Is Anybody There? Does Anybody Care?" Pp. 171–84 in *Debates on Evaluation,* edited by Marvin Alkin. Newbury Park, CA: Sage. Reprinted American Evaluation Association keynote address originally published in *Evaluation Practice* 9(1):5–19.

_____. 1981. "Measuring the Use of Evaluation." Pp. 17–34 in *Utilizing Evaluation: Concepts and Measurement Techniques*, edited by James Ciarlo. Beverly Hills, CA: Sage.

_____. 1980. "Knowledge Creep and Decision Accretion." *Knowledge: Creation, Diffusion, Utilization* 1(3):381–404.

_____. 1977. "Introduction." Pp. 1–22 in *Using Social Research in Public Policy Making,* edited by Carol H. Weiss. Lexington, MA: D. C. Heath.

_____, ed. 1972a. *Evaluating Action Programs.* Boston, MA: Allyn and Bacon.

_____. 1972b. *Evaluation Research: Methods of Assessing Program Effectiveness.* Englewood Cliffs, NJ: Prentice Hall.

_____. 1972c. "Evaluating Educational and Social Action Programs. A 'Treeful of Owls.'" Pp. 3–27 in *Evaluating Action Programs,* edited by Carol H. Weiss. Boston, MA: Allyn and Bacon.

_____. 1972d. "Utilization of Evaluation: Toward Comparative Study." Pp. 318–26 in *Evaluating Action Programs,* edited by Carol H. Weiss. Boston, MA: Allyn and Bacon.

Weiss, Carol H. and Michael Bucuvalas. 1980. "Truth Tests and Utility Tests: Decision Makers' Frame of Reference for Social Science Research." *American Sociological Review* 45(April):302–13.

Weiss, Heather B. and Jennifer C. Greene. 1992. "An Empowerment Partnership for Family Support and Education Programs and Evaluations." *Family Science Review* 5(1, 2):145–63.

Weiss, C. H., E. Murphy-Graham, and S. Birkeland. 2005. "An Alternate Route to Policy Influence: How Evaluations Affect DARE." *American Journal of Evaluation* 26(1):12–30.

Westinghouse Learning Corporation. 1969. *The Impact of Head Start: An Evaluation of the Effects of Head Start on Children's Cognitive and Affective Development.* Bladensburg, MD: Westinghouse Learning Corporation.

Westley, Frances, Brenda Zimmerman, and Michael Q. Patton. 2006. *Getting to Maybe: How the World Is Changed.* Toronto, ON, Canada: Random House Canada.

Westley, Frances and Philip Miller. 2003. *Experiments in Consilience: Integrating Social and Scientific Responses to Safe Endangered Species.* Washington, DC: Island Press.

Westover, Theresa. 2006. *What Gets Measured Gets Done—For Better or Worse.* EvalTalk listserv, July 31.

What Works Clearinghouse. 2006. *Evidence Standards for Reviewing Studies.* Washington, DC: U.S. Department of Education's Institute of Education Sciences. http://ies.ed.gov/ncee/wwc/overview/review.asp.

White House. 2006. *Overview of the President's 2006 Budget.* Washington, DC: Government Printing Office. http://www.whitehouse.gov/omb/pdf/overview-06.pdf.

Whitmore, Elizabeth, ed. 1998. *Understanding and Practicing Participatory Evaluation. New Directions for Evaluation*, No. 75.

_____. 1988. "Empowerment and Evaluation: A Case Example." Presented at the

American Evaluation Association annual meeting, New Orleans, LA.

Whitmore, E. and P. Kerans. 1988. "Participation, Empowerment, and Welfare." *Canadian Review of Social Policy* 22:51–60.

Wholey, Joseph S. 1994. "Assessing the Feasibility and Likely Usefulness of Evaluation." Pp. 15–39 in *Handbook of Practical Program Evaluation*, edited by Joseph S. Wholey, Harry P. Hatry, and Kathryn E. Newcomer. San Francisco, CA: Jossey-Bass.

Wholey, Joseph S., Harry P. Hatry, and Kathryn E. Newcomer, eds. 2004. *Handbook of Practical Program Evaluation.* 2d ed. San Francisco, CA: Jossey-Bass.

Wholey, Joseph S., Harry P. Hatry, and Kathryn E. Newcomer, eds. 1994. *Handbook of Practical Program Evaluation.* San Francisco, CA: Jossey-Bass.

Wholey, Joseph S., John W. Scanlon, Hugh G. Duffy, James S. Fukumotu, and Leona M. Vogt. 1970. *Federal Evaluation Policy: Analyzing the Effects of Public Programs.* Washington, DC: Urban Institute.

Whyte, William F., ed. 1991. *Participatory Action Research.* Newbury Park, CA: Sage.

Wildavsky, A. 1985. "The Self-Evaluating Organization." Pp. 246–65 in *Program Evaluation: Patterns and Directions*, edited by E. Chelimsky. Washington, DC: American Society for Public Administration.

Wildermuth, Cris. 2005. *Diversity Training.* Alexandria, VA: ASDT Press.

Williams, Bob. 2005a. "Quality Assurance." P. 350 in *Encyclopedia of Evaluation*, edited by S. Mathison. Thousand Oaks, CA: Sage.

———. 2005b. "Systems and Systems Thinking." Pp. 405–12 in *Encyclopedia of Evaluation*, edited by S. Mathison. Thousand Oaks, CA: Sage.

———. 2003. "Getting the Stuff Used." Pp. 196–213 in *Evaluating Policy and Practice: A New Zealand Reader*, edited by Neil Lunt, Carl Davidson, and Kate McKegg. Auckland, New Zealand: Pearson Prentice Hall.

Williams, Bob and Iraj Iman. 2006. *Systems Concepts in Evaluation: An Expert Anthology.* AEA Monograph. Point Reynes, CA: EdgePress.

Williams, Jay. 1976. *Everyone Knows What a Dragon Looks Like.* New York: Four Winds Press.

Williams, Walter. 1976. "Implementation Analysis and Assessment." Pp. 267–92 in *Social Program Implementation*, edited by W. Williams and R. F. Elmore. New York: Academic Press.

Williams, Walter and Richard F. Elmore. 1976. *Social Program Implementation.* New York: Academic Press.

Williams, Walter and John W. Evans. 1969. "The Politics of Evaluation: The Case of Head Start." *Annals of the American Academy of Political and Social Science* 385(September):118–32.

Winberg, A. 1991. "Maximizing the Contribution of Internal Evaluation Units." *Evaluation and Program Planning* 14:167–72.

Wisler, Carl, ed. 1996. *Evaluation and Auditing: Prospects for Convergence. New Directions for Evaluation*, No. 71.

Wolf, Robert L. 1975. "Trial by Jury: A New Evaluation Method." *Phi Delta Kappan* 57(3):185–87.

World Bank, The. 2006. *Reducing Poverty on a Global Scale: Learning and Innovating for Development.* Washington, DC: The World Bank.

World Bank, The. 2005. *Maintaining Momentum to 2015? An Impact Evaluation of Interventions to Improve Maternal and Child Health and Nutrition in Bangladesh.* Washington, DC: Operations Evaluation Department, The World Bank.

World Food Programme (WFP). 2006. *Monitoring and Evaluation Guidelines.* Rome, Italy: WFP. http://www.wfp.org/operations/evaluation/guidelines.asp?section=5&sub_section=8.

Worley, D. R. 1960. "Amount and Generality of Information-Seeking Behavior in Sequential Decision Making as Dependent on Level of Incentive." Pp. 1–11 in *Experiments on Decision Making*, Technical Report 6, edited by D. W. Taylor. New Haven, CT: Yale University, Department of Industrial Administration and Psychology.

Worthen, Blaine R. and James R. Sanders, eds. 1973. *Educational Evaluation: Theory and Practice.* Worthington, OH: Charles A. Jones.

Wortman, Paul M. 1995. "An Exemplary Evaluation of a Program That Worked: The High/Scope Perry Preschool Project. *Evaluation Practice* 16(3):257–65.

Wright, William and Thomas Sachse. 1977. "Survey of Hawaii Evaluation Users." Presented at the annual meeting of the American Educational Research Association. New York.

Wye, Christopher G. and Richard C. Sonnichsen, eds. 1992. *Evaluation in the Federal Government: Changes, Trends, and Opportunities. New Directions for Program Evaluation*, No. 55.

Wysocki, Robert K. and Rudd McGary. 2003. *Effective Project Management: Traditional, Adaptive, Extreme.* 3d ed. Hoboken, NJ: Wiley.

Yin, Robert K. 2002. *Case Study Research: Design and Methods.* 3d ed. Thousand Oaks, CA: Sage.

_____. 1994. "Evaluation: A Singular Craft." *The Qualitative-Quantitative Debate: New Perspectives. New Directions for Program Evaluation* 61:71–84.

Zadeh, Lofti A., King-Sun Fu, Kokichi Tanaka, and Massamichi Shimura, eds. 1975. *Fuzzy Sets and Their Applications to Cognitive and Decision Processes.* New York: Academic Press.

Zeng, Douglas Zhihua. 2006. *Knowledge, Technology and Cluster-based Growth in Africa: Findings from Eleven Case Studies of Enterprise Clusters in Africa.* Washington, DC: Knowledge for Development (K4D) Program, World Bank Institute.

Zimmerman, Brenda, Curt Lindbery, and Paul Plsek. 2001. *Edgeware: Insights from Complexity Science for Health Care Leaders.* Irving, TX: VHA.

Author Index

Subject Index